Entrepreneurship

Wiley Series in Management

Entrepreneurship

John G. Burch
Northeast Louisiana University

JOHN WILEY & SONS
New York Chichester Brisbane Toronto Singapore

Cover designed by John Hite

Library of Congress Cataloging in Publication Data:

Burch, John G.
  Entrepreneurship.

  (Wiley series in management)
  Includes bibliographies and index.
  1. Entrepreneur.   2. New business enterprises.
3. Small business.   I. Title
HB615.B87   1986   658.4'2   85-12455
ISBN 0-471-82522-0

Printed in the United States of America

10 9 8 7 6 5 4 3 2

To Joel and Seth,
budding entrepreneurs

PREFACE

To survive in the business world and contribute to economic growth, students must not only become well grounded in conventional business principles, but they also need to develop entrepreneurial attitudes and skills and the determination to face tough business realities. They must understand that the marketplace is global and learn how to compete in it. They will need to understand both the enormous competition that has recently developed from Asian and European nations and how a strong entrepreneurial economy will meet this stiff competition.

Strong entrepreneurship is the key process needed to meet economic challenges and to make a nation economically competitive. This textbook not only gives students entrepreneurial attitudes and understanding, but it also provides the necessary skills to become an entrepreneur.

This textbook is divided into six parts. Part One delineates entrepreneurship, its role in nations' well-being, and conditions that foster it. An entrepreneurship model is presented that brings together all components necessary for an ideal entrepreneurial economy. Furthermore, a profile of entrepreneurs is presented along with the risks and rewards of becoming an entrepreneur. The intrapreneur, a corporate entrepreneur, is also discussed. Part Two describes how entrepreneurs create products and services for the marketplace. Part Three deals with the means of going into business—start-up, buyout, or franchise. Part Four presents a constellation of venture opportunities, including mail order and international trade, with emphasis on exporting, moonlighting, shopping center development, technology transfer, and so forth. Part Five treats the legal and financial aspects of becoming an entrepreneur, which include the legal structure of a business venture, its protection, and its sources of financing. Part Six gives tips on how to write and prepare a business plan, describes its elements, and delineates pointers on how to present it to financing sources.

After studying this textbook and answering some, if not all, of the questions at the end of each chapter, students should be able to prepare and present a business plan for their venture idea. The ideal outcome would be for them not only to prepare a business plan but also to raise capital and launch a successful new business venture. The basic aim of this textbook is to present the necessary steps to help put venture building blocks together and keep them together.

ACKNOWLEDGMENTS

Thanks are due to all the people who directly or indirectly contributed to this textbook. I would particularly like to thank Glenda, my wife, for all the extra work she did to get the final manuscript in order. Special thanks go to Betty Stewart, Barbara Pace, Linda Parker, and the late Barbara Beeman, who unflaggingly bore the responsibility for typing the manuscript. For preparation of assignment material, special thanks go to Alfredo Salas, Zulfiquar Ahmed Dogar, and Yuet Yee Lam.

Special recognition and thanks are also due Rick Leyh, editor, for his support. Moreover, I gratefully acknowledge reviews and suggestions offered by the following:

Gibb Dyer
Brigham Young University

Roger Hutt
Arizona State University

Arthur Kuriloff
Management Consultant
Taos, New Mexico

John Kline
University of Colorado

Harold Welsch
De Paul University

CONTENTS

CONTENTS

PART ONE

ENTREPRENEURSHIP AND THE ENTREPRENEUR

CHAPTER 1

Analysis of Entrepreneurship

INTRODUCTION

The drive to venture and start new businesses is a strong thread running through the American fabric. Entrepreneurs and suppliers of risk capital are the star players in entrepreneurship. But for entrepreneurship to survive and prosper, a number of conditions must exist. Moreover, to give birth to new businesses in today's complex world, entrepreneurs need skills in accounting, law, finance, management, and marketing and also support from a variety of groups. The objectives of this chapter are the following.

1 To define entrepreneurship.
2 To identify conditions favorable to entrepreneurship.
3 To present a model of entrepreneurship.

DEFINITION OF ENTREPRENEURSHIP

Entrepreneurship is the act of being an entrepreneur, a derivative of the French term *entreprendre*, which means "to undertake; to pursue opportunities; to fulfill needs and wants through innovation and starting businesses." The entrepreneur is the one who does this; he or she is a person who undertakes a venture, organizes it, raises capital to finance it, and assumes all or a major portion of the risk. A person who invests in this undertaking is called a venture capitalist. Entrepreneurs bring to the deal talent, product-service venture ideas, know-how, and usually some of their own money. The venture capitalist provides risk capital, which can be start-up or seed capital or first-, second-, or third-round financing. If it is start-up capital that the venture capitalist furnishes, then both parties launch a business venture that they hope and believe will produce large returns.

Entrepreneurship Examples

Columbus, a true entrepreneur, started America's development with backing from Queen Isabella, a venture capitalist. From all over the world, aspiring entrepreneurs of different religions, cultures, and ethnicities, many of whom were penniless, came to America and played a major role in its development. The entrepreneurial thread is, indeed, tightly woven into the fabric of American society.

Today the entrepreneurial beat goes on, played by entrepreneurs such as Edson de Castro, founder of Data General; An Wang, founder of Wang Laboratories; Steven Jobs, cofounder of Apple Computer; L. J. Sevin, founder of Compaq Computers; and Fred Smith, founder of Federal Express. Literally thousands of other successful entrepreneurs could be mentioned. The point is that these people and others like them provide a variety of job opportunities and also serve as role models to inspire new generations of entrepreneurs. Moreover, they have reaped huge rewards for themselves and the venture capitalists who had the foresight to back them.

Entrepreneurship Initiates Changes

Some may think that entrepreneurship is simply a form of management when, in fact, the essence of entrepreneurship is the initiation of change as opposed to management, which involves controlling and planning within a given structure. For example, when someone develops a new product, such as a human-intelligent computer, this constitutes an innovative change and hence involves entrepreneurship. But once the production of this new computer begins, then management takes over and coordinates and organizes for the continuing production of it in a well-defined structure. Entrepreneurship reappears, usually from outside the present structure (many large companies have, however, established venture or entrepreneurship departments), to initiate change in the computer or in the way it is produced. Once that change is initiated, management again takes charge of the production and distribution process.

Entrepreneurship Spawns Entrepreneurship

Entrepreneurship generates additional entrepreneurial opportunities. The advent of personal computers opened up a vast software market, and young computer wizards have developed marketable computer software packages while sitting at their home computer terminals. William Gates, III, cofounder of Microsoft, exemplifies this budding group of entrepreneurs—the new tinkerers and "in-the-garage" inventors.

Many hardware niches remain to be filled. Kevin Jenkins, an accounting graduate, with his two friends, founded Hercules Computer Technology with $23,000. The company quickly grew from nothing to a $30 million enterprise by providing graphics boards for retailers who sell IBM personal computers.

Furthermore, personal computers create a number of supplementary niches. Users need training, computers require maintenance and repair, and soon there will be a vast used-computer market. The same situation exists in any new industry, such as biotechnology, telecommunications, robotics, and so forth. They all generate the need for thousands of small new businesses to fill niches in the marketplace.

On the lighter side, Rich Tennant makes a profit by poking fun at computers and serious users. His quirky cartoons and illustrations are displayed in a number of computer magazines. A group of entertainers wrote and presented a comedy show called *Up Your Computer!* for a consumer electronics convention. Also, some enterprising publishers gave birth to *Confuserworld*, a *Computerworld* parody. They were sued, however, by a humorless IBM when Mark Florant, one of the founders, wrote a story called "IBM Calls It Quits," the theme of which indicated that IBM was going to call it quits because business was too successful and boring.

It is not all high-tech entrepreneurship and its spinoffs, however. Observe the niches produced by shopping centers. For example, special niches favoring the taste buds of hungry and thirsty shopping center frequenters offer many opportunities. Entrepreneurs across the country have "gotten in the way" of these shoppers to offer them everything from specially prepared orange juice to delightfully stuffed potatoes. An entrepreneur can become a millionaire by setting up lemonade stands!

INFLUENCE OF ECONOMIC AND NONECONOMIC CONDITIONS ON ENTREPRENEURSHIP

Entrepreneurship just does not happen in a vacuum. So, at this point, we need to consider the influence of economic and noneconomic conditions on entrepreneurship. Many scholars argue that entrepreneurship flourishes in countries where particular economic and noneconomic conditions are most favorable. In these countries, people are motivated to maximize various rewards such as profits. Therefore, entrepreneurship emerges, and economic growth and development results. On the other hand, if economic and noneconomic conditions are not favorable, entrepreneurship dries up and the country's economy stagnates.

Comparative Analysis of Economic and Noneconomic Conditions of Great Britain and France

Wilken[1] made a comparative and historical study of six countries to help show what causes economic growth and development in these countries, that is, both the economic and noneconomic conditions that must be present to cause the emergence of entrepreneurship. We use a summary of Wilken's studies on Great Britain and France (results of other countries are similar) to help us decide if entrepreneurship is the key causal factor in the process of a nation's economic growth and development and if the amount and strength of entrepreneurship within a nation rests on the degree of favorability of economic and noneconomic conditions present in that nation. If you agree that Great Britain has had more and better entrepreneurs and has enjoyed better economic growth and development than France, then the influence of economic and noneconomic conditions summarized from Wilken in the following list is evident. Bear in mind that these conditions are Wilken's interpretations and that they existed in the eighteenth and nineteenth centuries. Maybe, however, we can learn from this presentation and construct sensible strategies for the future that will ensure that conditions favorable to a strong entrepreneurial economy will always prevail.

[1]Paul H. Wilken, *Entrepreneurship—A Comparative and Historical Study* (Norwood, N.J.: ALBEX Publishing Corp., 1979). The summary of Wilken's studies of Great Britain and France is used with permission.

Great Britain	France
Economic	Economic
1. Strong investment propensities existed in Great Britain because investors had a good chance to make high profits. Wealthy Britishers invested heavily in Great Britain's industries and new technologies. British investors also put capital into foreign countries, but their main investments went to British entrepreneurs, who exploited domestic or foreign (i.e., colonial) ventures.	1. The propensity of French investors to provide capital for industrial activities in France was weak. These investors poured money into land, government securities, and trade in commodities and currency, none of which created wealth for the nation. Most of the other capital flowed to foreign countries. Fortunately, this outflow of capital was balanced by an inflow of foreign capital, thus creating the paradox of French capital being used to develop Russia at at the same time that Belgian capital promoted French economic development. In addition, foreign investment by French capitalists benefited domestic entrepreneurs by increasing foreign demand for French goods.
2. Entrepreneurship received moderate support from the aristocracy.	2. The French aristocracy had a usurer and renter orientation and did not support entrepreneurship.
3. Good banking existed with available credit.	3. France had a poor banking system. Its banking system maintained a reserve of gold and silver that was five times greater than in the English system. Some economists estimated that the French annual growth rate could have been increased by as much as 100 percent if it had operated with the same fractional reserves as did the British banking system.
4. Early on, the corporate form of business was legalized. This move gave the investor limited liability and greater mobility of capital.	4. The principle of limited corporate form was not legalized until 1867.
5. Entrepreneurs, in addition to investing their profits back into their enterprise, actively sought outside capital.	5. Entrepreneurs showed an unwillingness to reinvest their profits in their enterprises; they consistently showed a strong preference to invest in land.
6. Entrepreneurs were successful in market innovation, both domestic and	6. The French had a poor market. Moreover, the domestic market was

(continued)

Great Britain	*France*
Economic	*Economic*
foreign. To be sure, the British colonies provided a strong market.	rural with a low level of per capita income.
7. The nation had a large middle class who demanded substantive goods rather than luxuries.	7. A large gap between the rich and poor existed in France.
8. Great Britain enjoyed an adequate supply of skilled, productive, and conscientious workers. Based on good performance, workers enjoyed a degree of upward mobility. Hiring and promoting were based on merit rather than on family affiliation for the most part.	8. France had a limited labor supply with low labor mobility. Workers remained close to the land, moving into industry during prosperous times and back into agriculture in depressed periods. Definitions of status were tighter than those in Great Britain.
9. The British adopted good management techniques.	9. France did not have strong managers.
10. Business endeavored to produce better-quality and lower-cost goods and services.	10. The French, on the whole, were behind Great Britain in producing better-quality and lower-cost goods and services with notable exceptions in fashion, wine, and cattle.
11. Great Britain had access to a plentiful supply of raw materials.	11. France never enjoyed a large supply of raw materials; their loss of Alsace-Lorraine in the Franco-Prussian War aggravated this disadvantage.
12. Many entrepreneurs developed and exploited new technologies. National technology expositions were held, and prizes were awarded to inventors.	12. France was slow to develop and use new technologies. French entrepreneurs, however, were encouraged to travel to England to obtain technology secrets.
13. Compared to the rest of Europe, Great Britain practiced free trade with limited tariffs.	13. France implemented strong tariffs.
14. England implemented strong legal support for private property for anyone.	14. France's legal support for landowners was strong, especially for the aristocracy.
Noneconomic	*Noneconomic*
15. England had a good transportation system.	15. France's transportation system lagged behind.
16. It can be argued that a general rise in need-achievement imagery in British literature between 1700 and 1800	16. Need-achievement literature similar to that of Great Britain did not appear to any great extent in France in the

Great Britain	France
Economic	*Economic*
preceded an increase in entrepreneurship.	eighteenth century.
17. Many of the entrepreneurs succeeded in becoming upwardly mobile, thus creating a strong belief in the possibility of upward mobility.	17. Many of the French entrepreneurs did not achieve upward mobility.
18. Entrepreneurs had nothing to fear from government; they felt secure.	18. Entrepreneurs did not seem to have a lot of faith in the pendular effect of French government; sometimes the government supported entrepreneurship, but other times it did not.
19. Great Britain had a good educational system.	19. France had a fair-to-poor educational system, especially for the masses. Many of the upper class were educated in England.
20. The Protestant religion fostered the work ethic.	20. No evidence exists as to whether the dominant Catholic religion stifled the work ethic.
21. At the university level, Great Britain has developed outstanding research and educational programs. In some universities, its business curriculum is at least on a par with American state-supported universities.	21. France simply does not have a widespread university system. Moreover, its business curriculum is woefully lacking, and what exists is 10 to 20 years out-of-date.
22. England is strong in research and innovation (e.g., drugs and machinery).	22. France lags far behind England in this area.

Government's Impact on Entrepreneurship

In Great Britain the economic and noneconomic conditions were favorable, and, hence, entrepreneurship emerged proportionately. Indeed, British entrepreneurs are hailed as models par excellence. In the eighteenth and nineteenth centuries, nowhere in the world was the venturesome spirit greater than in Great Britain. Fresh innovations and successful entrepreneurs went against the stranglehold of the aristocracy. Vertical mobility by anyone was a possibility. The steam engine, the iron rail, the spinning jenny, and thousands of other inventions made Great Britain the bastion of entrepreneurship. As many historians have said, "it was the workshop of the world." Today conditions in Great Britain do not seem exceedingly favorable, but changes are under way, and a major turnaround is expected soon.

A major part of the blame for the relative unfavorableness of conditions for strong entrepreneurship in France must rest on its government. Its "robbing-Peter-to-pay-Paul," central-government, and strong-regulation policies frustrated entrepreneurship. At times, French entrepreneurs were *too* secure in the belief that the government would bail them out if they got into any difficulties. Certainly, the consistent inability of the French economic system to eliminate inefficient producers has attracted wide comment. Unquestionably, overt activity of the state, either in promoting or restricting entrepreneurship, was less in Great Britain than in France. It is interesting to note that Great Britain had a *weaker* aristocracy, a *limited-interventionist* government, and a *stronger* economic system; today one can argue that it has a *stronger-interventionist* government, but a *weaker* economic system. Even so, the British economic system is still stronger than France's and few deny that France's government vacillates between socialism and near-communism. But in France today these conditions are also changing.

Current Conditions in Europe

Strong signals on the European business and political horizons indicate that a major entrepreneurial turnaround is imminent. Political leaders throughout Europe are now adopting probusiness, anti-interventionist principles whether they are socialists or right-of-center. Leaders in France, for example, are trying to expand France's capital markets and encourage small-company growth.

Moreover, Europe's people are a civilized, energetic lot, well mannered and innovative. They strive for the good life. Where else can you travel by subway to the theater, enjoy a sumptuous dinner afterward; and return to your hotel after midnight by subway in absolute safety? And despite what has been written about their welfare state, recession experimentation with socialism, runaway Keynesian economics, and the like, the entrepreneurial urge is returning with a concomitant renewal of institutions, infrastructures, and businesses. Paralleling this is a strong work ethic that is still intact. Europeans know how to work and are willing to work. For the most part, workers are competent and dependable; they take pride in what they do. Workers such as electricians, painters, plumbers, carpenters, and so forth, work a 12-hour day. Indeed, Europe will soon be a major, if not dominant, competitive force in the world again.

Some believe that the economic growth will double or triple in the next few years in West Germany and Great Britain. Even France and Italy are expected to have strong gains. Beginning to take place Europewide is a decline in inflation, lower budget deficits, increased monetary growth, and large investments in new technologies, such as automation and robotics. ICL from Great Britain, Compagnie de Machines Bull from France, and Siemens from Germany have set up a joint research center to spread the inhibitive costs of leading-edge research and development. Moreover, all the major European data-processing and electronic companies are taking part in a politically motivated program, ESPRIT (European Strategic Program for R and D in Informational Technologies). European countries, indeed, plan to become globally competitive players in high tech. France, for example, has already made major strides in artificial intelligence through its Prolog program.

The Current Status of Entrepreneurship in Other Selected Countries

Observe the following situations in selected countries and determine if they refute or add credibility to Wilken's analysis.

Mexico.   No aggressive American businesspeople in their right minds with money to invest would think of going to Mexico to open a business where Mexican nationals would, by law, be required to own 51 percent voting control of the business, especially when American investors have a much better opportunity in their own country with better laws and a more stable economic system.[2] Mexico lacks entrepreneurial skills, spirit, product know-how, and marketing skills. This is why Mexico cannot even join the bottom rung of the industrial nations.[3]

Some countries, on the other hand, have a good image and a receptive attitude. For example, Jamaica has a good English-speaking labor force, a stable government, and a very attractive location (90 minutes by air from Miami and two days by container freight from U.S. gulf ports). However, it lacks the entrepreneurial spirit and the right products. If Jamaica can somehow supply the missing essentials, she could ship all day long into the biggest, richest market in the world of 200 million buyers on her doorstep, just a few hours away—just like Puerto Rico.[4]

Peru.   Throughout Latin America, capitalism is still a dirty word. It is to the advantage of the rich to maintain a wide gap between them and the poor. Where capitalism and entrepreneurship flourish, the standard of living rises, and a strong middle class emerges. In Peru, strong barriers, indeed, exist against entrepreneurship. Even in spite of these barriers, however, a healthy underground economy is developing.

If entrepreneurs try to play it straight in Peru, they soon run into a frustrating exercise in futility. Access to the legal marketplace is barred by a dense bureaucracy that favors entrenched businesspeople of the traditional private sector. After actually going through the required 130 legal steps to set up a small clothing enterprise, the aspiring, but frustrated, Peruvian entrepreneur will have to work 40 hours a week for more than 6 months to pay 8 unavoidable bribes just to register to do business. The equivalent process in Florida takes four hours.[5]

---

[2]Lawrence Taylor, ''Mexico No; Jamaica Ole!'' *The Market Chronicle*, 17:13 (April 7, 1983), p. 2. The material is used with permission.

[3]Ibid.

[4]Ibid.

[5]Claudia Rosett, ''How Peru Got a Free Market Without Really Trying,'' *The Wall Street Journal*, January 27, 1984, p. 23. The material is used with permission.

Rather than to subject themselves to bribe demands, bureaucratic barriers, and legal morass, most entrepreneurs, understandably, go underground. Even in the underground, entrepreneurs still have to spend 15 percent of their income bribing bureaucratic officials to look the other way.

In some areas, the informal economy is more efficient than the legal sector. The market test of this efficiency is the awesome amount of underground business carried on profitably, without government planning or aid. Illegal buses provide 85 percent of Lima's public transportation, and illegal taxis provide 10 percent more. Underground activity accounts for 90 percent of the clothing business and 60 percent of housing construction, including relatively sophisticated structures up to six stories high. Underground entrepreneurs assemble cars and buses, build furniture and make high-precision tools.[6]

The Two Chinas.   Taiwan enjoys a classic Schumpeterian economy. Only 110 miles west of Taiwan, across the Taiwan Strait, is another world economically and politically—China, the world's largest Communist country. In Taipei, capital of Taiwan, one sees no waves of bicycles, as in Beijing, but swarms of cars and motorcycles; no bored shopkeepers with little to sell, but thousands of well-stocked food shops and bulging department stores; no ideologically pure "revolutionary opera," but throngs of middle-class families flocking to the Tung Wang Restaurant for a fashion show and a concert of very hard rock.[7]

Through the centuries, rulers of mainland China have traveled the road to feudalism, then to socialism, then to communism. Along the way they built the Great Wall to keep out invaders and new ideas. In this century, China reached the ultimate in communism—slavery. The people of China are slaves to the state and grim, blank-eyed bureaucrats; most labor is performed by hand; they suffer from wretched poverty, hopelessness, and shortages of food, clothing, housing, transportation, medical care, education, and entertainment; they are slaves to a system that is intolerant of innovation, change, and freedom of expression, a system that lobotomizes the mind and deadens the soul. To be sure, entrepreneurship does not, will not, and cannot thrive in this kind of environment. Indeed, the practice of Marxism and Leninism as developed by Mao Zedong promised the people freedom but gave them slavery.

Recently, from Beijing, however, new currents of change are flowing with a mix of Maoism, free enterprise, and the marketplace. Political slogans pasted on billboards have given way to advertisements extolling the virtues of TV and washing machines. Indeed, leaders are employing extreme measures in an attempt to throw off the debilitating economic system they have been enslaved to for centuries. They want to bring China's one billion people into the twentieth century by application of American business education, including management, marketing, and accounting;

---

[6]Ibid.

[7]Lawrence Minard, "The China Reagan Can't Visit," *Forbes*, May 7, 1984, p. 36. The material is used with permission.

a variety of technology; and, yes, entrepreneurship. But growth in industry and jobs must occur to increase significantly a per capita income of less than $400 where razors and cigarettes are considered luxuries.

If China's leaders establish conditions favorable to entrepreneurship, China could, in this century, become a major player in the world economy. Indeed, under the right conditions its entrepreneurial potential is truly impressive. The country is certainly blessed with energetic and hardworking people. Chinese who have moved to other countries with conditions more favorable to entrepreneurship have become strong entrepreneurs, especially of the small-business, merchant variety.

ENTREPRENEURSHIP MODEL

At its essence, entrepreneurship is the process of giving birth to a new business. But the question is this: What are the key components that work together to conceive of and give birth to new businesses? An entrepreneurship model is displayed in Figure 1.1, which helps answer this question.

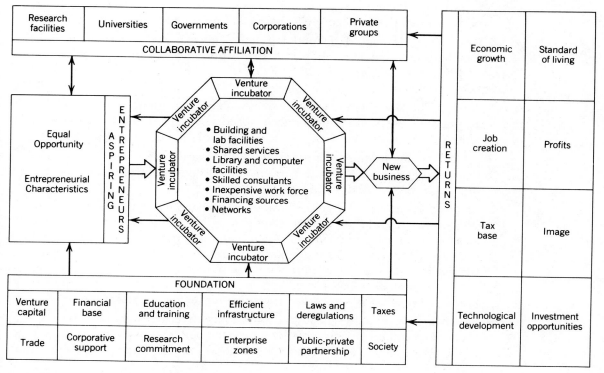

FIGURE 1.1 *The entrepreneurship model.*

Foundation

The foundation provides the environment and general support that help foster entrepreneurship. The major elements are these.

1 *Venture capital.*   Venture capital that is readily accessible provides the catalyst for starting risky ventures.

2 *Financial base.*   In addition to venture capital, a variety of financing sources, both debt and equity, should be made available at reasonable cost. The cost of capital is often too high for aspiring entrepreneurs and small-business people. These people simply cannot generate enough cash flow to service capital costs. Therefore, they are doomed before they can get started. Banks *and* governments must become more involved in financing new business ventures at reasonable rates.

3 *Education and training.*   These programs should be available to all people all the time to provide the knowledge and expertise to achieve their personal goals and learn new skills.

4 *Infrastructures.*   Adequate public and private infrastructures should be in place to provide efficient telecommunications systems, transportation, distribution networks, and general services that make the flow of commerce smoother.

5 *Laws and regulations.*   Further deregulation, such as that which occurred in the telephone and transportation industries, provides a significant stimulus for new business development. Moreover, outdated antitrust laws should be modified or deleted.

6 *Taxes.*   The tax system should be overhauled for simplification and equity. In addition, taxes should be generally reduced, especially for new businesses and older businesses that invest in research and plant modernization.

7 *Trade.*   Strong trade regulations, quotas, and tariffs are normally counterproductive. Elimination of trade barriers causes domestic businesses to become more competitive and eventually stronger.

8 *Corporative support.*   Large corporations' sponsorship of new business development to support their product lines through technology licensing nurtures a steady stream of new products. Also, many corporations have products that they are not currently manufacturing or marketing or both. The transfer of this technology out to entrepreneurs establishes a flexible and varied manufacturing-marketing base. Furthermore, corporate cultures should be conditioned to accept and support in-house entrepreneurs—intrapreneurs.

9 *Research.*   For moving ahead and improving, free investigations and experimentations must be made to discover new and better ways of doing things. One of the chief goals of entrepreneurship is to develop product-service ideas that will fill a new need or want in the marketplace.

10 *Enterprise zones.*   The major goal of setting up enterprise zones is to create jobs. The enterprises should be new businesses, however, not XYZ Company moved from a nonenterprise zone. Such a movement is a zero-sum game.

11 *Public-private partnership.*   Both the public and private sectors should work together to resolve conflicts and problems. Furthermore, strategies should be hammered out to meet international competition.

12 *Society.*   Trend leaders of a society, such as writers, reporters and commentators, teachers, politicians, clergy, parents, and so forth, should extol hard work, discipline, and risk-reward. They should encourage and nurture a creative, positive spirit. In today's world, some of this seems a bit old-fashioned, even trite. But the fact remains that without the attitudes that these virtues create and without positive stimuli from society, entrepreneurship dies.

Aspiring Entrepreneurs

The raw energy and talent for venturing comes from aspiring entrepreneurs who are dedicated, hardworking, and knowledgeable people. They are analyzed in the next chapter. Entrepreneurs come from universities, corporations, research labs, and the general community. They differ in age, sex, race, and creed. They all have an equal opportunity to become entrepreneurs.

Some aspiring entrepreneurs are tinkerers and inventors. Some are good at putting things together and making the result work; they are good organizers and take-charge people. Still others are opportunity-sensitive and can readily spot viable business opportunities. They all have a yen to venture. These people, supported and connected to the other components in the entrepreneurship model, create a synergism for an explosion in new business birth and growth.

Collaborative Affiliation

To a great extent, entrepreneurship is an intellectual endeavor. The collaborative affiliation component, made up of research centers, parks, and consortia; universities; governments; corporations; and private groups, cooperates with entrepreneurs and venture incubators to give general guidance, expertise, and research support. This collaborative affiliation represents a tightly connected partnership. The goals of this support group are to generate economic growth and diversification, to improve the standard of living for all members of the society, to create jobs, to broaden the tax base, to improve image and stature, to produce new technologies, and to generate additional investment opportunities. Specifically, the elements of this component are the following.

1 *Research facilities.*   These research facilities include research centers, technology and science parks, and research consortia. Establishment of these facilities represents a new wave of commitment and intensity to achieve a position of preeminence in new technologies. In some instances, these facilities are built through a linkage between universities, governments, and the private sector, where there is a balanced interplay of funding and effort. Examples are the Microelectronics and Computer Technology Corporation (MCC) in Texas, the Science and Technology Foundation in New York, the Ben Franklin Partnership Fund in Pennsylvania, the High Technology Council in Iowa, the Technology Park Corporation in Massachusetts, the Tennessee Technology Corridor Foundation in Tennessee, and the Research Triangle Park in North Carolina.

2 *Universities.* Many universities also play a major role in research. Moreover, many universities provide education in general business, accounting, marketing, management, and entrepreneurship to educate people who are not only entrepreneurially motivated but who also have the knowledge required to start and manage a business. Furthermore, traditionally disparate groups, such as law, engineering, medicine, computer science, and business, are working together not only to provide entrepreneurs guidance and expertise but also products and services that have commercial potential through licensing.

3 *Governments.* Federal, state, and local governments are taking a proactive, noninterventionist role to seek out and fund technological efforts from conception to full commercialization. Also, more efforts are being made to transfer technology from the laboratories and shelves of agencies, such as NASA, to consumers.

4 *Corporations.* Some of the vast financial resources of corporations can be marshaled to provide equity or debt capital for investment or for the development of new products and services that would be supportive of these corporations' own operations. For example, a large manufacturer may choose to back an inventor of a robot by providing engineering, lab, and production facilities for product development and to fund the venture to full commercialization. The large manufacturer could license the robots, eventually buy the company, or become a major customer of the new robotics firm. Exxon, GE, and Citicorp are examples of large corporations that have set up venture capital funds.

5 *Private groups.* A number of private groups can develop close ties with venture incubators, such as accountants, attorneys, and banks, to provide the professional expertise necessary to start a new business. Moreover, a number of successful businesspeople provide entrepreneurial services to aspiring entrepreneurs.

In addition to a collaborative affiliation, a number of the groups just described have established their own venture incubators. The University City Science Center, a nonprofit organization in Philadelphia, has a university-research incubator whose "owners" include universities and hospitals. Rensselaer Polytechnic Institute started its incubator unit in 1980, which provides entrepreneurs inexpensive floor space for operations and access to university resources. The Georgia Advanced Technology Center is a state-sponsored program that runs a full-service venture incubator that includes venture capital sources. Mississippi has an incubator called the New Enterprise for Women, whose goals are to generate jobs and retain homegrown talent. Indiana has an organization called the Indiana Institute for New Business Ventures, which helps in the formation and support of small technologically orient-ed, new-business entrepreneurs. Similar incubators have also been established in other states.

Control Data Corporation is a good example of a corporation that has estab-lished an incubator. A private firm, the Rubicon Group, is a venture incubator that was founded by an entrepreneur who has used his wealth to help aspiring entre-preneurs. Rubicon typically takes 20 to 60 percent of a new business' equity for capital and services and plans a two-year turnover of all its member entrepreneurs. The assumption is that each new venture within two years will fail, grow large enough to make it on its own, or expand outside the incubator with downstream financing available if needed. Also, a number of CPA firms have established entre-preneurial services to aid an entrepreneur in financial analysis and the preparation of a business plan. On occasion, the CPA firm, because of business contacts, can also help in bringing entrepreneurs and investors together.

Venture Incubator

The venture incubator provides an ideal place to ''hatch'' new businesses. Entre-preneurs, with foundation stimulation and support and also affiliation with a variety of helpful groups, bring to the incubator unit their abilities and product-service ideas. To bring these product-service ideas to full commercialization, however, requires a wide variety of skills and support, such as capital, professional expertise, labor, and so on. In addition to providing linkage to the foundation and collaborative affiliation components, the venture incubator specifically provides the following.

1 *Building and lab facilities.* Incubators provide floor space with necessary stor-age, office, and work space plus lab facilities and equipment as required.

2 *Shared services.* Shared services include secretaries, word processors, office supplies, telephone, shipping and receiving, and fabrication shops.

3 *Library and computer facilities.* These facilities are made available for entrepre-neurs who need to perform research and store and process large volumes of data.

4 *Skilled consultants.* Incubators have the ability to tap a wide variety of ex-perts for consultation. These experts include accountants, attorneys, market-ers, engineers, computer scientists, government officials, physicians, biotech-nologists, metallurgists, geologists, and the like.

5 *Inexpensive work force.* If the incubator is located close to a university, most stu-dents are willing to work part-time for relatively low wages and for the exper-ience. Such an agreement is beneficial for both the students and entrepreneurs.

6 *Financing sources.*   Once a product-service concept is ascertained to have market potential, capital is provided to launch a business structure that supports it.

7 *Networks.*   Entrepreneurs learn from, and are motivated by, each other. Close association with fellow entrepreneurs in the incubator can lead to a lot of cross-fertilization and creative dynamics. While in the venture incubator, entrepreneurs can also establish a number of business connections with future suppliers, bankers, accountants, attorneys, and even potential customers.

New Business

All the components are brought together to hatch the new business. A board of directors is selected, a management team is formed, legal and accounting work is started, an accounting information system is implemented, construction of a building is completed or one is leased, employees are hired, equipment is installed, inventory is bought, a marketing program is implemented, and customers are contacted. The "chick" has been hatched and is ready to start "scratching for business."

Returns to All the Components

All components of the entrepreneurship model are looking for definite returns, such as these.

1 *Economic growth.*   A healthy economy is one that grows at a good, steady pace without causing high levels of inflation. In essence, new businesses create wealth that is eventually distributed to all members.

2 *Standard of living.*   All the stakeholders in a country's economy want economic growth coupled with an improved standard of living that includes clean air and water, safety and security, peaceful relations, equal opportunity, and quality products and services at reasonable prices.

3 *Job creation.*   Clearly, new businesses create jobs, a significant return to all members of a society.

4 *Profits.*   The key stakeholders in the whole process are entrepreneurs, venture capitalists, and other investors. They all expect—and deserve—a substantial profit from their new businesses.

5 *Tax base.*   Clearly, all governments need ways to expand their tax base to support various programs. Some would argue that the tax base is already too broad and deep. The point here is that new businesses become taxpayers, thus returning revenue to governments and indirectly to other groups such as universities.

6 *Image.*   Research centers and universities are interested in enhancing their stature in order to attract topflight researchers and professors. They also want to secure funds to support a variety of research-educational programs.

7 *Technological development.* Global competition dictates that great strides be made in technological development. To do so requires massive amounts of capital and long lead times, which, in turn, call for public-private partnerships. Japan's Ministry of International Trade and Industry (MITI) and the Institute for a New Generation of Computer Technology (ICOT) are examples of such a partnership. In the United States, the Defense Advanced Research Project Agency (DARPA) supercomputer project bears directly on the development of artificial intelligence, one of the new entrepreneurial areas for the future, which will result in a variety of spin-off niches in which a number of entrepreneurs will become involved. As we have learned from earlier analysis, too much government intervention, however, can stifle entrepreneurship. On the other hand, a number of technologies would not exist today without government funding.

8 *Investment opportunities.* The success of one new business produces many additional entrepreneurial and investment opportunities. Or the creation of technology, such as transistors, fiber optics, computers, lasers, television, cellular phones, and so forth, propagates thousands of investment opportunities and new businesses.

The preceding model and analysis present only one proposal on how to develop an entrepreneurially strong economy. Bits and pieces of this model are already in place and working in many areas of this country and in other countries as well. Good returns are being produced by application of it or similar models. Furthermore, the model illustrates how different components of a country can work together to foster entrepreneurship and create a number of new and diversified businesses. If such an interconnected model of entrepreneurship is unavailable but with many of the components in place and scattered, then entrepreneurs will have to pull them together to meet their specific needs. For example, the entrepreneur will have to seek out equity capital from one source, loans from another, professional consultation from another, and so forth. Therefore, as most aspiring entrepreneurs will not have access to a formal venture incubator, they will have to build one themselves, and this is the assumption on which the rest of this book rests.

SUMMARY

Entrepreneurship is the act of starting a business. The entrepreneur is the actor, enterpriser, initiator, innovator, risk taker, and coordinator. Essentially, the entrepreneur sees an opportunity to fill a need or meet a want in the marketplace and then brings together all the expertise, labor, materials, and capital required to meet these needs and wants. Generally, when one business is launched, this will create investment opportunities for other supplementary businesses.

For entrepreneurship to flourish, a number of conditions must be in place, such as ample financing sources, strong educational and training facilities, efficient infrastructures, uniform commercial law and limited regulations, equal opportunity, low taxes and tax incentives, free trade, support from large corporations, research, enterprise zones, public-private partnership, and encouragement and support from society. In those countries where most of these conditions exist, entrepreneurship is strong. In countries where most of these conditions are absent, entrepreneurship is virtually dead, or entrepreneurs have gone underground.

An entrepreneurship model brings together all the foundation conditions that foster and encourage entrepreneurship, entrepreneurs, collaborative groups, and venture incubators in a concerted effort to hatch new businesses. The goals of these model components are economic growth and diversification, improvement of the standard of living, job creation, profits, a broader tax base, image enhancement, technological development, and new investment opportunities.

ASSIGNMENT

1   How does entrepreneurship create jobs and raise the standard of living in a country?
2   List and discuss five economic conditions that you believe have the strongest positive influence on entrepreneurship. Do the same for noneconomic conditions.
3   List and discuss the things that a government should and should not do to help foster entrepreneurship.
4   Give your impression, based on other courses, of how Schumpeter's theory differs from those of Marx, Malthus, and Keynes. Also, refer to the Bibliography.
5   As an investor, would you invest in Mexico? Why? Why not? Would stronger capitalism help or hurt Mexico's people? Explain.
6   Determine the current economic status of Germany and France. Are they becoming more or less entrepreneurial?
7   Based on your best research, determine if China's attempt at free enterprise and capitalism is succeeding.
8   Assume that you are starting a new country on a large island somewhere in the South Pacific. Give three economic and noneconomic conditions that you think must be established in this country. Explain why. What economic theories and teachings would you follow in setting up economic policies? Would you try to foster an entrepreneurial spirit in your country? If so, how would you go about doing this? If not, why not?
9   An economic analyst said that "for a country to work, its people must work." What do you think he meant? Explain.
10 List and explain all the components in the entrepreneurship model. How do they work together in launching new businesses?
11 What are the returns generated by entrepreneurship? Of what value are they? To whom?

BIBLIOGRAPHY

Backman, Jules, ed. *Entrepreneurship and the Outlook for America*. New York: The Free Press, 1983.

Baldwin, William. "City Hall Discovers Venture Capital." *Forbes*. February 16, 1981.

Baty, Gordon B. *Entrepreneurship for the Eighties*. Reston, Va.: Reston, 1981.

Behar, Richard. "Tempting the Gods." *Forbes*. February 25, 1985.

Benoit, Ellen. "Serving a Niche." *Forbes*. February 25, 1985.

Brandt, Steven C. *Entrepreneuring*. Reading, Mass.: Addison-Wesley, 1982.

Caruso, Denise. "Laughing at Computers." *InfoWorld*. July 16, 1984.

Casson, Mark. *The Entrepreneur*. Totowa, N.J.: Barnes & Noble, 1982.

Drucker, Peter F. "Why America's Got So Many Jobs." *The Wall Street Journal*. January 24, 1984.

Drucker, Peter F., *Innovation and Entrepreneurship*. New York: Harper & Row, 1985.

Frank, Allan Dodds. "Road Too Narrow." *Forbes*. April 30, 1984.

Freeman, Roger A. *Socialism and Private Enterprise in Equatorial Asia: The Case of Malaysia and Indonesia*. Stanford, Calif.: The Hoover Institution on War, Revolution, and Peace, copyrighted by the Board of Trustees of the Leland Stanford Junior University, 1968.

Gevirtz, Don. *Business Plan for America: An Entrepreneur's Manifesto*. New York: Putnam's, 1984.

Guldbert, Ove. "What's Rotten in Denmark." *The Wall Street Journal*. April 24, 1984.

Guroff, Gregory, and Fred V. Carstensen, eds. *Entrepreneurship in Imperial Russia and the Soviet Union*. Princeton, N.J.: Princeton University Press, 1983.

Incubator Times. Washington, D.C.: U.S. Small Business Administration, Office of the Private Sector Initiatives, October 1984.

Kozmetsky, George, Michael Gill, and Raymond Smilor. *Financing and Managing Fast-Growth Companies: The Venture Capital Process*. Lexington, Mass.: Lexington Press, 1985.

Landreth, Harry. *History of Economic Theory, Scope, Method, and Content*. Boston: Houghton Mifflin, 1976.

Landreyev, Igor. *The Noncapitalist Way*. Moscow: Progress Publishers, 1977.

"Marx Defrocked." *The Wall Street Journal*. September 5, 1984.

Minard, Lawrence. "The China Reagan Can't Visit." *Forbes*. May 7, 1984.

Murphy, Thomas P. "Hatching Promises." *Forbes*. June 4, 1984.

"A New Burst of Business Enthusiasm Over China." *Business Week*, April 30, 1984.

"A New Chairman Tries to Trim 'Le Grand Thomson' into a World-Class Fighter." *Business Week*. April 30, 1984.

Phalon, Richard. "University as Venture Capitalist." *Forbes*. December 19, 1983.

"Planting U.S. Seed Money in Japanese Start-ups." *Business Week*. April 23, 1984.

Ronen, Joshua, ed. *Entrepreneurship*. Lexington, Mass.:D. C. Heath, Lexington Books, 1983.

Rosett, Claudia. "How Peru Got a Free Market Without Really Trying." *The Wall Street Journal*. January 27, 1984.

Safire, William. "Loss of Spirit Cripples Industriousness of Once-Stalwart West Germany." *New York Times News Service*. January 1984.

Schumpeter, Joseph A. *The Theory of Economic Development*. New York: Oxford University Press, 1961 (originally published in 1934).

———.*History of Economic Analysis*. Edited from a manuscript by Elizabeth Boody Schumpeter. New York: Oxford University Press, 1954.

Taylor, Lawrence, "Mexico No; Jamaica Ole!" *The Market Chronicle*, 17:13 (April 7, 1983).

"Trying to Set the Entrepreneurial Spirit Free." *Business Week*. April 23, 1984.

Wilken, Paul H. *Entrepreneurship—A Comparative and Historical Study*. Norwood, N.J.: ABLEX, 1979.

CHAPTER 2

Analysis of
the Entrepreneur

INTRODUCTION

In the preceding chapter, entrepreneurship was analyzed from the viewpoint of conditions that foster and augment it and from an evaluation of its degree of activity in selected countries. Moreover, an entrepreneurship model was presented in which the entrepreneur was the key component. The subject of this chapter is the entrepreneur. The objectives of this chapter are as follows.

1 To give a general description of entrepreneurs.
2 To discuss how entrepreneurs use innovation.
3 To provide a comprehensive profile of entrepreneurs and a method of self-analysis.
4 To consider risk and its impact on entrepreneurs.
5 To determine stress on entrepreneurs and present ways to cope with it.
6 To describe corporations' use of entrepreneurs.

GENERAL COMMENTS ABOUT THE ENTREPRENEUR

Clearly, entrepreneurs are the main actors in entrepreneurship. But can they be defined, and where do they come from?

Overview

The term *entrepreneur* seems to have been introduced into economics by R. Cantillon, but the entrepreneur was first accorded a degree of prominence by J. B. Say in the nineteenth century and then later by J. A. Schumpeter. In America today, many view the entrepreneur as the hero of capitalism and the free enterprise system. He or she can rise from humble origins to a position of power and status by personal merit and skills.

The entrepreneur is, indeed, the change agent, the source of innovation and creativity, the schemer, the heart and soul of economic growth. But the entrepreneur remains a partly charted universe and really cannot be fully defined. Why, for example, does one person see an opportunity when another does not? Why do some people have strong entrepreneurial tendencies when others have little to none? No doubt, these questions intrigue scholars. It is indeed a mystery. But more has been learned about entrepreneurs in the past 20 or 30 years than in all previous history. What is known is informative and helpful; what is still unknown is tantalizing.

Typically, the entrepreneur is seen as an individual who owns and operates a small business. He or she is far beyond this. Simply to own and operate a small business or a big business does not make one an entrepreneur. If an individual is merely a caretaker involved in ordering, scheduling, and administration, then he or she should be considered a manager. If this individual is a true entrepreneur, then new products are being created, new ways of providing services are being implemented. The entrepreneur can be described as anyone who takes the risk to develop and implement an enterprise from a small, one-employee shop run on a part-time basis to a new high-tech firm. An entrepreneur can be the ramrod of innovation in a large corporation. Entrepreneurs are often the ones who go where others fear to tread. Therefore, by seeking out and accepting new risky ventures, they are often operating on the frontier of business.

Moreover, a number of people who are not considered businesspeople can act entrepreneurially. Accountants and lawyers can offer new, innovative services to their clients; teachers can use and experiment with a number of techniques, such as video, sketches and role playing, and theatrical props, to enhance communications; pediatricians can dress in clown suits to gain a better rapport with little patients. Malcolm Forbes flies balloons across continents and rides motorcycles into China and Russia. These exploits probably help to increase the circulation of *Forbes*, but they also satisfy Malcolm Forbes's entrepreneurial yen. Certainly, one does not have to "open shop" to be entrepreneurial.

Supply of Entrepreneurs

Where do entrepreneurial talent, know-how, and dedication come from? Are people born with entrepreneurial skills? Can entrepreneurs be taught? What gives them the incentive and energy to exploit opportunities? All these questions are puzzling because entrepreneurs cannot be standardized and reduced to a mechanical model.

The supply of entrepreneurial talent is subject to a number of both internal and external forces. Entrepreneurs are, to some extent, a product of genetics, family influences, peer pressure, cultural conditions, educational systems, strength of the work ethic, religion, and so forth. Moreover, the would-be entrepreneur must perform within, and be motivated by, the same conditions in which entrepreneurship itself is embedded. And obviously impediments to entrepreneurship such as taxes, regulations, and other unfavorable conditions covered in the last chapter tend to dry up the supply of entrepreneurs. Alternatively, favorable conditions tend to spawn entrepreneurs. Still entrepreneurial talent may exist in countries that have unfavorable conditions for entrepreneurship and vice versa. In the former situation, underground economies usually develop. In the latter, outsiders come in to exploit entrepreneurial opportunities.

The existence of a favorable environment will not by itself ensure entrepreneurial activity, not any more than the existence of a soccer field guarantees soccer games and players. The goal of a country should be to have the conditions and facilities for entrepreneurship plus the commitment to do everything possible to develop entrepreneurs as the entrepreneurship model illustrated in the preceding chapter.

THE ENTREPRENEUR AND INNOVATION

Simply being a caretaker or administrator of a business will not result in economic growth and diversification. Innovation is a major factor for meeting the changing needs of society. Clearly, an important tool of the entrepreneur is innovation.

Types of Innovation

Five types of innovation are distinguished: (1) introduction of a new product or service that is an improvement in the quality of the existing product or service; (2) introduction of a new method that increases productivity; (3) the opening of a new market, in particular an export market in a new territory; (4) the conquest of a new source of supply of raw materials, half-manufactured products, or alternative materials; and (5) the creation of a new organization.

The entrepreneur does not perform well in bureaucracies. Innovation, therefore, made by entrepreneurs usually occurs outside large corporations. For example, credit cards were not developed by banks; xerography was not created by a large office equipment company; Atari, by a computer vendor; or Weed Eater, by a lawn equipment manufacturer. These were the innovations of entrepreneurs who grasped an idea, developed it, and pursued its success with unflagging efforts.

Innovation Goal

Entrepreneurs are always looking for something unique to fill a need or want. They may or may not be inventors, but they have the ability to see the economic potential of an invention. They spend a lot of time asking: "What if?" and "Why not?" Others around entrepreneurs are exposed to the same opportunity, and yet it may not be seen by any of them. Or, if they recognize an opportunity, they may not have the ambition and guts to take advantage of it.

Innovation does not necessarily mean developing something earthshaking and profound; it does not always have to be a "new" gadget, tool, or service. A simple adjustment to something old can do the trick. For example, game rooms and penny arcades were flourishing before the turn of the century. Nolan Bushnell saw an opportunity to convert this old idea into new whizbang entertainment centers. Indeed, he plunked down his last $500 to start a company named Atari. A few years later he sold out for about $30 million. He simply made an electronic adjustment to an old idea based on pinball machines and other gaming devices one could have found a few years ago in many restaurants, pool halls, and penny arcades across the country.

The man who created the video-game boom struck again. After Bushnell sold Atari, he developed Chuck E. Cheese's Pizza Time Theatre. Again, Bushnell saw an opportunity and acted. He had noticed that patrons of pizza parlors spent a lot of time drumming their fingers on their tables and staring into space while waiting 15 to 25 minutes for their pizzas. Bushnell had the imagination to see this dead time as an opportunity, not a problem (*note:* many innovations stem from turning a problem into an enterprise). So he built a pizza parlor, named it after a rat, and filled it with video games, small amusement park rides, and choruses of performing robots. Now, instead of drumming their fingers, patrons happily feed a constellation of coin-gobbling machines while waiting for their pizzas.

In January 1984, Nolan Bushnell stepped down as chairman of Pizza Time Theatre. This was the second time in six years that he had relinquished the chairpersonship of a multimillion dollar company he founded. Bushnell's actions point out a key characteristic of strong entrepreneurs; they start a company, nurture it, get it to a high level of success, and bail out; they really do not make good managers. They are better at innovating and starting new ventures than they are at managing them.[1]

For another example of how slight modifications are sometimes innovative, consider the late Ray Kroc of McDonald's. He certainly did not invent the hamburger, but he did invent a new way of delivering it to the customer. Furthermore, Henry Ford did not invent the automobile, but he applied new ways of mass production that turned out cars cheaply enough so that most people could afford them. So Ford performed not only manufacturing and product innovation but also market innovation. Indeed, some entrepreneurs may spend too much time involved with the product and not enough time in looking at the market differently.

Innovation, then, is doing something different from the herd. To open another junky welding shop, grocery store, service station, shoe store, TV repair shop, and so forth, is the same as working for wages and maybe worse. If, however, an innovative twist could be applied to the grocery business to service the market differently, then entrepreneurial profit could be generated. For example, look at no-frill, warehouse markets or grocery shopping by phone.

The point is this: Go into something where the profits are not squeezed out, such as a computer dating and roommate and commuter matching service; a newspaper enterprise that gives quality, colorful coverage of the local community; a recording studio that provides music, props, direction, and choreography to aspiring entertainers; new and efficient forms of health care delivery systems; adult entertainment centers; computerized medical diagnosis; special training centers, for example, a chef's school; software packages for business analysis and banking; pollution control devices; waste treatment procedures and locations; an inexpensive, one-person airplane; self-shining shoes; and so forth.

How to Innovate

For making these or other innovations, systematic and logical thinking can lead you just so far. For thinking innovatively, imagination is more important than knowledge. Imagination and the ability to think creatively come from the right side of the

---

[1]Carrie Dolan, "Bushnell Resigns Pizza Time Post; Kennan Is Named," *The Wall Street Journal*, February 2, 1984, p. 36. This material is used with permission.

brain. There we can learn to think intuitively and creatively and learn how to deal with fuzzy, messy problems.

Mintzberg says in an article[2] that scientific research shows that the human brain is specialized; the logical, linear functions occur in the left hemisphere, and the holistic, relational ones occur in the right. He also says that a major thrust of development in organizations ever since Frederick Taylor began experimenting in factories has been to shift activities out of the realm of intuition toward conscious analysis. Moreover, educational systems are devoted to the left side: terminology, techniques, and analysis. Mintzberg believes that we need to develop both sides.

Edward de Bono says that logical thinking is vertical thinking that follows the most obvious line, proceeding straight up or down. On the other hand, creative thinking and the generation of new ideas are lateral thinking. Lateral thinking seeks to get away from the pattern that is leading one in a definite direction and to move sideways by reforming the pattern. Lateral thinking constructs ways to develop them. De Bono further states that it is frightening (or exciting) to contemplate how many new ideas are lying dormant in already collected information that is now put together in one way and could be rearranged in a better way.[3]

PROFILING THE ENTREPRENEUR

The objective of this section is to summarize and synthesize reams of research and empirical observations to provide an entrepreneurial profile. It does not necessarily follow, however, that one who fits an entrepreneurial profile will become an entrepreneur or that, if he or she does fit the profile, success is guaranteed. Fitting such a profile, however, probably increases the probability of entrepreneurial success, and common sense suggests that emulating this profile is putting everything in favor of would-be entrepreneurs.

Characteristics

A galaxy of personality traits characterize individuals who have a high propensity to behave entrepreneurially. Nine of the more salient ones are listed as follows.

1 *A desire to achieve.* It is safe to say that all entrepreneurs must have a desire to achieve. They all have the push to conquer problems and give birth to a successful venture.

[2]Henry Mintzberg, "Planning on the Left Side and Managing on the Right," *Harvard Business Review*, July–August 1976, pp. 49–58. Summary of this article is used by permission of the *Harvard Business Review*, copyright © 1976 by the President and Fellows of Harvard College; all rights reserved. Also see Jacquelyn Wonder and Priscilla Donovan, *Whole Brain Thinking*, (New York: William Morrow, 1984).

[3]Edward de Bono, *New Think*, (New York: Avon, 1967), copyright © 1967, 1968 by Edward de Bono. Summarized by permission of Basic Books, Inc., New York. Also see De Bono's "Information's Processing and New Ideas—Lateral and Vertical Thinking," *Guide to Creative Action* (New York: Scribner's, 1977).

2 *Hard workers.* Most entrepreneurs are workaholics; they have to be in many instances to achieve their goals.

3 *Nurturing quality.* Entrepreneurs take charge of and watch over a venture until it can stand alone.

4 *Accept responsibility.* Entrepreneurs accept full responsibility for their ventures. They are morally, legally, and mentally accountable.

5 *Reward oriented.* Entrepreneurs want to achieve, work hard, and take responsibility; but they also want to be rewarded handsomely for their efforts. And reward can be other things besides money, such as recognition and respect.

6 *Optimistic.* Entrepreneurs live by the doctrine that this is the best of times and that anything is possible.

7 *Excellence oriented.* Often entrepreneurs desire to achieve something that is outstanding and something that they can be proud of—something that is first-class.

8 *Organizer.* Most entrepreneurs are very good at bringing together all the components of a venture to make it achieve its goals. They are normally thought of as take-charge people.

9 *Money oriented.* As surprising as it may seem, money takes a back seat to the desire to achieve and the nurturing quality. Enterpreneurs want to make a profit, but the profit serves more as a meter to gauge their degree of achievement and performance.

Stereotypes

Richard M. White, Jr., performed a study that summarizes venture capitalists' preconceived opinions on 34 entrepreneurial stereotypes. Venture capitalists like entrepreneurs who are seeking capital to fit this profile before they invest their dollars in them, their ideas, and their capabilities. A summary of this profile follows.[4]

Entrepreneurs grow less tolerant with mediocrity, slowness, inefficiency, and dishonesty as they grow older; and most either quit or have been fired with fireworks from at least two companies. They all have high energy levels. Most have deep interests in the aspects of their lives over which they have control and tend to shun all subjects over which they have no control. All have a high degree of self-confidence, and all religiously follow their own standards. All want to gain control of their own destinies. Approximately half have been divorced. The other half have wives whom they either totally dominate or totally ignore. All are extremely organized, communicate well, and delegate authority well. All are extremely goal directed. All love chal-

[4]A list summarized from Richard M. White, Jr., *The Entrepreneur's Manual* (Radnor, Pa.: Chilton, 1977), pp. 220–24, copyright © 1977 by the author. The material is used with the permission of the publisher Chilton Book Co., Radnor, Pennsylvania.

lenges. Almost all place complete confidence in their fellow founders and support them well. All have an extremely low tolerance level with failure. None will tolerate dishonesties of any nature. Most consider money only as a tool with which to accomplish goals and never as an end in itself. Almost none feel that they need support from their venture capitalist except periodic cash injections. They are true researchers and perpetual students. They are splendid problem solvers. Most average one movie every two years, watch television perhaps an hour a week, and read trade journals perhaps ten hours a week. Many are true introverts. Most do not care if you like them, but they want and command respect. Most do not appreciably change their at-home life-styles. Almost all have excellent references. All show understanding for those who work with them and for them. In college, they probably had two minor jobs and several personal profit centers to keep them in cash. All are fast learners. Almost all had a personal hero from the time they were very young, and they imitated this hero. A large percentage prefer one-to-one sports over team sports. Almost all have a real zest for life. Most consider profits as their essential measurement of performance. All are impatient. They tend to keep their venture capitalist over-informed. Relationships with their venture capitalist do not cease when the business deal ends. Most are stable and likable people.

Tendencies

Characteristics and stereotypes that seem to describe the entrepreneur have just been presented. Tendencies toward entrepreneurial activity provide another way to show one more facet of the entrepreneur (see Fig. 2.1). There is a continuum of entrepreneurial activity, from almost no entrepreneurial tendencies to very strong ones. In this presentation, the laborer is the least entrepreneurial, and the inventrepreneur is the most entrepreneurial. In fact, the inventrepreneur is the epitome of entrepreneurial activity. This special entrepreneur has the ability both to invent a new product or service *and* to bring it successfully to the marketplace. The bureaucrat, lender (bank loan officer), professional, and manager tend to be nonentrepreneurial. The copycat entrepreneur simply imitates someone else's product or service and business. He or she has fairly strong entrepreneurial tendencies except in innovation. The opportunistic entrepreneur has fairly strong overall tendencies toward entrepreneurial activity, especially the tendency toward spotting and exploiting opportunities. Venture capitalists are not entrepreneurs, as such, but are a primary source of equity financing for business ventures, especially for start-ups and early-stage expansion. They have a strong wealth-seeking tendency. Both the innovative entrepreneur and the inventrepreneur have very strong overall tendencies toward entrepreneurial activity.

Generally, this analysis in Figure 2.1 is helpful in calibrating the strength of entrepreneurial activity based on tendencies. Or, putting it another way, if you have tendencies toward entrepreneurial activity as indicated in Figure 2.1 and you are working as a laborer, you may be wasting your time and talent, not to mention the effect on your self-satisfaction and frustration levels.

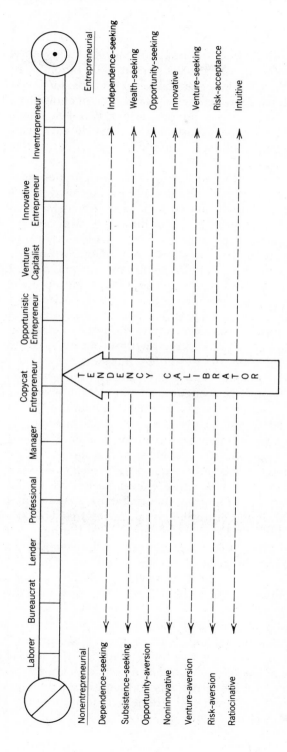

FIGURE 2.1 *Continuum showing tendencies toward nonentrepreneurial or entrepreneurial activity.*

Specifically, if you are independence-seeking, you want to be your own boss and self-governing, not subject to control by others or reliance on others for your livelihood. You are a loner, an individualist, a person who wants to do his or her own thing. You have a strong desire for freedom of choice to make your own decisions. On the other hand, if you are dependent, you welcome influence and control from others. You are more comfortable in a subordinate role. You probably seek institutions and group affiliation. Clearly, these tendencies are anathema to entrepreneurial activity.

One of the key reasons to engage in entrepreneurial activity is to gain wealth. If you strive for wealth, abundance, and the so-called good life, then your tendency is clearly toward entrepreneurship. Subsistence-seeking has no entrepreneurial pull. Here you are interested in the minimum to support life. You work only for basic necessities and are completely satisfied with a day-to-day existence.

Entrepreneurs are alert to unnoticed opportunities. They make it a practice always to be on the lookout for an opportunity and a way to exploit it. People on the other end of the continuum do not look for entrepreneurial opportunities.

The tendency to innovate is a strong propensity to introduce new things, effect change, and broach bold ideas. The person who leans toward the noninnovative end of the continuum is lacking in new thoughts and ideas. A person, however, can become a successful entrepreneur without strong innovative tendencies. Innovation is very desirable but not absolutely imperative. For example, copycat and opportunistic entrepreneurs do not have strong innovative tendencies.

Engaging in entrepreneurial activity, to a large extent, means venturing. So you should have a zeal for the new and a passion for novelty. You should be able to travel an uncharted course. If you abhor routine, are restless, and are drawn to new venture and quests, you have a strong tendency toward entrepreneurial activity. Alternatively, if you automatically say no to almost anything new, thrive on routine, will not leave the tried and true, and are totally satisfied with the status quo, then your inclination toward entrepreneurial activity is weak.

Entering into an entrepreneurial activity is tantamount to accepting risk. Remember that being entrepreneurial means that you are irresistibly drawn to the unknown, the untried, the new quest, and the new venture. Clearly, this means risk. It is the lure of the new and the quest, however, and not the lure of risk. But the entrepreneur will accept risk. The tendency of the nonentrepreneur is toward risk-aversion. He or she is not willing to take a chance or be exposed to loss, especially financial. He or she will not enter the tunnel until a clear light can be seen at the other end.

A great deal of research indicates that persons who engage in entrepreneurial activity are quite logical but also possess ready insight and tend to rely on this insight more than on elaborate quantitative analysis. They tend to have strong instincts and can readily make decisions under uncertainty. On the other hand, the tendency to depend on quantitative analysis and logic alone points away from entrepreneurial activity. The person who is extremely reluctant to guess, to make assumptions, to brainstorm, and to accept anything until all the parameters are known and completely measured is going to feel insecure in venturing.

Of course, nothing is ironclad about the preceding analysis. It simply shows tendencies toward entrepreneurial activity that, in some instances, may be open to debate. For example, people other than entrepreneurs can make decisions under uncertainty, the laborer or the lender, for example. They also can and do bear risk whether they want to or not. Also, in specific cases, people who are on the non-entrepreneurial end of the continuum can overnight move to the entrepreneurial end of the continuum. For example, a laborer can invent a construction tool and develop a successful business venture from it. Or a loan officer can create a new banking service. A manager can open a new market. A physician can develop and introduce a computer-based diagnostic system.

Tools of Self-analysis

The continuum shown in Figure 2.1, helps calibrate your tendencies toward or against entrepreneurial activities. For further self-analysis, refer to Figure 2.2, which includes stereotypes and characteristics. A strong pull toward the left in the tendency continuum and the absence of more than two or three characteristics and more than ten of the stereotypes would imply a low suitability for entrepreneurship. On the other hand, a strong pull toward the right of the continuum, and six to seven characteristics, combined with 20 to 30 stereotypes, indicate a good potential for entrepreneurship.

RISK TO THE ENTREPRENEUR

Generally, people are either risk takers or risk avoiders. In all cases, starting or buying a new business involves risk because money is invested today for profits tomorrow. Usually, the higher the reward, the greater the risk.

Overview of Risk

Few, if any, entrepreneurs have escaped failure. Most have seen the wild beasts of failure trample on their rose garden. Success is, however, not necessarily to the brave, but to the persistent. Persistency does not necessarily lead to success in a world of chance, but it helps. F. A. Woolworth went broke six times with his five-and-dime stores; on the seventh try, he made it. Indeed, persistency will nearly always beat the risk of failure. Adam Osborne, founder of Osborne Computer Corporation, who once met regularly with prime ministers and ambassadors and who was the darling of Silicon Valley, lost it all. He is regrouping his forces and psyche on the software side. His innovative twist is to market software packages

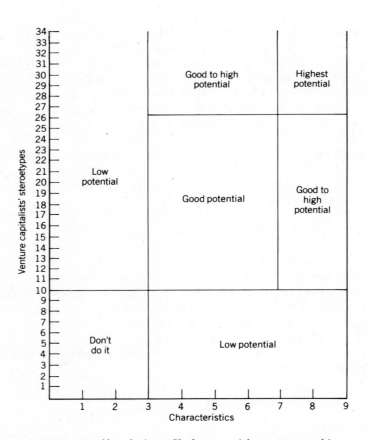

FIGURE 2.2   *A self-analysis profile for potential entrepreneurship.*

through bookstores, not through computer retailers. According to Osborne, software packages should look, feel, and smell like a book.

The worst advice ever given to entrepreneurs are the words of Ralph Waldo Emerson, who said, "Build a better mousetrap, and the world will beat a path to your door." This advice is utter nonsense. The entrepreneur must develop a business plan, develop a prototype, raise capital, put together an organization to manufacture and market the better mousetrap, deliver it, and provide postsale support—all of which involve risk. An enterprise, especially one out of control, can bow your head, break your heart, and scar your soul. It can enslave you to disloyal, complaining customers; incompetent and uncaring workers; vindictive competitors; mercenary bankers; and a complaining, thankless family.

The antithesis of the entrepreneur is a person who never loses because he or she never puts himself or herself at risk. One cannot be criticized for what one writes if one never writes anything. An individual cannot go bankrupt if he or she does not go into business. One must go into the arena to gain victory or suffer defeat. One must jump from the cliff to know the freedom of flight. The hog must root to find the acorn. It is not a taste for risk that is operative but a willingness to accept risk as the inevitable price of satisfying the tendency toward entrepreneuring. Some entrepreneurs are seduced by high-reward, high-risk ventures even if they have to assume the risk of ruin.

Risk Areas

According to Liles,[5] risk covers a multitude of areas, all of which aspiring entrepreneurs should understand. Briefly, these are the four critical risk areas.[6]

1 *Financial risk.*   In most new ventures, the individual puts a significant portion of his or her savings or other resources at stake. This money is risked and will in all likelihood be lost if the venture fails. The entrepreneur may also be required to sign personally on company obligations that far exceed his personal net worth. The entrepreneur, therefore, is exposed to personal bankruptcy. Many people are unwilling to risk their savings, house, property, and salary to start a new business. They are not entrepreneurs at heart.

2 *Career risk.*   A question raised by would-be entrepreneurs is whether or not they will be able to find a job or go back to their old one if their venture should fail. Sometimes reentry is difficult.

3 *Family and social risk.*   Starting a new venture uses most of the energy and time of the entrepreneur. Consequently, his or her other commitments may suffer. Entrepreneurs who are married and especially those with children expose their families to the risks of an incomplete family experience and possibly even to permanent emotional scars from inattention, quarreling, and bitterness. In addition, all friends may vanish because of missed get-togethers.

   On the other hand, starting a new business may afford the opportunity to bring the spouse and children into the business. Old friends may become investors; new friends may be developed because of a widening business and social circle. And the time the entrepreneur does spend with these people will be quality time.

4 *Psychic risk.*   The greatest risk may be to the well-being of the entrepreneur. Money can be replaced; a new house can be built; the spouse, children, and friends can usually adapt as long as they understand what everyone is working

---

[5]Patrick R. Liles, *New Business Ventures and the Entrepreneur* (Homewood, Ill.: Richard D. Irwin, 1974), pp. 14–15. The material is used with permission.

[6]Ibid.

toward. But if you fail, can you live with this failure? The sword cuts from both sides; it is great to win, but some people never recover from defeat.

STRESS ON THE ENTREPRENEUR

Some of the goals that entrepreneurs strive to achieve are independence, wealth, and satisfaction from their work. A study by David P. Boyd and David E. Gumpert[7] of entrepreneurs shows that the successful ones who achieve these goals pay a high price. More than a majority of those surveyed had back problems, indigestion, insomnia, or headaches. To continue to achieve and build on their goals, they are, however, willing to tolerate these results of stress. There seems to be a love-hate phenomenon where the entrepreneur loves what he or she is doing but hates the emotional and physiological effects of doing it, and anxiety and exhilaration run neck and neck through the entrepreneurial experience. The rewards of being an entrepreneur, stresses that the entrepreneur is under in achieving these rewards, and ways to cope with this stress are treated in this section.

Benefits of Ownership

As Boyd and Gumpert point out, for entrepreneurs who survive the start-up stage, the financial and psychological rewards can be great. The respondents to their study indicate two quite positive aspects of business ownership.[8]

1 *Financial rewards.* Nearly three fourths of the respondents earn more than $40,000 annually; 59 percent over $50,000; and 20 percent, over $100,000. Moreover, going into business offers the *opportunity* to create substantial and profitable financial enterprises.[9]

2 *Psychic rewards.* Independence and freedom of decision making were among the benefits the entrepreneurs mentioned most frequently.[10] A survey conducted by Chemical Bank indicated that the most compelling reason for going into business was to gain the freedom of being one's own boss.[11] Many respondents declared that they wanted control of their future, and they didn't want to be subservient to a godfather. The need to achieve was also very high on their list.

[7]David P. Boyd and David E. Gumpert. "Coping With Entrepreneurial Stress," *Harvard Business Review,* March–April 1983, pp. 44–64. A summary of this article is reprinted by permission of the *Harvard Business Review,* copyright © 1983 by the President and Fellows of Harvard College; all rights reserved.
[8]Ibid.
[9]Ibid.
[10]Ibid.
[11]"Chemical Bank Finds Small Business Optimistic," *The Market Chronicle,* October 13, 1983, p. 7. The material is used with permission.

Sources of Stress

In their study, Boyd and Gumpert identified four causes of stress.[12]

1 *Loneliness.*   Though entrepreneurs are usually surrounded by others—employees, customers, accountants, and lawyers—they are isolated from persons in whom they can confide. Long hours at work prevent entrepreneurs from seeking the comfort and counsel of friends and family members. Moreover, they tend not to participate in social activities unless there is some business benefit.

2 *Immersion in business.*   One of the great ironies of being in business is that successful entrepreneurs make enough money to partake of a variety of leisure activities, but they cannot take that exotic trip or vacation because their business will not allow their absence. Most entrepreneurs are married to their business; they work long hours; they have little time for civic organizations, recreation, or further education.

3 *People problems.*   Being your own boss is not quite the way it works because the entrepreneur must depend on and work with partners, employees, customers, bankers, and professionals. Most entrepreneurs experience great frustration, disappointment, and aggravation in their experience with these people. Because of irreconcilable conflict with partners, many partnerships are dissolved. Successful entrepreneurs are to some extent perfectionists and know how they want things done; often they spend a lot of time trying to get lackadaisical, incompetent employees to perform and make it happen. One entrepreneur seemed to summarize the whole work-ethic and people-problem malaise by saying, "I know in advance other people are going to disappoint me. If you don't expect too much from them, then you're delighted. You're surprised, if by chance they do well."[13]

4 *The need to achieve.*   Achievement brings satisfaction. In the course of the Boyd and Gumpert study, it became clear to them that a fine line, however, exists between attempting to achieve too much and failing to achieve enough. More often than not, the entrepreneur was trying to accomplish too much. Many are never satisfied with the job that they have done no matter how well it was done. They seem to recognize the dangers (e.g., health) of unbridled ambition but have a rough time tempering their achievement need; if they stop or slow down, some competitor is going to run up their back, and everything they have built will fall apart. At least, this is what they think.

Another source of stress that could be added to the preceding list was presented in the Chemical Bank study as a main local problem that could be called government

---

[12]Boyd and Gumpert, op. cit.
[13]Ibid.

and infrastructure problems. As Chemical Bank's respondents see it, crime, followed by lack of affordable commercial space and neighborhood cleanliness and by traffic congestion and parking, deteriorating neighborhoods, and lack of local government support are problems that cause a great deal of consternation and stress. These entrepreneurs simply do not believe that governments—county, state, and federal—are doing a good job fostering a healthy climate for small businesses.[14]

Coping Mechanisms

Boyd and Gumpert made a significant contribution in defining causes of stress, but what makes their study complete is the presentation of stress-reduction techniques, ways by which entrepreneurs can improve the quality of their business and personal lives. They acknowledge the classical stress-reduction techniques, such as transcendental meditation, biofeedback, muscle relaxation, and regular exercise.

Although such methods are probably helpful in reducing stress, Boyd and Gumpert suggest that another step entrepreneurs can take is to clarify the causes of their stress. Given the causes, entrepreneurs can combat excessive stress first by acknowledging its existence, second by developing coping mechanisms, and third by probing their unacknowledged needs. Boyd and Gumpert state that the search for causes of stress might begin with the four areas of vulnerability that their survey uncovered—loneliness, business immersion, people problems, and obsessiveness about the need to achieve. They, of course, recognize that additional factors may be at work, including family conflicts and financial difficulties. Following are ways that entrepreneurs can cope with these causes:

1 *Networking.*   One way to relieve the loneliness of running a business is to share experiences with other business owners. The objectivity gained from hearing about the triumphs and errors of others is itself therapeutic.

2 *Getting away from it all.*   The best antidote to immersion in business, said those entrepreneurs interviewed, is a good holiday. If vacation days or weeks are limited by valid business constraints, short breaks may still be possible. Such interludes allow a measure of self-renewal.

3 *Communicating with subordinates.*   Entrepreneurs are in close contact with subordinates and can readily assess the concerns of their staffs. The personal touches often unavailable in large corporations, such as companywide outings, flexible hours, and small loans to tide workers over until payday, are possible. In this setting, employees may often be more productive than their counterparts in large organizations.

4 *Finding satisfaction outside the company.*   Countering obsessiveness in the need to achieve can be difficult because the entrepreneur's personality is inextricably bound up in the fabric of the company. Entrepreneurs need to get away from the

---

[14]"Chemical Bank Finds Small Business Optimistic," op. cit.

business occasionally and become more passionate about life itself; they need to gain some other perspectives.

5 *Delegating.*   To implement the coping mechanisms requires time to implement. Therefore, the entrepreneur is going to have to delegate tasks. Entrepreneurs find this difficult because they think they have to be at the business all the time and involved in every task and operation. If delegation is to save time and thus relieve stress, appropriate delegates must be found and trained.

BIG CORPORATIONS' USE OF ENTREPRENEURS

Large corporations soon become risk-averting and cautious and are run, not by innovating entrepreneurs, but by bureaucratic committees. These bureaucratized giants eliminate the entrepreneur and replace him or her with cautious and conservative managers who are, at best, maintainers. Therefore, the most discouraging fact of life in these corporations is the loss of the very thing that made them big and successful in the first place. Many of the well-managed, progressive companies, however, are doing everything they can to encourage entrepreneurship and make it thrive within the corporate structure.

The Classic Scenario

Many bright, young people who possess many of the entrepreneurial characteristics already discussed go into large corporations with expectations of doing great things. Soon these expectations collide with the bureaucratic corporate culture that discourages, squelches, and even ostracizes these innovative, motivated people. They are ignored, shelved, or fired, and the corporation consequently loses one of its most valuable resources of new business development and growth.

The corporations begin to drift; their revenue shrinks; the bureaucratic management panics; consultants are called in. The consultants' prescription is to get back on a growth track by acquiring other companies. Buyouts and takeovers are made, some hostile, requiring protracted litigation and management attention. Finally, the takeovers are brought into the bureaucratic conglomerate, and the acquisition plans are achieved, but the goal of real growth and profitability are not. Consultants are brought in again. The recommendations, this time, are to divest, become lean and mean. Soon, the company divests itself of the acquisitions, but the old problems still remain.

Meanwhile, the bright, innovative people who were squeezed out have started their own companies and are highly successful because they offer products and services that consumers want and need. So the corporations that threw out their brains and innovators helped create their competitors. Even in smaller companies, entrepreneurs often leave and start their own businesses more from feeling victimized by former employers than from seizing a business opportunity.

Entrepreneurs in Corporations

A number of large corporations are trying to recruit and groom entrepreneurs, called "intrapreneurs," to breathe innovation back into the company. These companies are looking for people who do more than think of new things to do, but actually do new things; people who have the guts to take the responsibility for converting the idea from the mind to the marketplace. There are usually a lot of ideas floating around any organization, but ideas are useless unless put to use. The intrapreneur is the one who does this through innovation and looking at products, services, and markets with a fresh eye.

Intrapreneurs damn the bureaucracy and take full responsibility for maneuvering their projects through the organization, out the door, and into the marketplace. These people are highly decentralized and are given a great deal of autonomy. They get full support from a venture team. The intrapreneur is not a blue-sky dreamer or an intellectual giant. He or she may even be a product-service idea thief or may be impatient and egotistical. But most of all, such people get the job done. And when they do, they are feted in style with lights flashing and big rewards.

SUMMARY

Innovation is necessary to reap entrepreneurial profit. In some instances, innovation may be revolutionary; in other instances, it may be nothing more than adding a minor twist to an old product or service. Most entrepreneurs perform better when innovating and starting new ventures; they normally do not make good managers, especially those managers who are caught up in a lot of detail work and committee meetings. A study of entrepreneurs indicates that they do much of their thinking from the right side of their brain with governing influences from the left.

Furthermore, entrepreneurs show many other characteristics, such as a need for achievement, desire for responsibility, preference for risk, stimulation by feedback, being hard workers, being future oriented, being excellence oriented, and having skill in organizing and getting the job done.

Venture capitalists have a better chance to observe the actions of entrepreneurs and have formed some strong opinions as to how entrepreneurs conduct themselves. Stereotypes most often mentioned by these venture capitalists include being easily frustrated; high energy levels; being in control; self-confidence; loving challenges; being intolerant of dishonesty, incompetency, and triviality; treating money as a tool; studying and keeping on top of things; low entertainment need; striving with success to gain others' respect and usually being fast learners; expecting professionalism from others; being competitive; seeking sound, close business relationships.

People seem to have or develop tendencies toward entrepreneurial activity, which include independence-seeking, wealth-seeking, opportunity-seeking, innovation-searching, venture-seeking, risk-accepting and intuition-deciding. Such tendencies indicate a strong pull to initiate the entrepreneurial process.

Entrepreneurship doesn't always result in fun and glory. One drawback to becoming an entrepreneur is the constant presence of risk. There are four areas of risk: financial, career, family and social, and psychic. Also, success breeds stress, which comes from loneliness, total immersion in business activities, people problems, and the constant need to achieve. Ways to cope with this stress include networking, getting away from it all, communicating with subordinates, finding other forms of satisfaction outside the business, and delegating.

Many progressive corporations are trying either to hire or develop internally people who can work as entrepreneurs within the corporate structure. Through extreme decentralization and autonomy, these organizations are trying to recapture the entrepreneurship that got them started in the first place.

ASSIGNMENT

1 Interview at least one person who has started a business and, if possible, a member of this person's family. Take about an hour to gather insights into the entrepreneur's rationale for starting and owning a business. Also, determine his or her background and view of risks, rewards, and pitfalls; goals; and personal characteristics. Find what the single biggest problem was in getting started. What are personal qualities that stand out? What motivated this person to become an entrepreneur? What particular skills does this person possess? What are the three or four most important things in this person's life? In what ways, if at all, did this person's family or life situation influence his or her career decision and ability to become successful? What conflicts did he or she face? What roadblocks or setbacks did he or she have to overcome? Outside his or her family, who helped the entrepreneur most in getting started? How many hours does he or she put in each week now and when he or she first started?

2 You are planning on investing $10,000, one half your net worth, in a new venture. What are some of the characteristics you *want* and *not want* the entrepreneur starting this new venture to have?

3 Assume you are planning to marry an entrepreneur. What would be your expectations of your spouse concerning such things as hours of work, income, raising children, time with children, household duties, vacations, amount of business travel, time at home, and association with the opposite sex?

4 Complete the sentence: I would/would not like to start/buy my own business someday because _____

_____

5 Using Figures 2.1 and 2.2, rate your potential of becoming an entrepreneur. Summarize your strengths and weaknesses.

6 What do you find least appealing about being an entrepreneur? What do you find most appealing?

7 Explain why corporations are trying to hire entrepreneurs? Do you see a paradox in an entrepreneur working in a corporation? Explain.

BIBLIOGRAPHY

Ballas, George C., and David Hollas. *The Making of An Entrepreneur—Keys to Success*. Englewood Cliffs, N.J.: Prentice-Hall, 1980.

Baty, Gordon B. *Entrepreneurship for the Eighties*. Reston, Va.: Reston, a Prentice-Hall company, 1981.

Boyd, David P., and David E. Gumpert. "Coping with Entrepreneurial Stress." *Harvard Business Review*. March–April 1983.

Brandt, Steven C. *Entrepreneuring*. Reading, Mass.: Addison-Wesley, 1982.

Casson, Mark. *The Entrepreneur*. Totowa, N.J.: Barnes & Noble, 1982.

"Chemical Bank Finds Small Business Optimistic." *The Market Chronicle*. October 13, 1983.

De Bono, Edward. "Information Processing and New Ideas—Lateral Vertical Thinking." *Guide to Creative Action*. New York: Scribner's, 1977.

———. *New Think*. New York: Avon, 1967.

Dible, Donald M., ed. *Winning the Money Game*. Santa Clara, Calif.: Entrepreneurial Press, 1975.

Dolan, Carrie. "Bushnell Resigns Pizza Time Post; Kennan is Named." *The Wall Street Journal*. February, 2, 1984.

Liles, Patrick R. *New Business Ventures and the Entrepreneur*. Homewood, Ill.: Richard D. Irwin, 1974.

Mancuso, Joseph R. "What Drives the Entrepreneur? And Do You Have It in You?" *Across the Board*. July–August 1984.

McClelland, David C. *The Achieving Society*. New York: The Free Press, 1961.

———, and David Winter. *Motivating Economic Achievement*. New York: The Free Press, 1971.

Mintzberg, Henry. "Planning on the Left Side and Managing on the Right." *Harvard Business Review*. July–August 1976.

Peters, Thomas J., and Robert H. Waterman, Jr. "Corporate Chariots of Fire." *Across the Board*. May 1983.

———, and ———. *In Search of Excellence: Lessons from America's Best Run Companies*. New York: Harper & Row, 1982.

Ronen, Joshua, ed. *Entrepreneurship*. Lexington, Mass.: D.C. Heath, 1982.

Schollhammer, Hans, and Arthur H. Kuriloff. *Entrepreneurship and Small Business Management*. New York: Wiley, 1979.

Schumpeter, Joseph A. *Business Cycles*. Vol. I. New York and London: McGraw-Hill, 1939.

Timmons, Jeffry A., Leonard E. Smollen, and Alexander L. M. Dingee, Jr. *New Venture Creation—A Guide to Small Business Development*. Homewood, Ill.: Richard D. Irwin, 1977.

White, Richard M., Jr. *The Entrepreneur's Manual*. Radnor, Pa.: Chilton, 1977.

Wilken, Paul H. *Entrepreneurship—A Comparative and Historical Study*. Norwood, N.J.: ABLEX, 1979.

Wonder, Jacquelyn, and Priscilla Donovan. *Whole-Brain Thinking*. New York: William Morrow, 1984.

PART TWO

PRODUCT-SERVICE CREATION AND EVALUATION

CHAPTER 3

Product-Service Ideas

INTRODUCTION

Every successful business was a product-service idea in the beginning. This chapter gives some guidance in developing product-service ideas and suggestions on how to make them survive in an inconstant marketplace and a hard-boiled, sophisticated competitive arena. Specifically, the objectives of this chapter are as follows.

1 To show how changing relationships, needs, and wants create a demand for new products and services and to present the characteristics of successful ones.
2 To present sources of new product-service ideas.
3 To describe ways to generate new product-service ideas.
4 To discuss ways to help product-service ideas survive in the marketplace.

ANALYSIS OF PRODUCT-SERVICE IDEAS

A market-driven economy is always calling for new products and services. The rapidly shifting economy is producing an array of opportunities for new businesses fueled by new needs and wants of consumers stemming from increased affluence, leisure time, growth, and life-style changes.

Need and Want—The Twin Mothers of Invention

Not everybody needs an ice-cream sandwich with chocolate chips embedded around the edges, but if you had "invented" this junk food delight, it would have made you a small fortune because a lot of people wanted them (they are called Chipwich in New York) when they hit the market. Carry-on luggage is something that a lot of travelers needed but didn't really want. However, because of bitter experiences with lost luggage caused by incompetent, don't-give-a-damn baggage handlers, many travelers felt it necessary to buy luggage that was designed to carry a lot of personal belongings in one package that could be taken on the plane without too much difficulty.

Opportunities abound for identifying new needs and wants for new markets. Growth and change create these needs and wants, and filling them, in turn, creates change that stimulates even further growth. Table 3.1 suggests some typical interacting influences among growth, change, and needs.

A Few Examples

Many examples of products or services can be cited based on a clear perception of a need or want that requires fulfillment. These range from simple to complex, from inexpensive to costly, from serious to comical, and from significant to trivial.

For years, animal scientists have developed ways to breed animals artificially

TABLE 3.1
Relationship of Growth, Change, and Needs

Typical Areas of Growth	Areas of Change	Typical Areas of Change	New Needs	Typical New Needs	Growth Areas
Population	Urban living Youth markets Housing Privacy	Employment	Higher skills— more training Retraining Labor saving	Waste disposal	Creation of by-products New processing methods Recycling
Service industries	Travel Education Entertainment	Developing countries	Food supplements Know-how Training	More hygienic environment	Antismog devices Antipollution measures for water sewage disposal
Personal income	Use of disposable income Swimming pools Second homes Recreation	Raw materials	Use of less scarce materials Synthetics Ecological preservation and renewal	Personal safety	Burglar alarms Nonlethal personal, protective weapons Safety devices Limited access devices
Life span	Health services Retirement facilities Activities for senior citizens			New sources of energy	Solar energy technology Geothermal energy technology
Knowledge	Continuing education Educational methods Information storage and retrieval Liberty methods			Energy-saving devices	High efficiency fuel atomizer Engine knock sensor to increase fuel economy of automobiles

Source: Hans Schollhammer and Arthur H. Kuriloff, *Entrepreneurship and Small Business Management* (New York: Wiley, 1979), p. 44. This material is used with permission.

and transfer embryos from donor to recipient. Work is being done now to assign sex to embryos, that is, breed for male or female. In recent years, human medical personnel have begun using this same technology to produce "test-tube" babies. Many spin-offs will occur from this field of genetic engineering and artificial breeding, especially when these related fields are combined. Many entrepreneurs are already beginning to "see" the opportunities.

On the low-tech or no-tech side, a traveling businessperson who stayed in countless motels, through personal experiences, saw the need for motel rooms with adequate lighting and sufficient work space to do paperwork and set up a computer terminal. Based on this fundamental need, this businessperson started a motel chain that caters to traveling businesspeople and provides them with the facilities to meet their needs for proper lighting and work space. This service differentiation made this man millions.

There are many needs not only in products and services but also in packaging. Innovations in packaging include French's switch from a tapered jar to one with straight sides. After 61 years and a lot of customer complaints about the difficulty of removing all the mustard from the tapered jar, some smart person got the bright idea to switch. Many other packaging innovations are coming out almost daily. Dairy products can be placed on shelves without refrigeration. In the past, nearly all products were contained in packages that cost more than the product; that is, the customer was actually buying the package and getting the contents "free." Also, special handling, maintenance, and processing tacked on more costs to the consumer. The aim of innovative packaging and handling is to cross over the line so that the consumer is paying for the product with negligible costs for the package.

Simple product innovations include the erasable pen, especially the kinds with quality writing ability that sell for less than a dollar. Another breakthrough is the nutcracker that uses pneumatically fired, reusable bullets to shatter the shell without breaking the meat. The savings to the nut industry, especially for pecans, walnuts, and filberts, is expected to be tens of millions of dollars.

For the parents who buy toys for their children and see the toys destroyed or forgotten in a day or two, some entrepreneurs have opened toybraries. For example, Jerice Bergstrom and her husband run a toybrary out of a clapboard house in Norwich, Vermont. They put about $70,000 in their Toybrary with about 1000 lendable toys. These include such children's and adult's amusements as teeter-totters, board games, home computers, telescopes, a potter's wheel, and a grand piano. Members pay $60 a year to borrow items for three weeks at a time. The Bergstrom's predict their toybrary will become profitable with about 700 members. Normal wear and tear is expected on most items, but a few costly ones require a $100 deposit and extra rental. Borrowers provide their own transportation.

Because of the number of women today who have children and also work, there is a crying need for thousands of day-care centers.[1] In fact, the changing patterns of

[1]Sabin Russell, "Being Your Own Boss in America", *Venture*, May 1984, p. 40. Copyright © 1984 Venture Magazine, Inc., 521 Fifth Avenue, New York, N.Y. 10175. By special permission.

work in America provide many entrepreneurial opportunities in clothing, personal services, transportation, and food just to name a few.

Other entrepreneurs take traditional, small retail businesses to where the traffic is. For example, many entrepreneurs move from the Frost Belt to Florida and open gift shops, women's and men's stores, and service businesses (e.g., hairdressers). They open these businesses in hot resort areas such as Naples, Marco Island, Miami Beach, Sanibel, Fort Myers, Tampa, and so forth. They don't make much money, and, in some cases, their downside risk is big, but they look at profits as including sun, fun, and a relaxed life-style.

Taking something that is well established, possibly even to the point of decline, and significantly differentiating it from others often works wonders. For example, up until a few years ago, most junk dealers were viewed as pretty crude, low-life "business" people. But Gary Blonder of Newington, Connecticut, is changing that image. He is a junkyard tycoon and is making big profits by simply reshaping and renovating a seedy old business, once his father's 15-acre junkyard, into a well-managed emporium of clean, tested auto parts. Customers can now shop for these parts in a well-lighted, supermarket atmosphere rather than wade around in weeds and mud looking for that scarce part. Blonder also uses computers and telephone hot lines to locate and sell hard-to-get parts.

The entrepreneur who develops the first marketable gopher house (under-ground house) with a proved resale value is going to make millions. To decrease costs, some are using old boxcars for the main structure. Resale potential of these houses, however, is open to question.

A big backlog of postwar science is now maturing, hungering for application in commercial products. Plowing through the gadgets and black boxes developed back then provides a virtual gold mine of ideas for new business enterprises.

To reiterate, developing something new and making a success of it is based on satisfying a need or want. Apparently, George Lucas, the driving force behind the *Star Wars* trilogy, understood the want of boys 6 to 12 years old who make up the majority of the *Star Wars* market segment. When they are 13, their interests take other forms.

Anyway, Lucas was able to combine whizbang, high-tech special effects with good-triumphing-over-evil themes to provide a "new" source of entertainment. His third movie of the *Star Wars* trilogy, *Return of the Jedi*, along with his toy spin-offs, is suppose to gross over $1 billion. Because the main market segment is from 6 to 12 years of age, you can rest assured that another *Star Wars* movie will be produced in about 3 years to capture another cluster of the "automatic audience" and another billion or so dollars.

Marvin Minsky, who is something of a philosopher, says, "In the future, there will be only one industry: entertainment." This statement may seem outrageous, but it has more than a little truth in it. Nolan Bushnell says, "The only intelligent business to be in is the fun business." Based on this assumption, he aims to provide an alternative to the public school system. What this alternative will be is anybody's guess. Certainly, one wonders because he predicted that the personal robot will take the place of the family dog, being able to fetch the newspaper, guard the house, watch and amuse the kids, all without fleas, feeding, or housebreaking.[2]

Characteristics of Successful Product-Service Ideas

A successful business idea should have most, if not all, of the following characteristics.[3]

1 It should have a relative advantage over existing products or services. For example, the innovation allows one to perform a task in less time.

2 The innovation must be compatible with existing attitudes and beliefs. It shouldn't require a drastic change in the buyer's behavior.

3 It shouldn't be so complex that the buyer has a difficult time understanding how to use it.

4 The results or benefits of the innovation must be easily communicable to potential users.

5 It is helpful if the innovation is divisible, which means that users can try the innovation without incurring a large risk. The distribution of samples, or trial users, would allow potential buyers to use the innovation without risking a purchase.

6 The innovation must be readily available for purchase once the buyer decides to make a purchase.

7 The buyer must also believe that the innovation satisfies one of his or her needs by giving some immediate benefit.

SOURCES OF PRODUCT-SERVICE IDEAS

Sources of product-service ideas are virtually everywhere. Some come from formal publications, private groups, and government agencies; others stem from internal analysis after proper observation, study, and stimulation are made.

Internal Sources

According to Schollhammer and Kuriloff, every person stores knowledge over the years. This knowledge is composed of data of various kinds: ideas, concepts, principles, images, and facts. These internal resources are used as follows: First, the

[2]Richard A. Shaffer, "Robots Become More Mobile as Navigational Hurdles Fall," *The Wall Street Journal*, May 18, 1984, p. 29. This material is used with permission.

[3]Everett M. Rogers and Floyd Shoemaker, *Communication of Innovations* (New York: The Free Press, 1971), pp. 50–51. This material is used with permission.

concept is analyzed until it is sharply defined, including outlining problems that need to be solved. Next, the memory is searched to find similarities and elements that seem related to the concept and its problems. Finally, these elements are recombined in new and useful ways to solve the problems and make the basic concept practicable.

The creative act demands work from both sides of the brain. The idea is allowed to surface in the right side, and then the left side subjects it to careful scrutiny and critical analysis. A "new" idea is often nothing but another combination of existing ideas. New information about something combined with knowledge that an individual has is the mulling over or analysis stage. Many people give up at this stage because they begin to develop a feeling of hopelessness owing to roadblocks and frustration. But frustration is good; in fact, one should analyze to a point of total frustration and then go off and do something else. The conscious state should be given a rest from the problem, and the subconscious should be allowed to take over. More often than not, one will receive a burst of illumination from one's subconscious, sometimes when one least expects it. Remember, though, for this scheme to work, a person must get worked up over a problem to begin with; just to sit passively around and wait for a business idea to pop into one's head won't get the job done.

Maxwell Maltz[4] states that the subconscious mind is a goal-striving servomechanism consisting of a brain and a nervous system that the mind directs. The inner mechanism is impersonal and will work automatically to achieve goals that the individual sets for it. It must, however, have a clearly defined goal before it will go to work. Give it a concrete goal, and it will literally move heaven and earth to reach that goal.

External Sources

Opportunities are like seeds in the wind, and entrepreneurs are always prepared to capture a good seed, plant it, and nurture it until it takes root and thrives. Examples of sources of these idea seeds follow.[5]

1 Newspapers, trade journals, and professional publications tell about trends in social usage, changing customs, and developments in specific fields of activity.

2 Specialty magazines address particular interests such as sports, camping, food, fashion, and hobbies.

3 Trade shows, fairs, and exhibitions display new products and innovations in processes and services.

4 Government agencies provide information on patents open to public use.

---

[4]Maxwell Maltz, *Psycho-Cybernetics*, (North Hollywood, Calif.: Wilshire, 1975). Copyright © 1960 by Prentice-Hall, Inc., Englewood Cliffs, New Jersey 07682. The material is used by permission of the publisher.

[5]Schollhammer and Kuriloff, *op. cit.*, pp. 28–29. This material is used with permission.

5 Patent brokers furnish information on patents or patentable ideas that may be bought for commercial use.

6 Consumer groups may be brought together for open discussion of a potential product or service.

7 In a going concern, the members of the company can be encouraged to propose concepts worthy of commercial development.

The U.S. government is one of the largest suppliers of technical information. Moreover, it provides grants and loans to entrepreneurs as well as educational literature and seminars.

First, you can obtain a list of approximately 300,000 booklets and pamphlets on a wide variety of subjects by writing to the superintendent of documents, Washington, D.C. 20230. From this list you can order any pamphlet you think might prove helpful. There are also some other departments that you will find useful.

The Library of Congress offers services that can be extremely helpful. The National Referral Center, for example, offers a free service that will find you a free expert on any topic—an expert who can answer one or more questions better than probably any referral source. Write to National Referral Center, Science and Technology Division, The Library of Congress, Washington, D.C. 20540. In addition, the National Referral Center Resource File will provide the names and addresses of organizations willing to provide scientific, technical, and sociological information.

The Food Consumption Research Group, Agricultural Research Service, U.S. Department of Agriculture (USDA), 377 Federal Building, 60505 Belcrest Road, Hyattsville, Md. 20782, conducts studies and issues reports on the kinds and amounts of food consumed by households.

In addition, each fall, the Department of Agriculture sponsors a free four-day conference you may attend (contact the department for the exact date), where agricultural experts expound on food prices, land use, family characteristics, and other subjects. Copies of the proceedings are available free. Contact the USDA, ESCS Publication Service, Room 0054, South Building, Washington, D.C. 20250.

The Bureau of Economic Analysis, Department of Commerce, Washington, D.C. 20230, publishes a *Survey of Current Business Conditions*, a *Business Conditions Digest*, a bulletin entitled *Measuring and Analyzing the U.S. Economy*, and other publications. The Bureau of Domestic Business Development, Department of Commerce, has many experts who can supply information on specific industries.

The Small Business Administration (SBA), 1441 L St., N.W., Washington, D.C. 20416, will provide a computer literature search of the research and development of other agencies. The SBA publishes pamphlets about various types of retail businesses and conducts seminars and small-business courses for anyone interested. The agency also makes loans to businesses under certain conditions. For information on any of these activities, contact the Small Business Administration at the preceding address.[6]

---

[6]The sources are from Duane Newcomb, *Fortune-building Secrets of the Rich* (West Nyack, N.Y.: Parker, 1983), pp. 59–61 and are used with permission.

License rights, distributorships, and joint ventures are available for a wide array of new products in agriculture, the automotive and chemical industries, computer technology, electrotechnology, energy, industrial equipment, and other industries. A superb source for this information is *International New Product Newsletter*, Six Saint James Avenue, Boston, Massachusetts 02116 (phone: 617-426-6647).

A vast number of inventions are available for licensing in the fields of mechanical equipment, chemistry, nuclear technology, biology and medicine, metallurgy, electrotechnology, instruments, optics and lasers, ordnance, and food technology. A leading source of this information is *Government Inventions for Licensing, An Abstract Newsletter*, from the U.S. Department of Commerce, National Technical Information Service, 5285 Port Royal Road, Springfield, Va. 22161.

In your own community, there is a wide variety of sources that you can use. The local chamber of commerce can provide you with a list of businesses that exist and may be able to indicate local needs. Moreover, many business people are willing to give you advice and direction even if you plan to compete with them.

Newcomb[7] gives the following good advice about bankers. Many bankers possess a surprising amount of business knowledge and can answer such questions as how big a population base is needed to support a successful drugstore, bookstore, or florist's shop; the minimum amount of capital needed to open any of these; which local shopping center offers the best location for a particular business; and dozens of other questions. Some banks have experts on retailing, mail order, agriculture, and similar subjects. Others publish monthly newsletters or bulletins that offer useful business information.

To tap this source, write down the financial or business question that needs an answer, go to your local bank, and tell the manager you are considering going into business and would like to ask a few questions. Most bank managers will be glad to help you. Others will refer you to one of the bank's other experts.

METHODS OF GENERATING PRODUCT-SERVICE IDEAS

A number of authorities have devised methods to get the "creative juices stirring" to help an aspiring entrepreneur generate viable business ideas. Some of these methods are presented now.

Market Gap Analysis

Market gap analysis is a powerful method used to uncover areas in the market in which the needs and wants far exceed the supply.[8] This method has a hopper or

---

[7]Ibid., pp. 61–62.

[8]This section on market gap analysis is summarized from Richard M. White, Jr., *The Entrepreneur's Manual* (Radnor, Pa.: Chilton, 1977), copyright © 1977 by the author. This material is used with the permission of the publisher, Chilton Book Co., Radnor, Pennsylvania.

gathering effect of converting everyday information into bunches of lucrative product and service gaps that few have thought of before. A condensed version of how gap analysis works follows.

1 *Step 1.* Lay out your objectives as your reference point. For example, say that your broadbrush objectives are these.

   (a) You want to address a long-term growth industry (in this example, the leisure industry).
   (b) You want to manufacture a low-tech product for this industry.
   (c) You want a minimum of a 20 to 1 markup.
   (d) You want a minumum market potential of 1 million units per year.
   (e) You want no viable competition immediately.
   (f) You want a new product but do not want the pioneering efforts that many new products require. In other words, you want immediate customer acceptance.
   (g) You want to sell through already existing sales networks. You want these networks to stock enough (on their dollars) so that no front money is required for your company.
   (h) You want a minimum of six different venture capital avenues open to you. You want to give the image of a growth company.
   (i) You want to produce a low-technology product that can be produced by a minimum of 12 jobbers (manufacturers who produce for other firms) in your area. You will develop in-house capabilities when sales and profits warrant it.

2 *Step 2.* Segment your industry into its major components. The following examples show several ways to segment the leisure industry.

   (a) Adult—children—family
   (b) Male—female—both
   (c) Active—passive—combination of both
   (d) Spring—summer—winter—fall
   (e) Economic levels
   (f) Educational levels
   (g) Ethnic groups, and so on

3 *Step 3.* In step 3, follow the first leg of the first segment, and explore only adults. Segment each of the major components of step 2 into its major subsegments. For example, the major subsegments of the *leisure—adult* segment can be divided into the following.

   (a) Workdays
   (b) Weekends
   (c) Vacation
   (d) Retirement
   (e) Holidays
   (f) Other

4 *Step 4.* Segment the major subsegments of step 3 into their minor subsegments. For example, following on the *leisure—adult—workdays* leg, the minor subsegments are these.
  (a) Postwork/predinner
  (b) Dinner
  (c) Postdinner/prebed
  (d) Bed
  (e) Awake/prework
  (f) Coffee breaks
  (g) Lunch periods
  (h) Others

You'll note that so far the work has been to focus, magnify, refocus, remagnify, refocus again, remagnify again,—until the large growth industry is divided into handleable portions. An industry like the leisure industry is so large that you cannot begin to see it until you segment it down to its subsections. You are now just beginning to see the trees in the forest. The more complex an industry is, the more you have to divide, redivide, and reredivide.

5 *Step 5.* Eliminate those areas that do not meet your specifications outlined in step 1.

6 *Step 6.* List the problems that exist in each area of step 4. There are hundreds, but, for example, some of the problems of *leisure—adult—workdays, postwork/predinner* are these.
  (a) When work ends, people are tired.
  (b) Traffic frustrations are encountered on the way home from work.
  (c) Feet are hot and tired.
  (d) Clothes are rumpled, seem to cling, and are uncomfortable.
  (e) Wife or husband is tired and grouchy.
  (f) People experience postwork blahs.
  (g) Grocery store seems crowded and slow.
  (h) Parents must shout at children to get them in for their baths.
  (i) People who have dogs must walk and curb them.
  (j) Perhaps the dog is female and in heat, and every stray mutt within a mile is making passes.
  (k) Predinner cocktails are needed to unwind.
  (l) The TV news is depressing.
  (m) Lawn needs mowing; garden, weeding; roses have to be clipped; and so on.
  (n) Kids are grouchy and hungry.
  (o) Dinner preparations are slow, noisy, and smelly.
  (p) Telephone solicitors are irritating.

Now list these problems along the left-hand side of a work sheet, leaving ample room on the right for evaluations.

7 *Step 7.* Eliminate those problem areas whose solutions do not conform to objectives defined in step 1. For example, retain only (c), (h), and (j) for our example.

8 *Step 8.* On the sheet of paper in which you listed the problem areas along the left-hand side, along the top, place the numbers of your objectives in step 1.Place a check mark in each column where the solution to the problem would meet your requirements.

9 *Step 9.* Along the far right-hand side of your work sheet, list probable solutions to each of the problems. For example, *leisure—adult—workday, postwork/pre-dinner* items (c), (h), and (j) generate the following solutions:

(c) *Feet are hot and tired*. Approximately every adult who must stand or walk on concrete complains of this problem. Consider a pair of comfortable slippers with a vibrator to massage the feet as a person relaxes after work. Each slipper, of course, would be battery operated so that the wearer could walk without electrical cords. This gap should be explored further.

(h) *Parents must shout at children*. Have you ever noticed that even the most petite and feminine wife sounds like a baseball umpire when she tries to catch Junior's attention to come in for his evening bath? And how women hate this task! Consider an electrical chime (or whistle) whose volume can be varied to beckon Junior even five blocks away. You could allow each woman customer to program her own 10-bar tune so that her call is unique from all others. Or use a beeper.

(j) *Walking dog*. Consider, if you will, an electronic chastity belt that will allow the female dog to perform her usual body functions but will keep amorous males at bay.

10 *Step 10.* Select the best gap or gaps, and begin verifying them in testing. Will they sell, or are you chasing mirages?

Observation

Find a new value or use by looking at things differently; look for put-togethers; look for holes in the marketplace; look for once-successful products and services for recycling; look for new ways to do something. Hop in your car, take a trip, and look at what is being done in other parts of the country that are ahead in a given area, and see if you can do the same in your home town.[9] Fly to other parts of the world for the same purpose. Both coasts of America are hotbeds of new ideas that are eventually geographically translated and modified to fit other areas of the country. For exam-

[9]Paul B. Brown, "It's the Thought That Counts," *Forbes*, May 21, 1984, p. 99. This material is used with permission.

ple, anyone driving up and down the coast of California 15 years ago would have seen the future of fast-food businesses that are now thriving from coast to coast.[10]

Another approach is to look systematically at any business to find what makes it work and then ask what might happen if some things changed in the product or service or marketplace.[11] For example, look at regular life insurance with two components, savings and protection. This is an example of putting together, or building, two services. Some people, however, want only the protection. So, un-bundle the traditional life insurance policy to give this protection, and you have term insurance.[12] Or take a decreasing term insurance policy, and relate it to the amortization of a mortgage on a house, and call it mortgage-protection insurance. And so on.

Look at things that used to be done very well but aren't done any more. Remember the upscale, attractive movie theaters with plush decor and reserved seats that showed the blockbuster movies first? It worked for a while. Why doesn't somebody try it again?[13] Or how about the old-fashioned, all-male barbershops with sturdy leather and steel chairs and marbeled shelves adorned with varied-shaped bottles holding green, red, and yellow hair tonics and shaving lotions to brace the patrons and give them a manly odor?

Notebook and Idea-Board Method

One good way to energize your idea-generating powers is to make the ideas visual. If, for instance, you place a trigger idea where you constantly see it, you will subconsciously begin to generate others around it. If you also make those visual, you will begin almost automatically to generate additional subsidiary ideas.

To use the visual idea board on your business idea, you can start with a bulletin board of any size. Simply write your central idea in big letters on a piece of cardboard, place it in the middle of your board, and start bubbling out your own ideas. They can be anything visual: hand-printed slogans, newspaper clippings, magazine and newspaper pictures, hand sketches, or anything else.

It's also a good idea to link a notebook habit to your visual idea board. Any time you find an idea you feel will be useful to a bulletin board project, jot it down in the notebook, and transfer it to the bulletin board when you have time.[14]

Life-Style Analysis Method

Entrepreneurs can use life-style analysis effectively for product-service ideas. As an example, one important market pattern of attitudes and activities that has relevance

[10]Ibid.

[11]Ibid.

[12]Ibid.

[13]Ibid., p. 102.

[14]Summarized from: Newcomb, op.cit. Used with permission.

to a health and beauty aids manufacturer can be called a woman homemaker's life-style role as family physician. In this role, the homemaker is acting, thinking, and feeling like a nonprofessional practitioner of nursing and medical functions. Many of her concerns are the same as those of medical doctors and registered nurses in a hospital environment. But because she is in the home, the homemaker must deprofessionalize them. Profitable new-product opportunities exist for entrepreneurs who can commercialize the homemaker's needs within the context of this life-style role—who can, in other words, get inside the role with her, act it out and emotionalize it with her, and look for commercial opportunities in health care products and information services that they otherwise might not have seen or might not have seen as vividly.

The same concept of a market as in the life-style role of nonprofessional family physician can be useful to generate food product ideas. Food processors are accustomed to relating to their market of women homemakers as these play their role of family dietician. When many of the same women are newly considered in the light of their physician-in-the-home life-styles, product ideas can be generated for functional foods that contain a health or nutritional market benefit. This approach can yield seasonal foods to prevent winter health problems, foods designed for people who are recovering from major illnesses, foods that provide quick energy, or foods that give added values to people when they need to react under stress. In a similar manner, product developers for insurance companies or for manufacturers of furniture or disposable wearing apparel can use the concept of the family physician life-style as an analogous development base. A few more examples of the needs of a woman homemaker are (1) the homemaker in her life-style role as personal beauty and grooming care manager, (2) the homemaker in her life-style role as family entertainment director, and (3) the homemaker in her life-style role as child trainer and educator.[15]

SURVIVAL OF PRODUCT-SERVICE IDEAS

Generally, product-service ideas fail because consumers won't buy them or the new business venture cannot meet or beat competition or both. Entrepreneurs must have both a market and a competitive orientation; they must have one eye on the consumer and the other one on the competition. Each requires distinctive analysis, yet both are intertwined. Assuredly, if you have something that consumers don't want or need, you certainly have no base on which to be competitive, and you will fail. By the same token, you will fail if you have a product or service that consumers want but can't meet or exceed the competition. In short, to be successful, the entrepreneur must adhere to the fundamentals of business: Give the customer

[15]This whole life-style analysis method is summarized from Mack Hanan, *Venture Management* (New York: McGraw-Hill, 1976), pp 295–303 and is used with permission.

what he or she wants, control costs, work productively, and differentiate your product-service.

Market Orientation

Too often entrepreneurs conceive an idea for a new product or service and promptly become enamored of it. They concentrate on the development of the idea and on its conversion to actuality. They invest time, money, and energy in developing the idea without thought of identifying the customer and the customer's needs and willingness to buy. The entrepreneur's orientation is inward to personal ego needs and his or her own satisfaction. This approach is usually disastrous. Indeed, the result is often a product or service, perhaps cleverly worked out and produced, that few will buy.

To be sure, the entrepreneur's orientation must be to the customer. As stated earlier, the design of the product or service comes from finding out what potential buyers want and need and what they will pay for. In the final analysis, any enterprise is not really in a product or service business; it is in, or it better be in, the customer-satisfying business. Thus, the entrepreneur must understand his or her customer, the market, and the life cycle of the product-service idea that is about to be introduced to the marketplace.

An attempt to appeal to a mass market is generally unsuccessful. Alternatively, entrepreneurs must learn to target their markets by geography, income, life-style, and so forth. In fact, they must use computer and information technology for sophisticated market research and efficient distribution patterns for precision marketing and for responding quickly to changing tastes.

An entrepreneur must understand market dynamics and how he or she is going to be involved in these dynamics. Study of the product-service–market matrix,[16] shown in Figure 3.1, will indicate ways to enhance a specific market or expand into a new one. The matrix gives a way of cross-checking the possibilities of existing and new products or services against existing and new markets.

The matrix consists of four sections. It reflects the scope of alternatives in a company's product-service–market strategies. As the upper left section shows, the enterprise can choose to emphasize the sale of an existing product or service in an already developed market. What have we already said about this area? Often this market is stagnant and beginning to dry up like an old fishing pond during a dry summer. Or it is just sitting there at equilibrium with all the profits squeezed out. If the enterprise doesn't respond, the existing market can fade away. The enterprise can hang on by penetrating and increasing demand through price reduction. It can stay competitive for a while by being more productive and efficient. But, for the most part, the enterprise cannot depend indefinitely on its traditional market for exis-

---

[16]The idea of the product-service–market matrix was taken from Schollhammer and Kuriloff, op. cit. 38–51 and is used with permission.

Markets Products or Services	Existing	New
Existing	Increased demand and penetration	Market diversification and geographic expansion
New	Product or service modification and diversification	Pure invention of new product or service for a new market

FIGURE 3.1 *Product-service—market matrix. (Source: Based on Schollhammer and Kuriloff; op. cit., pp. 38-51. See note 16.)*

tence. Innovation is mandatory for survival. The safest block to be in is to use innovation that results in extension of the product or service.

The upper right section suggests the possibility of market diversification by finding new uses for an existing product or service. Small changes or improvements in existing products or services may appeal to a new segment of customers. Old-time arcade games were "computerized" to appeal to the Atari generation. The digital thermometer, in which the temperature is displayed directly in numbers, offers a welcome improvement in this instrument. "Love Boat" cruises are becoming popular again. Change may be directed at features other than change in the product itself. New packaging that uses color and clever art work can widen the appeal of a product. Old material can get a new lease on life. Polyester, a practical and durable material, in recent years almost died because of its undeserved tacky image. Some fashion designers have given it new life and appeal by using it in high-fashion wearing apparel.

Another opportunity to exploit is the addition of a new product or service for an existing market, as shown in the lower left section of the matrix. These may be true innovations. The development of "expert systems" (through the use of artificial intelligence) represents some true innovations. Schlumberger, for example, is an old-time oil service company. Its basic business is collecting data from oil wells drilled by other contractors. Schlumberger's goal is to help its clients locate 1 of 50 or so kinds of known trapping (a stuck drill bit) situations and to evaluate its hydrocarbon potential. To do so, Schlumberger has developed a family of electrical, acoustical, and nuclear probes, which are lowered into wells by a wire cable. The measurements are recorded on long pieces of paper known as well logs and are interpreted by human experts skilled at inferring geological information from masses of squiggly lines. Schlumberger's ability to generate new measurements currently exceeds—and threatens to exceed by orders of magnitude—the ability of the human interpreters to process those measurements. Artificial intelligence offers a major new approach to a problem that Schlumberger absolutely has to solve.

The final category in the product-service–market matrix concerns new products for a new market—true invention. This area has the greatest risk but also potential for the greatest profits. The need to develop instrumentation for monitoring and regulating the quality of water used in industrial processes is an example. Robots for household use is another. Genetic engineering is still another.

Often, however, the entrepreneur who is most successful is the one who follows the original innovator as quickly as possible. This way requires exceptional skill in research and development to learn from the mistakes or deficiencies of the innovator and to bring a production prototype ready for sale rapidly. Some not-too-ethical entrepreneurs even sell their prototype before it has been produced (or maybe even before it's ready for production) and then make the customer wait for delivery.

Furthermore, to be the first is not always the best strategy. Harry Dumont was the "first" with television but died a pauper. Robert Widener, the "Father of the Corporate War Room," was the first to apply graphics to computers for businesses. Other Johnny-come-latelies have been more successful, however, in raising venture capital and reaching a wider market. The electronics field is full of examples of this kind of follow-the-leader development and success.

The life cycle of a product or service is important to its success in the marketplace. The stages that a product or service can go through are development, introduction, early growth, late growth, maturity, and decline into obsolescence. Sales volume and profit margins are influenced by the various stages in the product's life cycle. In most cases, no product or service is immediately profitable, nor does its success last forever. For some products or services, the life cycle may be quite short; for others, it may last for years.

To be first in a field is risky because of the possible hesitancy of the market to accept a new product or service. On the other hand, being first can produce huge entrepreneurial profits. Usually, however, the cream of the market is between early and late growth. During maturity, sales volume plateaus, more competitors enter, and top prices are difficult to maintain because of intense price competition. In the declining stages, these conditions become even more severe until at some point the product or service dies. In some cases, with innovation and renewal, a new life cycle can be initiated. Clearly, then, timing is critical. Action taken too soon before the market is ready or too late when the market is declining will result in failure.

Competitive Orientation

The entrepreneur enters a world of government blunders and intervention, unpredictable monetary and fiscal policy, business cycles and recessions, changes in trade policies, domestic and foreign competition, political and social dysfunctions, crosscurrents of change in the marketplace, and rising labor costs. All these, then, form the competitive arena in which entrepreneurs must survive. There are three broad opportunity areas that will allow them to do so: (1) productivity, (2) product-service differentiation, or (3) both. This opportunity space is represented in Figure 3.2.

Entrepreneurs involved in fashion design, gourmet food, health spas, and the like, can do a lot to differentiate their products or services but little in the productivity area. At the other extreme, products or services in agriculture and other commodity areas allow little room for differentiation, but productivity can be improved. In the big middle are a number of products or services from manufacturers, banks, airlines, insurance, and so forth, that permit the opportunity to do both.

Product-service differentiation includes such things as access, price, quality, utility, image, uniqueness, maintenance, and warranty. At present, many organizations are being clobbered by better differentiated products or services from foreign competition. In a sophisticated and affluent society, consumer demands shift from more to different. People want style, individuality, quality, and quicker service. Outdated products or services cannot compete in the marketplace even if they are offered at favorable prices.

Computers and information technology are important factors contributing to productivity. This technology extends the muscle and brainpower of all workers, from the factory floor to the executive suite. Technologies tied together by telecommunications will include computers and workstations, data bases, automated office systems, computer-aided manufacturing (CAM), robots and expert systems, computer-based message systems, automated warehouses and inventory control systems, and electronic shopping systems.

A few examples of how products or services are being differentiated and produced more efficiently follow.

1 *Manufacturers.* Some manufacturers are tops in their industry in either productivity or product quality or both. They use flexible automation with pro-

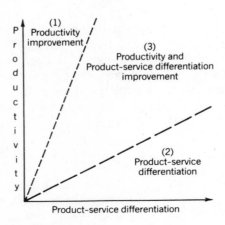

FIGURE 3.2 *The entrepreneur's opportunity space.*

grammed and numerically controlled machines that makes it possible to use the same machines to process different parts. Design and manufacturing data are stored in computer memories and communicated from one machine to another. The results are less labor needed, less material waste, and higher quality products.

2 *Suppliers.*   American Hospital Supply is using computers and telecommunications to connect their system to their customers' purchasing system for on-line teleordering. They cannot do much to differentiate their products, but they do a terrific job in differentiating their service.

3 *Airlines.*   Some people think transportation is a commodity and, therefore, cannot be differentiated. Not only have some airlines been successful in improving productivity, but they also have differentiated their service. For example, they have used information technology for faster fare updates; international pricing; and direct links with hotels, car rental agencies, and banks. Some of the more progressive airlines have extensions of their information systems embedded in travel agencies. Clearly, this tie-in with travel agencies increases the airline's business.

4 *Hotels.*   Some hotels have automated front-desk systems that offer guests 45-second check-in time. This is excellent service differentiation for those bone-weary travelers who dread standing in snail-paced lines to find at the other end a desk clerk who is often a new employee unfamiliar with check-in procedures.

5 *Retailers.*   Interactive technology gives retailers unlimited opportunities to provide outstanding customer service. The use of "infomercials" is a powerful way to present products without time restrictions. The customer can enjoy a leisurely and full explanation of products or services, alternatives, newest features, warranties, and complete demonstrations in their homes via a television set or computer terminal. The customer can then order items electronically.

SUMMARY

From needs and wants, members of a society thirst for new product and service ideas, yet do not always welcome them. Still, some ideas bear fruit, and successful business ventures flourish because of these ideas. Good ideas do not necessarily have to be based on inventions; old ways of doing things applied to existing computer technology provide a virtual gold mine of business opportunities, for example. One has to be, however, more than an idle dreamer. The odds against entrepreneurs are tremendous, and for every idea that may come to fruition on schedule, there are hundreds of frustrated entrepreneurial dreams.

The classic entrepreneurial riddle is how to look to the future, determine needs and wants of the society, and develop viable ideas that meet these needs and wants; and from such endeavors, the entrepreneur hopes to become wealthy. Among other things, the prospect of such financial success and independence are what motivates visionary entrepreneurs to battle the odds.

Sources of product and service ideas are all around us. Some of the ideas can be ferreted out of formal sources, such as publications and government agencies. Other ideas come from within the entrepreneur through creativity, innovation, and vision. Methods that can support and enhance the idea generation process are market gap analysis, observation, notebook and idea-board, and life-style analysis. The final and critical test of any product-service idea is its fit in the marketplace, its salability, and its ability to meet stiff competition.

ASSIGNMENT

1 Explain how changes in population, education, and entertainment bring about changes in needs and wants.

2 From one of the publications noted in the chapter, select a product idea that you believe is viable. Explain why. Does it meet characteristics of successful product-service ideas?

3 From a combination of internal and external sources, generate at least three product or service ideas that you think have merit.

4 Using market gap analysis, generate a viable product or service idea. Do the same, using life-style analysis.

5 Give an example of a "good" idea but one that is not marketable at this time. Explain.

6 Give an example of a successful product or service that is a rehash of an old idea and one that is a slight modification of a new idea.

7 Take one of your product-service ideas, and determine its fit in the market matrix, its stage in the life cycle, and its competitive advantage relative to productivity and product-service differentiation.

BIBLIOGRAPHY

Artificial Intelligence Applications for Business. Sponsored by New York University Graduate School of Business Administration, New York City, May 18–20, 1983.

Brown, Paul B. "It's the Thought That Counts." *Forbes*. May 21, 1984.

Conwell, Russell H. *Acres of Diamonds*. New York: Harper & Row, 1915.

Hanan, Mack. *Venture Management*. New York: McGraw-Hill, 1976.

International New Product Newsletter. Six Saint James Avenue, Boston, Massachusetts 02116.

Kindel, Stephen. "The Workshop Economy." *Forbes*. April 30, 1984.

Maltz, Maxwell. *Psycho-Cybernetics*. North Hollywood, Calif.: Wilshire, 1973.

Newcomb, Duane. *Fortune-building Secrets of the Rich*. West Nyack, N.Y.: Parker, 1983.

NTIS®. *Government Inventions for Licensing, an Abstract Newsletter.* U.S. Department of Commerce. National Technical Information Service, 5285 Port Royal Road, Springfield, Va. 22161.

Rogers, Everett M., and Floyd Shoemaker. *Communication of Innovations.* New York: The Free Press, 1971.

Russell, Sabin. "Being Your Own Boss." *Venture.* May 1984.

Schollhammer, Hans, and Arthur H. Kuriloff. *Entrepreneurship and Small Business Management.* New York: Wiley, 1979.

Sexton, Donald L., and Philip M. Van Auken. *Experience in Entrepreneurship and Small Business Management.* Englewood Cliffs, N.J.: Prentice-Hall, 1982.

Shaffer, Richard A. "Robots Become More Mobile as Navigational Hurdles Fall." *The Wall Street Journal.* May 18, 1984.

Welsh, John A., and Jerry F. White. *The Entrepreneur's Master Planning Guide.* Englewood Cliffs, N.J.: Prentice-Hall, 1983.

White, Richard M., Jr. *The Entrepreneur's Manual.* Radnor, Pa.: Chilton, 1977.

Winter, Ralphe E. "Acme-Cleveland Is Making Risky Changes to Survive in New Machine-Tool Industry." *The Wall Street Journal.* May 17, 1984.

CHAPTER 4

Product-Service Idea
Analysis and Evaluation

INTRODUCTION

After the generation of several product-service ideas, the next critical step is to evaluate their feasibility of becoming successful. Often an idea that appears to have promise early on soon loses favor on closer scrutiny. Conversely, some ideas that appear to have little merit can sometimes prove to be winners. The following material helps to push your idea through an analysis and evaluation screen that will indicate its worthiness as a business enterprise. Specifically, the objectives of this chapter are as follows.

1 To provide insights and questions that help determine a product-service idea's initial feasibility.

2 To present formal evaluation processes.

3 To describe ways to perform market research.

THE REAL VALUE OF AN IDEA

Once product-service ideas are generated, the next step is to determine what they are really worth. Following is a section on some ideas that may or may not have value; the next section lists questions to which these and other product-service ideas should be initially subjected.

Examples of Useful (Useless) Product-Service Ideas

A product-service idea is just that; it is an idea. Following are a few that may or may not have merit.

1 Mobile repair of anything, such as cars, lawn mowers, and houses.

2 Mobile service, such as lawn care, health care, child care, and so forth.

3 Disposable anything, for example, wearing apparel, hospital bedding, and cooking and eating utensils.

4 A full line of clothes, cosmetics, and physical health care (psychological or beauty or physical) for pets.

5 Aerosol peanut butter.

6 Camelot for lovers.

7 Repair-rental service for personal computer hardware and software.

8 A light, portable barge with amenities on a large lake with small explorer boats for fishing, sightseeing, and partying.

9 A safety saddle using safety-belt technology for small children who ride horses.

10 A restaurant that specializes in vegetables.

11 Get a used tire, tie a rope on it, and sell it as a "new" children's swing.

12 Open a campground that provides sing-alongs and campfire ghost stories.

13 Combine hand-held video-audio technology to develop educational systems for children, for example, a picture of a bear; the spelling of B-E-A-R; the pronunciation of *BEAR*; and a brief, amusing explanation of bears.

14 Combine computer and telecommunications technology to provide shop-at-home services, for example, groceries.

15 Take the old brainteasers (years ago, these logic games were regular features in magazines), and program them for personal computers.

16 Buy an established business, and do something innovative with it, for example, add a fun center to a washateria.

17 Start a jojoba farm.

18 Breed, train, and rent guard dogs for joggers, people who work late, and so on.

19 Buy 1000 acres of "cheap" woodland, and develop pedal-tours for cyclists who want exercise and the outdoors for their vacation.

20 Market a lightweight bulletproof vest for executives, druggists, and professors.

21 Gather a number of items indigenous to your state, package them in decorative baskets, name them "Touch of *(name of your state)*," and market them by mail order.

Let's not worry too much about how "good" or "bad" the preceding product-service ideas are at this stage; simply think what you would have to do to translate any of them into a business opportunity, a business concept, and eventually into a business enterprise. What general questions would you use to address the initial viability of any product-service idea? This is the subject of the next section, and it serves as an initial, quick-screen test of your product-service idea.

So you come up with a business idea. What next? Following is a list of preliminary questions that you should ask about your idea.

1 Is it a new product-service idea? Is it proprietary? Can it be patented or copyrighted? Is it unique enough to get a significant head start on the competition, or can it be easily copied?

2 Has your prototype been tested by "tiger teams" (independent testers who try to blow the system or rip the product to shreds)? What are its weak points? Will it stand up? What level of research and development should it receive over the next five years? If it is a service, have you actually tested it on guinea pig customers? Will they pay their hard-earned money for it?

3 Have you taken it to trade shows? If so, what reactions did you get? Did you make any sales? Have you taken it to distributors? Have they given you any orders for it?

4 Is your product or service easily understood by customers, bankers, venture capitalists, accountants, lawyers, and insurance agents?

5 What is the overall market? What are the market segments? Can you penetrate these segments? Are there special niches that you can exploit that big companies are ignoring? Will it sell in these niches? Can you get customers committed? Can you meet schedules and sales?

6 Have you done sufficient market research, or is your view of the market based on a hunch? Who else is in the market? How big is the market? How fast is it growing? What are the trends? What is the projected life cycle of your product or service? What degree of penetration in the market will you be able to achieve? Do you have any testimonials from customers and purchasing agents? How do you plan to advertise and promote it?

7 What distribution and sales methods do you plan to use: jobbers, independent sales representatives, your own sales staff, direct mail, door-to-door sales, supermarkets, service stations, your own stores? How do you plan to transport it: your own trucks, common carriers, postal service, or air freight?

8 Exactly how are you going to make it, and how much will it cost? For example, will it be made in-house or by others? Is production by a job shop or a continuous process? Can you show the efficiency and effectiveness of the production method you have chosen relative to other methods? What is the present capacity of your facilities? What is your break-even point? Can you show cost at different levels of volume?

9 Are you going to develop the business concept and license to others, or do you plan to develop the concept and sell completely?

10 Can you get—or do you already have lined up—the necessary skills to operate the business venture? Who will be your workers? Are they dependable and competent? How much capital do you need now? How much in the future? Have you developed major stages in financing?

At the idea stage, you will not be able to answer all the preceding questions fully. But you should at least begin to think about such questions because sooner or later they will have to be answered fully. Really, at this stage you are trying to determine if the idea represents a product or service around which a profit-making business can be built. See, for example, in the next section how fairly simple ideas have been translated into successful businesses.

Examples of Product-Service Ideas Translated into Business

The following examples show how product and service ideas become successful businesses.

The Shrink-wrap Idea.   An entrepreneur developed a patented process for covering boats with shrink-wrap, plastic sheeting that tightens when treated with hot air and is used for protection during winter storage. This shrink-wrap sheeting is much less expensive than canvas, and in many cases it can eliminate the cost of winter warehousing. It is also used in container freight protection.

The developer of this new product for small-boat protection felt he had a winner, but his big problem was figuring out how to tell prospective customers about it. His marketing solution was to haul his boat wrapped in shrink-wrap sheeting everywhere he drove to get attention, especially at marinas.

He concluded that there was a sizable market in boat protection. He figured that just 10 percent of the U.S. recreational boat market would amount to annual retail sales of about $80 million. The market seemed quite receptive to the product. Some marine owners said that the plastic would reduce their costs up to 75 percent compared with tarpaulins and even more compared to indoor storage. Moreover, the shrink-wrap covering protects against diesel fumes, road salt, and ice, which can make a new boat on the road look like a used boat when it arrives.

This entrepreneur made several mistakes in getting started, however. For example, he delayed looking for business until he could rent a house close to the shore in the early fall at off-season rates. He hadn't considered that, by then, marinas already would have made their storage plans for the winter. He also erred by taking the time to cover customer's boats himself rather than speeding development of the do-it-yourself kits his company now sells.

Competitors are also selling shrink-wrap and equipment kits to marinas. But other market segments are being penetrated as new uses of shrink-wrap sheeting are thought of, such as wrapping aircraft and oil-drilling equipment. Also, development is under way for a homeowner's kit that will enable people to shrink-wrap their own boats, as well as cars, air conditioners, bikes, lawn furniture—even piles of fire-wood. These kits will be sold through marinas and by mail order.[1]

Home Services Idea.   A new, fast-growing service market is created by the needs of thousands of professional and executive women, both with and without children. These women have little time for household and other chores, but they earn enough to hire others to do them. A number of entrepreneurs are tapping into this vast market to provide everything from take-out meals for their dinners to after-school sports for their children.

Some large service companies, some of which are offering franchises, began as small ventures operated out of someone's home. A large Chicago company will send a maid to prepare breakfast, make the beds, touch up the bath and kitchen, do a complete cleaning once a week, and, if necessary, pick up children from a day-care center or take them to the doctor. A San Francisco-area company contracts to shop

---

[1]The shrink-wrap example is summarized from Richard Koenig, "Fledgling Boat Firm Survives on Resourcefulness of Owner," *The Wall Street Journal*, May 21, 1984. p. 29, and is used with permission.

for groceries, clean houses, baby-sit, do household accounts, drive children to dance lessons, and perform a lengthening list of other tasks.

THE EVALUATION PROCESS

In some instances, the entrepreneur may be a dreamer chasing mirages and elusive dreams or numbskulled, half-baked ideas that have no chance at becoming a successful business enterprise. Consequently, a critical task in starting a new business enterprise is a bare-knuckle analysis and evaluation of the feasibility of the entrepreneur and his or her product-service idea's getting off the ground in the first place and also a cold-blooded analysis of the product-service idea's sales potential if it ever gets to the marketplace. It is imperative that entrepreneurs put themselves and their ideas through this analysis to find the "fatal flaws" if any exist, and they usually do. Otherwise, the merciless marketplace will do this after it's too late and after a lot of time and money has been spent and wasted.

Also note that product-service ideas are selected today for tomorrow. No matter how much you try to evaluate, you will never have perfect knowledge about an idea. The challenge is to make a strong effort toward "complete" evaluation, knowing that at some point you will have to make a decision with incomplete information, less than scientific accuracy, and more than stargazing.

To do so, first get a conceptual feel of your idea, its level of innovation, its degree of risk, its ability to be properly evaluated, and its profit potential. Then test the technical feasibility of it. Next subject it to various evaluation criteria.

Conceptual Evaluation

As alluded to several times before, a business is not always started on new or original ideas. To be sure, many businesses are based on old ideas that have been modified or updated; current ideas that have been repackaged for a new market; copycatting (reverse engineering); extension of existing product or service; product or service to satisfy a special market segment; or simply buying an existing business or a franchise operation.

Let us simplify by stating that all product-service ideas fall into one of the following categories: (1) The term *new invention* means it is virtually "new under the sun." It is something created for the first time through a high degree of innovation, creativity, and experimentation. It may or may not be useful, or it may be useful but not perceived as such because it is ahead of its time. Examples are fiber optics, bubble memory, and laser surgery. (2) The term *highly innovative* means that it is somewhat new and not widely known or used. Examples are cellular-based phones and high-speed train systems. (3) The concept *moderately innovative* represents significant modification of an existing product or service or the clever combination of different areas of technology, methods, or processes. Examples include microprocessors used to control fuel injection systems or one-person cars. Or the term could mean the redesign of bicycles to make them easier to ride by adults past their athletic prime, thus developing a new market. See, for example, recumbent bikes. (4) The term *slightly innovative* means that a clever twist is made to an established product or service, such as water slides. Or the phrase could mean the rejuvenation of an old product or service such as designer jeans or return to birth at home using midwifery. (5) *Copycatting* is simply imitating another's business idea; it is a me-tooer. Hundreds of examples exist in the general retail business.

An interesting and meaningful exercise is to see how these categories stack up against the following conditions: (1) *Risk* is the probability of something's failing in the marketplace and includes the financial, career, family and social, and psychic risks explained earlier in this text. (2) *Evaluation* is the determination of something's worth or significance by appraisal and by estimating pitfalls in technical feasibility, production, marketing, distribution, general acceptance, legalities, and so forth. (3) *Profit potential* is the level of return or compensation to the entrepreneur for the assumption of risks in translating the product-service idea to a business enterprise. In Figure 4.1, these opportunity conditions are related to levels of product-service innovation.

These relationships may not always hold, but, at least, this analysis gives you a conceptual base from which you can start your evaluation. To be sure, there are many other variables that dictate a product-service idea's success or failure.

The conclusions reached based on this analysis is that new inventions are risky and difficult to evaluate, but, if accepted in the marketplace, they can return monopolistic profits until competitors enter. Note that these relationships continue as expected until we reach the copycat category. Here risks are very high because there is little chance of succeeding with a complete imitation. Others would argue that old-line products and services may reduce risk significantly by giving a safe harbor to the tried-and-true. Where the entrepreneur brings other skills to the business enterprise, such a relationship may be valid. But it normally holds true, however,

Opportunity Conditions / *Levels of Innovation*	New Invention	Highly Innovative	Moderately Innovative	Slightly Innovative	Copycat
Risks	Very high	High	Moderate	Moderate to low	Very high
Evaluation	Very difficult	Difficult	Somewhat difficult	Easy	Easy
Profit potential	Very high	High	High to moderate	Moderate to low	Low to nil

FIGURE 4.1 *Opportunity conditions related to levels of product-service innovation.*

that this category means no growth and little profit above wages. In any event, the fact remains that a *pure* copycat approach is not really even an "idea" and, certainly, is not entrepreneurial.

In the past, inventions or highly innovative product-service ideas were difficult to bring to the marketplace, maybe because of poor entrepreneurial skills. Moreover, many "failed" when first introduced. Carlson, a lawyer and innovator of dry copying, produced poor copies from the first dry-process Xerox machine. The first commercially successful Xerox machine was not on the market until 20 years and almost $100 million later. Others have had similar plights. Bell and Edison had some notable problems and failures. So did Birdseye (frozen foods), De Forest (vacuum tube), Fleming (penicillin), Rust (cotton picker), Land (Polaroid), Judson and Sundback (zipper), Hobbs (automatic transmission), Whittle and Ohain (jet engine), Carrier (air-conditioning), Davis (power steering), and Biro (ballpoint pens).

Nowadays we are able to practice better entrepreneurship and, therefore, can get the product or service to the marketplace sooner and reduce the missteps and frustrations of the earlier entrepreneurs. There are many reasons for this, a number of which we will treat throughout this text. The main one, however, is our communication system. We are simply a better-informed society. And a better information flow can, in some instances, reduce the risks inherent in introducing a new product or service and can help to evaluate it better.

Technical Feasibility

Every new product or service must be subjected to technical analysis and testing to see if expectations of prospective customers are met. Some of the more important technical requirements are these.

1 The best and by far the number one technical requirement is this: KEEP IT SIMPLE, STUPID (acronym KISS). Keep it simple to build; keep it simple to transport; keep it simple to maintain; and, above all, keep it simple to use (e.g., an elevator is simple to use—this is good human engineering, a great subject for another course).

2 Make it flexible. The 3M company's brassier cups didn't sell, so the company sold them as protective face masks for workers. Now this product is one of 3M's big sellers.

3 One of the most "innovative" things a would-be entrepreneur can do in America today is build a product that will work and not fail. IBM's old policy is SELL–SERVICE–PRODUCT. They have now moved to strong quality assurance and aim virtually to eliminate the need for SERVICE. This is a good lead for the American entrepreneur to follow. Consumers are becoming fed up with shoddy American merchandise and are spending their money elsewhere. In the future, American entrepreneurs, to meet worldwide competition, are going to have to make products that are durable, reliable, safe, and easily maintainable.

Moreover, those products must be modularly designed with standard, interchangeable parts.

If a product doesn't meet these basic technical requirements, then it should be redesigned or scrapped. Some wise individual once said: "Never underestimate the stupidity of the American public and their desire for junk services, entertainment, and products." There is probably a lot of truth in this statement, but as consumers become more educated and as they have more options, quality of products or services will become a number one requirement.

The key approach to testing a product is to subject it to all conditions that have the potential of making it fail. Put it in a cage with a gorilla, or let a "tiger team" have a go at it. In addition to this kind of testing, traditional engineering studies should be made along with the evaluation of alternative materials. Various breadboard models and prototypes should be built for production operation, and market testing.

Generally Accepted Evaluation Methods

A number of evaluation methods can be used by the entrepreneur to find the big winner. Some are simplistic; others are mechanistic and complex. Some entrepreneurs operate with a single criterion and select viable products or services based on this one criterion, such as this: "Because we sell through supermarkets, the products of any venture we get into must also be marketed there."

Some aspiring entrepreneurs might use Proctor & Gamble's approach. Their belief is that the common denominator for any new products that they develop must have the ability to be flushed down a drain or toilet after use. Other entrepreneurs look solely at the financial side, where a product-service idea must have a minimum upside potential of 12 times their investment in 5 to 6 years of venturing. Obviously, there is no one, foolproof method, but any method that forces you to take one more critical look at your idea will be beneficial. Following are some methods that you may find helpful. You will notice some overlap and similarity between the methods. Please combine and modify to fit your needs.

Criteria-Ratings Matrix   Criteria should be selected that are important to the product-service idea's success. Examples of these criteria are ease of operation, quality and maintainability, marketability, ability to raise capital, return on investment, proprietary status, size of the market, simplicity of the manufacturing process, advertising and promotion potential, and growth potential. To make a proper evaluation, use a ratings matrix as shown in Figure 4.2. Get responses from as many "experts" as you can. In the figure, it is assuemd that 10 experts in accounting, marketing, manufacturing, and so forth, responded to the survey. Further, assume a weighted average on a scale of 3.0 for excellent, 2.0 for good, and 1.0 for fair. Note that negative ratings are not used with this method because general, first-level screening has indicated that a rating of 1.0 is at the very least needed to pursue a business concept.

The results of the ratings matrix of Figure 4.2 seem to indicate a fairly strong

| | Ratings of Experts | | | Weighted |
Criteria	Excellent	Good	Fair	Average
Ease of operation	8	2	0	2.8
Quality and maintainability	6	2	2	2.4
Marketability	7	2	1	2.6
Ability to raise capital	5	1	4	2.1
Return on investment	6	3	1	2.5
Proprietary status	9	1	0	2.9
Size of market	8	1	1	2.7
Simplicity of manufacturing	7	2	1	2.6
Advertising potential	6	2	2	2.4
Growth potential	9	1	0	2.9

FIGURE 4.2   *Example of criteria-ratings matrix.*

belief by the 10 evaluators that the product-service idea has a good chance of success. The only "weak" criterion is the ability to raise venture capital. This can probably be overcome by the presentation of a business plan and demonstration of the product or service to a variety of venture capitalists and other investors.

The Westinghouse Method.   Westinghouse has worked with a venture-rating system based on a "formidable formula" that represents the estimates and knowledge of several contributors. The formula, which acts like a primitive model, reads like this:[2]

$$\frac{\substack{\text{Chance of} \\ \text{technical} \\ \text{success}} \times \substack{\text{Chance of} \\ \text{commercial} \\ \text{success}} \times \substack{\text{Average} \\ \text{annual} \\ \text{sales} \\ \text{volume}} \times (\text{Price} - \text{Cost}) \times \substack{\text{Venture} \\ \text{life}}}{\text{Total costs}} = \substack{\text{Priority} \\ \text{category}}$$

The chances of the technical and commercial success of a venture are expressed as percentages, with 100 percent equaling 1. Average annual sales volume is expressed in units. Price is the net sales price per unit in dollars. Cost is the total dollar cost per unit. Venture life is the estimated number of years of life of the venture business over which the average annual sales volume in the formula can be expected to remain approximately the same. Total costs are the total dollar investment in development, including research, design, manufacturing, and marketing. The

[2]Mack Hanan, *Venture Management* (New York: McGraw-Hill, 1976), pp. 65–66. The material is used with permission.

higher the priority category the formula yields, the stronger the venture idea's claim to success.

An example will illustrate how the formula works. Assume that the engineering and research departments of a firm estimate that the chance of actually developing an acceptable venture product is 80 percent. Marketing estimates the chance of commercial success at 60 percent. Average annual sales are estimated at about 20,000 units per year during a nine-year life cycle. Net selling price will be about $120. Cost per unit, including materials, labor, and overhead, will be about $87. Research, as $50,000; design, as $140,000; manufacturing, development, tooling, and facilities, as $230,000; and marketing development, including advertising and promotion, as $50,000. Total investment is $470,000. Thus we have the following.

$$\frac{0.8 \times 0.6 \times 20{,}000 \times (120 - 87) \times 9}{470{,}000} = \text{Priority category 6}$$

This formula is especially helpful where several product-service ideas are being evaluated to select the best of the lot. For example, a venture idea that rated a "category 6" would be a better candidate for venturing than those of lower category values.

Hanan's Potentionmeter. Hanan[3] has developed what he calls a "potention-meter." This method permits a quick screen of each product-service idea's business potential according to a standard set of weighted checkpoints. He admits that his or any selection tools are essentially subjective. He further states that a quantified screening system focuses attention on the underlying judgmental beliefs of the venturers who create and operate it. This in itself is, however, well worth the exercise. Each criterion on the potentionmeter has been assigned values ranging from +2 to −2. The higher the value, the greater the potential of the idea. Only product-service ideas that pass the quick screen with a minimum of 15 are to be considered further. An example follows.

1 Contribution to before-tax return on investment
   +2 More than 35 percent
   +1 25−35 percent
   −1 20−25 percent
   −2 Less than 20 percent

2 Estimated annual sales
   +2 More than $250 million
   +1 $100,000,000−$250 million
   −1 $50 million−$100 million
   −2 Less than $50 million

[3]Ibid., pp. 98−100.

3 Estimated growth phase of life cycle
   +2 More than three years
   +1 Two or three years
   −1 One or two years
   −2 Less than one year

4 Estimated start-up time to high-velocity sales
   +2 Less than six months
   +1 Six months to one year
   −1 One or two years
   −2 More than two years

5 Capital investment payback
   +2 Less than six months
   +1 Six months to one year
   −1 One or two years
   −2 More than two years

6 Preemptive positioning potential
   +2 Technical or marketing preemptive capability
   +1 Short-term or partial preemptive capability
   −1 Initial preemptive capability but susceptibility to easy knockoff
   −2 No preemptive capability

7 Business cycle effect
   +2 Impervious to business cycles or countercyclical
   +1 Reasonably resistant to business cycles
   −1 Normally subject to business cycles
   −2 Strongly subject to business cycles

8 Premium-price potential
   +2 Superior perceived benefits that justify premium price
   +1 Superior perceived benefits that may not justify premium price
   −1 Equal perceived benefits that justify parity price
   −2 Equal perceived benefits that justify only lowest competitive price

9 Ease of market entry
   +2 Scattered competition that makes entry easy
   +1 Mildly competitive entry conditions
   −1 Strongly competitive entry conditions
   −2 Entrenched competition that makes entry difficult

10 Test-market time frame
   +2 Moderate testing required
   +1 Average testing required
   −1 Significant testing required
   −2 Extended testing required

11 Sales-force compatibility
+2 Moderate or no sales force training required
+1 Average sales-force training required
−1 Significant sales-force training required
−2 Extended sales-force training required

Baty's Selection Criteria   If your product-service idea meets six or fewer of the following criteria,[4] it is probably not feasible. If, on the other hand, your product-service idea meets seven or more of these criteria, then you are ready to make a proposal to topflight venture capitalists.

1 *Is it proprietary?*   This is the first question an investor will ask. It doesn't have to be patented (although patents provide great window dressing), but it should be sufficiently proprietary to permit a long head start against competitors and a period of extraordinary profits early in the venture to offset start-up costs.

2 *Are the initial production costs realistic?*   If your first product is plastic canoes, perhaps they are. If it is seagoing LPG tankers, perhaps they aren't.

3 *Are the initial marketing costs realistic?*   A specialized scientific instrument may, measured in this way, be a better first product than a new razor.

4 *Does your product have potential for very high margins?*   This is almost a necessity for a fledgling company. By this measure, a "new" cosmetic product might be less of a risk than a new machine tool. Note that gross margins are one thing that the financial community really understands.

5 *Is the time required to get to market and break even realistic?*   If you have no idea how long it will take to get there, then you can't even estimate how much money you'll need. In most cases, the faster, the better.

6 *Is the potential market enormous?*   For potential market, look ahead three to five years. By this gauge, keyboards for computer terminals will have an enormous market. It is projected that, within three years, 50 million keyboards will be sold. Over 80 million households are in this country. Some experts predict that over half of these households will have at least one personal computer. That is a lot of computers and keyboards.

7 *Is your product the first member of a growing family?*   So much the better if it requires a lot of high-margin accessories or supplies. Most of the best growth companies have products with large doses of this characteristic.

8 *Do you have some ready-made initial customers?*   It is certainly impressive to financial backers when you can list your first 10 customers by name.

[4]Criteria from Gordon B. Baty, *Entrepreneurship, Playing to Win* (Reston, Va.: Reston, 1974), pp. 33–34. The summary is used by permission of Reston Publishing Company, a Prentice-Hall Company, 11480 Sunset Hills Road, Reston, Virginia 22090.

9 *Are the development cost and calendar time realistic?* Preferably, they are zero. A ready-to-go product gives you a big leg up over competitors. Save your jazzy product development efforts for your second, third, or fourth product.

10 *Are you in a growing industry?* This is not absolutely essential if the profits and company growth are there, but there is less room for mistakes.

11 *Can your product and the need for it be understood by the financial community?* A good product in this respect may be a portable, heart-monitoring system for post-coronary monitoring. Probably over half of the people who will hear your presentation have already had coronaries.

MARKET RESEARCH

It is tough to get a product-service idea from the mind to the marketplace. But once it is there, it may be even tougher to gain acceptance and make sales. Indeed, gathering and analyzing market data about the marketability of the new product-service idea is key to determining the potential success of the venture.

Marketing Questions

The basic marketing question that must be asked over and over again is, "Will it sell?" Many aspiring entrepreneurs are so in love with their product-service idea that they ignore the market; they assume it will sell. And, on the other side of the street, more precisely Madison Avenue, is the "run-it-up-the-flagpole-and-see-who-salutes-it" crowd, who think that if it is advertisable, it is marketable. The market road is strewn with product-service ideas that were heavily—and many times cleverly—advertised and went bust.

The Edsel car was driven to the marketplace with great flourish, fueled by millions spent on splashy advertising and mass media hype. It immediately collided with consumer ennui and suffered the largest wreck in automotive history. Indeed, Edsel is synonymous with a colossal marketing fiasco. One can also wonder how many "Will it sell?" questions were asked about imitation leather shoes, odor-enhanced movies, and the Susan B. Anthony dollar. Remember that advertising and promotion are parts of market strategy, not market research.

Other important questions related to the "Will it sell?" question are these: Does the product-service idea fit customer needs or wants? Is there a real difference (or possibly a perceived difference) between your product-service idea and those of your competitors that will cause customers to choose yours over your competitor's? How many ways can you differentiate your product? Can you produce it for less than your competitors to give you a price advantage? What are your main market segments? What is the number of customers in these segments? What percentage of these customers can you capture? What distribution and sales channels will you use? How much is it going to cost for market research, salespeople's salaries (if your own salespeople are used), commission representatives, regional sales offices, advertising, application and service engineering, customer training, warranty repairs, manuals and other documentation, hand holding, and telephone and general communication? How long will it take to get sales representatives in the field? Can you call by name (not the name of the company, but the name of the *person*) at least 20 bona fide, high-volume customers? Can you call by name at least 100 well-researched customer prospects, not suspects?

Here are ways to answer these questions and perform market research: (1) do your own studies; (2) get studies from private research firms; (3) gather reports and surveys from trade associations; (4) obtain government reports (e.g., census); and (5) use university bureaus of business research.

Use of Your Own Market Survey

Your own market survey is research designed specifically for your product-service idea to get information about market opportunities, customers' preferences, and marketing requirements. These surveys are conducted as personal and telephone interviews or by mailed questionnaires.

When the basic features of the product-service idea are not well known, a personal field interview may be the only way to gather market information. Drawings, diagrams of models, or prototypes are used to explain the produce or service. Such interviews help to stimulate interest and gather names of bona fide customers. It is the best way to get information because you can probe and interact. It is, however, the most expensive.

Telephone interviews are used as a source of market information when the basic features of the new product are well defined and do not require an on-site demonstration of how it works. A prepared telephone questionnaire is used to guide the interviewer during the telephone interview. This technique is considerably faster and less expensive than personal field interviews, but it is less versatile. Eight minutes is the norm of effective interview time.

Mail surveys are used for a general investigation of potential customers' receptiveness to a new product-service idea. A mail survey includes a detailed description of the product or service, a letter requesting the cooperation of the addressee, and a questionnaire to be answered and returned in a self-addressed stamped envelope. This technique is limited because the questions are closed-ended, most respondents will not spend more than five minutes on your questionnaire, rarely can you expect more than 5 percent to respond within three weeks, and many of these responses may be inaccurate. Moreover, there is no way to explore and get feedback.

One of the more effective ways of overcoming the drawbacks of telephone and mail interviews is to combine them. First, write the person you wish to interview, and tell him or her who you are, what you are doing, why you need the information, and the questions you need answered. Then tell the individual that you will telephone him or her at a specific time on a specific date. Using this technique saves precious telephone time because introductory remarks are not needed. Also, your respondent has had enough time to read, digest, and think about your questions; and you will discover that such a person's answers are clearer and more accurate than if you catch him or her cold.

Library research is a strong, yet inexpensive way to learn basic information about the industry you are entering. Mountains of data are available from the Census Bureau, Department of Commerce, the Small Business Administration, stockbrokers, investment bankers, Standard & Poor's, Moody's, and so forth. If you live in or near a major city, use your library's professional researchers. These expert library researchers are free and can gather in-depth information for you in one-tenth of the time it will take you.

An excellent directory of market research reports, studies, and surveys, is *FINDex*, published by FIND/SVP, Information Clearing House, Inc., 500 Fifth Avenue, New York, New York 10110; telephone (212) 354-2424; Telex 148358. It is an annual service with a midyear supplement and update-by-phone service.

Another excellent publication is a book entitled *Where to Find Business Information* by David M. Brownstone and Gorton Carruth, published by John Wiley & Sons, Inc., 605 Third Avenue, New York, New York 10158. This book shows where current business information is located and how to get it.

Place an advertisement in a magazine or paper, and see who orders or shows interest. Return all checks and orders with a cover story, but keep accurate records because you will want to contact these people when you have the final product or service to sell. Or, better still, rent a booth at a trade show, and attempt to presell from preliminary sales literature and prototype samples. Frequently, the caliber of information gathered from the professionals who visit your booth and answer your questions is equivalent to years of personal interviews.[5] These techniques, however, stretch good, ethical conduct.

Another very effective research technique and one that is ethical is to pull "buddy calls" with salespeople who contact customers in your market segments. This technique gives you a great opportunity to get responses from valid potential customers in a real sales setting. If you know how to conduct yourself in front of these customers, they will help you collect your information.[6] Also, you may make some sales.

Use of Market Research Firms

The American Marketing Association can give you the names, addresses, and research specialties of hundreds of private research firms eager to supply you with information about the markets you intend to serve. In many cases, these firms have mass-produced market surveys available to anyone who has the price of purchase.

---

[5]Richard M. White, Jr., *The Entrepreneur's Manual* (Radnor, Pa.: Chilton, 1977), pp. 68–69. This material is used with permission.

[6]Ibid.

Other market research firms provide their services only on an individual client basis. Some examples of market research firms are these.

Stanford Research Institute
333 Ravenswood Avenue
Menlo Park, California 94025

Arthur D. Little, Inc.
25 Acorn Park
Cambridge, Massachusetts 02140

Business Communications Co.
471 Glenbrook Road
Stanford, Connecticut 06906

Theta Technology Corporation
Peer Building
530 Silas Deane Highway
Wethersfield, Connecticut 06109

Frost & Sullivan, Inc.
106 Fulton Street
New York, New York 10038

Morton Research Corporation
1745 Merrick Avenue
Merrick, New York 11566

Use of Trade Associations and Journals

Almost every industry has a trade association and a journal, and these represent some of the best sources of data about a specific industry. Trade journals include on a regular basis market surveys and forecasts. Moreover, the advertisements in trade journals provide excellent sources of information about competitors and their products. Attendance at trade shows and conversations with sales representatives can also be good ways of investigating competitive products and services. The trade associations and journals of various industries can be found in the following.

Encyclopedia of Associations
National Organizations of the U.S.
Gale Research Company
Book Tower
Detroit, Michigan

Ayer Directory of Newspapers, Magazines, and Trade Publications
Ayer Press
West Washington Square
Philadelphia, PA 19106

Examples of trade journals are *Electronic News* or *Railway Age*. The material published in trade journals such as these normally deals with product improvements or process descriptions; little direct information on markets or marketing is included, but the indirect statements and summaries are useful.

General business journals can provide good sources for market research. Examples of these are *Business Week, Forbes, Money, Fortune, Inc., The Wall Street Journal, Venture, Entrepreneur,* and *The New York Times.* Articles in these publications describe existing companies or proposed products or processes, and they present general information on customers or markets that can be useful for market research by aspiring entrepreneurs.

Use of Government Reports

The U.S. government prints tons of data that can be used in market research. Here are some of these publications.

U.S. Census Reports
Census of Business
Census of Housing
Census of Population
U.S. Industrial Outlook
    all from
U.S. Department of Commerce
Government Printing Office
Washington, D.C.

The U.S. government publications are summarized in the *Statistical Abstract of the United States,* which is probably the most useful, for it provides basic background information on income levels, employment figures, industry outputs, and so forth. *The Statistical Abstract* is available in nearly every library.

Material that is prepared specifically for smaller business firms is listed in *A Survey of Federal Government Publications of Interest to Small Business,* available from the Small Business Administration. Much of the needed background information for small business market research is available through government publications.

Within each state, a Department of Commerce exists—or the equivalent—which will provide a list of businesses, generally broken down into industry, size, and geographic location, that operate within the state. In addition, the Department of Commerce may also publish reports on the more important industries operating in the region; although these reports are prepared to further industrial development, they do contain data on wage rates, material supplies, and so forth. The reports may be obtained from the state capitol. The Chamber of Commerce within each major city usually publishes a list of companies located within the area; this list is very useful for industrial sales information.[7]

Use of University Bureaus of Business Research and Experiment Stations

Most of the flagship universities throughout the country provide experiment and research centers that gather a wealth of information for dissemination to the public. For example, The Texas A&M University System supports the Texas Engineering Experiment Station that investigates a variety of leading-edge innovations or conducts bootstrap studies. Examples include (1) finding ways of making exotic foods from glandless cottonseed, (2) studying wind loads for semisubmersible offshore platforms, (3) studying the direct use of coal and lignite in internal combustion engines, and (4) studying the production and marketing of synfuels.

Moreover, some of these research centers have a venture division that assists innovators and entrepreneurs by looking at the technical feasibility of an idea, cost of production, potential markets, and the potential of financial success. For example, the Texas Engineering Experiment Station (TEES) established in 1982 the Institute for Ventures in New Technology (INVENT), which helps the would-be entrepreneur-inventor make his or her product-service idea successful by eliminating design flaws, advising on market strategy, and securing financial backing. INVENT is a collaborative effort linking researchers in engineering, business administration, and other academic disciplines.

INVENT reviews all ideas submitted and selects unique, promising developments and then works with the entrepreneur-inventor to help create a business enterprise to capitalize on these developments. For each innovation selected for development, the team researchers investigate the appropriate interrelated questions: Is there a market for it? Will it work? Are patent or copyright actions necessary? Can it be produced at a reasonable cost? How should it be marketed effectively? How much financing is needed to launch the product or service? What kind of organizational structure and resources are needed?

The answers to these questions are compiled into a business plan to implement the commercialization of selected ideas. Once research analyses have been conducted to ascertain the viability of the innovation, complete recommendations from such analyses can aid in establishing the product credibility and business plans for the entrepreneur to acquire the resources necessary to compete successfully in the marketplace.[8]

---

[7]LaRue T. Hosmer et al., *The Entrepreneurial Function* (Englewood Cliffs, N.J.: Prentice-Hall, 1977), p. 80. This material is used by permission of Prentice-Hall, Inc.

[8]The Institute for Ventures in New Technology, Texas Engineering Experimental Station, The Texas A&M University System, College Station, Texas 77843. This material is used with permission.

SUMMARY

All businesses at their beginning started based on product-service ideas. The relatively easy part of entrepreneurship is the generation of ideas; the hard part is making a thorough evaluation of them and, of course, eventually making them succeed in the marketplace. During the evaluation process, many questions must be answered, ranging from "Will it sell?" to "Can we produce it for a profit?"

Product-service ideas range from inventions to copycatting although one could argue that copycatting is not an idea per se. Normally, the more innovative the idea, the higher the risks, and the more difficult it is to evaluate, but the greater is the potential for high profits. With better entrepreneurial skills, more timely flow of information, comprehensive evaluation methods, and thorough market research, the risks of introducing a product or service can be reduced.

ASSIGNMENT

1 Either from firsthand knowledge or from library research (e.g., *Moody's, Standard & Poor's, The Wall Street Journal, Barron's*), describe at least two companies that failed and tell why.

2 Develop a venture that you would like to go into based on one of your product-service ideas, and list the questions you would subject it to.

3 Assume that the shrink-wrap business or service to professional women had been your product-service idea. Explain what preliminary questions you would have asked about them. What evaluation method would you have used? What market research would you have performed? Be specific.

4 Give a product-service idea for each of the following: invention, highly innovative, moderately innovative, slightly innovative, and copycat. Explain each one's risks, evaluation, and profit potential.

5 Define the criteria-ratings matrix. Give two additional criteria that you believe should be included. Evaluate one of your ideas with it. What are the results? Explain.

6 Test one or your ideas for technical feasibility. Is it feasible? Why? Why not? Explain.

7 Use Westinghouse's formidable formula to evaluate several product-service ideas. Which one has the highest category?

8 Use Hanan's potentionmeter to evaluate one of your ideas. How did it score?

9 Subject one of your ideas to Baty's selection criteria. What are the results?

10 Explain how you would set up a "tiger team" to test your product-service idea.

11 Describe in-depth how you would formulate a market research program for your product-service idea.

BIBLIOGRAPHY

Baty, Gordon B. *Entrepreneurship, Playing to Win*. Reston, Va.: Reston, 1974.

Hanan, Mack. *Venture Management*. New York: McGraw-Hill, 1976.

Hosmer, LaRue T., et al. *The Entrepreneurial Function*. Englewood Cliffs, N.J.: Prentice-Hall, 1977.

Koenig, Richard. "Fledgling Boat Firm Survives on Resourcefulness of Owner." *The Wall Street Journal*. May 21, 1984.

Peters, Thomas J., and Robert H. Waterman, Jr. "Corporate Chariots of Fire." *Across the Board*. May, 1983.

Schollhammer, Hans, and Arthur H. Kuriloff. *Entrepreneurship and Small Business Management*. New York: Wiley, 1979.

Silver, David A. *The Entrepreneurial Life: How to Go For It and Get It*. New York: Wiley, 1979.

Smith, Randy Baca. *Setting Up Shop*. New York: McGraw-Hill, 1982.

The Institute for Ventures in New Technology. Texas Engineering Experiment Station. The Texas A&M University System, College Station, Texas.

Welsh, John A., and Jerry F. White. *The Entrepreneur's Master Planning Guide*. Englewood Cliffs, N.J.: Prentice-Hall, 1983.

White, Richard M., Jr. *The Entrepreneur's Manual*. Radnor, Pa.: Chilton, 1977.

PART THREE

MEANS OF ENTERING BUSINESS

CHAPTER 5

The Start-Up

INTRODUCTION

The three means of entering business are (1) the start-up, which is a new business enterprise started from scratch; (2) the buyout, where the buyer acquires an established business; and (3) the franchise, where franchisees operate units of franchise operations as if they were their own with certain restrictions and guidance from franchisors. If the product-service ideas are truly innovative, the start-up is the only means by which entrepreneurs can enter business. The content of this chapter centers on the start-up; the next chapter deals with the buyout; the chapter after next presents the franchise. Note, however, that if an entrepreneur developed a new product-service idea and connected it to a franchise operation as a *franchisor*, the business would simply be a form of start-up. The objectives of this chapter are as follows.

1 To summarize the entrepreneurial process and show how the start-up fits into this process.
2 To present reasons why start-ups fail. Many of these reasons also apply to buyouts and franchises.

ENTREPRENEURSHIP REVISITED

Examples abound of entrepreneurs from all over the country who are developing start-ups, both large and small. For doing the same, an entrepreneurial process should be followed.

Entrepreneurs Are Spawning Start-Ups

Today entrepreneurs are coming from the ranks of corporations, or they are career-minded housewives, or they are top business or engineering school graduates. They generate thousands of start-ups across the country.

Donald Burr is founder and president of People Express Airlines. Steven Jobs and Stephen Wozniak started Apple Computer with money raised by selling a Volkswagen microbus. Aryeh Finegold emigrated from Israel and started Daisy Systems, a company specializing in the development of engineering work stations. Morris Seigel turned his taste for herbal tea into multimillion-dollar Celestial Seasonings. Heather Evans makes high-fashion dresses for executive women. Steve Solms pioneered converting old cast-iron buildings into apartments.

Indeed, we may very well be entering the Golden Age of Entrepreneurship. Society is growing; the baby boomers are beginning another baby boom; the society is more affluent, more discriminating, more mobile, more urban, and better educated. This growth, combined with a widening array of technologies, has given entrepreneurs opportunities that simply did not exist before.

For example, thoughout our society there is a dire need for owners of personal computers to learn more about them. Obviously, the service idea is to form a venture to train people in their homes how to use their computers more effectively and fully.

Ideally, if an entrepreneur chose a location close to a large university, trainers could be recruited from a large number of students to form a cadre of whizbang computer jocks fresh and willing to help others learn more about computers. Call these trainers "computer tutors," dress them in special uniforms, design hats as replicas of magnetic discs, and supply adornments made from computer circuitry. Provide your trainers with flexible scheduling with so many contact hours per week.

Once this start-up is set up and thriving, natural opportunities for additional product-service ideas arise, such as selling software packages, computer repair service, and special seminars. It takes the true entrepreneur, however, to take the risk and put it all together, to perform the market research, develop tutoring packages, prepare the business plan, raise the capital, find the right location, set up the accounting system, recruit the tutors, devise marketing tactics and strategies, sell and answer complaints, schedule tutors, and sweep the floor at night. In addition, he or she must be available 24 hours daily, 7 days a week.

For another example, can anyone think of a worse business to be in than the "tennis shoe" or "sneakers" business? What a staid old industry, athletic footwear. What a dumb idea to develop athletic shoes for joggers, tennis players, and so forth. Right? Wrong. Nike went from a start-up several years back to over $700 million in sales. It met the unsatisfied need and want for better-engineered and better-styled athletic footwear. Previous industry companies had ignored these needs and wants, and their failure to innovate resulted in an industry that was, at least temporarily, slow growing and mature. Even financial analysts who poured over reams of business statistics concluded that the industry was mature and offered little investment opportunity.

This same explosion of growth occurs regularly in segments of one of our oldest industries, clothing. Designer blue jeans, active sportswear, panty hose, and Western clothing have shown that a new idea in a mature industry can cause dramatic growth for the committed entrepreneur. In addition, volume increases can be on a much larger scale than is possible in an embryonic high-technology industry where the market is still relatively small and undeveloped.

For alert entrepreneurs in a mature industry, the growth opportunities derived from new product-service ideas compare favorably with those in the so-called high-tech areas. The main reasons are these.

1 Mature industries provide a much larger array of new idea opportunities.

2 If the idea is successful, the market is usually much larger to support greater sales and profit.

3 Usually the raising of capital is easier because bankers and others understand the product-service idea more readily, and the industry is normally well serviced by a number of financial institutions.

4 Some believe that it is the easiest and best place to make money.

5 Because many entrepreneurs are trying to get in the high-tech area, there is less competition to find opportunities.

6 In some mature industries, conglomerates cannot give every product or service sufficient attention. This is where the entrepreneur can take one or two items and do a much better job with them than the conglomerate can do. This alternative, however, indicates a buyout, the subject of the next chapter.

These and other opportunities, combined with people who have a passion for individual expression, achievement, self-reliance, risk taking, and autonomy from bureaucratic mishmash, generally spell success. Certainly, a number of venture capitalists are willing and able to bankroll such people in their start-ups, assuming such start-ups are valid business concepts.

The Entrepreneurial Process and the Start-Up

In some ways, the person who buys a going business has an advantage over the one who starts from scratch. For one thing, there is more information concerning a buyout candidate or a franchise; they are easier to evaluate and to predict results and perform market research about. The start-up is simply riskier, especially for the first year or so. To be sure, the entrepreneurial process is especially applicable to a start-up. This process as it relates to this text and the real world is summarized in the form of a flowchart depicted in Figure 5.1.

Obviously, to become an entrepreneur, you must embark on an entrepreneurial search, systematically looking for business opportunities and generating product-service ideas. Such ideas must be evaluated to determine if they represent a viable business concept. If they don't, they may be scrapped or reevaluated. Or they may be modified, also for further evaluation. Or you may give up if none of your first ideas is viable. Or you may go back to the drawing board and generate more ideas.

If a product-service idea has merit, then a statement of the business concept should be prepared, for example, "The ABC Company will develop, manufacture, and sell to distributors, marinas, hardware stores, and home furnishing centers, a do-it-yourself kit to wrap and protect boats and household items that are subjected to weather and other abuses."

One of the keys to, and danger points of, any venture idea is the assumptions one has to make about one's product-service idea, especially during the evaluation phase and while performing market research. The advice, therefore, is this: When you make your assumptions—and you will have to make them—be sure they are made on current, relevant, and complete information.

Another critical point where well-informed, sane assumptions must be made is during preparation of the business plan and before the "GO" decision is made. These critical assumptions are the key to success or failure. When they are wrong, the business venture will fail. Many simulations should be performed, and hard what-if questions should be asked about the product-service idea again at this stage.

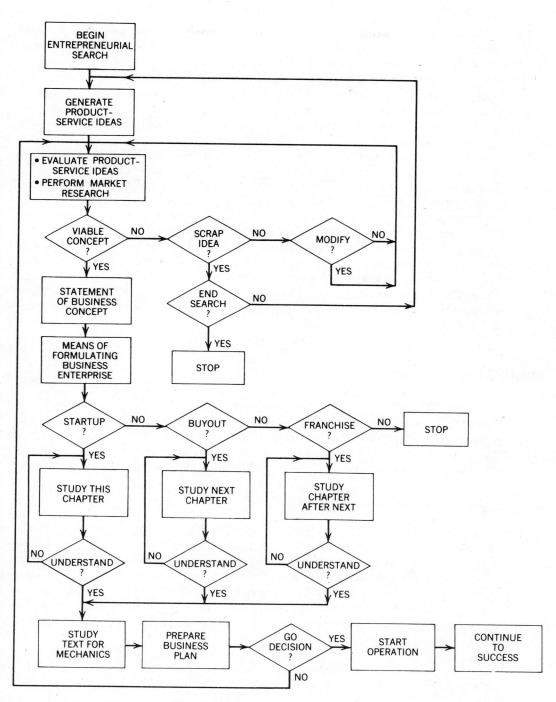

FIGURE 5.1 *Flowchart of the entrepreneurial process.*

Good assumers are rare birds. Often the "experts" make some real boners. Gillette, a leader in the razor blade industry, assumed that the stainless-steel razor blade was a trivial innovation. Wilkinson saw its profit potential. As a result, Gillette's market share fell from 70 to 55 percent in less than 18 months. Addressograph-Multigraph thought they had the best labeling machines in the industry and refused to move into computer labeling. They stuck by their metal-labeling machines, and one of the oldest and largest companies in the office equipment area is now a weak contender.

A big, significant part of becoming an entrepreneur involves coming to grips with a number of the mechanics of entrepreneurship. These mechanics include selection of the entrepreneurial team, selection of the board of directors, choosing legal structure, choosing and registering name and logo, obtaining business licenses and permits from governmental agencies, preparation of a business plan, and raising capital. These mechanics are presented later in the text.

Starting operations is more a managerial process than entrepreneurial; certainly, this is true after the business has been in operation for several years. Critical factors for success include continued product-service differentiation from competition and increased productivity. These critical success factors stem from good management, management information systems, market strategy, sufficient capital base, competent personnel, and so forth.

WHY START-UPS FAIL

The history of starting up any new business venture is not too good. Statistics indicate that out of every 10 start-up businesses, three will fail miserably; three will break even and eventually fail or will get a recharge from new management, more capital, or a new product or service; and three will trudge along being marginally profitable. Only one will score big. Following are some reasons why start-ups fail.

How Venture Capitalists Weight a Start-Up

The following data prepared by White graphically illustrate the importance of the management team (which is often also the same as the entrepreneurial team). These weightings surprise most people because they show that if you simply attract topflight managers and address a growth industry, you stand between a 70 percent and 90 percent chance of succeeding even before you develop your product-service idea. Or, if you look at it another way, no matter how great your product-service idea is, if you attract weak, incompetent people, you only have a fifty-fifty chance of making it—maybe less.[1]

[1]Richard M. White, Jr., *The Entrepreneur's Manual* (Radnor, Pa.: Chilton, 1977), pp. 15–16. Copyright © 1977 by the author. This material is used by the permission of the publisher, Chilton Book Company, Radnor, Pennsylvania.

The Manufacturing Start-Up	
Category	Percent Weighting
The management team	50−60
The growth industry addressed	20−30
The product idea	10−20
The marketing and finance plans	5−10

The Nationwide Industrial Service Start-Up	
Category	Percent weighting
The management team	60−90
The key employees	10−30
The growth industry addressed	10−20
The service idea	10−15
The marketing and finance plans	1−5

The Local Retail Sales or Retail Service Start-Up	
Category	Percent Weighting
The management team	30−50
The location	40−50
The product-service idea	5−10
The marketing and finance plans	1−5

Source: Richard M. White Jr., *The Entrepreneur's Manual* (Radnor, Pa.: Chilton, 1977), p. 15−16. Copyright © 1977 by the author. Reprinted with the permission of the publisher, the Chilton Book Company, Radnor, Pennsylvania.

The conclusion from these revealing data is that a venture capitalist would rather have an average product-service idea with a top management team than a good product-service idea with a mediocre team. Horse-racing enthusiasts have always known that it is wise to bet on a good jockey and a mediocre horse; not on a good horse and a mediocre jockey. The probability of a good horse's bringing home the poor jocky is slim to none. The probability of a poor management team achieving success is even less.

The Entrepreneur

The worst enemy of would-be entrepreneurs, at least in the short run, may be the entrepreneurs themselves. Often their wills are not strong enough to stick with their product-service idea until it's in the marketplace and making money, or their wills are strong enough, but they leap before they look.

Some entrepreneurs are enamored of their ideas and tend to jump to conclusions rather than think to conclusions. Would-be entrepreneurs delude themselves with goofy, get-rich ideas, and their foolish schemes fall through the bottom like a rock through a spiderweb. Ideas may soar in the mind, but sooner or later these ideas must meet the reality of the marketplace, and the marketplace does not pardon mistakes; its yes is yes, and its no is no.

Normal Pitfalls of a Start-Up

A famous quote that seems to summarize the whole market is attributed to Marshall Field, an expert merchandiser. He supposedly said, "Give the lady what she wants." This quote was the major objective of Field's renowned stores. Lack of sales is one of the obvious, but a major, reason why most ventures fail. Not determining whether or not the product or service will sell stems from inadequate market research and testing, market segmentation, weak marketing tactics and strategy, and improper pricing or a combination thereof.

Another major reason why ventures fail, especially those started by individuals who have a little nest egg and who want to quit their job, go into business, and be "their own boss," is undercapitalization. These people take their money out of the bank, make an additional loan, quit their job, and are down the tube in a year or two. They forget that they must maintain at least a semblance of their old life-style, which may take $20,000 to $30,000. Where is this money going to come from? They forget that bankers want their money on time. Where does this money come from? They forget that inventory vendors may have to be paid before the product is sold or, if it is raw material, before it is converted into a finished product. Where does this money come from? These poor would-be entrepreneurs lose the fruit tree before it has time to take root and bear fruit.

Incompetent management and operations employees can ruin a start-up more quickly than anything. Any of these boneheads can mess up and destroy in a few minutes what took the entrepreneurs a lifetime to build. If your venture is labor-intensive, the probability is high that you will fail simply because you cannot get the work done. The advice is not to go into any business unless you can control much of it yourself or unless you are sure that you can put together a close-knit, loyal management team supported by a dedicated, highly trained group of employees.

Lack of inventory control is a classic reason why many businesses fail. For new ventures, many entrepreneurs don't know how to buy. Here is a good piece of business advice: "The right item bought is an item already half sold." That is, if you buy the right style, color, size, and so forth, you can be fairly confident that you will be able to sell it.

Poor credit control and an inadequate accounting system are common reasons why many businesses go broke. My simple advice is not to give credit unless the item can be repossessed intact, or the customer has assets much greater than the item purchased or both. Moreover, before you ever open the doors, have your accounting system in place.

The would-be entrepreneur must be realistic. In some instances, the competition is simply too strong, and it costs too much to set up production facilities and enter the market. For example, many enterprises have fallen trying to enter the automobile business.

Sometimes the venture idea meets all evaluation criteria, but it cannot be made and sold at a price that is profitable. That is, it can be manufactured without a problem, and people will say that they want or need it; but when it comes to the sale's being made, the potential buyer simply will not pay the price necessary for the entrepreneur to make money. An example of this was a protective suitcase for skis.

Another pitfall that is sufficient to deal a fatal blow to the enterprise is the inability of suppliers to provide components or raw material needed for the product at a reasonable price or a relatively consistent price. Many entrepreneurs have met eventual failure because they were dependent on, and at the mercy of, suppliers who would not or could not meet the enterprise's needs. The same applies to entrepreneurs who acquire equipment and later find out, to their regret, that the vendor has gone out of business or is still in business but will not provide appropriate maintenance and service.

Going Against the Probabilities

Because of poor advice, inadequate planning, or misguided hunches, many aspiring entrepreneurs go into businesses that have a high probability of failure. These poor souls literally become members of a revolving "pool of fools." One will open a gas station and six months later is out of business; then another well-meaning but misguided would-be entrepreneur opens the same station and in six months or less is also broke. Information about such losers can be obtained from bankers, knowledgeable investors, and the Small Business Administration. Certainly, budding entrepreneurs need all the probabilities in their favor. Therefore, unless they can come up with an innovative twist to one of the traditional losers, entrepreneurs should consider instead a product-service idea in another, more profitable area.

According to Small Business Administration statistics, the following represent 10 winners and 10 losers.[2]

The *winners* are building materials stores; auto tire and accessory stores; liquor stores; sports, recreation, and health clubs; funeral homes; seed and garden stores; sporting goods manufacturing; engineering and laboratory equipment; hardware stores; and office supplies and equipment.

The *losers* are laundry and dry cleaning, used-car lots, gas stations, local trucking firms, restaurants, infant's clothing stores, local bakeries, machine shops, grocery stores, and car washes.

[2]Summarized from Randy Baca Smith, *Setting up Shop* (New York: McGraw-Hill, 1982), pp. 8–12, and used with permission.

SUMMARY

There are three ways to enter business; the franchise, the buyout, and the start-up. A start-up is a new business started from scratch and usually based on a new product-service idea. It is the purest form of entrepreneurship. And the entrepreneurial process is certainly a crucial task of start-ups, especially as it relates to assumptions and evaluations made about their feasibility and potential success in the marketplace.

Anyone investing in a start-up is taking a big risk but also looking for huge rewards. Yet many people disdain the risk and strike out on their own to test their entrepreneurial mettle. For sure, increasing entrepreneurial activity will produce more start-ups of all kinds. But many will fail. Why? Some of the reasons are failure to follow an entrepreneurial process, poor management team, faulty assumptions, misguided entrepreneur, inadequate marketing, insufficient capital, incompetent and sorry employees, poor inventory control and improper buying, loose credit controls and weak accounting system, deficient competitive strategy, and lack of service from suppliers and vendors. In some instances, entrepreneurs choose businesses that have little probability of succeeding no matter what the entrepreneur does. These losers are the black holes of the business world. Stay away from them.

ASSIGNMENT

1 What are the three basic ways to enter business? Give an example of each.

2 Briefly describe how a start-up differs from a buyout and from a franchise operation.

3 If you had developed a product-service idea and converted it to a franchise operation as the franchisor, would this be a start-up? Why or why not?

4 In your opinion, do you believe we are entering the Golden Age of Entrepreneurship? Why? Why not? If so, will this mean more start-ups? Explain.

5 At this point in the text, without reading ahead, try to explain why a start-up is normally riskier than buyouts and franchises.

6 Give the key points of your product-service idea at each stage in the entrepreneurial process flowchart through "Means of Formulating Business Enterprise." Does it appear at this point that your business enterprise will be a start-up, buyout, or franchise?

7 Give an example of what you think were poor assumptions made by the entrepreneurs of a product or service.

8 Why do venture capitalists give more weight to the management team (it is often also the same as the entrepreneurial team) than to the product or service idea?

9 In your opinion, how could the entrepreneur be his or her own worst enemy?

10 List and briefly describe the normal pitfalls of a start-up.

11 Based on your own research, explain why one of the Small Business Administration's winners (your choice) is a winner and why one of the losers (your choice) is a loser.

BIBLIOGRAPHY

Hanan, Mack, *Venture Management*. New York: McGraw-Hill, 1976.

White, Richard M., Jr. *The Entrepreneur's Manual*. Radnor, Pa.: Chilton, 1977.

Smith, Randy Baca. *Setting Up Shop*. New York: McGraw-Hill, 1982.

CHAPTER 6

The Buyout

INTRODUCTION

In a number of instances, buying a business offers an attractive way of becoming an entrepreneur. The leveraged buyout (LBO) is a popular way to buy many companies and is the main method discussed in this chapter. The objectives of this chapter are as follows.

1 To compare buyouts with start-ups.
2 To show how to find the right candidate for buyout.
3 To define the major players in the buyout transaction.
4 To describe financing sources and packages.
5 To discuss how to value the buyout, negotiate the price, and close the deal.

THE BUYOUT VERSUS STARTING FROM SCRATCH

To some, buying another company may be like buying someone else's car. Why buy a lemon or someone else's headaches? Certainly, starting your own business from scratch has advantages, but so does going the buyout route.

Advantages of the Buyout

Usually, with a buyout there are more sources of financing. As a matter of fact, in many instances the seller may become the biggest financing source. Moreover, bankers and other lenders are more willing to lend to an established business with several years of performance behind it.

The business is established, and it has a track record. Its earnings yield, its customers, its cost to sell or manufacture, its employees, its assets, its book value—all are known. Therefore, better forecasts can be made.

The target company is already operating. It has gone through the pitfalls of a start-up. All its components are in place. Often the first year or two of any business are the riskiest. It can take two or three years to reach the break-even point with a start-up.

Life for the owner of a start-up is usually tense and hectic. A well-defined strategy must be developed, the product or service must be produced and made available, and customers must be attracted and convinced to buy from an unproved firm. Meanwhile, capital must be raised, and cash flow, managed. Legal and accounting requirements must be met, and employees must be recruited and trained. Sometimes service businesses break even within a few months or even weeks, but the failure rate is high. Manufacturing companies have a slightly lower failure rate depending on the business, but it may take one or two years or more to break even. Before the break-even point is reached, it can be a tough time for entrepreneurs and their families.

It may be true in some cases that the entrepreneur who buys a business may be acquiring problems; but he also buys an ongoing business, a reputation, and, if he is lucky, a following of customers who will immediately give orders and generate a healthy cash flow.

In some situations, an entrepreneur may be able to buy a business for less than its book value and a price-earnings ratio of significantly less than 10 to 1. It's possible to buy existing businesses for much less than it would take to duplicate the same assets in a start-up. An entrepreneur who believes in his or her skills as a manager may buy a sick or unprofitable business at a huge discount and then turn it around. Note, however, that the rate of failure in businesses that need turning around when they are acquired is much higher than in businesses that are profitable at the time of acquisition. It often happens that the reasons the business is unprofitable are beyond the control of the buyer.[1]

Advantages of Starting from Scratch

A certain zest and spirit characterize the individual who starts his or her own business from scratch. To many entrepreneurs, the greatest thing about going into business in the first place is creating a start-up to match precisely a business model of size, location, customer base, employees, suppliers, plant and equipment, and product-service idea. Obviously, if the product-service idea is unique, the entrepreneur is pretty much compelled to start from scratch anyway.

The entrepreneur can start fresh without being shackled to an old way of doing things. The culture is already established in most businesses, and if this culture is negative, the entrepreneur may not be able to change it. In fact, this may be a reason why the seller wants to get out of the business. Moreover, if the business has a bad reputation, this, too, will be hard to change.

Hunting and finding a buyout target that meets the buyer's criteria can take a long time, maybe as long as three to four years. Many buyers, unless they are professional buyout specialists or investment bankers, don't have this much time to spend. One of the worst pitfalls in pursuing a buyout target is that often the buyer spends time and money in due diligence, researching, securing financing, negotiating, and so forth; the seller then may back out of the deal at the last minute, thus causing the buyer to pay large legal and accounting fees, not to mention incalculable opportunity costs.

The Leveraged Buyout

The leveraged buyout is a special means of acquiring a company, and it has been popular during the last few years. It is especially applicable to investment groups and qualified entrepreneurs. Simply put, a leveraged buyout is the layering of a debt

[1]LaRue T. Hosmer et . al., *The Entrepreneurial Function* (Englewood Cliffs, N.J.: Prentice-Hall, 1977), p. 484. The material is used with permission.

and other securities, which are senior to a relatively small amount of common equity, to finance the acquisition of a buyout target. Generally, the buyout candidate will be an established company with a visible and dependable record of cash flow, and this continued cash flow will be used to service the debt. Also, the buyout company often has a high ratio of fixed assets to total assets to provide the collateral security necessary for the debt financing. The classic leveraged buyout candidate has the following key criteria.[2]

1 An established, long-standing, predictable cash flow from operations that provides adequate debt service coverage for potential lenders.

2 A heavy preponderance of total assets represented by older, fully depreciated fixed assets, such as plant, property, and equipment, which have a worth significantly in excess of their *book* value.

3 Operations in a relatively mature marketplace with an anticipated moderate growth in revenues. This minimizes future capital expenditure requirements, frees up cash flow for debt service and avoids potential dislocations from rapid changes in technology.

4 An in-place product line and management team. This should allow a continuation of earnings in the future without surprises and changes when the company is sold.

5 Low existing current and long-term debt to allow significant new acquisition debt to be put on the books for the buyout.

Imperatives of a Buyout

The following conditions should exist when you consider the buyout route.

1 Entry via a buyout should be free of unfavorable legal implications and contingent liabilities.

2 You should be able to make a significant contribution in several of the following areas:
  (a) Marketing expertise.
  (b) Engineering and technical expertise.
  (c) Financial and accounting expertise.
  (d) Information system.
  (e) Long-term capital formation.
  (f) Product-service development.
  (g) Ability to organize, take the "bull by the horns," and get the job done.

[2]Abridged from Nicholas Wallner, J. Terrence Greve, and Michael Podolny, *The Directory of Financing Sources for Buyouts and Acquisitions* (San Diego, Calif.: Buyout Publications, 1982), p. 11, and used with permission.

    (h) Inventory control.
    (i) Fat cutting.
    (j) Cash managing (imperative in leveraged buyouts).
    (k) Credit managing.
    (l) International trade developing.
    (m) Hustling and promoting.

3 The business should have a record of profit and growth.

4 The present managers, if they stay on, must be compatible with you or the investor groups.

FINDING THE RIGHT COMPANY

Good buyout candidates are hard to find. Before the right one is found, a lot of "spade work" and time are required. First, you must understand fully your circumstances and financing sources. Next you should develop a fairly comprehensive profile of your target company based on fairly specific criteria. Then you must embark on a search strategy.

Ideal Profile for a Leveraged Buyout

Following are a few parameters that are particularly applicable to the leverage buyout.[3]

1 *Proved earnings performance.* Buyouts are financed by conventional lenders, so traditional theories of credit evaluation apply. Three to five years of at least constant sales and profit are a minimum. Often an ideal situation, however, is to find an underachieving company that is earning less than it should be and infuse it with managerial talent that increases earnings even higher. Another important point is to look for companies that grow enough to keep up with GNP, inflation, market size, but not much more. It costs to service increased sales, and this diverts cash flow, which, in turn, puts a strain on debt service. Also, earnings cannot be too cyclical because the average earnings must, at a minimum, support debt service.

2 *Low capital intensity.* Any buyout that looks as if it will require considerable amounts of R and D expenditures, capital equipment, or working capital to perpetuate the earnings stream is generally avoided. Any company that is either development sensitive or capital sensitive or both is a poor candidate for leveraging. Seasonal businesses that require significant working capital increases, particularly for inventory buildup, are usually avoided.

[3]Parameters from Nicholas Wallner and J. Terrence Greve, *Leveraged Buyouts* (San Diego, Calif.: Buyout Publications, 1983), pp. 75–86, and used with permission.

3 *Mundane product lines.*   Look for boring and ugly companies. Stay away from high-technology companies because high technology implies rapidly changing market, obsolescence, high mobility of management, and other factors that can spell disaster for a highly leveraged buyout. In some instances, however, high-technology deals can often become excellent leveraged buyout candidates because of the lack of buyers with technical backgrounds. Moreover, the sellers will frequently do a lot of the financing, thus reducing the risk to the buyer and other lenders.

4 *Dominant market position.*   The higher the leverage, the greater the financial risk; a strong market position serves as a strong safety factor.

5 *Quality management team.*   In a leveraged buyout, the balance sheet is loaded with debt. The number one objective is to amortize this debt; there is little margin for error. A buyout management team must be astute enough and psychologically able to handle the pressure from the risk of a lot of debt. Key management tools are budgeting, planning, cash flow forecasting, and cash management.

6 *Asset-based companies.*   The prime leveraged buyout candidate is a dull manufacturer of a proprietary product that is a leader in its industry with a physical plant carried at far below its real market value and with at least 10 years of remaining useful life. Distribution companies are not excluded, however, especially those with recognized stable product lines, strong market positions, tight credit and collection policies, and high inventory turnover. Service companies are the hardest to leverage because their primary asset other than accounts receivable is usually goodwill, assuming they have any goodwill.

7 *Strong balance sheets.*   To a leveraged buyer, a clean balance sheet means an abundance of good and adequate ''hard'' assets for collateral for loans and a high degree of liquidity. Because the assets of the corporation are the area where the leveraging takes place, ''hard'' assets, including accounts receivable, inventories, machinery and equipment, and real property, should be unencumbered by pledges to lenders or to third parties. Moreover, little debt should be present before leveraging.

8 *Excess and hidden assets.*   A fine point to consider in leveraging is the prospect of asset redevelopment. Many times the deal includes assets that can be spun off to reduce debt. These include real estate, excess machinery and equipment, obsolete and excess inventories, product lines, divisions, and so forth. Remember that paying off a buyout is difficult, and buyers should look for a number of ways to increase cash flow. You should not count on hidden assets to make the deal, but look for them, and, if they exist, convert them to cash.

9 *Resalability.*   Most seasoned entrepreneurs will readily tell you that it is easier to get in a deal then to get out. The trick is to pick a company that larger companies or other investors are likely to be interested in and devise a bailout plan *before* going into the deal.

10 *Size.*   Individual entrepreneurs buy companies ranging in size from very small to very large; it simply depends on who the buyer is, his or her vision, and the depth of his or her pockets.

A summary of an excellent article[4] that captures the essence of a leveraged buyout (LBO) follows: The first key is that the entrepreneur puts in precious little cash. The equity is then leveraged or "empowered" 10, 20, or even 50 times with debt. All senior funding is secured by the buyout's own assets. Lending limits, for example, might be 90 percent of receivables, 50 percent of inventories, and 25 percent of plant and equipment. A middle layer of subordinated debt is taken back by the seller or bought by a third-party investor.

The touchstone of LBOs is cash flow. Almost nothing else matters. All that counts is whether, when, and with what safety you can meet interest demands in the near term and pay back principal in the long term. But tax benefits help. The buyer writes up company assets, generating higher write-offs for depreciation to go with already hefty interest deductions.

With LBOs, small downdrafts in business can cause pneumonia overnight, even death. Sensitivity analysis is a must. "What-if" games are not games. You had better be awfully sure you can weather any storm. Default sits right over the horizon, especially in the initial years. A slight change in market, pricing, margins, overheads, even the economy—and in blow the banks with liens in one hand and auction blocks in the other. Or do they? When you owe small money, you have a creditor; when you owe big bucks, you have a partner.[5]

Matching the Buyer to the Buyout Candidate

Many buyers simply select the wrong kind of business; they don't match their needs and characteristics with the buyout company to determine what business they are best suited for. The following story illustrates this point.

> *Eric got excited about a Volkswagen dealership, but the deal fell through at the last minute. Next he pondered a Chinese restaurant; then, displaying versatility, he considered buying a chain of pizza parlors. Unable to make up his mind, Eric pursued a beauty supply wholesaler, then a plastic engineering firm. Finally, he found his perfect opportunity and forked over $85,000 for Puppy Land, a large retail pet and pet supply store.*
>
> *Three weeks later Eric limped back to our office. "Sell the business. And fast."*
> *I asked him what went wrong. "Oh, it's a profitable business," he admitted, "but it's not for me. I can't stand the endless stream of people who think Puppy Land is*

---

[4]Robert L. Kuhn, "Curing the Healthy," *Texas Business* (June 1984), pp. 31–32. The materials is used with permission.

[5]Ibid.

the mall's answer to the zoo, and the cats are the last straw." "The cats?" I asked. Peering through puffy eyes, he sighed, "Yeah, it turns out I'm allergic to cats."[6]

To build a buyers' business profile, Goldstein[7] uses the five following essential questions.

1 Can you *earn* from the business? Realistically assess the earnings potential of the target, and match it to your earnings goal.

2 Can you *manage* the business? Many buyers look for a business they have no prior experience with. No business is as easy as it looks, and going into one that you know nothing about can lead to failure.

3 Can you *enjoy* the business? Don't buy any business; find the one that will motivate you and put a gleam in your eye—one that you hate to walk away from at night.

4 Can you *afford* the business? What business you can afford depends on many variables: financing sources, negotiating ability, and luck are only three. Goldstein's guideline calls for available cash equal to at least 10 percent of the projected purchase price.

5 Can you *find* the business? You probably won't find a business that precisely matches your selection criteria, but do draw boundaries.

Target Company Profile

Finding the right company to buy is a tough job; it takes patience and persistence. The entrepreneur should first develop a "target company profile" describing the preferred buyout in terms of the following criteria: industry type of business (manufacturing, retail or wholesale, distribution and warehousing, petroleum, transportation, communication, entertainment, mining, and so on), type of product or service, location, size, and financial characteristics. Example of a target company profile is illustrated in Table 6.1.

Search Strategy

It takes time, patience, and persistence to land the right target instead of tired, shopworn, and overpriced leftovers that shrewd buyers have already bypassed.[8] For example, take note of the following case.

[6]Arnold S. Goldstein, *The Complete Guide to Buying and Selling a Business* (New York: Wiley, 1983), p. 19. The material is used with permission.

[7]Ibid.

[8]Goldstein, op. cit., p. 37.

TABLE 6.1
Example of Target Company Profile

Criteria	Prefer	Will consider

1. Company size
    Book value
    Annual sales
	$1–$1.5 million
	$10–20 million
		$0.5–$1.5 million
		$10 million plus

2. Company location	Southeast Southwest	Anywhere except upper Midwest
3. Type of business	Manufacturing Processing	Wholesale distribution
4. Type of products	Valves and Measurement devices	Industrial supplies
5. Industry (industries)	Chemical Petroleum Pulp and Paper	Any relevant to process control experience

6. Incumbent
    management
    requirement
	Sales and marketing
	Financial
		——

7. Ownership
    Participants
      Current owner
      Incumbent mgt.
      Outside investors
	
	No
	Yes
	No
		
		Yes
		Yes
		Yes

8. Other criteria
    Company must have proved record of consistent earnings and be in good financial
    condition.		

Source: Nicholas Wallner and J. Terrence Greve, *How to Do a Leveraged Buyout or Acquisition,* (San Diego, Calif.: Buyout Publications, Inc., 1982), p. 15. Used with permission.

Buying too soon and rushing in too fast spelled trouble for Craig H., whose goal was to buy a liquor store south of Boston. After scanning the ads in the Boston Globe *and placing a phone call to one local business broker, Craig uncovered 5 leads. "That's plenty," he thought. After three days of superficial investigation, Craig eagerly settled for a run-down liquor and wine shop with a hefty $80,000 price tag. "Don't buy just yet," I cautioned Craig. Flipping through the telephone directory yellow pages, I counted 600 liquor stores in Craig's area. "How many of these stores are for sale right now?" I asked. "I don't know. At least five," he replied. Knowing that 15 percent to 20 percent of all businesses in a given industry are for sale at any given time, I told Craig he could have his pick of 100 liquor stores. Why settle for 5? Craig, the overanxious buyer would not listen. Two weeks after he purchased his overpriced business, he came across another liquor store with double the sales and profits and a bargain $60,000 price tag.[9]*

[9]Ibid, p. 38.

Set realistic goals. Know your profile; know the target company profile. Do they match? Do you really know what you are hunting for? Are you hunting tigers with a BB gun? Are you hunting for deer when you should be hunting for quail? Are you hunting for alligators in the desert? Are you wasting expensive ammunition on frail game that won't "put meat on the table"? Do you shoot at anything that moves?

It is assumed that by now these questions have been answered. The next step is to search out and find prospective deals. The more deals that the buyer is exposed to, the better are his or her chances for success. Following are some of the methods the entrepreneur can use in finding the right deal.

1 *Direct approach.* Go directly to the source in person, and ask if the company is for sale. Or use telephone or letters. Use trade journals or other advertising media and run ads. Keep them simple, for example: BUYER WANTS SMALL BUSINESS WITHIN 30 MILES OF DALLAS. CALL PRINCIPAL AT XXX-XXX-XXXX.

2 *Indirect referrals.* Use people such as accountants, lawyers, bankers, and trust officers. Many of these people have an inventory of buyers and sellers. Other referral sources include suppliers, creditors, competitors, customers, distributors, and salespeople. Most of these people are in the information mainstream and are the first to know if an owner is contemplating a sale.

3 *Publications.* There are a number of publications that identify potential sellers, such as those published by Buyout Publications, Inc.[10]

4 *Professionals.* These are intermediaries who bring buyer and seller together. They include investment bankers, sponsors, brokers, attorneys, and accountants.

THE MAJOR PLAYERS

This section deals with the various players in the leveraged buyout transaction. The players are the seller, the buyer, financing sources, and other third parties.

The Sellers

Many established businesses of all kinds and sizes are for sale. Some buyout specialists estimate that as many as 20 percent of the businesses in any industry are for sale at any given time and that even more would be for sale if they were actively sought after. Why are businesss for sale? It may be any of a large number of reasons, some of which are these: The owner has a flop and is simply trying to unload it; the owner has a health problem; the owner simply wants to cash out and re-

[10]For a complete list, see Wallner and Greve, *Leveraged Buyouts,* pp. 89–93.

tire; somewhere in the business (e.g., between partners, between owners and employees, between owners and suppliers), there is a major disagreement; the target business is a subsidiary of a conglomerate and simply does not fit and is, therefore, being divested.

There are three seller groups.

1 *Public shareholders.* The public shareholder is far removed from the actual buyout transaction. Managers or an investment group simply buy for cash the stock of the company from the widely dispersed public shareholders to gain complete control of the corporation. Usually, the public shareholders are given a price well above the current market value of their stock. This kind of buyout is not of particular interest in this text.

2 *The corporate seller.* Usually a corporation is simply trying to divest a subsidiary that no longer fits into the total economic entity. For example, the product line does not match or is approaching obsolescence, the business is not growing at the desired rate, it is not earning enough, or earnings are erratic. In some instances, the seller is getting rid of mistakes and bad deals.

A problem that the entrepreneur may have in buying a divestitute is that the corporate seller looks for clean, simple transactions for cash. That means no seller financing, which is a key component of many buyouts made by private entrepreneurs. Moreover, an issue of significance to the corporate seller is the ongoing treatment of employees of the divested company. The obligation to meet contracts and meet equivalent wages and benefits for the employees who stay on is normally standard contract language for most corporations.

3 *The private seller.* Normally, this seller is the old entrepreneur who started the company years ago and is now thinking about cashing out and retiring. These sellers afford the greatest number of buyout opportunities, especially for the small entrepreneur. Normally, the private seller's reasons for selling are personal rather than corporate. Also, private sellers have a tendency to sell their companies when business is good.

The Buyers

Buyers come in many forms. These include corporations, individual entrepreneurs, management groups, employee groups, and buyout specialists.[11]

1 *The corporate buyer.* During favorable economic conditions where large non-financial corporations have suddenly and hugely increased their cash positions, they become acquisition-hungry and begin to hunt for buyout targets, especially middle-sized companies. Their aim is to diversify their asset base through

[11]Noted buyout specialists are Kohlberg, Kravis, Roberts, and Company and Forstmann Little and Company.

buyouts. They believe that it is cheaper to buy than to build. In short, they divert their massive cash funds from modernization and expansion to acquisitions.

2 *Individual entrepreneurs.*   Unlike corporations, this group is in the market to buy all the time except during severe economic dislocations. If they depend primarily on lenders, they are curtailed only when interest rates reach levels of 18 percent or more and when credit is tight.

Often the majority of these buyers are taking the plunge for the first time. Their deals are usually put together with a down payment, and the balance of the purchase price in the form of a note or notes paid out over a period of time. In many instances, the seller is the largest noteholder. This text deals mainly with this kind of buyer.

3 *Management groups.*   More and more management groups are participating in buyouts. Corporate sellers are finding out that management buyouts can be a viable option when the corporation knows and trusts the buying management group. As stated in earlier chapters, lenders and venture capitalists believe that the most important intangible in backing a venture is the quality of the management team. Therefore, investors are usually enthusiastic about backing former managers who form a buyout group to takeover and run the company. Moreover, these backers believe that when the managers have some of their own money in the deal and are owners, this situation provides strong motivation to perform. On the other hand, an owner who was a former manager may not be a better manager in the new deal. Having money at risk does not necessarily mean an improvement in managerial abilities.

4 *Employee groups.*   As with management groups, employees form groups to buy out the company they are working for. OTASCO, Incorporated, a home, outdoor, and automotive supply company, was acquired by its employees in 1984 and represents a good example of an employee buyout. This leveraged buyout was financed by a group of banks; the equity portion was financed by the OTASCO Employees Retirement Trust. The employees now feel that they are in control of their destiny and have an opportunity to succeed on their own. Clearly, the decisions they make and how they work are very personal. They are, indeed, working for themselves. Other employee buyouts usually involve a deal that is based on job survival rather than entrepreneurial activity. For example, several steel mills have been bought by blue-collar employees; otherwise, these mills would have been shut down. Other buyouts include building supply companies and various small manufacturing firms.

5 *Buyout specialists.*   These are large companies that combine their skills as buyout specialists and operating managers. They normally own outright several private companies. The total aggregate value of these companies may be several billion dollars. Also, some of these companies, in addition to buying companies for their own accounts, put buyout packages together for private entrepreneurs and management groups.

Financing Sources

The following list classifies each firm or institution into the one of three groups that best reflects its role in the buyout financing process. Although there are some firms that have characteristics of more than one of the groups, most can be clearly separated into one particular class of financing player.

1 *Senior lenders.* These are primarily larger financial institutions such as banks and commercial finance companies. The latter group, which are also known as "asset-based lenders," may be independent. In some cases, an insurance company will act as a senior lender by purchasing senior notes in a leveraged buyout. Regardless of its corporate structure, the senior lender almost always functions as a "pure" lender with no residual interest in the equity of the borrowing company. As a result, lenders in this group derive their return strictly from the interest charges on their loans and desire to take the least risk of all the financing participants. To minimize their risk, senior lenders often take a security interest in some or all of the assets of the acquired or the acquiring company. Such collateral usually consists of accounts receivable, inventory, machinery and equipment, and real estate.

2 *Subordinated lender-investors.* Participants in this group consist of insurance companies, pension funds, small business investment corporations (SBICs), and private venture capital pools.[12] As the name implies, these sources can function either as a lender or equity investor or both. Regardless of which securities are purchased, participants in this group almost always take some equity in the acquired company. The interest in the equity ownership requires this type of lender or investor to take more risk and subordinate his or her investment to that of the senior lender. As a result, the subordinated lender who is "sandwiched" between the pure debt and pure equity layers in the capital structure is often called a "mezzanine" lender.

Within this group, firms may have widely differing risk profiles and appetites for various securities. Some may want to take minimum risk and invest only in yielding securities with small equity options. Others may participate only in common stock. Still others may invest in several different securities of the newly capitalized buyout or acquisition. Typically, insurance companies, pension funds, and SBICs will seek interest-bearing securities whereas the venture capital pools are more likely to participate at the pure equity level. Needless to say, this group of investors is very important to the overall financing, especially if the corporate or private buyer lacks sufficient equity capital to do the deal only with senior lenders.

Mezzanine investors typically get a rate in the low teens with an equity kicker thrown in to sweeten the deal. Much of this kind of financing is really thinly disguised preferred stock, but it is called "debt" because interest pay-

---

[12]Two traditional lenders are General Electric Credit and Prudential Insurance.

ments are tax-deductible to the payer, but stock dividends are not. This mezzanine money allows the buyer to make riskier deals because senior lenders are more lenient and open to deals since they look at the mezzanine money as a buffer that protects their loans.[13]

3 *Sponsor-investors.* This group comprised of investment bankers and venture capital firms, is different in that one of its main functions, in addition to investing funds, is to provide services that are vital to making the deal happen. Although most of these activities are related to financing the buyout or acquisition, they also include activities such as matching a management team with a suitable corporate vehicle, negotiating with the seller, coordinating legal and accounting activities, closing the deal, and monitoring the operations after closing.

Other Third Parties

Once you have decided on financing sources, you should also be sure that you get the very best in other professional advisers. You can normally retain local lawyers and accountants for a fraction of the fees charged by more prestigious and experienced firms; however, you should always go with the most experienced firms. Without exception, the better, more experienced lawyers and accountants will enable the transaction to proceed more smoothly and rapidly. Remember that you are about to embark on one of the most important and largest investment decisions of your life. You can bet that the best talent will be represented on the seller's side.

Among legal information and documents are copies of contracts; evidences of ownership; copies of patents, trademarks, trade secrets, and copyrights; organizational documents; liens; chattel mortgages; conditional sales agreements; assignment of accounts; tax returns; zoning ordinances; building codes; court records; and so forth. A thorough investigation of these documents should be made by the lawyer to ensure transfer of good title and ownership and to relieve the buyer from the risk of contingent liabilities.

A special responsibility of some accountants is to attest to the reliability and fairness of financial statements. Moreover, accountants can be hired to make detailed analysis of accounting data and interpret this analysis. Accountants can serve as auditors to review the accounting procedures and the system of internal control. Tax returns for the life of the company should be reviewed. The specific tax treatment or IRS interpretation of both tangible and intangible assets' values or lives must be established.

If the buyout target is a manufacturer, cost records should be analyzed as to material, labor, and overhead costs; scrap sales; spoiled and defective items. If the buyout is going to be highly leveraged, cash flow becomes extremely important to

---

[13]Allan Sloan, "Luring Banks Overboard," *Forbes*, April 9, 1984, p. 43. The material is used with permission.

the buyer to meet debt obligations. Therefore, the accountant should prepare detailed cash-flow statements of past operations and provide projections over the next several years.

Most buyouts, particularly those that are highly leveraged, are dependent on asset financing. Commercial banks or other lenders use the underlying assets as security for funds extended to make the buyout. The services of a skilled, professional appraiser are imperative during this phase because lenders typically require current market values in orderly exchange for the assets and also a forced liquidation value should they be required to sell these assets piecemeal over a short timespan. The postbuyout of the price paid to the assets acquired has substantial tax and economic consequences. A detailed valuation is required to support the book and tax depreciable basis of the "new" company.[14]

A Typical Leveraged Buyout

Good Foods, Incorporated, has decided to sell its Tasty Pickle Division. You want to buy Tasty Pickle, and you agree to pay a price of $1 million.

You locate a venture capital firm, Sprouts, Incorporated, that will help finance the deal with subordinated debt and a 50 percent equity interest. The seller, Good Foods, also takes part of the subordinated debt. You put up your money of $100,000, or 10 percent of the total purchase price.

After a lot of negotiation, a financing package is arranged consisting of a $200,000 collateralized note from your bank, a subordinated note of $100,000 from Good Foods, a subordinated note of $500,000 from Sprouts, $100,000 of equity capital from Sprouts, and $100,000 from you. On the closing of the deal, the division's assets and recorded liabilities are transferred to a new corporation, Tasty Pickle, Incorporated.

Advantages and Disadvantages of Giving up Equity

Assuming you bought Tasty Pickle, why should you relinquish 50 percent of your equity to Sprouts? The reason is that giving up a portion of the pie is often a safer and better course of action. Indeed, this approach often provides many advantages, such as the following.[15]

1 The financial risk is less. You have a greater cushion in the event of a downturn in business.

[14]David R. Blaine, "Appraising the Appraisers," *The Journal of Buyouts and Acquisitions*, 2:2 (December 1983). The material is used with permission.

[15]Advantages and disadvantages are taken from C. William Steelman, "Pitfalls in Medium-Sized Leveraged Buyouts," *The Journal of Buyouts and Acquisitions*, 2:1 (October 1983), p. 20 and used with permission.

2 Because your company has a greater net worth, your banker will be far more willing to ride through the difficult times with you.

3 You will be able to move much more quickly. If you come into a bank with a solid base of equity, coupled with a solid cash flow and financeable assets, a decision can be quickly made—typically within two or three weeks. You should never lose sight of the fact that once the decision to sell is made, the first buyer with a solid offer has an advantage. This is particularly important in buying a private company because it is not at all unusual to see the seller get cold feet. You do not want to give him or her any opportunity for second thoughts.

4 In working with an experienced venture capitalist, you pick up an invaluable resource. A highly competent business person has made a decision to invest in you and will want to serve on your board. He or she has been through the process many times and will be an ongoing source of advice and counsel. Also, should good business so dictate, additional capital is, in most cases, readily available.

What, then, are the disadvantages of seeking out a venture capital partner?

1 You do give up a sizable chunk of equity. However, experience has proved that 50 percent of a good deal is better than 100 percent of a shaky one.

2 More important, the venture capitalist has ultimate control of the situation and, if necessary, can remove you and your management team. Although this prospect may be distressing to some, it is not a great worry for competent managers. In considering an investment, the venture capitalist considers the most important criterion to be the quality of management. If there is doubt about management's abilities, the investment is not made. Therefore, you should be primarily concerned with eliminating your own mistakes that would depress business profits. If you fail to do so, the business would be in trouble regardless of how the acquisition is financed.

Testing the Financial Package

An integral part of devising the proper financial structure is to test it against the target company's ability to generate sufficient earnings and cash flow. For any given financial package to be feasible, it is necessary to demonstrate clearly that the demands imposed by the proposed financing on the company's present and future financial resources can be satisfied. The procedure for verifying this fact is the preparation of pro forma financial statements (income statement, balance sheet, and cash flow), which are based on assumptions developed in the analysis, valuation, and financial structuring of the deal.

This involves a considerable amount of forecasting and "number crunching" by the buyer. Although this is a very laborious process, especially if it is necessary to run several different iterations or "what-if" analyses, it is an absolutely essential step in the deal process. To make decisions and commitments without performing these analyses is a significant gamble on the part of the buyer. In fact, it is unlikely that the transaction could be consummated without these analyses because lenders and investors almost always want to see the impact of projected cash flow on their investments.[16]

In addition to their vital role in testing the financial package, pro forma financial statements are also important tools in other aspects of the analyses, financing, and negotiation of the acquisition. First, they enable the buyer to analyze the impact of possible contingencies on the company and the investments of the financial participants. Such "what-if" analyses should show the effects of lower sales, increased labor or material costs, rising interest rates, and so forth, on earnings and cash flow. Another key reason to have pro forma statements is that they form the cornerstone of the "financing package," the most important tool used to sell the lenders and outside investors on the deal.[17]

Finally, these projections will be a starting point in an operating plan against which the company's progress can be measured after the deal has been closed. Of course, there will be periodic updates and revisions to the initial plan. But any successfully operated business is characterized by prudent financial planning. And the time to start is now—before the deal is closed.[18]

Goldstein's Financial Pyramid

A somewhat different slant to building a financial package is shown in Figure 6.1. This pyramid shows you how you can find your own financing building blocks.[19] Key points to remember are these.

1 Don't fall victim to a seller's "cash down" demands. You can probably buy with considerably less.

2 Always build your financial pyramid starting with bank financing and letting the seller provide secondary financing.

3 Why not assume the seller's liabilities, to be deducted from your down payment?

4 Your suppliers offer an excellent source of down payment money.

5 Can you tap cash flow to get the seller his or her money without digging into your pocket?

6 Brokers can lend.

7 Look for hidden assets you can presell to supply your down payment.

[16]Nicholas Wallner and J. Terrence Greve, *How to do a Leveraged Buyout or Acquisition* (San Diego, Calif.: Buyout Publications, 1982), p. 157, and used with permission.

[17]Ibid.

[18]Ibid.

[19]Goldstein, op. cit., pp. 150–51. This material is used with permission.

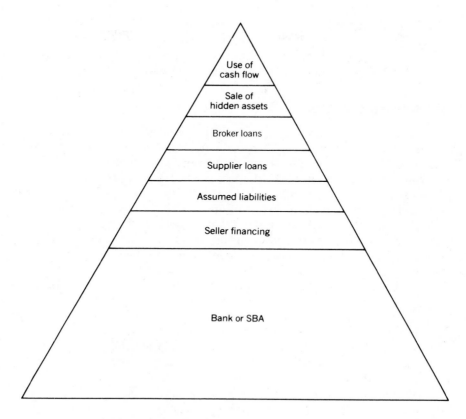

FIGURE 6.1   *The financial pyramid. (Source: Goldstein, op. cit., pp. 150–51. Used with permission.)*

8 Don't accept expensive partners unless you know you can't raise the funds elsewhere.

9 Don't be afraid of leverage. Remember that today's liabilities can be tomorrow's net worth.[20]

VALUING THE BUYOUT, NEGOTIATING THE PRICE, AND CLOSING THE DEAL

Don't forget that a buyout is fundamentally an investment, and the old money manager maxim of "buy low, sell high" should not be forgotten.[21] But what is its

[20]Ibid.

[21]Kent P. Dauten, "The Importance of the Purchase Price in Leveraged Buyout Transactions," *The Journal of Buyouts and Acquisitions*, 2:3 (February 1984) p. 9. This material is used with permission.

value to you? What price should you pay to make a desired rate of return on your investment? What valuation yardstick can you use? Is price the same as value? How do you set a price? What are important terms to include in the contract at closing? This section will help answer these questions.

Quantitative Measure of Value

Unfortunately, there is no such thing as a magic formula that you can use to crank out a value of the buyout target. A business value is a composite of hundreds of variables, some of which are qualitative and others of which are quantitative. Valuing a buyout is part art, part science, and part wild-eyed guesses. Indeed, seldom is it strictly numbers that move the buyer and seller to close the deal. A lot of it is based on psychological factors and simple human motivations. The deal could be struck simply because the buyer wants to get in for ego-achievement reasons and the seller wants to get out because he or she is tired and wants a change. In fact, nonquantitative factors can add confusion and disorder to a quantitative valuation process.

The astute entrepreneur will use a number of valuation methods to drive a range of values that can be adjusted and weighted as specific circumstances indicate. This approach is called "correlating the values" and can give a clear indication as to what the purchase price should be for the deal to be profitable.

Morevoer, application of quantitative methods help to take some of the "smoke" and fantasy out of the minds of both buyer and seller and return them to reality. "Putting the pencil to the deal" and seeing how the numbers look are imperative in any deal. Following are two methods that will help you do this. They are (1) asset values and (2) earnings and cash flow values.

Asset Values.   The first question to ask early on is what assets are to be transferred? The assets most commonly purchased in a buyout transaction are merchandise inventory, supplies, furniture and fixtures, leaseholds, buildings, real estate, equipment, and accounts receivable if they are guaranteed by the seller. Clearly, then, valuing a company this way is the sum of assets, especially tangible assets.

The simplest way to estimate a company's value by using this method is to take the net book value as it appears on the current balance sheet. Another way to use the balance sheet is to revise it to reflect the appraisal value of the items included, especially the tangible fixed assets. With this method, accounts receivable should be stated at amounts estimated to be realized. Inventories should be restated at current market values. Land, buildings, and equipment items may require special appraisals in arriving at their present replacement or reproduction values. Intangible assets, such as patents, copyrights, and secret formulas, should be included at their current values. Special care and investigation should be done to determine that all liabilities are fully entered and recognized. Although a better indicator of value than book value, the method of appraised asset values still ignores many other important valuation factors.

Incidentally, some evaluators try to establish a value of the buyout candidate based on a price paid for a "comparable" business with a similar asset base and within a reasonable time frame and equivalent location. Indeed, this technique is used extensively in real estate appraisal work and in large franchising operations where there is a high degree of uniformity. With most companies, however, especially smaller, private ones, little comparability exists from one company to another. No two businesses are alike; each is tied to its own unique economic potential, especially to the influence of its owner-managers. The only reason for looking at other buyouts is that the comparable method will give a point of reference and will let you see what is going on in the marketplace and derive some value indicators.

Earnings and Cash Flow Values.   Valuation by assets is not as relevant as estimated earnings and cash flow, especially in a leveraged buyout. The value of a company is not necessarily the sum of its assets. The value comes from the potential of the assets to make money; assets are useless without profit potential.

The normal earnings of the past are used as a basis for estimating earnings of the future. Economic and business conditions, the business cycle, sources of supply, incumbent management if available, continued demand for the company's products or services, price structure, competition, and so forth, must be studied in developing data that make it possible to convert past earnings into estimated future earnings. But a word of caution: What earnings the seller had does not necessarily mean that you will have the same earnings. You need to derive your own numbers. If you do use past earnings to help forecast future earnings, do so without rose-colored glasses.

An extremely good indicator of value is based on the capitalization of future earnings. Capitalized value is the value that would bring the stated earnings at a specified rate of return, and this rate is usually the current rate of return for investments involving a similar amount of risk. The capitalization technique is based on the following formula.

$$\text{Value} = \frac{\text{Estimated earnings}}{\text{Capitalization rate}}$$

The capitalization rate is derived by considering the relative risk of an investment in the company versus that associated with alternative investments. For example, if an investor can get a 15 percent return on marketable long-term government bonds, he or she should obviously demand more (a higher capitalization rate) from an investment in a company with no liquidity and an irregular earnings pattern. A higher capitalization rate might be offset if the company has excellent growth prospects and consequent potential for capital appreciation.

Assume that estimated earnings of a buyout target are projected at $50,000 per year for the next five years. If the investment is as safe as a government security, the buyer should be willing to pay $333,333 ($50,000 ÷ 0.15). Very few buyout targets, however, have as low a risk factor as this investment. As a rule of thumb, 20 to 40 percent is considered a normal range for buyouts. Therefore, where a buyout target has a projected earnings stream of $50,000, the price for it could range between $250,000 (20 percent or five times earnings) and $125,000 (40 percent or two and one half times earnings).

Goodwill

Goodwill is generally regarded as a summation of all the special advantages, not otherwise identifiable, related to a going business. It includes such items as a good name and reputation, capable staff and personnel, high credit rating, good service, superior product or service, favorable location, and the ability to earn above-normal profits as a result of these factors.

A number of methods may be employed in arriving at a goodwill figure. Following is an example of one of these methods.

Assume projected net earnings:

19X1	$130,000
19X2	90,000
19X3	85,000
19X4	95,000
Total	$400,000

Average net earnings for period:
$400,000 ÷ 4 = $100,000

Assume appraised value of net assets
as of 19X4 before recognizing
goodwill as $430,000.

If, in the preceding example, a return of 22 percent were required on the investment, the buyout would be valued at $454,545 ($100,000 ÷ 0.22). As net assets, with the exception of goodwill, were appraised at $430,000, goodwill would be valued at $24,545.

Strictly from the buyer's viewpoint, goodwill means one thing: The buyout will make money. The truth is that few buyout targets are producing excess profits or have other features that create goodwill. Moreover, a business that is sold is never really the same as it was. Usually profits fall off after the change of ownership.

Negotiating Price

You calculate value and negotiate price. Negotiating a price involves running all the variables through the minds of the buyer and seller to end up with an outcome:

agreed-on price. Negotiating is a back-and-forth process; each negative feature is weighed against each positive feature.

In addition to valuations as discussed earlier, negotiation dynamics has a lot to do with financing terms discussed in the following section. As a rule of thumb, price goes down as down payment by the buyer goes up. Bluntly stated, buyers with high aspirations but little cash will normally pay a premium for the opportunity to buy their own business. Moreover, high aspirations and big dreams can cloud objectivity and create a vulnerability for an inflated price.

Again, the valuation methods presented earlier should be heavy in the mix of variables used in setting the price. The payback period should help to put a lid on the price. Furthermore, it is imperative that the price be limited to a price that the business can afford to pay back out of *its own earnings and cash flow*.

Fundamental Rules of Negotiation.   The fundamental rules of negotiation for the buyer in a buyout are (1) view the negotiating process as a "win-win" rather than a "win-lose" situation; (2) identify your own needs, strengths, and weaknesses prior to engaging in negotiations; (3) try to determine the needs, strengths, and weaknesses of the seller and other parties with whom you will be negotiating; (4) get a competent deal attorney who is adept at working with the attorneys of the seller and lenders; (5) negotiate only where you are prepared, and do not allow yourself to be drawn into premature negotiations, especially with regard to price and terms; (6) enter into the negotiations with high, but not unreasonable, aspirations; (7) in making concessions, do so as late as possible in the negotiations, and always get something in return; (8) when the other party makes a concession, take it and avoid any further negotiations on that particular point; (9) don't put yourself in the position where you "must have the deal," or, if you really must have it, don't let the seller know it; (10) know your limits, and be prepared to "take a walk."[22]

In the process of buying a company, many things will occur that cannot be controlled or anticipated. In fact, one principle that always seems to hold true is to "expect the unexpected." During the time between reaching an "agreement in principle" and the closing, one or more unexpected things happen that often threaten to blow the deal up. Many aspiring buyers, who are otherwise very capable, often lose the deal and their investment of time and money because they are unable to cope with these disappointments. The professional dealer, however, expects the unexpected and, unless it is clearly not in his or her best interest, finds creative solutions to any unexpected problems.[23]

These unexpected and usually unpleasant surprises may include poor interim operating results, a better offer from another buyer, negative inputs from the seller's legal and accounting advisers, the seller's remorse, corporate politics, lowball lender

---

[22]Wallner and Greve. *How to do a Leveraged Buyout or Acquisition*, pp. 257–58.
[23]Ibid.

appraisals, and reduced lender advance rates. The key is to make the necessary adjustments, assuming the deal still makes sense from an investment perspective.[24]

Game Playing by Sellers.   Sellers come in all shapes and sizes, and they all play predictable games. You're bound to meet the following, camouflaged by their own smokescreen.[25]

1 *Ms. Just Testing.*   This "seller" advertises and even negotiates but never closes a deal.

Why do such sellers persist in wasting your time and money? For several reasons. Some want only to reassure themselves that their businesses are valuable. Others enjoy dickering with buyers. Finally comes the seller who figures she'll put her business on the market at a ridiculously high price to see if one poor sucker might take the bait.

How can you smoke out the testers? They never call in their accountants or lawyers because accountants and lawyers cost money and make their hobby very expensive. Whenever you suspect you're up against a tester, ask her to have her accountant work with your accountant to go over the books. That's when the tester usually backs out.

2 *Ms. I Don't Really Want to Sell.*   This character sits behind a big desk with her hands behind her head, saying "My business isn't really for sale, but I'll entertain an interesting offer." This master intimidator wants you on the defensive while maintaining the upper hand. But this same seller has beaten the bushes for the past three years looking for a buyer. Let such a seller know early in the game that you don't really want to buy. The phone call will come.

3 *Mr. In Demand.*   This seller's strategy is to get you bidding against yourself by believing every buyer is banging down his doors. Last week he had three offers that he's still considering, and tomorrow he expects two more. Mr. In Demand, is a very busy man sifting through all his wonderful offers. But because he's the benevolent type he'll add yours to the growing pile.

How should you react? First, tell him you don't care about other buyers or what they offer. Your only concern is what the business is worth to you. Next let him know you can't be rushed because you have too many other businesses to consider.

4 *Mr. Desperate.*   This cunning creature peeks out from behind his smokescreen to entice you to take advantage of his desperation. "I've got to sell—and—fast," he tells you, recounting his problems with his lower back. Maybe it's the broker handing you this yarn, but you see the message. Snap it up before it gets away. Today's your lucky day.

---

[24]Ibid.
[25]Summarized from Goldstein op. cit., pp. 155–56.

Mr. Desperate is seldom desperate. He just wants a fast offer to get the ball rolling so that he can spend the next four months negotiating you up to his price when he's not busy playing golf with his bad back.

How can you be sure Mr. Desperate's not in trouble? It's easy. If he were, he wouldn't be playing Mr. Desperate. He'd be called instead—

5 *Mr. Who's in Trouble.*   Now here's where you'll find the *real* Mr. Desperate. Bill collectors are closing in, the landlord's about to throw him out, and the sheriff's hanging auction signs outside his door, but there he sits pretending he's on top of the world.

Faced with the seller who has to sell, but isn't likely to admit it, you can use only one strategy. In fact, this strategy can work wonders in bringing any of these game players out from behind their smokescreen. Make a bogus offer. Start high, and the seller begins to dream his wonderful dreams and become psychologically committed. The trick is to work his dreams down slowly until you reach the price and terms you want.

Closing the Deal

If the participants have successfully cleared all the hurdles and dealt with all the unexpected surprises, the day they have all been waiting for finally arrives. It usually takes about five to six months from inception to the close of the transaction. By that time, everyone is generally tired of the deal but very happy to see finally some tangible results from the intensive efforts. The closing session itself is usually orchestrated by the attorneys with a multitude of documents that require appropriate signatures.[26]

The terms of the contract are of utmost importance to a solid, problem-free transfer of ownership. The old adage "good paper makes good deals" is certainly true in a buyout transaction. Goldstein provides a definitive list of terms that should be included in the contract to protect you. Here they are.[27]

1 *What assets are to be sold?*   The asset description should be detailed so that no confusion or misunderstanding exists as to what is being acquired. For example, an itemization may include merchandise inventory existing at time of sale; furniture and fixtures, equipment, tools, signs, supplies; and customer lists.

2 *What assets are to be retained by seller?*   Frequently, these include cash on hand and on deposit at the time of transfer, personal vehicles, tax rebates, insurance proceeds, prepaid deposits, and so forth.

3 *How will accounts receivable be handled?*   If the buyer is to acquire accounts receivable, their valuation must be decided. Rather than arbitrarily discount

[26]Wallner and Greve. *How to do a Leveraged Buyout or Acquisition*, p. 258.
[27]The list is summarized from Goldstein, op. cit., pp. 174–82.

older receivables, it's best to acquire them at face value. Those uncollected after a specific time period should be transferred back to the seller for full payment.

4 *What is the purchase price?*   Allocate the total purchase price among the assets being sold in order to establish the acquisition price of depreciable assets. The aim of the buyer is to place as much of the purchase price as possible on depreciable assets, such as furniture and fixtures, vehicles, equipment, and so forth.

5 *How will the purchase price be paid?*   This should be spelled out in the financing package. Counsel should prepare all finance documents such as notes, assumption of liabilities, amounts, liens, and so forth, and make them exhibits to the contract.

6 *How will inventory adjustment be made?*   The valuation of inventory should be conducted by physical tabulation immediately prior to the sale. Both parties should agree on a professional inventory tabulation firm to tabulate and value the inventory impartially. The objective is to buy at the seller's net acquisition price. All unsalable items should be rejected.

7 *What about other adjustments?*   Examples of items adjusted and prorated are insurance premiums, rent, deposits, payroll, fuel oil, inventory sold after tabulation, and prepayments.

8 *What about the seller's liabilities?*   If the buyer is to acquire the assets without assuming seller debt, the agreement will expressly state "assets are being sold free and clear of all liens, encumbrances, and liabilities or adverse claims." Examples of additional protection include notification to the seller's creditors of the intended sale not less than 10 days prior to the sale, a check of mortgages and liens, obtaining tax waivers, insistence on an indemnity agreement whereby the seller will pay or protect the buyer from any claims made by the seller's creditors, and additionally requiring the seller to place a sufficient portion of the purchase price in escrow as security to protect against unsettled creditor claims.

9 *What other warranties should the seller make to the buyer?*   A buyer should insist on each of these additional warranties:
   (a) The seller owns and has good and marketable title to all the assets to be sold. (If any items are not owned but leased and held on consignment, on loan, or on conditional sale, they should be set forth on a disclaimer list attached to the contract.)
   (b) The seller has full authority to sell and transfer the assets and to undertake the transaction.
   (c) The financial statements (or tax returns) shown to the buyer are accurate in all material respects. The tax returns or statements should be attached to the agreement.
   (d) No litigation, governmental proceedings, or investigation against the business is known to be pending.

(e) The seller has no knowledge of any developments that would materially affect the business.

10 *What are the rights of the seller to compete?*   The covenant of the seller not to compete should define a geographic radius and duration. It's enforceable to the extent that is reasonable to protect the goodwill. For businesses where the specific customers can be defined, the covenant should prohibit solicitation of these customers by the seller.

11 *What if there is casualty to the business prior to the closing?*   The contract should provide that on any casualty (fire, water, or sprinkler damage, and so on) to the premises or to any material part of the assets, the buyer should have the right to rescind the agreement.

The casualty clause should extend to the shopping center or other major adjoining tenants relied on to draw customers.

12 *What restrictions should be imposed on the seller in operating the business prior to closing?*   The minimum conditions should be that the seller will do the following:
(a) Maintain customary business hours.
(b) Not change prices beyond the ordinary course of business.
(c) Not terminate employees without good cause.
(d) Not conduct a going-out-of-business or liquidation sale.
(e) Not discontinue charge accounts, deliveries, or other existing service policy.
(f) Not terminate relations with suppliers.
(g) Preserve the goodwill of the customers, suppliers, and others having business relations with it.

13 *What conditions should attach to the agreement?*   The buyer should make the agreement conditional on any external factor on which full performance is dependent. The most common examples are these:
(a) Lease: The buyer would make the obligation to close conditional on his or her obtaining an acceptable lease for the premises. The terms of the proposed lease should be negotiated with the landlord in advance of the closing and even in advance of the negotiations. Therefore, a copy of the intended or required lease should be appended. The seller would agree to terminate his or her present lease on sale, with acceptance of termination by the landlord. If the seller's lease is to be assigned, the contract would be conditional on the landlord's assent to the assignment and acknowledgment that the lease is in good standing.
(b) Financing: If the buyer is relying on outside financing to fund the acquisition, the terms of the proposed financing should be spelled out. The seller should insist that the condition be satisfied by a certain time prior to the sale, or the contract may be voided. This protects a seller from waiting until the date of closing to find out that the financing condition hasn't been satisfied.

(c) License transfers: If the buyer is obligated to obtain new licenses to operate the business, the contract should be conditional on the buyer's obtaining the licenses. As with all conditions, the buyer should agree to use best efforts.

(d) Transfer of contract rights: If the buyer is relying on a transfer of contract rights (franchises, distributorships, or other third-party contracts), the agreement should be conditional on acceptance of the transfer.

14 *What happens to the books and records of the business on closing?* Under a transfer of assets, the financial and tax records would remain the property of the seller. Records relating to the goodwill of the business should be transferred to the buyer. These would include customer lists, trade secrets, pricing information, catalogs, and invoices relating to assumed liabilities. The seller should deliver any warranties on any equipment being transferred.

15 *How should disputes under the agreement be resolved?* The American Arbitration Association, with offices in every major city, will hear and resolve disputes within a matter of months; and their findings have the same authority as a court judgment if the parties agree to it in the contract.

16 *When should the closing be?* Buyers should be aware that even when a contract specifies a closing date, the parties have a reasonable period of time thereafter to perform. The buyer should insert a provision stating "time for performance is of the essence" if he or she intends to hold the seller to the exact closing date.

SUMMARY

The two extremes of going into business are the buyout and the start-up. In buyouts, many advantages exist for the would-be entrepreneur, and, consequently, this way of going into business should be seriously considered. The key advantage of a buyout is that all components are in place and operating. The main disadvantage is that the buyer may be acquiring a loser.

An attractive way for an entrepreneur to acquire a company is by using the leveraged buyout method. The simple formula of a leveraged buyout is this: leverage a lot of debt, generate cash flow to support it, write up assets and take depreciation to reduce taxes, use the kinds of selection criteria and company profile that give downside protection, and bring on board the kind of management that can run a highly leveraged company (i.e., management with good cash-flow skills).

No matter how one acquires a company, however, it is imperative that the buyer have something to contribute to it. Hunting for and buying a business may be similar to a dog chasing a car: What is the dog going to do if he catches it?

To help find the "right" company, the buyer should establish a list of selection criteria that meet his or her needs to find the target company. Finding the company in a reasonable time requires the development of a search strategy.

There are four parties to any buyout: buyer, seller, financing sources, and other third parties. The main buyer considered in this text is the private entrepreneur who buys for the first time. The main sellers are owner-managers and corporations. These two sellers provide a large and varied inventory of buyout candidates. Financing sources and other third parties are needed to finance and facilitate the deal, for example, investors, lenders, lawyers, accountants, and appraisers. Obviously, the key third parties are the ones who provide financial backing, both equity and debt.

A key to negotiating a price of a buyout and also determining if a buyout can meet its debt service is the value of it, especially from an earnings and cash-flow viewpoint. Both determining value and negotiating a price require the application of qualitative and quantitative methods.

During negotiations, sellers typically become game players, which retards at best and at worst stops the closing of the deal. If the deal is closed, the buyer must be sure that a number of protections are written into the contract.

ASSIGNMENT

1 List the advantages of a buyout. Compare and contrast these with the advantages of starting from scratch.

2 Which way would you rather go into business by buyout or start-up? Explain why.

3 Define a leveraged buyout. What are its main features?

4 What particular skills or expertise should the buyer bring to a leveraged buyout?

5 Develop a profile of a buyout target that would match your personal profile. What are your selection criteria? What special skills or talents would you contribute to your buyout? What methods would you use in finding your buyout candidate?

6 Who are the major players in a buyout?

7 Describe a typical financing package for a leveraged buyout. Be specific. Explain the advantages and disadvantages of both debt and equity financing.

8 What do price, cash flow, earnings, and appraised value of assets have to do with the financing package, especially from the viewpoint of servicing the debt?

9 Explain how one uses asset values and capitalization rates to value a company. Give an example.

10 Define goodwill. Give an example.

11 Assuming you have found a buyout, explain how you would go about negotiating a price for it. How do you counteract a seller's game playing?

12 Explain how accountants and lawyers facilitate the buyout.

13 List terms that should be written into the contract. Explain, from the buyer's viewpoint, why they are important.

BIBLIOGRAPHY

Blaine, David R. "Appraising the Appraisers." *The Journal of Buyouts and Acquisitions*, 2:2 (December 1983).

Dauten, Kent P. "The Importance of the Purchase Price in Leveraged Buyout Transactions." *The Journal of Buyouts and Acquisitions*, 2:3 (February 1984).

Goldstein, Arnold S. *The Complete Guide to Buying and Selling a Business*. New York: Wiley, 1983.

Greif, Lloyd. "Razing the Ivory Tower: How to Select and Use an Investment Banker." *The Journal of Buyouts and Acquisitions*, 1:5 (June 1983).

Hosner, LaRue T., et. al. *The Entrepreneurial Function*. Englewood Cliffs, N.J.: Prentice-Hall, 1977.

Kuhn, Robert L. "Curing the Healthy." *Texas Business*. June 1984.

O'Boyle, Thomas F. "Steel Entrepreneurs Seek Profits in Plant That Big Firm Discarded as Uneconomical." *The Wall Street Journal*. May 15, 1984.

Sloan, Allan. "Luring Banks Overboard." *Forbes*. April 9, 1984.

Steelman, C. William. "Pitfalls in Medium-Sized Leveraged Buyouts." *The Journal of Buyouts and Acquisitions*, 2:1 (October 1983).

Wallner, Nicholas and J. Terrence Greve. *How to Do a Leveraged Buyout or Acquisition*. San Diego, Calif.: Buyout Publications, 1982.

———, and ———. *Leveraged Buyouts*. San Diego, Calif.: Buyout Publications, 1983.

———, ———, and Michael Podolny. *The Directory of Financing Sources for Buyouts and Acquisitions*. San Diego, Calif.: Buyout Publications, 1983.

CHAPTER 7

The Franchise

INTRODUCTION

A cross between a start-up and a buyout is a franchise. Just about any product or service can be franchised, and, therefore, this means of going into business offers many entrepreneurial opportunities to both franchisor and franchisee. The content of this chapter, however, is directed toward the franchisee. Specifically, the objectives of this chapter are as follows.

1 To present an overview and definition of franchised businesses.
2 To disclose the advantages and disadvantages of them.
3 To describe how to find and select the right franchise.
4 To give some viable franchise examples.

THE FRANCHISED BUSINESS

Is a franchised business a good way to become an entrepreneur? It depends on the entrepreneur, his or her desires, level of experience, and need for freedom of choice and independence. A franchised business offers many opportunities, but there are also pitfalls.

Overview

Generally speaking, there is a franchising opportunity to fit any desire, capacity, or financial ability. In most cases, a lot of experience is not necessary although, in most cases, a good sales and business background is a plus.

With a franchise, you are starting a new business at the same time you are buying an existing one. Or putting it another way, as a franchisee, you are going into a proved business instead of starting from scratch. You are using the experience of others rather than going through a trial-and-error-phase in which many start-ups fail. If the franchise operation is 20 years old and has been successful, then you have 20 years of vast experience to draw from, not to mention the strength and resources of the parent organization. You should not, however, expect to have the franchisor do everything for you. A franchised business epitomizes a give-and-take, combined venture.

Clearly, then, you are reducing risks of a start-up to go with a proved success formula and get the shelter and support of the franchisor to instruct you on what to do, how to do it, when to do it—all for goal congruency and to make a success of the operation. If you are, however, the very independent-minded entrepreneur, you may not want the close relationship and guidance of the franchisor.

Definition

A franchised business has a unique relationship between a parent company, the franchisor, and you, the franchisee. Franchising occurs when the franchisee markets a product or service developed by the franchisor under an agreement and license to do so.[1] Normally, the franchisee pays a fee to operate under the franchisor's trade name and established procedures, as well as paying a royalty percentage of sales.[2] Depending on the agreement or license, the franchise is operated as if it were part of a large chain and uses the franchisor's trademark, layouts, equipment, logos, standard product or service, and so forth. To derive a precise definition of a franchise, however, is impossible.

A franchise is normally not a trade, profession, or industry. But even attempting to state what a franchised business is not is a problem because attempts are being made to franchise plumbing, carpentry, and complete mechanical services; dentistry, medical care; and storefront legal, accounting, financial, and tax services. Obviously, these businesses certainly represent some parts of a trade or profession. (Note the trouble one gets into when trying to draw boundaries around entrepreneurial endeavors.)

For some more help in deriving a definition, we turn to the California Investment Law, which describes franchising thus: "A contract or agreement, either expressed or implied, whether oral or written, between two or more persons, by which: a franchisee is granted the right to engage in the business of offering, selling or distributing goods or services, under a marketing plan or system, prescribed in substantial part by a franchisor and the operation of the franchisee's business pursuant to such a plan or system substantially associated with the advertising or other commercial symbol, designating the franchisor or its affiliate."[3]

Franchise arrangements can be subdivided into two broad classes: (1) product distribution arrangements in which the dealer is to some degree, but not entirely, identified with the manufacturer-supplier; and (2) entire business format franchising, in which there is complete identification of the dealer with the buyer. Some prefer a subdivision into three broad classes thus.[4]

1 Establishing a selective and limited distribution system for particular products (for example, automobiles, bicycles, gasoline, tires, appliances, cosmetics) to be distributed under the manufacturer's name and trademark.

[1]Arnold S. Goldstein, *The Complete Guide to Buying and Selling a Business*, (New York: Wiley, 1983), p. 77. This material is used with permission.

[2]Ibid.

[3]David D. Seltz, *How to Get Started in Your Own Franchised Business* (Rockville Centre, N.Y.: Farnsworth,1980), pp. 7–8. This material is used with permission.

[4]Peter G. Norback and Craig T. Norback, *Guide to Franchises*, rev. ed. (Homewood, Ill.: Dow Jones-Irwin, 1982), p. 2. The material is used with permission.

2 Franchising of an entire retail business operation, including the license of a trade name, trademark, method, and format of doing business, sometimes called "pure," "comprehensive," or "entire business format" franchising (for example, fast-food restaurants, schools, and so on);

3 Trademark and brand name licensing for processing plants (for example, soft drink bottlers), which combine some elements of (1) and (2).[5]

Types of Franchises

There are three types of franchises: sales-type, service-type, and store-type.[6]

1 *Sales-type franchise.* This franchise is applicable to all types of products and all types of sales approaches, such as homes, industry, offices, and institutions. The franchisee operates either as a sales manager, recruiting and managing a sales staff from his or her office, or as a salesperson, doing his or her own selling. This type of franchise is obviously for the extrovert, the motivator, the true salesperson. Moreover, this type of franchise requires minimum outlay, expenses, and overhead.

2 *Service-type franchise.* The main advantage of this type of franchise is that it requires little or no inventory. The key attribute required of the franchisee is a desire to work with his or her hands and solve customer problems. Included are such franchises as muffler and transmission shops, general auto repair, lawn-care services, sewer cleaning, appliance repair, furniture and carpet cleaning, grooming services, and health care.

3 *Store-type franchise.* The varieties of store-type franchises are extensive. They vary from foods to books to hardware. Unlike the other two types of franchises, a store-type franchise is characterized by the following factors: selection of a proper site, large investment and sufficient working capital, large inventories, personnel, and large overhead and a high break-even point.

Advantages of a Franchised Business

In many instances, the overall advantage of a franchised business is that the franchisor can do more for you than you can do for yourself. Certainly, there are some significant advantages that a strong, successful franchise operation can offer the would-be entrepreneur. As is true of the buyout discussed in the preceding chapter, having an established and accepted product or service with proved operations can minimize the risk of failure. In essence, you are capitalizing on someone else's experience.

No two franchises are identical, but normally if you go with a proved franchise, you gain benefit from the franchisor's expertise. A franchisor will educate you on

[5]Ibid.

[6]This section is summarized from David D. Seltz, op. cit., pp. 107–9.

how to run the business and give you continuous guidance. You will be able to take advantage of and use a success formula that has met the test of time and has won in the marketplace. The franchisor will provide you with proved sales, promotional, and advertising techniques. Normally, you will attend a training center for several weeks (you may have to pay your own expenses, travel, accommodations, and meals). In a fast-food franchise, for example, the franchisor will teach you proper preparation and serving of all the franchise's products, counter etiquette, selling techniques, accounting procedures and financial management, personnel management, marketing, and equipment operation and maintenance.

Many franchisors will help you with site location, which includes site criteria and assistance in selecting your site. Once the site is chosen, the franchisor's location experts will prepare a feasibility study that examines population trends, traffic counts, proximity of shopping areas, visibility, and accessibility of your site. In addition, some franchisors provide some of the financing necessary to help you get started.

If you start fresh, it may take years of promotion, trial and error, and large investments to reach a comparable level of product-service recognition and goodwill. With a franchise, you start with a pretested, well-known, and accepted product or service. Moreover, the franchisor will provide building plans that result in structures and layouts where every square inch is used efficiently and effectively. Also, economies of scale, volume buying, and cooperative advertising can significantly reduce the franchisee's operating expenses.

A proper and successful store opening is required to get your business off to a good start. Many franchisors have store-opening specialists who will assist you in this important task. In addition to advertising and promotion, the opening involves a lot of detail like training employees, contacting suppliers, ordering inventory and supplies, and running the business for the first week or two.

Once your store is opened, you will receive manuals and other material to help you manage the store along with guidance from supervisors out of headquarters. You will also be able to attend national and regional conventions where you can learn from others and get firsthand information about plans and new products. To be sure, a progressive franchisor is continually engaged in product-service research and development along with trying to find new ways to increase sales and profits.

Disadvantages of a Franchised Business

For independent-minded entrepreneurs, becoming franchisees reduces freedom that they would otherwise enjoy if they went into business on their own. A franchisor can dictate every aspect of the business: recipes, colors, store layouts, uniforms, lighting, store hours, signs, decorations, advertising, and other operating details. All McDonald's french fries taste that way because all its franchisees have to prepare them the same way. Standard operating procedures must be followed precisely. If you don't follow the dictates of the franchisor, then your franchise will be terminated.

Even after signing restrictive contracts, franchisees usually think that they are independent business people. It does not take long to realize that being a franchisee really borders on being an investor-employee, especially after you have dealt with numerous supervisors from franchise headquarters. Take this advice: if you are not willing to run your franchise by the franchisor's rules, don't go into franchising.

Franchise operators often work harder than regular employees, putting in 10 to 15 hours a day, 6 days a week, with low to moderate "salaries." On the other hand, if a franchise begins to pay off handsomely, the franchisor may move in to get a piece of the bonanza. Many franchisees feel that territorial encroachment is one of the worst problems. Indeed, a number of franchisors do not give territorial protection to their franchise holders and thus feel free to move in on them.

Through fees and royalties, you pay for the advantages discussed earlier. Generally, it will cost you more to buy a franchised business than a comparable nonfranchised business. In addition to paying for traditional things, such as inventory, supplies, equipment, building and land, fixtures, and so forth, you will have to pay thousands in fees and royalties of 5 to 15 percent on sales. Moreover, you never completely own a franchise during the franchise period. Also, the franchise agreement may prohibit you from selling to a third party or even leaving it to your family on death. In some instances, a franchisor may attempt to terminate prematurely the franchise agreement or arbitrarily refuse to renew it.

Selection of a bad franchisor who fails to fulfill contractual commitments can spell disaster. Such franchisors may slough off shoddy supplies and inventory on unsuspecting franchisees. In some instances, franchisor operations may have started because a major manufacturer needed a regular outlet for a product. For example, a meat-processing plant may start a hamburger franchise to develop its own market. The franchisee may be required to use only meat supplied by the meat-processing plant. The quality of the meat may be low but priced several times over the market price. To make matters worse, the franchisor may make late deliveries or deliveries containing more than the quantity ordered; either way, the franchisee has business disruption and inventory control problems.

Such sole-source clauses are common in franchise agreements, so proceed with caution. A better way is for the franchisor to give you a list of approved products and specifications. Then you can buy products and supplies from the vendor of your choice. As a special service, the franchisor should also provide you with a list of companies and warehouses throughout the country whom it knows can supply all the items that meet required quality control standards.

HOW TO FIND AND SELECT THE RIGHT FRANCHISE

Your first contact with a franchisor may be as a customer, through advertisements, or through various publications.[7] Gather enough information about a prospective

[7]Two excellent sources of franchisors are Peter G. Norback and Craig T. Norback, *Guide to Franchises*, rev. ed. (Homewood, Ill.: Dow Jones-Irwin, 1982) and David D. Seltz, *How to Get Started in Your Own Franchised Business* (Rockville Centre, N.Y.: Farnsworth, 1980).

franchisor to determine if you and the franchise operation will be compatible. As in a marriage, the franchisor and franchisee are bound each to the other for mutual prosperity. Indeed, like partners in a good marriage, each must expect to give and take on a number of issues in addition to those that are spelled out in the franchise contract.

Be skeptical of franchisors whose major activity is the sale of franchises and whose profit is primarily derived from sales or from the sale of franchise equipment or services. To be sure, stay away from pyramid schemes. Go with a franchisor who has a long, steady record of success with a proved product or service and not with a gimmick. Not going with a proved winner can result in a financial disaster like in the now-defunct Minnie Pearl chicken franchise operation. In this fiasco, both franchisor and franchisee lost; some of the franchisees lost their life's savings.

Moreover, many seemingly successful franchise operations can go sour or at least suffer untoward setbacks. To the dismay of many franchisees who opened Chuck E. Cheese's Pizza Time Theatres, the parent company, Pizza Time Theatre, has filed for protection under Chapter 11 of the Federal Bankruptcy Laws. The main purpose of this move is to give the company a chance to get organized and to get its bills paid. Many units are doing quite well regardless; however, such a move does put a cloud over the entire operation.

For another example, drastic changes can occur that the franchisee has little control over and may or may not be in favor of. The entrepreneur who made Church's Fried Chicken the "Cinderella" of fast-food franchise operations has been brought out of retirement to help the company fight four consecutive years of declining sales. To turn Church's around, he has made some major changes. One was the development of both ministores that have no sit-down capacity and cutback menus. He has also placed more of these stores in a given market. It is difficult to tell how the original franchisees will benefit from these and other changes.

Getting Information About the Franchise

You can get more information about a franchise than any other business. One way to get started is to send for a franchisor's "kit" that describes the business, when it was founded, the number and location of franchises, the required capital and financial help, training and managerial assistance, and the contractual requirements.

For questions about a specific franchise or about franchising in general, contact the International Franchise Association (IFA) at 1025 Connecticut Avenue, N.W., Washington, D.C. 20036 (telephone: (202)659-0790). The IFA is the only franchise association in the United States and is the oldest and largest in the world. Other organizations that you can contact are the Small Business Administration, the Better Business Bureau, your local Chamber of Commerce, Dun & Bradstreet, and your banker.

Federal law, through regulation by the Federal Trade Commission, requires that franchisors provide a disclosure statement to all prospective franchisees. The kind of information disclosed includes the following.[8]

[8]Peter G. Norback and Craig T. Norback, op. cit., pp. 25—26.

1 The identity of the franchisor and of its directors, principal officers, or general partners; their business backgrounds and certain criminal convictions; civil judgments; bankruptcies; and administrative orders involving any of them.

2 The business and franchising experience of the franchisor, a description of the franchise offered and the goods, training programs, supervision, advertising, and other services to be provided by the franchisor.

3 The franchisor's trade names, trade or service marks, and other commercial symbols to be licensed to the franchisee and of any restrictions on or litigation involving the franchisor's and the franchisee's rights and obligations relative to such trade names and trade or service marks.

4 All initial and continuing fees that the franchisee will be required to pay, how fees are determined if not uniform, the extent to which fees are refundable, and an estimate of the total investment to be made by the franchisee.

5 The number of franchised and franchisor-owned outlets currently operating, a list of names and addresses of existing franchises, and the number of projected franchises.

6 Whether the franchisee is required to purchase or lease goods or services from the franchisor or suppliers designated by the franchisor, whether the franchisor derives income from any such requirement, and, if so, the means by which the franchisor derives this income.

7 Whether the franchisee is required to purchase goods or services in accordance with specifications of the franchisor or from suppliers approved by the franchisor and a description of any specification or approved supplier program.

8 The conditions under which the franchise may be terminated or renewal refused, the franchisee's rights and obligations on expiration and termination, any option or right of first refusal that the franchisor has to acquire the franchise, a description of any covenant not to compete to which franchisee will be subject, and the franchisee's right to assign and otherwise transfer the franchise.

9 A description of any financing offered by the franchisor, including any waiver of defenses contained in a note, contract, or other obligation of the franchisee and whether the franchisor has in the past assigned or expects to assign any obligation containing any such waiver.

10 Limitations on the goods or services that the franchisee may sell.

11 A description of the territorial protection that the franchisee will have.

12 Compensation paid to a public figure whose name is used in the franchise or who endorses the franchise.

13 The data and methods used by the franchisor in preparing any projected sales, expenses, or income of the franchised business.

14 Copies of the most recent balance sheet and profit-and-loss statement of the franchisor audited by an independent certified public accountant.

Disclosure statements, copies of the franchise contract, and all other agreements that the franchisee must sign to acquire the franchise must be given to the prospective franchisee from two to seven days, depending on the state's law, in advance of the signing of any agreement or payment of any money to the franchisor.[9] To be sure, never sign any agreement without legal counsel.

In addition to reviewing the franchise contract, get out and investigate existing franchises and observe their operation, their customers, their employees, and so forth. Ask the franchisees questions that will help to validate material in the disclosure statement, such as effectiveness of the training, supervision, and advertising programs; level of sales and profit figures; performance of suppliers; loyalty of franchisor in meeting contractual obligations, such as territorial protection.

Possibly more important than interviewing *existing* franchisees is to check with *former* franchisees. Obviously, an additional question to ask this group is why the business failed or why the agreement was terminated. Moreover, suppliers are a good source of information. The point of all these questions is to determine if the promises of the franchisor match the performance.

The Franchise Contract

Request the franchisor to give you a specimen contract. If you do not fully understand everything in the franchise contract, have your accountant and attorney go over it thoroughly to make sure it meets your objectives. And—like the marriage analogy used earlier—signing a contract is like taking the marriage vows. There is a finality about it, and once you have signed on the line, you have a contractual commitment, one that is permanent and not easy to change.[10] The stipulations and legalities in the contract are for your attorney to review; the major tenor of the contract and the franchise opportunity itself depend on your judgment. In assessing the franchise contract, ask yourself if it seems fair? Does the contract contain a preponderance of negatives and bureaucratic controls? Does it seem to facilitate progress or restrain it? Are you going to become a true entrepreneur or a wage earner? Is the franchise contract a one-way street with the franchisor receiving all the benefits, profits, and rights while you do all the work?

The basic provisions that should be contained in the franchise contract are general definitions; duration and termination of the contract; licensor representations and warranties; obligations and duties of the franchisor; description of the property to be licensed; trade names and trademarks; use of property and hours of operation; the total cash investment required, including financing and terms of financing; lease and leasehold improvements; fees, royalties, and start-up costs and how they are determined; territorial protection; performance quotas; materials, support, and services furnished by the franchisor; terms under which the franchise

[9]Ibid.
[10]Seltz, op.cit., p. 49.

can be sold to someone else by the franchisee; advertising and promotion and requirements, if any, to participate; and responsibility for liability insurance.

SOME EXAMPLES

Almost any business you mention, especially in the retail trade, is probably franchised. There are endless examples that characterize the franchising field. They range from multimillion dollar giants to small service-type enterprises. Both the automobile business and automotive aftermarket are thoroughly franchised. Clearly, there are literally hundreds of food businesses—fast and slow service, stand-up and sit-down, full-menu or specialty, ornate or austere—that are franchised. Franchising can also cover a gas station, a municipal transportation system, a sports team, or a bottling works.[11] Moreover, franchises can be domestic or foreign. The following material will help you to get at least a real-world flavor of some of these opportunities.

Examples of Domestic Franchise Opportunities

When Californian Berry Fowler abandoned his six-year teaching career, he cited public school salaries and declining student performance in the basic skills as the key reasons for his departure.[12] But instead of switching professions, he started a franchising business to help the millions of Americans who need remedial reading and math tutoring. His franchise operation is called Sylvan Learning Centers, and he has sold over 100 to investors in 48 cities.

Sylvan is believed to be alone in offering remedial education franchises although its centers face competition from tutoring operations run by groups of teachers and psychologists or individuals. Fowler believes there is a huge market for his business, citing government figures that show 20 percent of all school children are performing below grade level.[13]

Sylvan, which charges $27,000 per franchise and requires investors to add $18,000 to $19,000 for equipment and materials, reaps royalty fees of 6 percent of a franchisee's sales. Fowler says a "good, strong" center should gross about $16,000 a month and reap monthly profits of about $10,000 from 100 students who attend two tutorials a week.[14]

[11]Ibid., p. 8.

[12]Gail Gregg, "Franchises Teach Johnny to Read," *Venture*, May 1984, p. 161. Copyright © 1984 by Venture Magazine, Inc., 521 Fifth Avenue, New York, N.Y. 10175. This material is used by special permission.

[13]Ibid.

[14]Ibid.

Sylvan's long-term business plan is anything but modest. The company anticipates licensing 600 new franchises over the next three years with 1400 to 1700 centers its eventual goal. And it has recently entered into the furniture manufacturing business, which could add substantial profits if franchising plans succeed as projected. Sylvan requires all centers to use the same furniture and equipment. By making its own, Fowler says, Sylvan can ensure quicker delivery and better-quality products while it earns a 20 percent markup for the company.[15]

Another example is Aamco Transmissions, Inc., 408 East Fourth Street, Bridgeport, Pennsylvania 19405. This company conditions and rebuilds transmissions for all cars, and there are nearly 900 in the 50 states and Canada. A total investment of $85,000 is required to open a franchise. A total of $75,000 is required in a secondary market. Aamco can arrange financing for one half of total requirement if the franchisee has good credit references. Franchisees have the option to arrange their own outside financing. A comprehensive six-week course is provided at company headquarters. In addition, field training is offered at the opening of the operation to launch the franchisee properly. A consulting and operation division continually works with each center on a weekly basis to ensure proper day-by-day operation. Also, monthly area meetings are held.[16]

Western Auto, 2107 Grand Avenue, Kansas City, Missouri 64108, is a large franchisor specializing in retailing of automotive parts, hardware, sporting goods, tools and wheel goods, appliances, televisions, radios and other electronics, housewares, paint, toys, and furniture. There are over 3400 in all states except North Dakota. The minimum capital required is $50,000. Financing is available on store fixtures. Floor planning of major items and deferred terms on some seasonal merchandise are offered. Financing of retail customer installment sales is also offered. Other financial assistance is extended depending on personal statements on prospects. A two-week training course in a modern, electronically equipped training facility prior to opening a store provides instruction in store operation, display, bookkeeping, product information, advertising, and credit management. Company personnel continue to offer training, counseling, and sales meetings after the formalized training school course is completed. The dealer is contacted periodically in the store by company personnel, such as the territory sales manager and the territory credit manager, offering counseling on sales, credit, and store operation.[17]

Hertz System, Inc., 660 Madison Avenue, New York, New York 10021, is a large franchisor whose business is automobile and truck rental. Hertz has over 1100 units in 48 states. Required capital varies according to the franchise location. The company, however, does not give any financial assistance. A zone system manager trains each new franchisee before the operation opens with a Hertz Starter Kit (the kit includes all forms needed to run a location). Visits are made by the zone system manager on a periodic basis. Manager rental representative training classes are

[15]Ibid.
[16]Norback and Norback, op. cit., p. 34.
[17]Ibid., p. 53.

provided. Manuals and guides for running a location are issued. A corporate training class is available to franchisees. Annual business meetings are held. Accounting and operational guides are provided to run the franchise. Visits by zone system managers are made to act as a liaison between the corporate and licensee locations. All forms and training classes are provided as needed. Contact is furnished directly to corporate management for all areas of rental business (e.g., insurance, advertising, and accounting).[18]

Muzak Corporation, 888 Seventh Avenue, New York, New York 10019, provides music programs for businesses of all kinds. Sound systems and related communication systems are included on a lease or sale basis to customers. There are approximately 300 franchises in the United States and 25 in foreign countries. The required capital varies according to the particular franchise, with no financial assistance from Muzak. Orientation sessions are held regularly in New York City. Continuing sales training sessions are held at various sites around the United States. Field visits by company staff provide evaluations, assistance, and progress reports. National advertising, sales brochures, and equipment specification sheets are provided continuously.[19]

Orange Julius of America, 3219 Wilshire Boulevard, Santa Monica, California 90403, is a fast-food franchisor specializing in scrumptious fruit drinks with over 500 units in 16 states, Canada, Europe, Australia, the Philippines, and Japan. The required capital is from $30,000 to $50,000 with a total investment of $80,000 to $110,000 eventually required. This amount is dependent on the size of the store, menu selection, and type of equipment required. The franchisees are required to arrange their own financing. On-site training, approximately 10 days, including preopening training and training subsequent to initial opening of the franchise, is provided. Managerial and technical assistance is provided for site selection, construction, equipment purchase, training of personnel, and management. Ongoing supervision is provided.[20]

Examples of Foreign Franchise Opportunities

What is the feasibility of investing in a foreign franchise? Are foreign-based companies worth considering? Without doubt, foreign franchises offer many innovative products and services, and their numbers are spreading throughout the country. But this situation must be weighed against the drawbacks of low product-service recognition; remoteness of the home office; possible cultural and language differences; costs of calling, traveling, and correspondence; and general logistical problems.

In any event, the same scrutiny and assessment of contractual, financial, and operational conditions discussed earlier are also certainly applicable to foreign

[18]Ibid., p. 57.
[19]Ibid., p. 73.
[20]Ibid., p. 177.

operations. Something worth considering is that you may be able to strike a better deal with a foreign franchisor than you can with an equivalent American firm.

But for some of us, having to do hard work may be the biggest barrier of all. Let's face it. Many of us have become soft; we are simply not accustomed to hard work. The Japanese, on the other hand, epitomize a strong work ethic. They are an industrious, resourceful people, and they expect the same from their franchisees. For example, Dosanko Foods, 43-30 38th Street, Long Island City, New York, 11101, is a Japanese restaurant chain that is now launching an aggressive American franchise expansion drive.

The management, however, expects its franchisees to participate *personally* in the daily operations of the business, even the scrubbing of floors and washing of windows. Management and office personnel, in turn, visit new franchises and work in taking orders, packing take-out orders, or doing whatever else needs to be done.[21]

Another example is Tidy Car, 5205 Timberlea Boulevard, Mississauga, Ontario, Canada L4W253. This franchisor has 750 outlets in the United States and 100 in Canada. Tidy Car franchisees, depending on the size of their investment, offer rustproofing, installation of theft protection devices and sunroofs, and repairs to glass and vinyl. Tidy Car plans to roll out as many as 300 new franchises in the United States over the next two years.[22]

Although some foreign franchisors appear to want to take the United States by storm, others plan to enter the market more gradually. Descamps, 200 West 57th Street, New York, New York, 10019, a French company that designs and sells bed linens, has only recently sold franchises in New York, Chicago, Miami, and Los Angeles. The Paris-based company also owns outlets in Japan and throughout Europe. Descamps plans to open franchises in San Francisco and other major cities throughout the United States. A Descamps franchisee can expect annual revenues of $250,000 to $300,000.[23]

SUMMARY

Franchising is a unique relationship between a parent company; the franchisor; and you, the franchisee. For a number of reasons, a franchised business normally requires considerably more investigation and analysis than other ventures. In other businesses, it is you and the customers primarily; with a franchise, it is you, the franchisor (the parent or controlling partner), and the customers. The more you know about the franchisor, the better before you sign a franchise contract.

[21]Richard Barbieri, "Buying a Foreign Franchise," *Venture*, May 1984, p. 1982. Copyright © 1984 Venture Magazine, Inc., 521 Fifth Avenue, New York, N.Y. 10175. This material is used by special permission.

[22]Ibid.

[23]Ibid.

The major caution is to make sure you *actually* get what you *thought* you would get. Thorough investigation, analysis, counsel from your accountant and attorney, questions asked of present and past franchisees and suppliers, and on-site observations will help narrow this gap. Gathering a lot of this information is easier than it sounds because, by law, you can obtain access to more information about a franchise operation than any other business.

Briefly, the benefits of going the franchise route are these: less risk; use of the franchisor's expertise, training, guidance, and general support; a proved business formula, product, or service that is widely recognized and accepted; effective and efficient operations; ongoing research and development; and strong marketing techniques.

On the other hand, the disadvantages of a franchise are going with a bad franchisor, payment of fees and royalties, a never-ending partnership, and less freedom and autonomy to make your own decisions.

A key aspect of a franchise operation is the franchise contract. Indeed, do not try to translate the legalese in this contract yourself, but enlist the aid of an accountant and attorney before signing anything. Although there are commonalities in all franchise contracts, no two are the same. Certainly, the franchise contract should be a two-way street, and presumably those prepared by the more established and reputable franchisors are. Nonetheless, because they are prepared by the franchisors, they are, without doubt, written to protect them. Consequently, if the provisions do not meet with your approval, negotiating new terms may be in order even though most of the better-known franchisors will normally not budge much from basic contract terms.

The final test as to whether or not a franchise operation is for you is really based on your sense of the general fairness and positive tendencies of the contract and representatives of the franchisor and on the compatibility between your characteristics and those of the franchise operation. If any of these aspects are missing or do not seem right, then you should direct your entrepreneurial sights in other directions.

ASSIGNMENT

1 Compare and contrast a buyout and a start-up with becoming a franchisee.

2 List and give a specific example of the three types of franchises.

3 Give the advantages and disadvantages of a franchise operation from the franchisee's viewpoint.

4 What do you believe to be the greatest advantage of being a franchisee? The greatest disadvantage?

5 Describe how you would go about investigating, analyzing, and selecting a franchise operation.

6 List the provisions that you believe to be most important in a franchise contract. Explain why.

7 Discuss the drawbacks of investing with a foreign franchisor. What are the advantages?

BIBLIOGRAPHY

Barbieri, Richard. "Buying a Foreign Franchise." *Venture*. May 1984.

Goldstein, Arnold S. *The Complete Guide to Buying and Selling a Business*. New York: Wiley, 1983.

Gregg, Gail. "Franchises Teach Johnny to Read." *Venture*. May 1984.

Norback, Peter G., and Craig T. Norback. *Guide to Franchises*. rev. ed. Homewood, Ill.: Dow Jones-Irwin, 1982.

Seltz, David D. *How to Get Started in Your Own Franchised Business*. Rockville Centre, N.Y.: Farnsworth, 1980.

Smith, Randy Baca. *Setting Up Shop*. New York: McGraw-Hill, 1982.

PART FOUR

PROMISING ENTREPRENEURIAL OPPORTUNITIES

CHAPTER 8

The Mail Order Business

INTRODUCTION

The mail order business is as old as the nineteenth century and as modern as tomorrow. The entrepreneurial opportunities in mail order are virtually limitless. This chapter attempts to cover the mail order field and to describe how to enter it. Specifically, these are the objectives of this chapter.

1 To present an overview and definition of the mail order business.
2 To describe the types of mail order and its future.
3 To discuss how to get started in the mail order business.
4 To present advertising strategies used in mail order.
5 To disclose legal aspects of mail order.

ANALYSIS OF THE MAIL ORDER BUSINESS

The mail order business represents an ideal way to market almost anything. Today it may offer one of the greatest opportunities to become an entrepreneur.

Overview

Today the mail order industry in the United States is growing at about double the rate of retailing. Tomorrow, with social changes and new communicating technology, the growth should be even greater. Mail order is one of several direct marketing methods as well as a definite and distinct kind of business. Fortunes are made in mail order just as in other businesses, but there are no shortcuts to such wealth. However, "[w]ith the help of computers, phones, show business, shrewd merchandising and your friendly postman, some smart entrepreneurs are restoring shopping to what it used to be before the advent of rude clerks, jammed parking lots and sales taxes."[1]

Mail order is an excellent way to market products and services to people across the country in both cities and remote, out-of-the-way places. Historically, the mail order business has been a vital marketing link between manufacturers, and widely scattered consumers; today it is an even stronger part of this country's marketing and distribution system. Indeed, mail order can virtually satisfy any consumer demand anywhere without the hassle of traffic and store shopping and the cost and time of traveling long distances. Normally, the customer can place orders from the comfort and convenience of his or her home or office without face-to-face contact with a salesclerk. Moreover, mail order businesses that service millions of customers

[1]Richard Greene, "A Boutique in Your Living Room," *Forbes*, May 7, 1984, p. 86. Used with permission.

range from part-time operations being run out of the basement of the operator's house to gigantic catalog houses.

Definition

Mail order deals with customers at a distance without face-to-face selling but instead sells products and services through various media, such as ads in magazines or newspapers, direct mail, telephones, radio, and television. Because of the diverse media used in this kind of business, the term *mail order* is somewhat archaic. Indeed, some have relabeled it ''direct marketing,'' but direct marketing includes house-to-house, canvass-type selling, which mail order does not include except in special situations where agents are used. Aside from house-to-house selling, however, the terms *mail order* and *direct marketing* are pretty much synonymous and can be used interchangeably. Throughout this chapter, however, *mail order* will be used because of its wide acceptance in practice.

Types of Mail Order

Before deciding on the mail order product or service, you must decide on what type of operation you are interested in and what type fits you best. Following are the more important types.

One-Shot Items. A one-shot item is a product for which no companion product exists or, if it exists, that cannot be sold in significant quantities to the same customer.[2] The one-shot product is probably what most would-be mail order entrepreneurs think is the mail order business. You advertise in a magazine or newspaper or through direct mail, and customers send you money; you mail the product; the deal ends for that customer, and you do the same thing over with other customers.

With this type of mail order, you know fairly quickly whether you have made money or not. The one-shot product also gives you back your investment in the shortest possible time and has the potential to be a ''get-rich-quick'' way of doing business.[3]

Some mail order experts say, however, that the one-shot approach is the toughest, most competitive part of the business. It is easy for you to get into business, and it's just as easy for your competitors to imitate you if they detect you are making a killing, and they can tell because your business is hard to conceal; there are few secrets in mail order.[4] Your success is easily detected by the fast-buck boys and they immediately close in.

[2]Jack Lander, *Make Money by Moonlighting* (Wilmington, Del.: Enterprise Publishing, 1982), p. 173. Used with permission.

[3]Julian L. Simon, *How to Start and Operte a Mail-Order Business*, 3d ed. (New York: McGraw-Hill, 1981), p. 26. The material is used with permission.

[4]Ibid.

If you can find a special niche for a staple one-shot product with a high-enough price, say over $10, then you may be successful. Or if you are lucky enough to advertise the "hot" fad that will sell furiously in display ads until the market is saturated, then you have a good chance of becoming a millionaire virtually overnight. Otherwise start with repeat items.

Repeat Items.   After you sell the first product to your customers, you continue to sell the same or similar products to them over a long period of time. The big cost in mail order is the cost of getting a customer. So once you get the customer, the customer keeps coming back, thus reducing significantly the cost of customer acquisition per sale. Normally, the mail order operator who deals with repeat items will have a full line of products. In fact, the first sale that is made opens up selling opportunities for follow-up products or services. As many mail order experts say, your last customer is your best customer.

Normally, repeat items are more of the middle-of-the-road kind like cigars, fine steaks, coats, hunting equipment, office supplies, and so forth. Operating this kind of business requires more than operating off the kitchen table; it requires more capital and inventory. Also, it takes more time and money before you can tell whether or not you are going to make a go of it.

Catalogs   Catalog sales are a special form of repeat business because your customers order again and again from your catalogs. Some of the big general catalog companies are Sears, Montgomery Ward, and Spiegel. Specialty and gift catalog people include Spencer Gifts, JS&A, L. L. Bean, Lillian Vernon, Omaha Steaks International, Heathkit, Hammacher Schlemmer, Law Enforcement Associates, The Gift Horse, Gadgets™, Ecclesiastical Arts Catalog, and The Sharper Image Catalog.

This kind of mail order can be quite profitable; however, you should be smart to begin with few items and expand the size of your catalog as you gain experience and capital resources for expansion. Some experts like Julian Simon advise newcomers to mail order to forget this type of business because it requires the entrepreneur to overcome extraordinary difficulties and to have unusual talent and a keen sense of the market, not to mention a sizable front-end investment. Few businesses are as entrepreneurial as catalogs, and it takes three or more years to determine if a catalog operation is a success by getting enough repeat business.

The mail order operator mails a catalog to a select list of customers. Typically, catalogs let these customers "see" the offerings; purchases are delivered by United Parcel Service (UPS) or by mail.[5] For many products, the target market is widely scattered. Some of the giant merchandisers like Penney's, Sears, and Ward's, also operate catalog counters in their stores and catalog offices in small communities where customers can go and examine the catalogs and place their orders. The order

[5]E. Jerome McCarthy and William D. Perreault, Jr., *Basic Marketing*, 8th ed. (Homewood, Ill.: Richard D. Irwin, 1984), p. 400. This material is used with permission.

is shipped from central warehouses to these catalog desks, and when it arrives, the customer is phoned and is asked to pick it up.[6]

Mail Order Combined with Agents.   Some mail order firms have to employ house-to-house salespeople to go out and find prospects for the product or service and sell it directly. Often these agents are themselves recruited through mail order ads in magazines and newspapers. This kind of deal should require little investment for the agent, offer lightweight products that are easy to carry and not obtainable in stores, and give a commission of 60 percent or more. This method is used for products or services that require face-to-face selling and demonstration, such as shoes, cosmetics, encyclopedias, insurance, and correspondence schools.

Why People Buy via Mail Order

It is lunchtime. A woman from Colorado telephones Lillian Vernon, a successful catalog mail order company, and is greeted by a pleasant "Can I help you?" The customer gives the item number, price, and page number—all the necessary order information. Quickly, Lillian Vernon's employee puts these and the customer's credit card number on a computerized order form. Then the salesperson makes a sales pitch about other items and says, "Good-bye."[7] In all, a very pleasant transaction. No hassle with parking. No time wasted trying to get help from a salesperson. No time wasted finding the right size, model, or color. No lines at the register. Many direct mail orders can be processed as quickly as a conventional retailer can run a credit check.[8]

Demographic and social trends favor mail order's continued growth because the customer is as near to specialty or regular products and services as the telephone or post office. People have better things to do than drive all over town trying to get their shopping done. They would rather be at the tennis court or poolside. Moreover, the women who used to do the shopping are now working full-time. For example, a husband and wife, both of whom have jobs, may do their shopping in bed by going through a pile of mail order catalogs.[9]

Spiraling energy and transportation costs and crime-plagued shopping areas make mail order an ideal alternative way to shop. Also, department stores have dropped many specialty items, thus creating opportunity niches for mail order operators to sell these items. And, finally, the advent of toll-free numbers, computers, and credit cards, as well as the 24-hour day, 7-day week service, makes it easy for the customer to shop at his or her convenience. Furthermore, the customer

[6]Phillip Kotler, *Principles of Marketing* (Englewood Cliffs, N.J.: Prentice-Hall, 1980), p. 471. This material is used with the permission of Prentice-Hall, Inc.

[7]Greene, op. cit., p. 88.

[8]Ibid.

[9]Ibid., p. 86.

is out of the weather. And if customers order from some states, such as New Hampshire, they can avoid state sales taxes.

There is a lot of truth in the old saying that "if it can be sold, it can be sold by mail." And many people love to shop for all kinds of products and services by mail; they get a thrill when the mail carrier brings their packages. Moreover, many people want things that are different from what their friends and neighbors have, such as novelties like robot kits, gaming tables, gold lamé dresses, or miniature horses. Also, there are many hobbyists, such as gardeners and stamp or coin collectors. Then there are those people who are looking for discounts for a price advantage. Still, a few buy via mail order to avoid embarrassment that certain products or services may cause if bought through conventional retailing.

History of Mail Order

Mail order is as old as the mail system. It originated in the mailed order of customers to a manufacturer or merchant for a product to be mailed back to them. Indeed, selling people things that they could not get anywhere else was the way mail order got its start.

After the Civil War, merchants sought customer orders by mailing catalogs to people living in remote areas. A. Montgomery Ward, established in 1872 in a Chicago hayloft, is popularly considered the first major mail order company and was followed 14 years later by Sears Roebuck & Co.[10]

The classic mail order story is about Richard Sears, a Minnesota railroad agent, who in 1886 bought a shipment of $25 watches for $12 each. He sold them to agents along the line for $14. Soon Sears was offering a variety of goods, mostly to people who lived half a day away from the nearest big store.[11] Indeed, the rest is history.

By 1918 these two companies conducted giant catalog mail order businesses, and there was a total of some 2500 other mail order houses.[12] In the 1930s and 1940s, however, many retailers discontinued their mail order operations as the chain stores opened branches in smaller towns and brought more merchandise to the inhabitants and as the number of automobiles and good roads increased. Today the mail order industry is undergoing a resurgence.[13]

Future of Mail Order

One of the greatest barriers to great growth and opportunity in the mail order business is a lingering image of mail order operators as rip-off artists or "snake oil" salespeople, out to make a fast buck by selling get-rich-quick schemes, dangerous

---

[10]Kotler, op. cit., p. 471.
[11]Greene, op. cit., p. 89.
[12]Kotler, op. cit., p. 471.
[13]Ibid.

weight-loss plans, fraudulent work-at-home schemes or job opportunities, and outright gyps. Such operators will have to clean up their act or be put out of business or put in jail or both. The Federal Trade Commission (FTC) and United States postal inspectors are the major watchdogs, and in the past few years laws against mail order abuse have been passed that give these agencies the teeth to put the bite on unlawful mail order operations.

On the brighter side, rapid growth is expected to continue in mail order, especially for those specializing in "at home" retailing. Experiments are now under way with two-way cable television systems whereby a customer can see and read about a product advertised on TV and order it by pushing a button. Videotapes and discs or signals from satellites to televisions or home computers may be the "catalogs" of the future.[14] The computer makes it possible to gather and store the same information and more on millions of customers that the small retailer had on several hundred customers. In this way, the mail order operator can have an individualized relationship with every customer with valuable, up-to-date information at his or her fingertips.

Because of the advent of computers and sophisticated software, interactive TV, and faster delivery systems, this country, without doubt, will go through a major change in the way product-service information is gathered and how merchandise is advertised and distributed to customers. To be sure, all this technology will be integrated to form a more efficient and effective direct marketing system. Indeed, the entrepreneurial and promotional opportunities are truly breathtaking.

There are many opportunities for entrepreneurs to develop themes, concepts, or niches. Technologies will help lower overhead and give greater efficiencies, which, in turn, provide opportunities to start discount mail order firms. For another example, products are often returned to the manufacturer for refurbishing, a task that the manufacturers may or may not want to do, or if they do it, they may not have a marketing outlet. A mail order operator may take over all or a part of refurbishing and market the products as refurbished items. Furthermore, our economy is becoming more service-oriented in that people seek information and guidance from a variety of experts. An example of an opportunity here is to bring together expert knowledge in health care, nutrition, and so forth, with exercise products and become a leader in health and fitness.

HOW TO GET STARTED IN MAIL ORDER

With determination, commitment, and common sense, anyone, young or old, black or white, woman or man, can make a go of it in the mail order business. To be sure, for some, mail order is the most desirable business to be in. As is true of any other venture, however, going into mail order takes guts, desire, and a little or a lot of

[14]McCarthy and Perreault, op. cit., p. 401.

money, depending on which type you go in. You can start part-time at your kitchen table or in the basement on that proverbial "shoestring." You can spend several thousand dollars on trying to move a one-shot item and lose it all overnight or receive a flood of orders and money for an item that you just advertised a few days earlier. Or you can go whole hog and go into the catalog business with distribution centers and large inventories.

Most of all, the mail order business can be fun. Indeed, what a wonderful feeling and thrill you will get when people start responding and you know that you have hit on the right product, at the right price with the right sales message. Many who have done it say it's magic.

Preparation

Learn as much about the mail order business as you can. The key published material that you should get a copy of immediately is *Standard Rate and Data Services*, from 5201 Old Orchard Road, Skokie, Illinois 60076. Also write the Direct Mail/Marketing Association, 6 East 43rd Street, New York, New York 10017. In addition, read textbooks on mail order; immerse yourself in catalogs and advertising copy; visit mail order companies; maybe even go to work for one.

Furthermore, if you are selecting a product, a sleep-inducing device, for example, order several samples from the manufacturer, test them on yourself and your friends, go to the manufacturer and absorb all engineering specifications and other documents, and then determine why it is built the way it is and why it works. Become an expert on sleep. In this body of knowledge that you gather is the information that you will eventually use to prepare advertisements, the key to successful mail order.

If you are convinced that you are prepared to enter the mail order business and you are sold on the product yourself, then test its marketability. Put an ad in *The Wall Street Journal* in a test market, for example, the Southwest edition, and see what happens. If the response meets your test standards, then run it in other editions. Furthermore, run it in magazines that fit a particular profile of customers who may need a sleep-inducing device, such as executives, traveling salespeople, shift workers, professors, and so forth.

Advantages of the Mail Order Business

William A. Cohen believes that the mail order business is a perfect place to make your fortune as an entrepreneur and gives the reasons why.[15] They are summarized and paraphrased as follows.

---

[15]William A. Cohen, *Building A Mail Order Business* (New York: J. Wiley, 1982), pp. 4–6. This material is used with permission.

Low Barrier to Entry.   If you want to enter the mail order business or employ mail order techniques to assist a business you already have in operation, there is little to prevent your entry. You don't have to pass a test, reach a specific level of education, or be experienced, although all these may help.

Low Capital Requirement.   Although you cannot get into mail order without some money, the initial investment is low compared to that in other businesses. You can test the marketplace with your toe, not your whole body. Such a test may run $2000 or less, and you may become established in two or three months. To open a hardware store may take from $200,000 to $300,000 and two or three years to get established. A retail store, for another example, requires not only an outlay for the store itself but also for fixtures, inventory, and sales personnel. In mail order, you may run a dry test, advertising before you have the product in inventory. If the results of this test do not meet your expectations, you return the money with a letter stating that you are "out of stock."

Dry-testing, however, if not unethical, may be against the law, a problem discussed later in this chapter. Through drop-ship arrangements, where you have no inventory cost whatsoever, you can run a test where the costs will be limited to your ads and mailings, if any. In any case, if you have a winner, you can move quickly to expand. If it's a loser, you can drop it at once, and your only cost is the cost of your test. Another advantage of testing is the ability to target a specific market, for example, for accountants, engineers, expectant mothers. You can also test other things such as different prices.

Ability to Move Fast.   If you have a winner, you need to be fast on your feet and exploit it quickly. If you have a retail business selling a certain item, for example, a special wrist radio, and if you advertise, your customers must come to you to purchase your item through your retail outlet, which is a stationary structure on which you probably have a mortgage or lease. But in mail order, if you are successful with a certain item during a test, you expand your promotion rapidly and nationally to get to the entire market. Furthermore, you can time your promotion through the mail to coincide with other promotional activities. For example, if you are selling a special item at a trade show, a direct mail campaign can be started, promoting this item to coincide with the show. This two-way promotion can increase your sales dramatically.[16]

Starting Part-Time.   One of the truly great advantages for the budding mail order entrepreneur is that he or she can start part-time. There are no schedules to meet, no interference with your job, and you can start at your kitchen table. Moreover, if you are just starting in business, it is usually wise to start part-time. Mail order is a rough,

[16]Ibid.

tough business, and you can't learn it overnight. Learning will be much less painful if your livelihood and that of your family don't depend on immediate success.[17]

Kinds of Products and Services That Sell

In mail order, you can sell virtually anything, such as airplanes, your skills, employment services, or tombstones. As stated before, success equals the right product or service, at the right time, at the right price. One of the first things that you must determine about the product or service is the legality of it. A number of items advertised are skating close to the edge of legality. Some have gone over the edge. Many of the mail order operators offering these items will be closed down by the Federal Trade Commission or U.S. Postal Service or assailed by the Better Business Bureau. The obvious advice is to stay away from these kinds of products or services.

After considerations of legality, the number one criterion for product-service selection is to choose those that you like and believe in or will have fun selling and also something you are an "expert" about. Also, try to find a product or service that has a story element inherent in it where interesting and appealing advertising copy can be written. Does it have utility, special beauty, value? Does it fit a particular life-style? Also, get an item in the growth phase of the life cycle.

Jack Lander recommends six major products that are sold successfully by mail order.[18]

1 The well-known product that can be offered at less than the going retail store price. (film, vitamins)

2 The subscription product. (magazines, books, collectibles, records or cassette tapes)

3 Clothing of all kinds sold to certain customers who find shopping in retail stores inconvenient or abhorrent.

4 Specialty items not generally carried by retail stores. (grandfather clock kits, gourmet foods, special edition paintings or other artwork, burglar alarms, patterns and plans, decorating items, special car parts, and so on)

5 New products and those that must be explained in detail in order to convince the buyer to act. (books, new tools or devices, correspondence courses, and so on)

6 Catalogs for specialty products. Some are offered free. (catalogs for seeds, hobby items, hardware items, special tools—anything in the five preceding categories)

Simon says that if a product falls into one of the following classes, it is a very poor mail order prospect.[19]

[17]Simon, op. cit., p. 2.

[18]Lander, op. cit., p. 44.

[19]Simon, op. cit., p. 59.

1 Standardized and branded goods unless you can offer a substantial price advantage.

2 Goods whose characteristics are hard to communicate in ads, such as perfume and high-style women's dresses.

3 Goods sold on a small profit margin, for example, coffee and food (except gourmet food).

4 Goods that don't lead to profitable repeat sales.

Simon also gives example of products that sell well by mail order, *but are not likely to constitute a business unless you combine them with a line of similar goods* (emphasis mine).[20]

blackhead remover	Confederate money
cuckoo clock	one-way-glass formula
address labels	shrunken heads
closet organizer	magnets
cleaning cloths	supermarket cost counter
huge balloon	hand vacuum cleaner
needle threader	pocket calculator

A sampling of other successful mail order products and services follows.[21]

fountain pens	insurance
frozen food	gifts
dancing lessons	magazine subscriptions
schools by mail	childcare and nursery items
shorthand system	collectors' items
tea bags	devices and gadgets
alarm clocks	greeting cards and stationery
book clubs	sports and outdoor equipment
hobby and craft items	entertainment
housewares	records and tapes
automobiles	gelatin capsules
cosmetics	vacuum cleaners
foods	chewing gum

---

[20]Ibid., p. 443.

[21]Items selected from Cohen, op. cit., pp. 77–79.

Sources of Mail Order Products-Services

William C. Cohen has developed a comprehensive list of sources of new mail order items. These sources are summarized and paraphrased as follows.[22]

1 *Copy others.* Start with currently successful items, but be careful because you may be copying a failure, or you may not have the talent or resources to market the same item.

2 *Attend inventor shows.* At inventor shows you will see hundreds of new products that the inventors would like to license to you for a royalty or perhaps sell outright.

3 *Check foreign products.* Foreign products not available in the United States can frequently be outstanding products for sale by mail. Foreign countries will assist the entrepreneur to sell their products in the United States. Some publications that will help you are: *The International Commerce Magazine Weekly*, published by the U.S. Department of Commerce; *American Register of Exporters and Importers*, published by the American Register of Exporters and Importers Corporation, 38 Park Row, New York, New York 10038; Overseas Trade Opportunities section of *American Import Export Management*, published by North American Publishing Company, 401 N. Broad Street, Philadelphia, Pennsylvania 19108; and *International New Product Newsletter*, Six Saint James Avenue, Boston, Massachusetts 02116.

4 *Read business opportunity sections of newspapers and magazines.* Frequently, individuals who have a product or mail order business to sell will advertise in publications, such as *The Wall Street Journal*.

5 *Call local manufacturers.* Every manufacturer has created a product at one time or another that was not successful for his or her particular line of work but that might be appropriate and successful for a mail order product.

6 *Government inventions for licensing.* Get a copy of the NASA publication *Tech Briefs*, published periodically by the National Aviation and Space Administration. It describes new ideas, concepts, and patents for new products that are by-products of the space program. To get a copy, write the National Technical Information Service, U.S. Department of Commerce, 5285 Port Royal Road, Springfield, Virginia 22161.

7 *Contact major corporations in the United States.* Just as NASA has by-products from the space program, almost every large corporation that has a research and development division will, on occasion, develop products for which it has no use. As a result, most major corporations have established special offices to market the licensing of their patents to individuals outside their companies. Also, get a copy of *Thomas' Register of Manufacturers*. You will find not only

---

[22]Cohen, op. cit., pp. 65–70.

names and addresses but also products and the individual to contact about obtaining them. Every page is a potential source of a new mail order product.

8 *Distressed or refurbished items.* If you see distressed merchandise that is identified as such because it has been greatly reduced in price, it may be an excellent mail order product, but be careful. Another tactic, as mentioned earlier, may be to sell items refurbished by the manufacturer or to take over both the refurbishing and the marketing process. Many manufacturers would probably be quite amenable to this kind of deal.

9 *Patents.* Many earlier patents are never even put into production but may be ready for the marketplace now. Furthermore, expired patents are in the public domain and are a ready source of new product ideas for mail order. For further information, write U.S. Department of Commerce, Patent and Trademark Office, Washington, D.C. 20231.

10 *Overseas trade publications.* These publications are excellent sources for importing new products into the United States. Two examples are: *Hong Kong Enterprise*, Third Floor, Connaught Center, Connaught Road Central, Hong Kong; *Made in Europe*, P.O. Box 174027, D-6, Frankfurt-am-Main, West Germany.

11 *Trade shows.* Like inventor shows, trade shows will have hundreds of products, some of which will be outstanding for mail order. To find out about trade shows, get a copy of the *Directory of the United States Trade Shows, Expositions, and Conventions*. Write to the United States Travel Service, U.S. Department of Commerce, Washington, D.C. 20230. Also, contact your local Chamber of Commerce.

12 *Rework items from old magazines.* If a product was a great mail order seller years ago, it may well be ready for a comeback. Get some old magazines and catalogs, read them, and use your imagination.

13 *Personalize items.* People like to see items with their names on them, and many have become successful mail order items, from card cases to briefcases. If you can figure out a new twist or way to personalize an item, you have a good possibility for a winner.

14 *Write a book or a correspondence course.* Again, the movement toward a service economy makes the mail order business ripe for the marketing of expertise, instruction, and information.

It is true that nearly anything can be marketed via mail order, but some items are more practical than others for this type of marketing. For example, is your product lightweight and easily handled by the postal service or other package-handling firms? Don't start with a mailing handicap. A book is a good example of an ideal mail order item. It enjoys a cheap postage rate, it is easily handled, and there is no breakage or spoilage. Conversely, products such as tombstones and lobsters have been sold successfully through mail and delivered by other means. Does your product sell at a price three or four times its cost? In addition to the cost of the product, there are costs of packaging, mailing, advertising, and so forth, all of which must be covered to make a profit. Also, try to select an item that sells for $200 or less; otherwise, you may have to offer credit, which can crimp your cash flow and spell disaster for a business struggling to get started. Also, select an item that is non-seasonal and an item that can be easily understood.

Copycatting

By definition, a copycat is one who slavishly imitates the practice or procedures of others. According to the copycat principle in mail order, you simply copy another's product, advertisements, and methods as closely as you can. Precise copying is not recommended for several reasons. For one, it is probably unethical and, in some instances where copyrights are used, it is illegal. From a logical viewpoint, you will be going for the same market, and at best profit from this market will be diluted. Another problem with copying exactly what another has done is that you may be copying another's mistakes, or the operator is pushing a loss leader to help generate sales on other, more profitable items.

The sensible way to use this principle is to build on the idea of someone else's and put your own twist to it. If the product or service is a success, it has already met the trials of the marketplace. Offering a totally new, unique product is extremely risky because the more unique and original your product or service is, the greater are your chances for failure in converting it to sales. Moreover, with limited resources, it is impossible to create a market for a new, unique product or service. Indeed, don't toy with the perpetual motion machine; apply your inventiveness and originality to the marketing side of your venture.

Ways to Get Started

What are you doing now? What are your hobbies? Is there something you are knowledgeable about or have an interest in already that you could market rather than start from scratch? You may, for example, already be in the retail business that caters to extra large people. Why not combine your walk-in trade with mail order and reach out to capture a larger market? You are already in business with the goods and expertise. If you are an avid fisherman, why not market your favorite lures and expertise through mail order? Or why not go into a joint venture with a manufacturer or retailer to market some of their products through mail order? You furnish the marketing expertise, and they furnish the products. Begin by advertising in local newspapers, then in regional media, and finally in national media.

Costs and Pricing Considerations

The obvious costs in mail order are for product or service, advertising, handling and packaging, and shipping. Advertising, for example, may be as much as 50 percent of total costs. Moreover, if you are in the catalog business, printing and distribution are a major cost of doing business. Each catalog can cost from $.50 to more than $1.00 to print and mail and even more for some of the fancy ones.

Other costs for any mail order operation include order processing and labeling; storage; correspondence, billing, forms, and office supplies; costs to cover returned, lost, or damaged merchandise; telephone and utilities; bank service charges and interest; accounting and legal services; bad debts; labor, salaries, and *your* salary (don't forget to pay yourself); and automobile, insurance, licenses, and rent.

Certainly, costs are important to consider when setting prices because if revenue fails to cover *all* costs, then in the long run, your firm will not be able to survive. In purely economic terms, the best price for a product or service is the price that maximizes the difference between total revenue and total costs.

A product's or service's price elasticity is a key concept in any pricing decision. Price elasticity measures the degree to which the volume of sales is affected by a change in price per unit. Demand for a product or service is price inelastic if a change in price has little or no effect on the volume of units sold. Demand is price elastic if a change in price has a substantial effect on the volume of units sold. Certainly, whether demand for a product tends to be price elastic or price inelastic can be a crucial factor in a decision relating to a change in price. Measuring the degree of elasticity is extremely difficult.

In some instances, the market price may already be set for your product or service, and customers will not pay more than this price. If you are in a market where you can set your own price, then a pricing strategy is an important consideration. Indeed, setting such a price is both a marketing and a financial decision.

The common approach to pricing standard products is to use a cost-plus formula. Compile and compute a cost base, and add to this base a markup to derive the target selling price. In some situations the percentage markup is more or less standard and has developed over years of experience and trial and error. Even after a number of calculations, however, the final selling price may be shaded up or down according to competitive forces in the marketplace. The question then arises, if you set the price according to how you sense the market, why bother with cost calculations? The answer is that costs give a point of departure and a floor, which guards you from pricing too low and thereby incurring losses.

Pricing a new, unique product or service presents a more challenging pricing problem. Test marketing can help. You simply introduce the new product or service in selected areas at different prices. Then data can be gathered to help indicate the best price to select. For example, a $2.00 price may produce 80 percent more sales than a $2.20 price. Or, on the other hand, a $2.00 price may actually do much better than a $1.98 price because of even-dollar pricing.

Further, pricing strategies include skimming, penetration, and loss-leader pricing. Many new products like house robots or miniature horses have a scarcity or novelty appeal that causes demand to be somewhat price inelastic. With these kinds of products, skimming pricing can be used whereby a high initial price is set with a progressive lowering of the price as time passes and as other competitors enter the market. Penetration pricing is just the opposite whereby the initial price is set low to gain quick acceptance in the market. Loss-leader pricing is similar to penetration pricing except that the main purpose of this kind of pricing is to price a product or service at a substantial discount to attract customers to your firm to build valuable mailing lists and to entice your customers to buy other, higher-profit items. What pricing strategy you choose depends on what you are trying to accomplish.

ADVERTISING STRATEGIES

The objective of advertising is to sell your ideas and product or service and to gain acceptance. As the cliché goes, "It pays to advertise." In mail order, you have to advertise because most, if not all, of the selling is done via the media. Consequently, advertising copy should explain why the product or service is better and how it works. Moreover, many of the items involve new technologies or they are expensive or both, so the customer wants hard facts about the item and full explanation about all its features. And if you can do all of this in an entertaining fashion, so much the better.

Selling through advertising copy is the most challenging way to sell. You can't get by on political or family connections or by being a charming, nice guy or a smooth talker. You have got to do it through what Joe Sugarman, owner of JS&A, calls "literary persuasion."

Choosing Advertising Media

For effective promotion and advertising, specific target customers must be reached. Unfortunately, not all potential customers read all the media, so not all media are equally effective. What, then, is the best medium? It depends on (1) your promotion and advertising objectives, (2) what target markets you want to reach, (3) the funds available for advertising, and (4) the nature of the media, including whom they *reach*, with what *frequency*, with what *impact*, at what *cost*.[23] Table 8.1 shows some of the pros and cons of major kinds of media.[24] As an advertiser, first you must specify your target market, and then match the media with this market where most of your potential customers will hear, read, or see your advertising message.

Classified Advertising

Generally speaking, newspaper classified ads will not pay off for mail order operators. The exceptions to this rule-of-thumb are such nationally distributed newspapers as *The Wall Street Journal* and *The New York Times*. There are also a large number of magazines that are good media for classified ads.

[23]McCarthy and Perreault, op. cit., p. 536.
[24]Ibid., p. 537. (partial table)

TABLE 8.1
Advantages and Disadvantages of Major Kinds of Media

Kinds of Media (listed by sales volume)	Advantages	Disadvantages
Newspaper	Flexible Timely Local market Credible source	May be expensive Short life No "pass-along"
Television	Offers sight, sound, and motion Good attention Wide reach	Expensive in total "Clutter" Short exposure Less selective audience
Direct mail	Selected audience Flexible Can personalize	Relatively expensive per contact "Junk-mail"—hard to retain attention
Radio	Wide reach Segmented audiences Inexpensive	Offers audio only Weak attention Many different rates Short exposure
Magazine	Very segmented audiences Credible source Good reproduction Long life Good "pass-along"	Inflexible Long lead times
Outdoor	Flexible Repeat exposure Inexpensive	"Mass market" Very short exposure

Source: McCarthy and Perreault, op. cit., p. 537.

What is true for all advertising copy is especially true of classified ads—the copy must be concise, and every word must tell. Your ad must compete with other ads for the reader's fullest attention as he or she skims through the classified section. Attracting attention is done in display ads by the headline, the layout, and the artwork. Your classified ad has no artwork and no layout other than the standardized block of type. The whole job of getting your reader's attention must be done by the first word or words. Then the promise is made, such as "$100 extra weekly income." Next tell what the product or service is, such as "Farms and Ranches." Also, call to the prospect with the lead word, if appropriate. For example, use terms like "Real Estate Salespersons," "Inventors," and "Writers." After the lead words, the good classified ad will contain whatever descriptive words are necessary to tell enough about your product or service to make the prospect want it and to convince him or her you are telling the truth. Then state the price, guarantee, key, address, plus a call for action ("Write today").[25]

Display Advertising

A display ad is space in a medium such as a magazine or newspaper in which advertising is placed.[26] A display ad is placed to offer a product or service that can be ordered immediately by a potential customer through the use of a coupon. Generally speaking, you get your volume business this way and build up a large customer data base.

Advertise in the same magazines that your competitors are using. These publications have a readership who are most likely to be interested in your product or service. Different responses can be expected depending on whether your ad appears on the back cover, near editorial matter, in the upper part of the magazine, or on the outside. Generally, the back cover is almost universally acclaimed as the best position. Coupon ads do not do well on the inside front cover because people don't like to cut the cover. It is better to be near editorial matter than near other advertisements. The upper part of the page does better than the lower part, and the outside of a page is better than the inside column.[27] Also, colors ads generally do better than those in black and white.

Direct Mail

Direct mail is the rifle approach to mail order marketing. To be sure, it is the most specific medium because you are selling directly to target customers via their mailboxes. You are sending a specific message and offer to a specific list of people. A typical direct mail package includes the outside envelope with an eye-catching message, the letter message and offer, the coupon and order form, brochures, and a postpaid reply envelope. This package is mailed to a special list of people who are on mailing lists rented from mailing list brokers or to a list of customers compiled by the operator himself or herself.

The keys to this approach are personalization of the letter and a mailing list containing prime customer prospects. The better the prospects on the mailing list, the better the response. For example, suppose you are selling sports-car ski racks in Minnesota. An extremely effective and appropriate mailing list for your direct mail venture could be created as follows: "Match the list of (Minnesota) motorists who own sports cars that will accommodate ski racks (readily available from the state's department of motor vehicles) with the list of zip codes for relatively affluent areas (from the Census Bureau) with the list of *Ski Magazine* subscribers."[28]

---

[25]Summarized from Simon, op. cit., pp. 148–49.

[26]Cohen, op. cit., p. 161.

[27]Simon, op. cit., pp. 207–8.

[28]Greene, op. cit., p. 61.

The advantages of direct mail are accuracy and personalization, speed in getting to your market, concealing information from your competitors, and being able to provide much more advertising and sales copy than you can in any other type of advertising.[29] The disadvantage is that your package is perceived as "junk mail."

Catalogs

Bill Abrams has written: "Last year, Americans bought an estimated $45 billion of merchandise from catalogs that clogged their mailboxes. The Direct Marketing Association calculates that the average U.S. home receives 80 catalogs a year, but anyone with a history of buying by mail could receive two or three times as many."[30]

There are several kinds of catalog businesses. One is the catalog showroom retailer who offers discount prices to walk-in trade and delivers a large number of the items in the catalog from the backroom warehouse. Price saving is the big attraction on items such as jewelry, gifts, luggage, and appliances. This kind of catalog operator offers few services.

General merchandise mail order firms such as Sears carry a full line of merchandise and send out millions of catalogs annually to a select list of customers. These giants also operate catalog counters in their stores and catalog offices in small communities where customers can go and examine the catalogs and place orders. The order is shipped from central warehouses to these catalog desks, and, on its arrival, the customer is phoned and is asked to pick it up.[31]

Specialty department stores, such as Neiman-Marcus and Bloomingdale's send catalogs to a select list of customers with discriminating taste for exotic and high-quality items. Some of these catalogs have become popular collector's items; consequently, firms such as Neiman-Marcus charge several dollars per copy.

Most catalog mail order firms rent mailing lists from other catalog marketers, list brokers, magazines, and credit card companies. Additional names come from their own list of past customers and people who have asked to be put on the firm's mailing list. The wave of the future will be electronic catalogs connected to customers' video display terminals (VDT) and push-button ordering.

To be sure, it is difficult to break into the catalog mail order business. The safest way is to let a small repeat-item business evolve to the catalog business, using brochures and direct mail as an interim step.

Using Other Media

Three media that show great potential for mail order are television, radio, and telephone. These media can be used to create a sale, generate leads, or support other

[29]Cohen, op. cit., p. 218.

[30]Bill Abrams, "Entrepreneur's Slick Catalog for Affluent Is Pacing the Growing Direct-Mail Business," *The Wall Street Journal*, Section 2, March 1, 1984, p. 27. This is used with permission.

[31]Kotler, op. cit., p. 471.

advertising programs. One major disadvantage of television and radio is the absence of a coupon where the potential customer can easily place an order. The use of credit cards and two-way television help to alleviate this disadvantage.

To be sure, interactive TV gives the mail order operator unlimited opportunities because of the ability to segment and target a market. The use of infomercials will provide mail order operators with a powerful way to present products without the time restrictions of general commercial TV. The potential customer enjoys a leisurely and full explanation of the product or service, alternatives, newest features, warranties, and complete demonstrations. The customer can use a toll-free number to place a credit card order with billing, electronic transfer of funds, and delivery on the same day.

Mail order operators are increasingly using the telephone to sell a variety of products and services. The toll-free number and the telephone combined with direct mail catalogs and broadcast media make a strong marketing program. Indeed, the telephone is a blessing for the impatient customer and for mail order operators who no longer have to wade through mountains of letters and make trips to the post office. The advent of cellular phones will really open up even more mail order opportunities.

Some telephone marketers have developed computerized phoning systems where households are dialed automatically and automatic voice systems give the message. This kind of telephone selling, however, has incurred the wrath of several consumer groups, and they, in turn, are proposing laws to ban it. On the other hand, automatic dialing is put to good use by large catalog houses such as Sears to dial customers to let them know that their order has arrived. Also, an interesting new twist uses taped messages from famous people for testimonials that the operator plays to prospective customers before asking them for an order.

How to Write Advertising Copy

First, to write good advertising copy, you must know *what* you are selling *to whom*.[32] This is basic, and without this knowledge, your advertising copy will not work. Assuming you have this knowledge, the challenge is to prepare advertisements that sell your product or service to the target market on a one-to-one relationship; I want *you* to buy from *me*. Don't try to be like everyone else. Establish a rapport in your copy; and make it exciting, entertaining, and stimulating. Indeed, the key to selling via mail order is good advertising copy that grabs the reader's attention, lures him or her into and through the message,ʹ and drives the reader to action.

To start learning how to write copy, read books on copywriting to get the basic principles. Two excellent texts are *Tested Advertising Methods* by John Caples and *A Short Course in Copywriting* by Victor O. Schwab. Also, study ads written by success-

---

[32]Sandra Linville Dean, *How to Advertise* (Wilmington, Del.: Enterprise Publishing, 1980), p. 120. This material is used with permission.

ful copywriters. Then start writing and *rewriting* your own to see how it stacks up against the experts.

Although copywriting experts have applied many innovative twists to their advertisements, all copy includes the following elements. This, then, becomes your guide to writing successful advertising copy.

1 *Get the prospective customer's attention.* Develop a key word or headline or picture that grabs the readers by the eyeballs. If you don't get their attention, they are not going to read the copy. Most experts will agree that the headline is the most important part of most advertisements. A good headline appeals to the reader's self-interest and stresses the most important benefit of the product or service. Here are some successful headlines: "How to Win Friends and Influence People," "Why Some People Almost Always Make Money in the Stock Market," "Whoever Heard of a Woman Losing Weight—And Enjoying 3 Delicious Meals at the Same Time."

2 *Increase interest.* The attention-getting headline must lead the potential customer into the next part of the copy, which increases interest by explaining advantages and benefits. There are four ways to do this: a story; a startling, shocking, or unusual statement; a quotation; or news.[33] No matter what you say about benefits or advantages of your product or service, the reader must believe it. Moreover, once you have gotten the reader's attention, you must hold it; if a pretty, sexy girl is used in getting attention, but has nothing to do with the copy, the reader will flip to something else.

2 *Create desire.* Promise of additional benefits or advantages are made by the use of testimonials from satisfied customers. You now have a third party supporting your claims. This part of the ad must convince readers that the product or service will meet their need—emotional, social, intellectual, and financial.

4 *Call for action.* A good salesperson always asks for the order. So should you. Tell the readers what action you want them to take and how. For example, in a display ad, you end the copy by saying: "Clip this coupon and mail a check today." "For free information, fill out the following form and drop in the mail today." "Enter my subscription and bill me later."

Testing

One of the greatest advantages about the mail order business is that you can test products or services, markets, advertising copy, and media before going full steam ahead. The rule of thumb is that if it won't work in a test, it probably won't work. Often the mail order operator has a hunch about something or has become intrigued with a new product or his or her nose tells him or her to advertise something a certain

[33]Cohen, op. cit., p. 272.

way. Testing is the way to find out if the hunches are correct or if your nose was on a hot trail.

Dry-testing is a strong technique that helps the mail order operator to determine if a product will sell before stocking it. Such testing gives the mail order operator a big advantage because he or she does not have to purchase the product until certain that it will sell, how many it will sell, and at what price. This technique may seem to be unethical, but the worst thing that can happen is that the customer wastes some time and possibly some postage. Or if you stock or drop-ship the product, the customer may have to wait a few extra days for it. It should be known that a number of large, reputable firms use this technique. The legality of it is covered later in this chapter.

Besides the product or service, other important things to test include advertising copy and media. You may use a split run to test two different ads in a single issue, or you may run the same ad in different publications. Along with testing advertising copy and media, you can also test different prices.

The use of keys is necessary to differentiate ads and media. Almost anything can be used as a key, a fictitious department number or name, for example. If you use mailing lists, a key should also be used to test their effectiveness. Once your keys are assigned, it is imperative that mailing labels on the return envelope contain the appropriate key for tabulation.

LEGAL ASPECTS OF MAIL ORDER

The mail order business has received a bad rap, some of it deserved. To be sure, this area of business has had more than its share of con artists and crooks. Because of these past transgressions, laws have been passed to curb them. Regulation and control are exercised by the Federal Trade Commission (FTC) and postal inspectors. As in anything, however, your aim should be to not offer anything by mail that violates the basic decency of business. Rather than worry about what you can get by with, work toward fair deals, honest offers, and money-back guarantees; then chances are good that you won't have to be concerned about the following material.

Importance of the Law in Mail Order

The law is more stringent in mail order because it is easier to cheat the customer. Indeed, it makes no difference whether you have satisfied customers or not; you have their money. Practically speaking, the customer has a tough time in getting back at the mail order operator. Some crooks have been quick to take advantage of these vulnerabilities. Many work-at-home and pyramid schemes are usually fraudulent. Examples of other gyps include these: An advertised engraving of George Washington for $.50 is a $.02 postage stamp; for the secret of making big money, send $2, and the customer gets a pamphlet with a message to "work hard"; a cigarette roller is a stick with instructions to place the cigarette on a flat, smooth surface and place either end of the stick at the middle of cigarette and push normally, and the cigarette will roll; a dependable way to hang clothes for $5 gets the customer an eightpenny nail.

The best advice to you is to be straight and honest; running a racket can get you time in jail and wipe you out financially. Your advertising must not fool even the most gullible person; the customer must get what the most trusting person would expect. You must be truthful in the spirit and the letter of the law. Moreover, you must be able to back your claims with strong evidence. If you sell a CPA correspondence course and claim that 50 percent of your clients pass the CPA exam the first time, then you better have clients who have done so. Also, you should be aware of products or services you cannot sell via mail order no matter how honest you are. These include lotteries, pornographic material, chain letters and pyramiding schemes, and new and unproved drugs.

The Direct Mail Marketing Association publishes a list of no less than 28 operating guidelines for ethical business practice for all direct response marketers whether they are selling products or services or raising funds for nonprofit organizations. Perhaps the basic guideline is this one:[34] "Direct response marketers should make their offers clear and honest. They should not misrepresent a product, service, publication, or program and should not use misleading, partially true, or exaggerated statements. All descriptions and promises should be in accordance with actual conditions, situations and circumstances existing at the time the promotion is made. Direct response marketers should operate in accordance with the Better Business Bureau's basic principles contained in the Better Business Bureau's Code of Advertising and be cognizant of and adhere to the Postal Laws and Regulations and all other laws governing advertising in transactions of business by mail, telephone, and the print and broadcast media."[35]

Price Comparison

The FTC has set forth guides and advisory opinions that should be followed when comparative pricing claims are used. They are these.[36]

1 No comparisons should be made or implied between the price at which an article is offered for sale and some other reference price unless the nature of the reference price is explicitly identified and the advertiser has a reasonable basis for substantiating its accuracy. Items compared must be identical or substantially similar.

---

[34]Ibid., pp. 39–40.

[35]Ibid.

[36]Robet J. Posch, Jr., *The Direct Marketer's Legal Adviser* (New York: McGraw-Hill, 1983), pp. 15–16. This material is used with permission.

2 When former-price comparisons are made, bona fide sales must have been made by the advertiser at the advertised former price in the recent past. If the article was offered for sale but no sales were made at that price or any other price in the recent past, the fact must be disclosed in connection with any mention of the former price. This test is important. The seller must be able to demonstrate that the product was openly and actively offered for sale, for a reasonably substantial period of time, in the regular course of business, honestly and in good faith. Again, sales records, checks, invoices, and even correspondence will be helpful here.

3 The guidelines concerning "sales" noted earlier must be geographically comparable over the entire marketplace and not merely isolated or unrepresentative geographic comparisons.

Delivery of Product or Service

One of the most important rules affecting mail order operators, is the FTC's Thirty-Day Delay Delivery Rule. In essence, it says that if there is a reasonable basis to believe that the product or service you are selling will not be shipped within 30 days of receiving a properly completed order, your ad must include a clear and conspicuous notice of the time in which you expect to make shipment. If you make no statement, the rule requires you ship within 30 days.

The 30-day period does not begin until a properly completed form is received. If the form is incomplete, the customer should be notified immediately. If you cannot ship the product or service within 30 days, you must let the customer know and give him or her the right to cancel the deal. You include a postpaid reply form, and give the customer an option to delay or cancel the order and receive a full refund. If the customer fails to respond, you can assume the no-response as a consent to another 30-day delay. If the delay is going to continue beyond the second 30-day delay, you must have the customer's consent on record. The postpaid reply form that you sent the customer must clearly state that this is the situation, and unless you receive a response rejecting the delay, the customer consents to a delayed shipment.

You can avoid the 30-day rule if you clearly state in your advertisements the delay period. For example, if it is going to take 60 days, then state "60 days from receipt of order." Furthermore, the 30-day rule pertains to cash, check, money order, or electronic funds transfer. If you bill the customer or use a credit card but do not charge the account until shipment of the product or service, then you can avoid the rule.

Endorsements and Testimonials

When we were discussing how to write effective advertising copy, the use of endorsements and testimonials was advised because they lend credibility to your product or service and increase sales. The statements, however, must be true and correct and quoted verbatim. Get a signed release to use the endorser's name, all comments, photographs, and illustrations. Do not use endorsements from persons who no longer use the product or service.

The FTC's guidelines for using endorsements and testimonials in advertising are as follows.[37]

1 Every endorsement must reflect the honest view of the endorser and may not use statements in endorsements that could not be supported if presented in the advertiser's words rather than the endorser's.

2 The advertiser may not distort the endorser's opinion or experience with the product by rewording the endorsement or by presenting it out of context. Furthermore, the advertiser may continue to use the endorsement only as long as he or she has good reason to believe that the endorser continues to subscribe to the views presented.

3 Where the advertisement represents that the endorser uses a product, the endorser must actually be a bona fide user of the product. Furthermore, such endorsement may be used only as long as the advertiser has good reason to believe the endorser continues to be a bona fide user of the product.

4 Endorsements that reflect the experience of an individual consumer will be interpreted as representing the typical performance of the product under similar circumstances. If the represented performance is atypical, the advertisement must disclose what typically would be in the depicted circumstances.

5 Advertisements that represent endorsements of "actual consumers" must use actual consumers or disclose that the persons appearing in the advertisement are professional actors appearing for compensation.

6 Endorsements concerning the effectiveness of drug products shall not be made by laypeople.

7 When there is a connection between the endorser and the seller that might materially affect the weight or credibility of the endorsement, such connection must be fully disclosed.

Advertising Copy

Understanding the compliance issues affecting endorsements and testimonials is facilitated by an understanding of the FTC's attitude toward advertising regulations. The FTC attempts to follow the ideal that its regulation serves two objectives: to provide truthful data and to maintain effective and fair competition. To this end, the FTC applies the following standards to advertising.[38]

---

[37]Quoted from Cohen, op. cit., p. 43.

[38]Quoted from Posch, op. cit., pp. 42–43.

1 Advertisements will be considered in their entirety—the advertisement's total *net impression* governs.

2 Literal truth will not save an advertisement if it is misleading when read in the context of the entire advertisement.

3 The advertisement is false if any one of two possible meanings is false.

4 Expressions of subjective opinion (puffery) are not actionable (that is, the FTC won't come after you!) unless they convey the impression of factual representations or relate to material terms.

5 An advertisement is generally tested by the impression it is likely to have on the "general populace," the "ordinary purchaser," or an "appreciable segment of the public" (though advertisements directed at special audience groups will be interpreted on the basis of their meaning to that group).

Dry-Testing

Dry-testing is a valuable technique that permits the mail order operator to test the salability of a product before he or she purchases it. A retailer, on the other hand, has to stock items before selling them, and if he or she purchases "dogs," then he or she suffers a loss. The FTC has issued an advisory opinion in which it allows dry-testing under strict guidelines to ensure that the potential customer is in no way misled about the terms of the offer.[39]

You must not, however, be in conflict with the 30-day rule. You can avoid restrictions of this rule if you bill by credit card or charge account and do not charge the customer until shipment of the product has been made. Also, you can protect yourself from the rule's provisions by stating the number of days before it will be shipped. Furthermore, as the FTC is not totally clear about this matter, the final best advice is to disclose fully to the prospective customer conditions of the offer and allow customers to cancel their orders if they choose to do so.

As always, if you are unsure about the legality of your promotion, consult an attorney, the FTC, and the U.S. Postal Service. Finally, use your common sense. Are you trying to mislead or cheat a prospective customer? If the answer is maybe or yes, don't do it.

Unordered and Substituted Merchandise

The federal law about unordered merchandise is fairly clear and concise. This law forbids not just blatant sending of unordered merchandise, but also sending of merchandise "on approval" without a customer's *prior* permission. Only two kinds of merchandise may be sent through the mails without prior consent: free samples, which must be labeled as such, and merchandise mailed by charitable organizations. Even merchandise mailed by charitable organizations is sent "on approval" and

[39]Cohen, op. cit., p. 46.

need not be paid for. When in doubt, don't dun; if an innocent error is made, write off the order.[40]

Where you have received an express order for an item, you may substitute if the substitution involves merchandise of equivalent or superior quality. Where a valid substitution is offered, the customer must be given the opportunity to return the item postpaid.[41]

FTC Negative Option Rule

The offer is one of the key parts of a sale. There are an endless number, including free trial, bill me later, free gift, discount, refund certificate, seasonal sale, time limit, free sample, limited edition, trade-in, reduced down payment, and so forth. A special type of offer is the club and continuing offer made by artistic clubs, book clubs, record clubs, and other mail order operators who sell repeat products over a period of time. One option is the positive option whereby the customer is notified every month of the monthly selection. To order, the customer must initiate the order. Another opinion is called the negative option whereby the customer is notified in advance of the new selection, and this selection is automatically shipped unless the customer returns a card that rejects the offer by a certain date.

An operator using negative option offers must comply with the following regulations. All promotional material must clearly and conspicuously state the material terms of the plan, including the following.[42]

1 That a negative option plan is being used.

2 The full obligation to purchase a minimum amount of merchandise.

3 That the member may cancel his or her membership any time after completion of the agreement to purchase the minimum amount of merchandise specified.

4 Whether billing charges include postage and handling.

5 That the member will be given 10 days to notify the seller that the selected merchandise is not desired or that he or she wishes to order alternative merchandise being offered. If the member receives less than 10 days, the account will be credited for returned merchandise. The seller must give full credit and pay the return postage for merchandise sent to members who have not been sent a proper form or who have not been given the required time to respond.

6 The frequency with which the advance announcement or merchandise will be sent to the member (i.e., the maximum received in a 12-month period).

7 A statement to the effect that introductory, bonus, or premium merchandise or a combination must be shipped within four weeks of the order unless otherwise disclosed.

[40]Posch, op. cit., p. 8.
[41]Ibid.
[42]Ibid., pp. 10–11.

8 A form contained in or accompanying the announcement clearly and conspicuously disclosing the procedure required to reject the selection.[43]

SUMMARY

The mail order business offers an excellent way for the entrepreneur to go into business. Some may think it is an old-fashioned way of doing business, but it is growing at a rapid rate, and with the evolving use of broadcast media and computers, its future seems extraordinarily bright. Furthermore, more and more customers are turning to mail order as the most efficient and convenient way to "shop."

Types of mail order include one-shot items, repeat items, catalogs, and mail order combined with the use of agents. For the entrepreneur starting from scratch, the one-shot and repeat items are more feasible than the catalog or agent business. The advantages of mail order are ease of entry, low investment, flexibility, and one can start part-time.

Just about anything can be sold via mail order; however, some items are more successful than others. Sources of products or services range from inventors to imported items.

Some mail order operators start by trying to copy the success of others. Exact copying is not recommended; however, if you can add an innovative twist to an already successful approach, then you increase your own chances for success.

The two biggest costs in mail order are for the product and advertising. There are, however, many other costs that must be considered and budgeted for, from postage and handling to bad debts. Often costs have little to do with the price you can charge because the dynamics of the marketplace are the ultimate price setter. The mail order operator, however, should perform cost analysis and test to help determine the "best" price to charge.

Advertising and promotion are the key parts of the mail order business. Available media include newspapers, magazines, television, direct mail, telephone, radio, catalogs, and so forth. Writing advertising copy that sells is imperative. Most copy includes these elements: Get the reader's attention, increase interest, create desire, and call for action. Both advertising copy and media should be tested to determine their effectiveness.

The laws and regulations that govern mail order are probably more stringent than those for most other businesses. The reason for this is because of the abuses and excesses of some mail order operators and consumer vulnerability. Full disclosure, honesty, money-back guarantees, and quick delivery will generally be enough to keep the mail order operator from running afoul of the FTC, postal inspectors, and other watchdogs who administer mail order laws and regulations.

[43]Ibid.

ASSIGNMENT

1 Define mail order. How does it differ from store retailing?

2 What are the types of mail order? Give what you believe would be a good example for each type.

3 Why do people buy through mail order? Why would you buy or not buy via mail order?

4 In your opinion, what is the future of mail order?

5 Draw up a plan for going into the mail order business. What product or service did you choose? What are your costs? What price will you charge? What advertising media will you use?

6 List the sources of mail order products and services.

7 What is copycatting? What is wrong with it? Can it be used effectively? State how, and give a specific example.

8 List the advertising media? Give the advantages and disadvantages of each.

9 Compare and contrast display and classified ads. Write copy for each ad on a product or service of your choice.

10 What are the elements of good advertising copy? Give an example of each.

11 Why are the laws and regulations that govern mail order important to you as an aspiring entrepreneur, to the average consumer, and to the industry?

12 Explain how a mail order operator abides by regulations of price comparison, delivery of product or service, use of testimonials and endorsements, advertising copy, dry-testing, unordered and substituted merchandise, and negative option rule.

BIBLIOGRAPHY

Abrams, Bill. "Entrepreneur's Slick Catalog for Affluent Is Pacing the Growing Direct-Mail Business." *The Wall Street Journal*. Section 2. March 1, 1984.

Cohen, William A. *Building a Mail Order Business*. New York: Wiley, 1982.

Dean, Sandra Linville. *How to Advertise*. Wilmington, Del.: Enterprise Publishing, 1980.

Greene, Richard. "A Boutique in Your Living Room." *Forbes*. May 7, 1984.

Kotler, Philip. *Principles of Marketing*. Englewood Cliffs, N.J.: Prentice-Hall, 1980.

Lander, Jack. *Make Money by Moonlighting*. Wilmington, Del.: Enterprise Publishing, 1982.

McCarthy, E. Jerome, and William D. Perreault, Jr. *Basic Marketing*. 8th ed. Homewood, Ill.: Richard D. Irwin, 1984.

Posch, Robert J., Jr. *The Direct Marketer's Legal Adviser*. New York: McGraw-Hill, 1983.

Simon, Julian L. *How to Start and Operate a Mail-Order Business*. 3d ed. New York: McGraw-Hill, 1981.

CHAPTER 9

International Trade

INTRODUCTION

It is good strategy for some entrepreneurs to view the world as their marketplace. Although many opportunities exist throughout the world, entrepreneurs must be aware of vast differences both within and between nations. Clearly, entrepreneurs who plan to enter the international arena should be aware of these differences and know how to adapt to them. The objectives of this chapter follow.

1 To present a brief history of international trade and describe its current conditions.

2 To disclose economic, cultural, competitive, political, and legal aspects of international trade and also various barriers to such trade.

3 To outline what opportunities exist in international trade markets and what must be done to enter and be successful in them.

THE INTERNATIONAL TRADE SCENE

Not too many years ago, the United States was a major exporter. Today she is a major importer with a mounting negative trade deficit. A turnaround may be under way, and, therefore, opportunities for entrepreneurs entering world trade may be greater now than ever before. Clearly, the opportunities are great for both export and import. But the big opportunity, especially because of government support programs, is in the export area. Also, once an entrepreneur begins export operations, import or countertrade opportunities soon follow.

Recent History

After World War II, everything in the world was in short supply. If it was available, however, the United States had it. Many Americans flocked into the export business to supply a worldwide market that was insatiable. Exporters were making from 100 percent to over 500 percent profit on many items. After a few years, production started up in other countries, and the American exporters found themselves being squeezed out. Moreover, the American manufacturers who ignored their export markets because the domestic market was so huge, who refused to adapt any portion of their product or service to fit foreign needs, who were unreliable, who were unethical, who would not give service, and who would not sell anything unless it was on confirmed irrevocable letters of credit—these U.S. exporters found themselves up against European and Japanese teams of government-producers-bankers-traders-carriers who took the play away from them.[1]

---

[1]Leonard Shaye, "Playing Export Games," *American Import Export Management*, April 1983, pp. 22, 63. This material is used with permission.

Indeed, American exporters began to lose out in the international markets. Big American trading companies became rare. Imports far exceeded exports. Big business and labor lobbied for import quotas and protectionism. Because of the deteriorating conditions in international trade and significant decreases in exports, the American business community in recent years has been presented with a wide array of export arrangements and programs. The Export Trading Company Act of 1982, for example, has been debated and passed. Multinational manufacturers and retailers have formed export trading divisions, and it has been stated again and again that nonexporting American businesses need to get on the export bandwagon. Studies by the Department of Commerce and others indicate, in a nutshell, that of the 300,000 United States manufacturers that were judged to have products with export potential, fewer than 25,000 actually were exporting. Moreover, about 85 percent of all exported goods were produced by fewer than 250 companies. To be sure, ways are being established to help exporters get their fair share of the international market.

Present Conditions

International trade means the movement of products or services or both across national borders by exporting and importing. Do American entrepreneurs need to think internationally? Although there are many barriers to trade and a variety of different factors to contend with between nations, there are many reasons for answering yes. One general reason is that we are in a world economy; we are becoming more and more interdependent. No country is an island unto itself; no country can long survive as an isolationist. New entrepreneurs and old established businesses need to enter the world marketplace. Indeed, nations trade with each other because they find they are better off by trading than going it alone. Even Communist nations are now exporting and importing more than ever before.

Also, American entrepreneurs must learn how to compete in a world economy. Competition is increasing from countries that only several decades ago did not have much of an economy, such as Hong Kong, Japan, South Korea, and Taiwan. Others, such as Brazil, South Africa, and Australia, will represent major competition in the future. Indeed, competition is coming from big, rich industrial nations; small, developing nations; and from a variety of countries that span the economic, cultural, political, and legal spectrum.

But the exciting thing about all this is that competition and the increasing wealth of nations produce massive market opportunities for entrepreneurs. People all around the spaceship *Earth* are becoming more affluent and, therefore, consumers of a wide array of products and services. Consumers mean markets, and 95 percent of the world's population lives outside of the United States with over 75 percent of the world's purchasing power, both of which are increasing. To be sure, such statistics mean a vast potential market for American products and services.

Implications of International Trade

Entrepreneurially, trade occurs internationally for the same reason that it does domestically. The basic goal of exporters and importers is to service a market and make a profit—to be better off after the trade then before. In macroeconomics, economists use the theory of comparative advantage to explain how the gains from trade are distributed among nations. They reason that most nations are not self-sufficient and cannot, therefore, supply all their needs from domestic resources. It is, consequently, to their advantage to specialize in products or services or both that they produce efficiently and to trade for things that other nations supply efficiently. Through international trade, nations can get more and different products and services than are available domestically, thereby increasing their standard of living. This, of course, is the key argument favoring free trade—trade without regulations, barriers, or restrictions—among nations.

Export. Export entrepreneurs see foreign markets as a basis for expanding sales beyond the limits of the domestic market. Exports allow entrepreneurs to keep their labor and capital employed more fully and continuously, to expand and lower operating costs, and to smooth out business cycles. Moreover, some export sales may produce greater profits than the sale of identical products in a highly competitive home market. Often the exporter will find that a product that is at maturity in the domestic market may be in its growth stage in a foreign market.

Today it is certainly easier to export because of improvements in transportation, storage, containerization, and communications, along with more legislation that encourages exporting. Moreover, there are more export intermediaries, bankers, and insurance agents, all of whom are becoming more experienced and adept at getting the goods to the buyer; providing financing, payment, and collection methods; and offering protection of goods.

Import. Import entrepreneurs purchase foreign products for use or sale in the home market. Importing involves searching foreign markets for acceptable or different products and sources of supply, providing for the transfer of the products to the home market, arranging financing, negotiating the import documentation and customs procedure, and developing plans for use or for resale of the product or service.[2] The reason for importing is to gain a comparative advantage over one's competitors in the home market.

Trade Deficit

A trade deficit is an interesting yet negative phenomenon that can happen when nations export and import. A trade deficit simply means that a country is importing more than it is exporting. In earlier times, Americans were known as "Yankee

---

[2]Ruel Kahler and Roland L. Kramer, *International Marketing*, 4th ed. (Cincinnati, Ohio: South-Western Publishing, 1977), p. 344. This material is used with permission.

traders," and America enjoyed a favorable trade balance. But today a flood of imports and feeble export sales have pushed the United States merchandise trade deficit to record highs—annualized trade deficits of well over $100 billion. And the red ink continues to spread.

Unfortunately, the grim fact is that each $1 billion lost in export sales costs approximately 25,000 American jobs. The good news for the average American consumer is, however, that competition from cheaper imports forces domestic prices to stay in line. And because of the soaring trade deficit, the good news for would-be export entrepreneurs is that government policymakers are making a determined effort to create favorable export programs and legislation to encourage exports in order to reduce the monstrous trade deficit.

Why do we have such a trade deficit? A very quick, simplistic answer is the strength of the American dollar that discourages foreigners from buying American products and services. Others, however, chalk it up to the American lack of experience and expertise in developing foreign markets. Marketers on the global scene feel Americans are rank amateurs, and such amateurism and inexperience lead to inflexibility and unreasonable demands. As some say, American exporters always want the "three ins," which means *in* advance, *in* gold, and *in* Zurich.[3] Such marketing narrow-mindedness may manifest even a broader and more important problem—an absence of savoir faire and human skills in the international arena, that is, the inability to create and maintain personal relationships with foreigners. Those who are skilled in international trade know that you don't go into a country, get an order, and come out the next day. You must be familiar with the people; their trade practices; their customs, culture, laws, and politics; and the needs of that country. If such criticism, however, seems to be too strong and even unfair, remember that the United States is far behind other much smaller countries in the export business. For example, Great Britain's manufacturers export over twice as much to Third World nations as the United States does. Such an amazing situation does make one pause for reflection.

FACTORS AND BARRIERS IN INTERNATIONAL TRADE

To be successful in international trade, entrepreneurs must understand how international markets differ from domestic markets. Also, because there is really no such thing as "free trade," barriers to trade must be understood.

Different Factors in International Trade

To a great extent, an entrepreneur's export program is constrained and shaped by economic, cultural, competitive, and political and legal factors; and each factor

---

[3]Steve Weiner and Robert Johnson, "Export-Trading Firms In U.S. are Failing to Fulfill Promise," *The Wall Street Journal*, May 24, 1984, p. 14. This material is used with permission.

differs between nations and regions. In Table 9.1, these factors are shown, along with their effect on marketing ingredients, such as product, price, distribution, and promotion.

Economic Factors.   The first concern of the export entrepreneur is the size of the market and the income of the people in that market, both of which affect the kinds of products and services offered and their price. Two income measurements are per capita and gross national product (GNP). Exporters who market consumer goods are interested in per capita income; those who market industrial goods are interested in GNP. Infrastructure conditions are also very important as they relate to distribution, communications, and media availability. As far as the size of the market is concerned, over 25 percent of the world's nations have a population of 10 million or more. But populations differ in many ways. For example, China has over 1 billion people with a small per capita income. On the other hand, Kuwait has a small population of under 2 million with a large per capita income.

Age and geographic distribution are also important considerations. Consumers, obviously, have different needs and purchasing power over their life cycle. Many developing countries have 40 or more percent of people under 15 years of age; this group may be widely scattered, dependent, and economically inactive. In Western Europe, by contrast, only 25 percent of the population fall into this group; most people are clustered within major cities and are economically active. Therefore, countries, with a similar population size, can have different product-service needs.

TABLE 9.1
Factors and Marketing Ingredients in International Trade

Obstacles to Uniformity	Marketing Ingredients			
	Product	Price	Distribution	Promotion
Economic factors	Varied income levels	Varied income levels	Different retail structures	Media availability
Cultural factors	Consumer tastes and habits	Price negotiation	Shopping habits	Language, attitude differences
Competitive factors	Nature of existing products	Competitors' costs and prices	Competitors' monopoly of channels	Competitors' budgets, appeals
Political and legal factors	Product regulations	Price controls	Restrictions on distribution	Advertising and media restrictions

The table material is adapted from Vern Terpstra, *International Dimensions of Marketing* (Boston, Mass.: Kent Publishing Company, 1982), Chapters 1 and 2. Copyright © 1982 by Wadsworth, Inc. Reprinted by permission of Kent Publishing Company, a division of Wadsworth, Inc.

Cultural Factors.   *Culture* is the distinctive way of life of a nation's people. All people throughout the world have essentially the same basic needs, but they do not all seek to satisfy them in the same way. Cultural variations among the nations provide an intriguing and fascinating diversity, but, in many instances, a difficult problem and challenge for exporters. For example, people in Asian cultures are fatalistic and do not seek instant gratification. Buddhists believe that human suffering is caused by desire, and the major goal in life is to extinguish this desire. Mohammed said, "All innovation is of the Devil." People in some Muslim countries have helped to reinforce this belief by throwing out television sets and ridding themselves of many material possessions. Women have dropped out of universities to resume their traditional role and garb. Indeed, culture is important to all people, and entrepreneurs must understand and respect others' cultures.

Language differences are important with regard to communication decisions in marketing that range from the choice of a brand name to packaging and labeling to the writing of a service manual or advertising copy for direct selling. What is a positive in one culture may be a negative in another. Amazonians laugh when injured; many others around the world cry. In some cultures, death is a cause for joy; in others, it is a cause for mourning and sorrow. In some cultures, wine is drunk by individuals of all ages during meals; in other cultures, there is a ban on the consumption of all liquor. What is considered funny in one culture is considered obnoxious in another. In some cultures, the father is the head of the household and makes all purchasing decisions. In other cultures, the children may make many of the buying decisions. And so it goes.

Americans should be especially wary of different cultural factors because they have been criticized for the way they bring their products and services and marketing methods into countries with cultures different from that of the United States. Sometimes Americans have been accused of cultural imperialism. To be sure, consumer behavior is culture bound and differs from country to country and even among subcultures within a single country. Such a factor poses significant stumbling blocks for the entrepreneur to overcome, but, at the same time, such differences provide real opportunities.

Competitive Factors.   Obviously, the exporter must be aware of his or her competitor's products and services, costs and prices, and channels of distribution, but, as stressed throughout this text, the fundamental way to meet and beat competition anywhere and anytime is by increasing productivity and product-service differentiation. Certainly, Americans have the wherewithal to be competitive. A staggering array of technology permits massive increases in productivity. And the innovative, creative, and managerial abilities that are available enable product-service differentiation.

Political and Legal Factors.   What are the political influences in the nation to which you plan to export? Are there political unrest and turmoil? Is the country Communist, capitalistic, socialist, or xenophobic? In some countries, the trade doors are opened; in others, they are closed. In some countries, the United States is under attack for political and economical reasons. Some products and even some services are politically sensitive in some countries. For example, drugs, liquors, cigarettes, television sets, and educational services are attacked in a few countries. Obviously, then, relevant and timely political intelligence is a key part of export planning.

Legal factors are basically the political expression of a nation. Indeed, politics and the law are intertwined, both stemming from a nation's culture. Certainly, the exporter must consider both the laws of the United States and the laws of candidate countries. Unfortunately, the laws covering the same product or service and the same marketing activities differ from country to country. Some countries do not allow door-to-door selling, others do not allow radio and television advertising, some products and services are under price controls, some countries have stringent noise and emission standards, and so on.

Barriers to Trade and the Challenge

Most international traders prefer to operate in a totally open, free market, where competition is the determinant of success. They prefer to follow Thomas Carlyle's formulation: "A fair field and no favor and the right will prosper." But the world is probably too complex and provincial to follow such grand ideals. Each country, in fact, affects the salability of foreign products and services in its domestic market, using methods to support demands of its own industries or its political and economic policies.[4] Such policies may be called barriers to your product.

Generally speaking, barriers to trade are categorized into two major divisions: tariff barriers and nontariff trade barriers. Naturally, there is a subjective aspect to barriers because what is a "barrier" to one party seems more like a "needed protection from unfair competition" to another party.[5]

Tariffs, or tax barriers, are the easiest to understand. Import duties or tariffs on goods arriving at a destination country are virtually universally used except at free ports or in free-trade zones. So the precedent for some tariff is strong and generally accepted. The imposition of tariffs becomes a "barrier" when the amount of the tariff becomes large (relative to the sale price or cost of the goods) and acts to make the imported goods essentially noncompetitive in the market of that country. Although there has been a resurgence of this type of barrier in the last year or so (by the United States and others), it has generally been perceived to be a nonproductive tactic, as quite often it forces the overall price structures upward, destabilizing the market and contributing to inflation.[6]

Of much wider diversity and greater subtlety and, therefore, harder to detect and anticipate are nontariff barriers. These can come in a variety of forms but have

---

[4]*Exportise* (Boston, Mass.: The Small Business Foundation of America, Inc., 1983), p. 88. This material is used with permission.

[5]Ibid.

[6]Ibid.

the overall net effect of screening out a product from a market or making it extremely difficult to gain a market foothold. They may also cause a product or service to be noncompetitive in price. Such nontariff barriers include (1) safety-environmental standards that make compliance difficult and expensive, (2) final assembly restrictions where the product can be sold only if final assembly is conducted in that country, (3) quality standards that stipulate peculiar quality standards to which the product must conform and inspections where the outcomes are uncertain, (4) quotas and import restrictions that simply limit the amount or type of certain products, (5) a "buy domestic" policy whereby products and services are bought from home sources to the exclusion of all else, (6) currency limitations that restrict buyers from purchasing foreign goods because of limited availability of hard currency, (7) native language content, which means that the product or service must use extensive native language, (8) ownership stipulations that the right to any product imported belongs to the importing country or its agent (who may also require royalties or comanufacturing rights), and (9) payoffs and kickbacks that can mean that in some countries payments will be demanded for facilitating the sales of product or services.[7]

There are many other nontariff barriers to trade, and the United States indulges in some as well as its trading partners. But, in general, these barriers are of less concern to smaller firms because they simply will steer their efforts to other countries when they encounter stiff barriers of this type.[8]

The United States must itself be careful not to throw up more restrictive trade barriers and curtail the flow of foreign-made goods from automobiles and steel to clothespins and orange juice. Protectionism in whatever form it takes merely invites more of the same. If the United States closes its doors, the rest of the world will be inclined to do the same, and real opportunities for economic expansion through growth in exports will be inhibited.[9] From the national government, there is a need for balance and consistency in direction and policy. For example, assurances must be forthcoming that contracts with foreign buyers of grain and other commodities will be honored without fear of embargo or other disruptive administrative action.[10]

From a strictly business viewpoint, the challenge to increase exports falls on the shoulders of entrepreneurs throughout the country. They must change their reluctance to enter the export market and realize the enormous opportunities for the taking. The United States Department of Commerce estimates that only about 1 in 10 American firms with capabilities to compete in foreign markets now do so. This information, indeed, suggests a mighty potential for export expansion for people with entrepreneurial and opportunistic skills.

---

[7]Ibid.

[8]Ibid.

[9]J. Ron Brinson, "Fairness of Free Trade," *American Import Export Management*, September 1983, pp. 8–12.

[10]Ibid. This material is used with permission.

OPPORTUNITIES IN INTERNATIONAL TRADE

Some of the greatest opportunities for smaller entrepreneurs are in the Third World and in the Association of Southeast Asian Nations (ASEAN). An array of opportunities abound in exporting, importing, franchised operations, and so forth.

Opportunities in Third World Markets

Many believe that Third World countries in Asia, Africa, and Latin American constitute the world's real growth market of the future. Possible product-service export opportunities in such nations range from the most elemental to the most esoteric. Competitive pressures are less intense than in developed countries, and special trade incentives frequently exist. Small businesses may be better equipped than the large multinational corporation to devise relatively low-risk, profit-returning strategies for entering such markets. Furthermore, for those entrepreneurs who might consider some degree of local manufacture or assembly in these nations, there are bountiful resources and a cheap labor supply. Many of these countries are anxious to attract capital and technology; consequently, they offer varying trade and investment incentives not to be found in developed nations.[11]

Difficulties encountered in such markets include fragmented markets, poor transportation systems and communications, language and cultural barriers, widespread illiteracy, and political instability. High rewards, however, come from risks. To be sure, the potential is there; the Third World market sprawls over three continents and embraces half the world's population.[12]

On the basis of a market segmentation model, it is possible to identify the most appropriate market targets and opportunities in terms of individual countries or regions and the ways they are pursuing their development, such as the following.[13]

1 *Basic needs countries.* The aim in these countries is to raise peasant living standards. Development priorities favor agricultural productivity, manufacture or importation of utilitarian consumer goods, expansion of small-scale local enterprise, and the mass dissemination of public health services and educational opportunities. A few examples of countries following this development course include China, Colombia, Costa Rica, and Peru. Some export opportunities include meat substitutes, synthetic fabrics, generic drugs, educational hardware and software, farm implements, high-yield seeds, insecticides and fungicides, battery-operated radios, bicycles, clothing, soap, writing instruments, and basic tools.

[11]Leslie M. Dawson, "Opportunities for Small Business in Third World Markets," *American Journal of Small Business*, 7:1 (Summer 1982), pp. 19–26. This material is used with permission.

[12]Ibid.

[13]Ibid.

2 *Appropriate technology countries.*   The development strategy here is away from bigness toward a lower, basic level of technology to maximize work opportunities. Workplaces are small and simple, and production is for local markets. Some examples are India, Bangladesh, Indonesia, and the Philippines. Some opportunities include construction of brick factories, hand-powered washing machines, foot-powered sewing machines, clay stoves to replace open-fire cooking and heating, windmill power systems, and dirigibles for freight movement.

3 *Isolationist countries.*   Policymakers for these countries believe that meaningful progress and self-reliance are accomplished only by means of complete isolation from the international economy. They want to be insulated from the "evils" of the world and be free to pursue their own path to progress and resist any domination by the superpowers. Examples of countries committed to this course include Albania, Algeria, Cuba, Iran, and Uganda. Obviously, exporting to these countries is severely limited. Nonetheless, they cannot be totally self-sufficient, and some possible areas of product-service opportunities include processes and equipment for mining, harvesting, milling, fishing, drilling, and canning; automotive parts; medicines, tools and dies, computers; and education systems.

4 *Indigenous modernization countries.*   Advocates of this approach pursue a course of modernization emulating none of the superpowers. They attempt to select the best of the developed countries and block out those things they consider detrimental. They seek to be innovative and aggressive, exploiting native resources to the maximum and capitalizing on their better ability to respond to the needs of their own people. Examples include Brazil, Egypt, Mexico, Saudi Arabia, and Venezuela. Export opportunities include computer hardware and software, precision instruments, optical devices, plastics, electronics, all forms of management consulting, roads, irrigation systems, communications, hairdressing, interior decorating, minor and major appliances, jewelry, furniture, clothing, advertising and promotion, and art.

Regardless of political orientation or choice of development mode, the animating characteristic of Third World thinking is for a "greater piece of the action." From the host country's point of view, this translates into a maximum degree of local manufacture, distribution, and management. Many Third World nations prohibit the importation of fully assembled products or require a minimum percentage of local ownership of operations. Whether or not such formal constraints are found to exist in a given market, an entry plan will appear far more acceptable if it seeks to demonstrate that, rather than compete against local enterprise, the entry is likely to stimulate the growth and development of local businesses. It may be found possible to incorporate some locally produced components in the final product or to enlist the aid of local firms in the distribution and servicing function.[14]

[14]Ibid.

For many small firms, the ideal solution to local enterprise participation is the joint venture: a business partnership based on a sharing of manufacturing, marketing, or management responsibility. Although such an arrangement reduces the United States firm's equity in the overseas operation, the trade-off may be highly beneficial in terms of securing an immediate market position and a benevolent, helpful attitude on the part of the host country's government.[15]

ASEAN Opportunities

Many regions and nations of the world provide excellent opportunities for the exporter (and importer). One region, however, that seems to offer an abundance of opportunities and one that is profiled in this chapter is the Association of Southeast Asian Nations (ASEAN), comprising Indonesia, Malaysia, the Philippines, Thailand, and Singapore—the Pacific Rim countries. ASEAN offers incredible opportunities for investment—export; import; franchise, joint venture, or license arrangements; or on-site businesses or manufacturing facilities. The amazing thing is that American business people have not seized these opportunities. Some fear that Americans may lose these opportunities to Japan and Great Britain by default.[16]

ASEAN includes a population of over 270 million consumers with increasing buying power and growing demands and expectations. Indeed, these people want to improve their standard of living. As a direct result of the Export Trading Company Act of 1982, Bancorp's International Division has started up First Interstate Trading Company. It is moving aggressively into the whole Asian market region, including China. Its services for the exporter include analysis of product-service marketability, packaging, freight forwarding, and financing.[17]

A brief profile of each country's import needs follows.[18]

1 *Indonesia.* The government is constructing or is planning major projects in refineries, petrochemicals, power (both distribution and transmission), mining (particularly in coal), cement, and the forest products and paper industries. The private sector interest in cement, forestry, and wood products is especially pronounced and offers excellent sales opportunities for American firms.

The government is encouraging investment in backward and forward linkages in areas such as automotive manufacturing, agribusiness, and marine

---

[15]Ibid.

[16]Julian Weiss, "Marketplace Southeast Asia: ASEAN," *American Import Export Management*, June 1983, p. 60. This material is used with permission.

[17]Willy T. B. Tjen, "Five Nations with Increasing Buying Power and Growing Demands," *American Import Export Management*, February 1984, pp. 30, 32, 34. This material is used with permission.

[18]"1984 Prospects for U.S. Exporters Throughout the ASEAN Five," *American Import Export Management*, February 1984, pp. 35–36. This material is used with permission.

products. Electronics and textiles are other industries undergoing government-sponsored assessments and expansion encouragement. There is considerable American private investment interest in many of these areas that would likely increase the chances for American follow-on sales.

2 *Malaysia.*   Despite the current belt-tightening, substantial Malaysian government outlays for infrastructure development and other major projects should yield opportunities for U.S. exports. Allocations under the Fourth Malaysia Plan include about $1.8 billion for transport, $950 million for energy, and $600 million for telecommunications. Other sectors likely to provide export opportunities include defense; petroleum production and refining; and industrial projects to produce petrochemicals, cement, paper and pulp, iron, and steel. Significant demand will also exist for engineering and architectural services.

3 *The Philippines.*   Several areas of export opportunity here include energy development, major industrial projects, infrastructure development, telecommunications, computers and peripherals, security and safety equipment, mining and extraction equipment, and a variety of consumer goods.

4 *Singapore.*   The outlook here is favorable for industrial and office products that increase productivity. These include computers and word processors; process control equipment; and other equipment for the automation of manufacturing, assembly, raw material processing and packaging, and warehousing and cargo handling.

5 *Thailand.*   Potential U.S. exporters and investors should watch carefully as the Thai government pushes ahead with plans for extensive development of the eastern seaboard area. Import needs include food-processing and agri-business equipment, electric power-generating equipment, electronic components for further assembly, telecommunications equipment, computers and business equipment, pharmaceuticals and other chemical products, manufacturing equipment and raw materials for plastics, and medical equipment.

Foreign Market Entry Strategies

A variety of strategies are used in entering world markets. Table 9.2 summarizes the major strategies available for tapping world markets.

The most traditional entry to international markets is through exporting. Some companies merely fill orders from abroad without any marketing effort on their part. Some smaller companies may sell to larger companies who, in turn, export these products. Other companies use export management companies (EMCs) who act as intermediaries to reach overseas markets. Some companies use licensing or joint ventures or both to gain many of the benefits of exporting. Still others, such as multinationals, set up complete marketing and production facilities abroad. Engineering and construction companies export their talent and expertise to foreign countries to build a number of facilities such as hydroelectric dams on the Amazon. Professors and research scientists go around the world to educate people on a variety

TABLE 9.2
Foreign Market Entry Strategies

Term	Definition
Exporting	Marketing goods in one country that were produced in another.
Foreign licensing	Method of foreign operation whereby a firm in one country agrees to permit a company in another country to use the manufacturing, processing, trademark, know-how, or some other skill provided by the licenser.
Joint venture	An enterprise in which two or more investors share ownership and control over property rights and operations.
Wholly owned subsidiary	Company completely owned by the parent firm.
Turnkey	The contractor agrees to provide the buyer with a complete operating plant in the foreign country. The contractor agrees to design and build the physical plant and to train local personnel in its management and operation.
Management contracts	Contracts involving the sale of management services for operation of the overseas facility.

This table is adapted with permission from Kahler and Kramer, op. cit., p. 74.

of subjects or consult with officials on the establishment and management of many projects, ranging from irrigation systems to reforestation. Obviously, you are not bound by a single strategy for entering international markets. Indeed, conditions vary greatly among the several world markets, so you may have to develop more than one strategy.

THE PRODUCT-SERVICE CONCEPT IN INTERNATIONAL TRADE

The concept of a product or service used in marketing is broader than that of a mere assembly of physical or chemical components in a certain size, shape, and color combination. Cosmetics and perfumes are not chemicals to the buyer but are adventure, hope, and love. Motorcycles in one part of the world may represent a vastly improved form of transportation for a family; in other parts of the world, motorcycles are thrills and excitement. Successful marketers surround their product or service with an array of value satisfactions that differentiates it from competitors.

Such marketers' views of product or service are especially applicable to exporting to foreign markets. Generally, exporters cannot merely extend their domestic product or service to foreign markets. Various kinds of adaptations may be necessary. The product or service is everything the customer receives when making the purchase, such as the physical product, the package, the label, the brand, the service, and the support.

Product-Service Adaptation

When a new-to-export entrepreneur starts to sell in a foreign market, he or she faces several policy questions: What existing products or services should be sold abroad? Are adaptations needed? The rationale of market testing is well known. Obviously, you want to know that customers will buy your product or service. The foreign market, however, is vast and marked with significant differences. Just as test-market cities are used in the United States, test countries could be used to test international markets. For example, Colombia could be used for market testing Latin America; Belgium, for Europe; and Malaysia, for Asian countries. Or even a small region within a country could be used to market-test several nations.

Export services provided include advertising, management consulting, educating, transportation engineering, insurance underwriting, telecommunications and computer consulting, and franchising. With these exports, as with products, there is also a need to consider the *total service*. For example, U.S. advertising agencies operating in other countries have found that it is necessary to offer clients more than media space purchasing, art and copy ideas, and production facilities. They may differentiate themselves from local and other foreign competitors through services such as marketing research, public relations, and sales promotional aids.[19]

There are a number of instances where the standard domestic product is sold in foreign markets without the necessity for adaptation. Pepto-Bismol, Perrier, Coca-Cola, and Kodak film are examples. There are many more cases, however, where some form of adaptation of the product and service is necessary. Adaptation can be described in two ways: mandatory and discretionary.[20]

Mandatory Adaptation.   If exporters want to be in the foreign market, they have no choice but to modify their product or service. One such factor for U.S. firms is the metric system. The United States is the only major country in the world still using British units of measure. So, to be effective in export activity, the exporter must at least be familiar with metric measurement. If a product is sold abroad for which measurement is an important variable, then it must go metric. Moreover, all brochures, catalogs, specifications, and correspondence must be prepared in metric units.

Differing electrical systems are another factor. Electrical power characteristics are not standard worldwide. The volts, current, and cycles differ significantly between countries; and consumer and industrial products run by electricity are very sensitive to these variations in the power supply. Clearly, the kind of electrical power system used in foreign markets should be carefully researched, and plans made to adapt to them.

The major foreign market factor forcing product adaptation is, of course, government intervention for consumer protection and product regulation. For example,

---

[19]Ibid., p. 221.
[20]Terpstra, op. cit., pp. 87–97.

in the United States, we have the Food and Drug Administration, the Environmental Protection Agency, and so forth. The United States, as well as many other countries, regulates emissions, noise levels, percentages of sugar in food products, phosphates in detergents, safety features for all kinds of equipment and automobiles, the amount of water in canned vegetables and fruit, and so forth.

Discretionary Adaptation.   Here, exporters decide whether and how to modify their products. Indeed, a number of factors exist that might encourage exporters to adapt their products to seize market opportunities. For example, different levels of income mean that consumers in all countries cannot afford to purchase the same items. Consequently, the sewing machines Singer sells in Africa are simple, basic, powered by hand, and inexpensive. This process of developing simpler products is sometimes called reverse engineering or inventing backward.[21]

Differing consumer tastes are an important factor in inducing product adaptation. For example, Campbell had trouble trying to sell U.S. formula soups in Europe. After some years of red ink, Campbell was induced to adapt to European soup tastes and come out with a tomato soup based on an Italian recipe, a tomato soup based on a British recipe, and so on. Campbell is now making profits in Europe.[22]

Another important factor that may encourage firms to modify their products is the level of education and technical sophistication in foreign markets. Consumers in affluent countries are advanced commercially, industrially, and scientifically. In such countries, there is almost no limit to the complexity and sophistication of products that can be offered to consumers or to industry. In many other countries, with lower levels of education, affluence, and technical sophistication, consumers and workers simply cannot handle, operate, or maintain technically complex or sensitive machines or gadgets.[23]

An excellent checklist that helps evaluate the degree of adaptation necessary for foreign markets is shown in Table 9.3 and serves as an excellent summary of the adaptation problem for exporters. Thirteen environmental factors are considered along with their potential adaptation implications.

Additional Product Features

Consumers everywhere are concerned with the complete product, which includes features in addition to the physical product such as packaging and labeling, brands and trademarks, and warranty and support.[24] These features are now discussed.

Packaging and Labeling.   One obvious purpose of packaging, especially in exporting, is the protection of the product during its long journey from point of

[21]Ibid.
[22]Ibid.
[23]Ibid.
[24]Terpstra, op. cit., Chapter 5.

TABLE 9.3
Adaptation Implications of Environmental Factors

Environmental Factors	*Product Adaptation Implications*
Level of technical skills	Product simplification
Level of labor cost	Automation or manualization of the product
Level of literacy	Remarking and simplification of the product
Level of income	Quality and price change
Level of interest rates	Quality and price change (investment in quality might not be financially desirable)
Level of maintenance	Change in tolerances
Climatic differences	Product adaptation
Isolation (heavy repair difficult and expensive)	Product simplification and reliability improvement
Differences in standards	Recalibration of product and resizing
Availability of other products	Greater or lesser product integration
Availability of materials	Change in product structure and fuel
Power availability	Resizing of product
Special conditions	Product redesign or invention

The table is taken and adapted with permission from Kahler and Kramer, op. cit., p. 227.
Source: Richard D. Robinson, "The Challenge of the Underdeveloped National Market," *Journal of Marketing*, October 1961, p. 22.

production, through many transfer points, through different climatic conditions, to the final point of use. Another purpose is to put labeling on the packaging that serves as a promotional tool and informs and protects the buyer. An important point is that labels must remain attached to the package. In some instances, the same package can be used in a number of countries with minor modifications to take into account the local language, tradition, and governmental requirements.[25]

The package must be compatible with, and meet the requirements of, a total transportation and distribution system; and it must be easily handled and displayed. Moreover, the design of packages and labels should be compatible with differing cultures. The symbols, words, and colors used may have different meanings in different cultures. For example, white conveys mourning to the Chinese whereas in Ghana it expresses joy.[26] Generally, the colors of a nation's flag are safe colors.

Legal requirements must be complied with in the various countries where such requirements include regulation of stated size of packages and the amount of contents; promotional claims; label content; and "no return" bottles, cans, and plastics. In some countries, laws have been enacted to force the use of returnables

[25]Kahler and Kramer, op. cit., p. 233.
[26]Ibid., p. 236.

and biodegradable packaging. Such ecological controls are likely to increase in the future.[27]

Brands and Trademarks.   If the product is to be advertised and promoted, the consumer must be able to identify the product by name, term, sign, or symbol and to separate it from those of the competition. As in any market, domestic or foreign, that is the purpose of a brand. The trademark is that part or all the brand that has been given legal protection.

For the big international firms such as Coca-Cola, Singer, and Mercedes-Benz, international brand names and trademarks are imperative because these companies do a lot of promotion on a wide scale. For many commodities sold in international trade and for the new-to-export entrepreneur, brands and trademarks are probably of little significance.

Warranty and Support.   From the consumer's point of view, a warranty is part of the product in that it guarantees the integrity of the product and of the exporter's responsibility for the repair or replacement of defective parts to make the product right. Not surprisingly, what consumers expect from a product will vary from country to country, but this is changing. In spite of the fragmentation common in international warranty policy, there are occasionally internationally uniform warranties. Otis elevators and Boeing aircraft obviously can't have much difference in warranty between countries. Furthermore, there are various pressures for greater uniformity. Growing international competition, economic integration (as in the European Common Market), increased international travel and tourism, and the continued expansion of multinational firms all are forces promoting greater international uniformity in warranties.[28]

Postsale service and support form a critical part of the total product for such consumer goods as automobiles and appliances and for industrial goods such as computers and capital equipment.[29] This support is sometimes referred to as "life-cycle support," and it can be subdivided into the following categories:[30] (1) Training includes onetime training courses at the factory or on-site, training of customer personnel on a periodic basis, and training the customer in new applications of the product during its life cycle. (2) Maintenance includes both preventive maintenance and repair services. These services are performed under warranty and after the warranty has expired or when it is not applicable. This category can also include repair of repairable parts for return to the customer's inventory. (3) Spares and repair parts concern the supply of both "standard" spares and "peculiar" spare parts and assemblies. (4) Tools and test equipment involve the supply of standard and special tools or test equipment (or both) required to operate, troubleshoot, or

[27]Ibid., p. 237.
[28]Terpstra, op. cit., p. 98.
[29]Ibid.
[30]*Exportise*, op. cit., p. 173.

repair the product in the field. (5) Documentation provides handbooks, instructions, and specifications, all properly translated, about the product.[31]

Any foreign sale must, at least, address the various life-cycle support elements as well as the basic product being sold. Foreign customers are very sensitive to the support elements of a sale and will normally ask the U.S. supplier a number of questions regarding it. Over the years, this has been one of the most difficult areas for small businesses to address, especially if they had not considered it ahead of time. The degree of complexity involved with the support of a product varies dramatically from one item to another and according to the nature of the customer. The information in Table 9.4 gives some examples of products and typically what might be expected by purchasers in the life-cycle-support area. The new-to-export firm should carefully consider its product or products, try to "fit" it or them into the chart, and then compile a list of support services that could be required. At this point, the exporter can assess options regarding the methods of supplying the services and develop costs and so forth.[32]

TABLE 9.4
Typically Required Life-Cycle-Support Services (Customer)

Product	Training	Maintenance	Spares and Repair Parts	Tools and Test Equipment	Documentation
Simple toy or other similar consumer item	None	Limited warranty (replacement)	None (whole item replaced)	None	Operating instructions
Household appliance	None; may have to train distributors	Warranty; return to plant or repair station for repair	Generally more; if certain elements are of limited life or expendable, some spares may be included with product	None	Operating instructions; handbook for uses of appliance; list of repair stations and instructions for repair
Large powered tool; industrial machine, such as lathe, milling machine	Some; on-site familiarization, safety briefing, operating demonstration; if customer will maintain, must	Warranty; minor repairs on-site; major repairs at depot or on-site by factory	Limited-life parts are spared with delivery; other parts supplied by factory according to	Special tools provided; usually no test equipment needed beyond that built into the products;	Extensive operating instructions and guide, including hints and warnings; installation

[31]Ibid.
[32]Ibid.

TABLE 9.4 *(Continued)*

Product	Training	Maintenance	Spares and Repair Parts	Tools and Test Equipment	Documentation
	conduct maintenance (probably on-site)	representative or customer	schedule; failed large parts are repaired by factory or factory rep. and then returned to customer inventory	some customers may request standard tools needed as well	guide; lists of parts and sources; if customer will repair, must supply detailed maintenance handbook
Medium ADP installation for business use; numerical-controlled industrial machine; power-distribution equipment; small motor vehicle; and so on	Factory training frequently required; on-site training of customer operators and maintenance people commonly required	Warranty; most repairs on-site by customer or factory rep.; rarely would product be shipped back to factory	Inventory of critical parts often maintained on-site; parts inventory replenished by factory on order or according to plan; initial spares usually delivered with product	Special tools provided with product; some customers will want factory to supply standard tools also; test equipment also may be required, especially test software-diagnostics	Extensive operating and maintenance instructions, including those needed for tools and test equipment; extensive software documentation (functional descriptions, source code, and so on)
Larger ADP installation; aircraft; large flight simulators; large motor vehicles; electrical generator; power loom	Factory training frequently required; on-site training of operators and technicians; demonstration of operation (also, sometimes of reliability); safety training may require presence of factory rep. on-site for a	Warranty; most repairs on-site by customer or factory rep.; multiple-level maintenance schemes common; often requirement for more extensive built-in test equipment (BITE); preventive maintenance common	Inventories of many parts (critical and otherwise) maintained on-site; parts replenished by factory on order or according to plan; initial sparing (usually a year's worth) delivered with product; back-up	Most tools and test equipment-software delivered with product; inventory of these and/or parts for these also often maintained	Extensive, detailed operating and maintenance instructions required; same for special tools, test equipment-software; detailed software documentation required including specs, coding, flow charts, and so on, in some instances

(continued)

TABLE 9.4 (Continued)

Product	Training	Maintenance	Spares and Repair Parts	Tools and Test Equipment	Documentation
	period after delivery		software discs or tapes often required		may require life-cycle support plans and analyses
Major ADP installation; turnkey training center; air traffic control center; power-generation system; and so on	Factory training and on-site training required for operators and maintenance technicians; extensive demonstrations of operations and trouble-shooting; safety demonstrations; often requires on-site training support for extensive period after delivery or periodically during life cycle; reliability demonstration also required at times; training programs must accompany system changes	Warranty for period after delivery; repairs of major items on-site via tiered maintenance plan; smaller items returned to intermediate repair facility or factory; extensive requirements for BITE and fault isolation-diagnostic features and software; often require customer to perform life-cycle repair according to reliability assurance warranty based on supplier's reliability estimates	Extensive parts inventories and supplies of consumables maintained on-site; parts and consumables replenished on order or by plan from factory; initial sparing (usually 1–2 years delivered with product; back-up software and tapes required, including those for test equipment or any other special facilities; factory repaired parts are used to replenish on-site inventories	All tools and test equipment-software delivered with product; inventory of these maintained on-site and at factory; changes in software are delivered and integrated on-site	Extensive, detailed operating, installation, and maintenance instructions required; same for tools, test equipment-software; detailed hardware and software documentation required, including detailed interface drawings; life-cycle support plans required, including analyses for maintainability, sparing, configuration control, and so on

Source: Exportise (Boston, Mass.: The Small Business Foundation of America, Inc., 1983), p. 174. This table is used with permission.

SUMMARY

Because of a mounting trade deficit and increasing competition, both private and public sectors are encouraging and giving support to entrepreneurs who wish to enter international trade, especially as exporters. In addition to gaining this support, the entrepreneur must also have the ability to deal with economic, cultural, competitive, political, and legal factors in other nations or regions and to overcome a variety of trade barriers.

Although the challenges and barriers to entering international trade are great, the payoff can be rewarding. Many trade opportunities exist throughout the world. Those areas that seem to hold abundant opportunities for smaller entrepreneurs are in some of the Third World and Southeast Asian nations.

Before entering the international market, entrepreneurs will likely have to perform both mandatory and discretionary adaptation to their product or service. Additional product or service features include packaging and labeling, brands and trademarks, warrant, and postsale support.

ASSIGNMENT

1 What is meant by comparative advantage among nations?

2 How can the standard of living of all people be increased by international trade?

3 List and explain the different factors among nations and their impact on international marketing.

4 List and describe the barriers to trade.

5 Do you believe there are export and import opportunities in Third World markets? Why? Why not?

6 Pick one of the ASEAN countries, and, from additional research, prepare an export profile of this country.

7 Explain the strategic ways to enter foreign markets.

8 Explain and give examples of mandatory and discretionary adaptation. Also explain and give examples of additional product features.

BIBLIOGRAPHY

A Basic Guide to Exporting. Washington, D.C.: United States Department of Commerce/ International Trade Administration, 1981.

Barovick, Richard L. "The Washington Front." *American Import Export Management.* October 1983.

Brinson, J. Ron. "Fairness of Free Trade," *American Import Export Management.* September 1983.

Casey, William R. "A Forwarding Prospective." *American Import Export Management.* November 1983.

Daiboch, Alfred F. "Have You Won Your Share of Federal Export Support?" *American Import Export Management.* February 1984.

Dawson, Leslie M. "Opportunities for Small Business in Third World Markets." *American Journal of Small Business*, 7:1 (Summer 1982).

Dooley, Brian J. "NVOCCs." *American Import Export Management*. June 1983.

———. "Export Management Companies—Your 'Outside' Export Office." *American Import Export Management*. May 1984.

Everett, Carl E. "Making a Thief's Job Harder: An Export Packing/Security Story." *American Import Export Management*. April 1983.

"Eximbank Gives You the (Small) Business." *American Import Export Management*. December 1983.

Exportise. Boston, Mass.: The Small Business Foundation of America, Inc., 1983.

Farrell, Kevin. "Ex-Im Gets Serious About Small Business." *Venture*. May 1984.

"FTZ Homes?" *American Import Export Management*. March 1983.

Holt, Walter B. "Break the Payment Mold: Try a Mixture of Methods." *American Import Export Management*. March 1983.

Kahler, Ruel, and Roland L. Kramer. *International Marketing*. Boston, Mass.: Kent Publishing Company, 1982.

"1984 Prospects for U.S. Exporters Throughout the ASEAN Five." *American Import Export Management*. February 1984.

O'Leary, Paul A. "ETC Act: Helpful or Harmful?" *American Import Export Management*. November 1983.

Shayne, Leonard. "Playing Export Games." *American Import Export Management*. April 1983.

Terpstra, Vern. *International Dimensions of Marketing*. Boston, Mass.: Kent Publishing Company, 1982.

"The 'Pro' Side to ETCs." *American Import Export Management*. June 1983.

Tjen, Willy T. B. "Five Nations with Increasing Buying Power and Growing Demands." *American Import Export Management*. February 1984.

Weiner, Steve, and Robert Johnson. "Export-Trading Firms in U.S. Are to Fulfill Promise." *The Wall Street Journal*. May 24, 1984.

Weiss, Julian. "Marketplace Southeast Asia: ASEAN." *American Import Export Management*. June 1983.

Welsh, Ellen. "'How to' . . . Finance a South American Deal!" *American Import Export Management*. February 1984.

Werner, Tom. "Air Cargo Can!" *American Import Export Management*. September 1983.

CHAPTER 10

The Export Business

INTRODUCTION

A number of export programs and services are in place today for entrepreneurs who plan to become exporters. The new-to-export entrepreneur must learn not only about these programs and services but also how to go about exporting. The objectives of this chapter follow.

1 To present groups, agencies, and publications that provide counsel and support to export entrepreneurs.

2 To explain how to market products or services in a foreign market.

3 To detail the mechanics of exporting.

IMPORTANT FACTORS IN STARTING AN EXPORT BUSINESS

Some of the key questions confronting the new-to-export entrepreneur are, Where do I begin? Where do I go to get counsel and ideas? Where are the sources of publications and reports on exporting? Where do I go to get financial assistance and insurance protection? The following material will help to answer these questions.

Stages of Exporting

To many, going into exporting is an all-or-nothing proposition. It does not have to be. It may be combined with other ventures, or it may evolve through several stages, paced by the capabilities and capacity of you and your company, or both. Typically, these are the stages.[1]

1 *Introductory stage.* This is the "getting your feet wet" stage. It is often brought about by participation in a small company trade mission, a Department of Commerce program, or targeted programs such as the Smaller Business Association of New England (SBANE)/Massachusetts Port Authority (MASSPORT) —Small Business Export Program. And lately some businesses have been introduced to the idea at small business development centers. During this introductory phase, small company executives get an inkling that there may be a potential for foreign sales of their products or services. They may follow this up by more investigations, marketing research, and so on to arrive at a better sense of this new sales potential.

2 *Opportunity stage.* In some instances the opportunity stage may occur first owing to the arrival of an unexpected request for quotation from a foreign source. In this stage, the smaller company begins to respond to overseas tender

---

[1]*Exportise* (Boston, Mass.: The Small Business Foundation of America, Inc., 1983), pp. 2—3. This material is used with permission.

offers (requests for quotations) but has no well-defined program of pursuing export sales. If its bids are successful, the orders are filled.

3 *Maturing stage.* Here the exporter begins to develop more formal arrangements for sales, marketing, and physical distribution of products and services. First, the company may call on an export management company (EMC) to assist in this area. Gradually, new exporters evolve their extended sales force overseas, and it begins actively seeking new customers and generating requests for quotations. This stage endures through the maturity of a company's export program, perhaps ultimately resulting in the formation of branch offices or subsidiaries in foreign markets. Because professionals are involved, the risk of "surprises" is minimized. Some companies, however, operate completely through EMCs, with their attendant simplicities and reduction of risk. They are quite satisfied to achieve lower profits on export sales, choosing instead to look on these sales as a contributor to better utilization of an undercapacity operation.

Counsel for Exporters

The first steps in setting up an export business are the most difficult because the new exporter lacks experience. Where should one begin? Fortunately, many counseling and assistance sources are available that will help answer this essential question—first of all to determine if a given venture has export potential.

The United States Department of Commerce and its 47 district offices, located in industrial and commercial centers throughout the United States, provide excellent assistance and counseling for the new exporter. They can tell you about foreign markets for American products and services, financing aid to exporters, tax advantages of exporting, international trade exhibitions, export documentation requirements, economic facts on foreign countries, and export licensing and import requirements.[2]

The local district office should be the starting point for any entrepreneur who needs international marketing assistance or technical product information. A district office brings together for local business people all the Commerce Department's varied resources and services.[3]

In addition to the services of its district offices, the United States Department of Commerce gives the entrepreneur direct contact with business people experienced in all phases of export trade through its district export councils. These councils assist in many of the workshops, seminars, and clinics on exporting arranged by the district offices in cooperation with chambers of commerce, trade associations, banks,

---

[2]*A Basic Guide to Exporting* (Washington, D.C.: United States Department of Commerce, International Trade Administration, 1981), p. 1. This material is used with permission.

[3]Ibid.

trade schools, colleges, and the Small Business Administration. The councils also arrange for private consultation between experienced and prospective exporters.[4]

The International Trade Administration can provide commercial and economic information on specific countries in which an entrepreneur may be interested. This "country-specific" assistance can be obtained primarily from the following two sources.[5]

1 *Office of Country Marketing (OCM).* This office offers professional business counseling and commercial information on a geographical basis for major overseas marketing areas of the non-Communist world. The OCM staff will provide general briefings on how to do business in particular markets and assist in resolving problems that U.S. firms have encountered overseas.

2 *East-West Trade (EWT).* Recognizing both the great potential of Communist markets for U.S. exporters and the special economic-political-commercial considerations that they require, East-West Trade offers American companies advice and assistance in developing their export trade with Communist countries.

Readers interested in the role played by state development agencies in promoting and supporting exports may wish to write to the National Association of State Development Agencies (NASDA), 444 North Capitol Street, Washington, D.C. 20001 (telephone: (202) 624–5411).

Exporters have a wide choice of financial institutions that provide them with marketing assistance as well as international financing. More than 250 U.S. banks have qualified international banking departments with specialists familiar with specific foreign countries or various types of commodities and transactions or both. These banks, located in all major U.S. cities, maintain correspondent relationships with smaller banks throughout the country. This banking network enables exporters to find export financing assistance for themselves or their foreign customers. Larger banks also maintain correspondent relationships with banks in most foreign countries or operate their own overseas branches, providing a direct channel to foreign customers.[6]

The counseling services that a commercial bank may perform for the exporter include the following.[7]

1 Advice on export regulations.

2 Exchange of currencies.

3 Assistance in financing exports.

[4]Ibid.
[5]Ibid., pp. 9–10.
[6]Ibid., p. 4.
[7]Ibid.

4 Collection of foreign invoices, drafts, letters of credit, and other foreign receivables.

5 Transfer of funds to other countries.

6 Letters of introduction and letters of credit for travelers.

7 Credit information on potential buyers overseas.

8 Credit assistance to the exporter's foreign buyers.

Many other groups, both in government and the private sector, stand ready to lend experienced, expert guidance to companies that are starting an export trade. For instance, country desk officers at the U.S. Department of State can brief your firm's representative on the political and economic climate in the countries they monitor. The State Department's Office of Commercial Affairs can offer assistance in contacting appropriate offices within that department. The address is Office of Commercial Affairs, Room 3638, EB/OCA, U.S. Department of State, Washington, D.C. 20520 (telephone: (202) 632−8988).

Industry trade associations are useful both for the special services they offer members and for the opportunity they provide to meet companies with previous export experience. Experienced firms—sometimes even direct competitors—are, in fact, among the most valuable sources of information for beginning exporters.

Normally, trade consultants will have specialized knowledge of one type or another relating to international trade. They are retained by companies that typically have a specific problem or goal to be addressed or desire a personalized approach or both. The areas of expertise of trade consultants are as broad as the field itself. Here are some examples of specialties for which one might be sought out.[8]

1 Specific knowledge of, and contacts in, a certain market area, such as Saudi Arabia or Southeast Asia.

2 Expertise in structuring overseas joint ventures, licensing arrangements, or comanufacturing.

3 Familiarity with, and access to, difficult markets, such as the USSR or China.

4 In-depth knowledge of the use of advertising in a country or region.

5 Provision of general training in international trade for novice companies.

Publications for Exporters

Selected publications that can help entrepreneurs identify foreign markets and plan their general export strategy include (1) *Foreign Trade Report, FT410: U.S. Exports—Commodity by Country*, which provides a wealth of statistics on shipments of all merchandise from the United States to foreign countries. Write to Superintendent of Documents, U.S. Government Printing Office, Washington, D.C. 20402. (2) *Market*

---

[8]*Exportise*, op. cit., p. 19.

Shares Report, which provides basic data needed by exporters to evaluate overall trends in the size of markets; measure changes in the import demand for specific products; compare the competitive position of U.S. and foreign exporters; select distribution centers for U.S. products abroad; and identify existing and potential markets for U.S. components, parts, and accessories. For a free catalog, write to National Technical Information Services, 5285 Port Royal Road, Springfield, Virginia 22161. Also get a copy of Official Export Guide, North American Publishing Co., 401 N. Broad St., Philadelphia, Pa. 19108.

A comprehensive series of international marketing reports are published by the U.S. Department of Commerce's International Trade Administration (ITA). These reports offer the U.S. business community pertinent data on foreign market conditions, export opportunities for U.S. suppliers, useful exporting techniques, and other topics. Many of the reports in this series summarize research conducted "on site" in foreign markets by overseas contractors of the State Department's U.S. Foreign Service or by economic or commercial officers of the U.S. Foreign Service or the Department of Commerce. The following publications in the series are available on a continuing basis.[9]

1 *Overseas Business Reports (OBR).*   These reports provide basic background data for businesspeople who are evaluating various export markets or considering the possibility of entering new areas.

2 *Foreign Economic Trends and Their Implications for the United States (FET).*   This series of country-by-country reports gives in-depth reviews of current business conditions; current and near-term prospects; and the latest available data on the gross national product, foreign trade, wage and price indexes, unemployment rates, and construction starts.

3 *Global Market Surveys (GMS).*   These extensive market research studies are conducted in selected foreign countries for specific U.S. products and industries with marked export growth potential.

4 *Country Market Sectoral Surveys.*   Each of these in-depth reports covers the most promising export opportunities for U.S. firms in a single country. About 15 leading industrial sectors are usually examined in each survey.

The Commerce Department also offers a number of trade-promotion programs that can help you explore foreign markets and evaluate your export potential in specific geographical areas. The following are especially useful to new exporters because they can provide immediate business leads with only minimal investment of resources and without committing your firm to large-scale exporting efforts. For the same reasons, these programs are excellent tools for locating agents or distributors and generally for developing your export operations.

---

[9]*A Basic Guide to Exporting,* op. cit.

1 *Trade Opportunities Program (TOP).* Export opportunities, originating from either private or government sources overseas, are transmitted daily to the TOP computer in Washington, D.C., by U.S. Foreign Service posts around the world. As subscribers to TOP, American business firms indicate the products or services they wish to export, their countries of interest, and the types of opportunities desired (direct sales, overseas representation, or foreign government tenders). The TOP computer matches product interests of foreign buyers with those indicated by the U.S. subscribers. When a match occurs, a "trade opportunity notice" is mailed to the subscriber. Foreign trade opportunity notices include descriptions of the products or services needed, their end uses, and the quantities required; information about the foreign buyer; transaction requirements and preferences; trade and credit references; bid deadline dates; and other pertinent information.[10]

2 *New Product Information Service (NPIS).* This program provides worldwide publicity for new U.S. products available for immediate export. This exposure enables foreign firms to identify and contact U.S. exporters of specific products, thereby giving the American company direct indications of market interest and often generating substantial sales, agent contracts, and other benefits.[11]

3 *Export Contact List Services.* The Commerce Department collects and stores data on foreign firms in a master computer file designated as the Foreign Traders Index (FTI). Covering 143 countries, this file contains information on more than 140,000 importing firms, agents, representatives, distributors, manufacturers, service organizations, retailers, and potential end-users of American products and services. Newly identified firms are continually added to the FTI file; information on listed firms is also updated frequently.[12]

Finance and Insurance for Exporters

A number of complaints are voiced about the accessibility of federal export funding programs to small and midsized companies. The key to any federal export support program is the participation of local banks and their willingness to develop the capability of providing quality trade banking support. Indeed, small exporters not in close proximity to a bank with a strong trade capability are essentially disenfranchised from United States government export programs. True access begins at your banker's doorstep.[13]

Recent changes, however, in small-business programs of the Foreign Credit Insurance Association (FCIA) and the Export-Import Bank of the United States

[10]Ibid., pp. 7–11.

[11]Ibid.

[12]Ibid.

[13]Alfred F. Daiboch, "Have You Won Your Share of Federal Export Support?" *American Import Export Management*, February 1984, p. 24. This material is used with permission.

(Eximbank) make these agencies more attractive than ever as sources of trade financing for the small to midsize company. The most important change is the new distinction being made between a "Small Business Exporter" as used by Eximbank and the "New-to-Export" trader at FCIA.[14] *Small* means any company with a minimum net worth of $2 million.

FCIA has removed the guidelines on maximum net worth for an exporter to qualify for its new "New-to-Export" policy. Any exporter, irrespective of net worth, that qualifies in all other respects is eligible for this enhanced coverage. At Eximbank, access to its small business program has also been made easier. These programs are now available to any company that qualifies as "small" under the size guidelines of the Small Business Administration (SBA). To explain these revisions and to find out about other programs available to you as a would-be exporter, telephone Eximbank's Small Business Hotline at (800) 424–5201.[15] The main address is 811 Vermont Avenue N.W., Washington, D.C. 20571 (telephone: (202) 566–8990).

Eximbank programs especially geared to small exporters include the following.[16]

1 Guarantees of short-term working capital loans. A commercial bank applies to Eximbank for a 90 percent guarantee for a loan used to produce and then market the product. The loan must be collateralized, but Eximbank has recently expanded its definition of *collateral* to include second mortgages on plant and equipment, inventory, and accounts receivable.

2 Fixed-rate, medium-term export loans from small manufacturers' commercial banks to their foreign buyers that can be obtained at competitive interest rates with the assistance of Eximbank's discount loan program.

3 Credit insurance available through a "New-to-Export" policy from the Foreign Credit Insurance Association (FCIA). Even start-ups are eligible. Eximbank offers no deductible terms and will cover up to 95 percent of the commercial risk and 100 percent of the political risk if the deal goes sour.

Officials at Eximbank, through the Small Business and Export Trading Programs division, expect to have a sizable impact on many businesses in addition to reducing the trade deficit and to be able to fulfill Eximbank's small business mandate. Indeed, the Eximbank programs that offer working capital, guaranteed loans, and export insurance to small companies for the first time are certainly a boon to entrepreneurs who expect to enter the export market.[17]

[14]Ibid.

[15]Ibid.

[16]"Eximbank Gives You the (Small) Business," *American Import Export Management*, December 1983, p. 8. This material is used with permission.

[17]Kevin Farrell, "Ex-Im Gets Serious About Small Business," *Venture*, May 1984, p. 178. Copyright © 1984 Venture Magazine, Inc., 521 Fifth Avenue, New York, N.Y. 10175. The material is used by special permission.

EXPORT MARKETING PROGRAMS

Promotion of your product or service is just as important in foreign markets as it is in your home markets. Similar advertising media are available. In addition, a number of programs such as trade fairs and exhibitions are available worldwide to provide you with on-site selling opportunities. For overall marketing and distribution of your products or services, two important intermediaries are available in the form of export management companies (EMCs) and export trading companies (ETCs). For the manufacturer who intends to import components, assemble, and reexport, the Foreign Trade Zone (FTZ) approach offers significant opportunities. FTZs also offer a number of other services and facilities for the nonmanufacturer exporter-importer.

Promotion of Export Sales

There are many ways to promote export sales of your products or services. You can advertise in foreign magazines and newspapers, for example, or on radio and television. Or you can participate in international trade fairs and other overseas marketing events. Selected programs include these.[18]

1 *Promotion in publications and other media.* A large and varied assortment of magazines covering international markets is available to U.S. exporters through American publishers. These range from specialized international magazines relating to individual industries such as construction, beverages, and textiles to worldwide industrial magazines covering many industries. Many and varied consumer publications produced by U.S.-based publishers are also available. A number of these are produced in national language editions and also offer "regional buys" for specific export markets of the world.

Television, radio, and specially produced motion pictures are also used, depending on the country. In areas where illiteracy may be high and programs may be seen and heard in public places, these offer one of the few means of bringing an advertising message to great numbers of people. In many countries, particularly those in Latin America, various forms of outdoor advertising (billboards, posters, electric signs, and streetcar and bus cards) are widely used to reach the mass audience. The International Advertising Association, Inc., 475 Fifth Avenue, New York, N.Y. 10017, is a good source of names of domestic agencies that handle overseas accounts.

2 *The export development offices (EDOs).* The U.S. Department of Commerce maintains offices and personnel abroad that stand ready to assist American exporters through a variety of programs. Services include market research; buyer identification; shipping and customs assistance; exhibition design and mounting; and organization of trade fairs, trade seminars, and special promotions.

[18]*A Basic Guide to Exporting*, op. cit., pp. 72–77.

3 *International trade fairs.* In today's international market, trade fairs are "shop windows" in which thousands of firms from many countries display their wares. They are marketplaces in which buyer and seller can meet with mutual convenience. Some fairs, especially those in Europe, have a history that goes back for centuries. The Department of Commerce sponsors participation in these and other selected international trade fairs worldwide. The cost to the U.S. participant varies by country and event. Here, however, is all you need for participation: Provide your products or services for display, supply technical and promotional handout literature, ship products to the exhibition site, and assign a representative qualified to staff the booth and transact business.

Export Management Companies (EMCs)

The export management companies (EMCs) together form one of the most important ways for the new-to-export entrepreneur to reach foreign markets. They are U.S. firms that specialize in marketing U.S. products overseas. EMCs generally specialize in particular product categories, which allows them to perform extensive market research with a small staff. They are able to operate under their own letterhead as distributors or under the letterhead of a represented firm, acting as an export department for the client. EMCs often assume credit risks and have a thorough knowledge of the financial needs of their overseas market sector. They provide market research and handle government regulations and restrictions in the foreign market. They are able to consolidate shipments for savings and arrange for transportation of goods, and they make use of extensive overseas market contacts and foreign language proficiency to aid their marketing-advertising efforts. Unlike the Japanese general trading companies, the EMCs are product area specialists, which allows them to take advantage of unique markets despite their smaller size. Some also handle imports and countertrade—though generally on a limited basis.[19]

The common advantages of working with an EMC are these.[20]

1 You are relieved of demands on your time while you are developing overseas sales.

2 The EMC has the contacts, distribution network, and know-how to produce sales.

3 There is essentially no risk.

4 You are able to market test your product or service without major investment.

5 You learn from the EMC and begin to develop your own expertise.

The common disadvantages of working with an EMC are these.[21]

---

[19]Brian Dooley, "Export Management Companies—Your 'Outside' Export Office," *American Import Export Management*, May 1984, p. 48. This material is used with permission.

[20]*Exportise*, op. cit., p. 90.

[21]Ibid.

1 You may lose a certain amount of control in pricing, promotion, and distribution of your product or service.

2 EMC sales may not be as profitable as domestic sales because of the discount arrangement. Furthermore, use of EMC adds cost, so your product or service may suffer competitively.

3 At times, your EMC may be financially strained.

4 EMCs sell multiple items and tend to devote more effort to the more profitable items.

5 EMCs sometimes favor certain countries and ignore others owing to built-in biases.

6 The EMC could be perceived as an "intermediary" by some customers who would rather deal directly with the exporter. For example, the Saudis do not generally like intermediaries in their business dealings.

Export Trading Companies (ETCs)

The Export Trading Company (ETC) Act was passed in 1982, and many look forward to a new era of American foreign trade based on it. In essence, it creates a new tool to open new markets for American business. This act was intended to form export trading companies patterned after certain large trading companies of Japan, West Germany, France, Great Britain, Korea, and Hong Kong. Such trade organizations do the exporting for groups of firms who might otherwise be discouraged by a complex maze of export regulations, shipping costs and techniques, foreign tariffs and standards, and language and cultural differences.[22] Clearly, an option would be available to smaller firms that hesitate to sell overseas on their own. Instead, they could hire or join an export trading company to handle all the complicated details of exporting. They, in effect, would have a one-stop export service.[23]

This ETC Act is also designed to attract producers of products and services (engineers, accountants, architects, and lawyers), manufacturers, banks, and export service businesses into an effective joint effort to develop foreign markets. It accomplishes this by a new form of antitrust protection and by new authority for banks to own an interest (a key feature of the act) in exporting ventures.[24] The key to its success is creative combinations of a wide range of businesses, all directed toward international trade. The impetus for such combinations will come from entrepreneurially minded individuals in banks, exporting companies (including EMCs), freight forwarders, customhouse brokers, marine insurers, technical service companies, trade associations, and governmental export promotion offices.[25]

---

[22]"The 'Pro' Side to ETCs," *American Import Export Management*, June 1983, p. 14. This material is used with permission.

[23]Ibid.

[24]Ibid.

[25]Ibid.

Selling Directly

The business customs, channels of distribution, and type of product or service have a lot to do with the selling method used. There are a few industries where it is possible, even preferred, to sell directly to the customer. These opportunities usually occur in product areas that are fairly uniform throughout the world, as in commercial aviation, machine tools and capital goods, and space-related technology. In these instances, the customers are limited in number and very knowledgeable.[26]

In other instances, the customers of many countries prevent, in effect, most direct contacts between the U.S. exporter and the foreign customer unless they are arranged in some fashion by native intermediaries. The degree of severity of these business customs varies widely from virtually none in some Western European countries to absolute prohibition in Soviet-bloc countries.[27]

So, although there are exceptions, the new-to-export entrepreneur is likely to encounter much difficulty dealing with customers directly. Also, because the new exporter is typically unfamiliar with many international trade procedures, the wisest move is to enlist the aid of knowledgeable partners during development of foreign sales. Later, after customer relationships have been developed, it is more common to deal with customers directly for follow-on orders.[28]

The Use of Foreign Trade Zones

Foreign Trade Zones (FTZs) were authorized by the United States Congress under the Foreign Trade Zone Act of 1934. To the general public, a zone appears merely as another warehouse in Brooklyn or a wharf terminal in New Orleans, but to the entrepreneurs involved in international trade, it has special significance.

Geographically and legally, the zones are within the United States, but for customs purposes, they are outside. They are operated as public utilities established under grants of authority from the Foreign Trade Zones Board and are supervised by the United States Customs Service. They are situated in major port cities as well as in inland locations. The zone program does not entail any federal, state, or local agency funding.

Foreign Trade Zones facilitate import and reexport businesses. For example, the services of a zone are ideal for a manufacturer who has an "importing for exporting" situation.[29] The manufacturer can avoid duty payments and enjoy flexible manufacturing practices. The imported goods can be held in the zone without being subject to customs entry, payment of duty or tax, or bond. Such goods or components may be stored, sold, exhibited, repacked, assembled, sorted, cleaned, mixed with other

---

[26]*Exportise*, op. cit., p. 86.

[27]Ibid.

[28]Ibid.

[29]"FTZ Homes?" *American Import Export Management*, March 1983, p. 18. This material is used with permission.

foreign and domestic items, or manufactured in the zone. Later, the goods may either be exported or transferred into customs territory. If the finished goods are entered for consumption in domestic commerce, the duty rate is lower than it would have been in importing the raw material outside a zone and paying the duty immediately. No duty payments are involved with manufacturing for export, and virtually unlimited time is available for manufacturing, storage, and export when using a zone. The zone has facilities for loading and unloading, for warehousing goods both foreign and domestic, and for reshipping goods. The manufacturer may set up operations within the zone or may request multisites or subzones.

The economic advantages of the FTZ are numerous, both to the company making use of it and the region. Here is a listing of the advantages.[30]

1 U.S. quotas, duties, and bonds are not applicable within the zone. Therefore, goods can be landed and stored quickly without full customs formalities.

2 Cash flow can be improved because duty is not paid until goods leave the zone. If goods are exported, U.S. customs-duty payments are not required. Also, merchandise may be withdrawn in partial amounts.

3 Insurance on goods in zone storage can be limited to value alone plus ocean freight rather than including duty and taxes.

4 Merchandise may be displayed in the zone's showroom, where potential buyers may inspect and sample goods before purchase and payment of duty.

5 Goods can be repaired, altered, relabeled, or remarked to meet federal or local requirements. They can also be processed to qualify for lower duty or freight charges.

6 For products manufactured in a zone, a choice is offered: The rate of duty or quota limitation on the finished product entering U.S. trade channels may be applied to the finished product, that is, to the percentage of it that is of foreign origin, or to the foreign materials in the finished product.

7 Salvage or repair of damaged goods may be carried out to maximum market advantage, free of duty and quota.

8 Certain bonded merchandise may be transferred to the zone for export, canceling the bond or time limit applicable to bonded warehouses and making possible immediate recovery of taxes already paid.

9 On goods destined for export, recovery of U.S. customs duty or of certain state taxes can be made on entry into the zone.

10 Goods subject to import quotas may be held within the zone until the next quota period. Storage also allows the businessperson either to hold goods until market conditions improve within the United States or to ship the goods abroad if U.S. buyers are not found.

[30]*Exportise*, op. cit., pp. 94–95.

In considering the use of an FTZ, some entrepreneurs will need only to lease floor space in a multi-user warehouse processing facility that zones provide as a part of their public services. In this way, a zone's benefits are available to companies even when their principal facilities are outside the zone's boundaries. When a decision is made to locate the manufacturing facility within a zone, the industrial-type FTZ offers open land under long-term lease.[31]

MECHANICS OF EXPORTING

Preparing products for shipment abroad requires special attention and specific procedures. For the exporter, details cannot be overlooked. Some of the more important details include pricing; preparing quotations; using appropriate communication procedures; receiving payment; packing and marking; shipping and insuring; preparing export documentation; understanding government regulations, tax ramifications, and tariffs; and financing exports.

Pricing

Pricing is not easy for domestic markets; it is even more difficult for foreign markets owing to export price escalation and currency fluctuations. In exporting, more transportation and insurance services are required as well as longer distribution channels of more intermediaries. Furthermore, there are additional charges for export documentation and import duties. And the importer-distributor has to have a higher margin than the domestic wholesaler because of the extra work done in clearing the imported goods. All these items add up to the phenomenon known as price escalation in exporting.[32] An example of export price escalation is shown in Table 10.1, where the final consumer price for the foreign market is 50 percent higher than the domestic price.

In other instances, export price escalation may be less or more. For larger-value shipments, such as industrial products, the costs of freight and insurance will normally be a lesser percentage of the cost. A major additional consideration, however, for industrial products is the level of service and support required. For consumer products, some experts state that the retail price in the average European market would be about five times your FOB (free on board) price. This estimate is considerably more than that shown in Table 10.1. The important point to remember, however, is that there are far more variables in the proper pricing of your products for foreign markets than for your home market. Examine all these variables *before*

[31]Ibid.

[32]Vern Terpstra, *International Dimensions of Marketing* (Boston, Mass.: Kent Publishing Company, 1982), p. 140. This material is used with permission.

TABLE 10.1
Export Price Escalation

	Domestic Sale	Export Sale
Factory price	$ 7.50	$ 7.50
Domestic freight	.70	.70
	8.20	8.20
Export documentation		.50
		8.70
Ocean freight and insurance		1.20
		9.90
Import duty (12% of landed cost)		1.19
		11.09
Wholesaler markup (15%)	1.23	
	9.43	
Importer-distributor markup (22%)		2.44
		13.53
Retail markup 50%	4.72	6.77
	14.15	20.30
Final consumer price	$14.15	$20.30

Source: Vern Terpstra, *International Dimensions of Marketing* (Boston, Mass.: Kent Publishing Company, 1982) p. 141. Copyright © 1982 by Wadsworth, Inc. Reprinted by permission of Kent Publishing Company, a division of Wadsworth, Inc.

your price is set because the price must be high enough to return an adequate profit.[33]

In some instances, export price escalation may be large enough to make the firm's product noncompetitive in some export markets. In trying to overcome the problems of price escalation, the firm can consider several possible strategies, which include[34] (1) shipping modified or unassembled products that might lower transportation costs and duties; (2) lowering its export price at the factory, thus reducing the multiplier effect of all the markups; (3) getting its freight or duty classifications or both changed for a possible lowering of these costs; or (4) producing within the export market to completely eliminate the extra steps.[35]

In some instances, an exporter may be able to sell a product for less in a foreign market. Price at the factory may be set on direct costs only with a margin added to cover exporting costs and still give a small return to help cover administrative, advertising, and factory overhead expenses. With this way of pricing, the foreign market is seen as a marginal market. Quoting prices at levels lower than domestic prices, however, is technically known as dumping, which is against the law in a number of industrial countries. Antidumping laws generally require

[33]*Exportise*, op. cit., p. 13.

[34]Terpstra, op. cit., p. 141.

[35]Ibid.

that products be offered for sale at prices that are no lower than those in the country of manufacture.[36]

Export price quotations may be made in terms of the currency of the exporting country, of the importing country, or of a third country. The selection of a currency to use in quoting a price is an important pricing issue. Indeed, in today's world of floating exchange rates, the value of other currencies in terms of the dollar is constantly fluctuating. If you price your product at $1.00 and quote in a foreign currency equivalent to the $1.00 and if the foreign currency value vis-à-vis the U.S. dollar declines 20 percent by the time you receive payment, then, in effect, you have gotten $.80 for your product.

The importer may favor price quotations in the currency of the exporting country if an additional speculative profit is foreseen owing to an expected exchange fluctuation before settlement or because the importer believes that the assumption of exchange risks will affect the price quotation favorably. The importer frequently prefers purchasing at prices quoted in the importer's national currency, however; and in order to promote sales, the exporter may grant the request. Quotations in the currency of the importing country shift the risk of exchange fluctuations to the exporter. They enable the importer to compute profits, to announce resale prices promptly, and also more readily to compare price quotations received from the competitive exporters of different foreign countries. Custom, moreover, may largely determine the prevailing practice in particular trades, and the danger of nonpayment of bills owing to unfortunate exchange speculation by importers may cause the exporter to favor foreign currency price quotations.[37]

The practice of quoting prices in the currency of a third country is at times dictated by custom, but when the currencies of both the exporting and the importing country are unstable or when the banking facilities of a third country are depended on for financial settlement, it may be rational to quote prices in the currency of a third country. For over 50 years, the United States has been the third-country choice of most marketers.[38]

Preparing the Quotation

Price quotations represent an important part of exporting because they establish the legal responsibilities of buyer and seller and specify when the title to the goods changes hands. All quotations should include a description of the product, the price for that product at a specified delivery point, the time of shipment, the terms of payment, and delivery terms. A description of the product should include the total gross and net shipping weight and the total cubic volume packed for export, as well as other basic dimensions. This information is necessary so that buyers may deter-

---

[36]Ruel Kahler and Roland L. Kramer, *International Marketing*, (Boston, Mass.: Kent Publishing Company, 1982), p. 274. This material is used with permission.
[37]Ibid., pp. 279–80.
[38]Ibid.

mine if special handling or loading equipment will be needed. It will also enable them to compute transportation charges. In some countries, import duties or taxes or both are assessed on the weight of the shipment rather than on its value; the buyer must be able to calculate this in advance.[39]

Often a pro forma invoice must be submitted with the quotation. These invoices are not for payment purposes. They are only models that the buyer will use when applying for an import license or arranging for funds. In fact, it is good business practice to include a pro forma invoice with any internal quotation whether it has been requested or not. When exporters prepare final collection invoices at the time of shipment, it is advisable to check with the Department of Commerce or some other reliable source for special invoicing requirements that may prevail in the country to which they are shipping.[40]

The time of shipment or shipping schedule can be important to a prospective buyer. It should always be specified whether the time quoted for shipment is from the factory or the port of export. The estimated shipping date from the U.S. port of export is always preferable because the overseas buyer has no way of estimating inland transit time in the United States.[41]

Delivery terms are very important; a simple misunderstanding about delivery terms may prevent exporters from meeting contractual obligations or make them responsible for shipping costs they sought to avoid. Obviously, the buyer and seller have different preferences for the manner in which the duties and responsibilities are to be split. The key legal points are (1) when title passes and (2) who is responsible for the arrangements for shipping and insurance. For example, buyers may prefer to have the seller accept all responsibility for the shipment until it arrives at the buyer's place of business whereas the seller, on the other hand, might prefer FOB plant terms.

A complete list of important terms and their definitions is contained in *Incoterms*, a booklet that can be ordered from: ICC Publishing Corporation, 801 Second Avenue, Suite 1204, New York, N.Y. 10017. It is comprehensive and explains fully how buyer and seller divide risks and obligations in specific kinds of international trade transactions. The following are a few of the more common delivery terms used in international trade.[42]

1 *Ex-factory*.   An ex-factory contract means that the buyer takes possession of the merchandise at the factory of the seller and bears all risks and expenses from there on. This limits the exporter's risks and responsibilities but places a great burden on the foreign buyer. This is not a recommended price quotation except when dealing with large foreign buyers who have representation in the exporter's country, as, for example, a Japanese trading company.

---

[39]*A Basic Guide to Exporting*, op. cit., p. 24.

[40]Ibid., p. 25

[41]Ibid.

[42]Terpstra, op. cit., pp. 144–45.

2 *FOB (free on board) named inland carrier.*   An FOB quotation like this is not much different from an ex-factory quotation. All the seller does in addition is to see that the merchandise is loaded on a train or truck outside his or her factory. From the marketing viewpoint, it has the same shortcomings as the ex-factory quotation. Nevertheless, it is a popular price quotation with American exporters because they use it domestically and because it limits their responsibility.

3 *FAS (free alongside) vessel, named port of shipment.*   With an FAS quotation, the exporter maintains ownership of the goods and responsibility for their handling until they are placed alongside the ship at the port of embarkation. In this quotation the exporter has greater risk (owning the goods for a longer time) and greater responsibility (arranging inland transportation in the foreign country), but it lessens the burden on the foreign buyer. The FAS quote is higher than the FOB quote because inland freight is included.

4 *CIF (cost, insurance, freight) named port of destination.*   A CIF quotation transfers title to the buyer once the merchandise is loaded aboard the ship or plane. However, the exporter assumes responsibility for arranging for and paying for transportation and insurance all the way to the foreign port. This means more work for the exporter but greater convenience for the foreign buyer. The CIF quotation is higher than others, of course, because it includes ocean shipping and marine insurance.

FOB Ardmore, Oklahoma, would probably not mean much to prospective foreign buyers. The buyers would have no way to determine with any accuracy what the export costs would be in Ardmore and would not know the freight charges from Ardmore to the port of export.[43] Indeed, foreign buyers often complain about U.S. exporters' frequent use of FOB plant pricing. Good general advice to the exporter is always to quote CIF. It means something to foreign buyers; it shows the foreign buyer what it costs to get the U.S. exporter's product to a port in or near the desired country. If assistance in figuring the CIF price is needed, an international freight forwarder will be glad to help. Furnish a description of your product with its weight and cubic measurement when packed; the freight forwarder can then compute the CIF price. There is usually no charge for this service.[44]

International Communications

Knowing how to communicate internationally is basic to successful exporting. Your first contact with a prospective customer or agent in a foreign country will probably be by letter, and letters will probably remain one of your major means of communication. However, the use of telegrams or cables (TELEX) have become standard in

[43]*A Basic Guide to Exporting*, op. cit., p. 27.
[44]Ibid.

international business as have telephones. Following are helpful checklists for all three models of communications.[45]

1 *Checklist for letters.* Answer inquiries promptly and in the language of the inquirer, if possible. Include the abbreviation U.S.A. in your letterhead in the address, cable information, and name of your bank. Be polite, courteous, and friendly; and add a personal touch to your letter. Avoid slang. Personally sign your letters; form letters are not satisfactory and may be considered an insult. Send letters by airmail, and use stamps rather than a postage meter because an array of colorful stamps gets attention.

2 *Checklist for cables.* Include your cable address on all correspondence. Draft the cable before sending it to make sure it is clear and covers all points you intended. If there is urgency that the foreign party receive the cable and a terminal is not available, you can request that Western Union notify the party immediately, even hand-carry the cable if necessary. Use the buyer's system of measurement and money values.

3 *Checklist for telephones.* Check the number and name of the party you are calling. Be aware of time differences, and time your call accordingly. Remember, for example, that when it's 12:00 noon in New York, it is 12:00 midnight in Djakarta, Indonesia. Determine if direct dialing is available and feasible. Be prepared with notes handy before you call. Speak clearly, and identify yourself and your company. Be tactful, polite, and helpful. Take notes during your conversation. Include the date of the call and the name and title of the person to whom you spoke. Before hanging up, confirm and clarify all pertinent matters. You may also wish to acknowledge the phone conversation by letter.

Receiving Payment

Traditional payment terms include cash in advance, open account, documentary collection, and letter of credit.[46]

1 *Cash in advance.* With this term of sale, the seller receives cash payment from the buyer prior to shipment. From the seller's viewpoint, this is the least risky. Buyers will normally reject this method because it ties up capital until the goods are received and resold. Furthermore, the buyer does not know if the goods will actually be shipped.

2 *Open account.* This method is opposite to cash in advance. It is a procedure whereby a seller ships goods to a buyer for payment at a later date. Unless the

---

[45]Ibid., pp. 29–30.
[46]Ibid., pp. 33–38.

buyer is of unquestionable integrity, an open account can be extremely risky for the seller. Moreover, the seller's capital is tied up until payment is received.

3 *Documentary collection.* This method of payment can be defined as payment on delivery of certain documents, wherein goods are turned over to the buyer only on receipt of a cash payment. Under this method, the goods are consigned through a carrier in such a way that the buyer cannot obtain the goods without payment. The seller's major risk is nonpayment and the costs of freight both ways. Common documents used for this method are sight draft, time draft, date draft, delivery orders, and so forth.

4 *Letter of credit.* This is frequently used to receive payment. It is a document issued by a bank at the buyer's request in favor of the seller. Letters of credit may be revocable or irrevocable; the seller is advised to insist on irrevocable letters of credit. This means that once the credit has been accepted by the seller, it cannot be altered in any way by the buyer without the permission of the seller. The bank will accordingly pay regardless of the wishes or financial ability of the buyer. In this manner, the seller trusts the reputation of a third party financial institution. It may, therefore, be desirable to have the buyer confirm the letter of credit through a U.S. bank. Through this means, the U.S. bank accepts responsibility to pay regardless of the financial situation of the buyer or foreign bank.

Today many buyers and sellers are breaking away from tradition and employing payment procedures that are a combination of the preceding or variations thereof. For example, the seller may wish to have a 30 percent cash in advance down payment with the balance of 70 percent payable on an open account basis. Another illustration would be a 20 percent cash in advance down payment with a 60 percent collection item completed by 20 percent in open account.[47]

For smaller exporters, one of the best ways to insure payment is to use bank-owned export trading companies. With the advent of the Export Trading Company Act of 1982, banks may now take title to goods and engage in nonbanking transactions through their own trading company. This is important to the exporter because the bank, using its extensive network of customers, is able to eliminate time and risk for U.S. exporters by working with them to find markets for products while facilitating payment more quickly than if the exporters actually took possession of the goods and sold them themselves.[48]

For added protection, the exporter can pay for the services of the Foreign Credit Insurance Association (FCIA), which offers insurance coverage of commercial credit risks. The new exporter should consider this protection carefully before entering into credit transactions. FCIA policies, however, provide payment only after the exporter has exhaused every reasonable means of obtaining payment.[49]

---

[47]Walter B. Holt, "Break the Payment Mold; Try a Mixture of Methods," *American Import Export Management*, March 1983, p. 24. This material is used with permission.

[48]Ellen Welsh, " 'How to . . . Finance a South American Deal!' *American Import Export Management*, February 1984, p. 42. This material is used with permission.

[49]*A Basic Guide to Exporting*, op. cit., p. 37.

Packing and Marking

Two functions closely related to packaging and labeling are packing and marking. Packing is the task of putting the packages in a container or shipping crate for shipping, and marking refers to symbols, words, or numbers that appear on the cargo to help in identification for appropriate handling.

There are four problems that must be kept in mind when designing an export shipping crate: breakage, weight, moisture, and pilferage. In addition to the normal handling encountered in domestic transportation, an export order moving by ocean freight will be loaded aboard vessels by a sling, in a net with other items, by conveyor, chute, or other method, putting added strain on the package. In the ship's hold, cargo may be stacked on top of the crate or come into violent contact with it during the course of the voyage. Overseas, handling facilities may not be as sophisticated as in the United States; the cargo may be dragged, pushed, rolled, or dropped during unloading, while moving through customs, or in transit to the final destination.

Moisture is a constant problem because cargo is subject to condensation even in the hold of a ship equipped with air-conditioning and a dehumidifier. The cargo may also be unloaded in the rain, and many foreign ports do not have covered storage facilities. In addition, unless cargo is adequately protected, theft and pilferage are constant threats. One way to deter pilferage is to avoid mention of contents or trade names on packages. Strapping and seals may also discourage theft. A very effective means of eliminating both moisture and pilferage is "shrink wrapping," which involves sealing the merchandise in a plastic film.[50] Here are some tips: (1)Heavy crates should be skidded and have provisions for forklift trucks. They should also have notches to facilitate use of slings. (2) Cement-coated nails are recommended because they hold better. Packages should also be strapped because this gives them added strength. Plywood sheathing is economical and strong. (3) Avoid overpacking because customs duties in some countries are assessed on the gross weight, rather than on the value, of the package. Added weight will also result in higher inland freight charges in the United States and abroad (not to mention the cost of packing itself). (4) Use waterproof inner liners, moisture-absorbing agents, and rust-inhibiting coatings (on finished metal parts).[51]

One increasingly popular method of shipments is the use of "containers" obtained from carriers or private concerns. Varying in size, material, and construction, these can accommodate most cargo but are best suited for standard package sizes and shapes. Some containers are no more than truck bodies lifted off their wheels and placed on a vessel at the port of export. These are then transferred to another set of wheels at the port of import for movement to an inland destination.[52]

Normally, shipments by air do not require as heavy packing as ocean ship-

[50]Ibid., p. 22.
[51]Ibid.
[52]Ibid.

ments, but they must still be adequately protected. In many instances, standard domestic packing is acceptable, especially if the product is durable in nature and there is no concern for display packaging. In other instances, "high test" (at least 250 pounds per square inch) cardboard or triwall construction boxes are more than adequate.[53]

In the case of both ocean and air shipment, carriers can advise on the best packaging. Marine insurance companies also are available for consultation. If your firm is not equipped to package for export, there are professional firms that will perform this task at moderate cost.[54]

Pilferage while containers are en route is also likely if the container has been damaged or not properly maintained. Proper attention to sealing with tamperproof seals and maintenance of accurate seal records, including noting seal numbers and the reason for any breaking of seals, will do much to reduce the instance of pilferage en route. Good maintenance practices are also the first line of defense against such pilferage, and shippers should be careful to reject any damaged or defective container offered for the transportation of their cargo.[55]

Usually, the buyer will specify special export marks that should appear on cargo to facilitate identification on arrival. These marks will also help the carriers to identify the cargo to ensure that it arrives at the correct destination.[56]

Legibility is of the utmost importance. Letters should be at least two inches high; stenciled in black, waterproof ink; and fully exposed. Packages should be marked on at least two adjacent sides—and preferably on the top also. Sacks should be marked on both sides prior to filling. Drums should be marked on both the side and top.[57]

As mentioned earlier, to avoid pilferage, avoid showing trademarks or other clues indicating the contents of the cargo. Old marks on packages should be completely obliterated to avoid confusion. If new marks are to be imprinted over old ones, care should be taken to use a light color markover paint or ink. The paint should be completely dry before the new marks are applied.[58]

In addition to port marks, customer identification code, and indication of origin, the marks should include the package number, gross and net weights, and dimensions. If you are shipping more than one package, be sure to mark the number of packages in the shipment. Also include any special handling instructions on the package. It is a good idea to repeat these instructions in the language of the country of destination. Standard international shipping and handling symbols should also be utilized.[59]

[53]Ibid.

[54]Ibid.

[55]Carl E. Everett, "Making a Thief's Job Harder: An Export Packing/Security Story," *American Import Export Management*, April 1983, pp. 52–53. This material is used with permission.

[56]*A Basic Guide to Exporting*, op. cit., p. 22.

[57]Ibid., p. 23.

[58]Ibid.

[59]Ibid.

Shipping the Product

Obviously, an important part of exporting is providing a way to get the product to the customer. International shipping requires special attention because of rules and regulations not encountered in domestic shipping. In addition, because the goods are traveling across international boundaries, special care must be taken to meet all requirements. Fortunately, you can call on professionals to assist you with the many complexities of getting your product from your site to the buyer's site safe and sound. Following are some ways to get this done.

Nonvessel Operating Common Carriers (NVOCCs). These transportation specialists fill an important transport niche for small exporters who ship less than container load overseas. The freight consolidation of NVOCCs has grown hand in hand with containerization. The NVOCCs serve the needs of less-than-container-load (LCL) shippers. They serve as intermediaries between the containership lines and the small shipper. Their primary business lies in packing containers by consolidating the LCL loads of several shippers into one container. This allows the shipper to take advantage of low container rates without having to fill a container; it also allows the shipping lines to fill their vessels and make efficient use of precious space.[60]

International Freight Forwarder. Full service freight forwarders can handle almost all the paperwork, shipping, and insurance arrangements for the exporter. Indeed, they are specialists in the mechanics of international trade. Because their expertise is combined with the economics of scale gained from serving many clients, freight forwarders are used by many larger exporters as well as smaller firms. The customhouse broker serves U.S. *importers* in much the same way. Most firms do both and are, therefore, interchangeable.

Freight forwarders can assist with an order from the start by advising the exporter of the freight costs, port charges, consular fees, cost of special documentation, and insurance costs, as well as their own handling fees—all of which will help in preparing the quotation. They can also recommend the degree of packing that should be considered to ensure that the merchandise arrives in good condition at its destination. If it is desired, freight forwarders can even arrange to have the merchandise packed at the port or to have it "containerized." The cost for their services is a legitimate export cost that may be figured into the contract price charged to the customer.[61]

When the order is ready to ship, they will review the letter of credit, packing list, and so on, to ensure that everything is in order. If it is desired, they can also reserve the necessary space aboard an ocean vessel.[62]

[60]Brian J. Dooley, "NVOCCs", *American Import Export Management*, June 1983, p. 24. This material is used with permission.

[61]*A Basic Guide to Exporting*, op. cit., p. 39.

[62]Ibid.

When the cargo arrives at the port of export, the forwarders make the necessary arrangements to clear it through customs and have it delivered to the pier in time for loading aboard the selected vessel. They may also prepare the ocean bill of lading and any special consular documentation that may be required. After shipment, they forward all documents directly to the customer or to the paying bank with instructions to credit the exporter's account accordingly.[63]

Ocean Carriers.   There are three categories of ocean carriers available to you for shipment of your goods: (1) Ocean-freight conference carriers are those that have joined together to establish common freight rates and to set shipping conditions standards. If you expect to ship steady volumes of goods via these carriers, you can achieve rate reductions by becoming a "contract shipper," entering into an agreement with the conference carriers to use their lines whenever possible. (2) Independent-line carriers, as the name indicates, quote individually to any shipper desiring the movement of goods overseas. No agreement need be signed, and they will often quote competitively, especially if they feel you have also asked conference carriers to bid. (3) Tramp vessels have no established schedules and normally carry only bulk cargo. For these reasons, except for a few cases, it is not likely that a new exporter would use tramp vessels.[64]

Roll-on, Roll-off (Ro-Ro).   Direct drive-on and drive-off of wheeled cargo vehicles on specially designed oceangoing ships is commonly referred to as roll-on, roll-off (Ro-Ro) capability. Ro-Ro offers the shippers an alternative method for removing cargoes to consignees overseas. The lowboy trailers and railcars utilized for Ro-Ro transportation enable shippers to load their cargoes right at the plant or warehouses, move the vehicles to the piers, and load them directly on the vessels. Mafi-trailers are used to move cargo on and off the vessels at the port.[65]

By rolling cargo on board these vessels and rolling it off at its destination, shippers can reduce not only the number of times their cargo is handled but significantly speed up and make easier the loading and unloading process. Port confusion and congestion can often be reduced or avoided by using Ro-Ro because no cargo-handling gear is necessary. One only needs a suitable ramp-landing area.[66]

Air Carriers.   Although ocean carriers account for the largest percentage of tonnage of goods moved in international trade to and from the United States, the air carriers have long provided a significant alternative for many exporters (or importers), especially those shipping products that have a high value relative to their weight and that are perishable or otherwise need the flexibility and speed of air distribution.

[63]Ibid.
[64]*Exportise*, op. cit., p. 126
[65]Ibid., p. 127.
[66]Ibid.

Innovations in the air cargo industry include advanced airplane technology, nose-loading features, and logistical superiority, which combine to win over more and more shippers. Joined to air carrier technology are improved airport facilities, which have increased their airfreight capacity and ground handling equipment.[67] Indeed, Dallas/Ft. Worth, landlocked cities, plan to become a major force in international trade, and one of the main reasons is DFW Airport with its massive and efficient freight-handling facilities.

International Marine Insurance.   Shipment of goods to foreign markets should be insured against loss or damage by adequate insurance. By common convention, this insurance is referred to as "marine" or "ocean marine" insurance regardless of the mode of carrier—land, sea, or air.[68]

Basically, there are two types of marine insurance, normal and contingency. Normal insurance is the type usually contracted with an insurance company and provides broad coverage to protect the cargo. Contingency insurance provides the same coverage but is used only as a backup in transactions where the customer is supposedly responsible for purchasing insurance coverage. Thus, these policies would pay damages only to the extent that adequate coverage is not provided by the customer.

Export Documentation

Because of the greater time and distance, the extra transportation and insurance required, the greater number of intermediaries (which may include the Eximbank and FCIA), and the fact that two or more political jurisdictions are involved, the amount and kinds of documentation are much greater for exporting than for domestic shipping. Two general kinds of documentation are required: commercial documents for shipping, forwarding, collecting, and insurance; and documents for the government, such as a shipper's export declaration, a consular invoice, or a certificate of origin. An average shipment requires over 40 documents and several hundred copies. Documents are needed to leave the exporting country and to enter the importing country and for all those who will handle the goods in both countries. This paperwork is considered the most onerous task in exporting. Of course, many firms pass on this burden to freight forwarders and customhouse brokers.[69]

Documentation requirements and other regulations imposed by foreign governments vary from country to country, and it is vital that you be aware of those that apply to your own operations and transactions. Most governments require consular invoices, certificates of inspection, health certification, and so forth. In certain cases, your failure to observe foreign trade documentation requirements may prevent your

---

[67]See Tom Werner, "Air Cargo Can!" *American Import Export Management*, September 1983, pp. 20, 21, 63.

[68]*Exportise*, op. cit., p. 129.

[69]Terpstra, op. cit., pp. 131–32.

customer from taking possession of your shipment. It may then be impounded for sale at public auction or returned to you on a costly freight collect basis. Shipping delays, loss of sales, and other costly problems may also arise from inadvertent violation of trade regulations.

Government Regulations and Tax Incentives

The ebb and flow of trade regulations and restrictions are tough to get a handle on. Today some in the U.S. Congress are concerned over technology leakage to the Soviet Union and consequently press for tighter laws and more restrictions on high-technology exporters. Then there is the difficulty of even defining high technology. Other congressional representatives, remembering the Soviet pipeline sanctions and billions of dollars lost by American exporters, want to protect exporters against unpredictable and restrictive controls. Still others want to create an Office of Strategic Trade, an independent agency, which would take over all export-import controls from the Commerce Department. Indeed, there are major disagreements everywhere.

In any event, besides obtaining the required shipping documentation, exporters should be careful to meet all international trade regulations established by specific legislation or other authority of the U.S. government. The import regulations of foreign countries must, of course, also be taken into account. Some of the basic regulations that you will need to understand are summarized below along with tax incentives offered by the U.S. government.

1 *Limitations on technology export.* The Export Administration Act of 1979 requires the approval of the Department of Commerce for exports that may adversely affect national security by contributing to the military potential of unfriendly foreign countries. The act focuses on the export of technology or goods that contribute to technology transfer. Although framed as an export-licensing statute, the act can be interpreted to consider as an "export" information or processes disclosed within the United States and carried to a foreign country inside someone's head.[70]

The second major statute affecting technology transfer is the Arms Export Control Act, which provides that the proposed export of defense articles or defense services be submitted to the Department of State for licensing. Although this statute is primarily aimed at arms sales, it also prohibits the unlicensed export of technical data of military significance.[71]

2 *Antidiversion clause.* To help ensure that U.S. exports go only to legally authorized destinations, a "destination control statement" is required on shipping documents. Exceptions to the use of the destination control statement are

[70]*Exportise*, op. cit., p. 147.
[71]Ibid.

shipments intended for consumption in Canada and shipments being made under certain general licenses.[72]

3 *Foreign Corrupt Practices Act (FCPA).* The Foreign Corrupt Practices Act of 1977 makes (among other things) certain payments, offers of payments, and gifts to foreign political parties or foreign political candidates illegal if made corruptly for the purpose of obtaining, retaining, or directing business to any person. It also establishes recordkeeping and internal accounting control requirements for all publicly held corporations whether or not these corporations are engaged in international business.[73]

Selected tax incentives especially applicable to the exporter are the following.

1 *Drawback of custom duties.* Drawback is a form of tax relief in which a custom duty, lawfully collected, is refunded or remitted wholly or in part because of the particular use made of the commodity on which the duty was collected. American firms that import materials or components that they process or assemble for reexport may obtain "drawback" refunds of all duties paid on the imported merchandise, less 1 percent covering customs costs.

2 *Domestic International Sales Corporation (DISC).* This is a category of corporation added to the Tax Code by the Revenue Act of 1971 in an attempt to increase American exports. DISCs are really nothing more than paper corporations that shelter a portion of earnings from taxes as long as earnings are invested in export-related projects. There is much foreign opposition to DISCs. For example, the European Economic Community protested that DISCs constituted an illegal export subsidy, and an international tribunal agreed. Now the administration is proposing a replacement that would be more acceptable to U.S. trading partners. The replacement is called the FSC, or Foreign Sales Corporation, an export subsidiary that would be situated outside the United States. International rules appear to permit tax exemption when export income comes from outside the country.

3 *Webb-Pomerene Associations.* Under the Webb-Pomerene Act of 1918, specific exemption from the prohibitions of the antitrust laws is provided for associations that are formed for the sole purpose of engaging in export trade and that are actually engaged solely in such trade.[74]

4 *Free Port and Free Trade Zones.* To encourage and facilitate international trade, more than 300 free ports, free trade zones, and similar customs-privileged facilities are now in operation in some 75 countries, usually in or near seaports or airports. Many American manufacturers and their distributors utilize free

---

[72]*A Basic Guide to Exporting*, op. cit., p. 51.

[73]Ibid., p. 53

[74]Ibid., p. 55.

ports or free trade zones for receipt of shipments of goods that are then reshipped in smaller lots to customers throughout the surrounding areas.[75]

5 *U.S. Foreign Trade Zones.* Exporters should also consider the customs privileges of U.S. foreign trade zones. These are domestic sites that are considered outside customs territory and are available for activities that might otherwise be carried on overseas for customs reasons. For export operations, the zones provide accelerated export status for purposes of excise tax rebates and customs drawback.

Tariffs

The effect of the tariff is to make imported items more expensive and to reduce their ability to compete with local products. Substantial progress has been made recently in reducing tariffs,[76] as the following examples show.

1 *The General Agreement on Tariffs and Trade (GATT).* This is a multilateral agreement that sets out the rules for world trade. It establishes a forum for negotiating multilateral tariff reductions among member nations. The basic tenets of GATT are that (1) countries should consult together to overcome trade problems; (2) domestic industry should be protected only with customs duties and tariffs, not through quantitative restrictions and other nontariff measures; and (3) tariffs should be reduced through multilateral negotiations and considered then a "ceiling" against future increases.[77]

2 *Most-favored nation (MFN) treatment.* Most-favored-nation (MFN) treatment is a commitment that a country will extend to another country the lowest tariff rates it applies to any third country. All contracting parties undertake to apply such treatment to one another under Article I of the General Agreement on Tariffs and Trade (GATT). When a country agrees to cut tariffs on a particular product imported from one country, the tariff reduction automatically applies to imports of this product from any other eligible for most-favored-nation treatment.[78]

3 *Generalized system of preferences (GSP).* This is a system of nonreciprocal tariff preferences for the benefit of developing countries. It is one element in a coordinated effort of the industrial trading nations to bring developing countries up to certain dollar values or import percentage limits.[79]

[75]Ibid.
[76]*Exportise*, op. cit., p. 154
[77]Ibid.
[78]Ibid.
[79]Ibid.

Financing Exports

Several sources of financial assistance are available to exporters. A few of the more noted sources are now briefly described and summarized.[80] Further information may be found in the publication entitled *A Guide to Financing Exports*, which can be obtained free of charge from Export Communications Section, Room 3056, International Trade Administration, U.S. Department of Commerce, Washington, D.C. 20230.

1 *Export-Import Bank (Eximbank).* This government-owned corporation assists the financing of exports. It offers direct loans, guarantees, and insurance in a variety of programs. Insurance against commercial and political risk is handled through the Foreign Credit Insurance Association (FCIA) on behalf of Eximbank. Write to Eximbank, 811 Vermont Avenue, N.W., Washington, D.C. 20571.[81]

2 *Private Export Funding Corporation (PEFCO).* PEFCO is owned by more than five dozen investors, mostly commercial banks. It lends only to finance the export of goods and services of U.S. manufacture and origin. Write to PEFCO, 280 Park Avenue, New York, New York 10017.[82]

3 *Small Business Administration (SBA).* The SBA is actively involved in helping and encouraging small businesses to export. There are three major areas in which SBA contributes: management assistance, financial assistance, and cooperation with other government agencies. For more information or assistance, contact your nearest SBA office.[83]

SUMMARY

The stages of exporting are introductory, opportunity, and maturity stages. The first two stages especially call for counsel from government, financial sources, and private consultants. Also, various publications, export programs, and financial-insurance groups give the new exporter a wide array of services and information.

A key part of exporting is a proper marketing program, which may include advertising in various foreign media, the use of government-sponsored programs, and trade shows. Firms that perform direct marketing and facilitation services include export management companies (EMCs) and export trading companies (ETCs). The exporter can try to sell directly, but such an approach is normally not recommended for the new exporter. For some exporters, the use of Foreign Trade Zones

[80]Ibid., pp. 113–15.
[81]Ibid.
[82]Ibid.
[83]Ibid.

(FTZs) may be beneficial for marketing as well as for providing certain tax and duty advantages.

Mechanics of exporting include pricing, quotation preparation, conducting proper communications, receiving payment, packing and marking, shipping, and export documentation preparation. Other factors include government regulations and tax incentives, tariffs, and financing sources.

ASSIGNMENT

1 List the stages of exporting.

2 List and explain counseling sources for exporters.

3 What are the publications available to exporters?

4 What finance and insurance services are available to exporters?

5 Gather information about the Eximbank, and write a short report on how it aids small, new-to-export entrepreneurs.

6 Write a short report on the following: EMCs, ETCs, FTZs, and international trade shows.

7 Write a report on how the United States Department of Commerce and the International Trade Administration help small, new-to-export entrepreneurs. Get some of your research material from your district office of the Commerce Department.

8 List and give complete examples of the mechanics of exporting.

BIBLIOGRAPHY

A Basic Guide to Exporting. Washington, D.C.: United States Department of Commerce/ International Trade Administration, 1981.

Barovick, Richard L. "The Washington Front." *American Import Export Management*. October 1983.

Brinson, J. Ron. "Fairness of Free Trade." *American Import Export Management*. September 1983.

Casey, William R. "A Forwarding Prospective." *American Import Export Management*. November 1983.

Daiboch, Alfred F. "Have You Won Your Share of Federal Export Support?" *American Import Export Management*. February 1984.

Dawson, Leslie M. "Opportunities for Small Business in Third World Markets." *American Journal of Small Business*, 7:1 (Summer 1982).

Dooley, Brian J. "NVOCCs." *American Import Export Management*. June 1983.

———. "Export Management Companies—Your 'Outside' Export Office." *American Import Export Management*. May 1984.

Exportise. Boston Mass.: The Small Business Foundation of America, Inc., 1983.

Everett, Carl E. "Making a Thief's Job Harder: An Export Packing/Security Story." *American Import Export Management*. April 1983.

"Eximbank Gives You the (Small) Business." *American Import Export Management*. December 1983.

Farrell, Kevin. "Ex-Im Gets Serious About Small Business." *Venture*. May 1984.

"FTZ Homes?" *American Import Export Management*. March 1983.

Holt, Walter B. "Break the Payment Mold: Try a Mixture of Methods." *American Import Export Management*. March 1983.

Kahler, Ruel, and Roland L. Kramer. *International Marketing*. Boston, Mass.: Kent Publishing Company, 1982.

"1984 Prospects for U.S. Exporters Throughout the ASEAN Five." *American Import Export Management*. February 1984.

O'Leary, Paul A. "ETC Act: Helpful or Harmful?" *American Import Export Management*. November 1983.

Shayne, Leonard. "Playing Export Games." *American Import Export Management*. April 1983.

Terpstra, Vern. *International Dimensions of Marketing*. Boston, Mass.: Kent Publishing Company, 1982.

"The 'Pro' Side to ETCs." *American Import Export Management*. June 1983.

Tjen, Willy T. B. "Five Nations with Increasing Buying Power and Growing Demands." *American Import Export Management*. February 1984.

Weiner, Steve, and Robert Johnson. "Export-Trading Firms in U.S. Are to Fulfill Promise." *The Wall Street Journal*. May 24, 1984.

Weiss, Julian. "Marketplace Southeast Asia: ASEAN." *American Import Export Management*. June 1983.

Welsh, Ellen. " 'How to' . . . Finance a South American Deal!" *American Import Export Management*. February 1984.

Werner, Tom. "Air Cargo Can!" *American Import Export Management*. September 1983.

CHAPTER 11

A Potpourri
of Opportunities

INTRODUCTION

The earlier chapters in this part deal with special umbrella opportunities that embrace a broad range of specific opportunities. Mail order can be used to market almost any product or service imaginable. Export opportunities abound, especially with new emphasis and programs by government agencies, bankers, and business-people across the country.

This chapter concludes our discussion of entrepreneurial opportunities by giving a potpourri of additional opportunities that range from moonlighting ventures to inventrepreneurship. The aim of all these chapters is to make you aware of the vast number of opportunities that are available to you—their advantages and disadvantages and the pitfalls—and, at the same time, to stimulate you to exploit them or to use them to derive your own special opportunity.

Clearly, entrepreneurship covers a wide range of businesses. You may become an entrepreneur who establishes a manufacturing facility in space; you may develop a cost-effective waste disposal method; you may become an exporter of low-value, plentiful hardwood products of this country to countries where such products are scarce; you may buy out a small manufacturing firm and contribute to its rejuvenation and success; you may develop a 2-million-square-foot shopping center with dazzling architecture and create innovative shopping methods; you may write a computer software package for business analysis; you may upgrade old homes and resell them at a substantial profit in your spare time; you may develop an interactive video catalog system for a mail order operation; you may rent a stall at the local flea market for a moonlighting operation; or you may open a designer jean boutique from a little-used room of your home.

The point is that there are opportunities that fit your skills and tastes. You don't have to create another IBM or Exxon to be a success. If you sell heart-shaped pillows at the local flea market on weekends and if you believe you are successful, then clearly you are. The real bottom line of your venture is to have fun with it, gain fulfillment, and relish what you are doing. Whether you make $5,000 or $5 million a year with your venture is, to a great extent, irrelevant. Following are some opportunities that you might consider pursuing. The objectives of this chapter are these.

1 To cover a number of moonlighting opportunities.

2 To present the shopping center as an entrepreneurial opportunity for both the developer and tenant, but especially for the developer, and also to disclose a number of details that the developer and tenant should know about.

3 To discuss the need for new technology; for the inventrepreneur, a special entrepreneur; and for ways to finance technologies in their embryonic stage.

4 To introduce a variety of entrepreneurial role models.

MOONLIGHTING OPPORTUNITIES

A moonlighter is a person who holds a second job or who goes into a spare-time business venture while holding a regular full-time job. Many think that moonlighting is part-time, door-to-door selling or working at a gas station at night. It certainly can be. But there are all kinds of part-time jobs and business ventures for one who wants to pursue them. A professor, for example, set up an auctioneering business which he works on weekends. A lawyer became a wine steward and works at it two nights a week. A stockbroker opened an escort service for authors. In this section, we consider spare-time business venture opportunities that could evolve into full-time businesses, depending on your goals.

Why People Moonlight

Many people want to make more money than they are presently making and do other things with their lives, but they don't know how. Still others fall short because they think that they don't have the time to take on a part-time venture, or they simply don't have the guts and commitment to make a venture work. Some people sell themselves short; they simply don't believe that they can do anything out of the ordinary and, consequently, have nothing to offer that anyone would buy. A number of people want to go into a venture, but they won't pursue it because they think one has to have a lot of money to get started.

These reasons are invalid. Many psychologists say that most of us use only about 10 percent of our brainpower and work capacity. Furthermore, professionals who know about such things say that many of us have vast amounts of untapped moneymaking potential lying dormant waiting to be unleashed. Certainly, a lot of moonlighters who started with almost nothing have made millions selling ordinary, or even wacky, products or services to customers who were willing to pay hard-earned money for these products and services. In fact, two appealing reasons to go into a moonlighting venture are that (1) it takes little front-end money, and (2) the venture enables you to do "your thing." The pet rock, for example, turned the country upside down and made millions for its nearly broke originator. Knitted ski caps, started as a kitchen enterprise, created several millionaires.[1]

What are some other reasons why people start moonlighting ventures? A very practical reason is that it gives you a way to go into business without quitting your present job. Or, if you look at it from another viewpoint, the venture provides you with a fallback position if your present job goes sour. Moreover, in many instances, it gives you tax write-offs that you would not have with an ordinary job. And if you have bigger goals in mind, it sets a base for a full-time business. As a matter of fact, a very sensible and risk-reducing way to go into business is via moonlighting; you can get one foot wet without the fear or possibility of drowning. From the moneymaking

[1]Duane Newcomb, *Fortune-Building Secrets of the Rich* (West Nyack, N.Y.: Parker Publishing Company, 1983), p. 15. This material is used with permission.

side, some moonlighting venturers don't merely want to keep up with the Joneses; they want to get far ahead of them. Or at least they are trying to earn a little more money to be able to partake of and enjoy life's little extras.

Are there any psychological reasons why people become moonlighters? Yes. Number one: It's fun. Normally, if you go into a venture that you really love, it is not a hardship; it may actually relieve negative stress and create positive stress. Clearly, it gives you a change of pace and a different way to relax. You meet new people and exchange ideas. You gain a sense of satisfaction and achieve fulfillment. In a more serious vein, some people feel trapped in a dead-end job, and a moonlighting venture gives them a vehicle to break away. These people are simply tired and fed up with things as they are. They are weary of doing everything the way others want them done. They want to call some of the shots. Indeed, they are looking for more recognition, freedom of choice, and success.

Selected Opportunity Examples

Following are examples of how you may start a part-time venture. You may be able to imitate some of them, depending on your goals, tastes, and skills. Some of these ventures require the ability to work with your hands. Others require marketing and good communication skills. You may have a full-time job at night and have to operate your part-time venture during the day or on weekends only. At the very least, the following opportunity examples may generate ideas for your own special moonlighting venture whether you work out of your home, your shop, or your office.

Free-lance Disc Jockey.   Develop your own, unique theme, concept, and music or other entertainment format. Determine who your audience is, their needs, and the demographics. Fit your format to this audience. Line up businesspeople who service your audience, and commit them to advertising time. Then negotiate with the management of the local radio station for a 60-minute slot for each weekend. If you get the advertisers committed and the format worked out, you can get the slot and a slice of the advertising revenue.

Bicycle Rental and Repairs.   Young and old alike are riding bicycles all over the place. Bicycling for pleasure, exercise, or racing has certainly increased in popularity in recent years. Many bikers don't do it full-time, don't want to own a bicycle, and don't know how to or choose to repair them. This situation provides a great opportunity to open a bicycle rental and repair shop to service these people. A member of your family or someone else could take care of rentals during the weekdays, and you could make repairs at night and during weekends.

Picture Framing.   If you like to work with your hands, this moonlighting opportunity gives you a clean, well-defined environment in which to work. Picture framing can be both satisfying and profitable.

Shoe Bronzing. Many parents want to have mementos of their recently born children. These children's shoes are bronzed to give the parents a permanent memento of the early years. Also, bronzed shoes have decorative value and can be used as paperweights or bookends. Investment in supplies and equipment is minimal, and good returns can be made. Prospective customers can be obtained through hospitals, birth announcements, direct mail, newspaper ads, and so forth.

Shoeshine Service. Don't laugh. You may not make much more than $8.00 per hour, but you may have a lot of fun. This could be an ideal change of pace. Set up your shoe shine service where there is a lot of traffic around hotels, shopping centers, theaters, and so forth. Put a little pizzazz into your work, and you will get all the business you can handle.

Making Stained-glass Windows. Making stained-glass windows is a personal choice. Not only would this venture be profitable, but it would also be extremely satisfying—working with your hands and building something beautiful at the same time. Moreover, a lot of contractors and private builders are using more and more stained-glass insets or windows in condominiums, houses, and other structures. The easiest way to do it is to install the glass in the customer's frames and then let the customer actually install the frames in the building. To get started, you would be well advised to study as an apprentice under the tutelage of an experienced worker before going into business for yourself.

Escort Service. Many visitors in town would like to have local escorts as dinner or theater companions or as expert guides to show them around town and accompany them to special meetings. For example, a stockbroker in New York serves as an escort for authors of several publishing houses. She guides these authors to special points of interest and serves as their companion at the obligatory cocktail parties and promotional sessions.

Wine Steward. On Monday and Wednesday nights, a Houston corporate attorney leaves his office and heads for the Confederate House restaurant, where he serves as the restaurant's wine steward. He moonlights five hours each night, guiding diners through the most extensive wine list in Houston. He averages $40 to $50 a night in tips alone. But his main kick comes from the younger customers who know nothing about wine and are willing to experiment.[2]

Limousine Service. Many affluent people want and can afford the amenities of being picked up graciously and chauffeured to their destination without the hassle of traffic and finding one's way from one point to another. These people want to travel in style. A variation to this venture—and one that does not require an

[2]Excerpted from William C. Banks, "You're Not Alone in the Moonlight," *Money*, April 1984, p. 219. This material is used with permission.

investment in limousines, high insurance premiums, and so forth—is to serve as a chauffeur only. In this way, you drive the client's automobile to the airport, shopping trips, or whatever, and pick him or her up at scheduled times.

Mobile Repair or Maintenance. As stated several times earlier, any kind of mobile repair and maintenance service has a high probability of being successful. For example, Ms. Fix-Up, has a home repair and painting business in Santa Cruz, California. She does everything from carpentry and painting to gutter cleaning. A few tools, business cards, and liability insurance represented her start-up investment. She distributed her cards in Laundromats, grocery stores, and paint and hardware stores. She also placed a classified ad in the local newspaper. She started getting calls and business is booming. She also teaches home repair at a community college. Her future plans include turning her start-up into a franchise operation and selling franchises nationwide.[3]

Bringing Back Old-style Movie Theaters. There is something nostalgic about independently owned, grand old movie theaters with fresh popcorn with real butter, fresh-brewed coffee, candy, apple juice, and cookies. But nostalgia is not the only reason why small independent theaters such as the 140-seat Bijou Theatre in Eugene, Oregon, are starting up and surviving. The fact is that the businesses fill a niche, offering films the chains don't—old films but classics, foreign films, and contemporary popular ones.[4]

Typing and Word-processing Service. Almost everyone needs a letter or report typed at one time or another. The advent of computers and software and their combination with various typing mechanisms and fonts have given the technicians fantastic abilities to create, store, and modify—through electronic cutting and pasting and duplication—virtually any kind of letter, manuscript, and document in any style, quality, and format.

Making and Repairing Dolls. Many people of all ages around the world collect dolls and are known as "dollers." Indeed, collecting dolls is one of the largest hobbies in the world—and still growing. Dollers will pay several thousand dollars for original or antique dolls. These prices eliminate many dollers from this market, which opens a good market for quality reproductions that may sell for $200 or more. The main component for doll reproduction is the head, which is cast in China, porcelain, or ceramic. Repairs involve general structural repair, such as restringing, washing and curling hair, sewing or replacing clothes, replacing glass eyes, and filling in cracks.

[3]"New and Growing," *In Business*, February 1983, p. 11. This material is used with permission.
[4]Martha Wagner, "Good Times at the Bijou," *In Business*, February 1983. This material is used with permission.

Selling Food Specialities from Secret Recipes.   When ballet master Louis Chalif left the czar's court and came to the United States at the turn of the century, he brought along his secret mustard recipe. Today his descendants market blue-and-white jars of Chalif Hot 'n' Sweet mustard in the finest gourmet food stores across the country.[5] Tom and Mary Lynn Thompson have turned their croissant recipe into a successful mail order business. They sold croissants to local restaurants in Allentown, Pennsylvania; packaged them as executive gifts for Prudential Bache in Philadelphia; and advertised in the local paper, offering a special Christmas gift of home-delivered croissants in fireside baskets. Business grew, and today the Thompsons are full-time mail order operators of C'est Croissant.[6] If you, your father or mother, grandfather or grandmother, or any other relative or acquaintance of yours has a special knack for creating mouth-watering delights, you may have an item ready for full commercialization, or, at the very least, you may be able to sell such items to local restaurants.

Mobile Pet Grooming, Accessories, and Training.   Washing and grooming the family pet is a real hassle. Most people are not set up for it. Considering the size of the pet population, this venture seems to present an excellent moonlighting opportunity. Moreover, follow-on sales would include ribbons, collars, clothes, toys, special reward foods, wormers, and certain shots. The drawback is the initial investment in a van and grooming equipment. The generation of extra revenue, however, could come from additional service such as personal protection and obedience training.

Seminar, Training, and Tutoring Programs.   If not an expert, you probably are quite knowledgeable on several subjects or know how to do something that the average person cannot do but would like to know more about. At the very least, you can become the "local expert" and do an adequate job introducing your "class" to your subject or skill and point them toward further material and development. To get started, you first need a strong interest in your subject and a desire to work with people and teach. The place you do it in can be your home, motel, high school classroom during off hours; you can teach also through continuing education at a community college or university, at the YMCA or YWCA, or similar community organizations. Payments for the use of most of these facilities are made by some split of the course fee, usually payable at the conclusion of the course. The key to getting the necessary number of attendees (usually 10 to 20 is the break-even point) is an appropriate mailing list and publicity and directed advertising. In some cases, if your courses are successful, you can use them as a springboard for other opportunities such as consulting. For example, two women in California started Inner Gourmet by offering gourmet classes out of their kitchen. Since then, they have di-

---

[5]John Meislin, "Hot Stuff in a Mustard Jar," *In Business*, February 1983, pp. 42−44. This material is used with permission.

[6]"New and Growing," op. cit., p. 11.

versified their business to include European tours, TV shows, food styling, and writing and publishing.[7] Another example is Dr. Paul Mandala, who makes his living as chief of pediatrics at Good Samaritan Hospital in West Islip, New York. Mandala noticed that his friends were asking him about wines almost as often as they tapped him for free medical advice. Two years ago, he decided he had answered enough questions for free, so he designed a wine-appreciation course and offered to teach it on weekends and Wednesday nights in his office near the hospital. He charges $175 a person for a beginner's class and $250 for an advanced course. Mandala is looking forward to establishing his wine-tasting and appreciation venture on a full-time basis in a dozen years or so, when he retires from medical practice.[8]

Writing.   Here is a venture you can do in your spare time and at home. Most people can learn to write well. If you can combine your writing ability with a fertile imagination and flair for telling a good story, then you are prepared to enter the field of writing, especially fiction writing. There is good money in both articles and books, and it seems that the market is insatiable. Extra money can also be earned by writing nonfiction articles for trade and business magazines. Interview enterprising merchants or manufacturers in your area who are doing something with a new twist, make notes about what they are doing, gather personal and background facts, take pictures, and sell your articles to appropriate trade magazines. Start an entertainment directory that reports on what is happening around town. Prepare job letters and résumés for people seeking employment. Local newspapers are always looking for interesting stories to fill space. Write and submit interesting stories on local people and events. If you live in a large apartment complex, start your own local newspaper about the people and families living in the apartments. Make it personal and provide information that is especially relevant to the tenants. If you have a knack for literary persuasion, sell your talent to advertisers, and write advertising copy for them. Write a journal about local weddings, newlyweds, births, job changes, or whatever; and sell advertising space to various businesses. If you have an artistic flair and a talent for storytelling, develop a cartoon strip for the local newspaper. If it catches on, you may go into full syndication. Or if you have strong opinions and a credible background in a particular subject, start by writing a column for the local newspaper. A large readership will evolve into more newspapers, wider coverage, and more money. Write "how-to" books on any subject from piquant recipes to flying airplanes.

Design and Produce Work Clothes for Special Industries.   Clothes design and sewing take a special talent, but for those with this talent, lucrative niches can be exploited in a variety of fields, especially the affluent ones. For example, Nurse

---

[7]Rill Ann Goldstein, "Carving a Niche in Gourmet Foods," *In Business*, February 1983, pp. 32–44. This material is used with permission.

[8]Banks, op. cit., p. 220.

Leslie Green hates the "pukey green potato sack" she has to wear in the Buffalo General Hospital operating room. Scrub suits have traditionally been made of bedsheets dyed green and cut into baggy unisex patterns. Where are the need and the want? Fashion scrubs. Offer scrubs that are stylish, colorful, with matching accessories. Design something that will make the nurses look good against the gray operating walls. Nurses and physicians should look like professional workers rather than janitors or houseworkers or joggers.[9] Get a sewing machine, tools and supplies and start with a small, local hospital.

Construct a Racketball Facility.   Construct a building with racketball courts; saunas, massage facilities, showers, and dressing room facilities; warm-up room; lounge and bar; and office. Make it clean and colorful. Open it at least 60 hours per week. Hire someone to operate it during the day. Then you can come in on evenings and weekends to catch up on paperwork, supervision, and various other duties. Once your format catches on, you may devote yourself full-time to your venture, possibly developing it into a franchised operation.

Security Systems.   At night and weekends, sell and install burglar alarms and home security systems. You may also sell some of the devices through mail order.

Flea Market.   Rent a booth at the local flea market. You may start and raise seed capital by selling items from your attic or your relatives' or neighbors' attics and garages for a commission. Once you raise your seed money, buy one or two of your favorite items for retailing. Better yet, combine vacation travel abroad with importing exotic items that can be sold domestically at a substantial markup.

Become a Part-time Farmer.   Acquire a small plot of acreage (you don't need more than five acres), and grow vegetables such as tomatoes, kale, and cucumbers. Select crops that have different growing and harvest seasons, that is, early spring, late spring, summer, and fall. Much of your cultivating and planting can be done in the cool of the evenings. Your marketing can be done at roadside stands, in a farmer's market, or through grocers. If you don't have a green thumb, you might consider raising capons, pheasants, or turkeys for local restauranteurs.

Become a Consultant.   Consultants are in the problem-solving business. Consulting, indeed, is both a business and a profession. Consultants are people with an above-average knowledge or a not commonly available skill who have a strong drive and a willingness to hustle. Consulting, for most aspirants, should be started on a part-time basis; the nature of consulting allows schedule flexibility and is, therefore, clearly ideal for the moonlighter. Generally, becoming a consultant does not require a special license or passing a qualifying exam, such as that for a certified public

---

[9]Angelo B. Henderson, " 'Pukey Green' Fast Loses Ground to Mauve in Hospital Scrub Suits," *The Wall Street Journal*, Section 2, June 20, 1984, p. 31. This material is used with permission.

accountant. Some jurisdictions, however, require a mercantile license for anyone offering goods and services for sale. Most require licensing of certain professions, such as accounting, engineering, appraising, and so on.

In addition to your technical-professional skills, you must be proficient at marketing your services and receiving sufficient payment for such services. Moreover, you must be adept at both writing and making oral presentations. In most instances, you will have to write reports about your work and present them orally, using visual aids. To market yourself, develop a contact base by joining professional societies and trade associations. Become as visible as possible. Use direct mail, write articles about your speciality, and give speeches and seminars to groups who represent potential clients. Most qualified consultants clearly know how to apply their expertise, but many fail because they do not know how to present and market it. Without doubt, the first aim of an aspiring consultant is to establish himself or herself as a credible, recognizable figure in the field.

Generally speaking, you do not have to have a string of degrees or several decades of experience to be a successful consultant. Become fairly skilled and knowledgeable in an area, learn how to present and market this skill, charge for it, and you are on your way. Some consulting opportunities include wardrobe selection; vacation planning; information systems analysis; advertising writing; commercial art; testing for water pollution; tutoring and training; tax specialization; alcoholism counseling; word-processing specialization; industrial engineering; location specialization by putting together industries wanting to build plants with cities wanting such plants; development and production of film and video productions, training programs, new product introduction, and razzmatazz for companies' annual conventions and meetings; interior decorating; office design; physical therapy; and gourmet expertise.

To go into consulting, you require little investment; at minimum, all you need is yourself and a space in your home. To be sure, do not undertake expenses that are not absolutely necessary, and do not undertake long-term commitments like expensive advertising agreements, a big office lease, acquisition of elaborate furniture and fixtures, and hiring of an office staff. Start part-time from your home with an answering service. Also, get a plastic zipper-type case for papers, a typewriter, and a few business cards and several boxes of stationery with an appropriate letterhead.

Obviously, you need to get paid a fee for your expertise and information. Beware of those clients who believe in "doing business on a handshake." Get a written agreement, making clear the nature of the engagement, work to be performed, scheduled dates for performance and completion, cost, and the basis for computing your fee. When accepted by the client, the agreement represents an executory contract between you and your client. In setting a cost, you must consider the time required by the engagement. Most consultants develop a per hour or per diem fee. In addition to this fee, clients are charged for direct costs for travel, special report processing, and extraordinary out-of-pocket expenditures. Fee rates vary considerably among consultants because of the demand for certain services, the reputation and experience of the consultant, different sections of the country, and so forth. As a rough rule of thumb, most consultants earn upward of $300 per day. It is reputed that some internationally known consultants earn as much as $10,000 for a half-day seminar—no recording devices allowed.

In some agreements, payment schedules require one third of cost on signing an agreement, one third at some identified midpoint, and one third after final acceptance of services rendered. Some corporations, however, will not pay any portion of an advance, but, at least, they should be required to make specific progress payments at 2-week or 30-day intervals. For fee calculations, you may use the following scheme:

Basic labor or wage rate paid by the industry for the same or equivalent skill	$40.00
Equivalent fringe benefits (e.g., 30 percent)	12.00
Overhead (office space; answering service; typing, copying, and word processing; and office supplies—e.g., 25 percent of base rate)	10.00
Administrative, marketing, accounting, and advertising expenses (e.g., 15 percent of base rate).	6.00
Profit (e.g., 15 percent of aggregate amount)	10.20
Fee per hour	$78.20

SHOPPING CENTER DEVELOPMENT OPPORTUNITIES

The shopping center is a significant part of American consumers' buying experience. These appealing complexes of retail stores draw the traffic to an atmosphere of excitement caused by sparkling lights, periodic firework displays, beautifully decorated display windows, eye-catching motifs (e.g., old-world bazaar motif or Western theme), a variety of interesting exhibits scattered throughout the mall, the beat of music coming from record shops, and the aroma of tempting foods and drinks coming from restaurants.

Many shopping centers, especially the larger ones, contain malls that are weather-protected. Shopping centers are built to provide a variety of products and services in one complex for shopping convenience. They represent a fine balance and mix of multitenants who offer a wide variety of products and services. Indeed, successful shopping centers represent a perfect synergistic marketing facility. They offer more than convenience, comfort, a broad selection of goods and services; they also appeal to customers' emotions and make shopping fun and entertaining.

The development of a shopping center offers good entrepreneurial opportunities to you. But the shopping center is also an umbrella opportunity that offers a variety of specific retail opportunities for the entrepreneur who wants to open a small store. Whether you plan, however, to become the entrepreneur who develops the shopping center or the one who becomes a tenant, you should find the following material helpful even though it is slanted toward the shopping center developer.

Types of Shopping Centers

The modern shopping center has its roots in the retail bazaars similar to the ones found in Asia today. Also, many aspects found in today's shopping center can be traced to farmers' markets and flea markets of older civilizations. Today, shopping centers can be divided into the following five types.

1. *Neighborhood.* Neighborhood centers feature convenience items or services, such as cigarettes, bread, milk, drugs, or hairstyling. They serve a neighborhood of 10,000 to 20,000 people. Customers walk to the center or get there within a 10-minute drive. There are usually no more than 10 stores with the center being anchored by a supermarket and drugstore or, possibly, a cafeteria. Generally, at least a 10-acre tract of land is needed for the center, building, customer parking, employee parking, truck-loading docks, and rear access driveways. Few neighborhood centers have weather-controlled covered malls connecting the stores.

2. *Community center.* The community center serves from 20,000 to over 100,000 people and is located within a 20-minute drive of its customers. It is anchored by a supermarket and a junior department store or regular variety store. Convenience and shopping goods and services are offered by 10 to 20 stores. The developer will locate the center in a central business district near large residential complexes, in any central city area near major residential populations, and in the suburbs where the center is surrounded by residential buildings of all kinds: single-family house, two-family house, garden apartment, and high-rise apartment. In most cases, at least 25 acres of corner property are needed for driving convenience and for the advertising value of visibility from two or more thoroughfares. Also, additional acreage should be bought for restaurants and theater chains that may desire space adjacent to the community center because there is a good traffic flow in and out of the center.

3. *Regional center.* The regional center serves well over 100,000 people who are within a one-hour drive. Sufficient acreage is necessary to provide space for 30 to 60 tenants and the necessary parking and service space. Also, the developer may acquire additional acreage for satellite businesses, such as bank branches, supermarkets, theaters, restaurants, office buildings, and so forth. The major draw is several major, full-line department stores. Other stores include shopping stores, specialty shops, pet stores, convenience shops, and so forth. The complex usually has a weather-controlled mall connecting the stores. These centers are normally located at the intersection of two or more major highways; few of them are built in a major urban area. Most of the new ones are built in outlying suburbs where large, appropriately zoned parcels of land exist.

4. *Superregional centers.* A shopping center that contains three or more major, full-line department stores is classified as superregional. These centers contain over 100 stores built with a weather-controlled mall, located at a major intersection. These centers are, indeed, integrated retail complexes offering a wide variety of convenience stores, shopping, and specialty goods and services. The developer usually acquires 40 or more acres required for the shopping center along with

additional adjacent land that is leased or sold to complementary businesses to give the developer extra profit and to ensure him or her land use control. A super-regional center attracts customers from a wide radius. On Fridays and Saturdays, people may drive over an hour to reach these centers for a day of shopping and entertainment.

5. *Specialty center.* The specialty center concentrates on specialty goods and services. Customers will drive long distances to acquire the goods and services offered by specialty center merchants, who cater to these customers' discriminating tastes and affluence. This kind of center may be anchored by a high-class firm like Neiman-Marcus. Products and services offered at these top-of-the-line pricing centers include gourmet food, exotic gifts, wineshops, camera equipment, personal photography service, art galleries, picture framing, antiques, and so forth.

A different kind of specialty center is a discount center that houses a number of discount outlets. These centers are, in reality, closed-in flea markets. With improvement in quick-erection buildings (e.g., Butler buildings), flexible partitioning, and low construction costs, this kind of shopping center format offers a real opportunity for the entrepreneur who is planning his or her first shopping center venture. Also, advances in tent technology may offer an innovative way to provide tenants space for their retail stalls. Moreover, the use of tents can add a modular aspect for easy expansion or contraction, depending on the level of business and needs and wants of the marketplace. For example, you could have a main tent for the staples with smaller satellite tent clusters that would house specialized goods and services, such as handicrafts, various cuisines, T-shirt lettering, and so forth.

Size of Shopping Centers

The average size of shopping centers is around 300,000 square feet of gross leasable area (GLA). The mall area can require as much as 20 or 30 percent additional space. For example, a superregional center may have 700,000 or more square feet of GLA and 150,000 square feet of mall area. Specialty centers range from 50,000 to 300,000 square feet of GLA. The neighborhood and community centers range from 25,000 (very small) to 700,000 square feet of GLA. A rule-of-thumb of land utilization is 25 percent of acreage for the shopping center building and 75 percent for parking space.

Some shopping center developers are constructing mixed-use configurations that contain office-building–hotel complexes located next to superregionals with over 1 million square feet of GLA. Such complexes require at least 60 to 100 acres of land. Another similar kind of complex may contain several office buildings, a luxury hotel, and a specialty shopping center with no major, full-line department store. In areas where land is scarce, the developer will have to build multilevel, integrated, vertical complexes within the confines of, for example, a block. Such a configuration may contain one or two major, full-line department stores, a specialty center, a luxury hotel, office space, and underground parking.

Parking Space Ratios

The results of a recent study of the Urban Land Institute with funding from the International Council of Shopping Centers recommend the following ratios for adequate parking for a typical center.[10]

1 An average of 4.0 spaces per 1000 square feet of gross leasable area (GLA) for centers having a GLA of 25,000 to 400,000 square feet.

2 An average of 4.5 spaces per 1000 square feet of GLA for centers having a GLA of between 400,000 and 600,000 square feet.

3 An average of 5.0 spaces per 1000 square feet of GLA for centers having a GLA of over 600,000 square feet with some possible downward adjustment of the parking index for centers over 1.2 million square feet of GLA.

Previous shopping center studies indicated somewhat different ratios. For example, earlier industry standards called for 5.5 car spaces per 1000 square feet of GLA. The reasons given by the Urban Land Institute study for the lower ratios included these:[11] (1) a greater tendency by shoppers to avoid centers at peak hours, (2) intensified center competition, (3) an increase in carpooling and mass transit use, and (4) the fact that customers make fewer trips to centers than they previously did.[12]

Tenant Mix

Tenant mix has two aspects: (1) the balance between national and local chains and independent stores and (2) the balance among the various storeroom classifications. Over 80 percent of the gross leasable area of superregional centers is occupied by national chain store units. Another 15 percent of the superregional GLA is occupied by local chain stores. The national chain stores represented a little less of the GLA of regional centers, whereas local chain stores represented a little more of the GLA of these centers. Independent stores, therefore, represent 10 percent or less of regional shopping centers. These chain stores represent about 90 percent of the sales of the regional and superregional centers, but they pay a little less of the total rent and total charges on a proportional basis. In like manner, the independent stores pay 13 to 17 percent of the total rent and total charges.[13]

---

[10]Mary Alice Hines, *Shopping Center Development and Investment* (New York: Wiley, 1983), p. 92. This material is used with permission.

[11]Ibid.

[12]"Lower Parking Ratios Are Recommended," *Shopping Centers Today* (New York: International Council of Shopping), June 1981, pp. 1 and 2. This material is used with permission.

[13]Hines, op. cit., p. 113.

Gross Leasable Area

Most of the space of superregional and regional centers is devoted to general merchandise units, including major department stores. In the mall buildings alone, about a quarter of the gross leasable area is devoted to clothing stores; and about 15 percent of the GLA, to general merchandise stores. Another 15 to 20 percent of the GLA is devoted to food and food services. Many other types of stores offering convenience stores, shopping, and specialty goods and services make up the rest of the GLA of the superregional and regional centers.[14]

In contrast, community centers devote about one third of their space to general merchandise stores, and neighborhood centers devote about the same amount of their space to food and food service stores. General merchandise stores comprise less than 10 percent of the GLA of the neighborhood center. Food and food-service sales make up two thirds of the sales of neighborhood centers but only 40 percent of the sales of community centers. One fourth of the sales of community centers come from general mechandise stores.[15]

From several sources of data, one might conclude that a center will cost from $27 a square foot of gross leasable area up to double that amount—as a general rule. Generally, the smaller the center, the lower the cost per square foot of GLA. The larger the center and the more complicated the construction, of course, the higher the cost. The larger regional and superregional centers may cost $50 to $70 a square foot of GLA. A vertical center built now in the crowded central business district of a major city would probably cost more than $70 a square foot. The land cost of the center city would add a large cost dimension to the overall cost of the center. Suburban land costs may be high but usually nothing like the extraordinarily high costs of central business district land. Foundation costs of high-rise centers are higher than the foundation costs of one- and two-story centers.[16]

Average sales per square foot of gross leasable area (GLA) yield, at best, a ballpark figure. Many experts give an average of $120 to $200 in sales per square foot of GLA *per year*. A polo shop in Dallas does $1,000 in sales per square foot of GLA per year. Stores in a specialty center dealing in high-price items may enjoy an average of $300 to $500 in sales per square foot of GLA per year. A jeweler dealing primarily in diamonds may do even $2,000 per square foot per year. Souvenir and gift shops in the EPCOT Center in Florida do $7,000 in sales per square foot.

Lease Payments

Rent is another figure that is difficult to estimate, but as a rule of thumb, it runs about 10 percent of sales. If, for example, a tenant's sales are running $150 per square foot

---

[14]Ibid.

[15]Ibid.

[16]Ibid., pp. 95 and 100.

of GLA, then his or her rent will be $15 per square foot. Or, if we look at it another way, if the tenant's sales are $300,000 per year, he or she will pay $3,000 in rent. But this is only a ballpark figure because there are many other factors that may dictate the amount of rent charged. These factors entail the location, the amount of store frontage, sales per square foot (as already mentioned), type of merchandise sold, the financial strength of the tenant, the number of built-in fixtures required, and simply supply and demand. A jeweler in a top location with a lot of plate-glass frontage may pay $50 or more rent per square foot. A small specialty food store with little frontage located off the beaten path may pay as little as $6 rent per square foot.

Lease Revenue

From expected sales per square foot of each of the merchants of the tenant mix, you can estimate your total lease revenue. This revenue has got to cover your mortgage debt service, operating costs, overhead, and profit. The base rent per square foot of GLA may start at $15, for example, and increase over time tied to an index, such as the Wholesale Index or Consumer Price Index. Indexed base rents are for your financial protection as the shopping center developer. Lease terms include such things as duration of lease; rent payments; indexed base rent formula, if applicable; definition of space; reciprocal easement agreements; operational rules, regulations, and default clauses; expansion provisions; sales reporting and bookkeeping; developer's right to audit tenant's books; tax payments; insurance coverage; common area maintenance responsibility; storeroom use and restrictions; subletting; promotion and advertising, including the grand opening; merchants' association; sign restrictions; alteration restrictions; and payment for fixtures.

Operational Rules and Regulations

The operational rules and regulations for the center include[17] store opening and closing for customer sales, center opening and closing times for public admission, truck delivery schedules for the loading docks, employee and tenant parking, supervision of storeroom and center management employees, holidays celebrated by the closing of the center, storeroom line of business restriction, required tenant advertising and promotional expenditures, contributions to the mall marketing fund, and attendance at mall management meetings.

Sources of Financing

Sources of financing for shopping center development come from the following sources: an investment group of people with high tax brackets, such as accountants, physicians, and lawyers; savings and loan associations; real estate investment trust

[17]Ibid. p. 146.

(REIT); life insurance companies; pension funds, endowment funds, and foundations; financial subsidiaries of industrial corporations, such as General Electric Credit Corporation; foreign investors; and commercial banks.

Site Analysis and Selection

What are the three main variables for success in the retail business? The answer is (1) location, (2) location, and (3) location. This answer is overstated, but not by much. With better transportation systems, location may not be quite as important as it used to be, but, clearly, a shopping center needs a better location than other kinds of business.

What constitutes a good location for your proposed shopping center? What are the drawbacks and constraints? Clearly, the strategic decision you must make is what type of shopping center you are going to build and where you are going to locate it. But availability of land, zoning regulations, and location characteristics will dictate what type of shopping center you build, and, on the other side, the type of shopping you want to build will dictate what site you look for. It is a trade-off situation. You must compare one against the other to derive an optimum decision.

Do not let the availability of a tract of land at a cheap price dictate where you locate your center. If the tract does not meet certain site selection variables, then it would be foolhardy to construct your center on such a tract, even if it were free. As stated earlier, finding the right location is crucial to the center's success and requires a systematic approach.

Demographics. One of the first things to do is to get a "feel" of the market area and community. Are people moving into the community or leaving it? Positive indicators of growth include land development projects; the presence of major businesses and new businesses moving into the community; the presence of well-kept homes, clean streets, and attractive storefronts; progressive citizen groups; and adequate public services.

Demographic information is certainly important. In addition to the size of the population, many other facts need to be known. What do people do for a living? What is the per capita income? What percentage is married? Single? Divorced? What is the average number of children per household? What is the number who rent and the number who own homes? What are the age and value of these homes? What is the number of air conditioners and other appliances? What is the number of automobiles in each family?

This demographic information can be obtained from census tracts and the chamber of commerce. For a more complete profile of the residents, analyze their life-styles. What do they like to do for entertainment? For hobbies? Do they ski or garden? What are their political preferences? Their traditions? Their culture?

What good is all this information? It helps you target your customers and determine what needs and wants they have. This information enables you to develop the right mix of tenants to serve these needs. A mismatch means failure. A shopping center, for example, with a number of tenants selling maternity clothes, sporting goods, toys, and so forth would not be successful in a retirement community no matter how numerous and affluent the residents might be.

Traffic Analysis.   If you like the community and the demographics seem to fit your shopping center concept, the next question to answer is, How do you get in the way of all those potential customers? Traffic analysis is the answer. What is the flow pattern? Is the traffic clustered during certain times? What are these times? Where is the beaten path? Where are the dead spots? What is the direction of the traffic? What will the customer need on his or her way to work? From work? If most of your business will come from customers coming from work and if the major traffic flow from work is on the west side and you locate on the east, then your center will probably fail. Get pedestrian and car counts from the city hall's planning and traffic engineering departments and from the county and city highway departments.

The key part of traffic analysis is to determine how the traffic passes, who passes, why they pass, when they pass, and where they pass. If most of the people who pass a potential site are teenagers on motorcycles and bicycles going to and from school, then the customer potential for a typical shopping center is nil. Or your traffic analysis performed in June may indicate all the right data for a sufficient number of model customers. But unknown to you is the fact that this traffic may dry up in November and December, the top shopping months. Clearly, the season, month, week, day, and hour should all be input into a traffic survey.

Data from thorough traffic analysis can give you some meaningful numbers. For a simple example, your analysis may show that the traffic generates 10,000 people passing the potential site each day and that 40 percent are potential customers who will spend an average of $10, and your center is open 360 days a year; then the average annual sales volume of the center would be $14.4 million. Once you have this figure, a number of ratios and computations can be applied to determine cost-effectiveness, ability to attract investors and tenants, debt service and payback, rent per square foot, and so forth. For example, if your plan is to build a shopping center of 100,000 square feet of GLA, then you are pretty much on target because the results of your traffic analysis, indicating $14.4 million in annual sales, gives $144 in sales per square foot.

The flow, amount, and nature of traffic may also indicate a special niche that a developer may want to fill. For example, traffic analysis of a downtown business district may indicate that some kind of specialty shopping center may be suited to cater to special traffic such as office workers. Analysis will probably show that peak shopping times are during the lunch hour and before and after work. A shopping complex to serve this traffic would include restaurants, bars, clothing and shoe stores, flower shops, gift stores, bookstores, hairstyling shops, travel agencies, and so forth. Peak shopping times would be during the week, with sales falling off during weekends.

As surprising as it may seem, some out-of-the-way places may serve as ideal sites for certain kinds of customers. A shopping center complex may contain, for example, fabric shops, seamstress and tailor shops, day-care centers and nursery schools, a neighborhood grocery, and hardware supplies for traffic on the back streets or secondary roads.

Infrastructure, Engineering, and Zoning Considerations.   Another important part of location selection includes highway, engineering, and zoning considerations. The proposed site for the center must be served by appropriate utilities, such as natural gas, electricity, telephone lines, cable television, and water and sewerage lines. The site should be well above the flood level with good and unrestricted drainage. The site must be easily accessible by traffic, both for ingress and egress; and traffic, before reaching the site, should not be impeded by stoplights, narrow roadways, and other such obstructions. Freeway ramps should be near the site and long enough to accommodate incoming or outgoing traffic without obstructing normal traffic flow. Moreover, the site must have high visibility.

Soil composition of the site must pass all percolation tests. The surface soils must possess load-bearing qualities. Subsurface conditions must be able to support foundation pilings. In addition, there are many other site regulations the developer must contend with. Cities, counties, and states are empowered to enact and enforce zoning ordinances, which regulate the size of structures, density of population, erection of signs and displays, adjacency to streets and other rights-of-way, parking, use of buildings, and construction materials and design. And if these regulations are not enough, the developer must deal with assorted groups concerned with ecological and environmental factors. These concerns center on land use, noise, pesticide, radiation, hazardous waste, and safety and health controls.

Location Within the Shopping Center

Incidentally, for those of you who plan to enter the retail business via renting space in a shopping center, location *within* the center is important. Normally, the best location is either adjacent to one of the major anchor stores or at the end of the center next to a major thoroughfare. If you are going into a business that requires late hours, such as a drugstore or liquor store, be sure you are located near plenty of internal and external lighting. Also, check the shopping center rules concerning additional store hours. Moreover, if you open a liquor store, drugstore, or convenience store, it is a good idea to locate near a main entrance for quick in-and-out service.

Furthermore, as a prospective tenant, be sure that you understand the lease, the merchant association rules and regulations, assessments for advertising and promotion, the formula for calculating rent, the store hours, renewal provisions, your right to sublet, any restrictions on your use of the property (including your right to hang out a sign or make alterations), or restrictions on installing any special fixtures or equipment. As far as fixtures are concerned, check to see who pays for the installation of special rooms, cabinets, and drapes that cannot be removed when you leave. If the fixtures are permanent and you pay for them, arrange a procedure to be written into the lease for selling these or any other improvements at the end of the lease period. Also, on your own, check local zoning ordinances and building, safety, health, and fire regulations before signing the lease.

Promoting the Shopping Center

An important aspect of traffic analysis is that rent is based on traffic count and the attractiveness of the location, which can be stated in terms of an advertising-rent ratio. With spotty or inadequate traffic, rent is low, and advertising expenses are high because you have to spend great sums of money on advertising to draw customers to your location. People simply don't pass by or come to such a location because it is out of their way, it is in a high-crime area, or highways leading to it are inadequate.

Rent-Advertising Ratio.   The rent charged per square foot of gross leasable area (GLA) in a shopping center ideally located may run, for example, $10, with advertising expenditures running $2, or 20 percent of rent. That is, for rent and avertising, the cost is $12 per square foot of GLA. Sales may run $150 per square foot of GLA. At a poor location, rent may be $5 per square foot of GLA, but it may take $10 or $15 per square foot of GLA to generate the same level of sales. Seldom is it the case, however, that higher advertising expenditures will draw customers to an area where they do not want to come.

Selling the Sizzle.   In any event, promotion and advertising are key functions for any shopping center no matter where its location may be. Even with an ideal location, it cannot be taken for granted that this location will automatically draw the customers. People may pass by your center and need the products or services that you are offering, but you still have to draw them into your stores and sell them. You have to appeal to their emotions. Often you are selling the sizzle, the complete product. Dresses are parties and sex appeal. Suits are good looks and success. Restaurants are well-prepared, tasty food, good service, and atmosphere. Pets are love, companionship, and entertainment. Durable goods and furniture make a house into a home.

Two identical shopping centers with equal locations can open at the same time and have different responses. One can run classical newspaper ads announcing its grand opening, run a few spots on radio and television, and offer low prices on some major items. This shopping center will draw reasonable crowds and enjoy average sales. If, on the other hand, the second shopping center runs newspaper ads offering bargain prices, runs radio and television spots, *and* "sells the sizzle," the center will be mobbed, and sales will skyrocket.

To put on a grand opening spectacular, use clowns to hand out goodies and entertain people; put on a fireworks display; strategically locate different singers, bands, and sound systems—punk rock, middle-of-the-road, whatever—on opposite sides of the shopping center; have local high school bands and cheerleaders display their talents; bring in experts to demonstrate how to garden, ski, golf, cook, repair, or whatever in front of appropriate stores; scatter exhibits—art, antique cars, boats—throughout the mall.

Continuing Advertising and Promotion.   Don't stop with the grand opening. Continue advertising campaigns and promotions. As a shopping center developer, do some of the general advertising and promotion on your own, but require certain levels of standalone and participative advertising by your tenants. If you have general purpose panel trucks that service the shopping center, paint them with symbols, letters, and displays that show the products and services offered at the center; your trucks are on the move up and down the highways and all around town. This approach gives you a lot of eye-catching, free advertising. Your tenants can do the same. A hamburger proprietor can secure a facsimile of a big hamburger on top of his or her service truck for the same reason.

Tie your business to worthy fund-raising promotions. Help sponsor worthwhile causes. Use open-house promotions, and give door prizes. Use gimmicks. For example, every time a sale of over $20 is made in a pet store, have a mechanical dog dig for a plastic bone in which goodies are contained, and give the bone to the customer. Or let the kids "go fishing," and catch plastic fish surprises. Attach inflated balloons that contain tags to a "surprise panel." Every time a customer makes a purchase, for example, a pair of shoes, he or she is allowed to puncture a balloon and receive the prize named on the tag that was in the punctured balloon. Sponsor contests that create a lot of publicity. For example, if one of your tenants owns a sporting goods store, suggest that he or she sponsor a marathon.

Use personalized ads in the newspaper. An ad may read: John Smith says, "I got a haircut my way at Cutter Joe's Barber Shop." Put exhibits about your center in the lobby of your bank or other places that draw additional traffic. Solicit business through mail order, using direct mail and display ads. This represents a great opportunity to increase sales significantly while making marginal expenditures. Other very successful businesses are doing it. For example, the Neiman-Marcus mail order business is growing by leaps and bounds. Use coupons in all your printed media. Demonstrate products in the home, in a supermarket, in the shopping center, or on the back of a flatbed truck. Distribute samples. Use handbills. Welcome newcomers. Where appropriate, use door-to-door salespeople.

Where suitable, personalize show windows. For example, take candid snapshots of passersby, and display them in your show window, and offer a prize to those who can identify themselves. Use tickler files for remembering customers' birthdays and other important events in your customers' lives. If your tenants send invoices, have them insert sales messages and brochures along with the invoice. This is a low-cost way to announce a sale, offer a discount, or a new product or service, or distribute coupons. Produce a shopping center newsletter containing personal and background information on tenants and their families. Also provide additional information about products and services. Give a lot of inside information along with handy tips. Also, join service clubs, and never pass up an opportunity to give a speech to any group.

Prepare a promotion calendar for at least six months ahead, and tie promotions to special days and events. For example, in January, run an after-Christmas sale; in February, run a St. Valentine's Day promotion; in March, run a St. Patrick's Day sale; tie a promotion to a special local event like Founder's Day; tie a rodeo event to selling Western apparel; open the center at a special time, say, early in the morning, for both local people and special transient groups who cannot shop during regular hours.

TECHNOLOGY TRANSFER AND DEVELOPMENT OPPORTUNITIES

The well-being of a country and the gains of its society to a great extent are measured by its technological development. The development of one piece of technology produces the need for other technology. It is a ripple effect, and the ripples expand throughout the society. This ripple effect stimulates conventional technology to improve, and it brings about a more dynamic society that can adapt to change, a society that is better off than its predecessors. This country is in need of people who have the ability and commitment to develop technology and to bring it to full commercialization. For the person who can do this, the entrepreneurial opportunities are virtually limitless.

Overview of Technology Development

We live and work in climate-controlled buildings; we bathe in warm, free-flowing water; we select from closets filled with beautifully designed clothes made from a variety of cloth; we eat fresh fruits, eggs, and bread and drink beverages, all delivered to our doorstep everyday; we have access to a variety of energy sources and a bewildering array of devices and machines that use this energy for our benefit; we are entertained by a constellation of shows beamed into our homes from around the world; we carry on conversations with people virtually anywhere on the globe or in space; within hours we can reach any vacation spot in the world; we can mow our lawns while sitting down; we have access to an infinite number of tools and devices to help us do any job imaginable; we speed in air-conditioned automobiles over highways paved with cement; new machines, drugs, and medical technology battle our diseases; new equipment helps farmers to plow, plant, and reap crops on more land a thousand times more quickly than they could do by hand or with horse-drawn equipment.

Surprisingly, people sometimes wonder whether new inventions benefit them. One often hears a person who is exasperated with a malfunctioning device utter a sarcastic phrase like, "Ah, the wonders of modern technology." Indeed, throughout history, some people have been against technological development. During the economic depression of the 1830s, for example, some persons in the United States demanded a law to end all inventing. They feared that new machines would put people out of work. But during this period, inventors developed the steam loco-motive, the sewing machine, the telegraph, the harvester, and the vulcanizing rubber process, all of which increased the number of jobs and improved the standard of living.

The Need for New Technology

The need for new technology never ends. Today many inventions are needed. For example, we need safe ways to dispose of waste materials; we need crash-resistant fuel tanks; construction workers, soldiers, and roughnecks in the North Sea need low-cost personal heating systems; manufacturers and processors need a viable thumb for robots; we need devices to reduce or eliminate acid rain; and so forth.

For a long time in this country, inventions were always forthcoming; you could always bet that whatever was needed would be invented in this country. Indeed, Yankee ingenuity flourished and provided a wellspring of inventions. This is no longer the situation. For the last several decades, there has been a decline in industrial innovation in the United States vis-à-vis other countries, such as Japan and Great Britain, thus, causing stiff competition for American businesses abroad and even in their own backyard. General Motors, for example, is buying most if its presses and machine tools from Japanese manufacturers. At one time, no one was even close to competing with American machine tool manufacturers. Many other examples could be cited. This unfortunate turn of events has helped cause a mon-strous trade deficit that, in turn, has caused major layoffs and high unemployment. Clearly, if this trend continues, the standard of living and affluence that we have taken for granted will vanish.

Current Malaise

Complacency is a problem. Business and labor enjoyed great successes coming out of World War II and into the early 1960s. They began to feel invincible and smug. Quality was de-emphasized. The United States began to fall behind in nearly all the smokestack industries. Consumers here and abroad wondered if "progress was our most important product." Granted, the momentum from the 1950s and 1960s was so great that we are still leading in some areas, but we lost in others. And some of the businesses that are around today will not be here 10 years from now.

Many of today's professional managers think in the short-term because their performance is measured that way. They are pressured to do those things that will increase return on investment and to pay dividends. Management must be able to sacrifice short-term opportunities for long-term ones. They must not be afraid of risk; indeed, they must be encouraged to take necessary risks to ensure a strong future.

Furthermore, both management and labor lobby for import quotas and tariffs to protect products and jobs from foreign competition. This artificial protection stifles the inventive spirit, gives a feeling of security and self-contentment, and, down the road, causes more problems than it solves.

On the government side, often it seems that policy and programs are adrift on a sea without a compass. Often we are involved in brushfire approaches like bailouts; import quotas and tariffs; export restrictions; and on-again, off-again mazes of regulations.

The Turnaround and Emerging Inventrepreneur

Because of competitive forces, progressive companies will return to an ongoing, strong commitment to research and development and commercialization of new technology. To be sure, a slight turnaround in research and development spending by some American businesses began to appear in the late 1970s and continues a steady climb, indicating a deepening commitment by managements of more progressive companies to R and D. These top companies' expenditures for R and D range from 15 percent to 30 percent of sales. Clearly, such commitment to R and D reflects American industry's concern that foreign competition is steadily eroding the technological lead of the United States. Today the United States is the world leader in R and D spending, especially in information technology and electronics companies, such as IBM, AT & T, GE, ITT, Hewlett-Packard, and Digital Equipment. Other leaders in R and D include General Motors, Ford Motors, United Technologies, Du Pont, Eastman Kodak, Exxon, Xerox, Dow Chemical, and Boeing. All these giants and many smaller companies are becoming more willing to tap into and support technological development outside their companies. Moreover, they show a strong inclination to license viable new technology from individuals.

The key person in this resurgence is a special kind of entrepreneur, called the "inventrepreneur." He or she possesses many of the same characteristics as the entrepreneur explained earlier. The inventrepreneur must have a bulldog commitment to success and the ability to deal with many setbacks. Moreover, the inventrepreneur must be able to work for months or years without much tangible reward or feedback, work in isolation, and reject conventional ways. He or she must have an insatiable urge to try something new. The inventrepreneur must be able to run the long gauntlet of criticism, frustration, and disappointment even before the invention is ready for production and commercialization—and sometimes afterward.

One of the big problems facing the inventrepreneur is that the technology that he or she derives will never be adopted and will lanquish on shelves because it is, in fact, infeasible. Still, many other potential inventions never see the light of day because the inventrepreneur cannot continue his or her work owing to a lack of funding or because he or she has developed something useful but does not have the necessary skills to bring it to full commercialization. The following material helps to solve these problems.

Technology Transfer and Commercialization

Inventrepreneurs have a deep understanding of their technology. So do classical inventors. What, then, is the difference between the two? First, inventrepreneurs will look for an end use for their technology. They will keep a business objective in mind. They will have a better understanding about how to get their idea from a breadboard stage to full commercialization. They will have an appreciation of financial, legal, management, and marketing assistance to get the technology produced and out into the marketplace. They will understand that they need a third party to provide these needs and to guide them to the business objective of sales for the technology. Two main groups that give this kind of assistance are technology transfer firms and developers of R and D limited partnerships.

Technology Transfer Firms.   The primary function of technology transfer firms is to help the inventrepreneurs license their technology and to provide them with funds for patenting, market research, preparation of a business plan, and so forth. The basic tools of licensing and technology transfer are market research, economic analysis, and a legal contract. Normally, technology transfer occurs in one of the following ways: Technology in one country is licensed to a manufacturer or agent in another country, one company licenses technology to another, or inventrepreneurs license their technology to a company that produces and markets it. In this chapter, we are primarily concerned with the latter situation.

Many companies are reluctant to license technology for a variety of reasons. Some simply do not want to deal with an individual. Stories abound where "inventors" have received huge rewards for tools or devices they allegedly developed but that were stolen by corporations. Some of this has happened both ways, where greedy lawyers with an inventor client take advantage of corporations, and corporations take advantage of inventors. Most corporations do not, for their own protection, negotiate directly with individuals. Another reason why corporations may not license technology is because they want to be known as innovators with strong research and development departments.

Alternatively, there are a number of corporations that search for technology to license. They do this for several reasons. First, it is a cheap, low-risk way to bring in technology. Second, a corporation may be looking for a quick, easy, and low-cost way to broaden its product line or may be wanting to establish a start-up division based on the new technology.

Naturally, the question arises as to why individual inventrepreneurs (or a company or a country) would want to license technology. First, they simply don't have the wherewithal to develop fully, produce, and market their invention. Second, they may be able to secure the necessary support to start a business, but they simply, for whatever reasons, don't want to operate a business because they would rather stay in the lab or garage and do what they do best—invent. Third, some inventrepreneurs have struggled for years to get their product to a prototype stage; they want some quick front-end money and to enjoy royalties. Fourth, many new devices, processes, chemicals, and drugs developed in the United States cannot be used in the United States because of various regulations. For example, it takes years to get approval from the Food and Drug Administration for the use of new pharmaceuticals and pesticides in this country. So the strategy is to license such products to a foreign country where the regulations are not as severe. Then, after a number of years, the product may be approved for use in the United States.

How does the licensing process work? The technology transfer firm furnishes a licensing team made up of a technological expert, a business expert, a negotiation expert, and a lawyer. In some instances, all this expertise may reside in one or two licensing professionals. Clearly, the technology must be understood by a disinterested, objective third party. Tough questions must be asked. Is the technology credible? Is the inventrepreneur credible and honest? Is the technology useful? Business and marketing analysis must be performed to determine production costs, projected profits, and end-user acceptance.

A skilled negotiator is certainly a key player in the licensing process. The relationship between the licenser and the licensee is usually a fragile one. The negotiator must know how to bring parties together in a pleasant setting, break the ice, and get people acquainted with each other. The negotiator must understand culture and tradition. The Japanese, for example, want pleasant and extended negotiations lasting several weeks with dinners and social interaction. They want sufficient time to pay attention to the details, to understand fully where you are coming from, and to size you up. People who think they can make a quick deal with the Japanese are in for an awakening. In addition to being aware of protocol, the negotiator must plan each step through the negotiating phase and be able to describe all aspects of the technology, its costs, its marketability, and so forth. Moreover, he or she must constantly test for understanding and agreement, that is, where each party is coming from, throughout the negotiation phase.

The main function of the lawyer is to explain the legal ramifications of the license agreement and draw it up. Key elements of this agreement contain boilerplate, which includes common legal covenants and stipulations; duration of license agreement; the amount of the advance or front-end payment; the amount of royalty payments and what they are based on (usually a percentage of sales); and grantback, which means that if the licensee builds onto the original technology, the licenser has a right to license back this developed technology.

Royalties are set during negotiations. No universal formula exists for calculating royalties, but a royalty rule of thumb may be similar to the following: 2 percent of sales for a new compound or chemical mixture, such as a new pesticide or cleaning solvent; a me-tooer, low-tech, or mid-tech device should command 2 or 3 percent of sales; a unique, one-of-a-kind device may command up to 6 or 7 percent of sales; and a new high-tech product may command as much as 25 percent of sales.

Another thing that technology transfer firms can do for the inventrepreneur is to give him or her guidance and advice that will prevent costly mistakes. For example, to protect themselves from someone stealing their invention and to prove ownership of the invention, inventrepreneurs should keep a log in a bound notebook in which entries are made on each page, dated, signed, and witnessed. The development of an invention is evolutionary; every activity, experiment, and change should be duly recorded for full documentation. In addition, inventrepreneurs should not discuss their invention with others, and they should be careful not to disclose information about it in published material. If it is thus disclosed, the inventrepreneur automatically loses his or her foreign patent rights and has one year to get a patent within the United States; otherwise, at the end of one year, U.S. patent rights are lost.

Another question that a prospective inventrepreneur may want to know is, At what stage can one get a technology transfer firm interested in handling the technology and in helping license it? There is a range of answers. In some rare cases, you may get some help while still in the garage. But at the very least, at this raw stage, the product must be patentable. At this stage, the risk is very high; and the value, very low, so one cannot expect much interest or help and, certainly, not much negotiating leverage in commanding a favorable royalty structure. Probably the ideal time to go for a license is when the technology is developed to a point where it is ready for full commercialization, patented, tested, and ready for production. The problem that the inventrepreneur has, however, is getting the necessary funds and support to reach this stage. That is the reason for the next section.

R and D Limited Partnerships. Research and development limited partnerships are fairly complex financial mechanisms by which investors help individuals perform the necessary work to bring technology to a point where it is ready for production and marketing. The investors, in turn, get healthy expense write-offs and a claim to future earnings in the form of long-term capital gains. The R and D limited partnership is that much needed bridge between the conception of an idea and the time that the idea becomes a start-up business. It helps the man or woman who has an idea but no money. These partnerships serve as both a substitute for, and a complement to, venture capitalists. Normally, venture capitalists will not finance any technology until it is ready for full commercialization.

The U.S. Supreme Court decision in 1974 in *Snow* v. *the Commissioner* removed the legal cloud over the tax deductibility of the investments as expenses and, consequently, touched off the current boom.[18] The mainstream R and D limited partnerships are generally unleveraged. An investor who puts $1 into the deal can typically expect a tax write-off of about $.85. To an investor in the 50 percent bracket, that saves $.425 cents in federal income taxes. In a leveraged R and D limited partnership, the investor puts up the same $1 in cash and, in one common variation, signs notes for another $2. Thus, the investor is deemed to have $3 "at risk" and is able to write off close to that full amount. The amount that can be written off is always subject to change, so investors should consult their tax accountants for the current tax rulings. One of the drawbacks is that with early-stage financing, it is

[18]Thomas P. Murphy, "Is There A Better Way?" *Forbes*, July 2, 1984, p. 201. This material is used with permission.

difficult to make reasonable financial estimates, so often the partnership ends up making a finite commitment to an infinite need.

Developers of R and D limited partnerships state that they serve the financial niche that other investors normally do not serve—the metamorphosis stage in which the caterpillar is changed into a butterfly; where the breadboard is changed into a marketable prototype. The R and D limited partnership does not take an equity position, but it expects that the technology developed will become the base for a full-blown business venture. The typical scenario would go something like this: An inventrepreneur brings his or her idea to a general manager or developer of R and D limited partnerships with a request for funding. A background check is made on the inventrepreneur. Credibility of both the inventrepreneur and the technology is established. Competitive and marketing analyses are made. Patentability of the technology is reviewed. Ideally, the technology is patentable at this stage or will be in the short-term. The inventrepreneur agrees to give up some portion of his or her rights to the technology and assign these to the partnership. Furthermore, he or she agrees that the aim of the technology development is to form a future business to produce and market it.

The R and D limited partnership is formed with an appropriate level of funding, and a research company is formed that may be nothing more than a lab stocked with necessary equipment. The general partner serves as chief administrator of the total project, making sure that proper tax-deductible expenditures are made and that the inventrepreneur receives sufficient administrative and financial support. The general partner also prepares an R and D plan, somewhat analogous to a regular business plan to serve as a road map for the development project.

When the end product is deemed ready for commercialization, venture capitalists or even some of the investors in the partnership are brought in to provide the necessary equity funding to form a start-up venture to construct the facilities for production and marketing. A typical financial package may consist of 10 percent royalties paid to the R and D limited partnership and an equal split of equity ownership between the venture capitalist and the inventrepreneur.

Even though R and D investors deal in the riskiest stage of entrepreneurship, they are still fairly conservative and practical about what they will fund. Logical questions asked include, Is your product idea trying to do too much for too many? Is it too ambitious? Is it overkill? Is it too much of an answer? Are you applying something that we already have and know about to problems to which we have no solutions, or are you trying to reinvent the wheel?

For example, postage-sized receptors can be attached at stress points on any structure, such as airplanes, bridges, buildings, and so forth to test for structural fatigue. Does it sound like a good idea? Maybe. But who is going to install such systems? Most state and federal agencies don't have enough funds to repair highways, let alone install stress-testing systems. Also, such a system probably results in overkill; there are just simply too many data to assimilate and analyze. This project would probably be turned down.

What about interfacing computers to a process that needs real-time feedback?

Take a computer and a visual graphics system, and monitor a series of moves made by a performer, for example, a bowler or football player, and play back the results for appropriate corrections. Or develop a system whereby a deaf person could "see" his or her voice pattern and continually correct it until it matches or fits a correctly pronunciated pattern. Will such ideas receive funding? Without doubt.

Radically new technology is not always better. For example, synfuels still wait in the wings. Energy from corn is a thing of the past. Other energy sources will be a long time in coming to commercialization. We often underestimate how much room for improvement is left in conventional technology and its ability to be adapted to many other uses. Enthusiasts, for example, predicted for years that AC adjustable drives would replace DC motors, but Exxon's abortive excursion into electrical motors demonstrated once again that such change is difficult. Similarly, enthusiasts have long been predicting that electronic controls would replace electromechanical controls in appliances. The transition has not yet occurred. Pneumatic control devices, highly touted during the 1960s, have found only limited application. Much the same is true of thermoelectric cooling.[19]

SELECTED ROLE MODEL PROFILES

Throughout this text and especially in the last several chapters, entrepreneurial opportunities have been presented and analyzed. A treatment of opportunities, however, would not be complete without the presentation of profiles on successful entrepreneurs. It should give you encouragement to see how others got their start, what battles they fought, what obstacles they overcame, and how they refused to accept failure. You should also learn from them and use them as your role models. Here are a few for your consideration.

Hello, Irene[20]

Irene Herlache has always been ahead of her times. Back in the late 1960s, for example, she was a frustrated bank administrator. But instead of complaining, Herlache rounded up $30,000 to buy a telephone answering business based on a back porch in the Chicago suburbs. She quit the bank four years later.

Now, at 68, Herlache has 1,650 customers, 75 employees, 2 offices, and annual revenues of over $1 million. But she's still blazing trails. Last month, for example, Herlache's Du-Page Answer Service installed the latest computerized switchboard

---

[19]Excerpted from Lowell Steele, "Managers' Misconceptions About Technology," *Harvard Business Review*, November–December 1983, p. 138. Used by permission of the Harvard Business Review. Copyright © 1983 by the President and Fellows of Harvard College; all rights reserved.

[20]This profile is an abridgment of the following article: Jeff Blyskal, "Hello Central, Give Me The Computer," *Forbes*, July 2, 1984, pp. 94 and 95. This material is used with permission.

equipment. How else to compete against corporate giants, many of which see the humble business of answering telephones as a land of opportunity?

Quiet corners in telecommunications are hard to find, and this $700 million-a-year backwater is unusually appealing. Pretax margins run to 50 percent of revenues, and the answering business is a fragmented collection of some 4,600 small companies. Customers—typically doctors, plumbers, or real estate brokers—buy basic service for as little as $30 per month.

We-deliver Tom[21]

Thomas S. Monaghan, president and founder of Domino's Pizza, Inc., is probably one of the most unlikely millionaires in the country. Raised in an orphanage, Monaghan worked as a laborer on a number of northern Michigan farms until he was 17, then joined the marines to get his life started. Discharged from the service a few years later and flat broke, he was determined to make it big.

Armed with a plan and hidden managerial abilities he'd never tapped, Thomas Monaghan and his brother borrowed $500 as a down payment and opened a small pizzeria near a Midwestern college campus. Although handicapped by the lack of a phone, the pizza delivery business still took in $99 the first week.

During that first year, Monaghan developed a strategy that allowed him to grow rapidly over the next few years: Establish outlets close to college campuses and military bases, where there was an insatiable demand for pizza, and open only during the peak hours of 4:30 P.M. to 12:30 A.M. or 1:30 A.M.. This would cut back on labor costs and ensure that the manager would be on the premises at all times.

Following this strategic plan, Monaghan opened successful pizzerias at several college campuses over the next few years plus a regional commissary to supply the outlets. Today Monaghan's pizza delivery chain is the largest in the country with 300 stores operating in 28 states.

Kapor's Caper

In the 1960s, Mitchell D. Kapor adored the Beatles, grew his hair long, and joined protest marches against the Vietnam War. In the 1970s he worked as a disc jockey for a rock radio station, taught transcendental meditation, and earned a master's degree in psychology. In the 1980s, Kapor became a millionaire.

Kapor is an example of baby-boomers who have turned from protests to profits. As president and founder of Lotus Development Corporation, Kapor has orchestrated one of the brightest success stories in the personal computer software market. Lotus' first product, a software package dubbed 1-2-3, which integrates computer graphics, information management, and spread sheet analysis, has

[21]This profile is an abridgment of a case in Duane Newcomb, *Fortune-Building Secrets of the Rich* (West Nyack, N.Y.: Parker Publishing Company, 1983), pp. 32 and 33, and is used with permission.

topped best-seller lists for more than a year. Symphony, which adds word processing and communications, is another successful product.

To help preserve Lotus' distinctive character, top managers recently drafted a statement of company philosophy. Among the key features are belief in the dignity of the individual, ethical behavior, and a sense of humor. The challenge Kapor faces is to keep his company's corporate culture as healthy as its financial performance. Says he: "It's a balancing act between people and profits."

A Conveyor to Success

Tom Loberg's firm began as Hydro-Controls in 1945. It manufactured hydraulic pumps, lawn mower parts, and other items. Loberg was the man who first experimented with a rotary blade on a lawn mower, the design used almost exclusively today.

Loberg's big innovation was, however, the conveyor he built for a friend's feed and seed operation in Wisconsin in 1947. Others in the feed, seed, and grain industry began to ask for the conveyors, and Loberg was on his way. The company really took off in 1964. That was the year the company devised the idea of shipping to a customer any standard conveyor system within 24 hours of order. "If it's late, we pay the freight" was the slogan the company used to guarantee that 24-hour shipping commitment.

Sales are over $40 million, and Loberg's customers range from family groceries that need a single section of conveyor to unload a produce truck at the back of the store to companies, such as Delta Airlines, Fisher-Price, Wal-Mart, Nike, and Texas Instruments. Besides the American market, the conveyors are exported to countries such as Brazil, Peru, Saudi Arabia, and the Soviet Union.

Handy Andy[22]

Andy Prokosh stumbled on the idea to package a home kit when his family built a vacation home designed by his father. It was easy and didn't require any particular skill. As a result, the family had a great time. Prokosh realized then that there were a tremendous number of people who wanted to build their own vacation cabins or homes, yet needed something that could be put together without any previous experience.

The idea stuck in his mind, and several years later he designed a house for the nonbuilder that can be put together like a paint-by-number kit. "The kit," Prokosh explains, "is designed for people who can't tell a nut from a bolt and aren't even sure which end of the hammer hits the nail." It contains all the needed tools, two ladders, two carpenter's aprons, and a booklet that includes full-size drawings of each nail and all screws. If unsure which nail to use, the beginning builder can compare it with the drawing. Because of his ability to see the needs of a large untapped group of

[22]This profile is an abridgment of a case in Newcomb, op. cit., pp. 77 and 78.

people and an economy that now promotes do-it-yourself projects, Prokosh is well on his way to a giant fortune.

I-Bought-the-Company Victor

Around the world and in over 15 languages, Victor Kiam announces to television viewers that he liked the Remington shaver his wife gave him so much that "I bought the company." What he does not say is that the deal was a leveraged buyout (LBO).

In 1979, Kiam put up less than $1 million of his own money, borrowed $24 million on the basis of the company's assets and projected cash flow, and bought Remington Products, Incorporated. He paid off all his bank debt in less than 12 months—some nine years ahead of schedule. The business has continued to grow rapidly, more than doubling its sales and its U.S. market share and exporting around the world—even to Japan.

In some respects, the deal was right out of a textbook. The company had a solid niche and a healthy market share. Kiam put up his own money and thus had great incentive. And the price was right: Remington sold at around book value, so Sperry Corporation was satisfied because it did not have to take a write-down. Kiam liked the price because it was not inflated by the Remington name, which he considered a valuable asset. Part of the debt was at a fixed rate. Sperry gave Kiam a $4 million mortgage loan on the Bridgeport, Connecticut plant and took back $3.5 million in subordinated debentures. Kiam did not have to pay the $6 million for Remington's foreign assets until the end of the first year.

As of 1979, Sperry's Remington Division had lost more than $30 million over the previous four years. In 1985, Kiam's Remington Products had sales approaching $200 million and a pretax profit of some $15 million, about 14 times Kiam's initial equity investment. Now Remington is expanding its product line and sales are growing by leaps and bounds. The risks may have been higher than those of many LBOs, but so are the rewards.

A Gadget Freak[23]

To compete, traders demand fast, accurate quotations from a wide range of dealers. And supplying those quotes is New York-based Telerate Inc., a little company and unique franchise operation that has been growing at a fast clip. Today Telerate's data base is the industry standard although it faces stiff competition from well-heeled competition such as Reuters, the London-based news and financial giant.

Neil Hirsch, founder and chief executive officer (CEO), had the idea for Telerate at the age of 22 and parlayed it into a company with a market of $700 million. A college dropout, with more time than money, Hirsch hung out at a Merrill Lynch

---

[23]This profile is an abridgment of the following article: Robert Barker, "Growing Pains, Telerate Faces New Rivals, Flattening Orders," *Barron's*, June 25, 1984, pp. 6, 7, and 16. This material is used with permission.

branch in Manhattan, fascinated by the electronic quote monitors. "I was always a gadget freak," explains Hirsch. After reading an article about how the dealers in the commercial paper market had to rely on telephone and telexes to trade, Hirsch got an idea: Why not link up the commercial paper markets electronically?

Hirsch no longer has time to hang out at his local brokerage firm. Instead, he runs things from his office on the 104th Floor of the World Trade Center, where a black-vested waiter regularly refills Hirsch's glass of orange soda. Hirsch believes the potential for future growth is "enormous." He is planning to export his services as well as adding other services.

Sell-the-Sizzle Joe[24]

Joseph Cossman, the millionaire and mail order genius, regularly uses the power of habit to help promote products. First, for every product he wants to sell, he puts out a new product release (a one-page description of the product along with its use), which is mailed to hundreds of magazines around the country. Second, whenever he travels, Cossman writes to the producers of television and radio shows in cities he plans to visit and offers to talk about his latest product or the mail order business in general. Third, Cossman regularly attends trade shows and at every one habitually attempts to create a unique selling atmosphere.

At one New York toy show, for instance, Cossman had a gun that shot bits of potatoes—the "spud gun." He rented a room and asked potato associations across the country to send him enough potatoes to fill that room. He then sent news releases to every editor, writer, columnist and television and radio station in New York City. He set up spud-gun displays in stores around the convention center and handed out spud-gun sheriff's badges to every person attending the convention. Cossman also contacted a local orphanage and offered the institution all the potatoes it could use if it would send him enough children to put on a spud-gun battle. He also had 8000 pounds of potatoes dumped on the sidewalks in front of the hotel and turned the children loose to put on a battle royal.

The result: Fifty thousand pounds of potatoes arrived from potato associations across the country, every newspaper and television station in New York City reported the promotion, the spud-gun battle made all the papers, and buyers swamped the Cossman suite, where they found a room full of potatoes and models in potato sacks serving coffee. At this particular show, Cossman oversold the spud gun by 400,000 units.

Head Gets Ahead[25]

In 1947, Howard Head, then an aerospace designer, metals expert, and ski enthusiast, began to design, build, and test metal skis. Working in his home shop, he

[24]This profile is an abridgment of a case in Newcomb, op. cit., pp. 128 and 129.

[25]This profile is paraphrased from James Brian Quinn, "Technological Innovation, Entrepreneurship, and Strategy," *Sloan Management Review*, Spring 1979, by permission of the publisher. All rights reserved.

would create a ski, produce a few, and then beg ski professionals to test them. Despite their disparaging comments and three years of work that produced nothing but broken and twisted skis, Head persisted. He was described as "possessed by his idea," a "fanatic" on the subject. After each test—and failure—he would redesign the ski, make some more, and take them out for tests. Head worked night and day out of his own home. He ran out of his own money, and his company, which he had incorporated with only $8,000, almost went under. A timely infusion of $60,000 (for 40 percent of the company) saved it. Only after seven years and scores of design failures did Head finally begin to make some money from his enterprise. Hundreds of others had tried to design metal skis, but had failed. Head's skis worked so well they were called "cheaters" by the trade. They sold for $100 in a market used to paying only $25 and helped create the ski boom of the 1950s.

One Who Stopped to Smell the Roses[26]

After Bob Lewellen of Kansas City made his bundle, he chose to leave the workaday world. His personal code of independence: if you've got it, don't flaunt it. "I'm not the sort to drive a $40,000 Porsche," says Lewellen, 46, a city councilman. "For me independence means being able to participate in community service." In 1962, with $500 of savings from his job as a TV director, Lewellen bought a Pizza Hut franchise. Later he formed a corporation that bought a Taco Bell franchise for $100,000. In 1972, he sold out at a profit of more than $500,000 and handed the money to real estate developers to invest for him. "The time came for me to stop building a war chest," he says. "A person can only eat and drink so much." Besides serving his city, Lewellen is secretary of the Leukemia Society of America. He also works part-time as an assistant director in ABC and CBS broadcast booths during baseball and football season. His favorite luxury: taking his three sons to sporting events around the country.

SUMMARY

This chapter covers a wide range of entrepreneurial opportunities from moonlighting ventures to the development of new technology. Moonlighting ventures provide an ideal way for the budding entrepreneur to enter a business venture in his or her spare time. It is a low-risk way of going into business. In addition, it generates extra income and gives the entrepreneur a change of pace from his or her regular job.

Development of a shopping center is an ambitious undertaking and presents opportunities for high returns on an individual's investment. Also, the shopping center embraces a number of specific opportunities for the smaller retailer. A shopping center developer can build a center to fit almost any market and location

[26]This profile is paraphrased from John Stickney, "The New March to Financial Independence," *Money*, June 1984, p. 74, and used with permission.

containing an appropriate mix of product-service retailers. Other key considerations include site selection, engineering and zoning regulations, and lease revenue calculations. For ensuring the success of a shopping center, innovative advertising and promotion activities are highly desirable, if not imperative.

Technology transfer and development opportunities are very special in that the key player is a person whom we refer to as the inventrepreneur. He or she is an inventor-entrepreneur, a person who has a strong technological expertise and a good understanding of business, marketing, and financing. This area of opportunity presents some of the greatest challenges but, at the same time, some of the greatest potential for high rewards. The need for new technology in the United States is great. Technology transfer firms and R and D limited partnerships will help the inventrepreneur meet this need.

Many people just like yourself have exploited entrepreneurial opportunities and become successful. A number of these people are presented to you for encouragement and inspiration and to show you the variety of opportunities available to you and the diversity of people who pursue such opportunities. These people, who serve as role models, are old and young, men and women, educated and uneducated, skilled and nonskilled, born with advantages, born without advantages, and so on. The point is that in their own way, they have achieved success.

ASSIGNMENT

1 List the reasons why people go into moonlighting opportunities. Explain why you would pursue such opportunities. Describe a moonlighting venture that fits your inclinations and talents. Explain.

2 Name and give an example of the types of shopping centers.

3 Why are shopping centers location-dependent? Explain how one selects a good location.

4 Based on a rule of thumb, what is the percentage of acreage devoted to parking space? To the building?

5 What does GLA mean? Why is it an important measurement in shopping center development?

6 Using a rule of thumb, explain what percentage of the building GLA and mall space are.

7 What is the general average of sales per square foot of GLA?

8 List three sources of financing for shopping center development.

9 Prepare a promotion and advertising plan for your shopping center opening. Do the same for the first year of operation.

10 In your own words, define *inventrepreneur*.

11 Explain why some countries, such as Japan and Great Britain, have moved ahead of the United States in technology development and why many of their products and services are outselling the United States technology both here and abroad.

12 Explain how the technology transfer firm helps the inventrepreneur.

13 Explain how licensing technology works.

14 Explain how R and D limited partnerships help inventrepreneurs.

15 Explain the gap that R and D limited partnerships fill.

16 Choose your favorite entrepreneurial role model, and prepare a report or profile about him or her.

BIBLIOGRAPHY

Banks, William C. "You're Not Alone in the Moonlight." *Money*. April 1984.

Barker, Robert. "Growing Pains, Telerate Faces New Rivals, Flattening Orders." *Barron's*. June 25, 1984.

Blyskal, Jeff. "Hello Central, Give Me The Computer." *Forbes*. July 1984.

Gillis, Phyllis. *Entrepreneurial Mothers*. New York: Rawson Associates, 1984.

Goldstein, Rill Ann. "Carving a Niche in Gourmet Foods." *In Business*. February 1983.

Henderson, Angelo B. " 'Pukey Green' Fast Loses Ground to Mauve in Hospital Scrub Suits." *The Wall Street Journal*. Section 2, June 20, 1984.

Hines, Mary Alice. *Shopping Center Development and Investment*. New York: Wiley, 1983.

Holtz, Herman. *How to Succeed as an Independent Consultant*. New York: Wiley, 1983.

Kanter, Rosabeth Moss. "The Middle Manager as Innovator." *Harvard Business Review*. July– August 1982.

Lander, Jack. *Make Money by Moonlighting*. Wilmington, Del.: Enterprise Publishing, 1982.

"Lower Parking Ratios are Recommended." *Shopping Centers Today*. New York: International Council of Shopping Centers, June 1981.

Meislin, John. "Hot Stuff in a Mustard Jar." *In Business*. February 1983.

Murphy, Thomas P. "Is There a Better Way?" *Forbes*. July 2, 1984.

Newcomb, Duane. *Fortune-Building Secrets of the Rich*. West Nyack, N.Y.: Parker Publishing, 1983.

"New and Growing." *In Business*. February 1983.

Parker, R. C. *The Management of Innovation*. New York: Wiley, 1982.

Quinn, James Brian. "Technological Innovation, Entrepreneurship, and Strategy." *Sloan Management Review*. Spring 1979.

Rubinger, Bruce. "Industrial Innovation: Implementing the Policy Agenda." *Sloan Management Review*. Spring 1983.

Schmidt, Allan H., and Ira Alterman. *Computing for Profits*. New York: Macmillan, 1984.

Seltz, David D. *A Treasury of Business Opportunities for the '80s*. Rockville Centre, N.Y.: Farnsworth Publishing Company, 1982.

Steele, Lowell. "Managers' Misconceptions About Technology." *Harvard Business Review*. November–December 1983.

Stevenson, Howard H. and David E. Gumpert. "The Heart of Entrepreneurship." *Harvard Business Review*. March–April 1985.

Stickney, John. "The New March to Financial Independence." *Money*. June 1984.

Wagner, Martha. "Good Times at the Bijou." *In Business*. February 1983.

PART FIVE

LEGAL AND
FINANCIAL CONSIDERATIONS

CHAPTER 12

Structuring the Business Venture

INTRODUCTION

You now have a basic product-service idea in mind; you may even have a prototype. You may have commitments from key people who will become members of the founding entrepreneurial team. You may be spending a lot of time on your venture while holding down a full-time job. Your market segments and their potential and your pro forma financial statements are still only "off-the-top" estimates even though you have performed some rigorous analysis. You may even have some venture capitalists and other investors lined up who *might* provide start-up capital. You have probably developed business relationships with an accountant, a lawyer, a banker, and an insurance agent. You are wondering whether to incorporate or take the sole proprietorship or partnership route. The objectives of this chapter are these.

1 To discuss how to build a winning entrepreneurial team and elect a top-notch, helpful board of directors.
2 To disclose how to select a legal business form, such as sole proprietorship, partnership, or corporation.
3 To describe how to comply with certain business formalities.

THE ENTREPRENEURIAL TEAM

As noted earlier, the key to success and winning is the "jockey, not the horse," which is another way of saying that the entrepreneurial team is the most important element in the venture creation process. General George Doriot, recognized by many as the father of the American venture capital industry, is well noted for his preference for "a Grade A entrepreneurial team with a Grade B idea."

Building the Entrepreneurial Team

Probably nothing in entrepreneurship is less understood than the dynamics of organizing and building an effective entrepreneurial team. In essence, building an entrepreneurial team is no different from building a great football team; get the right people for each position; get everyone to do his or her job while working together as a team, and you will have a winner. On the other hand, bring together a group of people where the chemistry is not right, where philosophies clash, where skills do not fit, and where there is little goal congruency, and your venture will fail no matter how good the product-service idea is.

The entrepreneur, as the founder, needs people around him or her who have the entrepreneurial spirit; the corporate types and nine-to-fivers won't do. The entrepreneur needs people who are dedicated, people who will work around the clock if need be, people who are enthusiastic, and people who will brainstorm and solve problems.

Formation of the entrepreneurial team is like getting married; it should be approached with great care and thought. Partners should be selected as one would an ideal spouse, and they should complement the founder's personal and business strengths; the chemistry should be right. Vibrations should be in tune, and the members should *respond* to each other. A prospective member's trust and commitment should be carefully measured. Expectations should be brought in line with realities and clearly delineated before anyone is officially brought on board.

An extended "mating dance" is needed among potential team members, preferably during a moonlighting period of planning the business and testing relationships and commitments prior to actually launching the venture. The courtship should be tested thoroughly before ownership and other commitments are solidified, for they are very difficult and costly to alter or revoke once established. Preparing the business plan, discussing and presenting it to potential investors, working on a prototype, and dealing with other prospective team members all provide unique opportunities to test the potential marriage.

How Investors View the Entrepreneurial Team

Both academic studies and venture capitalists' experiences seem to confirm that a team effort is more likely to succeed than is the individual effort. The team theoretically should include a complementary group of people whose specialized skills cover the major functional needs of a business enterprise, such as information systems and accounting, marketing, and engineering and production. If a business plan presented to venture capitalists and other investors is properly organized by an experienced entrepreneurial team, these investors will, at least, look further into the deal; if the entrepreneurial team appears to be inexperienced and perhaps naive, it is a safe bet that they will "pass" on the deal.

Most venture capitalists squeeze a business proposal through four test gates before giving any serious attention to it. These are (1) the quality of the entrepreneurial team, their business experience, and their relative strengths in various areas such as general management, marketing, and so forth; (2) the market, how big it is, how much of it is penetrable, who the competitors are, and methods and costs of distribution; (3) the product or service, what need or want it fills, what it replaces, how it is used, its ease of use, and patent protection if any; and (4) the business plan that shows over the next three to five years all aspects of the venture, how it all fits together, and the capital required; if the venture makes sense, the business plan will be a good distillation of it, and the entrepreneurs as well as the venture capitalists will be able to see one version of how the entire venture could get started.[1] If the business plan cannot make it through the first test gate, capital will be difficult, if not impossible, to raise.

---

[1]Donald M. Dible (ed.), *Winning the Money Game* (Santa Clara, Calif.: Entrepreneur Press, 1975), pp. 59–62. Adapted by permission of Reston Publishing Company, a Prentice-Hall Company, 11480 Sunset Hills Road, Reston, Virginia 22090.

Working Out a Fair Arrangement

Numerous sensitive issues relating to titles, salary, stock, and responsibilities can become explosive. All major issues must be resolved up-front. A faint consensus and hesitant commitments by team members will lead to poststart-up blues for all concerned. An essential first step is to help team members recognize the various factors that should influence their decisions concerning ownership and salaries. For example, these might include who generated the idea for the venture, sweat equity, expertise, track records relative to the needs of the business; potential contribution to the firm's goals; dollars available to invest personally; and effort in preparing the business plan. After the venture is flourishing, initially agreed-on salaries and stock positions can be adjusted, if necessary, to reflect actual contributions.[2]

Experience has shown that a "democratic team" is a hard way to go about organizing the business; democracy may be a sensible way to organize a political program, but it doesn't seem to be feasible for a young business. It is far better to have one person in the group as a clear leader. It is also a good idea when organizing the entrepreneurial team to consider the appropriate participation of the various members and set up a "management stock pool" in which stock is purchased by the founding members, vesting ownership with them over a period of three or four years.

Suppose it turns out after a short period of time that one of the founders finds the degree of commitment more than he or she can support and wants to back out. Then there is a prearranged plan for this individual to sell back at least a portion of his or her stock to the management pool, from which it can be resold to his or her replacement, who will also have to be a key member of the entrepreneurial team. It may even turn out after six months that the president, for one reason or another, wants to leave and take his or her stock with him or her. Obviously, a new president must be found who must be given proper incentives. This matter should be considered at the outset so that you avoid a built-in problem that careful planning might have otherwise detected.

The "buy-out provisions" that are sometimes established between the principals of a partnership are a similar method of avoiding conflicts and difficulties among close associates. In contemplating the details of such a separation, one is reminded of the parable of the two kids disagreeing over how to divide up the 50 percent ownership each had in a layer cake: "You cut it in half, and I get to pick which half."[3]

---

[2]Jeffry A. Timmons et al., *New Venture Creation—A Guide to Small Business Development* (Homewood, Ill.: Richard D. Irwin, 1977), pp. 346–47.

[3]Dible, op. cit., p. 69.

THE BOARD OF DIRECTORS

If the venture is incorporated, a board of directors will have to be formed. Each member of the board has a fiduciary duty to the corporation and its shareholders. Being fiduciaries, directors must act with the utmost good faith and are held accountable for any breaches of trust in their corporate dealings. Selecting competent, influential board members can be beneficial to the business venture in not only fulfilling fiduciary responsibilities but also in providing counsel, guidance, and practical assistance.

Selection of Board Members

One extremely important consideration, often given little thought by entrepreneurs who incorporate their venture, is selection of the board members. A small, closely held corporation usually has on its board the founder entrepreneur, a spouse or relative or friend, and perhaps three or four other acquaintances. By chance such a group may represent a good, viable board. Nevertheless, such boards are too often selected without thought and are of little use to the venture. Working directors should be selected who can make significant contributions to the new corporation.

Most ventures have a board of between five and seven people. Different theories exist among venture capitalists as to what constitutes the optimum composition of the board. One view holds that it is useful to have only one member of the entrepreneurial team on the board, preferably the president, with perhaps four or five outside people. With this approach, the board can then review the performance of anyone on the team with the president in complete candor. Others hold that this separation need not be so rigid and that, on a seven-person board, perhaps two or even three of the team should be represented. This representation of management will suffice in those cases where the predominant investment position or the controlling shareholder position or both lie outside the team. Obviously, that can be modified by the election of management nominees with a greater or lesser degree of independence where control rests with the management group.

How Directors Can Help

In some instances, entrepreneurs may want to have the fun of always being at bat without having to go in the bushes and retrieve the ball. They want to call all the shots. The investment objectives of the participants as well as the relative proportions of the board of directors are different in each venture, but most investors or lenders seem to favor ventures in which the outside investors have a majority ownership position with effective control of the board during growth periods even though the entrepreneurial team may have a substantial ownership and, in fact, run the company with little "interference."

Often, however, when the venture is getting started, entrepreneurs need all the help they can get. When the system functions properly, the entrepreneurs are not only pleased with the support their directors and investors can give but find there is a good deal of problem solving in which both groups can participate. Stories abound about fledgling entrepreneurs trying to get things done without success, such as getting goods shipped on time, credit from vendors or banks, urgent repairs made, orders from potentially big customers, and employment of top people. Often one phone call from a board member to a friend in high places can get more done than the entrepreneur could get done in months of chasing around and going up blind alleys.[4]

The relationships between the management team and the board of directors should be fairly straightforward. The management team runs the day-by-day operations of the company; the board does not. The board has a responsibility to the shareholders to see that management carries out its responsibilities properly. The entrepreneurial team looks to the board much as they might to an in-house management-consultant group. If the board of directors has been carefully selected, its members have "been there before." Here are some examples of questions with which an experienced board can help a management team: How do I arrange for a licensing deal in Japan? My controller says I should lease the equipment from the XYZ Company rather than the ABC Company—has the controller analyzed the trade-offs properly? We want to sell a big order to Xerox, but they say we have no financial backing. Can you help us convince them otherwise? How much business can we swing on the present capitalization? Are the operating ratios that we are encountering with respect to receivables, payables, and inventory feasible for our kind of business in our stage of growth? Are we getting a reasonable deal from our banks on receivables compared to other situations with which you are familiar?

The essence of the argument is that management may be "too close to the trees to see the forest," and it takes the objective viewpoint of a competent observer away from the pressures of the business to see the problems in proper perspective. If the directors have been picked properly, several of them will be familiar with businesses of comparable size in this field of activity and should be able to make useful comments on these matters. An important point to remember is this: The most useful members of the board of directors are often those who have had detailed operating experience with problems similar to those at hand. For a business with potential production or manufacturing problems, a board member with production experience might be preferred to the dentist who happens to be an investor and a friend of the president. The well-organized president will work out the essential issues with the management team and then propose alternatives to the board for their consideration. On key issues, management proposes, and the board disposes.

[4]Ibid., p. 72.

In the final analysis, if the management team performs badly, it is up to the board to recognize that a change in management is required and to act accordingly.[5]

INTRODUCTION TO LEGAL BUSINESS FORMS

The various legal business forms offer tax, legal, and financial advantages and disadvantages. Your entrepreneurial goals should be facilitated, not hindered, by your chosen business form. In the United States, a substantial body of law surrounds the legal forms of business organization. These forms include sole proprietorship; partnership, including general partnership, limited partnership, joint venture, family partnership, and syndicate; corporation; and trust, including real estate investment trust (REIT), business trust, and personal trust. In this chapter, however, we devote our attention to the sole proprietorship, the partnership, and the corporation.

A typical scenario would be for you to start as a sole proprietorship or partnership and sooner or later end up with a corporation. Many experts may, however, advise you to start as a corporation, elect Subchapter S Corporation tax treatment, and later convert to a regular corporation. The following material provides you with some major considerations that at least help you to gain a perspective on this very important business form decision. In areas like this, however, the caveat is always this: Consult your accountant and your lawyer.

SOLE PROPRIETORSHIP

The sole proprietorship is largest in number and smallest in dollar volume of sales. It is the pervasive form in the small-business area. The single owner of the business takes full legal, tax, and financial liability for the business. It is the oldest form of business and is the purest form of free enterprise and raw entrepreneurship. In a sense, it is the absence of a legal form of business. An individual creates a business by the simple act of "putting up a sign and opening the door." In some instances, permits or licenses are required, and if the proprietorship is conducted under a trade or created name, a small filing fee may be required. Otherwise, starting a proprietorship may cost nothing.

Although an entrepreneur may be personally satisfied to conduct his or her business as a sole proprietorship, it might be more advantageous for business and tax purposes to incorporate. Then again, if the business is small and earnings are less than, say, $25,000 and there are no intentions of attracting investors, the costs of

[5]Ibid., p. 73.

incorporation and the complexities involved in running a business in the corporate form may mitigate against such a decision. In the final analysis, the decision of whether to do business as a corporation depends on the size and nature of the entrepreneur's business, his or her expectations for future growth and the source of capital for this growth, and other positive characteristics of the corporate form.

Advantages of a Sole Proprietorship

Some distinct and significant advantages exist for this legal form of business. Here they are.

1 Unlike the situation in a partnership or corporation, no agreements are needed to create, manage, or terminate a sole proprietorship; it is a one-person show.

2 Because it is a one-person show, the owner is the only one who calls the shots. There are no committee meetings—no waiting on people from the home office to make up their collective minds; therefore, it is easy to make decisions. Indeed, it is the lack of control that discourages many entrepreneurs from switching from a sole proprietorship to a corporation or partnership.

3 Relatively few legal requirements exist such as maintaining extensive records, filing forms, or keeping minutes; and the cost of forming and operating the business is minimal. Compared with corporations, regulations are minimal.

4 The owner may borrow money on assets outside the business. And although it's not a good idea, assets can be easily comingled. For example, a cash sale from the business may be used to pay the house note.

5 There is no double taxation as occurs with corporations.

6 The owner can use expenses and losses of his or her proprietorship as tax deductions against personal income.

7 A sole proprietor is not an employee. Although he or she can set up a retirement plan for employees, the plan will be disqualified for tax purposes if the sole proprietor receives any benefits thereunder. However, he or she can set up a Keogh plan, which is a retirement plan for self-employed individuals. In the past, many sole proprietors incorporated their businesses as a means of establishing retirement funds that were far larger than those available to the self-employed under the Keogh Act. One of the things that the Employee Retirement Income Security Act of 1974 (ERISA) did was to make vast improvements in certain important features of Keogh pension and profit-sharing plans. These features not only allow a self-employed person to improve existing Keogh plan benefits for himself or herself but also encourage many self-employed businesspeople who are not incorporated to set up new Keogh plans.

Disadvantages of a Sole Proprietorship

Unfortunately, many significant disadvantages exist for those entrepreneurs who select the sole proprietorship business form.

1 Some would say that the major disadvantage of a sole proprietorship is the lack of continuity when the sole proprietor dies. Although business continuity is important for some, there are, however, other disadvantages just as severe.

2 As stated earlier, the proprietor and the business are a single legal entity. The proprietor, therefore, is wholly and personally liable for all his or her debts without regard to whether they are incurred for personal or business reasons.

3 The problem of obtaining credit and securing capital rests on the sole proprietor's personal credit standing and reputation. It is difficult to involve others in ownership because the prospective investors incur unlimited personal liability. Few wealthy people are willing to expose their personal fortunes to a struggling small business. Therefore, if the entrepreneur plans to raise capital from venture capitalists or other financing sources in the future, then he or she should avoid the sole proprietorship form of business.

4 Often the sole proprietorship has a "one-horse outfit" or "fly-by-night" image; consequently, many suppliers and companies do not want to deal with this business form.

5 The uncomplicated tax treatment of the sole proprietorship is one reason why this business form is popular. But in terms of special tax benefits, there is nothing special about it. Indeed, the advantage of not being subject to double taxation may diminish when one looks at other factors, such as the individual owner's tax bracket (which may exceed that of a corporation), the inability to deduct a salary paid to the owner as an expense, the inability to take advantage of certain fringe benefits, and the ability of a corporation to retain earnings for future expansion and not declare such earnings as dividends. Moreover, all normal profits of the business are usually taxed as ordinary income to the owner. If the proprietor sells his or her business, the tax law states that the proprietor has sold not a single asset but individual assets of the business and must allocate the purchase price to all the individual assets carried on the books, including goodwill. The proprietor must recognize an ordinary gain on some of the assets rather than report the whole gain as a capital gain, which he or she could do if he or she sold all the stock in a corporation.

PARTNERSHIP

The partnership form of joint ownership involves two or more persons or investment entities. In a *general* partnership, all partners have equal legal and financial responsibility for the debts of the business. The work contributions made by the partners may be unequal and the partnership agreement may specify unequal profit, cash flow, and depreciation distributions depending upon their respective equity contributions. A similar form called a joint venture is more limited in scope and duration, but, for all practical purposes, it is identical with a general partnership and is treated the same for tax purposes. A *limited* partnership is an association formed by one or more general partners and one or more limited partners. The limited partners have limited liability and are also restricted from participating in management of the partnership. A general partner or partners who manage the partnership have unlimited liability as in any ordinary partnership.

Please bear in mind that many of the advantages and disadvantages listed later can be modified by a partnership agreement. For example, if a new partner does not wish to be held liable for past obligations of the partnership, an agreement can be drawn up and signed by all partners to effect this stipulation.

A word of caution, however, is in order when drafting partnership agreements. Businesses that in substance more nearly resemble corporations than partnerships, for tax purposes, will be considered "associations" by the IRS and taxed as corporations. To avoid this kind of tax treatment, be sure that your partnership and the agreement have more noncorporate characteristics than corporate ones. The four basic corporate characteristics are (1) continuity of life; (2) centralized management, such as corporate headquarters; (3) limited liability of shareholders; and (4) ease of transfer of ownership.

Advantages of a General Partnership

The advantages of a general partnership are these.

1 Partners share in the management and profits of the business.
2 Partners receive indemnification for payments made on behalf of the partnership, and they receive interest on any advances.
3 Partners have ready access to accounting records and business affairs of the partnership.
4 The legal formalities of operation are less than with a corporation. The cost of formation is usually less although detailed partnership agreements designed to achieve specific tax or business purposes can be time-consuming and costly.
5 Each partner has a fiduciary obligation to other partners.
6 Regulations and reporting requirements are usually less than those for a corporation. Also, a partnership enjoys more privacy.
7 The more personal wealth the partners possess, the easier it is to secure credit and raise debt capital.
8 With careful drafting of the partnership agreement, flexibility and simplicity of operation can be achieved. Moreover, specific needs of each partner can be met.

9 The partnership does not pay taxes. A corporation is taxed as a separate *entity*. The income stream is then taxed again when it is distributed by the corporation to its shareholders in a nondeductible form such as dividends. On the other hand, a partnership is not treated as a taxpaying entity. This business form serves only as a nontaxable conduit of income and deductions to the partners. The partnership does, however, have a legal identity distinct from the partners, but only for formality and as a reporting entity for accounting purposes. The partnership is required to file a tax return, Form 1065, for information purposes only. A warning is, however, in order; the IRS can and sometimes does challenge the status of a partnership and attempts to tax it as a separate legal entity.

10 Losses are passed through to the individual partners. These losses can then be used by the partners to offset income from other sources. Partnerships are, therefore, a good way to organize new ventures because operating expenses usually exceed revenue in the early years of most new business ventures.

11 Unlike the sole proprietorship, a partner's interest in the business is considered a capital asset. Thus, partners generally realize capital gains or losses when their interests are sold.

Disadvantages of a General Partnership

A general partnership has these disadvantages.

1 Any partner has the right and power to sign contracts and obligate the other partners to third parties. Without an agreement to stipulate otherwise, new partners are generally held responsible for the obligations of the partnership arising before their admission. Because each partner is an agent of the partnership, any one partner can bind the entire partnership in a business arrangement even if it is contrary to the opinions of the majority.

2 Each partner is fully responsible for all debts incurred by the partnership, and such personal liability continues even after the firm has been dissolved. Regardless of the amount of capital contributed, general partners share profit, loss, and liability equally unless a specific agreement is made to the contrary.

3 Continuity of life can be a problem. Generally, the rule is that the death or withdrawal of one of the partners automatically terminates the partnership. An agreement can be drawn up to alleviate or reduce this problem by providing penalties for withdrawal. The agreement can also provide for an option or absolute obligation of the remaining partners to buy the deceased partner's interest.

4 Normally, an entrepreneur by nature is a strong-willed, take-charge person. Obviously, the addition of partners decreases the entrepreneur's control of his or her business. In a partnership, the majority rules unless the partnership agreement states otherwise.

5 Partners have little tax protection in the case of ordinary income. Moreover, the partners do not have the full tax benefits of the tax-deductible plans, including pension and profit sharing that are available to a corporation.

Some of the disadvantages of a general partnership can be overcome through the use of the limited partnership. The limited partnership is frequently used when the potential investors are seeking the relative security of limited liability and special tax advantages. A limited partner, however, may not take part in the control of the business without becoming liable as a general partner. The formation of a limited partnership requires the filing of a certificate with the appropriate state agency.

Advantages of a Limited Partnership

A limited partnership has several advantages.

1 The general partner or partners manage the operation; the limited partner or partners are investors only. The general partner has unlimited liability; the limited partner has limited liability.

2 The entrepreneur who is the general partner manages the partnership without interference from the limited partner or partners.

3 As with a general partnership, a limited partnership is not a taxable entity. The net income (or loss) is reportable on a partnership return but taxed at the individual partner's level. Without risking unlimited exposure, the limited partners are able to receive tax benefits of noncash losses.

4 The death of a limited partner does not dissolve the partnership, and the partnership agreement can empower a limited partner to substitute a new limited partner in his or her place.

5 The limited partner can sell his or her interest without the consent of all the other partners. Because a limited partner is simply one who puts up capital and shares in the profits (or losses), a new limited partner is merely one who is entitled to the share of the profits that would have been due his or her predecessor.

6 Investors pool their money in an R and D limited partnership to fund research and development by a sponsoring company. These investors receive up-front tax benefits plus results of the technology developed. In turn, the sponsoring, or recipient, company or inventrepreneur has capital with which to fund research work, with buyout options on any products or profits from the R and D.

Disadvantages of a Limited Partnership

Here are some disadvantages of a limited partnership.

1 The limited partnership normally requires more complex partnership agreements. It also must comply with more state laws and regulations to retain the

limited features of the partnership. To protect creditors who might otherwise assume that all members of a limited partnership are general partners, elaborate public records must be filed listing the limited partners and the extent of their potential liability. Obviously, more disclosure reduces privacy.

2 A limited partnership may be viewed as a corporation by the IRS and taxed accordingly. This form of business acts as a halfway house between the freedoms and dangers of a general partnership and the constraints and advantages of a corporation. In some instances, a tendency may exist to treat it more as a corporate entity; if so, the IRS will tax it that way.

3 The blocks of ownership are much less transferable and salable than shares in a publicly held corporation.

4 A limited partnership is illiquid; your money is tied up in it as long as the general partner sees fit.

5 A certificate of limited partnership must be properly filed and published. If this is not done, the limited partnership is technically a general partnership, and everybody is regarded as a general partner. The limited partners, therefore, lose one of the limited partnership's most attractive advantages—limited liability. If the limited partnership certificate contains a false statement, any person who suffers by virtue of relying on the certificate may hold any party signing the certificate liable.

6 The limited partnership, although similar to a corporation, still lacks flexibility in financing.

7 If the venture suddenly turns in a big profit, income of partners could be taxed at maximum rates.

8 In some instances, high front-end fees go into the pockets of the general partners, which reduces the amount of investment in the actual venture.

9 In some agreements, investors are subject to cash calls to sustain a project. This situation can create severe problems if investors thought they were in the deal only for the amount of the initial investment.

10 A crackdown on tax shelters by the IRS is always present if tax breaks are unreasonable. But more urgent than potential problems with the IRS is the business deal itself. Generally, the greater the tax breaks, the less likely it is that the deal is economically sound.

CORPORATION

The corporation is a legal business entity with an indefinite life that is directed by a board of directors and managed on a day-to-day basis by a management group. The corporation's net income is taxed by federal and state tax authorities. The shareholders receive their income through dividends paid by the corporation. Dividends to shareholders are also taxed. Because a corporation is a legal business entity, a corporation may act like an individual.

Overview of Incorporating

The general procedure for incorporating is to reserve a name for the corporation in one or more states. Once the name is reserved (usually for 30 days), the required documents from each state must be filed. Then, a corporate minute book, stock certificates, and corporate seal are ordered; and on notification of the filing, the first official, recorded meeting of the new corporation is held. An attorney can provide valuable assistance during incorporation, or the entrepreneur may do it all himself or herself. Normally, for the first-time incorporator, the use of an attorney is advisable.

If you plan to start a real growth business, one that will require several rounds of financing at major milestones in the future, incorporation is really the only sensible way to go. Remember that the main reason investors wish to own a piece of the company in which they invest is to get income or growth or both, and, at the same time, they do not want to be liable beyond their investment in the business venture. Note that a sole proprietorship or partnership has never been listed on the New York Stock Exchange or publicly traded over-the-counter.

General Advantages of Incorporating

The specific advantages of incorporating your venture are these.

1 The single most significant nontax advantage for incorporation is the concept of limited liability. The liability of shareholders to creditors and anyone else bringing suit is normally limited to the amount of the shareholder's investment. In some instances, creditors and others seeking enforcement of corporate obligations can use the alter ego doctrine that attempts to impute to the owner-shareholder the obligations of the corporation. This doctrine can work where the business venture was incorporated to defraud innocent, good-faith creditors. This defeat of the limited liability concept is also referred to as "piercing the corporate veil."

2 Most smaller corporations usually do not gain anything by incorporating in a state other than the one in which their main operations are located, especially if the business is an intrastate business. Only when corporations are national in scope and owned by many shareholders do considerations of incorporation in a nondomiciled state, such as Delaware, become important. The reason Delaware is mentioned as a state to incorporate in is because many, if not most, corporations incorporate there to take advantage of liberal statutes. Regardless of where a person lives or has a business, he or she can take advantage of Delaware Corporate Laws. Anyone can form a corporation as long as he or she completes the forms provided for that purpose; a lawyer is not needed. The Company Corporation, Corporation Center, 725 Market Street, Wilmington, Delaware 19801, provides all the services required for incorporation for a relatively small fee. If you wish, the Company Corporation will also furnish you a complete

corporation kit, including a record book, corporate seal, stock certificates, preprinted minutes and bylaw forms, and a complete set of forms and instructions to obtain tax benefits, such as a tax shelter under Section 1244 of the Internal Revenue Code.

3 The corporation is the only viable form for "going public." Moreover, many different financial methods can be offered to potential investors. You can divide the ownership of a corporation into millions of shares in any denominations, say $0.01 to $30.00, making it easy for a variety of investors to get a "piece of the action." Moreover, you can offer to the investment community some sophisticated and varied financing packages to fit different investment tastes and needs. For the entrepreneurial team, directors, and venture capitalists, voting common stock may be offered. For those investors who want preferred treatment and a little more safety, you can offer preferred stock. You can also make a series of preferred stock convertible so that investors acquiring this stock can enjoy the same upside potential and equity growth as the common shareholders because of a one-for-one convertibility ratio of the preferred into common. Other financing techniques that can be included in your financial package are convertible debentures and warrants. These financial instruments offer even stronger claims against the corporate assets than preferred stock because the investor is in a position to be a creditor rather than an equity holder. Regardless of what instruments you use, the corporate form offers more flexibility in preparing financing packages than a sole proprietorship or partnership.

4 Unlike the case with partnerships, the death or withdrawal of any shareholders will not affect the legal existence of the corporation. Continuity of ownership and unlimited life of the corporation permit you to transfer interest to your successors, to sell off interests to members of the family or key employees, or to ultimately cash out yourself by selling your interests to stock-market investors. In some instances, however, a closely held corporation's stock may not be marketable. In such cases, provisions should be drawn up to redeem the shares in the estate of a deceased shareholder or of a shareholder who wishes to withdraw.

5 The corporation is a legal entity and may acquire or sell property, enter into contracts, and participate in legal actions. Moreover, it has an image of power, size, and continuity.

6 If you are going to own multiple businesses, each should be set up as a separate and distinct corporation; the failure of one will not have any legal impact on the others. All the separate corporations are owned by your parent corporation that acts as a prime-holding company. Creditors can get access only to the single corporation that they sold to and cannot come in and collect from the other corporations. Moreover, the holding company can file one consolidated tax return for all the subsidiary corporations, so losses from one can offset profits of another.

Tax Advantages of Incorporating

The legal form of business you choose—sole proprietorship, partnership, corporation, or Subchapter S Corporation—can have a tremendous impact on the amount of taxes you pay. Sole proprietorships are easy to start, but they have legal disadvantages, as already noted, and can often result in your paying more taxes than you would if your business were organized as a corporation. In some instances, the Subchapter S Corporation is extremely useful; in other cases it is not. A regular corporation, in many instances, is your best way to go. As a matter of fact, if your company is making money and is operating as a business should, with sound entrepreneurial objectives, then a regular corporation is probably the appropriate choice. And clearly your responsibility is to keep expenses in line, which obviously calls for taking advantage of numerous tax-saving opportunities of the corporate form. Here are some of these tax advantages.

1. A corporation's federal income tax rates may be lower than the owner's individual tax rates, especially for a smaller company. Currently, the rates are as follows.

Corporation's Taxable Income	Corporation's Tax Rates
Up to $25,000	15%
$25,000–$50,000	18%
$50,000–$75,000	30%
$75,000–$100,000	40%
Over $100,000	46%

As a sole proprietorship and partnership, your rate may be as high as 50 percent (subject to change at any time). If, however, your rate is something less than 46 percent, maybe you are better off not to operate in a corporate form from strictly a tax viewpoint. Alternatively, many people are surprised to learn that while they are paying exorbitant taxes, a corporation's tax rates are relatively small. As can be seen by the figures just given, as you approach a 40 to 50 percent tax bracket, a corporation earning the same amount may still be in the 18 percent bracket.

By organizing your business as a regular corporation, you can shift earnings to its tax return, often cutting the overall tax bill on your earnings. For example, if your business earns $90,000 and you pay yourself a $40,000 salary and leave $50,000 in the corporation, you would owe around $16,000 (assuming a personal tax bracket of 40 percent) on your personal return, and your corporation would pay $9,000 (a corporate tax rate of 18 percent), or a total tax bill of $25,000. If your business were not incorporated, your personal tax bill on $90,000 would amount to $36,000, $11,000 more than if you split with your corporation.

2. One way to overcome double taxation of the regular corporation is to transfer cash you need out of the corporation as salaries, rent, interest, and royalties for work and assets you provide to the business. These payments are taxable to you, but they are deducted by the corporation. So they are taxed only once. Any of these methods of avoiding double taxation may be subjected to tests of reasonability by the IRS. This situation is discussed later.

3. A sole proprietorship or partnership can offer its owners company cars, limited retirement plans, and a few other tax perks. But neither business form can compete with the list of tax-free benefits of the corporate form. These fringe benefits give you additional ways to squeeze funds out of your corporation without suffering from the big tax bite. Clearly, deducting fringe benefits from your corporation gives you one of the few ways you can help yourself in a completely tax-free manner. When you pay for an item from your salary, you are buying it with disposable income, that is, what is left over *after* you are taxed. If, for example, you are in the 40 percent tax bracket, each $1.00 of earnings leaves you only $.60 to spend as you wish. Because various items that you want are deductible, your corporation buys the items *before* taxes, then deducts the expenses. When you move to higher brackets, the contrast between what something costs you and what your corporation pays for it can be even greater.

Your corporation can enjoy big tax advantages such as tax credits and excellent depreciation deductions from owning company cars and planes. Or you could personally buy such items, lease them to the corporation, and take all the tax benefits. Qualified stock options can give you a way to pay yourself a long-term, leniently taxed capital gain. Also, your corporation may be able to provide you with tax-free meals and housing that it can deduct. When your corporation owns the house in which you live, it may be able to deduct depreciation expenses along with other items such as insurance and utilities. The house, however, must be on the business premises. Another tax-free benefit your corporation can provide is the payment of premiums on health and accident insurance. The same applies to group term life insurance and pension and profit-sharing plans. For example, premiums paid by a corporation on up to $50,000 of group-term life insurance for each employee, including owner-employees, are tax-free compensation. If your policy is for more than $50,000, the premiums for the excess are taxable compensation.

If you have your own one-person corporation, you may be able to get tax-free reimbursements of your medical costs for both you and your spouse. The corporation, in effect, reimburses you and your spouse for any medical costs not covered by insurance and then uses these reimbursements as deductions. To increase the probability that you would receive such favorable tax treatment, prepare a written plan, and write it so that all covered employees are eligible for the same benefits, and be sure that you are in substance an employee of the corporation, not just a shareholder. Also, you cannot deduct the medical costs on your personal tax return. And, finally, if you travel a lot and wine and dine customers, you are doubly benefited because your corporation can deduct business entertainment, out-of-town meals, and lodging expenses.

4. Another significant tax advantage of a corporation deals with selling your assets to your corporation. Normally, when you sell something, you are taxed on any gain. Your corporation can buy assets from you without your owing taxes on the deal. The IRS asks only that you put your assets into the corporation in exchange for stock or other securities in the corporation and that you own at least 80 percent of all classes of stock immediately after the deal. The corporation may be a new one you just formed, an existing corporation you own, or an existing corporation you don't own. It does not matter whether you own 0 percent or 100 percent of an existing corporation before a deal just so long as you own 80 to 100 percent afterward.

5. Although you are taxed on all dividends you receive from your corporation or from investments in shares of stock, a corporation may not be. Only 15 percent of the qualifying dividends a corporation receives from most other domestic corporations are taxed to it. Letting your corporation own a part or all of your investments may result in substantial tax savings. The restriction, however, is that your corporation needs to generate income from business operations. If too much of its revenue is from "passive" sources such as dividends or interest, the personal holding company tax treatment could apply.

6. If your business is a sole proprietorship or partnership, selling it could be a tax disaster, because the gain is treated as ordinary income (although in most partnership sales, only part of the resulting gain would be ordinary income). On the other hand, shares of stock in a corporation are a capital asset, and if you have owned them for more than six months, selling them at a gain will result in long-term capital gains treatment.

7. The IRS always shares in your profits, so why not let them share in your losses if you have any? A little-known Section 1244 of the Internal Revenue Code allows you to deduct any loss on your investment as an ordinary loss. Have your attorney draft a provision in your corporate bylaws that the shares of stock fall under Section 1244 of the IRS Code. Without this provision, you can treat the loss only as a capital loss, and this saves you money only if you have a corresponding capital gain in the same year.

8. The income or loss of a Subchapter S Corporation is treated in the same way as that of a partnership, thus eliminating double taxation. We will say more about the Subchapter S Corporation later.

Disadvantages of Incorporating

The disadvantages of incorporating are as follows.

1 The expense of incorporating is usually higher than with other forms of business. But for most profit-making, growing businesses, this expense is insignificant. In any event, the main expenses are (a) those required at the time articles of incorporation are filed and prepayment of state franchise tax; (b) attorney's fees, if any; (c) costs for such things as a corporate minute book, corporate seal, and stock certificates. All these expenses, however, can be amortized against corporate income.

2 A corporation is created only by statute. In general, the statute requires a lot more "paperwork" and record keeping. Many believe that corporations are over-regulated, and the disclosure requirements destroy privacy because much of the corporation's information must be on public record. The owners of a corporation file two tax returns, individual and corporate. Moreover, the corporation must hold regular meetings of stockholders and directors, keep accurate records, develop an accounting internal control system, keep an accurate record of the minutes, register in states other than its domicile before transacting business in those states, and file financial information and tax reports. Most entrepreneurs do not like to keep records, but all the tax advantages of owning a corporation could be wiped out overnight without sufficient documentation and complete corporate minutes. If, for example, you do not have sufficient records to indicate expansion plans to justify accumulated earnings, then you may be forced to pay significant penalties. Further-more, banks, insurance companies, and various state and federal agencies, besides the IRS, all require notarized authorizations to grant loans, buy property and equipment, enter into leases, and even to sell assets.

3 As the corporation grows larger, the more likely it is that the founding entrepreneur and even the entire founding team may be reduced to the status of typical shareholders with little influence other than through the election of a board of directors.

4 Minority stockholders have legal protection against fraudulent or overly oppressive majority action as a function of state law. In a number of instances, how-ever, minority shareholders abuse their rights to the detriment of a corporation. Or putting it another way, minority shareholders can be a real "pain in the neck."

5 Double taxation is a big disadvantage of the corporate form of business. Although your corporation may pay a lot less tax on a specific amount of income than you would as personal or partnership income, some of that corporate income could end up being taxed twice. That is, when money that has already been taxed to the corporation is paid out to its owners as dividends, these dividends cannot be deducted as an expense by the corporation, and, on top of this, they are taxed to the shareholders. As mentioned earlier, the obvious way to lessen the burden of this disadvantage is to get the cash you need out of the corporation in the form of salaries, rent, interest, and royalties for effort and property you provide to the corporation as an expense. In this way, they are taxed only once. Of course, if you pay yourself too much salary, for example, traps in the law can be used to interpret this salary as, in substance, a dividend. You must be careful in avoiding these traps.

Closely held companies, especially, get close scrutiny from the IRS when they take corporate deductions for paying "reasonable compensation" for services rendered. Was the payment reasonable compensation for actual service rendered, or was it a *disguised dividend*? This is a critical question because if it is found to be a dividend, the corporate deduction is disallowed. Guidelines that the IRS follow are these: (1) how vital your role is in the corporation and your devotion to your work; (2) comparable salaries for positions like yours in similar corporations; (3) economic status, size, and complexity of the corporation; (4) possible conflicts of interest between you and the corporation; and (5) evidence of a reasonable, long-standing, consistently applied compensation plan.

For those who plan to start a moonlighting venture, whether you incorporate or not, beware of the IRS's tendency to regard a part-time operation as a hobby. Although business losses are fully deductible, those from what the IRS calls a hobby may be limited. So your best strategy is to turn any "hobbies" you or your spouse have into bona fide businesses. Examples are golfing, fishing, skeet shooting, and so forth, for prize money; animal breeding; weekend farming; and antique or coin collecting. If on your weekend farm, for example, you consistently reported losses and deducted them against profits from your regular business or salary, the IRS might enter and say that you have a hobby, allowing you to deduct interest, taxes, and casualty losses, but not depreciation, operating expenses, and so forth.

Subchapter S Corporation

Subchapter S Corporation treatment occurs by an agreement (IRS Form 2553) between you and the IRS. To the state in which you are incorporated, the S Corporation is just another corporation. The legal advantages of operating as a corporation remain the same, such as limited liability, ease of transfer of ownership, and continuity of life. But for tax purposes, the S Corporation is treated like a partnership. That is, profits or losses are passed through to owners' personal tax returns where losses can be used immediately to offset earnings that shareholders produce elsewhere rather than kept in the corporation for possible later use against corporate earnings. It is the ability to funnel tax-shelter losses to individual shareholders' personal returns that make S Corporation an ideal tax-saving vehicle.

Following is a simple example of the S Corporation's tax advantage:

	S Corporation	Regular Corporation
Corporation's tax return		
Corporation's loss	($20,000)	($20,000)
Loss passed through	all	none
Loss retained in corporation	($-0-)	($20,000)
Your tax return		
Other earnings	$55,000	$55,000
Loss from corporation	(20,000)	($-0-)
Your taxable income	$35,000	$55,000

As you can see from this example, the S Corporation's tax loss is funneled directly to your personal tax return. Losses from a regular corporation are retained in the corporation. If your business generates a profit, an S Corporation may still be preferable because S Corporation profits are taxed only once on shareholders' personal tax returns.

To elect Subchapter S Corporation treatment, a corporation must satisfy each of the following conditions.

1 It must be a domestic corporation that is not an ineligible corporation.

2 It must have no more than 35 shareholders. A husband and wife are normally counted as 1 shareholder for this purpose. If, however, a husband and wife divorce, splitting their stock, then they are counted as 2 shareholders. If there were 35 shareholders before the divorce, the stock split will increase the number to 36, causing the S Corporation to become a regular corporation and to be taxed as such.

3 Each shareholder must be an individual, an estate, or a specified type of trust. This requirement prevents a partnership with many partners or a corporation with many shareholders from becoming a shareholder in an S Corporation. Clearly, without such a requirement, the 35-shareholder limit could be circumvented. Also, no shareholder may be a nonresident alien.

4 An S Corporation can have only one class of stock issued and outstanding. Other classes may be authorized, but only one can be outstanding.

5 Keep your S Corporation clear of membership in affiliated corporate groups, such as parent-subsidiary relationships.

Congress has instructed the IRS to overlook some violations of these requirements. Excessive violations, however, could cause you to lose Subchapter S status for five years, which may, in turn, lock tax shelter losses into the corporation, which may have no profit to offset against them.

Like a partner in a partnership, each shareholder in an S Corporation takes into account his or her pro rata share of items of income, loss, deductions, or credits of the corporation. These items are included into each shareholder's personal tax return, subject to whatever rules, limitations, and so forth, apply to the shareholder's personal tax situation. The deduction an S Corporation shareholder can claim for a loss passed through to him or her by the corporation is limited to the sum of this shareholder's adjusted basis in the corporate stock he or she owns plus his or her adjusted basis in any debt the corporation owes him or her. Loss pass-throughs in excess of the currently deductible amount can be carried forward indefinitely and allowed in any subsequent year in which the shareholder has an adequate basis in his or her stock or in debt the corporation owes him or her.

If you are considering becoming an S Corporation, the IRS will generally require your company to adopt a calendar-year tax year unless you can show the IRS a sound business reason for adopting a different taxable year. The calendar-year requirement for S Corporations permits the corporations to serve as a link for passing through its income, losses, and credits to shareholders to be claimed on individual returns.

Therefore, to reflect S Corporation income accurately, shareholders and the corporation should have identical taxable years.

Generally, start-ups go through several years when they have losses. These new businesses are building facilities, purchasing equipment, advertising heavily to attract customers, paying accountants and lawyers organization fees, and the like. All this means more expenses than revenue and, therefore, a lot of front-end losses. This is where S Corporation treatment really comes in handy. As already shown, these losses are sent to your personal tax return rather than being held useless in the business. But when the business starts making money, in some instances, you may be better off taxwise to permit part of the income to be taxed to the corporation. This means giving up Subchapter S Corporation treatment and changing the business to regular corporate tax status. In any event, before making your decision, consult your accountant or attorney familiar with your tax situation, the tax law, and tax planning. The sooner you take the correct action, the better.

Although an S Corporation election gives you distinct tax advantages, it brings with it some disadvantages. As already shown, S Corporations may have only 35 shareholders. This restriction severely limits your raising capital from a large variety of financing sources. Moreover, since only one class of common stock can be issued, this eliminates many investors who seek preferred treatment over common shareholders, for example, preferred stock, warrants, and convertible debentures. If S Corporations receive too much of their income from passive sources, such as interest, dividends, and rents, they can lose their election. Most entrepreneurial companies are growth directed, which means reinvesting profits for expansion, but cash-flow problems may occur in S Corporations. Because shareholders are liable for tax on undistributed corporate profit, the S Corporation must distribute enough cash to enable shareholders to pay their taxes. So, S Corporations can only retain a limited amount of profit. Also, as mentioned earlier, you will probably have to operate on a calendar-year basis. If you have income from other sources, an S Corporation election can result in higher taxes. In addition, regular corporation deductions are generally more favorable than individual tax deductions. S Corporations are not eligible for these special corporate deductions. One of the most significant of these deductions is one that allows a regular corporation to deduct 85 percent of dividends received from other corporations. And, finally, one of the major disadvantages of an S Corporation election is that shareholders who own 2 percent or more of the corporation's stock are not eligible for tax-free benefits allowed to regular corporations. Such benefits include group-term life insurance, accident and health plans, and employer-provided meals and lodging.

Summary Comments About Incorporating

It is impossible for anyone to tell you with precision whether or not you should incorporate. The advantages, disadvantages, restrictions, and state and federal regulations—all must be weighed to derive an optimum decision for each specific situation. In general, from a tax viewpoint, businesses that generate large amounts of profit should be incorporated because corporate tax rates are lower than individual rates. Furthermore, corporations can retain profits that increase the value of stock. This feature converts ordinary income into a capital gain. In most cases, more favorable corporate deductions can be used to offset high profits. For businesses with operating losses, a partnership or S Corporation is a more suitable form because these losses pass through for immediate deduction on the partners' or shareholders' personal returns.

BUSINESS FORMALITIES

Anyone starting up a business venture must pay attention to certain formalities, procedures, and regulations. Such formalities include name selection; qualifying to do business; licenses, fees, and filings; and tax and insurance considerations.

Selecting a Name

One of the first formalities involved in starting your venture is the selection of a name for it. Obviously, the best name is one that succinctly describes your product or service idea and captures the essence of your business, like *Caterpillar Tractor Company*. Or the name may be memorable, but mean nothing, like *Exxon*. Your name will appear on advertising copy, your product, stationery, signs; it is a form of publicity for you, and it will be in sight more than any other aspect of your business. Therefore, try to create a name that is catchy and makes people remember it, like *Apple* for computers.

Probably it is not a good idea to use your personal name as part of the business name. Here are two reasons for this: If your business venture fails, your name will be associated with it. Also, if you sell your business later on and the buyer engages in practices you don't agree with, then your name is associated with these practices.

If you incorporate your business, you will have to submit your business name for approval to the appropriate state agency of the state in which you incorporate. If you intend to operate as a sole proprietorship or partnership, consult your bank or clerk of court's office to see if your business name should be registered. Often this formality is required if you are using a created name for your business.

The name picked for a new corporation, when it is submitted to the state in which it is incorporated, will be recorded as long as it is in proper form and as long as no one else is using the same name or one that is too similar prior to the application of the new corporation. The name must contain the word *association, corporation, club, foundation, fund, company, incorporated, institute, society, union, syndicate,* or *limited,* or one of the abbreviations *Co., Corp., Inc.,* or *Ltd.* Certain property rights under the law accrue to the original owners of a business name or to a corporation that originates a name. These businesses may legally prevent a new firm from using a name that is the same or similar to theirs.

Qualifying to Do Business

The initial requirements to qualify to do business in a state differ depending on whether the corporation is chartered within the state, which is a domestic corporation, or outside the state, which is a foreign corporation. Normally, all domestic corporations automatically qualify to do business within the state. A charter can be applied for by signing and verifying the articles of incorporation and filing them with the secretary of state. In most states, there is no fee or tax levied on the act of incorporation other than a filing fee, which is sent with the application. If the application is approved, a certificate of incorporation is issued.

Before a foreign corporation can transact business in another state, it must apply for a certificate of authority from the secretary of state of that state. A filing fee is usually required with the application. If the secretary approves the application and all taxes have been paid, a certificate of authority is issued.

Business Licenses, Fees, and Filings

A variety of business licenses, inspection fees, and filings are regulatory in nature besides serving to raise revenue. Most licensing and inspections are usually administered at the county and city level. A complete listing of compliance requirements can be obtained from appropriate county tax offices and city hall. Examples include these. If you handle food, a health department permit that can be obtained from a county health department is required. A sign permit is usually required by your city. Also, check county and state offices for regulations of signs and right-of-way. A business and occupational license is required for businesses like real estate firms and barbershops. Federal licenses are required for such businesses as radio and television stations. If your business has discharges into the air or water, your city may require an air or water discharge permit. Transportation businesses require a variety of permits and state authorities. Land use zoning is generally determined at the city or county level. The zoning departments of the respective city or county should be contacted to make sure that a potential business location is zoned for the particular type of business planned.

In addition, a federal employer identification number is required. Form SS-4 is used for the application and is filed with the Internal Revenue Service (IRS). Necessary forms may be obtained from the local office of the IRS. The filing of Form SS-4 will cause the registration of the company as an employer, and the federal government will automatically send the necessary payroll tax return forms, depository receipts, and other information to the taxpayer. The employer then becomes liable for federal withholding taxes and the Federal Insurance Compensation Act (FICA).

Tax and Insurance Considerations

Just as tax rules play a part in the form of business you select, they also play an important role in the decisions you make on how to operate your business. You will have to choose from a variety of special elections that can mean the difference between good tax planning and tax disaster. Basically, these elections deal with two factors. One is the way in which a business accounts for its revenue and expenses. Whether an expense is treated as made in one year or another will affect not only the profit for the year but also the amount of taxes paid. This is the basic timing issue. The other basic issue deals with the classification of revenue and expenses.

The timing issue is settled by the accounting method chosen—cash, accrual, or hybrid—and selection of the taxable year. It can be the calendar year (may be required with an S Corporation), a fiscal year, and the 52–53-week year. The tax law also permits the use of a short year in some special situations, such as the initial return of a business, its final return, or when it changes its accounting period. Even more important than the choice of a taxable year is the choice of the accounting method. The taxable year merely controls the opening and closing dates of the accounting period; the accounting method determines what revenue has been recognized, when it has been taken in, what expenses have been paid, or how much of either are reportable or deductible.

The classification of revenues and expenses and their deferment or acceleration can have a significant impact on your tax bill. Accounting methods used to defer revenue or accelerate expenses include installment sales, cash method, accrual method, percentage-of-completion method, various inventory valuation procedures such as last-in, first-out (LIFO) and first-in, first-out (FIFO), various depreciation methods, consignment sales, prepayments, and so forth. Moreover, various accounting elections should be made early on, such as reserve method for bad debts, amortization of organizational costs, method of treating research and development costs, and the like. Again, consult your accountant for methods and elections that give you maximum tax advantages.

Another tax consideration involves the collection of sales and use taxes for the state. In most instances, the state sales tax applies to the gross revenue of retailers from the retail sale of tangible personal property. Usually, all such property is subject to sales tax except certain foods, items taxed under other statutes, and other items specifically exempted by law. Use tax is imposed on the storage, use, or other consumption of property purchased from a retailer. Use tax is generally applied to purchases of property outside the state for use within the state. Before engaging in business, sellers are required to obtain a sales tax permit for each place of business in the state by filing an application with the state controller. This permit must be conspicuously displayed at the place for which issued and normally does not require renewal. The retailer bears the liability for collection and payment of sales and use taxes.

State franchise tax is a tax on corporations for the privilege of doing business in the state. Generally, specific exemptions from tax are provided for certain corporations, including qualifying nonprofit or cooperative corporations and state savings and loan institutions.

All real and tangible personal property is subject to property taxes. Generally, property is assessed at full fair market value and taxed at the aggregate of all levies for state, county, municipal, and district purposes. On notice from the appraisal district, the agent of a business must list all taxable property of the business. This list is to include property owned in other counties as well, but this property cannot be taxed in more than one county.

For business insurance requirements, consult with your insurance agent. At minimum, you will need the following types of coverages: for directors' and officers' wrongful acts, keyperson life insurance, business interruption, building and contents, criminal loss, and liability.

SUMMARY

The critical success factors of your business venture are the people you bring on board as the founding entrepreneurial team and the board of directors. All should play a definite role and provide certain management skills. The first challenge is to recruit these people; the second is to provide them with a fair piece of the action where all members will be satisfied.

Another important task in setting up your business is to choose an appropriate business form that will provide you maximum tax, legal, and financial advantages. Although there are a number of variations, the basic business forms you have to choose from are the sole proprietorship, partnership, and corporation. Each business form offers its own special advantages and disadvantages.

No matter where you plan to transact business, you will be required to go through certain formalities to do so. These formalities deserve serious consideration and include selecting a business name; qualifying to do business; licenses, fees, and filings; and tax and insurance considerations.

ASSIGNMENT

1 Complete the following Personal Survey form. If you have team members, also have them do the same. These surveys will help to determine strengths brought to the venture. They will also help to disclose deficiencies that will need to be corrected or recruited.

PERSONAL SURVEY

Entrepreneurial Tendencies and Characteristics	*Strong*	*Moderate*	*Weak*
1. Independence-seeking			
2. Wealth-seeking			
3. Opportunity-seeking			
4. Innovative			
5. Venture-seeking			
6. Risk-acceptance			
7. Intuitive			
8. Desire to achieve			
9. Hardworker			
10. Nurturing quality			
11. Accept responsibility			
12. Reward-oriented			
13. Optimistic			
14. Excellence-oriented			
15. Organizer			

Administrative Skills			
1. Accounting			
2. Marketing			
3. Management			
4. Engineering			
5. Law			
6. Production			
7. Distribution			

2 Have your team members determine together, the following points:
  (a) Responsibility and authority of each member. Give a fairly complete job description and title.
  (b) Share of ownership, perquisites, and other benefits.
  (c) Salaries paid and dividend payments.

3 From your tax course or from library research, become familiar with Section 1244 and Subchapter S of the Internal Revenue Code. What advantages do either of these elections give you? Are there any disadvantages? Explain.

4 Assume you incorporate your business venture. What kind of stock do you plan to issue? Also be specific about the amount authorized, the asking price, how you plan to sell it, and the amount left for the entrepreneurial team and board of directors.

5 Outline in detail the legal business form you have chosen for your business venture. Explain why this form gives you the most advantages. What are the disadvantages?

6 Select a name for your business venture. Explain why you chose this name.

7 Determine what licenses, permits, fees, and the like, you need to set up a business in your county and city.

BIBLIOGRAPHY

Ballas, George C., and Dave Hollas. *The Making of an Entrepreneur, Keys to Your Success.* Englewood Cliffs, N.J.: Prentice-Hall, 1980.

Baty, Gordon B. *Entrepreneurship, Playing to Win.* Reston, Va.: Reston Publishing Company, 1974.

Closely Held Business. Englewood Cliffs, N.J.: Institute for Business Planning, Inc. A publication from Prentice-Hall's Information Services Division, 1983.

Dible, Donald M. (ed.). *Winning The Money Game.* Santa Clara, Calif.: The Entrepreneur Press, 1975.

Frank, A. L. *A Guide for Software Entrepreneurs.* Englewood Cliffs, N.J.: Prentice-Hall, 1982.

Goldstein, Arnold S. *How to Save Your Business.* Wilmington, Del.: Enterprise Publishing, 1983.

Liles, Patrick R. *New Business Ventures and the Entrepreneur.* Homewood, Ill.: Richard D. Irwin, 1974.

Nicholas, Ted. *How to Form Your Own Corporation Without a Lawyer for Under $50.00.* Wilmington, Del.: Enterprise Publishing, 1981.

Schollhammer, Hans, and Arthur H. Kuriloff. *Entrepreneurship and Small Business Management.* New York: Wiley, 1979.

Shames, William H. *Venture Management.* New York: The Free Press, 1974.

CHAPTER 13

Protecting the Business Venture

INTRODUCTION

Besides being skilled in product-service innovation, marketing, production, and the organization of facilities and employees, you must be aware of a number of risks of loss and liability that your business is subject to—some significant enough to put you out of business. Protecting your business against risks is a process of preparedness, a process of becoming knowledgeable about these risks, and mobilizing policies and procedures to protect your business against them.

You can avoid some risks by knowing more about what they are and taking steps to keep them from happening; you can prevent some by doing things better and by taking the initiative to install countermeasures; you can shift some by transferring them to insurance and bonding companies. The objectives of this chapter follow.

1 To describe how to prevent loss of records and documentation.
2 To discuss how intangible assets are protected by patents, copyrights, trademarks, and trade secret agreements.
3 To disclose how to prevent loss from nonperformance by other parties.
4 To analyze how to guard against loss from a number of perils.
5 To discuss how bankruptcy laws help to protect businesses.
6 To state how to comply with various regulatory agencies.

BUSINESS RECORD KEEPING

A good record-keeping system is crucial to the success of your business venture. Actually, records and appropriate documentation should be kept even before the business starts its operations. This is why a good accounting and information systems person should be considered as one of the first members of the entrepreneurial team. To be sure, records are the memory, history, story, audit trail, and road map of the business and its transactions. The increasing size and complexity of businesses, as well as the growth of government regulation and the need to document transactions, have resulted in a need for more and more record keeping and for retaining these records over a greater time period. Unfortunately, despite the importance of record keeping, many small businesspeople use the "shoe box" approach to record keeping. Pieces of paper are thrown in a shoe box, and at the end of the year someone tries to analyze the contents of the box. This way of "keeping records" is asking for trouble.

Keeper of the Records

Generally, the authority and responsibility for the storage and disposition of records should be assigned to an individual, such as an accountant or information systems expert or both. Such a person has responsibility for creating, storing, and disposing of most of the business records—a "cradle-to-grave" responsibility. The record-keeping system designed should be simple to use and understand; accurate, up-to-date, and consistent; protected from hazards and misuse; and free from inactive and obsolete records.

A good keeper of the records knows which records to keep and how long to keep them. After a while, the sheer bulk of records become cumbersome and unmanageable. Every added file clerk and file cabinet and each additional foot of dead storage space emphasize the growing waste of space, time, energy, and money to meet the demands for the retention of records. You simply, however, cannot keep everything. Establishment of intelligent policies and procedures for the retention and destruction of inactive and obsolete records is imperative. One must be very careful because premature destruction of records may result in the loss of information essential to the effective defense or prosecution of lawsuits, the settlement of federal income tax matters, or the favorable disposition of many problems requiring documentary proof. Indeed, records are your chief protection against the claims of others just as they are essential as potential evidence for your own claims.

Factors Affecting the Retention of Records

Even though there may be considerable differences between businesses as to retention periods and procedures, there are several fundamental considerations in determining which records must be retained. These include the nature of the record itself, the statutes of limitation, the nature of the business, and governmental or statutory requirements.[1]

The nature of the record is obviously an important factor in determining whether it shall be kept. For example, the certificate of incorporation or the minutes of a meeting are in a category quite different from the third copy of a purchase order. Factors that influence the value of the record include the worth of the document in terms of future company operations, the availability of identical copies in other files, the extent to which the data are summarized on other available documents, and the extent to which the record is the original evidence.[2]

In such instances, as when the records are in the nature of contracts, notes or other evidence of indebtedness, or court judgments, the statutes of limitation may govern the retention period. Because these statutes fix or limit the period of court action, such documents may be retained until the right of action has passed. This period varies in different states and for various types of action; moreover, the statutes are subject to revision by legislative change.[3] For example, the minimum time you should keep promissory notes, open accounts, instruments and contracts

---

[1]J. Brooks Heckert and James D. Willson, *Controllership*, 2d ed. (New York: Ronald Press, 1963), p. 707. This material is used with permission.
[2]Ibid., p. 708.
[3]Ibid.

under seal, and ordinary contracts in Louisiana are 5, 3, 10, and 10 years, respectively. For Pennsylvania, it is 6, 6, 20, and 6 years, respectively.

If you are not absolutely sure how long you need to keep certain records, you might consider microfilming them. Generally, all the 50 states and the federal government accept microfilm or microfiche as a substitute for the original document. In some special cases, some documents may not be admissible as evidence in a microfilm format. Check state and federal statutes for exceptions.

The nature of the business also may be a factor in record retention. Thus, if a product must be aged several years before sale or use, the lot sheets attending the manufacture of wine, for example, would probably be retained much longer than the records incident to the fabrication of a piston. Then, too, the nature of the business may determine the type of governmental regulation applicable.[4] For example, a contractor working for the federal government on a fixed-price contract must retain records for a period of three years after final settlement under the contract.

Finally, governmental and regulatory requirements are of increasing importance. Under various laws, both federal and state bureaus or agencies have promulgated what kind of records should be kept and their retention requirements. Obviously, this situation affects a large share of the records of businesses.[5] For example, every business must keep records of accounts to establish gross income, deductions, credits, and other material required to be shown in federal or state income tax returns. These records are subject to examination and must be kept as long as they may be material under the tax laws. Apart from the protection such records afford, keeping these records is required by law.

Classifying Records for Retention

One of the first steps in the development of a record-keeping system is the classification of records according to those to be retained permanently; those to be retained for a long period of time, perhaps microfilmed, and then destroyed; and those to be preserved for a short time and then destroyed. Each type of record should be considered with respect to such probable future reference needs as the following: (1) supports title to property, (2) supports payments made to others, (3) supports claims against outside parties, (4) supports record requirements by governmental agencies, (5) provides protection against future tax claims, and (6) provides essential operating statistics.[6]

Classification of records include (1) vital or essential, (2) valuable, (3) important, (4) useful, and (5) nonessential or temporary records. *Essential* records are irreplaceable or are not replaceable immediately, and they are needed for the business's survival. Examples are deeds and leases; powers of attorney; minutes of shareholder

[4]Ibid.
[5]Ibid.
[6]Ibid., p. 708–9.

and director meetings; accounting records; blueprints and drawings; copyrights, patents, and trademark authorizations; laboratory notebooks; capital stock records. *Valuable* records are those necessary to prevent financial loss or to recover money or property. Some examples are an accounts receivable ledger, inventory records, insurance policies, securities, and audit reports. *Important* records are administrative tools that might be obtained after considerable effort or delay and that would not adversely affect essential operations to any serious degree. A few examples include cost reports, projections, shipping reports, manuals, and credit reports. *Useful* records are those that are not needed for current operations but are helpful for reference and similar purposes. Such records ordinarily would be destroyed when current usefulness ceases. The *nonessential* records are those that are available for destruction relatively soon and that do not have long-term value.[7]

Destruction of Records

It is obviously important to know how to create records, store them, maintain and update them, and protect them and also how long to retain them. This latter task deals with a timetable for destroying old, out-of-date records; otherwise, over time, a business will drown in a flood of records. With the use of classification procedures and retention periods, classes of records can be indexed, and these indexes can be set up in a tickler file. Then records can be destroyed pretty much on an automatic, routine basis. Before records are actually destroyed, however, it is recommended that you recheck to make sure that not only are the right records being destroyed but also that no change in retention regulations have been made since the earlier destruction date was set. For security and confidentiality, records should be shredded or cremated. In some instances, the federal government requires cremation certificates.

PROTECTING INVENTIONS AND KNOW-HOW

The most valuable single asset of your business may be an invention, a creative trademark, or special know-how. Such an asset gives you a competitive edge and goodwill; therefore, it is very important to protect this asset from being stolen and used by the thief as his or her own. Fortunately, the law promotes such creativity and innovation by allowing you to enjoy the exclusive use and profits of your inventive creations through legal protective measures, such as patents, copyrights, trademarks, and trade secret agreements. Before these legal measures are treated, steps of product-service development and keys of product-service commercialization are given.

[7]Ibid., pp. 709–10.

Model Development

Models go through various stages of development. The following terms are generally used as models go from the drawing board into three-dimensional representation.[8]

1 *Breadboard.* The first attempt at putting together a working unit is usually spread out, without too much concern about the relation of parts. More important is the convenience of the inventor and engineer to work on the subunits, make corrections and adjustments, and so on.

2 *Brassboard.* A more refined and improved version of the breadboard, reflecting the solution of problems learned from the building of one or more breadboards, is the brassboard. At this stage, commercial considerations are introduced. Such matters as availability of parts, nature of linkages, quality of materials, multiple suppliers, and the total cost of the product are considered.

3 *Prototype.* The arrangement of parts, subassemblies, and so on into a form as close as possible to the final commercial product produces the prototype.

4 *Production prototype.* This represents the design and production engineering and also the design and production models leading directly to a tooled manufactured product.

Example of Key Events in Commercializing a Product

Following in Table 13.1 is a good and clear example of how a successful entrepreneur of the Weed Eater—and now a multimillionaire—commercialized his product idea.[9]

Commercializing an Innovation or Invention

Here is a list of steps for an entrepreneur to follow when introducing a patentable product or service.[10]

1 Conceive of a problem statement, invent an answer, consider it in detail so that it is refined and defined, start a laboratory notebook, and keep careful notes of all the facts relating to the invention and its development.

2 Make a complete disclosure of the invention in your notebook, and have each entry witnessed by at least two individuals—that is, signed with their signatures and dated. The development data also should be noted, and the witnesses should indicate that the invention was explained to them and understood.

[8]William H. Shames, *Venture Management* (New York: The Free Press, 1974), p. 15. Copyright © 1974 by William H. Shames, president of Risers Fitness Laboratories, 5 Tudor City Place, Suite 1819, New York, N.Y. 10017, and used with the permission of the author.

[9]George C. Ballas and Dave Hollas, *The Making of an Entrepreneur, Keys to Your Success* (Englewood Cliffs, N.J.: Prentice-Hall, 1980), pp. 2–3. This material is used with permission.

[10]Ibid., p. 14.

TABLE 13.1

Key Dates and Events for the Weed Eater Venture

Year	Month	Event
1953		First conceived of the idea for a flexible line trimmer.
1971	June	Tested the idea with "popcorn prototype"
	October	Entered into agreement with machinist to produce working prototype
	December	Worked out the final working prototype design
		Applied for a patent
		Decided on the name "Weed Eater"
		Commenced work on the formation of the company
1972	January	Incorporated the company
		Applied for a patent
		Committed to manufacturer to produce the units
	April	Made first local television commercial
		Offered first unit for sale
	June	Arranged master distribution setup to distribute the Weed Eater units on a national basis
	September	Ended first fiscal year with sales of $500,000
	October	Arranged first volume sales to distributors
1973		Achieved sales of $2.7 million
1974		Achieved sales of $7.7 million
1975		Achieved sales of $16.5 million
1976		Achieved sales of $41.0 million
1977	January	Bought first national advertising during professional football's "Super Bowl"
	March	Sold the company
	December	Projected sales for year were $80 million (based on $54 million actual sales during first five months)

Source: George C. Ballas and Dave Hollas, op. cit. Used with permission.

3 The previous steps should be coordinated by consultation and disclosure to a qualified patent attorney to whom a written disclosure has been given.

4 Next there should be a reduction to practice by applying for a United States patent and the building of a working model.

5 An investigation of what is presently done in the area of the invention should be made through books, trade publications, and professionals and other people in the field and should include a search of the state of the patent art by a patent attorney.

6 Finally, the product should be commercialized by the inventor through his or her company, a new company he or she forms, or the licensing or selling of the idea to another firm.

Patents

Patents are issued by the commissioner of patents, U.S. Department of Commerce. A patent gives the inventor the exclusive right to make, use, or sell the patent for a period of 17 years in the United States, its territories, and possessions. Design patents for ornamental devices are granted for 3½, 7, or 14 years, as the applicant elects. Currently, patent rights also extend to over 80 countries, including the Soviet Union.

A patent grants the inventor the top ability to prohibit others from using a patented machine or device, chemical compound, formula, and the like without paying a royalty. The law, however, gets a little fuzzy when one moves from a physical machine to a formula or intellectual property such as a computer program. For example, only recently the U.S. Supreme Court upheld patents where a computer program was *part* of an industrial process. It seems at this point a computer program must be tied to something else (e.g., control of a robot) to be protected under a patent.

Some key points worth remembering about patents are these: (1) You are not protected by a patent until the validity of it is tested in a court, (2) the U.S. government does not help you defend your patent, and (3) most patents provide very narrow claims. Moreover, three conditions must be met to obtain a patent: (1) The invention must be new and not obvious, (2) it must not have been achieved previously by someone else or known to the public for more than a year before the date of application, and (3) it must have practical utility. A patent search is done by the U.S. Patent Office through a patent attorney. Normally, in the past you did not file for a patent until a prototype had been built and the technology had been developed; today, to meet the preceding standards, you do not have to make a model or prototype. You simply describe the art involved in your invention, so all you are patenting is the act or process of doing something. You can patent the process but not an idea.[11]

Surprisingly to many, having a patent properly registered with the Patent Office does not conclusively establish its validity. It creates only a presumption of validity. To test its validity, it must have its day in court, where protracted litigation can run over $1 million. And even more surprising is that in over half of these cases, the courts find the patents either invalid or otherwise unenforceable. Generally, however, it is better to have a patent than not.

In the past, courts did not effectively and consistently apply patent laws to protect inventions against infringers. This has recently changed with the installation of a 15-judge body called the Court of Appeals for the Federal Circuit (CAFC). This

[11]Ibid., pp. 134–43.

court is the ultimate arbiter of patent law. According to many experts in the patent field, the CAFC protects new inventions from idea thieves more effectively. This simply means that a patent is worth a lot more to the holder today than it was a few years ago. The inventrepreneur, therefore, will now have more incentive to invent and bring the product or service to the marketplace knowing that he or she enjoys much greater protection.[12]

Copyrights

The Copyright Office attached to the Library of Congress, Washington, D.C., offers protection to authors, composers, and artists from the pirating of their literary or artistic work, ranging from printed material to photographs to records and motion pictures. Copyrights, as with patents, trademarks, and service marks, provide a legal monopoly for the holder. The copyright protects a work from piracy for the life of the author plus 50 years.

To gain protection, the author or company must first make a claim by printing a notice in the front of the work. A standard form is the following: Copyright, followed by the year of publication, and the name of the author or company. Application for copyright is made to the Copyright Office, Library of Congress, after publication. If proper procedures are followed, the author may recover actual or statutory damages, attorney's fees, and any profits that the infringer has made. Illegally reproduced copies may also be seized.

Trademarks and Service Marks

A trademark is a distinguishing name or symbol identifying a product used in commerce and subject to regulation by the U.S. Congress. An example of a trademark is a multicolored apple with a bite (byte?) out of it. It can be protected against use by others for a period of 20 years by registration and may be renewed for an additional 20 years. Registration is a service provided by the commissioner of patents, U.S. Patent Office. Most states also offer trademark and service mark registrations. For further information about application procedures, write to the superintendent of documents, Government Printing Office, Washington, D.C. 20402, and ask for *General Information Concerning Trademarks.*

A trademark or service mark is a word, a name, a symbol or artistic figure, or a combination of these elements to identify your product or service and distinguish it from your competitors. A trademark or service mark gives your product or service unique recognition. It is even better if it is designed to catch the customer's attention. One of the most important decisions made early in starting a business venture is selecting a trademark or service mark.

The common law protects the use of trademarks, but since the Lanham Act of 1946, the principal protection has come from federal law. Trademark law recognizes

[12]David Henry, "Patent Absurdity No More," *Forbes*, September 10, 1984, p. 163.

that property rights extend beyond ownership of actual goods to the intangible aspects of goodwill that trademarks represent. In forbidding misappropriation of trademarks, the law prevents misappropriation of a company's goodwill and reputation. It protects both the company that owns the mark and the customers, distributors, or sales agents who rely on it.[13]

In practice, trademark laws, however, do not seem to be very effective. There are counterfeits of everything from designer blue jeans to auto parts. Penalties for infringements are slight, and counterfeiters, if they get caught, write them off as minor expenses of doing business. But strong, new federal anticounterfeiting laws are in the works that will make counterfeiting a felony, with convictions carrying jail terms and substantial fines. The existence of these new laws, trademark owners hope, will make counterfeiters concerned for the first time about what might happen if they get caught.

Trade Secrets

By definition, a trade secret may consist of any formula, pattern, device, or compilation of information that is used in a business and that gives an opportunity to obtain an advantage over competitors who do not know or use it. It may be a formula for a chemical compound, a process of manufacturing, treating or preserving materials, a pattern for a machine, or a list of customers.[14] Information that is of general knowledge cannot be a trade secret.

Obviously, some of your employees will have to have access to your trade secret information, and it is very likely that some of these individuals will eventually move on to other jobs with your secrets still fixed firmly in their heads. In most cases, the departed employees will pose no threat to your operation, but there is always the possibility that one of them will make your secrets known to a new employer who might be one of your direct competitors, so you must take protective steps.[15]

If someone does misappropriate your trade secret, you must show that it is, in fact, a trade secret and that someone confiscated it by breach of a special relationship. For example, to enforce trust that you give licensees or employees who work on or who may have developed the trade secret, you must have an agreement drawn up and signed that gives a precise definition of the trade secret and describes the confidentiality and proprietary nature of it.

Get your key employees to sign an agreement not to compete with your company after they leave your employ. If they, however, misappropriate your trade secret, you have two types of remedies available: (1) Apply for injunctive relief to restrain the employee, and (2) sue for damages.

---

[13]Robert N. Corley, O. Lee Reed, and Robert L. Black, *The Legal Environment of Business*, 6th ed. (New York: McGraw-Hill Book Company, 1984), p. 450. The material is used with permission.

[14]*Closely Held Business* (Englewood Cliffs, N.J.: Institute for Business Planning, a publication from Prentice-Hall's Information Services Division, 1983), p. 7971. This material is used with permission.

[15]Ibid.

If you are an entrepreneur who has left the employ of another company to start your own business, you may have another kind of trade-secret problem. Start-up businesses, especially high-tech ones, often get hauled into court by injured, vengeful, or worried former employers who accuse the start-ups of stealing trade secrets. Such a suit can hit the start-up at the worst possible time—when trying to raise money, when every available minute has to be spent in managing the new business, and so forth. In certain areas of the country, such as the Silicon Valley, trade-secret suits have become so common that many believe it is a ploy to stifle competition.[16] Beware of the jilted former employer!

Summary Example[17]

Chris Haney and Scott Abbott were waging a heated game of Scrabble on a bleak December day in 1979 when they had a bright idea. Forty minutes later they had mapped out the rules and design for a game they felt would be even more challenging than the coffee table classic they had been playing. Today the two former journalists are collecting millions of dollars in royalties from their creation, Trivial Pursuit, a board game that weaves a little strategy and a lot of obscure facts together into a rollicking mix of mind and minutiae. But having the idea for their game was only part of Haney and Abbott's winning strategy. The rest involved savvy marketing and an ability to tenaciously protect their rights to their own creation.

The first step Haney and Abbott took to guard their board was to copyright the 6000 questions that are at the heart of Trivial Pursuit. They did this almost simultaneously in the United States and Canada. But their vigilance did not end there. Last year they spent $100,000 in legal fees for prosecuting imitators. Also, they shielded the Trivial Pursuit name by applying for a registered trademark.

While securing a trademark and copyright, Haney and Abbott also sought a third mode of protection. The board's design, informally sketched by Haney and later polished by a professional artist, represents a unique graphic creation. As such, it may be guarded by a design patent. A design patent will cover only the shape and appearance of a product, not its function. It stays in force for 14 years and is not renewable.

For another example, consider the case of Anita Soffer, 47, a part-time business manager from Sherman Oaks, California. She does not expect the patent for the fruit picker she invented to be issued until next year, but she began manufacturing and selling the product herself early last year. Soffer grew tired of picking oranges from the trees in her backyard by hand. All the metal fruit pickers on the market seemed to her to be heavy and awkward. So in 1978 she solved her problem by designing her

[16]Erik Larson, "In High-Tech Industry, New Firms Often Get Fast Trip to Courtroom," *The Wall Street Journal*, August 14, 1984, pp. 1, 12. This material is used with permission.

[17]The material for this section is an abridgment of the following article: Andrea Rock, " 'Eureka!' But What Do You Do Next?" *Money*, May 1984, pp. 136–43. The material is used with permission.

own lightweight picker: a plastic cuplike device that attaches to a pole. Realizing she had invented a sorely needed product, Soffer decided to patent her idea.

After her patent attorney conducted a search and filed her application, Soffer set about marketing her invention. Two routes lay open to her. She could either start her own company or try to sell the rights to her fruit picker to an already existing firm.

Like most successful inventors, Soffer took advantage of one of the most valuable resources available: free advice from suppliers, manufacturers, and distributors in the line of business she planned to enter. To determine what her production costs would be, she talked to plastic manufacturers and plastic-mold makers. She conducted her own market research by calling on garden-equipment retailers to ask if they would be willing to buy her fruit picker at $9—a healthy markup from her estimated cost of $4.50 each. Says Soffer: "I just had to get up the guts to go into all of these places and ask a lot of stupid questions."

In the end, she decided to go it alone. She used a $20,000 Small Business Administration loan and about $10,000 from her savings to get started. She had to pay $13,000 to have a plastic mold made for her device. But after a year of sales, Soffer has grossed $45,000. Recently, she negotiated an agreement to sell her idea to a garden-supply company for a 5 percent royalty on sales. Soffer, like Haney and Abbott, who test-marketed their game in Canadian retail stores, realized the advantages of developing her product before trying to sell it to a larger concern. If fact, because of their own initiative, Haney and Abbott struck a deal with a U.S. manufacturer and distributor, Selchow and Righter Company (after being turned down by Milton Bradley and Parker Bros.) for a licensing agreement that pays them 15 percent of wholesale sales—triple the normal royalty for board games. Last year, those sales in the United States topped $20 million.

CONTRACTS

Every business enters into numerous contracts during its existence. These can range from a simple oral contract for someone to cut the grass every two weeks to involved written contracts with employees, suppliers, franchisors, franchisees, distributors, customers, and the like. It is through contractual relationships that employers, employees, and businesses associate and conduct business with each other. They perform services for each other, combine talents and facilities for a common business goal, distribute goods for each other, and so forth. Following are brief explanations of some of the relationships that exist and how contracts should fix stipulations and define provisions to avoid litigation and liability. Or, as the attorneys say, "Get it in writing!"

Employment Contract

Although most employment contracts for regular employees are oral, it is the best policy to have a contract in writing with members of the entrepreneurial team, other important executives, outside sales employees, employees engaged in research and development, professionals, and employees with access to trade secrets. The terms of the contract should include compensation and how it is to be paid, disability, retirement and death provisions; those provisions dealing with inventions, trade secrets, know-how, and confidential disclosures; and agreements not to compete.

Provisions must be carefully written to cover both the hiring *and* firing of the employee. This is especially true in the case of someone who has a large equity position because the courts generally look on forfeitures with disfavor. Avoid this litigation problem by including in the employment contract a well-drafted and generally self-enforcing termination and stock buy-back provision. Generally, employee contracts are terminated by inefficiency, insubordination, illness, discontinuance of business, sale of business, merger, and so forth.

If an employee leaves, you can protect the company from losing its prototypes, blueprints, laboratory notes, trade secrets, or confidential items such as a customer mailing list. If the employer develops new technology, the employee can be expressly obligated by contract to assign inventions and patents developed while on the job to the employer.

Employee agreements should include a carefully defined provision that deals with unfair competition. Generally, you cannot prohibit competition by former employees, but you can prevent *unfair* competition that would involve the misuse of a trademark or trade name, the misappropriation of trade secrets or patented positions or processes or know-how, or the misuse of customer lists and other inside information in other employment or business ventures. Also, for covenants not to compete to be enforceable, they must be reasonable as to duration and territory. For example, a covenant against competing in the same city for a period of three to five years will generally be sustained.

Marketing Contracts

Selling the product or service is one of the most important functions of the business, which may take many different forms. Is it to be done through employees of the business, commission agents, distributors who purchase the product for resale, consignees, or franchise arrangements? Generally, in developing the marketing contract, you will want to have maximum motivation, control, and business advantages in selling the product or service while avoiding possible legal liabilities, such as liability to customers for the acts of salespeople, for violation of federal trade regulation laws, to states for taxes applicable to doing business in those states, and for violations of federal antitrust laws.

Sales Warranties

A sales warranty is an implied or written guarantee of the integrity of a product or service and of the maker's or supplier's responsibility for the repair or replacement of defective parts or to make the service meet certain expectations. A seller's warranty may run to a party other than the buyer. To ascertain express or implied warranties, review the sales contract, intructions, labels, packages, advertisements, and so forth used in the sale and distribution of the product or service. A number of warranties and exclusions under the Uniform Commercial Code are summarized as follows.

If the sales contract uses language "as is" or "with all faults" or other language that calls to the buyer's attention the exclusion of warranties, then no warranty arises. If the buyer examines the goods or is given an opportunity to examine the goods and refuses, no warranty will arise as to defects the examination revealed or should have revealed. A sample or model, if part of the basis of the agreement, will create an express warranty that the goods delivered will conform to the sample. The service of food in a restaurant implies a warranty that goods will be merchantable and fit for consumption. The Uniform Commercial Code provides that a seller of consumer goods warrants not only to the buyer but also the buyer's family and guests that the goods conform to the warranty if it is "reasonable to expect that such persons may use, consume, or be affected by the goods."

Warranties that may be excluded by agreement entail express warranty by affirmation of fact or promise, warranty against infringement, course of dealing, and usage of trade. With warranty of title, the seller warrants that good title will be conveyed and that title will be free of any security interest or lien of which the buyer is unaware. Exclusion may be made by using specific language indicating that the seller does not claim title in himself or herself or that he or she is selling only that title or rights that he or she has. Exclusion of warranty of merchantability can be made only by language expressly mentioning merchantability. In a written contract, the exclusion must be conspicuous. If a merchant has reason to know any particular purpose for which goods are required and the buyer is relying on the seller's judgment or skill, he or she, therefore, warrants that the goods are fit for that purpose. Exclusion may be achieved by using conspicuous language, such as, "There are no warranties that extend beyond the description on the face thereof." If goods are sold by a description that becomes part of the basis of the transaction, there is an express warranty that they will conform to the description. The description will not be words but may be technical specifications, blueprints, and so forth. Language excluding warranties and descriptive language are to be construed as consistent with each other whenever reasonable. General language of disclaimer will not disclaim the warranties of description and the warranties that arise from a sale by sample if the disclaimer is inconsistent.

LESSENING THE RISK OF CONTRACTUAL LOSS

Whenever two or more parties enter into an oral or written contract, there is always the danger of nonperformance and its attendant risk of financial loss. Safeguards against such risk are surety bonds; consequential loss coverage; credit insurance; product-service protection; and the use of deposits, escrows, guaranties, and indemnities.

Surety Bonds for Protection

A large number of business transactions are guaranteed by suretyship in which an individual, partnership, or corporation lends its name or credit to obligations of other parties. That is, one has become legally liable for the debt, default, or failure in duty of another. A surety bond is a bond that guarantees performance of a contract or obligation. If a party is bound by a contract to perform for you, then requiring a surety bond may be a wise move. By the same token, if you are to perform for another party, surety bonds will allow you to compete on an equal footing with larger or better-known companies because your ability to perform is guaranteed by a bonding or insurance company. Through the bond such companies guarantee that you are honest and have the necessary ability and financial capacity to meet all the obligations required to complete the contract.

Consequential Loss Insurance for Protection

If you plan to produce your own product and for some reason lose your facilities and production capacity, you are obviously going to have trouble meeting your obligations and ability to deliver the product on time and in amounts agreed on. Your business, indeed, will lose money if it is shut down as a result of a disaster. Moreover, you will have to continue paying expenses, such as salaries, taxes, and other fixed costs even though no revenue is coming in. To protect yourself from consequential losses and, thus, running into a variety of contractual problems, you should carry a fairly comprehensive package of consequential damage insurance.

Credit Insurance for Protection

Credit insurance helps to protect you from losses when others cannot meet the payment part of their contract with you. Credit life insurance is generally used by retail businesses that sell on credit. This kind of insurance pays the outstanding debt of a customer in the event of death. Commercial credit insurance enables you to have an open account of credit that you can extend to buyers of merchandise for commercial purposes.

Credit insurance is particularly beneficial for those businesses whose sales are concentrated in a few accounts or in one line of business or in a particular region or who do custom manufacturing so that repossession of the product when an account goes bad would not be very helpful. You must, however, practice good credit management because credit insurance is granted on a year-to-year basis and will be canceled if you overextend credit. To be able to maintain credit insurance can significantly improve your borrowing power and credit rating.

A number of businesses are not appropriate for credit insurance. Examples of these are businesses that deal primarily with federal or state governments, businesses that do not have repossession problems such as those that sell products on conditional bills of sale or irrevocable letters of credit, businesses that factor their receivables where the factors assume the credit risks, and businesses that do mostly cash or COD business.

Product-Service Liability Protection

Two of the greatest hazards facing many businesses are having a large judgment brought against them for injury suffered from a product or service or having contracts rescinded because the product or service did not meet warranty terms. Ways to protect your business against the possibility of loss in these areas are warranty provisions and exclusions (discussed earlier), insurance, and preventive measures.

1 *Product liability insurance.* As a manufacturer or a retailer, you are protected by this insurance against injury or damage to a user of your product. Even though this kind of insurance is known as "product" liability insurance, services, too, can cause injury and damage and may be subject to product liability. This kind of insurance is expensive, but the awards in the event of injury or death caused by your product or service may be sufficiently high to make such insurance imperative.

2 *Preventive measures.* Following certain preventive measures can also protect you from product liability. These measures include making sure that the design and manufacture of the product are in accordance with trade, engineering, and legal standards; that the product is pretested at an independent laboratory to ensure viability and safety; that you implement a strong quality assurance program at points of input, at work in process, and at finished goods; that all critical parts of the product be properly identified and coded; that all instructions are clear and warnings conspicuously placed; that advertising be reviewed by engineers and attorneys; that records of fieldwork and service be properly signed and recorded; that you establish a method of handling claims; that a liaison be set up among safety, research, engineering, production, quality assurance, legal, sales, and insurance departments in the coordinated review and analysis of product liability claims; and that all personnel be properly trained and supervised.

Use of Deposits, Escrows, Guaranties, and Indemnities for Protection

The essential elements of common business arrangements like use of deposits, escrows, guaranties, and indemnities for protection are discussed briefly as follows.

1 *Deposits.* A deposit is money or property given as a pledge or a down payment to bind a transaction pending its final consummation or to ensure the performance of one or more conditions. Common examples of where deposits are given are these: on contracts for delivery of goods, on leases as security for a

tenant's performance of the terms and covenants in the lease, on purchase options, and under contracts of sale pending the outcome of tests. A deposit that is forfeited because the contract is not carried out or because of the happening of an adverse condition goes to the party to whom it is owed.

2 *Escrows.* An escrow is an arrangement wherein a disinterested third party, the escrow agent, serves to protect the interests of two or more contracting parties while a title transfer is being effected or after a default has occurred. According to the instructions of the escrow agreement, the escrow agent may collect all papers, releases, and money necessary to the transaction and effect the exchanges with full protection to all parties.

3 *Guaranties.* In practice, the main forms of guaranty are those of guaranty of payment and guaranty of collection. If the guaranty is a negotiable instrument, the Uniform Commercial Code spells out the meaning of "payment guaranteed" and "collection guaranteed" or the equivalent. It provides that the latter means that the signer will pay only after the holder "has reduced his claim against the maker or acceptor to judgment and execution has been returned unsatisfied, or after the maker has become insolvent or it is otherwise apparent that it is useless to proceed against him."

4 *Indemnities.* An indemnity is an agreement by which one person engages to secure another against anticipated loss or damage. As applied in product liability, for example, indemnification principles permit any seller who is compelled to pay the injured plaintiff to obtain full recovery from the party who sold the product to him or her. Thus, a retailer who is held liable can get indemnification from the manufacturer providing that the defect can be traced back to the manufacturer and the retailer is without fault for failing to conduct a reasonable inspection of the product.

RISK MANAGEMENT

Risk management is a term applied to that person who makes a systematic analysis of loss exposures, threat probabilities, and protection benefits. He or she calculates loss exposure and the most cost-effective way to reduce or eliminate risks. In some companies, risk managers recommend engineering standards, procedures, and physical devices as countermeasures against risk. Generally, however, risk management in most companies centers on the selection, purchase, and management of a business's insurance protection program.

Overview

There are many threats and perils to any business: some known, others unexpected. Examples include acts of God, fire, death or ill health of key employees, product liability, people being injured or killed by company trucks or automobiles, loss from hazardous employment, loss through failure to make timely deliveries, and the like. It is not a question if such losses will occur; it is more a question as to when and how often they will occur. So the best thing is to have the business adequately protected against the consequences of a variety of threats, which means a well-planned, comprehensive insurance program. Generally, risks fall into four categories: loss of property, loss of earning power, future expenses, and liability losses.[18]

Loss of Property

Property insurance protects against losses that may occur to your business property already owned. This includes real property or plant, equipment, and buildings; personal property, which includes machines, office supplies, furniture and fixtures, and computers; inventory; and so forth. This field is fairly well covered by insurance. As fast as new causes of loss become sufficiently important, new forms of insurance are devised to cover them.[19]

In addition, every individual or business faces a possible loss of property because of dishonesty or unfaithfulness. One's residence or business is robbed by a burglar, payroll checks are stolen and forged, customer mailing lists are stolen and sold to a competitor, money and securities are improperly handled by a trustee. Those contingencies give rise to a second group of insurance policies that protect against such losses of property. These are commercial and homeowners multiperil insurance, theft insurance, forgery insurance, and fidelity bonding.

Then, too, other persons are likely to fail in the performance of some expected act. A debtor may be unable to pay his or her debt, a contractor may be unable to complete a building, a supplier may be unable to furnish critical parts, or a person may buy a piece of property with a defective title. Individuals and businesses can protect themselves from such failures of others by credit insurance, surety bonding, and title insurance.[20]

Loss of Earning Power

The loss of earning power is the loss of property that will probably be acquired in the future. This is not property in existence now but the wages, interest, profit, rent, royalties, and operating expense that will be earned by future effort. The loss of earning power by persons may result from such events as death, illness, accident, old age, childbearing, or loss of employment. The branches of insurance covering these contingencies have not unfortunately acquired names in keeping with their purposes, so that death is a contingency covered by "life" insurance, and disease is a

---

[18]Robert Riegel, Jerome S. Miller, and C. Arthur Williams, Jr., *Insurance Principles and Practices, Property and Liability*, 6th ed. (Englewood Cliffs, N.J.: Prentice-Hall, 1976), p. 29. The material has been adapted by permission of Prentice-Hall, Inc.

[19]Ibid.

[20]Ibid.

contingency covered by "health" insurance. On the other hand, the earning-power loss may result from the loss of use of property suffering the direct losses of, for example, profits through interruption of business by fire and also loss of rents by reason of buildings remaining untenanted as a result of windstorm. Various forms of consequential loss insurance are available.[21]

Future Expenses

Future expense is another type of loss that frequently results from common perils. On a personal basis, for example, the public welcomed the opportunity to provide by insurance for future hospital expenses. In order to avoid a loss of earning power, a business may incur extra future expenses to continue operations when it suffers a property loss. A family may incur additional living expenses when it is forced to occupy rented quarters while its damaged home is being repaired. Insurance coverage includes medical expense insurance, extra expense insurance, additional living expense insurance, replacement cost insurance, leasehold insurance, and commercial and homeowners multiperil insurance.

Legal Liability

The likelihood of financial loss occurs because of legal liability for the consequences of certain acts or omissions. A poorly designed lawn mower injures the operator or an innocent bystander; a golfer hits a bystander with a golf ball; a salesperson is injured on defective stairs; one negligently injures a pedestrian while driving an automobile. In these cases, damages will have to be paid to the injured parties. Therefore, many forms of insurance have been devised to protect individuals and businesses from their liability at law for injuries to persons and damage to property.

BANKRUPTCY AND OTHER DEBTOR-CREDITOR ARRANGEMENTS

The objective under the bankruptcy law, Bankruptcy Reform Act (1978), is to provide benefits and protection to debtors and creditors alike. The debtor is free to perform in the future without pressure of previous debt. The creditor is protected by provisions for an equitable distribution of the bankrupt's estate or a reorganization of the debtor's business under court supervision. A large majority of bankruptcy proceedings are straight bankruptcies, which amount to the liquidation of the debtor's estate followed by a court-supervised distribution to creditors. Straight bankruptcies are covered by Chapter 7 (liquidation) of the Bankruptcy Reform Act. Chapter 11 (reorganization) of the act provides for the reorganization and legal resuscitation of sole proprietorships, partnerships, and corporations. Chapter 13

[21]Ibid., p. 31.

(adjustment of debts of an individual with regular income) of the act provides for working out the debts of an individual or sole proprietor whose income comes primarily from wages, interest, and other "regular" income. Composition and extension agreements are common-law arrangements to accommodate debtor-creditor relationships and resolve conflict.

Bankruptcy Proceedings

Bankruptcy proceedings begin with the filing of either a voluntary or involuntary petition to the bankruptcy court. A voluntary petition is one filed by the debtor; an involuntary petition is filed by one or more creditors of the debtor. An involuntary case may be initiated under Chapter 7 (liquidation) or Chapter 11 (reorganization) against an individual, partnership, corporation, or other business entity. Only the debtor's creditors may initiate an involuntary case, and they must have aggregate claims against the debtor of at least $5,000. Also, if the debtor has more than 12 creditors, at least three of them must join in the involuntary petition. If the court finds in an involuntary proceeding that the debtor is unable to pay his or her debts as they mature, the court will order "relief" against the debtor. Relief may also be ordered if someone has been appointed to control the debtor's property, such as a receiver, within the previous 120 days for the purpose of satisfying a judgment or order lien.

The "trustee in bankruptcy" is an important person in the bankruptcy proceeding. The trustee is someone elected by the creditors to represent the debtor's estate in taking possession of and in liquidating the debtor's property. Broad powers are granted the trustee. The trustee can (1) affirm or disaffirm contracts with the debtor that are yet to be performed; (2) set aside fraudulent conveyances, that is, transfers of the debtor's property for inadequate consideration or for purpose of defrauding creditors; (3) void transfers of property by the debtor to creditors that prefer certain creditors over others; (4) sue those who owe the debtor some obligation; and (5) set aside statutory liens against the debtor's property that take effect on commencement of bankruptcy proceedings. With the court's authorization, the trustee can also run the debtor's business during the liquidation process.[22]

On application, a debtor may be discharged from debt within 1 month and before the expiration of 12 months of having been adjudged a bankrupt. Discharge in bankruptcy will be refused when (1) the court discovers that the debtor had been allowed to plead voluntary bankruptcy within 6 years of the present petition; (2) the debtor has not given a satisfactory explanation of losses; (3) the debtor has issued false financial statements; (4) the debtor has transferred, concealed, or destroyed property within 1 year with the intent to harm creditors; (5) the debtor has falsified, concealed, or destroyed records; and (6) the debtor has not cooperated in supplying information requested by the courts.

[22]Corley et. al., op. cit., p. 408.

Chapter 7—Liquidation

Under Chapter 7, a court may appoint a trustee to operate the debtor's business temporarily if this is in the best interest of the debtor's estate and will aid in an orderly liquidation of the estate. A provision in Chapter 7 allows an individual who is a debtor to redeem certain personal property that is a personal, family, or household item. To redeem this kind of property, the debtor pays the secured creditor whatever the bankruptcy court allowed to discharge the debt. Individual states, however, may reduce the amounts of the federal exemptions through legislation. Under most statutes, however, the bankrupt is allowed the right to retain household furnishings to a certain appraised value; tools of the bankrupt's trade, also limited as to value; schoolbooks, the family Bible, and other items considered necessary to the bankrupt's survival and ability to continue working.

The purpose of bankruptcy under Chapter 7, from the debtor's viewpoint, is to obtain a discharge of further obligation to creditors. Certain debts, however, cannot be discharged in bankruptcy. They include those arising from taxes, alimony and child support, intentional torts (including fraud, breach of fiduciary duty, government fines, and debts not submitted to the trustee because the creditor lacked knowledge of the proceeding). Education loans that become due within five years of the filing of the bankruptcy petition are also nondischargeable unless "undue hardship" can be proved.[23]

Chapter 11—Reorganization

Under Chapter 11 proceedings, the bankruptcy judge may appoint a trustee only if a party who has an interest in the debtor's estate requests it "for cause," such as evidence of fraud, dishonesty, incompetence, or gross mismanagement on the part of the debtor, or if the appointment would be in the best interests of creditors, shareholders, or others with interests in the estate. Chapter 11 rejects the SEC's view that the "public interest" in large corporate reorganizations is so great that appointing a trustee should be mandatory. Section 1104 specifically excludes consideration of the number of a debtor's shareholders and the amount of a debtor's assets and liabilities from the definitions of "cause" and "best interests."[24]

The essence of the reorganization process is the plan of reorganization for financial and operating rehabilitation. The debtor—or a trustee, if appointed—is given exclusive right for 120 days to file a plan. The debtor has up to 180 days after the reorganization petition is filed to receive the necessary consents from the various creditors and owners, if relevant. The court, however, is given the power to increase or reduce the 120- and 180-day periods. If the debtor fails to meet either of these

---

[23]Ibid., p. 409.

[24]*Forms of Business Agreements and Resolutions*, Volume 2, (Englewood Cliffs, N.J.: Institute for Business Planning, a publication from Prentice-Hall's Information Services Division, 1982), p. 6411. This material is used with permission from Prentice-Hall, Inc.

deadlines or others established by the court, creditors and other interested parties may file a plan of approval.

REGULATORY AGENCIES

Because of a wide array of statutes and regulations dealing with employment practices, fair trade, labor relations, worker safety, environment protection, and investor protection, virtually every business, large or small, is subject to the jurisdiction of one or more of the many regulatory agencies. The direct day-to-day legal impact on business of the rules and regulations adopted by these agencies is significant—almost overwhelming. You as a prudent entrepreneur should be aware of these agencies and how you may be subjected to liability from them. With at least some background knowledge, you can spot potential problems and get counsel *before* an agency acts. Some agencies that may have significant impact on your business are now described, along with some suggestions on how to protect yourself and your business from noncompliance with their rules and regulations.

The Equal Employment Opportunity Commission (EEOC)

An important statute that strives to eliminate discriminatory employment practices is the federal Civil Rights Act of 1964, as amended by the Equal Employment Opportunity Act of 1972, as administered by the Equal Employment Opportunity Commission (EEOC). The act prohibits employment discrimination based on race, color, religion, sex, or national origin by employers, employment agencies, and labor unions. Discrimination by the federal government is also prohibited, but the Civil Service Commission has jurisdiction over this area. Discrimination for any of these reasons is a violation of the law except that (1) employers, employment agencies, and labor unions can discriminate on the basis of religion, sex, or national origin in those certain instances where these categories are bona fide occupational qualifications reasonably necessary to normal business operations, (e.g., female swimsuit model for male swimsuits, Baptist minister for priest in Catholic church, or vice versa); (2) employers working under government security program can deny employment to individuals because of their inability to obtain security clearance; (3) employers can establish different standards, compensation, terms, or conditions of employment if applied pursuant to a bona fide seniority or merit system or if they result from the fact that the employees work in different locations. But race and color can *never* be factors in evaluating an employee or applicant for employment because race and color are unrelated to an individual's ability to perform a job.

When you start advertising for job applicants, a preference, limitation, specification, or discrimination based on race, color, religion, sex, or national origin cannot be indicated. Of course, if religion, sex, or national origin is a bona fide business qualification, this may be mentioned in the notice or advertisement. Some state laws prohibit newspapers from publishing classified advertisements according to gender. In certain instances, an employer may give preferential treatment to groups such as veterans and American Indians.

Although the Equal Employment Opportunity Act does not expressly prohibit your asking prospective employees about their race, color, religion, or ethnic background, if you do, you are taking a risk. The Equal Employment Opportunity Commission looks on this line of questioning with extreme disfavor. Therefore, only when religion or national origin constitutes a bona fide occupational qualification may you make these inquiries. In fact, if such questions are asked and you can give no acceptable justification for doing so, this by itself constitutes strong evidence of discrimination.

The Equal Employment Opportunity Commission (EEOC) has adopted guidelines on affirmative action, and complying with them can relieve you of possible liability and penalties that you may incur in an unfair employment practice action. Appropriate affirmative action includes the following procedures: (1) Institute training programs that emphasize teaching skills to minorities and women; (2) actively recruit minorities and women; (3) eliminate all hiring standards that adversely affect minorities and women; (4) modify promotion and layoff procedures that previously adversely affected minorities and women; (5) monitor affirmative action procedure regularly to make certain they are effective, and change them if they are not; (6) avoid unnecessary restrictions on the work force as a whole; (7) maintain quota systems only until the goals of the affirmative action program are reached.

The Federal Trade Commission (FTC)

The basic objective of the Federal Trade Commission (FTC) is to maintain free competitive enterprise by preventing the economic system from being constrained and stifled by monopoly or eroded by unfair or deceptive trade practices. The FTC has broad, sweeping powers and a mandate to determine what methods, acts, or practices fall within the rather vague category of being ''unfair or deceptive.'' The FTC's decisions are made on a case-by-case basis. Generally, then, part of the FTC's responsibility is to safeguard competition whereas another part deals with consumer protection.

Cases before the FTC may originate through complaint by a competitor or consumer or from federal, state, or municipal agencies; or the FTC itself may initiate an investigation to determine possible violation of the laws administered by it. No formality is required in making application for complaint. A letter giving the facts with accompanying documentation is sufficient. If the complaint is valid and in the purview of the FTC's goals of maintaining competition and protecting consumers, an investigation is initiated. After the investigation, the FTC may issue a cease and desist order to prevent wrongful actions. The respondent can consent to the order without admitting any violation of the law. Or a party may apply to a United States court of appeals for review. Special cases, such as false advertising of foods, drugs, devices, or cosmetics that are injurious to health and where there is intent to defraud or mislead, can cause violators to pay up to $10,000 per day of noncompliance to a consent order and up to a year in jail or both.

In carrying out its duties, the FTC tries to make wide use of voluntary and cooperative procedures. To help businesses choose the voluntary route, the FTC periodically issues the following: (1) Advisory opinions are furnished as to whether a proposed course of conduct would be likely to result in further action by the FTC; (2) trade regulation rules set out the experience and judgment of the FTC concerning the substantive requirements of the statutes it administers; (3) industry guides are administrative interpretations of the statutes that the FTC enforces, and they provide guidance for both the FTC staff and businesses evaluating the legality of certain practices.

The National Labor Relations Board (NLRB)

The National Labor Relations Board (NLRB) was created pursuant to provisions of the National Labor Relations Act or NLRA (Wagner Act) of 1935. The NLRA, as later amended by the Taft-Hartley Act of 1947 and the Landrum-Griffin Act of 1959, protected by law the right of employees to organize and bargain collectively and select a union with exclusive power to act as their collective-bargaining representative or to refrain from such activities if they wanted to. The NLRA also prohibits certain unfair labor practices by employers and labor unions or their agents and authorizes the NLRB to designate appropriate units for collective bargaining and to conduct secret ballot elections to determine whether employees desire representation by a labor union.

Excluded employees are agricultural workers; supervisory personnel; domestic servants; persons employed by parents, spouses, or relatives; confidential employees; employees of state and federal governments; and persons subject to the Railway Labor Act; and persons who formulate, determine, or effectuate labor policy.

Excluded employers are any businesses not involved in interstate commerce, the United States government, wholly owned government corporations, Federal Reserve banks, states and political subdivisions, nonprofit hospitals, railroads and airlines that are covered under the Railway Labor Act, and, generally, any small business. Presently, the NLRB seems to concentrate on labor disputes involving larger nonretail businesses; large enterprises operating office buildings, hospitals, and hotels; transportation and communication companies; public utilities; and companies engaged in operations for the national defense.

A summary of unfair labor practices by employers include (1) interference with efforts of employees to form, join, or assist labor organizations or to engage in concerted activities for mutual aid or protection; (2) domination of a labor organization or contribution of financial or other support to it; (3) discrimination in hiring or tenure of employees for reason of union affiliation; (4) discrimination against employees for filing charges or giving testimony under the act; (5) refusal to bargain collectively in good faith with a duly designated representative of the employees; and (6) agreeing with a labor organization to engage in a secondary boycott.[25]

If the NLRB finds that an employer has committed an unfair labor practice, it issues a cease and desist order. Such orders are subject only to limited judicial review. Generally, on such review, the order will not be disturbed. Moreover, the NLRB may order reinstatement of an employee who has been wrongfully discharged, with back pay and restoration of full seniority rights. Even where a person buys out another business, the new owner may be required to reinstate an employee wrongfully discharged by the seller.

The Occupational Safety and Health Review Commission (OSHRC)

Congress, in an effort to lessen personal injuries and illnesses arising out of hazardous work situations, enacted the Occupational Safety and Health Act (OSHA) of 1970. The purpose of OSHA is to provide safe and healthful working conditions for employees working in companies engaged in interstate commerce. The Department of Labor is involved in the implementation of OSHA; the Department of Labor is empowered to conduct plant safety inspections either with the owner's consent or by a warrant if a warrant to inspect the premises is obtained prior to the inspection.

OSHA also establishes the Occupational Safety and Health Review Commission (OSHRC) as the forum for the adjudication of safety grievances and the review of inspection citations. Any business affecting interstate commerce comes within the scope of OSHA even if that business has one employee or even if it is exempt from other federal regulations.

Your aim and function as an employer is to provide all your workers with a safe and healthy work environment. This entails a business that is managed, operated, and maintained in such a way that it (1) frees the workplace from hazards that are likely to cause death or injury, (2) provides a clean and orderly workplace, (3) furnishes employees protective equipment, (4) supervises employees and prevents practical jokes and similar practices that endanger others, (5) provides regular safety meetings that inform everyone about proper safety procedures, (6) provides proper medical and first-aid facilities, and (7) keeps comprehensive logs and detailed records on all illnesses and injuries.

The National Environmental Policy Act (NEPA)

NEPA became effective in 1970. Since then federal courts have analyzed it in hundreds of cases, and the Council on Environmental Quality has interpreted it in several sets of guidelines. The act is divided into two titles. Title I establishes broad policy goals and imposes specific duties on all federal agencies, and Title II sets up

---

[25]Corley et. al., op. cit., p. 252.

the Council on Environmental Quality (CEQ). As the CEQ's role under NEPA consists mainly of gathering and assessing information, issuing advisory guidelines, and making recommendations to the president on environmental matters, this discussion centers on Title I.[26]

First among the broad policy goals enumerated in Title I is that federal agencies should recognize the complex interdependencies between human life and the environment and take them into account before making and implementing decisions. Other listed goals promote recycling depletable resources, balancing population and resource use to permit high standards of living, and fulfilling "the responsibilities of each generation as trustee of the environment for succeeding generations."[27]

Besides being a statement of policy goals, Title I of NEPA imposes specific "action-forcing" requirements on federal agencies. The most important of these requirements is Section 102 (2) (C). It requires all federal agencies to prepare an environmental impact statement (EIS) prior to implementing certain actions. An EIS must be included "in every recommendation or report on proposals for legislation and other major Federal actions significantly affecting the quality of the human environment." This EIS must be a "detailed statement" estimating the environmental impact of the proposed action. Any discussion of such action and its impact must contain information on adverse environmental effects that cannot be avoided, any irreversible commitments of resources necessary, and available alternatives to the action. Figure 13.1 shows the components of an EIS.[28]

Although the designated federal or state agency is responsible for preparing each EIS, it is to your advantage to aid in the preparation of the impact statement in whatever way possible if your company is planning a project that will require a permit from an agency. You may, for example, compile data included in the statement.

The Securities and Exchange Commission (SEC)

If you plan to operate your business as a corporation and issue stock to a large number of shareholders, you will need to become familiar with the Securities and Exchange Commission (SEC) because this agency enforces the federal securities laws that regulate the sale of securities to the investing public. The Federal Securities Act of 1933 regulates anyone who is involved with or who promotes the initial sale of securities.

From the point of view of your corporation, if it issues stock to the public, the Division of Corporate Finance is the most important division of the SEC. It has the responsibility for administering (1) the Federal Securities Act of 1933; (2) the registration provisions of the Securities Act of 1934; (3) the periodic reports filed, such as

---

[26]Ibid., pp. 493–94.
[27]Ibid.
[28]Ibid.

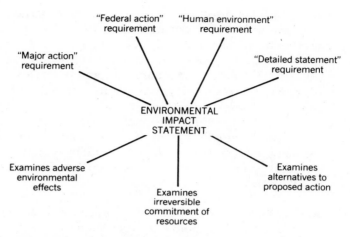

FIGURE 13.1. *Components of an environmental impact statement (EIS). (Source: Robert N. Corley, O. Lee Reed, and Robert L. Black, The Legal Environment of Business, 6th ed. New York: McGraw-Hill, 1984. Used with permission.)*

Forms 10-K, 10-Q, and 8-K; (4) proxy solicitations; and (5) the statements of beneficial ownership filed on Forms 3 and 4.

In your role as either a corporate director or a corporate officer or both, you have a broad scope of powers and responsibilities and, consequently, of liabilities. As a director, you have a duty to the corporation as an entity, not to any individual shareholder. You have the power to make policy decisions, to set the compensation scale of the officers and employees, and to supervise the running of the company from a goal-setting, strategic viewpoint. Generally, the officers of a corporation are authorized to act on its behalf. In most instances, the smaller the corporation, the greater the practical power of its officers.[29]

Liabilities You Face as a Director.   Because a director has such sweeping powers, there are many things he or she can do or agree with the other directors to do that are improper and that will cause the corporation or the director or directors or both to incur liability. Some of the liabilities you may face include (1) premature commencement of business; (2) paying out dividends improperly; (3) making improper compensation arrangements; (4) firing an employee who has a contract; (5) approving an action that is not within the corporate power; (6) patent, trademark, and copyright infringement; (7) failing to act as a steward and prudent person in behalf of the corporation and protest the actions of the board when it does something wrong; (8) improper handling of withholding taxes; (9) making other than arm's-length loans to the corporation; (10) securing improper loans from the corporation for

[29]*Closely Held Business*, op. cit., pp. 8012.9–8047.0.

yourself or other directors, officers, or shareholders; (11) subjecting the corporation to needless taxes; (12) inducing the corporation to breach its contract if the action is taken for personal profit; (13) performing wrongful acts that could also include malfeasance and in some jurisdictions, nonfeasance; (14) continual absence from meetings; (15) failure to safeguard corporate assets and investing corporate funds in speculative enterprises; (16) making gifts and contributions unless they promote the business; (17) unreasonable accumulation of earnings that leads to tax penalties; (18) liability of a director (who is in the position of holding a controlling interest in the corporation) to the corporation and other shareholders for an illegal sale of his or her controlling interest; (19) improper seizure by a director for himself or herself of an opportunity that belongs to, or should have been offered to, the corporation; (20) failure to file annual reports.[30]

Liabilities You Face as an Officer.   Officers have the power to run the corporation on a day-to-day basis; bind the corporation to agreements and contracts; sue in the corporation's name; make capital expenditures; and, in some instances, remove directors. Virtually anything you do in an offical capacity that is within your delegated powers as an officer will not be subject to liability, especially if it is done properly. What's more, even if it is done improperly, as long as it isn't negligent or fraudulent, you are entitled to make mistakes, and there will normally be no liability. But where you act outside the scope of your authority and your actions turn out badly, then you are going to be held liable to the corporation if someone complains.[31]

A word of caution is that, when you are dealing with third parties outside the corporation, make sure that they understand that you are doing business as a corporation. This is especially important in a small business that has incorporated after establishing itself as a proprietorship or partnership and built up customer relations over the years. There are a number of ways to indicate to people that you are doing business on behalf of the corporation, but probably the most important is the way you sign papers, contracts, and the like. Always sign the name of the corporation first, then the word *by* and your name, followed by your title; this makes it clear that you represent the corporation. If you merely sign your name, you are binding yourself personally. And if you sign the corporation's name and your own, with or without title, you may find that you have bound both the corporation and yourself as an individual.[32]

Fraud Liability.   When stock is offered to the public, it is no longer the rule of *caveat emptor* (let the buyer beware); it is *caveat vendor* (let the seller of stock beware). Under the SEC, it is unlawful for any person, directly or indirectly, by the use of mails or any other means of interstate commerce in connection with the purchase or sale of

[30]Ibid., pp. 8026–29.
[31]Ibid., p. 8030.
[32]Ibid.

any security (1) to use any device, scheme, or artifice to defraud; (2) to make any untrue statement of a material fact or to omit a material fact that makes the statement made misleading; or (3) to engage in any act, practice, or course of business that operates as a fraud or deceit on any person.[33]

Those standing in a fiduciary relationship, such as directors, officers, or a controlling shareholder, have a duty to disclose all material facts. One of the most important provisions of the SEC concerns insider transactions. To prevent "insiders" from profiting from information not available to the general public, the law prevents short-swing profits by insiders. Thus, if a director, officer, or major shareholder realizes profits on the purchase and sale of a security within a six-month period, the profits inure to and belong to the company or the investor whose purchase of a security from, or whose sale of a security to, an insider resulted in the insider's profit and the investor's loss.[34]

Suggestions on Avoiding Liability. Here are some general suggestions on protecting both yourself and your corporation from liability: (1) Rely on professional advice; (2) file your dissent, and continue to exert influence wherever possible to deter the corporation from embarking on a wrongful and improper course; (3) make sure that your objections are noted in the minutes of the meeting; (4) check for exculpatory clauses; (5) purchase officers' and directors' liability insurance; (6) get the facts into the record, and make a full disclosure of any conflict of interest; (7) keep the corporation a separate entity even if it is run by one person; (8) keep separate books and records; (9) don't be a big-shot braggart by making such announcements as, "*I* am the corporation—the corporation is only a name;" (10) don't become liable for unpaid wages of your employees; and (11) maintain a corporate image to strengthen the corporate veil.[35]

SUMMARY

If certain records are lost, a business may not be able to survive. Clearly, one of the first things to do to protect your business is establish a sound, well-protected record-keeping system.

If you have developed a new and useful product or service, created an artistic work, generated a distinctive trademark, or have trade secrets, methods should be employed to protect them from misuse by others. Protective measures include patents, copyrights, trademark registrations, and various agreements.

Contracts are a form of protection in that they permit parties to bind themselves to legally enforceable obligations not required under either federal, state, or the

[33]Ibid., pp. 8042–43.
[34]Corley et. al., op. cit., pp. 227–28.
[35]*Closely Held Business*, op. cit., pp. 8045–47.

common law. Once made, a contract obligates the parties to perform, and, if properly drawn, they will be enforced by courts. Additional methods that ensure performance include surety bonds; consequential loss insurance; credit insurance; product-service liability insurance; and the use of deposits, escrows, guaranties, and indemnities.

Moreover, someone in your company or you yourself should have the responsibility for determining those risks that can be transferred and the means and cost-effectiveness of transferring such risks. Usually, potential property loss, earning power loss, future expenses, and legal liability can be insured.

Bankruptcy proceedings, which wipe out the debt of a party considered insolvent, are part of the law that allows troubled proprietorships, partnerships, and corporations the opportunity either to reorganize for a second chance or to start over without the burden of a crippling indebtedness.

A number of regulatory agencies can impose penalties on you and your business if you violate their rules and regulations. The impact on your business of these rules and regulations adopted and enforced by the various agencies is probably greater than the impact of the courts or other branches of government. It, therefore, behooves you to know about these rules and regulations and make sure that your business is in compliance with them.

ASSIGNMENT

1 How does a record-keeping system help to protect the business venture?

2 List and explain the factors affecting the retention of records.

3 How can you classify records? What is the purpose of record classification?

4 Outline an appropriate procedure for record destruction.

5 Differentiate between a production prototype and a breadboard.

6 Define a patent. How does it protect an invention? In your opinion, what are the five most important questions about patents? List the answers to these questions.

7 Explain how a copyright can be used as a protective device.

8 What is the purpose of a trademark? In your opinion, what are the five most important questions about trademarks? List your answers to them.

9 How can you protect yourself against the pirating of trade secrets from your business?

10 What is a contract? How do contracts help protect your business? What additional measures can you use to help lessen the risk of contractual loss?

11 What is the purpose of risk management? What are the duties of a risk manager? What kinds of losses or perils are you subject to that you can transfer to an insurance company? Explain.

12 What are the reasons for bankruptcy law? What is the difference between involuntary and voluntary bankruptcy?

13 What is bankruptcy under Chapter 7? Under Chapter 11?

14 Outline bankruptcy proceedings.

15 Name the regulatory agencies described in this chapter, and state the basic function of each. Describe what steps you can take to be in compliance with their rules and regulations.

BIBLIOGRAPHY

Ballas, George C., and Dave Hollas. *The Making of an Entrepreneur, Keys to Your Success.* Englewood Cliffs, N.J.: Prentice-Hall, 1980.

Closely Held Business. Englewood Cliffs, N.J.: Institute for Business Planning, a publication from Prentice-Hall's Information Services Division, 1983.

Cohen, William A. *The Entrepreneur and Small Business Problem Solver.* New York: Wiley, 1983.

Corley, Robert N., O. Lee Reed, and Robert L. Black. *The Legal Environment of Business.* 6th ed. New York: McGraw-Hill, 1984.

Dible, Donald M. (ed.). *Winning the Money Game.* Santa Clara, Calif.: Entrepreneur Press, 1975.

Forms of Business Agreements and Resolutions. Vol. 2. Englewood Cliffs, N.J.: Institute for Business Planning, a publication from Prentice-Hall's Information Services Division. 1982.

Heckert, Brooks J., and James D. Willson. *Controllership.* 2d ed. New York: Ronald Press, 1963.

Henry, David. "Patent Absurdity No More." *Forbes.* September 10, 1984.

Jacobs, Sanford L. "Holding Patent Doesn't Keep Copycat Products off Market." *The Wall Street Journal.* Section 2, May 14, 1984.

Larson, Erik. "In High-Tech Industry, New Firms Often Get Fast Trip to Courtroom." *The Wall Street Journal.* August 14, 1984.

Riegel, Robert, Jerome S. Miller, and C. Arthur Williams, Jr. *Insurance Principles and Practices, Property and Liability.* Englewood Cliffs, N.J.: Prentice-Hall, 1976.

Rock, Andrea. " 'Eureka!' But What Do You Do Next?" *Money.* May 1984.

Shames, William H. *Venture Management.* New York: The Free Press, 1974.

Silver, A. David. *The Entrepreneurial Life, How to Go for It and Get It.* New York: Wiley, 1983.

CHAPTER 14

Financing Instruments and Venture Capital

INTRODUCTION

As "they" say, money is what makes the world go around. More specifically, money is necessary to finance, launch, and make your business venture a success. But to get this money, you will have to give something in exchange, either a promise to pay the money back plus interest or a piece of ownership and control. That is, you get your financing through debt or equity or both. The financing package you offer to lenders and investors contains financing instruments that serve as legal representations of your company's debt or equity commitments to your sources of financing. The objectives of this chapter are as follows.

1 To describe all financing instruments except a straight loan agreement.
2 To discuss stock offerings.
3 To treat venture capital and analyze venture capitalists.

FINANCING INSTRUMENTS AND PACKAGE

Five financing instruments are available to build a financing package and to obtain money for your business venture. These are pure debt instrument (discussed in the next chapter), warrants, convertible debentures, preferred stock, and common stock. On one end of the spectrum, there is pure debt and a senior claim against assets; on the other is equity giving the least claim against assets but ownership and control. Clearly, the least downside risk to the investor is a debt instrument, but the highest upside potential is given by owning common stock.

Financing Instruments

The financing instruments used to build a viable financing package are discussed as follows.

1 *Loan with warrants.* A warrant provides the investor with the right to buy stock at a fixed price at some future date. Terms on the warrants are negotiable. The warrant customarily provides for the purchase of additional stock, say up to 10 percent of the total issue at 130 percent of the original offering price within a five-year period following the offering date.

2 *Convertible debentures.* Convertible debentures offer a financing instrument that also offers a strong claim against business assets. An advantage to your business, if we assume the corporate form, is that interest paid on the debentures is a deductible business expense of the corporation. Dividends paid on preferred or common stock are not deductible. Because the debenture is a loan to your company that is convertible into stock, the conversion price, the interest

rate, and the provisions in the loan agreement are items that you will have to negotiate with the investor.

3 *Preferred stock.*   Especially for start-ups, preferred stock is an ideal financing instrument because it gives investors preferred treatment if anything goes wrong. You can also make the preferred stock convertible so that the preferred shareholders may enjoy the same upside potential and equity growth as the common shareholders, assuming a one-for-one convertibility ratio. At the same time, preferred shareholders are protected in their downside risk because if there is a liquidation, they are the first shareholders to participate in the distribution of assets.

4 *Common stock.*   Common stock is the most frequently used financing instrument for selling ownership in companies. Usually common stock (it can be voting or nonvoting) carries the right to vote on certain corporate actions. Common stock represents pure equity and ownership. In liquidation, common shareholders are the last to share in the proceeds from sale of assets of the corporation. If your company grows and is successful, shares can be sold to the public on several of the exchanges, such as Over-the-Counter Market (OTC), the American Stock Exchange (AMEX), or the New York Stock Exchange (NYSE).

Financing Package

The different financing instruments just described provide you with flexibility to put together a variety of financing packages for the investment community. For the entrepreneurial team and key managers, you can offer common stock. For private venture capitalists and various government financing sources, you can offer a combination of both stock and convertibles.

In essence, one of the most attractive instruments for both you and the investor is preferred stock. It offers a good balance. On the one hand, it is equity and provides a long-term capital base for the company's future growth; on the other hand, if properly structured, preferred stock can contain rights virtually equivalent to those in a debt instrument, thus assuring the investor of seniority in the case of a merger or liquidation and the ability to influence management via voting rights.

Making the financial package viable centers on satisfying your need for capital and the other investors' desire for a good return on their investment. The three chief controllable factors in most deals are (1) the percentage of equity given investors, (2) debt covenants and the amount of security given investors, and (3) interest rates and conversion privileges.

1 *Percentage of ownership.*   The amount of equity and the way it is divided depends on the total contribution of all parties and the level of risk assumed by each. Generally, the farther you are from the early stages of your business, the greater your share of equity.

2 *Covenants provided in the agreement.* Most investors demand that certain covenants be written into the investment agreement to protect them if things go sour. This is especially true with start-ups where the entrepreneur has not established a track record. The conventional covenants provide the capital investors a way to take control if one or all of these circumstances occur: (1) Working capital falls below certain limits, (2) sales fall below a specified level, (3) a target profit is not realized, and (4) retained earnings fall below a predetermined level. Other common covenants may prescribe how funds are spent and also that debt be secured with certain assets such as accounts receivable and inventories.

3 *Interest rate and conversion privilege.* Conversion privileges have been explained earlier. Interest rates and amortization of debt must be in line with the company's cash flow projections and its ability to meet debt service. A foolish thing for you to do and one that will spell disaster for your business venture is to attempt to build a capital base with short-term debt.

SELLING SECURITIES

Equity funds can be raised either through public or private offerings. You are required, however, to comply with the laws of the Securities and Exchange Commission (SEC) and the laws of the state in which your company is domiciled. Because the securities laws are complex and differ significantly between states, raising capital by selling securities can be a difficult and traumatic task, especially if you plan to go public with your stock offering. Some steps, however, have been taken to reduce some of the complexities and red tape. For example, Regulation D has made it easier for small businesses to raise money. Up to certain amounts, a business can make a single offering to an unlimited number of investors without having to register the offering. In addition, Regulation A exempts your company from certain filing requirements, such as the 10-K, 10-Q, or interim 8-Q forms if your company has fewer than 500 shareholders and less than $1 million in assets.

Advantages of Selling Securities

The advantages include the following.

1 Generally, securities will command a higher price. This means that equity capital can be raised with minimal dilution of the original owners' stock.

2 Selling securities is the only practical way of raising huge amounts of capital. And once the securities have gained favor in the marketplace, the mechanism is in place for additional capital to support a continuing growth program.

3 A public market provides liquidity for original owners and managers to raise cash for themselves by selling portions of their stock.

4 The marketplace sets a value on the company's stock, which helps in attracting management through favorable stock-option plans.

5 Being publicly held can increase a company's image to its customers, suppliers, bankers, and competitors.

Disadvantages of Selling Securities

Here are some of the chief reasons why owners of a closely held business might prefer to keep it that way.

1 Going public requires a detailed disclosure of the company's affairs in its offering prospectus. This disclosure reveals to suppliers, customers, employees, unions, competitors, and the public at large many private details of the company's business that it may want kept to itself.

2 The paperwork and reporting requirements are onerous. In addition to the requirements of the stock market and investors for continuing information about the company's operations, management must provide various reports for the SEC and maintain communication with analysts, portfolio managers, and the like. Moreover, officers, directors, and major shareholders have to report monthly on all transactions in the company's securities.

3 The management of a closely held business run it their way without fear of reprisal from shareholders. Moreover, they can make decisions more quickly. They are streamlined to take advantage of opportunities and act on a variety of proposals. A public corporation, on the other hand, must be concerned with shareholder reactions.

4 Shareholders are looking for a good earnings and dividend record plus stock value appreciation. They also scrutinize various expenses and become hostile if they believe salaries and other amenities for management are out of line. In essence, management now has a lot of shareholders to satisfy. If managements do not satisfy shareholders, they run the risk of ouster.

5 If a corporation has elected S Corporation treatment, this tax advantage will be lost with more than 35 shareholders.

6 The costs of the offering are significant. In addition to the investment banker's commission for underwriting the stock offering, there are costs for accountants, attorneys, and printing and distribution costs. For example, the mere printing of the prospectus and its distribution can amount to thousands of dollars.

Investment Bankers—Underwriters

Generally, if you sell stock, you will need an investment banker, more commonly called an underwriter. Underwriters are professional, experienced people who can do a much better job than you can do because they are better equipped to select the types of securities and set the price that will make the stock offering deal work. Moreover, investment bankers form a syndicate with other underwriters to offer your stock to a number of markets that one working alone could not reach. This helps to attract the right mix of investors. In addition to conducting a successful stock offering, investment bankers also maintain an orderly aftermarket.

Investment banking firms provide an array of services that include (1) equity financing, either through public or private placement; (2) debt financing; (3) asset-based financing, such as real estate and leasing; (4) quasi-equity financing through R and D limited partnerships; and (5) financial advice. Today a number of investment bankers are not just for the mature and large business; they are becoming instrumental in the growth and direction of small, emerging companies, especially those that demonstrate the potential of high growth. In the past, their main function was to take mature and large companies public; now they help secure debt and equity capital and provide full-scale investment and management counseling as well.

To take you on as a client, underwriters will want to review your financial statements. They will want to know about the industry in which your company does business and will evaluate the competition and the reputation of your company and its products or services. They will determine the growth prospects of your company. Moreover, for a composite evaluation, they will talk to customers, competitors, suppliers, and others who might know something about the industry in general and your company in particular. Where needed, they will use industry experts and independent appraisers. In addition, they will want to know what research and development efforts are being made to improve existing products and develop additional products. They will want to know your business philosophy, aspirations, and long-term goals and strategies for meeting these goals. They will want to know all about your managers, their experience and potential, as well as talk to all your key people. Furthermore, they will want to know what steps you have taken to hold key personnel by stock options and employment contracts, and they will want to make sure that these commitments are not unduly burdensome to the company and the shareholders. Underwriters will want to make sure that your business can stand a complete audit required by the SEC and will also want to see a complete accounting system established and all word-of-mouth arrangements reduced to writing. They will want all records, including minute books, brought up-to-date. Finally, they will want all insider relationships with the corporation formalized and put on a prudent, arm's-length business basis.[1]

Private Stock Offering

Some companies are simply too small to consider a public offering of their stock. But today they can, without too much trouble, sell securities in private placement.

[1]*Closely Held Business* (Englewood Cliffs, N.J.: Institute for Business Planning, Inc., a publication from Prentice-Hall's Information Services Division, 1983), pp. 6812–13. This material has been adapted with permission from Prentice-Hall, Inc.

Investor protection laws, as administered by the Securities and Exchange Commission (SEC), have required the preparation of extensive reports and financial statements so that prospective shareholders are properly informed. Such procedures have not made sense to the small business interested in selling small amounts of stocks to a few investors, such as relatives, friends, employees, suppliers, customers, and local professionals. So in April 1982 the SEC eased the rules for private placements. The new rules under Regulation D were introduced to help businesses raise capital.

With Regulation D, a company can have an offering with no limit on the number of investors and with no minimum investment. The regulation has made it possible for many companies to raise capital without the expense of disclosure statements. Regulation D has eased the definition of a "sophisticated" investor and is now using the concept of an "accredited" investor. Today many small companies are selling stock to employees and others using Regulation D's Rule 504, which permits offerings up to $500,000 to an unlimited number of investors.

Clearly, the objective of Regulation D was to make it easier and less expensive for small firms to sell stock. But many states have not kept pace with the eased rules. Consequently, many small companies still find it costly and time-consuming to try to clear their offerings in such states. Moreover, many companies are discouraged by the requirement of audited financial statements for offerings of $500,000 and over, which are cited under Rule 505 ($500,000 to $5 million) and Rule 506 (over $5 million). There are still some kinks to be ironed out, but Regulation D does a lot to simplify small-company financing.

SEC Registration for Going Public

The registration process consists of preparing and filing a registration statement with the SEC. A registration statement is generally comprised of two parts: (1) the prospectus and (2) a number of forms. By law, a company is not allowed to sell stock to the public until it files the registration statement with the SEC. After the SEC reviews it and makes sure that it complies with all regulations on fair and full disclosure, the company is given permission to proceed with the offering. The investment banker sends prospectuses to any individual who expresses an interest in the company.

The prospectus is suppose to disclose fully all pertinent information about a company and present a fair representation of the company's true prospects. All negatives are clearly highlighted and explained. Detailed information includes (1) the history and nature of the company, (2) the capital structure, (3) description of any material contracts, (4) description of securities being registered, (5) salaries and security holdings of major officers and directors and the price they paid, (6) underwriting arrangements, (7) estimate and use of net proceeds, and (8) audited financial statements. In addition, information is provided about the competition with an estimation of the chances of the company's surviving. Other disclosures include description of products, research and development, trade secrets, patents, and so forth. Profiles of management and customers are also disclosed.

Regulation A is a shortcut registration procedure provided by the SEC and is used exclusively by smaller companies to raise capital through the issue of stock. Successful clearing of the bureaucratic and legal hurdles does not, however, guarantee that the stock will sell. Many small companies, indeed, have gone to the trouble and expense of arranging this kind of offering only to find that potential shareholders would not buy the stock. Generally, Regulation A offerings are handled on a "best efforts" basis, and the underwriter usually wants a bigger price spread.

Reporting Responsibilities of Going Public

Moving from private to public equity financing involves not only a major strategy shift on the part of management but also a new style of management and a new, much stronger emphasis on record keeping and reporting. Management must be willing to share ownership, decision making, and control with outsiders. Moreover, because of the new stringent stewardship responsibilities, management must provide full disclosure of company operations and how capital funds have been used. The purpose of SEC reporting regulations is (1) to require disclosure of more meaningful information in the annual reports and (2) to improve the dissemination of the more technical 10-K report filed with the SEC.

Some of the more important disclosure requirements for annual reports are (1) audited financial statements that include the balance sheets for two years and income and funds statements for three years, (2) five-year selected financial data, (3) management's discussion and analysis of financial conditions and results of operations, (4) a brief description of the business, (5) line-of-business disclosures for the last three fiscal years, (6) identification of directors and executive officers with the principal occupation and employer of each, (7) identification of the principal market in which the securities of the firm are traded, (8) range of market prices and dividends for each quarter of the two most recent fiscal years, and (9) offer to provide a free copy of the 10-K report to shareholders on written request unless the annual report complies with Form 10-K disclosure requirements.[2]

A description of the most common forms prepared for the SEC and the information contained in each follow:[3] (1) Form S-1, which is information contained in the prospectus and other additional financial data; (2) Form 10-Q, which contains the quarterly financial statements and a summary of all important events that took place during the three-month period; (3) Form 8-K, which is a report of unscheduled material events or corporate changes deemed of importance to the shareholder and which is filed with the SEC within 15 days after the end of a month in which a significant material event transpired; and (4) proxy statement, which is information given in connection with proxy solicitation.

---

[2]K. Fred Skousen, *An Introduction to the SEC*, 3d ed. (Cincinnati: South-Western Publishing Company, 1983), p. 157. This material is used with permission.

[3]Ibid.

Blue-Sky Laws

The intent of the SEC is to ensure full and fair disclosure of all material facts concerning securities offered for public investment and to provide adequate information so that an investor can make an informed decision (though not necessarily a good decision). The federal law is not designed to protect investors from bad or speculative investments. The aim of state blue-sky laws is basically the same, but the methods used to achieve this aim vary from state to state. The categories include (1) fraud laws, which impose penalties for fraud in the sale of securities; (2) regulatory laws, which prohibit the sale of securities until an application is filed and permission is granted by the state; (3) registration of securities, securities dealers, and salespeople; and (4) certain "miscellaneous" provisions dealing with such topics as advertising, prospectus requirements, and reports, as well as civil and criminal penalties.

Pricing the Stock

The price your company gets for its stock is obviously an important part of raising sufficient equity capital. Following is a summary of pricing as told by an experienced investment banker.[4]

> *Now I'd like to get into one of the more interesting sides of this business—the pricing of securities issues. Basically, we use very standard guidelines of the kind you would learn in any college course in finance. We don't have a "secret formula." For example, if you had a $10 million company—let's say a small chain of retail stores—we'd like to find two or three other retail store operations in the same geographic area that also had sales of $10 million. Assuming that they were already public companies, we would look at the price-to-earnings ratio on the stocks of those companies and at their growth records over the last four or five years. We'd also look at the return on invested capital, the book value, and the total market value of the company's stock. We would compare earnings growth, size of the company, areas of distribution, market to book value, and profit margin ratios. We would then determine a statistical average on which to base a decision on the stock price at which your company should sell. There are always pluses and minuses in, making these evaluations. Maybe you've got a stronger management team, and you're growing faster. But bascially, we're going to compare your company to other companies in the public marketplace in order to come up with a realistic value for your company. You probably think that your company is the greatest in the world and that your stock ought to sell at twice the price-to-earnings ratio of your*

[4]This section is abridged from Edward C. Reed, "Financing Through an Investment Banker," in Donald M. Dible (ed.), *Winning the Money Game* (Santa Barbara, Calif.: Entrepreneur Press, 1975), pp. 252–54, and adapted with the permission of Reston Publishing Company, a Prentice-Hall company, 11480 Sunset Hills Road, Reston, Va. 22090.

competitors. That would be a tough thing for us to accept and justify to potential investors.

I grant you that there is a lot of subjective judgment involved in this. One factor is how well you sell yourself. Let's say that the president of a competing company is a poor public speaker. He'll probably get a few minuses on this. Maybe you're a super salesperson and can effectively communicate with the analysts, stockbrokers, and investors. Then we'll give you a little higher price. These are the kinds of things we're constantly weighing.

We have one other requirement in our firm. Let's say that we evaluate your company and decide that its worth $11 a share in the public market. Then we would tell you that we'd like to sell your stock to the public at $10 a share. We would sell your stock at slightly below market value because we want the public to make a little money, too. If we could price our deals perfectly, we'd price them at approximately 10 percent below the level at which we think they're going to sell. Then we'd hope that, immediately after the offering, this company would sell at $11 so that the initial investors would make some money, and the stock wouldn't drop below the offering price. The next time you want to raise money from the public, you'll have a lot of shareholders with whom you have created substantial goodwill who will want to buy more of your stock. If you don't structure the offering in this way and your initial price is too high so that your stock starts to go down, it will be extremely difficult to sell additional shares in the future.

We've turned down quite a few deals because the management of the company involved wanted $11 per share instead of the $10 per share that we recommended. We need investors who constantly want to buy stock in new companies. If they buy the stock and it doesn't go anywhere, they've got stale money. Then they're not going to want to invest in other companies that we bring public.

It usually takes a minimum of three months to prepare and market a public offering. One of the really tough parts of this business is in predicting what the stock market conditions will be three to four months from now. When we discuss the proposed price of your stock, we'll ask you for some estimates. Then we'll say, 'OK, if your estimates hold up, we'll take you public in three or four months at this kind of price based on the current conditions in the stock market.'' With the gyrations of the stock market, predicting what's going to be happening in three to four months can be a really difficult job that involves a lot of judgment.

Typical Sequence of Events of a Public Offering[5]

Although each individual case has its own characteristics and its own time schedule, a typical pattern might be as follows: The XYZ Company has reached a point in its

[5]This section was taken from Peter W. Wallace, "Public Financing for Smaller Companies," in Stanley E. Pratt (ed.), *Guide to Venture Capital Sources* 7th ed. (Wellesley Hills, Mass.: Capital Publishing, 1983), pp. 109–10, and is used with permission. Also see *Pratt's Guide to Venture Capital Sources*, 9th ed. (Wellesley Hills, Mass.: Venture Economics, Inc., 1985.).

growth where it recognizes the need for additional capital to finance growth in the year or two ahead. The company may have been in business for a number of years, and private investors who provided the initial capital are interested in seeing some degree of liquidity and a measure of value on their shares. In a series of meetings, the XYZ directors determine that it is appropriate for the company to seek a public offering. The management is directed to discuss this possibility with a number of underwriters and to ask those who appear to be both suitable and interested to make formal presentations to the board of directors. The proposed underwriters will each make visits to the company to become acquainted with management and operations prior to submitting their proposals. Finally, a selection is made by the board and management of the company and the formal process commences.

When the preparation of the underwriting is to begin, an "all hands" meeting is held involving the company management, the managing underwriter, company counsel, underwriter's counsel, and auditors. At this time, a time schedule is laid out for the demanding task of preparing the registration statement to be filed with the SEC as well as the subsequent events that will involve the marketing of the proposed issue. A part of the registration statement is the prospectus, which will be distributed publicly and which describes the company's history and operations in some detail. The preparation of the registration materials will typically take 30 to 60 days, a time period that may be extended, if necessary, to accommodate the completion of an audit.

Once the registration statement is filed with the SEC, the preliminary prospectuses are printed, and the marketing process commences. At this time, the underwriter will invite other investment banking firms into the underwriting syndicate, and the final syndicate may be composed of 50 to 70 firms. As these firms accept positions in the syndicate, their salespeople begin to talk with clients and furnish them with prospectuses. Meanwhile, the managing underwriter will typically organize a series of presentations by company management in various key cities where significant institutional or individual investor interest can be found. Perhaps a half dozen to a dozen cities will be visited over a period of one to two weeks.

At the same time the SEC processes the registration and ultimately responds (usually within 30 days) with a series of comments, questions, or requests for additional information. The prospectus is then modified as needed to conform with the SEC request, and when the SEC is satisfied with the content, it will permit the issue to become effective.

Immediately prior to the offering's becoming effective, the underwriter and the company have the last of a series of price discussions and set the price of the offering, which will then be incorporated into an amended prospectus. The revised prospectus with the price amendment then becomes a final prospectus that is printed and distributed after the offering has become effective. As soon as the offering is effective, sales can be confirmed by the members of the syndicate to their clients. Prior to effectiveness, they can do nothing more than take indications of interest.

The final step will be the closing, generally five business days after the offering becomes effective. At this time, the money changes hands and the offering is completed.

VENTURE CAPITAL

Entrepreneurs who seek venture or risk capital have diverse sources to choose from. Venture capital can be obtained from private venture capital firms, from government-backed agencies, from wealthy individuals, or from a number of associates such as employees, suppliers, relatives, and so forth. Such investors differ significantly in their taste for risk, ranging from investors willing to back unproved business concepts or inventions to those preferring later-stage financing for established businesses. Investors differ as well in the size of the investment they will consider; their exit horizons or level of patience for cash flow, dividends, and capital appreciation; their degree of personal involvement with a venture and level of ownership; and their rate of return requirements and the substitutability of non-financial for financial rewards.[6]

Advantages of Venture Capital Financing

The venture capital sources are the lifeblood of small businesses that need long-term equity or debt financing. Moreover, most venture capital firms have on their staff experienced people who can give you a wealth of help and guidance in steering your company from one stage to another. Pitfalls exist, and problems crop up. The venture capital staff have been there before, and they can, therefore, help you to avoid the pitfalls and solve problems. Furthermore, no matter what stage your business is in, you will need additional funds in the future because of growth demands or because of crises or unforeseen trouble or both. Nothing is more disastrous to a business than to run out of money and available financing sources midway into the venture. Reputable venture capital firms go into a deal generally anticipating that additional funds will be needed at various stages throughout the venture.

Besides money, a reputable venture capital firm provides a wide range of services to young, small companies. Specifically, some of the services provided include (1) market research and strategy for those businesses that do not have their own marketing departments; (2) management consulting functions as well as management audit and evaluation; (3) additional financing sources; (4) contacts with prospective customers, suppliers, and other important businesspeople; (5) negotiation of technical agreements; (6) help in establishing management and accounting controls; (7) help in employee recruitment and development of employee agreements; (8) help in risk management and establishment of an effective insurance program; and (9) counseling and guidance for the business in complying with a myriad of government regulations.

[6]William E. Wetzel, Jr., "Informal Investors—When and Where to Look," in Stanley E. Pratt (ed.), *Guide to Venture Capital Sources*, 7th ed. (Wellesley Hills, Mass.: Capital Publishing, 1983), p. 23. This material is used with permission.

Myths About Venture Capitalists[7]

There are a number of myths circulating about venture capitalists. These are dispelled as follows.

Myth 1. *Venture capital firms want to own control of your company and tell you how to run the business.* Nothing could be further from the truth. No venture capital firm intentionally sets out to own control of a small business. Venture capitalists seek more than 50 percent of a company when they need to have that much of the company in order to justify the amount of money they are putting into the business. Venture capitalists have no desire to run your business. They do not want to tell you how to make day-by-day decisions and have you report to them on a daily basis. They want you and your management team to run your company profitably. They do want to be consulted on any major decision, but they want no day-to-day say in your business operations.

Myth 2. *You must have an introduction to venture capitalists from one of their friends in order to obtain financing.* You do not need an introduction to venture capitalists from anyone. A business plan that is well prepared is the best introduction you can have. Gone are the days when you needed an intermediary to introduce you to a rich investor before he or she would invest money into your venture. Most venture capital firms are run by middle-class, nonelite individuals. They are interested in good investments. They are not interested in your social contacts or introductions. Later on in your relationship, if you have mutual friends or know people of similar background, such contacts will enhance your credibility; but there is no need to have an intermediary to get your idea across to the venture capitalist or to gain financing.

Myth 3. *Venture capital firms are interested only in new technological discoveries.* Most venture capital companies are not interested in revolutionary ideas that change the way people live. These kinds of ideas take 10 to 20 years to develop. It is doubtful that any professional venture capitalist would have backed the electric light bulb. It took a farsighted person to see that someday everyone would replace their oil lamps with light bulbs. Revolutionary ideas are very difficult to finance because the return on investment takes so long to realize. Venture capitalists are more interested in an add-on technology like a new type of computer, a new silicon chip, a new market technique, or something that will involve moderate change. It is true that venture capitalists tend to be oriented toward high technology, but a better way of viewing their orientation is to say that they are interested in companies that promise high growth. If you have a company that has a potential for high growth, then you can attract venture capital money.

Myth 4. *Venture capitalists are satisfied with a reasonable return on investments.* No venture capitalist expects a reasonable return on his or her investment. The truth is that these people expect very high, exorbitant, unreasonable returns. They can

[7]This section is abridged from David J. Gladstone, *Venture Capital Handbook* (Reston, Va.: Reston Publishing Company, Inc., a Prentice-Hall company, 1983), pp. 21–24, and adapted by permission of Reston Publishing Company, a Prentice-Hall company, 11480 Sunset Hills Road, Reston, Va. 22090.

obtain reasonable returns from hundreds of publicly traded companies. They can obtain reasonable returns from many types of investments not having the degree of risk involved in financing a small business. Because every venture capital investment involves a high degree of risk, there must be a corresponding high return on investment.

Myth 5. *Venture capitalists are quick to invest.* On the contrary, it takes a long time to raise venture capital. On the average, it will take six to eight weeks from the initial contact to raise your venture capital. If you have a well-prepared business plan, you will be able to raise money in that time frame. A venture capitalist will see from 50 to 100 proposals a month. Out of that number, 10 will be of some interest. The venture capitalist will read those 10 business proposals. Out of those 10, 2 or 3 will receive a fair amount of analysis, negotiation, and investigation. Of the 2 or 3, 1 may be funded. This funneling process of selecting 1 out of 100 takes a great deal of time. Once the venture capitalist has found that "one," he or she will spend a significant amount of time investigating possible outcomes before funding it. Your proposal will be weighed against the many alternate investment opportunities available. Make sure it stands out and is well prepared so you can receive your funds quickly.

Myth 6. *Venture capitalists are interested in backing new ideas or high-technology inventions. Management is a secondary consideration.* Venture capitalists back only good management. If you have a bright idea but have a poor managerial background and no experience in the industry, try to find someone in the industry to bring into your team. The venture capitalist will have a hard time believing that you, with no experience in that industry and no managerial ability in your background, can follow through on your business plan. You do not necessarily need a complete management team the day you write your proposal. Many venture capitalists have staff members who can help you with certain areas of your business. However, most of them would prefer that you have your management team pulled together before you get the venture off the ground. A good idea is important, but a good management team is even more important.

Myth 7. *Venture capitalists need only basic summary information before they make an investment.* A detailed and well-organized business plan is the only way to gain a venture capital investor's attention and obtain funding. If you think that you can hastily write a two-page summary and have a venture capitalist fund your investment, you are sadly mistaken. Venture capitalists want a good summary as a start, not as a substitute for a sound plan. Every venture capitalist, before becoming involved, wants the entrepeneur to have thought out the entire business plan and to have written it down in detail.

Checklist of What the Venture Capitalist Looks for in You

Here are some of the key personal qualities that venture capitalists look for or, to turn it around, the qualities you will want to project when seeking their aid.[8]

---

[8]*Closely Held Business*, op. cit., pp. 6745–46.

1 *Resourcefulness.* The ability to deal skillfully and promptly with new situations and problems is an indispensable quality. A prominent venture capitalist once offered a dramatic example of this quality in a man who owned a rat- and vermin-infested building scheduled for demolition—a virtual entomologist's paradise, well stocked with every variety of termites, cockroaches, lice, and so on, and unfit for human habitation. The idea: Rent the building to an exterminator for six months until demolition can begin. The exterminator would have a great laboratory for experimentation and could expect to get thousands of dollars' worth of free advertising through the newspapers. *Result:* $9,000 in cash for six month's rent for Mr. Resourceful.

2 *Self-discipline.* The venture capitalist must be concerned not only with whether the businessperson will have the self-discipline to work hard on a tight budget but also whether he or she will have the self-discipline to deal with prosperity. There is nothing so corrosive for some people as prosperity. At the first signs of a turnaround, they want to move up a notch in personal and business accoutrements. The problem, though, is that the cycle of rags to riches may move back to rags.

3 *Expertise.* The businessperson has to know his or her business. If the venture capitalist gets the feeling that he or she knows more about the business than the entrepreneur, you can be sure there's no "deal."

4 *Amenability to advice and suggestions.* Venture capitalists certainly don't want to do business with people who will follow advice and suggestions blindly, but they do want someone who is at least amenable to counsel on occasion. They don't care for someone who rejects an idea out of hand. It may, however, be all right if a week later the entrepreneur comes back with the original suggestion with an added twist of his or her own. Venture capitalists figure they may be able to live with that type, but the ideal would be a sound decision maker who will listen and modify his or her decision when someone comes up with a better idea.

5 *Confidence.* Venture capitalists look for someone who exudes confidence in himself or herself and his or her operation without being cocky and overbearing.

6 *Integrity and candor.* Venture capitalists look for people who are able to face up to reality with integrity and candor and who know their own strengths and those of their organization but also know their personal and company weaknesses and are willing to admit them and deal with them in a positive way.

7 *Compatibility.* Closely related to the qualities we've been speaking of is personal and company compatibility. The venture capitalist wants to be able to help you and your company if and when the need arises and will want to match his or her capabilities with your prospective needs. If, for example, the venture capitalist has strength in the marketing area where you may have a weakness—OK, he or she figures you're compatible in that respect. But if he or she doesn't have the required capability and doesn't see being able to develop it when the need arises, other factors will have to be very good if a deal is to emerge.

8 *Communication.* The venture capitalist looks for an entrepreneur who not only knows his or her business and problems but also can communicate effectively. Poor communications breed trouble in most any kind of marriage.

9 *Promoter vs. operator.* Starting up and running a business usually require different qualities, and this is apt to be reflected in attitudes toward risk. A willingness to take risks may be acceptable and, indeed, desirable in the start-up phase of a business; but once a business reaches a certain level, say, a volume of annual sales of $4 or $5 million, it may require a more conservative individual to bring the sales up to, say, $10 million and beyond. In this respect, then, the qualities that the venture capitalist looks for may vary depending on the development of the business at the time his or her help is sought.

10 *Planning and risk taking.* Closing a deal takes time—two to six months or more. If you've delayed making your move to raise venture capital until your condition is desperate, it indicates one of two things or possibly both: lack of planning or of a willingness to take risks. And, of course, desperation weakens your bargaining position.

11 *When the analysis takes place.* The analysis of your qualities takes place at every phase of the "mining" process, from the initial contact to the closing. It is going on in connection with the business plan (some venture capitalists call it the blue book) you make. It continues throughout all meetings, interviews, and written presentations.

Checklist for Choosing a Venture Capital Firm

Clearly, choosing a venture capital firm can be a crucial business decision. You will be choosing someone who will be working with you over a long period of time, who will intimately know how your business operates, and to whom you will have to submit periodic financial reports. The success of your expansion plans and perhaps even of your entire business will be closely tied to the manner in which your investor conducts his or her business. Make the following checks before making a final decision.[9]

1 *Reputation.* Choose a venture capital firm that has a good reputation for making money—both past and present. This will help you weed out the "nervous" investors who try to pull their money out when the first cloud appears on the horizon. The venture companies that have good profit records know that problems invariably crop up with each investment. They have learned to expect them and know how to deal with them. The successful venture capital firms stick through difficult times with their clients.

[9]Ibid., pp. 6748–49.

2 *Track record.* Check out the profit schedules of companies financed by the venture capital firm. Compare these profits to those made by the investor. You want a financing company that is interested not only in its own profit goals but also in the profits of the companies that it finances. Occasionally, you will find venture firms that make lots of money for themselves, but strangely enough the businesses they invest in don't do that well.

3 *Resources.* Make sure that the venture capital firm that you choose has enough and is willing to disburse additional funds to see your program all the way through to completion. We emphasized earlier the danger of obtaining less than the full amount needed to do the complete job. There will also be the need for extra money to help you through unforeseen problems. Do not neglect to talk over thoroughly the amount that the investor is willing to commit, making sure that you understand the conditions on which he or she will advance additional funds.

4 *Personnel.* Pick a firm that has enough personnel willing to help you with its investment in you and your program. Venture capital firms that are profitable will generally have the required number of people to work with you. If they have a large enough investment in your company, their opportunity for making a worthwhile profit will be another guarantee that you will be able to call on them whenever you need them. They will then be doing their best for you, for your success means their profit.

Slicing the Pie

Lenders think in terms of the capability of your business to meet the debt service and the security of their loans. Investors who provide risk capital use several variables to price the business venture: (1) the amount of money you are putting into the deal, (2) upside potential, (3) downside risk, (4) need for additional funds, and (5) getting out of the deal.

1 *The entrepreneur's investment.* How much money are you (or the entire entrepreneurial team) putting into the deal relative to the total amount invested by all investors? Clearly, the less of your money you invest, the less equity you will receive. In fact, in most cases, you are going to have to put in some of your own money; otherwise, no one will take you seriously. But with putting in no more than 10 percent of the deal, you may be in a position to negotiate 40 or 50 percent of the equity for yourself. If you handle 30 percent of the financing needs, you can probably negotiate 60 to 70 percent of equity. No rule, however, exists for setting equity ownership. It is based on other variables besides the amount of money you bring to the deal. Do you have a good, clear business plan? How revolutionary and innovative is the product or service? What are the track records of both you and your management team? What are your other financing sources?

2 *Upside potential.* Investors go into a deal to make a substantial capital gain. They want to know how much profit the business will generate. Most venture capitalists think in terms of a 5-year horizon, and they want to make at least 5 times their investment every 5 years, but really to get their attention, you are going to have to propose a deal that will give them 5 to 10 times their original investment in 5 years. Generally, however, the lower the risk, the lower their return on investment demands. Clearly, start-ups and turnarounds demand a higher return on investment than would a leveraged buyout. Generally, most venture capitalists expect their portfolio companies to offer a 35 to 45 percent return compounded annually—certainly never lower than 25 to 30 percent. The venture capitalist will usually invest in one or all of the following ways: common stock, preferred stock with conversion privileges, convertible debentures, and warrants.

3 *Downside risk.* In the event of bankruptcy or liquidation, the venture capitalist wants to know how much he or she would lose. Clearly, the higher the downside risk and the lower the liquidation value of the company, the more the venture capitalist will have to receive in equity ownership to compensate for the risk.

4 *Additional funds.* How many subsequent rounds of financing will the business need in the years ahead to continue operation and growth? It generally takes several rounds of financing either in public offerings of stock or private placement to bring the company from start-up to maturity. Clearly, each successive requirement for capital will cause dilution of ownership by existing shareholders unless the original venture capitalist is willing to put up his or her pro rata share each time. It is unlikely that the venture capitalist will continue to invest every time additional funds are needed; therefore, the more potential dilution, the more equity ownership the venture capitalist will want on his or her initial investment. The ideal situation is to get all the capital you need during the initial investment to take you from start-up to the stage of public offering.

5 *Exit from the deal.* The typical non-SBIC venture capitalist may look to bail out of the deal within three to five years. An ideal way to achieve this is to take the business public, which enables the venture capitalist gradually to sell his or her share of stock as desired. Unless a capital gain on the investment can be realized at some point, a venture capitalist has not made a successful investment regardless of how successful the business venture may be from your viewpoint. The point to remember is that a venture capitalist always wants to sell his or her position to you, another investor, or to the public no matter what percentage of the equity ownership he or she has. It could be that you would want to stipulate that you have the right of first refusal on the sale of any stock.

SUMMARY

Financial instruments legalize and formalize the financial arrangement between you and your financing sources. They represent obligations to a lender or ownership rights of an equity investor. These instruments include loan with warrants, convertible debentures, preferred stock, and common stock. You use these instruments in a way to make investment in your business attractive while at the same time meeting your financial objectives.

The chief way to obtain equity capital is to sell securities in a private placement or a public offering. Generally, a greater amount of money can be raised with a public offering, but it also requires stringent registration and reporting requirements monitored and enforced by the SEC and through state blue-sky laws. Because of their financial, legal, and marketing skills, investment bankers are typically used to handle both private and public stock offerings. These investment bankers take care of all the registration, reporting, and legal requirements; evaluate your company and the market and price the stock; set up syndicates; and, finally, market your stock.

Generally, in the early stages of your business venture, you cannot raise money by a public stock offering; there simply is not a market for your stock. You are not established; you are an unknown and considered a risk. You need start-up capital and second- or third-round financing, or you are trying to buy another company either as a leveraged buyout or a turnaround. You need risk or venture capital. This is where the venture capitalist comes into play.

ASSIGNMENT

1 List and give an example of the financing instruments used to develop your financing package.

2 Why isn't short-term or even intermediate-term debt a good source of capital financing? Explain. If this kind of debt is not appropriate for establishing your capital base, then what is it used for?

3 List and explain the advantages and disadvantages of selling securities.

4 Compare and contrast going public and private placement.

5 What are investment bankers? What purpose do they serve?

6 Research Regulation D, and explain how it helps small businesses raise capital.

7 Outline SEC registration requirements. Explain the reporting requirements.

8 What is the purpose behind the SEC's "full and fair" disclosure regulations?

9 What are blue-sky laws? Research your state's blue-sky laws, and determine if they restrict or aid the implementation of Regulation A and Regulation D.

10 Outline the sequence of events involved in a public stock offering.

11 What is a venture capitalist? What is his or her purpose?

12 What are the advantages in financing through a venture capitalist?

13 List and explain the myths about venture capitalists.

14 List and explain what the venture capitalist looks for in you.

15 What should you look for in selecting a venture capitalist?

16 How much ownership of your business venture should your venture capitalist get? Explain fully.

BIBLIOGRAPHY

Closely Held Business. Englewood Cliffs, N.J.: Institute for Business Planning, a publication from Prentice-Hall's Information Services Division, 1983.

Cohen, William A. *The Entrepreneur and Small Business Problem Solver.* New York: Wiley, 1983.

"Corporate Financing in the 80s." *Venture.* June 1983.

Dible, Donald M. (ed.). *Winning the Money Game.* Santa Barbara, Calif.: Entrepreneur Press, 1975.

Farrell, Kevin. "A Federal Program for Entrepreneurs." *Venture.* May 1984.

Feinberg, Andrew. "Funds for SBICs" *Venture.* May 1984.

Galante, Steven P. "Venture Capital Lures Foreigners." *The Wall Street Journal.* July 6, 1984.

Gladstone, David J. "SBA Programs for Financing a Small Business." In Stanley E. Pratt (ed.), *Guide to Venture Capital Sources,* 7th ed. Wellesley Hills, Mass.: Capital Publishing, 1983.

————. *Venture Capital Handbook.* Reston, Va.: Reston Publishing Company, 1983.

Hosmer, LaRue T., Arnold C. Cooper, and Karl H. Vesper. *The Entrepreneurial Function.* Englewood Cliffs, N.J.: Prentice-Hall, 1977.

Liles, Patrick R. *New Business Ventures and the Entrepreneur.* Homewood, Ill.: Richard D. Irwin, 1974.

Pratt, Stanley E. (ed.). *Guide to Venture Capital Sources,* 7th ed. Wellesley Hills, Mass.: Capital Publishing, 1983.

Reed, Edward C. "Financing Through an Investment Banker." In Donald M. Dible. (ed.). *Winning the Money Game.* Santa Barbara, Calif.: Entrepreneur Press, 1975.

Scott, Joseph. "Innovative Funding For Small Business." *American Way.* March 1984.

Silver, A. David. *The Entrepreneurial Life.* New York: Wiley, 1983.

Skousen, K. Fred. *An Introduction to the SEC.* 3d ed. Cincinnati: South-Western Publishing Company, 1983.

Wallace, Peter W. "Public Financing for Smaller Companies." In Stanley E. Pratt (ed.). *Guide to Venture Capital Sources.* 7th ed. Wellesley Hills, Mass.: Capital Publishing, 1983.

Welsh, John A., and Jerry F. White. *The Entrepreneur's Master Planning Guide.* Englewood Cliffs, N.J.: Prentice-Hall, 1983.

Wetzel, William E., Jr. "Informal Investors—When and Where to Look." In Stanley E. Pratt (ed.). *Guide to Venture Capital Sources,* 7th ed. Wellesley Hills, Mass.: Capital Publishing, 1983.

CHAPTER 15

Government, Banks, and Other Financing Sources

INTRODUCTION

Normally, not all financing needs are met by one source, such as venture capitalists, or from the general investing community. Or, in some situations, neither one of these sources will provide you with any funds. In either case, you can turn to government-backed sources, banks, or other financing sources. The objectives of this chapter follow.

1 To present some of the more popular government-backed financing sources.

2 To discuss banks as a means of financing your operations.

3 To list other ways to meet your financial needs.

GOVERNMENT-BACKED SOURCES OF FINANCING

There are a number of government-backed, flexible financing sources for furnishing both equity capital and long-term funds to enable businesses, especially small ones, to operate, grow, and modernize. Some of the more common sources of government-backed financing are discussed in this chapter.

Small Business Administration (SBA)

The Small Business Administration (SBA) assists small companies to finance a start-up, conversion, or expansion. The SBA also makes loans to purchase equipment, facilities, machinery, supplies, and materials or to acquire working capital. Loans are direct or in participation with banks. Also, in the event of disasters, individuals, businesses, and nonprofit organizations can get disaster loans. The same assistance is available for small businesses that suffer from economic injury resulting from (1) federally aided urban renewal or highway construction projects; (2) inability to market or process a product because of disease or toxicity resulting from natural or undetermined causes; and (3) United States trade agreements, especially those dealing with export.

Several thousand banks in the United States make SBA 90 percent guaranteed loans, and there are a few nonbank companies that also participate. Only several hundred lending institutions, however, *actively* make SBA guaranteed loans. Over the past few years, the SBA has selected the most active banks with the best loan records to be designated as "certified lenders."

As a certified lender, the SBA attempts to give three-day turnaround service. The paperwork necessary for a loan has been reduced substantially, thereby reducing the processing time dramatically. Thus, in these cases, an SBA guaranteed loan processed through a certified lender takes no longer to process than a regular loan. The small businessperson who wants to utilize a guaranteed loan is advised to contact his or her local SBA office for a list of certified lenders. This listing may also be obtained from the deputy director of finance, Small Business Administration, 1441 L Street N.W., Washington, D.C. 20416.

Small Business Investment Companies (SBICs)

SBICs are privately or publicly owned, government-chartered organizations that supply venture capital for start-up, for expansion financing, and for leveraged buyouts (LBO). The Small Business Administration is empowered to license and regulate SBICs. There is, however, a wide variation between the operations and objectives of different SBICs. It is possible to categorize SBICs, but even in these categories many differences exist.[1]

1 *Captive SBICs.* Captive SBICs are usually guided by the objective of the parent organization. The most common example is the bank SBIC, where emphasis is more often on grooming future bank customers than on making a capital gain. Other SBICs may be associated with larger venture capital outfits or even industrial concerns.

2 *Noncaptive SBICs.* Noncaptive SBICs are independent firms. Some are privately held by a few individuals; some, partially by institutions; and some, by the public through widespread distribution of their stock. These SBICs are usually more oriented toward capital gains and are more flexible than captive SBICs.[2]

In both categories of SBICs, there are those that tend to specialize in a particular industry, area, or type of risk. Most SBICs are interested in some form of equity participation; however, there are some that concentrate mostly or solely on lending money. Most are oriented toward 5- to 20-year investments. Generally, SBICs are more likely to come in contact with more low-technology business ventures rather than high-technology ones. Some examples of ventures they finance are shopping center development, broadcasting, fast-food franchises, movie production, grocery stores, and drug stores.

Moreover, many SBICs, limited in geographic area and management talent, invest in the smaller businesses located in their area. Indeed, their main advantage is an intimate knowledge of local business and sources of capital.[3] They, therefore, represent an excellent source of financing for businesses with more moderate growth prospects and lower potential risk. To receive a list of the most active SBICs, write to the National Association of Small Business Investment Companies, 618 Washington Building, Washington, D.C. 20005.

---

[1]Patrick R. Liles, *New Business Ventures and the Entrepreneur* (Homewood, Ill.: Richard D. Irwin, 1974), p. 462. This material is used with permission.

[2]Ibid.

[3]Ibid.

The typical types of financing made by SBICs in order of their frequency are as follows.[4]

1 *Loan with options to buy stock.* This is a loan for seven years, with three years interest only, then four-year amortization; 12 to 18 percent interest rates (subject to change); usually subordinated to institutional lenders, with stock options to purchase 10 to 30 percent of the company's stock at a low exercise price. This is usually a third-round financing.

2 *Convertible debenture.* A convertible debenture may be for eight years, five years interest only, then three years of amortization; 13 to 16 percent interest rates (subject to change), unsecured with conversion privileges to purchase 25 to 40 percent of the stock of the borrower at a reasonable price. This is usually a second-round financing.

3 *Straight loan.* This is a loan at 14 to 18 percent interest rates (subject to change) with a straight amortization over five to seven years, secured by specific assets. This is usually financing for a mature company secured by specific collateral.

4 *Preferred stock.* This stock is to be redeemable after 10 years, with a 10 to 12 percent dividend, with an option to convert to common stock of approximately 40 to 60 percent of the company. This is usually first-round financing.

5 *Common stock.* In recent years, SBICs have been more prone to purchase common stock equity in the business.

So the best advice to you if you intend to seek SBIC financing is to structure the proposed investment with a debt instrument with equity option rights or in a format as just set out. To structure the proposed financing any other way will risk a premature turndown by the SBIC.[5] Remember that an SBIC's motivation is growth participation rather than fast-in-fast-out lending.

Another angle on the types of investments SBICs make is determined by the stage of development of the business. These stages are as follows.[6]

1 *Start-ups or first-round financing.* These are the most difficult situations to finance through an SBIC because a new company needs equity and not debt. The new company needs to retain its cash flow in the initial years to use internally rather than pay interest on SBIC debt. Some SBICs will, however, invest a portion of their funds in early-stage financings, and approximately 25 percent of the funds invested by SBICs today are in new companies.

[4]David J. Gladstone, "SBA Programs for Financing a Small Business," in Stanley E. Pratt (ed.), *Guide to Venture Capital Sources*, 7th ed. (Wellesley Hills, Mass.: Capital Publishing, 1983), pp. 32–35. This material is used with permission. Also see *Pratt's Guide to Venture Capital Sources*, 9th ed. (Wellesley Hills, Mass.: Venture Economics, 1985).

[5]Ibid.

[6]Ibid.

2 *Second-round financing.* In this situation, the company has created a product or service and is marketing it with some degree of success. The company needs funds to finance the business's growth. In these cases, a convertible debenture is normally the structure. Most SBICs invest a large portion of their funds in second-round financings.

3 *Third-round financing.* Third-round financing is needed when a company is running well and has generally established profitability but needs growth capital. A loan with warrants will typically be the structure from an SBIC. Many SBICs invest funds in this area also.

4 *Public offering.* Sometimes an SBIC will purchase stock or a convertible debenture that is part of a public offering or a semipublic offering. In this instance, the company is usually well along in its development cycle, and investment risk can be clearly analyzed and managed. This is an infrequent area for SBICs to invest.

5 *Leveraged buyout.* In many cases, a company may be purchased by new owners with mostly debt. Often the current operating management participates in the purchase. Those businesses usually have demonstrated cash flow to service such debt. SBICs often provide subordinated debt in the form of loans with warrants. The SBIC debt, in fact, supports senior debt because it may be unsecured or so far down the ladder from security that a senior lender really thinks of it as equity. Most SBICs are eager to invest in leveraged buyouts because the cash flow is more easily predictable.

6 *Straight debt.* There are a number of SBICs that make collaterized loans for a simple, high interest rate. Usually, this is done when the SBIC has excess funds; however, there are a number of small SBICs that concentrate or specialize in this type of financing.

7 *Turnaround.* Some SBICs finance turnaround situations, companies in trouble (even bankruptcy) that need money and management assistance. Usually, a turnaround deal is structured as debt with equity options. Where possible, the SBIC will seek security for its investments. Not many SBICs are investing in turnaround opportunities.

Cousins to the regular SBICs are minority enterprise small business investment companies (MESBICs). These firms are licensed to provide financing to small businesses that are at least 51 percent owned by socially or economically disadvantaged persons, such as members of minority groups and United States Vietnam Veterans. Most MESBICs operate in a manner very similar to SBICs and pursue the common objective of adequate investment returns, but they also possess the added expectation that social benefits will result from successful investments.

In recent years, the National Association of Small Business Investment Companies (NASBIC) and the American Association of Minority Enterprise Small Business Investment Companies (AAMESBIC), which represent SBICs, want out of the congressional budget process. They want to sever their ties to the United States Congress and the Small Business Administration (SBA), which polices and doles out funds to them, and create a Corporation for Small Business Investment, a capital bank with federal agency status.

One of the chief reasons for this movement is that the SBA is unable to meet the 3-to-1 leverage factor; that is, SBICs are entitled to $3 of federal funding for every $1 of private-sector capital they obtain. The SBA cannot even come close to meeting this commitment because of the increased demand on venture capital within the past several years.

The financing vehicle that NASBIC and AAMESBIC are proposing would be an independent entity similar to the Federal National Mortgage Association, which raises capital by selling debentures backed by Federal Housing Administration mortgages. Initial capital for the bank would be raised by selling shares in the bank to SBICs, which would each purchase 2.5 percent of the bank. The bank would then sell stock to other financial institutions, institutional investors, and the public, as required, creating a secondary market in SBIC bank securities.[7]

Small Business Innovation Research Program (SBIR)

Increasingly, there are public and quasi-public risk capital programs for the technology-based inventrepreneurs and small firms. Small companies engaged in high-technology research and development have gotten a boost from the federal government through the 1982 passage of the Small Business Innovation Development Act, which established the Small Business Innovation Research Program (SBIR). This program is under the jurisdiction of the Small Business Administration (SBA) and will provide several billion dollars this decade to small companies and individuals for high-technology research and development. Specifically, the objectives of the SBIR program are these.

1 To increase the opportunities for small science or high-technology firms in federal research and development.

2 To stimulate technological innovation from government-funded research and development.

3 To couple SBIR support with follow-on venture capital or other private-sector funding.

4 To improve the economic and social return from federal research and development.

The program is already enabling inventrepreneurs to work on such disparate developments as laser tree trimmings and striped-bass habitats in thermal-waste waters. Funds have been awarded to (1) a company to develop computerized processing of the Chinese language; (2) a company that improves operations of industrial robots; (3) a company that is developing a diagnostic tool that offers an

---

[7]Andrew Feinberg, "Funds for SBICs," *Venture*, May 1984, p. 32. This material is used by special permission. Copyright © 1984 Venture Magazine, Inc., 521 Fifth Avenue, New York, N.Y. 10175.

alternative to radiological and surgical procedures; (4) companies involved in the development of sensory aids for the deaf and blind; and (5) a company working a hand-held device for computer-assisted position identification in natural terrain that will be used by soldiers, hikers, backpackers, and the like. If some of the thousands of research projects under way bear fruit, Americans will enjoy better export-import opportunities and better health, be able to cut concrete with water, buy X rays for one-twentieth of today's costs, clean up rivers with laser beams, measure the gripping force of robots, and partake of a wider array of recreational activities.[8]

The SBIR competition is structured in three phases. The six-month Phase I involves a solicitation of proposals to conduct feasibility-related experimental or theoretical research on described agency requirements. The objective of this phase is to determine the technical feasibility of the proposed effort and the quality of performance of the small firm. It is scheduled to last six months and may be viewed as the scientific and technical proof of concept. The maximum award for Phase I is $50,000.00. The more lengthy Phase II (up to two years) is the principal research and development effort. Funding of Phase II is based on the results achieved during Phase I and the scientific and technical merit of the Phase II proposal. The object of Phase II is to refine the concept and to develop a functional prototype. The maximum award for Phase II is $500,000.00. Phase III involves the use of private sector funds to pursue commercial application of the research funded in Phases I and II with federal funds. Phase III may allow for contracts with a federal agency for potential products or processes intended for use by the United States government.

Firms that win the awards are expected not only to attract private capital but to also create many new products and jobs. SBIR offers full worldwide commercial patent rights, subject to the rights for government use, and "march in" rights if the firm does not pursue commercialization within a reasonable time.

Small Business Revitalization Program (SBR)

Across nearly half the nation, economic development professionals (EDPs) are putting together financing for small businesses under the federal government's little-known Small Business Revitalization (SBR) program. To find out if your state is involved, contact your banker, or check with your state economic development office or governor's office, or call the National Development Council in Washington.[9]

Some authorities think that SBR is one of the best venture capital sources available to small businesses through the federal government. Some states, however, are reluctant to join in because they do not want Washington bureaucrats

---

[8]Joseph Scott, "Innovative Funding for Small Business," *American Way*, March 1984, pp. 149–52. This material is used with permission of American Airlines, Copyright © 1984 by American Airlines.

[9]Kevin Farrell, "A Federal Program for Entrepreneurs," *Venture*, May 1984, p. 188. This material is used by special permission. Copyright © 1984 Venture Magazine, Inc., 521 Fifth Avenue, New York, N.Y. 10175.

telling state officials what to do. Still others decline on political grounds because they do not want the opponent political party to take the credit for creating jobs.[10]

Basically, SBR is really a financial hybrid that combines existing programs, techniques, and options of the Small Business Administration's Guaranteed Loan Program and its Certified Development Company Program and the Department of Housing and Urban Development's Urban Development Action Grant (UDAG) Program. But none of this money is available for start-ups or companies without assets.[11]

The objective of the SBR program is to put together the financing partnerships that enable banks to lend at reasonable fixed rates for 15- to 25-year terms. Sometimes it requires a government-guaranteed loan that the SBA provides. At other times it may be that the community is eligible for loan guarantees under the Department of Housing and Urban Development's UDAG program. Or the business may qualify for a 100 percent guaranteed debenture under SBA's Certified Development Company Program. But each of these sources requires some private lending as well.[12]

International Financing

As already noted in other parts of this text, a variety of programs exist that help foster international trade, especially export. The Eximbank authorizes the Foreign Credit Insurance Association (FCIA) to issue policies that cover commercial or political risks or both on short- and medium-term credits extended by United States exporters to their overseas customers. An exporter can apply to his or her bank, and, in turn, the bank can get a guaranteed payment of medium-term export paper purchased without recourse. Exporters can get guarantees covering commercial and political risks involved in the performance of services abroad and in the leasing or exhibition of United States products in foreign markets. Overseas customers who do business with United States exporters or the actual exporter can negotiate loans for the payment of product and services. Moreover, the Eximbank will discount export debt obligations held by commercial banks, thus providing liquidity to banks financing United States exports.

The Overseas Private Investment Corporation (OPIC) offers a variety of services to private United States companies interested in establishing new businesses or expanding present facilities in less developed countries. These services include investment information and counseling; preinvestment and project development financing; project insurance against the risks of currency inconvertibility, expropriation, and war, revolution, or insurrection; and project financing through loan guarantees and direct dollar and local currency loans.[13]

[10]Ibid.

[11]Ibid.

[12]Ibid.

[13]*Closely Held Business,* op. cit., p. 6728.

Financing Through Sales to the Government

Clearly, the best way to raise money is through internal financing by selling your product or service. The federal government is constantly in the market for products or services. And, indeed, if you can meet the federal government's terms and conditions, you can create an excellent customer. But the federal government's needs are extremely complex and varied and subject to almost daily change.

To stay on top of everything and tell where you might fill the product or service needs of the federal government, get an annual subscription of the *Commerce Business Daily* from the superintendent of documents, United States Government Printing Office, Washington, D.C., 20402. This publication gives you a daily list of United States government procurement invitations, subcontracting leads, contract awards, sales of surplus property, and foreign business opportunities. The *Commerce Business Daily* covers everything from research and development sources to a list of every company awarded a contract valued at $25,000.00 or more. This latter feature gives you a dual benefit: (1) a look at your possible competition and (2) a lead for companies for whom you might do subcontracting.[14]

State and Municipal Government Financing

Many states and some municipal governments have organized development companies for the purpose of assisting small businesses to start or expand operations within their confines, to create jobs and produce economic activity. New York State, for example, has the privately financed New York Business Development Corporation, which makes long-term loans at reasonable interest rates. In addition, the state itself has authority to sell a limited number of bonds and make loans for certain projects. Examples in some of the New England states include the Connecticut Product Development Corporation, Maine Capital Corporation, and the Massachusetts Technology Development Corporation. In other areas, industrial foundations have been established, usually identified in some way with local boards of trade or chambers of commerce. Here are the most common methods that the states and other jurisdictions use to help finance business.[15]

1 *State development credit corporatons.*   Capital comes from sale of stock or loans made to the corporation by a pool formed by private financial institutions who become members of the corporation. With the creation of this type of structure, it is possible to spread the risk of a particular venture.

2 *State industrial development authorities.*   Public funds are used for loans to aid local development corporations in the construction of industrial buildings. The authority is an arm of the state government. In fact, some states guarantee financing of new plants.

[14]Ibid., p. 6729.
[15]Ibid., p. 6723.

3 *Municipal bonds.*   Many communities have authority to float a revenue bond issue to cover the cost of putting up a new plant. The revenue bond is secured by a specific plant or project, and the payment of interest and repayment of principal are derived from the plant's revenue.

4 *Tax concessions.*   Many states have legislation that exempts certain new operations from state or local property taxation for limited periods. Some states leave such arrangements to the discretion of community authorities. Tax inducements in this way become an integral part of the location agreement.

COMMERCIAL BANKS

Entrepreneurs often feel that the bank is or should be a source of risk capital for a new business venture. Banks are fiduciaries; they are not in the risk capital business. They are entrusted with your dear mother's savings, and you certainly don't want them using her savings to play the venture capital game. Their objective must necessarily be preservation of the assets entrusted to them. They, more than anyone else, must restrict the lending of funds to proved businesses.[16]

A bank is a lender and may not assume an equity position in the business of its borrowers. Basically, banks make loans to businesses for their short-term seasonal or cyclical needs and to supplement the capital investment of the owners of the business. Generally, a short-term loan is for three to six months. Loans are either secured or unsecured. Surprisingly, most bank loans are unsecured because the typical business borrower has a long and trustworthy relationship with the bank.

Five Loan Questions

When you decide to borrow money for your business, the typical lender will ask you five questions.[17]

1 *What do you plan to do with it?*   If you are planning to use the money to undertake a highly risky venture, you will probably be turned down. If the reason given, however, makes good business sense, you will probably get the loan *provided* you have the right answer to the remaining four questions.

2 *How much do you need?*   Surprisingly, some businesspeople go to their bankers with no clear idea as to how much money they need. All they know is that they need help. The more precisely you can answer this question, the more likely you are to get the loan.

[16]John A. Welsh and Jerry F. White, *The Entrepreneur's Master Planning Guide* (Englewood Cliffs, N.J.: Prentice-Hall, 1983), p. 180. This material is used by permission from Prentice-Hall, Inc.

[17]Donald M. Dible (ed.), *Winning the Money Game* (Santa Clara, Calif.: Entrepreneur Press, 1975), pp. 274–76. This material is adapted by permission of Reston Publishing Company, a Prentice-Hall company, 11480 Sunset Hills Road, Reston, Va. 22090.

3 *When do you need it?*   If you rush to your banker out of the clear blue sky and tell him or her that you need a substantial loan as of "yesterday," you have a problem. Such a request shows that you are a poor planner, and most lenders do not want to get involved with poor planners.

4 *How long will you need it?*   The shorter the period of time that you need the money, the more apt you are to get the loan approved. The time at which the loan will be repaid should correspond with some important milestone in your business plan, such as receipt of payment from one or more of your customers.

5 *How will you repay the loan?*   This is the most important question. What if your plans go awry, do you have other income that can be diverted to pay off the loan? Do you have collateral? Even if you have lots of fixed assets, the lender may be unimpressed because he or she knows, maybe from bitter experience, that assets sold at a liquidation auction bring only a fraction of their "value" in a going concern. Five to ten cents on the dollar is nothing unusual. So, if your banker offers to lend you money on a collateralized basis valuing your assets at from 5 to no more than 20 percent of book value, do not be surprised. Moreover, banks truly do not want to be in the foreclosure business.

Kinds of Loans

Remember, when you ask for a loan, that you are a *customer* of the bank; don't beg or put yourself in the position of asking for a favor. Know what you are entitled to, how much money your situation justifies, how much you should pay for the money, and what collateral, if any, you should give. Have the facts and figures ready, and be willing to lay the cards on the table. Be able to provide a complete business plan to the banker. Following are the more popular loan accommodations a bank is willing to extend.[18]

1. *Line of credit.*   Application for a line of credit is not an application for a loan, but simply an arrangement under which the bank agrees to make loans if funds are needed. As the borrower needs funds, he or she borrows against the line of credit. Advances are evidenced by short-term notes, which are periodically reviewed and repaid, reduced or extended.

2. *Term loans.*   A business loan that runs for a term of more than one year with provisions for amortization or retirement over the life of the loan is a term loan. Such a loan, even if secured, will depend on the bank's appraisal of the long-range prospects of the company, its earning power, and the quality of its management. The term is sometimes a maximum of 10 years but more often 3 or 5. These loans are particularly useful when the borrower needs to expand facilities, buy capital equipment, or respond to rapid growth in sales.

Many term loans are backed by collateral security, but the bank must still rely

[18]*Closely Held Business*, op. cit., p. 6762.

primarily on the ability of the company to repay the indebtedness out of earnings over the life of the loan. Therefore, the profitability of the business is far more important to the banker than the liquidation value of the security. Repayment of the loan can take several forms. Repayment may follow along seasonal lines, calling for a large payment when income is high. As a matter of fact, depending on the nature of the business and what stage it is in, the loan may be repaid on almost any agreed-on basis. For example, early payments can be small, with large final payments.

Term loans are usually covered by a formal, comprehensive agreement that includes definite operating policies. The agreement binds the borrower to maintain working capital at an agreed level and to secure bank approval before making capital expenditures over a certain amount, limits the amount to be paid in salaries and bonuses, keeps assets free of encumbrances, and applies a certain portion of net profits to loan repayments over and above the amount stipulated in the borrower's note.

3. *Short-term loans.*   Short-term loans are secured by an installment note or a series of promissory notes that have maturity dates calling for repayment within a specified period of time, usually a year or less, at which time they are reviewed, repaid, reduced, or extended. These loans are provided as working capital loans to help finance seasonal inventory or accounts receivable, unexpected capital needs, or short-term emergencies.

Yardsticks Bankers Use in Evaluating a Loan

To a large extent, bankers will base their loan decision on financial statements, including a balance sheet, income statement, and cash flow projections. These and other financial data will be subjected to analysis to determine the degree of solvency and profitability of your company. A business from a banker's viewpoint must be able to meet its debt obligations on a timely basis.

Bankers subject the financial statements to a number of ratios to ascertain solvency and profitability. Solvency can be determined by: acid-test ratios, working capital ratios, accounts receivable turnover, inventory turnover, number of days' sales in inventory turnover, ratio of fixed assets to long-term liabilities, and ratio of shareholders' equity to liabilities. Profitability analysis shows the ability of a company to earn income. This can be assessed by computing various measures, which include the ratio of net sales to assets, the rate earned on total assets, the rate earned on shareholders' equity, earnings per share on common stock, and the price-to-earnings ratio.

In addition, bankers want to know more about you and your entrepreneurial or management team. Are you reliable? Do you have a good credit record? Do your managers have the ability to run a business properly? Are disbursements for dividends, salaries, and bonuses in balance with sales, profits, net worth, and working capital? How effective are the salespeople? Can you meet competition?

Ways to Ensure Repayment of Loan

Sometimes your signature is the only security the bank needs when making a loan. At other times, the bank requires additional assurance that the money will be repaid. The kind and amount of security depend on the bank and on your situation. These are ways to pledge security.[19]

1 *Endorsers, comakers, and guarantors.* Borrowers often get other people to sign a note in order to bolster their own credit. These endorsers are contingently liable for the note they sign. If the borrower fails to pay the note, the bank expects the endorser to make good. Sometimes, the endorser may be asked to pledge assets or securities that he or she owns. A comaker is one who creates an obligation jointly with the borrower. In such cases, the bank can collect directly from either the maker or the comaker. A guarantor is one who guarantees the payment of a note by signing a guarantee commitment. Sometimes a manufacturer will act as guarantor for one of his or her customers.

2 *Assignment of leases.* A lease assigned as security is similar to a guarantee. It is used, for example, in some franchise situations. The bank lends the money on a building and takes a mortgage. Then the lease that the dealer and the parent franchise company work out is assigned so that the bank automatically receives the rent payments. In this manner, the bank is guaranteed repayment of the loan.

3 *Warehouse receipts.* Banks also take commodities as security by lending money on a warehouse receipt. Such a receipt is usually delivered directly to the bank and shows that the merchandise used as security either has been placed in a public warehouse or has been left on your premises under the control of one of your employees who is bonded (as in field warehousing). Such loans are generally made on staple or standard merchandise that can be readily marketed. The typical warehouse receipt loan is for a percentage of the estimated value of the goods used as security.

4 *Trust receipts and floor plannings.* Merchandise such as automobiles, appliances, and boats has to be displayed to be sold. The only way many small marketers can afford such displays is by borrowing money. Such loans are often secured by a note and a trust receipt. This trust receipt is the legal paper for floor planning. It is used for serial-numbered merchandise. When you sign one, you (1) acknowledge receipt of the merchandise, (2) agree to keep the merchandise in trust for the bank, and (3) promise to pay the bank as you sell the goods.

5 *Chattel mortgages.* If you buy equipment such as a cash register or a delivery truck, you may want to get a chattel mortgage loan. You give the bank a lien on the equipment you are buying. The bank also evaluates the present and future market value of the equipment being used to secure the loan. How rapidly will it

[19]Ibid., pp. 6773–75.

depreciate? Does the borrower have the necessary fire, theft, property damage, and public liability insurance on the equipment? The banker has to be sure that the borrower protects the equipment.

6 *Real estate.* Real estate is another form of collateral for long-term loans. When taking a real estate mortgage, the bank finds out (1) the location of the real estate, (2) its physical condition, (3) its foreclosure value, and (4) the amount of insurance carried on the property.

7 *Accounts receivable.* Many banks lend money on accounts receivable. In effect, you are counting on your customers to pay your note. The bank may take accounts receivable on a notification or nonnotification plan. Under the notification plan, the purchaser of the goods is informed by the bank that his or her account has been assigned to it, and he or she is asked to pay the bank. Under the nonnotification plan, the borrower's customers continue to pay him or her the sums due on their accounts, and he or she pays the bank.

8 *Savings accounts.* Sometimes you might get a loan by assigning to the bank a savings account. In such cases, the bank gets an assignment from you and keeps your passbook. If you assign an account in another bank as collateral, the lending bank asks the other bank to mark its records to show that the account is held as collateral.

9 *Life insurance.* Another kind of collateral is life insurance. Banks will lend up to the cash value of a life insurance policy. You have to assign the policy to the bank. If the policy is on the life of an executive of a small corporation, a corporate resolution authorizing the assignment must be made. Most insurance companies allow the policy to be reassigned to the original beneficiary when the assignment to the bank ends. When interest rates are low, some people like to use life insurance as collateral rather than borrow directly from insurance companies. One reason is that a bank loan is often more convenient to obtain.

10 *Stocks and bonds.* If you use stocks and bonds as collateral, they must be marketable. As a protection against market declines and possible expenses of liquidation, banks usually lend no more than 75 percent of the market value of high-grade stock. On federal government or municipal bonds, they may be willing to lend 90 percent or more of their market value. The bank may ask the borrower for additional security or payment whenever the market value of the stocks or bonds drops below the bank's required margin.

OTHER FORMS OF FINANCING

Besides selling stock or making long-term loans, there are a variety of ways you can get access to cash, especially for short-term use. These ways include financing from suppliers, customers, and receivables. Sources for long-term financing are equipment leasing and franchising.

Financing from Suppliers

Suppliers are always seeking an outlet for their products. Consequently, many will grant attractive credit terms to customers whom they believe to be good risks. The most frequently used source of credit from suppliers is trade credit whereby you receive the merchandise with invoices payable within 60 to 120 days. If you are a new business, the trade creditor must have some assurance of your integrity, a record of your past credit performance, your management and marketing skills, your financial condition (which may require the submission of financial statements), and the prospect of your business surviving.

If you, for example, intend to open a retail shoe store, a great portion of your financing may come from the shoe manufacturer. You could lease a building, build and install fixtures and shelves yourself (sweat equity), and go to a regional shoe market or have shoe salespeople call on you. With some negotiation and disclosure of financial and credit information, you may be able to stock your store with enough inventory to get started. Your chances are even greater if you deal exclusively with one full-line manufacturer, say, International Shoe Company.

So, by using trade credit, as much as 70 to 90 percent of initial financing is established. A warning: The trade creditor expects to be paid, so you must buy merchandise that will sell quickly, and you must sell your merchandise for cash; otherwise, it will be impossible for you to meet the payment terms. If you get an extension of time, say, an additional 30 to 60 days, you are only postponing the inevitable; sooner or later the supplier must be paid. If you do not pay, you will not be able to buy merchandise for the next season from your original supplier. Moreover, you will not be able to buy from any other supplier because the word will get around that you are a poor credit risk. Therefore, within a season or no more than a year, you are out of business. As pointed out several times in this chapter, debt especially if it is short-term, is not the best way to go into business. It is a valuable financing tool. Do not, however, abuse it or try to force it to serve as a long-term capital base.

Financing from Customers

Deposits are advance payments on contracts, such as on government contracts, and represent a significant source of financing for some companies. Often such advances can be used for working capital or to meet other short-term obligations.

The use of installment sales is another form of financing from customers. In some businesses, especially in the retail field, it is common to make sales on the installment plan. In the typical installment sale, the purchaser makes a down payment and agrees to pay the remainder in specified amounts at stated intervals over a period of time. Generally, you retain technical title to the goods or may take other means to make repossession easier in the event that the purchaser defaults on the payments. You take the installment sales contracts to a sales finance company or a bank and convert this paper, at a discount, into cash.

Use of Receivables in Raising Cash

Your business may use accounts receivable or notes receivable as a basis for a cash advance from a bank, finance company, or factor. For example, accounts receivable owned by you may be (1) pledged, (2) assigned, or (3) sold.

1 *Pledge of accounts receivable.* You make the collection and use this cash to meet your obligation to the lender. You may have to give the lender access to your records to determine whether remittances are being properly made on pledged accounts.

2 *Assignment of accounts receivable.* Lenders may agree to advance cash over a period of time as accounts receivable are assigned to them. The assignments carry a guarantee on your part to make up any deficiency if the accounts fail to realize required amounts. You are, in effect, selling your accounts on a recourse basis.

3 *Sale of accounts receivable.* Certain factors or finance companies purchase accounts receivable outright on a "without recourse" basis. Your customers are notified that their bills are payable to the factor, and this party assumes the burden of billing and collecting accounts. Factoring frequently involves a continuing agreement whereby a factor assumes the credit function as well as the collection function. Under such an arrangement, the factor grants or denies credit, handles the accounts receivable bookkeeping, bills customers, and makes collections. You are, consequently, relieved of all these activities. Your sales provide immediate cash. Generally, factoring is expensive (80 cents on the dollar), but it relieves you of a lot of accounting, credit checks, credit managers, and all the staff and credit system costs that a new business cannot afford in the beginning.

Life Insurance Companies

Even though life insurance companies are a major financial presence in the economy, their role in small-business financing is unusually limited. Most insurance companies have rather rigid criteria for the kinds of companies they will carry in their loan portfolio, limiting themselves to companies that have a high level of capitalization and offer only a nominal risk. Indeed, lending to small businesses is a small proportion of an insurance company's loan portfolio.

Nevertheless, to companies that qualify, insurance companies will provide commercial mortgages as well as unsecured term loans. The terms and conditions are similar to those offered by commercial banks.[20]

[20]"Corporate Financing in the 80's," *Venture*, June 1983, p. 72. This material is used by special permission. Copyright © 1983 Venture Magazine, Inc., 521 Fifth Avenue, New York, N.Y. 10175.

Equipment Leasing

Most businesses need capital equipment. There are three ways to get the equipment you need: (1) pay for it out-of-pocket, (2) borrow the money from a bank, or (3) lease the equipment. Probably the smartest way to obtain your equipment is by leasing. You do not have your cash tied up in equipment that you really want to *use*, not *own*. You are not paying for equipment in one lump sum, and you do not have to make a down payment. You simply pay for the equipment as you use it. Leasing, indeed, is an important and economically sound way to finance your equipment needs.

Franchising

One way a business can raise capital is to sell franchises. If your business is unique, new, or particularly marketable, this could be an ideal way to grow. Many small start-up companies have used franchises to increase their financial base. The franchisor sells, in addition to the product or service, a "success formula" that has been proved in the marketplace. Success stories range from fast-food franchises to the printing and copy services industry. Diverse examples include the Gymboree Corporation, a service business for babies to learn physical skills; the Computerland Corporation; and the Century 21 Real Estate Corporation.

One of the advantages of a franchise operation is that it creates a continuing inflow of capital into the franchisor company. This cash inflow usually comes from some or all of the following fees.[21]

1 *Initial fee.* Franchisors frequently get an initial fee from each franchisee. These fees vary greatly depending on the nature of the business and the strength of the franchisor. Fees run from $5,000 up.

2 *Royalty, operating, and service fees.* These fees are based on gross receipts, net income, and periodic rental fees for equipment, signs, or proprietary services.

3 *Advertising fees.* Franchisees are frequently charged a fee to support a national advertising effort. This advertising fee received from each franchisee goes into a national advertising fund to pay for an advertising campaign in magazines, radio, and television.

To start a franchising operation, as a franchisor, you should first develop a pilot operation. This pilot will serve as an experimental and proving ground for your franchise idea. Everything—location, building, product or service, hours of operation—should be as close to the future outlets as is possible. The pilot franchise should be run for at least six months and preferably longer in order to gather enough data on sales, costs, profits, and operating procedures. This information will be used to determine the kind of franchise package you eventually offer to prospective franchisees.

[21]*Closely Held Business,* op. cit., p. 6790.

SUMMARY

By far, the two major venture capital sources are private venture capital firms or government-backed organizations and programs, such as the SBA, SBICs, SBIR, SBR, Eximbank, OPIC, and various state and municipal programs.

A major source of short-term financing comes from your banker. This kind of financing is required because of the seasonal or cyclical nature of your business. Other funds are supplied via government-guaranteed loans through government agencies, such as the SBA, or term loans of three to six or seven years for financing equipment and capital goods.

Other sources of funds can be used as part of the financial package. These include suppliers, customers, factors, life insurance companies, and equipment leasing companies. An ideal way to raise money is to become a franchisor and sell franchising outlets.

ASSIGNMENT

1 Explain how the SBA serves as a source of financing.

2 What kind of financing are SBICs involved in? What kind of financing instruments do they use?

3 What is the purpose of the SBIR program? How could this program help you raise capital? How does the SBR program differ? Explain.

4 Explain how the Eximbank and OPIC help you in financing.

5 Explain how state and municipal governments serve as financing sources.

6 Explain the purpose of a commercial bank from a financing perspective. What kind of financing can you get from a bank?

7 List and explain the five loan questions bankers ask prospective customers.

8 How do bankers evaluate a loan, both secured and unsecured?

9 List and explain the ways you can ensure repayment of a loan?

10 Explain how you can obtain financing from suppliers and your customers.

11 Explain factoring. How does it serve as a financing source?

12 How does leasing help you in financing your business?

13 Explain how franchising can be used to provide financing. How can you as a franchisor use franchisees as financing sources?

BIBLIOGRAPHY

Closely Held Business. Englewood Cliffs, N.J.: Institute for Business Planning, a publication from Prentice-Hall's Information Services Division, 1983.

Cohen, William A. *The Entrepreneur and Small Business Problem Solver.* New York: Wiley, 1983.

"Corporate Financing in the 80s." *Venture*. June 1983.

Dible, Donald M. (ed.). *Winning the Money Game*. Santa Barbara, Calif.: Entrepreneur Press, 1975.

Farrell, Kevin. "A Federal Program for Entrepreneurs." *Venture*. May 1984.

Feinberg, Andrew. "Funds for SBICs." *Venture*. May 1984.

Galante, Steven P. "Venture Capital Lures Foreigners." *The Wall Street Journal*. July 6, 1984.

Gladstone, David J. "SBA Programs for Financing a Small Business." In Stanley E. Pratt (ed.), *Guide to Venture Capital Sources*, 7th ed. Wellesley Hills, Mass.: Capital Publishing, 1983.

————. *Venture Capital Handbook*. Reston, Va.: Reston Publishing Company, 1983.

Hosmer, LaRue T., Arnold C. Cooper, and Karl H. Vesper. *The Entrepreneurial Function*. Englewood Cliffs, N.J.: Prentice-Hall, 1977.

Liles, Patrick R. *New Business Ventures and the Entrepreneur*. Homewood, Ill.: Richard D. Irwin, 1974.

Pratt, Stanley E. (ed.). *Guide to Venture Capital Sources*, 7th ed. Wellesley Hills, Mass.: Capital Publishing, 1983.

Reed, Edward C. "Financing Through an Investment Banker." In Donald M. Dible (ed.). *Winning the Money Game*. Santa Barbara, Calif.: Entrepreneur Press, 1975.

Scott, Joseph. "Innovative Funding For Small Business." *American Way*. March 1984.

Silver, A. David. *The Entrepreneurial Life*. New York: Wiley, 1983.

Skousen, K. Fred. *An Introduction to the SEC*, 3d ed. Cincinnati: South-Western Publishing Company, 1983.

Wallace, Peter W. "Public Financing for Smaller Companies." In Stanley E. Pratt (ed.), *Guide to Venture Capital Sources*, 7th ed. Wellesley Hills, Mass.: Capital Publishing, 1983.

Welsh, John A., and Jerry F. White. *The Entrepreneur's Master Planning Guide*. Englewood Cliffs, N.J.: Prentice-Hall, 1983.

Wetzel, William E., Jr., "Informal Investors—When and Where to Look." In Stanley E. Pratt (ed.). *Guide to Venture Capital Sources*, 7th ed. Wellesley Hills, Mass.: Capital Publishing, 1983.

PART SIX

PREPARATION
AND PRESENTATION
OF THE BUSINESS PLAN

CHAPTER 16

Form of the Business Plan

INTRODUCTION

The document written to provide you with a management guide and to raise capital for your business venture is called a *business plan*. Clearly, great care should be exercised in its preparation. You may, indeed, have the greatest business idea since the riding lawn mower, but unless you gain the trust of others and communicate precisely what you intend to do, you will have great difficulty in ever launching your business venture. After all, if investors support your business venture, you will be spending *their* money. They want to know who you are and exactly how you plan to spend their money. Following is an overview of the business plan, some tips on how to write and put it together to gain the credibility you need and to get your message across to the ones who will invest in your venture. Specifically, these are the objectives of this chapter.

1 To present an overview of the business plan and reasons for preparing it.
2 To suggest ways to improve writing style.
3 To present some tips on how to make the content of the business plan more substantive, understandable, and attractive.

OVERVIEW OF THE BUSINESS PLAN

What is a business plan, and why should you go to the trouble of creating a written business plan? Whom should you get to help write your business plan? The following material answers these questions.

Definition of the Business Plan

The business plan is a written document prepared by the entrepreneur that describes the business venture, the product or service, the customers, the competition, the production and marketing methods, the management, the financing, and all those things necessary to enter business and make or sell the product or service. It is the *game plan* of the business venture. Some people call the business plan a prospectus or proposal or blue book or deal. No matter what it is called, the business plan is the culmination of all your research, ideas, analysis, late-night schemes, and dreams. If prepared properly, it is a clear picture of where you are, where you are going, and how you are going to get there. If you like an analogy, it is similar to one's résumé. It lays everything on the table about you and what you intend to do. It discloses the good, the bad; the strengths, the weaknesses; it is comprehensive but concise; it is a full and fair disclosure of your business venture.

You may already have a business and seek expansion financing, or you may be going into business for the first time. You may already be or plan to be a manufacturer or a wholesaler or a retailer or a contractor or a service operation. You may plan to enter business via a start-up, a buyout, or a franchise or joint venture. The legal form of your business venture may be a sole proprietorship, a partnership, or a corporation. All this makes little difference as far as the business plan is concerned. The length, complexity, and detail of business plans may differ, but the objectives of all business plans are the same—to raise capital and to provide a detailed formulation of a program of action to achieve certain goals.

Reasons for Preparing a Business Plan

A business plan is the most important business document that you will ever prepare. And it will also probably be the most difficult. It takes a lot of time, research, discipline, and commitment to complete. Indeed, there is a real temptation to try to accomplish your business objectives without it. But it doesn't matter whether you are going to open a booth at the local flea market or buyout Exxon, you still need a business plan.

Writing a good, complete business plan forces you to reassess every part of your venture and form a clearer picture of what you are really trying to do. It bakes the idea to well done vis-à-vis a half-baked idea. It makes you "dry run" the first few years of your venture on paper and develop an understanding of, and solutions to, many of the problems that will be encountered. One of the chief reasons why businesses fail is that poor assumptions were made early on, or something critical was overlooked. A comprehensive, well-researched business plan tests assumptions and uncovers a lot of things that may have otherwise been ignored. You may discover more about what you don't know than what you do know about your business venture. It is, indeed, what you don't know that can hurt you. What are the current and expected conditions in the industry? Is there an uptrend or downtrend? Is the market saturated? What are the profit margins for this kind of business? Are materials in short supply? Is there extreme price-cutting because of stiff competition? Is the product or service out of fashion? Are there excessive government regulations in the industry? Are there labor problems? What are sales and cash flow going to be? How much money is needed now and in the future?

Before beginning your first draft, you need to rethink what business you are getting into; you need to know thoroughly your product or service—its strengths and weaknesses and how it stacks up against the competition; you need to understand the market and specifically your market niche and how you will penetrate this market; you need to get commitment from your key employees (assuming you will have employees); and you need to understand accounting and financing conditions and requirements over the next four or five years.

Now is the time to ask yourself again some simple, yet important questions, such as these.

1 Does your business venture have a good chance to grow into a successful company?

2 Is your product or service going to sell? Do you have customers committed? Have you thoroughly researched the market to determine if there is a need for your product or service at a price that will be profitable to you?

3 Have you put together a good venture team that works well together?

4 Do you really understand that venture capitalists will invest in your venture only if they see a way to make big profits? The same question applies to other investors or your banker.

5 Have you discussed risks, rewards, commitments, and tasks lying ahead with your accountant, lawyer, banker, insurance agent, and family? Are you prepared to make the commitment necessary to succeed? Is your family behind you?

Once you decide that your business plan passes muster, then you can use it as the basis for raising capital and obtaining support for your venture. As Joseph R. Mancuso stated, "The business plan is the heart of the heart of the raising capital process."[1] Regardless of what you have heard about how money has been raised on the basis of business ideas scribbled on tablecloths or on the backs of envelopes, forget it. Anyone who invests money is generally professional and expects a similar degree of professionalism from entrepreneurs. Indeed, any knowledgeable investor expects you to be fully prepared and armed with a completely researched, well-written business plan for the venture you want financed or for any other support you are seeking.

In the course of gaining support and raising capital, a number of people will read your business plan, each with a slightly different perspective. These are some of the people.[2]

1 *Bankers.* Virtually every business needs the services of a commercial banker. As banks are an important source of loan money for any business, it's a good idea to develop a friendly and candid relationship with your banker at the earliest possible opportunity. The best way to start is by presenting him or her with a copy of your business plan as soon as it is completed. Your ability to meet sales and profit objectives specified in the plan will go a long way toward establishing your creditworthiness.

2 *Suppliers.* The survival and growth of almost any business depends on its ability to secure and maintain trade credit from its suppliers. Usually, suppliers will provide 30-day credit to their customers on an open account basis provided the customer can demonstrate creditworthiness. Even without substantial cash reserves, a small business may succeed in establishing a line of credit by

---

[1]Joseph R. Mancuso, *How to Prepare and Present a Business Plan* (Englewood Cliffs, N.J.: Prentice-Hall, 1983), p. 301. This material is reprinted by permission of the publisher.

[2]Donald M. Dible (ed.), *Winning the Money Game* (Santa Clara, Calif.: Entrepreneur Press, 1975), pp. 81–83. This material is adapted by permission of Reston Publishing Company, Prentice-Hall company, 11480 Sunset Hills Road, Reston, Va. 22090.

persuading the supplier that its chances of survival are good. In such a case, a business plan does the trick. The plan gives substance and form to what may only be an idea at the time the credit is established.

3 *Customers.* When a small company tries to land a big contract, there are often doubts in the customer's mind as to the ability of the small company to produce on schedule. Often small company bids are rejected out of hand on the grounds that their ability to produce is questionable. A well-executed business plan can show the steps and the time required to double or triple plant capacity and may prove to be just what the doctor ordered to win your customer's favor and get his or her order.

4 *Investors.* It is not only wise, but it's also a moral obligation to do anything and everything within reason to protect the money invested by backers. The conscientious preparation of a business plan goes a long way toward satisfying this obligation. Most often, the primary function of the business plan is to serve as a fund-raising document. No professional investor would consider putting money into a deal that was not documented with a business plan. Verbal presentations by the principals are considered important. However, the business plan is the information source on which the final investment decision is based.

5 *Employees.* Many small companies, operating in low-overhead facilities, have difficulty recruiting capable employees. In some instances, the goals and objectives of the company as set forth in the business plan can be an important factor in influencing a decision to join the firm.

The final reason why you should prepare a business plan is because it serves as a road map for your business venture once it is started. A slight modification of an old quote is applicable here: "If you don't know where you are going, it is going to be hard to get there." Any venture you undertake, like any journey you undertake, must depend on a road map and roadsigns for direction. The business plan will become an operating tool that will help you manage your business and drive it to success. You plan your venture and your work; then you work your plan.

Moreover, as stated earlier, the business plan serves as a valuable recruiting tool when hiring employees. In addition, it can provide these people with a sense of direction, goals to be achieved, policies, and a management tool. It lets everyone know how he or she fits into the organization and what is expected of him or her.

Who Should Prepare the Business Plan?

If you are beginning the business venture alone, you should be the one to prepare the business plan. If there is an entrepreneurial team, then each member should contribute his or her efforts to the project. Do not in any circumstances hire someone to write the plan for you. This does not mean that you should not enlist the aid of others and get help from outsiders, but the final plan should be written by you and your team members. The reason should be obvious: It is difficult to defend someone else's work. If you put it together, then you have a better understanding and feel for it. Your oral presentation and defense of it will ring true.

Outside sources that you may need to enlist to give you guidance and help you prepare your plan are listed as follows.

1 *Publications and general consultants.* Clearly, this chapter, the next two chapters, and the texts listed in the bibliographies of these chapters will give you the necessary framework to prepare a business plan. Moreover, a wealth of publications on how to write a business plan can be obtained from The Center for Entrepreneurial Management, Inc., 83 Spring Street, New York, New York 10012; (212) 925–7304. Also, write to Institute for New Enterprise Development (INED), 385 Concord Avenue, Belmont, Massachusetts 02178; (617) 489–3950. Or get in touch with your local SBA office. In addition, some business professors at your nearest university can help you prepare your business plan. In some instances, private business consultants can be an important source of help in preparing your business plan and in assisting you in securing financing for your venture. Anyone, however, can say he or she is a business consultant. Therefore, check references carefully before engaging a business consultant's services.

2 *Lawyer.* Competent legal advice, as stated throughout this text, should be sought at the outset. Sound legal advice is one of the critical elements in any business. Clearly, your lawyer will need to make input to all the legal aspects of your business plan, for example, the legal form of your business, financing instruments, patents, agreements, and so forth.

3 *Accountant.* An accountant needs to be brought on board early on. Accounting is the language of business, and all financial statements and forecasts should be prepared with the guidance of an accountant. Many investors also require that the financial statements be audited and accompanied by an opinion from the accountant. Moreover, all tax ramifications must be disclosed and explained.

4 *Banker.* Try to find a banker who is truly interested in seeing your business succeed. You may eventually have two bankers, one from a commercial bank and one from a Small Business Investment Company (SBIC). In addition to being valuable sources of financing, your banker or bankers can provide you with advice and counsel in evaluating all aspects of your business plan.

5 *Suppliers.* Suppliers can provide you with industry forecasts and surveys, availability of material, prices, and delivery schedules.

6 *Customers.* The customer can give you a wealth of information about competition. Moreover, customers can give you letters of intent to buy from you and specifications on current and projected product or service requirements.

7 *Advertising Agency.* If you plan to use an advertising agency, give it a complete overview of your business venture, product-service description, and target market. It, in turn, will be able to recommend advertising and marketing strategies and applicable costs.

8 *Insurance agency.* An insurance agent will be able to develop an appropriate insurance program for your company and also answer a number of questions regarding the overall protection of your business venture.

HOW TO WRITE A BUSINESS PLAN

Which is more important: style or substance? For business plans, to be sure, both are important. The next two chapters present the substance, the elements that should be included in the preparation of your business plan. This section deals with the style of your business plan, a primer, if you will, on how to improve your writing skills to help you put your thoughts down on paper more clearly and concisely and to create a more readable and appealing business plan.

Overview of Good Writing

Good writing is important for setting the tone and for effectively communicating what it is you want to say. The proper choice of words—sometimes even a single word—can make the difference between writing something that is clear or something that is obscure. A story is told about Truman Capote's secretary, who mildly scolded him for sitting at his desk all day and writing only one word. He said, "Yes, by God but it was the right word." The late Capote and other great writers have known that searching for the right word is searching for better vision—both for the writer and the reader.

As an entrepreneur, your writing skills must be sharp. Much of your time will be spent writing letters, analytical and evaluation reports, memorandums, narratives for financial reports, policy and procedure statements, interim reports, proposals, opinion statements, and newsletters. As an aspiring entrepreneur, you will find the most important piece of writing you will ever write is the business plan, a report that may mean success or failure, whether you fly or fizzle, whether you get the capital or don't get the capital.

Don't ever hire a word jockey to write your business plan. It won't work. Venture capitalists want to know facts and figures, but they also want to know your heart, mind, soul, and guts. They want to know what you really think about the venture you are proposing. To explain and defend someone else's report is like trying to ride someone else's horse; sooner or later, you're going to get bitten, kicked, or thrown.

To succeed, we all will have to become better communicators to explain new concepts and technologies. Complexities require that we must be effective senders and understanding receivers. We spend most of our working hours using words and responding to the words of others. The typical investor spends at least half of his working day and an extra hour or two at night reading letters, business plans, and publications. He or she will not tolerate ambiguous, inaccurate, extraneous, incomplete, and boring writing because it wastes time, leads to poor decisions, and, in the case of an aspiring entrepreneur, can result in the worst thing—no action.

The style of the business plan that you present to prospective investors, such as venture capitalists, should be *your* style. If you have a poor style, change it. Unfortunately, many people, especially with business and engineering backgrounds, erroneously think that business and technical writing does not need style. But stuffy and boring writing numbs the brain and glazes the eyes; it is a sure cure for insomnia.

This age of committees, staff meetings, and technocrats has produced some of the world's dullest writing. You have read (or not read): "The meeting was called to order by the president. The minutes were read. There was an attempt . . . Mr. Smith thought that, in his opinion, proper aspects should be brought to bear . . . The meeting was interrupted . . . In addition, Mr. Brown also . . . The reason is because . . . and so forth." Wake up!

On purpose, this section is mixed with examples of business writing and so-called literary writing. Good writing is good writing, no matter who does it. Good writing includes both style and substance. A pleasing and interesting style communicates to the reader almost as much as the message itself; for opening the door and getting the chance to present your business plan, style is far more important than substance.

The most difficult level of communication is one-way, such as a letter or a business plan. You are competing with hundreds of entrepreneurs, and you have one shot at the investor—no chance for explanation or clarification. You either accomplish your communication objective or you blow it. At this level of communication, neither immediate feedback nor the clear identification of accomplishing nonverbal cues, such as body language or eye movement, is possible. For success, you must be better than merely an average writer.

Do you think you are a poor to average writer? No one needs to write poorly; good writing is a skill that can be learned. Faulkner, Melville, Shakespeare, Dante, Homer, and all the other great writers came into this world ignorant and without writing skills. Writing didn't come easily to them. They developed and refined their writing skills over a period of years. Their key to success was learning the rules; writing, rewriting, and writing again; practice, practice, and more practice.

Study and emulate the style of effective writers whether they be George Orwell or George Odiorne. Remember this: Most of the great writers work through many drafts before the final one is completed. Peter Drucker even writes something he calls the "zero draft" that comes before the first draft. Hemingway liked to write a few new pages each day, but only after he had carefully reviewed all that he had written in the preceeding few days. By the time he completed a piece, he had reviewed most of it a hundred times or more.

The Payoff from Good Writing

Most business plans rest on a fine line between success and failure. For those of you who like a formal analysis of this assumption, take a look at the following matrix shown in Figure 16.1.

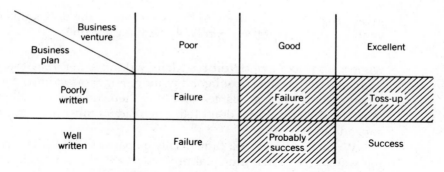

Business plan \ Business venture	Poor	Good	Excellent
Poorly written	Failure	Failure	Toss-up
Well written	Failure	Probably success	Success

FIGURE 16.1. *The payoff matrix from good writing.*

A poor business venture idea will fail no matter how well the business plan is written. The *Good* column is where most of us are. Therefore, as the shaded area shows, good writing pays off. Many venture capitalists look at several hundred business plans per month. A good venture idea dressed in a shabby suit is quickly ushered out the back door via a waste basket and eventually dumped in the incinerator. Normally, a good business venture idea with its Sunday suit on will, at least, get another once-over and probably get you an interview. Sometimes an excellent business idea presented in rags will not catch the eye of the investor and will be thrown away with the trash.

Some Important Writing Rules

The rules covered in this section will help you write a good business plan for your business venture. Study these rules, and apply them until they become second nature to you. Remember that writing is a skill that can be learned. Writing doesn't come easily to even the greatest of writers. They had to learn the same as you.

The Honesty Rule.   Honesty in writing, as in life, concerns more than not lying. Honesty means revealing what you actually think and feel at least as it may be significant and relevant to the business plan. To do so may mean telling "the whole truth, nothing but the truth, so help you God." It may mean getting in touch with thoughts and feelings that have been repressed because you want more than anything to start that new business. Be honest to yourself and to your fellow investors. If you go in blind, you will soon regret it, and the dream will turn into a nightmare; you may be chained to this nightmare for several years before you can wriggle free. In the process, you will lose one of your most prized possessions, credibility; once lost, it is almost impossible to regain.

One more note about honesty. Powerful writing is honest writing, always. An oral explanation and defense of your business plan will be forceful and effective if your writing is honest; it will flow smoothly; it will ring true. The prospective investor will react positively to this, and even if the decision is not to invest in the venture, this decision will probably be the right one.

Writing with Nouns and Verbs. Many writing experts say that choosing the right noun and verb is the crux of good writing. For greatest impact and clarity, seek the most concrete noun available—and only then consider modifiers. Then choose the most active verb; show, don't tell. The readers must hear and see with their own ears and eyes.

Write "flat broke" for "financially embarrassed." Write "gasoline in the drinking water" for "environmental problems." Mark Twain said, "The difference between the right word and the almost right word is the difference between lightning and the lightning bug."

Verbs are words that express action, occurrence, or existence. Choices of effective verbs make narratives forceful and lively. In business writing, they make process and causal analyses precise. Amateur writers rely too heavily on *to be, am, is, are, was, were, to have, to make, to go, to come, to move,* and *to get.* We have thousands of active verbs in our English storehouse, yet we write like deprived weaklings.

Weak:	The tractor went up a 3-to-1 slope.
Strong:	The tractor climbed a 3-to-1 slope.
Weak:	The houses on Montana Street were in need of complete overhaul.
Strong:	The houses on Montana Street stood in weeds and debris in total disrepair.

I, You, or They Rule. Unless you are a skillful writer, do not use the first person. The first person is *I*. The second person is *you*. The third person is *they*. Learn how to write with authority in the third person. This writing forces you to think clearly and logically; it makes you concentrate on your subject. Later, if you think you are good enough, return to the first or second person. Opinion is almost always more forceful and convincing if such opinion is written without the personal pronoun. It is weak to write: "In my opinion, I believe computers are here to stay. Instead, write: "Computers are here to stay."

Use of Transitional Words. Once you've started writing, lead your reader by the hand from one thought to another by using transitional words. Without them, we would write weak, conflicting statements; with them, the statements string together, and our meaning is clearer. Many transitional words are listed here.

Admittedly	In addition	On the other hand
And	In fact	Still
Assuredly	Indeed	The fact remains
But	It is true that	Therefore

Certainly	Moreover	Thus
Clearly, then	Nevertheless	To be sure
Consequently	No doubt	True
Even so	Nobody denies	Undoubtedly
Furthermore	Obviously	Unquestionably
Granted	Of course	Yet

Not: The systems project had value. It wasted time.
But: Admittedly, the systems project had value. But it wasted time.

Avoid Redundancies.   Cut any word that repeats a meaning or that pads without adding anything. Each of the italicized words or phrases that follow is redundant.

a *distance* of ten yards	*future* prospects
advanced *forward*	in addition, he *also*
an *actual* fact	inside *of*
another *one*	ouside *of*
at *the* present *time*	*past* history
equally as good as	retreat *back*
false illusion	small *in size*
few in *number*	*usual* custom
free gift	*young* teenager

Big Words and Small.   A good writing vocabulary needs to be big, but that does not mean that it should be made up exclusively of big words. Most particularly, it does not mean a vocabulary in which big words are substituted for perfectly adequate small words. Use those in parenthesis.

accompany (go with)	manner (way)
appeared to be (seemed)	obtained (got)
desired (wanted)	received (got)
implemented (follow up)	required (needed)
individual (he, she, man, woman)	securing (getting)
informed (told)	stated (said)

Outworn Expressions.   Nothing is grammatically wrong with the following expressions except they are simply tired expressions used in the business world.

along this line	are in receipt of
as a matter of fact	as the case may be
as to	as yet we have not heard from you
at an early date	
due to the fact that	avail yourself of the opportunity
in accordance with	

in terms of	in regard to
in the near future	in the event that
kindly	inasmuch as
relative to	previous to
we feel	take the liberty
we hope	we regret to inform
thanking you in advance	we trust
pursuant to your request	according to our records
hereto	in reference to your letter
herewith	hereinafter
trusting you will	under separate cover
attached please find	at your earliest convenience

Use Words Economically.   Many writers tend to use extra words that add nothing to the meaning of their expressions, resulting in overstuffed language. A few examples are listed here for your examination.

Don't Use:	*Use*:
exactly identical	identical
full and complete	full *or* complete
personal opinion	opinion
refer back to	refer to
whether or not	whether
as of this date	yet, still, now
at the present time	now
be kind enough	please
due to the fact that	due to, since, because
during the time	while
for the purpose of	to
in the month of March	in March
in order to	to
in reference to	about
in the event that	if
in the neighborhood of	about
in view of the fact that	since
not in a position	unable
until such time	when
with regard to	about
without further delay	now
you owe a total of $300	you owe $300
your check in the amount of $100	your check for $100
absolutely necessary	necessary
advance planning	planning

arrived at the conclusion that	concluded
at your earliest convenience	soon
on the grounds that	because
pursuant to our agreement	as we agreed
thanking you in advance	thank you
utilization	use
yours of a recent date	your letter
first and foremost	first
held a meeting	met

Use Words That Give a Clear Picture. Clarity is an important attribute of your business plan. Try to use words that will tell exactly what you mean. Here are a few examples.

Murky:	*Clear*:
Termination of your rental contract will be effective on December 31.	Your rental contract will expire on December 31.
We guarantee this tire to last longer than any other.	We guarantee this tire to last for 48,000 miles; no other manufacturer guarantees a tire to last longer than 40,000 miles.
Questionnaires were sent out to a number of our users regarding a special paint of ours.	We sent questionnaires to 1800 users of our Epoxy 2-D paint.
We want to try to market a dessert.	We intend to market standard size frozen apple pies.
Many outlets have examined our product.	One hundred outlets examined our product.
Eventually we will prepare our report.	You will have our report July 15.

Accentuate the Positive and Eliminate the Negative. Clearly, readers want to read positive statements. See how shifts in point of view creates positive messages in the following examples.

Negative:	*Positive*:
If I have not answered all questions . . .	If you have any other questions . . .
We close at six.	We are open till six.

Do not hesitate to call us.	Please call us.
Our shipments cannot be made until June 1.	Shipments can be made on or after June 1.
The report was not complete.	The report needs to include cost data.

Use Figurative Language.   Using figurative language is one of the best ways of making writing concrete and vivid. Including a little of it in your business plan will make it more expressive and distinctive. Using figurative language means that the expressions are taken in a figurative sense rather than a literal sense, and these expressions are known as metaphors and similes. A metaphor never explains; it creates an image, and the image explains itself. It is an implied comparison. A simile is a slowed-down metaphor; instead of jumping straight to its image, it arrives by way of an "as" or "as if" or "like."

If you feel the urge, try to sprinkle a few metaphors and similes throughout your business plan. Avoid, however, those that are tired and worn out, such as these: "All that glitters is not gold." "Birds of a feather flock together." "Hungry as a bear." "Feel like a million." Some good examples for your consideration are "His eyes are as hard and wary as a junkyard dog." "Joe's temper flared when Sue told him another Aggie joke." "After today's meeting with Mayor I. M. Portant, I can see that the wings of reason do not always fly true." "Those investors are on a flight to safety." "Too many controls are written into this agreement; we need some wiggle room." "Mary was not prepared for the meeting. The motions of her mind were as unpredictable as the flitter of a bird in the branches." "Highflyer Computers has a Kamikazi pilot sitting in the president's chair."

Some may think that more colorful writing does not sound the way they talk. The paradox of writing is that written sentences should *sound* like natural speech, but they *cannot be* natural speech. Why? Because natural speech is a lot more than words. Natural speech, in addition to words, includes tone of voice, inflection, facial expressions, gestures, manner, even the speaker's appearance. You simply cannot defend your writing on the basis of "That's the way I really talk." The objective of writing is to create something that is a lot more interesting, clearer, more specific, and more thoughtful in every way. But the underlying trick is to make it *sound* natural.

TIPS ON PUTTING TOGETHER THE BUSINESS PLAN

You will have to decide what information to include, what information to emphasize, and how to organize your business plan for maximum effectiveness. Following are some tips that will aid you in gathering information and in physically putting your business plan together.

Make Your Business Plan Legible

Legibility relates to how easy or difficult your business plan is to read once it's on the printed page. Keep these points in mind:[3]

1 Use good-quality paper heavy enough to make the typing stand out. Type your business plan on white bond paper, 20-lb. weight, 8½ x 11 inches.

2 If copies are required, make them by the best reproduction process you have available. Carbon copies are generally undesirable.

3 Maintain 1-inch margins all around.

4 If you're going to put your business plan in a binder, leave 2 inches of margin on the left-hand side.

5 If typed single-space, allow double-space between paragraphs, above and below headings, lists, long quotations, and graphics.

6 Use legible, nondistracting type. Avoid script and types with fancy lines and flourishes.

7 Use typographical elements to make words, phrases, and sentences stand out. Catch your reader's attention by using italics, all-capital letters, and different colors. But don't overdo such devices.

8 If the sequence of a list is random or arbitrary, use bullets (●) or dashes (—). If the order is important, use Arabic numerals (1, 2, 3 . . .).

9 Keep paragraphs fairly short (under 100 words) to break the page vertically.

10 Use pictures and graphs where appropriate. Include graphics in boxes.

Business Plan Format and Parts

A business plan needs a formalized presentation to save readers' time and effort and to prevent confusion. The formal parts help readers recognize the various units of the business plan, thus speeding up the retrieval process by highlighting important information. In the next chapters the content of a business plan is presented. In this section, the format and major parts of the business plan are presented without regard to content. The parts should include (1) letter of transmittal, (2) title page, (3) table of contents (4) summary, (5) body of the business plan, (6) appendixes, and (7) bibliography.

Letter of Transmittal.   The letter of transmittal officially presents the business plan to your reader. The letter is bound with the business plan; it explains the occasion for

---

[3]Thomas E. Pearsall and Donald H. Cunningham, *How to Write for the World of Work,* 2d ed. (New York: Holt, Rinehart and Winston, 1982), p. 97. Copyright © 1982 by CBS College Publishing. Copyright © by Holt Rinehart and Winston, Reprinted by permission of the publisher.

the business plan; it refers to the title; it explains the major features that may be of special interest to the reader. Close the letter by stating your willingness to provide additional information if the reader desires it.[4]

Title Page.   The title page gives identifying information about the business plan. It presents the title of the business plan, the name and position of the person or group for whom you prepared it, your name and position, and the date you submitted the business plan.

Table of Contents.   The table of contents is a list of the headings and subheadings of the business plan. It provides a handy outline overview of the business plan that helps your reader locate major sections quickly. The appropriate headings and subheadings that are appropriate to a complete business plan are presented in the next chapter.

Summary.   The summary may be the most important part of the business plan. Most investors are harried and hurried. The summary is the first thing that Mr. Deeppockets is going to look at. You are either going to catch his attention or lose him here. Mr. Deeppockets makes a quick first-pass perusal to weed out the obvious "whizzers." (A *whizzer* is a plan with no apparent merit that "whizzes" from the "In" basket to the trash can.) If the summary holds his attention, then he will go into the main body of the plan. Potential investors simply do not spend more than five minutes on it at first. A venture capitalist, for example, may receive over 100 plans a month, and he or she simply does not have enough time to read through each one in detail. The summary is the key to capturing the investor's attention within a five-minute span. You must, in a few paragraphs, give the essence of your plan and show how it is different from, and better than, the others.

The Body of the Business Plan.   Clearly, the body of the business plan is the longest part because it presents your detailed message. In essence, it answers the five *W*'s and the *H*: Who? What? When? Where? Why? and How? It takes no set organization, but its contents should be arranged in some logical, unified order. The arrangement must help the reader skim the business plan, read it thoroughly, or refer to specific parts of it by using heads and subheads, which separate the body into major divisions and divide each major division into sections. A rule of thumb is that one cannot have too many heads and subheads.

Appendixes.   The appendixes contain information or documents that, although useful, might disrupt easy reading of the body of the business plan. Appendix material has direct but secondary rather than primary importance to your reader.

---

[4]For excellent and concise instructions on how to write a business letter, see Malcolm S. Forbes, "How to Write a Business Letter." Order from International Paper Company, Department 1-A, P.O. Box 900, Elmsford, New York 10523.

Examples include drawings, patents, agreements, copies of questionnaires, related correspondence and reports, extended résumés, detailed financial information, and so forth.

Bibliography.   In writing your business plan, you may use information already made available by others in published or unpublished sources. When you refer to others' work, document the source you are quoting or paraphrasing by citing the source and by listing the source in the bibliography.[5]

Illustrating Your Business Plan

To communicate your message in the business plan effectively will require the use of devices in addition to words and sentences. The devices include charts, tables, and photographs. Of course, none of these devices should be used unless they add to the understanding of your business plan. Otherwise, they simply add clutter. The use of word-processing systems and hard copy of computer graphics can significantly enhance your business plan.

Charts.   Charts are layouts, graphs, or diagrams that pictorially represent some relationship, dimension, activity, or result of an operation or integration of a functioning whole. The organization chart, for example, provides information concerning reporting relationships of key personnel and levels of authority and responsibility. Physical layout charts depict the physical environment of an office, store, shop floor, and the like.

Other kinds of charts include line charts, bar charts, pie charts, and pictorial charts. Line charts show comparisons between two or more quantities and depict trends. The lines help the reader quickly grasp the results of comparative data. Bar charts also show trends and compare relationships. Each bar represents a quantity where the height or length of the bar indicates the amount of the quantity. Horizontal bar charts are often used to report quantities of time, length, and distance. Vertical bar charts depict heights, depth, and the like. Pie charts show percentages of a whole. Pictorial charts show quantity and comparison by using representations or visual images. The comparative number of people taking their lunch with them ("brown bagging") by regions of the country, for example, may show a drawing of a person carrying a lunch pail or bag, and each picture would represent 100,000 people. The appropriate number of pictures would be placed by each region, thus giving a graphic presentation of the number of people who take their lunch with them to work, school, or whatever, by region.

Tables.   Tables, if properly constructed, save words. They present, simply and clearly, large blocks of information without all the connecting devices needed in

[5]Pearsall and Cunningham, op. cit., p. 139.

writing. Tables, however, if not properly set up, can become the most confusing part of your business plan. To eliminate confusion, label each column and row to identify the data. If the space between columns is wide, use spaced dots or dashes as leaders.

Photographs.   A famous classical Chinese proverb says, "One picture is worth a thousand words." No doubt, appropriate photographs of quality inserted in your business plan can pay high dividends in communicating your message because the reader, seeing the photograph, can quickly and clearly receive the message and put it to proper use. The use of quality photographs is a most efficient way to increase the consistent and dependable transfer of information.

Moreover, drawings can be used effectively. Drawings, like photographs, show what objects look like. Unlike photographs, however, they can be made to show different aspects of an object. The four most commonly used views are external, cutaway, sectional, and exploded.

Computer Graphics.   Furthermore, the advent of business computer graphics has opened up a full range of information transfer that includes the entire range of data presentation and publication, for example, the written word, charts, graphs, drawings and paintings, photography, and films. Such a broad view of graphics can obviously permit you a *wide* range of possible presentations in the future. Indeed, the power of the computer has opened the entire range of the graphic art and presentation to the business community in general. Data will be presented, analyzed, and interpreted by using charts, graphs, pictures, words, and tabular presentations of numbers easily assimilated by the reader. Type fonts, page design, graphic formats, shadings, sentence and word spacing, underlines, headings, color, and so forth, will all be effectively and efficiently blended to achieve optimum message transfer.

Product Description

Another very important ingredient of your business plan is the product you will manufacture or sell or both. So it is necessary that you provide a product (or service) description that explains the purpose, appearance (use of photographs and drawings), physical structure, and operation of your product.

You must describe the features of your product and the reason or significance of such features. You will need to blend much functional description with visual description to acquaint your reader with the product fully. Again, this calls for the use of photographs and drawings. Here you may want to enlist the aid of a professional photographer and artist to help you prepare good pictorials.

In addition to pictorials, use analogies, especially when the product resembles something else with which your reader is more familiar. Analogies can be helpful in explaining shape, size, and structure. A common way to do this is to use metaphors of shape based on letters of the alphabet: A-frame, C-clamp, I-beam, O-ring, S-hook, T-square, U-bolt, Y-joint, and so on. Another way is to name parts of objects after parts of anatomy: head, eyes, ears, mouth, teeth, lip, throat, tongue, neck, shoulder, elbow, arm, leg, foot, and heel. Gears and saws have teeth; pliers and vises have jaws; needles have eyes. A third way is to use resemblances to other well-known objects: a mushroom-shaped anchor, a barrel-shaped container, a canister the size of a tube of lipstick.[6]

Analogies also can be used to suggest structure and size. Examples: "The simplest portable hair dryer looks a little like an oversized handgun in which a small fan blows hot air out of a screened nozzle." "The tape-recording head is a small C-shaped electromagnet the size of a dime." "The barometer case looks like a small metal shoe box with a glass lid." "The combustion chamber is shaped like a fat figure eight."[7]

If you can't make the comparison by using a well-known and easily visualized analogy, you can often compare a new mechanism with an older one or a more complex one with a simpler one. Examples: "Disposable syringes are just like rubber ones except that they are made of plastic and can be discarded after use." "An automobile battery is much larger and chemically different version of the battery that powers a flashlight."[8]

When a product or part of a product has an easily identifiable geometric shape, you can refer to that shape for description. Shapes include right angle, acute angle, obtuse angle, triangle, quadrilateral, pentagon, hexagon, circle, half-circle, oval, polyhedrons, cones, cylinders, spheres, and ellipsoids. Or, again, you can use well-known shapes, such as Hula-Hoops and face of a coin for circles; layout of a racetrack for ovals; dice or children's blocks for polyhedrons; nose cones on spaceships; jars, glasses, cans, and tubes for cylinders; tennis balls and marbles for spheres; and eggs or footballs for ellipsoids.[9]

Research Aids

Generally, most business plans require extensive research in addition to market research. You will have to gather a wealth of information from a variety of sources that may include on-site inspection, interviews, questionnaires, letters of inquiry, experiments, and libraries. Libraries are one of your most important sources for research. They are a veritable wealth of information. A sampling of useful references and source books includes these.

1 *Yearbooks.* These are published annually and contain information about the previous year. Nearly every major professional organization publishes a yearbook. Following are some examples that you may find useful: *Commodity Year-*

---

[6]Ibid, p. 221.
[7]Ibid.
[8]Ibid
[9]Ibid.

Book, Demographic Yearbook, The Municipal Year Book: An Authoritative Resume of Activities and Statistical Data of American Cities, Statistical Abstract of the United States.

2 *Almanacs.*   Whereas yearbooks are restricted to selected topics, almanacs contain enormous amounts of miscellaneous information, usually in the form of lists, charts, and tables. Much information pertains to the previous year, but a few contain historical information of a broader scope. Examples of some almanacs that you may find beneficial include *CBS News Almanac, Economic Almanac,* and *World Almanac and Book of Facts.*

3 *Biographical dictionaries.*   These dictionaries consist chiefly of brief, factual information about prominent persons. Some examples are *American Men and Women of Science, Who's Who in America,* and *Who's Who in Finance and Industry.*

4 *Encyclopedias.*   These are quick sources of a variety of information. Following are a few of the more general encyclopedias: *Encyclopaedia Britannica, The Lincoln Library of Essential Information,* and *McGraw-Hill Encyclopedia of Science and Technology.*

5 *Periodical indexes.*   A periodical index is a reference that covers a given number of magazines and journals and gives the author, title, volume number, page numbers, and date of issue for items published in the periodicals covered by the index. Some periodicals of a general nature are *Reader's Guide to Periodical Literature, Applied Science and Technology Index,* and *The Business Periodicals Index.* Examples of restricted subject periodicals indexes include *Accountant's Index* and *Business Education Index.*

6 *Guide to books and government documents.*   In addition to general and restricted subject indexes to periodicals, these guides serve the same purpose for books, pamphlets, and government documents. Examples are *A Guide to Science Reading, Energy Research Abstracts, Government Reports Announcements and Index,* and *United States Government Publications: Monthly Catalog.*

7 *Guides to book reviews.*   To help you determine if a book is applicable to your research, book reviews give you a quick evaluation. These book reviews are contained in *Book Review Digest, Book Review Index,* and *Technical Book Review Index.*

How to "Blow It"

To wrap up this section on how to write and put together your business plan, let's play a little game and summarize some of what has been presented by listing some rules on how to write a *bad* business plan.

1 Exaggerate and embellish everything in the plan, especially your credentials and the market potential of your product or service. Make outlandish promises. This lets the reader know that you are a real promoter and hustler.

2 Misuse or misspell words. Examples: "Lots 2 and 4 are contagious pieces of property that I own." "He told several amusing antidotes at the meeting." "One of the principle buildings on that lot is the warehouse." Misuse of words will not add to the credibility of you or your business plan, but it will certainly get the reader's attention.

3 Use poor grammar. This approach lets the reader know that you are a person of action and that you don't have time for grammar and other silly things.

4 Make your prospective investors think that you spent a lot of time on your business plan by padding. Here is a good example: "In my opinion, I believe, although I do not claim to be an expert on this complicated subject, the shaft-driven prototype, in most circumstances, would seem to be rather dangerous in many respects, or at least so it would seem to me."

5 When you get a chance, insert superfluous sentences or maybe entire paragraphs.

6 Make the reader dig for meaning by being obscure, especially in the summary.

7 Fill your sentences with deadwood and undergrowth. Begin a lot of sentences with such expressions: "There are . . . " "In my opinion, I believe . . . " "In the area of . . . "

Substitute:	*For*:
the question as to whether there	whether
is no doubt but that	doubtless
he is a man who	he
the reason why is that	because
owing to the fact that	since
in spite of the fact that	although

8 Ignore Professor Strunk's advice: "Vigorous writing is concise. A sentence should contain no unnecessary words, a paragraph no unnecessary sentences, for the same reason that a drawing should have no unnecessary lines and a machine no unnecessary parts. This requires not that the writer make all his sentences short, or that he avoid all detail and treat his subjects only in outline, but that every word tell."[10]

9 Use a lot of platitudes, such as the following: "Everything should work out real well if the right kind of variables come together and everything works out according to plan. If it does, then we will consider it quite a success."

10 Use stale remarks, lifeless words, generalities, and euphemisms. Use "nice," "circumstances," "instances," "factors," "eventualities," and so forth. Say, "revenue enhancers," for taxes.

11 Keep your reader alert by wandering aimlessly through the business plan. Jump abruptly from one topic to another without format or connections. Don't use

[10]William Strunk, Jr., and E. B. White, *The Elements of Style*, 3d ed. (New York: Macmillan, 1979).

any headings or subheadings; run everything together. It saves time and paper, and you don't have to think as much. Also, punctuation is a waste of time.

12 Use the first person. A rule of thumb is to use at least 10 "I's" per page.

13 Use the passive voice.

14 Be bold. The business concept is all that matters. Write your business plan "off the top of your head." Library and empirical research is a waste of time. You've got better things to do.

15 Strip vigor and style from your writing. Your business plan is supposed to be dry and dull. Most of that so-called good writing is just a bunch of flowery sentences thrown together. Anyway, it's sissy to write like Hemingway, Twain, Wolfe, Crane, or any of the rest of them. And if you become really educated, you can write statements like this: "In my opinion, I believe that there are objective considerations of contemporary phenomena that compel the conclusion that success or failure in competitive activities exhibits no tendency to be commensurate with innate capacity to establish the drilling rig at its proper location." At the very least, such writing will make a deep impression on the venture capitalist.

16 Write your business plan on spiral notebook paper. This approach lets your prospective investors know that you don't waste money.

SUMMARY

The business plan is the guts, nuts, and bolts of your business venture put down on paper. It is written for your benefit because it forces you to rethink your business venture totally and to put it into exact qualitative and quantitative terms. When your business venture is launched, it also serves as a critical document in managing your business.

If you plan to raise money from outside sources (most entrepreneurs do), the business plan is essential because venture capitalists, bankers, and the like, want to know everything about you and your business venture before they will give you any money. The more clearly they understand this, the more likely you are to get the money.

To ensure that your message is understood by all readers, you must use good writing skills. To be sure, good writing is a means to an end; it is the *written* business plan that must communicate and get people interested in backing you. Initially, it is the written business plan that must get the job done.

Writing the business plan is something less than a full-fledged art, but more than simple craft. Rigid standards apply to some aspects of your business plan and obviously should be followed, as by using quality paper, typing, margins, and the like. Other efforts used to write your business plan are somewhat creative, where no precise formulas apply. This chapter, however, points out some of the ways you can write and put together a better business plan ranging from proper word usage to physical layout and illustration. How imaginative you are in designing your plan is, to a great extent, up to you.

ASSIGNMENT

1 What is a business plan, and what are the reasons for preparing one?

2 Who should write the business plan? Explain fully.

3 Why is it important to practice good writing skills in preparing your business plan? Explain the payoff from good writing.

4 Explain and give an example of the writing rules presented in this chapter.

5 What is the purpose of transitional words?

6 Why is the phrase *center around* a logical impossibility?

7 What is wrong with the word *irregardless*?

8 Why is it impossible to be "more perfect"?

9 What is a trite expression?

10 Give an example of a redundancy in word usage.

11 Explain why written sentences should sound like natural speech but cannot actually be natural speech.

12 Why should you avoid the passive voice?

13 What is meant by using words economically? Give some examples not presented in this chapter.

14 Give an example of a murky sentence. Then rewrite it for clarity.

15 Why is it better to accentuate the positive in your writing?

16 State how you might put a little zip in your writing. Give examples.

17 List the ways to make your business plan more legible.

18 What are the major parts of your business plan? Explain each part's purpose. Also, explain why the "summary" may be the most important part of your business plan, at least in the early going.

19 According to an old Chinese proverb, one picture is worth more than a thousand words. How could you apply this proverb to writing your business plan?

20 Select a product or service of your choice, and describe it in writing for a naive reader. Use metaphors, analogies, and shapes in your description.

21 Go to the library, and review at least five of the references presented in this chapter. Write a synopsis on each.

22 List the ways to write a *bad* business plan.

BIBLIOGRAPHY

Burke, Kenneth. *Language as Symbolic Action*. Berkely: University of California Press, 1966.

Coe, Richard M. *Form and Substance*. New York: Wiley, 1981.

Cowan, Gregory, and Elizabeth Cowan. *Writing*. New York: Wiley, 1980.

Dible, Donald M. (ed.). *Winning the Money Game*. Santa Clara, Calif.: Entrepreneur Press, 1975.

Ehrlich, Eugene, and Daniel Murphy. *Basic Grammar for Writing*. New York: McGraw-Hill, 1967.

Forbes, Malcolm S. "How to Write a Business Letter." In "Power of the Printed Word." International Paper Company, Department 1-A, P.O. Box 900, Elmsford, New York 10523.

Himstreet, William C., and Wayne Murlin Baty. *Business Communications*, 3d ed. Belmont, Calif.: Wadsworth, 1969.

Jarett, Irwin M. *Computer Graphics and Reporting Financial Data*. New York: Wiley, 1983.

Leggeth, Glenn, C., David Mead, and William Charvat. *Handbook for Writers*, 8th ed. Englewood Cliffs, N.J.: Prentice-Hall, 1982.

Mancuso, Joseph R. *How to Prepare and Present a Business Plan*. Englewood Cliffs, N.J.: Prentice-Hall, Spectrum Book, 1983.

Opdycke, John B. *Harper's English Grammar*. New York: Fawcett, by arrangement with Harper & Row, 1965.

Payne, Lucile Vaughan. *The Lively Art of Writing*. New York: A Mentor Book from New American Library, Times/Mirror, 1965. The hardcover edition published by Follett.

Pearsall, Thomas E., and Donald H. Cunningham. *How to Write for the World of Work*. New York: Holt, Rinehart and Winston, 1982.

Strunk, William, Jr., and E. B. White. *The Elements of Style*, 3d ed. New York: Macmillan, 1979.

Thomas, Henry. *Better English Made Easy*. New York: Fawcett, by arrangement with Hawthorn Books, Inc., 1954.

Welsh, John A., and Jerry F. White. *The Entrepreneur's Master Planning Guide*. Englewood Cliffs, N.J.: Prentice-Hall, 1983.

CHAPTER 17

Elements of the
Business Plan—Part I

INTRODUCTION

Joseph Mancuso, president of the Center for Entrepreneurial Management in New York, has started a library that contains the original business plans for some of the country's better- and lesser-known companies, such as the business plan for Federal Express. Mancuso says, "These business plans are a real window into entrepreneurship. You can see the skeleton of the dream that materialized 10 years later."

Because the skeleton of a business plan is fairly extensive, this chapter and the next one are required to cover all its "bones." Specifically, the objectives of this chapter are these.

1 To give an outline of the business plan's complete skeleton for a total view.

2 To discuss all the elements of this outline up to the financing program, which is the principal subject of the next chapter.

COVER MATERIAL

The cover material for a business plan consists of a letter of transmittal and a title page. They are discussed as follows.

Letter of Transmittal

The letter of transmittal or covering letter provides some basic introductory statements. By letter, you are meeting and "shaking hands" with the prospective investor and telling him or her why you are "there." The letter officially presents the business plan to your reader. It (1) explains why you are sending him or her the business plan, (2) restates the title, and (3) points out special features of the business plan that are of special interest.

Know precisely what you want, and write it down: "My company is looking for $1 million to buy out Cronus Computer Systems." And please spell the investor's name correctly. Don't blow your chances before you get started. Tell what your letter is about in the first paragraph. Don't keep your reader guessing, and write the letter from the reader's point of view. Why should he or she be interested in taking a look at the business plan? What is in it for him or her? Imagine the reader sitting across the desk from you; then simply talk to him or her. Be specific and clear. Do not exaggerate. Be honest. Make your letter neat and appealing. Type it perfectly on top-quality 8½-by-11-inch stationery. Keep it short—a couple of paragraphs if possible; certainly no more than one page. The last paragraph or last few sentences should tell the reader exactly what you want him or her to do or what you are going to do: "I will be in El Paso next Tuesday. May I have an appointment with you then?" See the following letter as an example.

Mr. Fred Deeppockets
Venture Capital Company
One Plaza Suite
El Paso, Texas 79968

Dear Mr. Deeppockets:

    The accompanying business plan titled *Buyout Plan of Cronus Computer Systems* is submitted for your consideration. We are looking for equity financing of $1 million to buy out Cronus Computer Systems. Arrangements for debt financing of $2 million is in place with Fidelity Bank of Boston. We project that you will triple your money in three years. Cronus builds computers and develops software packages especially for the "bread and butter" work done by small accounting firms, such as write-up, financial statement preparation, and tax work. We intend to become the leading vendor in this special niche.

    If you have an interest in providing $1 million in equity financing for the Cronus buyout, I would be pleased to meet with you on Thursday the 15th at your office and explain in detail the business plan. Please call me if you have any immediate questions.

               Sincerely,

               John Goodfellow
               1040 Inland Drive
               Chicago, Illinois 60611
               (312) 777–1000

Title Page

The title page gives identifying information about the business plan. It contains the title of the business plan; your name, position, and address; the date you submitted the business plan; and private placement disclaimers. An example of a title page follows:

DEVELOPMENT OF CIELO MESA SHOPPING CENTER

(A business plan for the development of
a new 1,000,000-square-foot shopping
center in Atanta, Georgia)

Prepared by

Angi Milam, Owner
Land Developers, Incorporated
10 Leaseway Drive
Atlanta, Georgia 30339
(404) 222–7070
September 18, 19X8

PRIVATE PLACEMENT DISCLAIMER

THE STRUCTURAL SKELETON

All business plans, like any book, report, and so forth, need a table of contents. The following section discusses briefly the purpose of a table of contents for your business plan. Then the table of contents is used to display the structural skeleton of the business plan, which is the subject of the rest of this chapter and the next chapter.

Table of Contents

The table of contents is a list of the headings and subheadings of the business plan. It provides a handy outline overview of the business plan that helps your prospective lenders and investors locate any major section quickly. As a matter of fact, we will use this section to provide the skeleton of the rest of the business plan. The skeleton is as follows.

I.   Summary
  A.   Summary format
  B.   Added comments (not part of the business plan)

II.   Business Description
  A.   Name of business
  B.   General business description
  C.   History of the business
  D.   Business goals and milestones
  E.   Uniqueness of the business
  F.   The industry
  G.   The product or service

III.   Market Research and Analysis
  A.   Target market and customers
  B.   Market survey
  C.   Market position
  D.   Market size and share
  E.   The competition

IV.   The Marketing Plan
  A.   Sales and distribution
  B.   Advertising and public relations
  C.   Pricing

V.   Research and Development Plan

VI.   Manufacturing and Operations
  A.   Production characteristics
  B.   Labor force

      C. Suppliers
      D. Equipment
      E. Property and facilities
      F. Manufacturing cost data

 VII. The Key People
      A. Description of management team and directors
      B. Remuneration
      C. Shareholders
      D. Employment agreements
      E. Consultants

VIII. Overall Schedule, Major Events, and Risks

  IX. The Financing Program
      A. Reason for financing
      B. Sources of financing
      C. Financial package
      D. Timing and stages of financing
      E. Equity, control, and valuation-pricing

   X. Financial Plan and Projections
      A. The budget
      B. Key assumptions and estimates

  XI. Appendixes

 XII. Bibliography (if applicable)

I. The Summary

The summary is a pithy statement of your business concept. It should be no more than a three-page statement that defines and highlights the business plan. To be sure, the summary is the most crucial part of the business plan because you either capture the investor's attention here or you lose it. Virtually thousands of entrepreneurs are vying for capital in the financial community all the time. Investors place a high dollar value on their time. They are looking at hundreds of other new proposals, they are in the process of closing several deals, and they are on the phone daily with principals of each of their portfolio companies. They simply do not have the time initially to wade through a lot of details. By spotlighting the major features and opportunities, the investor will be able to decide quickly whether or not the venture is feasible and of interest. You should be able to explain in a few paragraphs what your venture is and why it will succeed. What will your product or service do? Why will it do well? Is it cheaper, better, faster, newer, more efficient, more convenient? What gap or special niche will you fill that is not currently being filled?

Obviously, the purpose of the summary is to entice the investor to read your business plan, to get you an interview, and eventually the backing that you need. In plain language, it is the bait, the lure, the come-on, the siren song. And why shouldn't it be? You are struggling to get backing, and, for sure, no one is going to back you unless they fall in love with your business venture. The essence of the summary must stress well-founded promises of opportunity, ability of management, credibility, and profit. Above all, however, the summary cannot promise more than is in the guts of the business plan, nor can the guts of the business plan exaggerate, puff, or lie. It must be based on honesty. It is not a tool for "financing by finagling."

Some entrepreneurs send their summaries to prospective investors without other parts of the business plan attached. They figure that if the investor indicates interest, he or she will request the complete business plan. Others send the complete business plan along with the summary. It is difficult to say which is the better way. Logic seems to argue for making available the complete proposal to the investor because if the summary sparks sufficient interest, he or she may spend a few extra minutes thumbing through the business plan. And if the business plan is well packaged containing eye-catching enclosures, good pictures, and unusual exhibits, this may be enough to get that vital interview with the investor.

A. Summary Format. Following is an example of a summary for a start-up registered beef cattle operation. The key aspect of this summary is the format that you can use for your own business concept.

The business.

Vista Hills Ranch, Incorporated
Whispering Pines Road
Texarkana, Texas 75502
Telephone: (214) 838−6666
Tom Jones, Owner/Manager
Date of this plan: March 19X0

Type of business. Vista Hills Ranch, Incorporated, will be the home of a new American breed of registered beef cattle developed by combining the best genetics from two top domestic breeds, Brahman and Hereford. This new breed will be called Braher™ (registered with the Patent and Trademark Office) and will carry one-half the bloodlines from each breed. Braher™ will be a powerful and distinctive new breed that combines the outstanding and special characteristics of Brahman and Hereford breeds. Brahman cattle are noted for longevity, foraging and efficient feed conversion, calving ability, and heat and disease resistance. Herefords are noted for their fertility, weight gain, and adaptability. Selective mating of the best genetics from well-known and outstanding bloodlines from both breeds will produce a new breed of beef cattle that will combine these performance characteristics, resulting in the complete "beef-producing machine," an animal that excels in *all* characteristics that make money for both the registered breeder and the commercial cow-calf operation. The business that we are in is to be the first to produce Braher™, and our motto will be: "Mating the best to the best."

The product. The product is Braher™ breeding stock, both heifers and bulls. This product is the progeny from our selective mating of Brahman with Hereford. The final product that will be offered in the market must meet highly stringent selection criteria, such as conformation, color, disposition, and hardiness. Moreover, the parents of this progeny must also live up to the performance characteristics already mentioned. Any parents or the progeny of said parents not meeting our idea of the "perfect beef machine" will be culled from our operation and will not be offered in the marketplace.

The market. The market will be made up of three segments: (1) those who are now in the registered cattle business but who want to change and get on the bandwagon and become registered Braher™ breeders, (2) those who are new to the registered cattle business and who are looking for a top breed to build their operation on, (3) commercial ranchers who produce weanlings and yearlings for the beef industry (meat processors) and who are always in need of top bulls to breed to their commercial cow herds.

The competition. Because Vista Hills will develop Braher™, no direct competition will exist in the short term. We will promote Vista Hills as the originator of Braher™, and obviously buyers will have to come to us for this breeding stock. General competition, however, will come from other established breeds, such as Angus, Simmental, Brangus, and so forth. We will meet this competition by promoting Braher™ as the "perfect beef machine" that combines in one breed all major performance characteristics. In the long run, others who also breed Braher™ will be in direct competition, but we see the expansion and competition as a positive thing, especially because Vista Hills will be recognized as the main source of outstanding Braher™ breeding stock, and, therefore, the prime source for such expansion.

Management. Tom Jones, Owner/Manager, was born on a ranch in Kilgore, Texas, and with the exception of four years in the United States Marine Corps, where he served as a captain, has worked in all phases of ranching. He is well known and respected in the registered beef cattle industry as a top breeder and also as one of the first successful breeders of Simbrah, an American breed that has enjoyed years of success in America and abroad. Tom has a degree in animal science from Auburn University. He is 35 years old.

Jerry Short, D.V.M., is a specialist in beef genetics and reproductive techniques, which he has practiced for over 12 years. He received his doctorate in veterinary medicine from Texas A&M. He serves as chief genetic and reproductive consultant at Vista Hills Ranch.

Capital requested. Subchapter S Corporation common stock worth $600,000 is offered for 30 percent ownership. A total of 100,000 shares is authorized; therefore, 30,000 shares are offered at $20 per share. The board has elected section 1244 stock tax treatment.

Use of capital. The sum of $500,000 will be used to buy 200 (100 head of Brahman; 100 head of Hereford) head of top brood cows from premier Brahman and Hereford registered purebred ranches in North America. This assembled herd of brood cows will become the foundation for the Braher™ breeding program. Each brood cow will be selectively mated by artificial insemination to the greatest sires of the respective breeds. A total of $100,000 will be used to promote and advertise the new Braher™ breed in trade magazines and to produce the first two production sales in 19X3 and 19X4. Moreover, once the performance of certain matings prove to be of superior quality, such matings will then be performed by embryo transfer techniques whereby from 5 to 10 offsprings can be produced during one gestation period per cow.

Collateral. Vista Hills Ranch includes 1500 acres of pasture land, four small lakes, perimeter and cross fences, three breeding barns, two houses, three trucks, four gooseneck trailers, two tractors, and various implements and equipment. The total operation is appraised at $1.6 million fair market value. Of the total 100,000 shares, Tom Jones owns 50,000 shares; Jerry Short owns 10,000 shares; Joe Ling, president of Fourth National Bank, owns 5000 shares, and Willie Starkoris, attorney, owns 5000 shares.

Financial projections.

	19X1	19X2	19X3	19X4	19X5
Sales	$ —0—	$ —0—	$1,000,000	$1,500,000	$2,000,000
Expenses	300,000	350,000	400,000	450,000	500,000
Net Income	(300,000)	(350,000)	600,000	1,050,000	1,500,000

It is also important to remember that a very attractive facet of this proposal is that breeding cattle are subject to investment credits and are depreciated over a five- to seven-year period. Moreover, profit from the sale of breeding cattle is subject to capital gains treatment. Also, the losses for the first two years are passed through on a pro rata basis to the shareholders to offset against other income on their individual tax returns. Roughly, because of these tax advantages, the $600,000 investment could, in real terms, be equivalent to $300,000 depending on specific tax brackets and other variables for specific tax treatment; however, a tax accountant should be consulted.

Exit for investors. Vista Hills Ranch, Incorporated, plans to go public in the year

19X6. If for some reason Vista Hills does not go public by the end of year 19X6, then the investors can exchange their common stock for $60 per share and be paid out at $20 per share over three years: January 1, 19X7, January 1, 19X8, and January 1, 19X9.

B. Added Comments. The preceding kind of summary with or without an attached detailed business plan is traditionally mailed to several selected venture capitalist where it is routed through the proper channels with the attendant time delay and red tape. In some instances, however, the art of seeking venture capital has entered the computer age as shown in the following abridged article.[1]

> *Folks with a cool $25,000 to invest have a hard time meeting guys with hot ideas. They rely on the old grapevine, tips on the links, even local bankers. But now investors and entrepreneurs are hooking up through blind dates.*
>
> *The outfit doing the match-making is Venture Capital Network, Inc., [VCN] a nonprofit corporation started by the Business and Industry Association of New Hampshire. It brings together individuals who dabble in the high-risk world of venture capital with founders of fledgling firms through the equivalent of a computer dating service.*
>
> *Whether boy meets girl or investor meets entrepreneur, the process is basically the same. Investors and entrepreneurs fill out multiple-choice questionnaires, supplying basic information about themselves and what they seek in a mate. Investors check off the types of businesses that interest them, geographical considerations, how much they're willing to invest, the age and track record of the firm they seek, their planned involvement in the company's operations and its minimum acceptable annual sales five years down the road.*
>
> *Entrepreneurs supply their vital statistics along the same lines, as well as a two-page summary of a business plan and a three-year past or prospective profit-and-loss statement. The profiles are entered into a computer, run by the Small Business Development Program at the University of New Hampshire, which spews forth matches.*
>
> *Informal risk capital investors who finance these small size ventures are a big chunk of the venture capital market. William Wetzel, Jr., professor of finance at the University of New Hampshire, whose research of individual venture capitalists in New England was the brainchild for VCN, says that collectively the informal investors, or "business angels," as he calls them, may represent the largest pool of risk capital in the country. Indeed, he claims that they finance as much as five times the number of ventures as the public equity markets and professional venture capitalists combined.*
>
> *Yet "a number of small entrepreneurs and emerging growth firms get caught in that gap," says William Cahill, VCN president, and have a rough time finding capital.*

[1]Elizabeth Sanger, "Mating by Computer," *Barron's*, September 3, 1984, p. 32. This material is used with permission.

Banks often snub them because they're shy on equity, while professional venture capital firms don't usually bother with such trifling amounts. As it happens, small-scale venture capitalists have an equally hard time finding likely-looking ventures in which to invest.

Once the computer flags an investor with a prospective venture, the investor reviews the entrepreneur's questionnaire—which is anonymous. If still interested, he's given the business summary and financials. Next step is for VCN to tell the investor and entrepreneur about each other. Then it's up to the two parties to pursue a partnership.

II. Business Description

This section covers a number of key topics that help the investor understand your business concept. Suggested key topics to include in this section are (1) the name of the business, (2) general business description, (3) history of the business, (4) business goals and milestones, (5) uniqueness of the business, (6) the industry, and (7) the product or service.

Your business concept will consist of one of the following: (1) a start-up (or possibly seed money to investigate a business concept); (2) buyout of an existing company, acquisition of a franchise, or creation of a franchise; or (3) expansion of an existing business. If it is a start-up, then obviously the history topic is irrelevant. Otherwise, the key topics discussed later are about the same for any business concept, and you should, indeed, be able to fit these topics to your own business plan.

A. Name of Business. In naming your business, you can be as creative or as conservative as you wish. One way is to develop a name that is derived from contractions of other words. Biogen, Diasonics, Computrac, Telecom are examples of this. Names can also be descriptive, such as Waste Management, Engage-a-Car, Toys-R-Us, Piezo Electronics.

Names can be unique and catchy, but they mean nothing (or have a hidden meaning): Lotus, Apple, Exxon, D-X. Or, you may want to name your business after yourself (not normally recommended). Examples of successful companies who have done this are Amdahl, Hewlett-Packard, Wang, Du Pont, Hughes, Sears, Penney, Smith International, and Fluor.

In naming your business, you may also want to consider how the name is likely to be shortened or abbreviated. Many companies prefer, except in the most formal circumstances, to use initials in place of a longer name, such as IBM, 3-M, ITT, GTE, GE, AT&T.

Whatever name you develop, be sure to find out whether or not the name is free of legal restrictions. In most states, you can telephone or write the commissioner of corporations or secretary of state's office for a thorough name check. This service is usually free or available for a nominal charge, but you should consult your attorney before using this service.

B.   General Business Description.   This section presents a general synopsis of the business that you are in or intend to start. For example, you might state, "Infotex now sells stock market videotex services to 500 subscribers in Spokane. Infotex networks existing personal computers to provide a wide range of market-watch services to investors or potential investors in the NYSE (New York Stock Exchange), AMEX (American Stock Exchange), and OTC (Over-the-Counter) markets. Infotex harnesses the enormous computing power now resident in personal computers and interconnects them with a vast array of electronic information services. Infotex enhances or replaces many of subscribers' traditional services, such as newsletters, stock guides, and financial newspapers. For our subscribers, electronic information retrieval has replaced the printed word."

C.   History of the Business.   In this section, trace the history of your business. Tell where it was formed; and state how and when its first products or services were chosen, developed, and introduced. Specify what roles each member of the entrepreneurial team played in bringing the business to where it is today. Relate who were the founding shareholders and directors. List and explain the most important milestones through which the business has passed, pointing out important changes in its structure, its management, and its ownership. Explain the major achievements the business has enjoyed to date. If the business, on the other hand, is a start-up or looking for first-stage expansion financing, it may not have enjoyed many successes, but rather a few setbacks and losses. If so, describe them, and explain how they will be avoided in the future. To be sure, do not omit any reference to past problems. Finally, keep the history of your business under two pages.

D.   Business Goals and Milestones.   State the goals of the business and critical milestones. The reader, indeed, wants to know how you plan to move from where you are today to where you intend to be in the future. You may explain that your company, Infotex, plans to take advantage of the demand for more information about the stock market and recommended securities by top market analysts. You may further state that Infotex will provide a network of market services for 2000 subscribers in Spokane by 19X6 and for 4000 subscribers in Orlando by 19X7 and that if these test markets indicate sufficient potential, you plan to go nationwide with a total of 800,000 subscribers by 19X9.

E.   Uniqueness of the Business.   What is your distinctive competence? What are your key success factors? This section provides potential investors with a clear picture of the reasons why you will succeed. Because you are competing against other entrepreneurs who offer excellent investment opportunities, you must show that your chances for success are better than these alternatives. Show how your product or service is unique or your management team or your marketing force or your production process, and so forth.

The key objective in this section is to make your business stand out from all the rest. No one wants to invest in a "copycat" or a "me-tooer;" they want to invest in a company that has a unique business position. You may state something along these lines: "Our software packages make it easy for subscribers to learn how to use Infotex services. The training manual is only *five* pages, and an average subscriber can be up and running with access to all of our services within 15 minutes of training. The conversion to Infotex services eliminates reams of paper that the subscriber would otherwise have to wade through and allows him or her to use a personal computer fully and cost-effectively."

F. The Industry. Present the current status and prospects for the industry in which the proposed business will operate. Describe any new products or developments, new markets and customers, new requirements, new companies, and economic trends that could affect the venture's business positively or negatively. List industry standards. Specify growth in sales and profits, backlogs, and foreign competition. Include all published forecasts. Indicate businesses that have recently left the industry and why. State the social, political, technological, and regulatory trends affecting the industry in general and your business specifically. Identify the source of all information used to describe industry trends.

The investor wants to know the key success factors of the industry and how your product or service fits into the industry. He or she wants to know what changes would affect sales and profits and if barriers of entry exist; that is, how easy or difficult it is for someone to get started in the same business that you will be in. Can future competitors enter with ease? If the start-up capital required is small and the skill level required modest, then many competitors will quickly enter the market. Most investors shy away from industries that are easy to enter.

Furthermore, investors want to know if the industry is in the doldrums, ready to make a turnaround. Or is it "buggy whips"? Or is it cyclical or somewhat stable with a consistent growth. Or is it "hot" ready for a shakeout or crash (e.g., the personal computer industry in 1984 and 1985)? Or is it unproved (e.g., genetic engineering)? Or is it now out of favor (e.g., synfuels, shale oil, and nuclear power)? Is it seasonal? Is it heavily unionized? Is the industry growing at a rate significantly faster (or slower) than the GNP?

G. The Product-Service. The purpose of this section is to describe your product or service, explain its unique characteristics or specific advantages, and convince the investor that it (they) will sell for a good profit. Obviously, the potential investor is vitally interested in what you are going to sell, what kind of product or service protection you have, and what the opportunities and possible weaknesses are. Describe how features of your product or service will beat the competition. Discuss any opportunities for the expansion of the product line or the development of related products or services. Also, disclose any product disadvantage or the possibilities of rapid obsolescence because of technological or styling changes or marketing fads. Include photographs, prototypes, or samples. If you get an interview, use demonstrations to improve understanding and heighten interest.

Stress any unique features of your product or service by spotlighting the differences between what competitors currently have on the market and what you have or plan to offer. Indeed, one of the major considerations used in evaluating products and services is their uniqueness. If a product or service is a copycat or a product falls into the "commodity" category, then it becomes subject to severe price competition, and its sale price ends up being the same as all the other products of its kind with most, if not all, of the profit squeezed out. Some of the characteristics that provide product uniqueness are size, service, convenience, ease of use, maintainability, quality, prestige, durability, safety, cost-effectiveness, style and appearance, and adaptability. And, believe it or not, packaging of the product in many instances may be more important than the product itself. Packaging differentiation is, indeed, an important consideration.

If your product can be patented, you should consider obtaining a patent on it. If your product or service is based on new technology or a special formula, a trade secret protection program is in order to enable you to retain a competitive edge. One of the world's best-kept trade secrets is the formula for Coca-Cola. A trademark prevents competitors from using your company's or product's name and will help build name identification. The Xerox name has become synonymous with photocopy machines; Kleenex is a product name that has become synonymous with facial tissues.

Describe any patents, trademarks, trade secrets, copyrights, or other proprietary features. Discuss any head start that you might have that would enable you to achieve a favored position in the marketplace. Place copies of copyrights, trademarks, and patents in the appendix. If there are any licensing agreements, enclose those in the appendix.

If you are a distributor, specify your major product lines, who manufactures them, and categories of customers who buy them. Also, disclose your greatest volume items and your big-ticket, high-profit items. If you are a retailer, your product may be T-shirts at the local flea market or a variety of products and services in a department store. In any case, items for a retailer are similar to those for the distributor and require the same disclosure. The same applies to the mail order business.

If you are a manufacturer, explain how the product works and what its unique characteristics are. Save the "bits and bytes" for the appendix, however. Describe significant materials and supplies, and list your principal suppliers. Specify your production facilities and any productivity advantages. In distributing, retailing, manufacturing, or any other business where inventory is a major part of the operation, give some inventory management indicators, such as shelf life, obsolescence, life cycle, turnover ratios, and inventory valuation methods.

On the service side, if you are a contractor, from mowing lawns to building suspension bridges, specify how bids are made and what special competencies your business has in the work that it does. Do the same for personal services that your business offers. For example, if you are, or plan to become, a restauranteur, describe special meals and drinks served. If you are a publisher, explain your specific features and how advertising is sold and subscriptions are achieved. If you plan to open a fitness center, explain how your services differ from other fitness centers.

Here are a few examples that will give you some guidance and flavor on how to write this section of your business plan.

A manufactured product.   Quik-Frez™ is a low-cost, long-life consumer product that is designed to freeze homemade ice cream within one minute after the ingredients are placed and mixed into the Quik-Frez™ stainless steel module. Quik-Frez™ represents a significant breakthrough in cryogenic technology as applied to consumer products. Currently, there is nothing else like it on the market. Its advantages are (1) superb convenience and efficiency, (2) low retail price at $109.95 for the one-quart size and $139.95 for the one-gallon size, and (3) an almost instantaneous freezing of the ingredients that captures the full flavor of all of them and gives a distinctive flavored bouquet and smooth-textured ice cream.

Quik-Frez™ has been test-marketed for six months in Columbus, Ohio. Results of this market research are exceedingly gratifying. Ninety-five percent of the test users report that the ice cream made by Quik-Frez™ is superior to other ice creams, including homemade ice cream made by traditional methods and ice cream from specialty stores and food markets. Users stress the full-bodied flavor and luxurious texture of Quik-Frez™ ice cream. The only disadvantage that we foresee at this time is the significant cost of penetrating other markets and advertising and promoting to "educate" consumers about Quik-Frez™ and gain its acceptance as *the* way to make ice cream.

Innovative Products, Incorporated, manufactures Quik-Frez™ as its major product and presently buys the cryogenic module from Cryogenic Technologies of Detroit, Michigan. A second source does not exist for this module. All other components are shelf items, readily available from a variety of sources.

Innovative Products, Incorporated, is truly an outstanding example of the "factory of the future." Its production facilities are fully automated, using the latest in computer-assisted manufacturing (CAM) and robotics. The vendor for this new manufacturing technology is Cincinnati Milacron, one of the premier machine tool manufacturers in the world. With the use of CAM and robotics, our break-even point is presently at $11.50, a decrease from $18.75 before automation.

Raw material components including the cryogenic module are ordered on an as-needed basis for each production run. Work in process per unit averages 10 minutes, and with the use of new production technology, defective units are zero. The finished goods inventory has a maximum shelf life of two weeks. Our accountant uses the last-in, first-out (LIFO) method of costing inventory.

Because of strong trademark and patent protection (copies are included in the appendix), and because of wholehearted acceptance from our test consumers, we believe the probability of obsolescence of Quik-Frez™ is quite low. Quik-Frez™ has been subjected to stringent durability tests, and the results of these tests indicate that a unit will remain serviceable, with minor maintenance, for an average of 10 years. Moreover, we continue to work alone and with all suppliers in both technological and market research to uncover any areas of improvement. We have sent you several samples of Quik-Frez.™ Enjoy!

Mail order product. Our mail order firm, New Horizons, Incorporated, plans to market throughout North America, No-Spill™, a product designed for people who drink while driving (preferably nonalcoholic beverages). No-Spill™ is a thermos container, designed on the basis of a child's training cup, that has a small opening slightly raised that permits the drinker to snuggle a smoothly contoured spout in his or her mouth and get a swig of beverage without spilling a drop. Slightly recessed within the opening is a check valve that is easily released by the thumb when one wants to drink, but automatically closes when not in use, thus preventing accidental spilling. No-Spill™ is made in pint and quart sizes and comes with a holder that can be securely attached to the interior of an automobile or truck cab. Suggested retail prices are $25.00 for the pint size and $35.00 for the quart size.

Zippy Products Company of Denver, Colorado, is the manufacturer of No-Spill™ and holds all proprietary rights. The president of Zippy, Nyad Snorkel, will grant us exclusive rights to market No-Spill™ via mail order if we will stock 50,000 of either size or any combination for $5.00 per container across the board. Our test marketing indicates strong acceptance of No-Spill™, and we believe that it is an extremely "hot" item that would sell like a robin after a worm. Our projections indicate that a 50,000-unit inventory with 75 percent quarts and 25 percent pints would sell out within 60 days after advertising. Our advertising program is scheduled to begin immediately and last for 30 days. The major disadvantage is that if the product does not sell, we will have limited outlets to dispose of it.

The two key practical selling points of No-Spill™ are safety and convenience. Furthermore, No-Spill™ offers a novelty aspect that we think will appeal to mail order customers. Several samples have been sent to you, and a schematic of how No-Spill™ works is in the appendix.

A service. Physio-Fitness Centers prepare individual exercise-nutrition programs for our fitness-conscious clients and update these programs on a daily basis. We give all our clients personal direction, feedback, and supervision for their complete fitness program. For example, we keep track of all of their goals, such as miles jogged, pounds lost, heart rate, and so forth. This service is extremely important because most businesspeople are goal-oriented, and most of our clients are or will be businesspeople, especially executive types.

The biggest excuse most people use for not working out is that they don't have a structured program just for them as individuals. To be sure, the strength of Physio-Fitness Centers is our structured programs and personalized service. Moreover, we provide gym clothes, shower facilities, masseurs and masseuses, saunas, and personal grooming shops. We also provide private or community exercise areas.

We move our clients quickly through customized routines of rowing, weight training, jumping jacks, leg lifts, treadmill, sit-ups, and bicycling where no one task becomes tedious. We also offer racquetball, tennis, and swimming for those so inclined. For most of our exercise programs, clients are in and out in less than one hour.

We offer a number of specialties, such as the "Early Bird" program for early-rising executives who keep their business clothes at our center. They do their workout, shower, and eat a light breakfast at our special dining room, where nutritious, low-calorie lunches and dinners are also served to clients on other programs. We also provide an attractive environment, where clients can relax, meet people, and socialize.

We plan to locate our centers close to large office complexes nationwide for easy access by our clients. We are also negotiating with several large companies to set up fitness programs for their executives either on-site or at our own centers.

Because of the very unique and customized architecture of the centers that we plan to locate nationwide, the principal risk of this venture is salability of these centers if the fitness programs become unprofitable. The centers are built expressly for our program. Their adaptability to other uses is quite limited. For our architect's rendition of the proposed centers and brochures describing in more detail Physio-Fitness Centers' services, please refer to the appendix.

III. Market Research and Analysis

In this section of your business plan, you need to present enough information to convince the investor that you can meet sales projections and deal with the competition. You must describe the total market and specify your segment or niche in this market and your market share. Your analysis of the market is based on market studies available from private research firms; trade associations; trade publications that may dedicate one or more issues a year to a review and analysis of marketing trends in the industry served; and discussions with distributors, dealers, sales representatives, customers, and even competitors. Be prepared to specify and disclose the sources of data and methods used to establish the market size and your share and the analysis of your competitors. Also, disclose the person or persons doing the market research and analysis and also his or her credentials.

A. Target Market and Customers. Specify your target market or markets clearly. Describe the major segments you will penetrate and how you will reach and sell to them. Usually, products and services serve some part of a larger market. For example, is your target market to sell sheepskin seat covers for the trucking industry marketed on a consignment basis at major truck stops across North America? Or do you plan to manufacture several sheepskin coverings that will transcend several markets, such as automobile, trucks, bedding, and furniture?

Analysis of market segmentation is a critical part of your business plan. Do not assume that the size of the customer is normally distributed. If the distribution is not normal, which is probably the case, 50 percent of the customers may not be above the average. If an "average-size" customer can afford the product, this may only be 10 percent of the total customer base. In many markets, 20 percent of the customers may represent 80 percent of the demand. Ignoring factors that prohibit penetration of this 20 percent may cripple the entire marketing effort.

Who and where are the major customers for your product or service in each market segment? What are their buying habits? What are the bases of their purchase decisions: comfort, price, convenience, quality, service, personal contacts, political pressures, status? Your price, for example, is determined by how much the market will pay for your product or service, not by how much it cost you to make and sell it. Price is a function of the marketplace, not of your cost. If you calculate the maximum selling price of your product and then find you cannot make, sell, and distribute it at a profit, you will have to modify your product's concept. You will need either to find a way to sell your product for more money or to make it a lower cost.

In many companies, the "customer" who says he or she will *use* your product or service is not necessarily the one who will *buy* your product or service. The real buyer, or purchasing agent as he or she is often called, looks for the best price. If your product or service stresses quality, durability, convenience, or any other criteria besides price, your potential users are going to have a tough time convincing the purchasing agent to buy from you. For example, a manufacturer of a high-quality metal primer sent a cadre of salespeople into the market to convince a number of *users* (e.g., tool pushers, yard supervisors, shop managers, maintenance supervisors) to use this primer. Its demonstrated ease of application, durability, and quality were enthusiastically received by *all* users without one negative reaction. When these users placed their orders, which were routed through purchasing agents, the reply was, "We can get all the primer we need for $6.00 a gallon." The high-quality primer sold for $7.50 per gallon. By trying to get the orders, the salespeople became tennis balls between the people in the field who wanted the new primer and the purchasing agents, where the controller served as line judge. Nearly all controllers, as you probably have already guessed, also opt for lower-cost items. In some instances, the one who is going to use the product or service is also the one who will buy it. In other cases, as described in the preceding example, you must specify both the user and buyer and be sure that you have purchase commitments from *both*.

Identify major buyers who are willing to make purchase commitments. Get purchase orders if possible. Also, disclose potential customers or lost customers who have shown no interest in or dropped your product or service, and tell why. Furthermore, explain what you are doing to overcome such negative reactions.

B. Market Survey. The market survey verifies the demand for your product or service and whether potential customers will pay the price. Following is an example of the results of a market survey.

Ron Stone, our marketing manager, called on six major truck stops in Dallas, Reno, Seattle, Buffalo, Miami, and Cleveland to obtain consignment agreements for CUSHY, our sheepskin seat covering for long-haul truckers. All truck stops signed agreements to take on consignment one CUSHY display rack containing 24 CUSHY seat covers, which retail for $50.00. The reorder point is set at eight, and to date all truck stops except Seattle have reordered once to replenish their inventory.

In addition, Ron contacted directly a minimum of 50 truck drivers at each truck stop. He sold, on an average, 25 drivers at each stop. The consignment profit of these sales was passed along to the managers of each truck stop.

Ron is in the field now, calling on other truck stops across the country, securing consignment agreements at the rate of two per day. The reception that Ron is getting for CUSHY has been exceedingly favorable. Our projections are for 1000 CUSHY display racks to be installed in major truck stops by September of next year.

C. Market Position. Determining where your product fits in the marketplace is called "positioning." Following are some of the questions you must answer to determine your position in the market: (1) Will your business be considered a technical leader, follower, or middle-of-the-roader? (2) Will your business be aggressive and take risks, or do you plan to grow carefully and slowly? (3) Will you build a strong reputation for fast and reliable service? (4) Will you be in the high-priced—high-quality end of the market, or will your company try to make an adequate product that can capture a large market share by selling at a low price?

D. Market Size and Share. Total sales volume in a given industry is generally a valuable measurement, but it is not enough. The really important measurement is the figure for *your* market share. This figure represents the percentage of the total market available that your business has captured or expects to capture. A table such as the following is helpful.

Year	Industry Sales ($)	Your Share (%)	Your Share ($)
19X5 (actual)	$50,000,000	0.5 of 1.0%	$ 250,000
19X6 (actual)	55,000,000	0.5 of 1.0	275,000
19X7 (projected)	62,000,000	0.75 of 1.0	465,000
19X8 (projected)	70,000,000	1.0	700,000
19X9 (projected)	82,000,000	1.25	1,025,000

To present estimated data, you use a table like the following. Assume projections over the next three years. A five-year projection may be even better.

		First Year				Year	
		1Q	2Q	3Q	4Q	2	3
Estimated total market	Units						
	Dollars						
Estimated market share	Units						
	Dollars						

Estimate the share of the market and the sales in units (e.g., billable hours for service, pounds, gallons, pieces, components) and dollars that you have ascertained based on rigorous, objective analysis of customer commitments, market size and industry trends, your competition, their offerings, and estimated share. These projections are, indeed, one of the keys to your venture's success. Everything else is directly or indirectly based on these figures. Consequently, potential investors will subject such figures to close scrutiny. Most investors have been bitten before by exaggerated sales projections, and most are more than twice shy. Be prepared to defend your projections.

E. The Competition. Nearly all businesses have competition, but if you don't think that you do, describe why, such as a patent, copyright, or trade secret position. If you foresee competitors entering in the future, then describe who they are, when they might enter the market, and their impact on your sales and market share. To be blunt, however, most investors are not going to believe that you don't have some kind of competition—if nothing else, competition that comes from product-service substitution.

Prospective investors expect you to know your competitors inside and out. They want to know who the competitors are, their strengths and weaknesses, and a comparative analysis of your strengths and weaknesses. They will ask straightforward questions, such as these: "Specifically, what advantages do you have over the competition?" "In terms of price, performance, service, warranties, and so forth, how do you compare with your competition?" "How can you beat the competition in price?" "Who is the pricing leader?" "Who is the quality leader?" "How will the competition react to you, the new kid on the block?"

Relative to the last preceding question, you should also give some consideration to your defensive strategy. Will your product or service threaten any of your existing competitors? If so, how will they fight back, and what will your reaction be? If your product represents a significant advance in technology or application, your competitors may seek to divert or at least delay your efforts until they catch up. Many people expect large, entrenched companies to react slowly to changes in the marketplace. When their primary market is seriously threatened, however, such companies can act swiftly and commit substantial financial resources to a competitive effort. If you don't believe this, take a look at what IBM did to the personal computer market.

An example of how the competition may be analyzed is shown as follows, starting with a comparative matrix.

Your company and the competition / GIZMO features	Price	Performance	Service	Warranties
YOUR Company	$4,950.00	9	10	8
ABC Company	$4,700.00	5	3	3
BIG Company	$5,000.00	10	9	10
XYZ Company	$4,400.00	4	4	4

Weights: 1 to 10, where 1 = poor and 10 = excellent.

The market segment served by YOUR Company is highly competitive in price, performance, service, and warranties, especially with stiff overall competition coming from BIG Company, the largest and most respected company in the market. XYZ Company is the price-cutter, but we and BIG have not lowered prices to meet XYZ's because of significant performance, service, and warranty advantages. It appears that ABC will have to meet XYZ's price; otherwise, they stand to lose a significant amount of sales.

All our competitors are larger than we are, have been in the business longer, and have greater financial resources. But our research and analysis shows that we can beat ABC and XYZ in pricing within the next 18 to 24 months. We are now beating BIG Company in price and service. We will be able to match BIG in performance and warranties within 12 to 24 months. Copies of both our present and proposed warranties are in the appendix.

Our major cost savings will result from installation of a computer-aided manufacturing (CAM) system the first of next year. The installation of CAM will make us competitive with BIG Company on all fronts. BIG is a fine business in all respects with good management and a stable, loyal work force, but its major weakness is its outdated production facilities analogous to the Bessemer process in the steel industry. We believe, therefore, that their break-even point will rise by 10 to 15 percent from its present base of $1,510.00. Because of their vast size and large-scale integration of production facilities, we do not believe that they will be able to modernize their plant and equipment for several years. In the meantime, we project a 20 percent decrease in our break-even point from $1,500.00 to $1,200.00, within 24 months. This decrease will result from the use of CAM in our production process, and we will, therefore, be able to price our GIZMO for as little as $4,000.00 and cover administrative and marketing expenses plus taxes and still produce a profit of 10 to 12 percent.

We have a good service team, and it is getting even better. We can provide immediate and superior service to all our customers. Our meantime to repair (MTTR) is 36 hours; BIG's is 30 hours. We project that within 12 months our MTTR will also be 30 hours. Our goal is to reduce our MTTR to 24 hours within the next three years. Both ABC's and XYZ's MTTR is around 64 hours, and trends indicate that it is increasing. Surveys disclose a lot of negative comments about ABC's and XYZ's service and warranties. Most respondents say that their service is "horrendous" and their warranties "are not worth the paper they are written on."

Neither ABC nor XYZ has introduced any new improvements to their GIZMO in three years. In many ways, their GIZMO design is nearing obsolescence; it lacks many of the modern characteristics of our GIZMO, especially instantaneous fire suppression systems. Moreover, the fuel injection system in our GIZMO is controlled by a microcomputer. Their fuel injection systems are mechanically controlled. We can, therefore, offer our customers a 10 percent cost savings in fuel, proved in field tests conducted and certified by Independent Labs of Los Angeles.

As of now, we have 10 percent of the market, ABC has 16 percent, BIG has 53 percent, and XYZ has 21 percent. In the 1970s, ABC was a fairly successful business, but it began tailing off in the early 1980s. Today it is weak on all fronts; it has weak management, labor problems, worn-out plant and equipment, poor credit rating, and a timid sales force. XYZ is a cutthroat operation, well managed with a low-cost labor force. It has the most aggressive salespeople in the market. Even though their GIZMO's overall quality is below industry standard, they have enjoyed some degree of success. They will continue to eat into ABC's customer base. As of now, BIG is the class of the market and will provide the stiffest competition. BIG's only weakness is its outdated production facilities; it will take us from one to two years to take advantage of this weakness. And, indeed, one would expect BIG to make significant changeovers to modern plant facilities over the next five to seven years.

We realize we are the new kid on the block and, therefore, believe our best defense is an aggressive offense. Both ABC and XYZ take their customers for granted and deliver a shoddy product and undependable service. We believe because of the quality of our GIZMO; our young, go-get'em salespeople; and our well-planned advertising and promotion program, we can take away at least 18 percent of sales from ABC and 5 percent from XYZ. Within two years, we will begin to chip away at BIG's customer base in addition to getting a lion's share of new customers.

IV. The Marketing Plan

Knowing about the customers and how the competition is reaching them provides a basis for proposing a marketing plan of action. With market research and analysis under your belt, you will be able to set up a marketing plan for your product or service. Bringing any product or service to the marketplace successfully requires the formulation of a marketing strategy for gaining a foothold for your product or service and winning a profitable share of the overall market. Specifically, the investor wants to know how you are going to move the product or service from your business into the hands of the customer. Typical questions are these: "Describe your channels of distribution." "What are your advertising and promotion plans?" "How much will it cost?" "What degree of market penetration do you project?"

A. Sales and Distribution.   Your market segment may be reached by a number of different channels of distribution. A sample of the channels available to you are these: (1) your own salaried or commissioned salespeople, (2) export trading companies, (3) export management companies, (4) full-service freight forwarders, (5) manufacturer's representatives and agents, (6) wholesalers and distributors, (7) jobbers and brokers, (8) direct mail and mail order, (9) retailers, (10) factory outlets, (11) direct salespeople, and (12) vending machines. Generally, most small businesses selling outside their immediate geographic region rely on commission salespeople or manufacturer's representatives as a sales force. Larger businesses set up their own salaried sales force.

Describe how your business will go about marketing its unique product or service. Who will sell? Will they be paid a salary or commission? Will they have to travel? Will they have an expense account? If so, describe the accounting and control for this expense account. If you plan to use your own sales force, how many salespeople will it take to meet your marketing plan? How long will it take a salesperson to book an order? What is your expected sales conversion rate; that is, how many sales calls will it take to get an order? How large is the average order? Who is the person in charge of sales? What are his or her credentials and experience?

If you elect to use sales agents or distributors for your product, you will have to include sales commissions or distributor sales discounts in your planning. You should also indicate how you will attract and arrange for distributors to sell your product. If your arrangement will permit agents or distributors to return unsold products after a specified time, you may also have to factor in product sales returns.

Your business plan should also address the issue of international sales. If there is a market for your product outside the United States, do you plan to sell to this market? If so, you should explain how you will go about it. Do you plan to use foreign agents and distributors, or will you set up your own foreign sales organization?

Specify current backlog and current shippable backlog. The backlog is to be produced. The shippable backlog can be shipped and billed immediately. Describe the purchase orders you presently have. What are your selling costs as a percent of sales. For example: "Our selling costs are 12 percent at an 8000-unit level; 10 percent at a 10,000-unit level, 8 percent at a 15,000-unit level; and 6 percent at a 20,000-unit level. Our goal for the next fiscal year is to sell 20,000 units. Presently, our backlog is 4000 units, and our shippable backlog is 3000 units."

B.   Advertising and Public Relations.   The advertising and public relations program of a product or service is as important as its technical features. In many instances, especially for the entrepreneur who is just getting started, it may be better to turn this program over to a professional agency or an in-house person who is well qualified to build a viable advertising, promotion, and public relations program. Whom are you trying to reach? What are the best media to use? How much money will be spent for brochures, catalogs, television, radio, newspaper, magazine, mailings, samples, billboards, and demonstrations?

Your advertising plan should take into account the availability of your product or service. New companies often make the mistake of advertising their product or service long before it becomes available. Customers then become disappointed when they cannot get the product or service right away. Premature advertising also serves to notify your competition of your intentions and gives them more time to react to your entry into the market.

Many companies overlook the value of public and press relations (PR) in disseminating news about their product or service. Editors and news directors are always looking for stories about new companies and innovative products. If you explain your idea and describe your product or service to such people, they may run stories about your company. Depending on your product or service, this "free advertising" can produce more sales than paid advertising. PR is also valuable in positioning your company in the market. The market will form an opinion about your company, your product, and your service based on what appears in the press.

Following is an example of a marketing plan of a fledgling manufacturing firm that has designed and produces a state-of-the-art fish-finder device called Fish-Meter.

Our marketing plan uses a number of "push-pull" techniques to achieve our sales goals. We "push" the Fish-Meter to get it in front of the customer, get it in the store, on the shelves, on prominent display. We have three jobbers in Florida and two in Louisiana who serve fishing camps and sporting goods stores throughout both states. We push these jobbers by offering prompt, overnight delivery of Fish-Meter and cash bonuses for signing up new retailers. We offer our retailers money-back guarantees and a variety of prizes for achieving sales targets. All this is backed up by weekly advertisements in *Fishing Products News*, the major trade publication for store owners and recreational fishing products jobbers and distributors. Furthermore, we have three salaried salespeople who travel the trade shows where they staff the Fish-Meter booth, passing out brochures, answering questions, and demonstrating how Fish-Meter works.

On the other side, "pull" techniques are applied to produce heavy consumer demand. Our three salespeople also attend fishing tournaments where drawings are held so fishermen can win a Fish-Meter. Coupons are given to people who answer silly questions, and a Fish-Meter is awarded to contestants who tell the best fish story.

Next month, we have a one-page, full-color display ad in *Fish Story*, the largest circulation recreational fishing magazine on the market. This display ad will show a happy fisherman with a full string of fish in one hand and a Fish-Meter in the other. The headline: "I ALWAYS GET MY LIMIT WITH FISH-METER," will sell the main idea. The ad will also show photo inserts of fishermen with their testimonials for Fish-Meter.

In the same issue of *Fish Story*, the Fish-Meter is mentioned in the "What's New" section. Furthermore, we have been promised a complete article about Fish-Meter in the March issue. If we like the response from *Fish Story's* display ad, we plan to sign an agreement with them to run 12 similar ads over the next year. Each ad costs $1,000.00.

Starting next month, we have two spots on "Fishing with Sam," a popular 30-minute weekly fishing show that is syndicated through Group-A, a cable station that feeds 40 major television stations in the Southeast. We plan to sign a contract with Group-A to run 104 spots over the next year. Each ad will cost $400.00 each. If we sign this contract, Sam Perkins of "Fishing with Sam" fame will interview six users of Fish-Meter and use these interviews on his program, where they will be free publicity for us.

We are presently advertising on KWKH radio in Louisiana. We have signed an agreement with them to broadcast three spot ads on each fishing update report at 6:00 A.M. and 5:30 P.M. daily for the next 30 days. They charge $20.00 per spot. If response from these ads is positive, we plan to use radio extensively in our marketing plan. We have made a tentative commitment to Magna Advertising Agency of New Orleans to handle our advertising on radio if we can expand our operations to all states in the Southeast as planned.

The number-one thrust and objective of our advertising and public relations program is to introduce recreational fishermen throughout the Southeast to Fish-Meter and increase demand for this product. Secondly, the program will help to recruit jobbers to push it and retailers to stock it. Coordinated advertising and public relations creates demand from jobbers and retailers who want to sell it and fishermen who want to buy it. Furthermore, we will hire two additional salaried salespeople to help in a planned demonstration and goodwill blitz at trade shows and fishing tournaments in all states within the Southeast.

Each salesperson is paid a salary of $500.00 per week plus $100.00 per diem travel expenses. Each is furnished with a van that contains the sales booth and paraphernalia. All vans are colorfully and professionally painted with signs and advertising copy about Fish-Meter. They serve as traveling billboards. Each fully equipped van costs $20,000.00. We project that each salesperson can book 40 orders per week with retailers on an average of 24 Fish-Meters per order. The wholesale price of Fish-Meter to retailers is $49.50 each. On an average, we project each company salesperson can sign up two new jobbers per week. An average initial order from jobbers is 100 Fish-Meters at $35.00 each. Each jobber is given a protected territory, and all retailers, both the ones they sign up and the ones we sign up, become the jobbers' customers and are serviced by them. Incidental retail sales are made at the tournaments of about 50 Fish-Meters per week at a retail price of $89.95. Customers at these tournaments, however, are encouraged to buy from the local sporting goods retailers who stock Fish-Meter.

Anticipating a move into other states and our "blitz," we have mailed brochures about Fish-Meter to 240 top jobbers and 3000 sporting goods retailers throughout the Southeast. We are also very active in getting publicity from the mass media in the major recreational fishing areas in the Southeastern states. We already have one story in the *Atlanta Times* and an interview on a local talk show in Birmingham. Such publicity will create consumer demand and excitement and will also showcase Fish-Meter, all helping both to push and to pull the project. Moreover, this coverage will augment our advertising program and trade show and tournament tours. We will also mail photographs, testimonials, and fish stories from satisfied customers to a variety of sports magazines and sports editors of newspapers in an attempt to gain additional free publicity and to puff Fish-Meter.

Mr. Charlie Perch is our marketing manager in charge of coordinating and executing our marketing plan. He has an M.B.A. from the University of North Carolina. He was marketing manager for Acme Sporting Goods, Incorporated, of Providence, Rhode Island, before joining up this year. His major marketing achievement was expanding the market of TROL-MOTO from a two-state market to the leading trolling motor in North America for Acme. He has budgeted $400,000.00 to implement the marketing plan for the next fiscal year.

Charlie has met recently with John Bass, owner of the largest chain in the Southeast of sporting goods retailers specializing in recreational fishing equipment. John has given us a purchase order for 8400 Fish-Meters for October delivery. Smith and Company, the largest jobber in the Southeast, worked with Charlie on this deal and will be the jobber who serves Bass Enterprises. A volume discount of 15 percent is given to Bass, and this discount is also passed along to Smith to serve the account.

Charlie Perch is also talking with JAWS, a major mail order firm, about becoming the exclusive direct marketer of Fish-Meter nationwide. JAWS would handle all advertising and mailing expenses. For an initial order of 10,000 units from JAWS, we will commit to an exclusive mail order agreement and would ship FOB destination at $29.75 per unit.

C. Pricing. Setting price is a key decision you must make to meet the competition, penetrate the market, maintain or increase your market position, and produce sufficient profits. If your major product or service differentiation is to be a price-cutter, then explain how you will do this and make enough profit to stay in business. Do you enjoy greater efficiencies in manufacturing and distribution? Do you have lower labor, material, and overhead costs? Following is an example of how pricing policies may be presented.

Cost Report for Fish-Meter (at 200,000 volume)

Manufacturing Costs per Unit		
Direct materials	$5.00	
Direct labor	3.00	
Factory overhead	2.00	
Other manufacturing costs	1.00	$11.00
Other Costs per Unit		
Administrative costs	$2.00	
Selling costs	6.00	
Other	1.00	9.00
Total Cost per Unit		$20.00

The suggested retail price for the Fish-Meter is $89.95. We sell some units at fishing tournaments to fishermen, but these retail sales are incidental because our main customers are jobbers and retailers. Once our market is established, we plan to deal mostly with jobbers and one major mail order firm. Our jobbers will serve retailers; the suggested price to retailers is around $50.00, but our jobbers will be free to work out their pricing arrangements with their retailers. The mail order firm will serve the catalog market segment, where the catalog price will be in the $85.00–$95.00 range. The pricing schedule for our distributors is displayed as follows.

Distributor Pricing Schedule

Volume (Units)	Discount	Price
Up to 100	None	$35.00
101 to 500	2%	34.30
501 to 1000	5%	33.25
1001 to 5000	10%	31.50
Over 5000	15%	29.75

Our projection for this fiscal year is 200,000 units produced and sold. Our unit cost to manufacture is $11.00 per unit, of which $9.00 is variable, and $2.00 is fixed. Other costs per unit amount to $9.00, of which $5.00 is variable, and $4.00 is fixed. Full cost at a 200,000-unit level is $20.00 per unit. If our long-term sales projections hold and we increase our output to a 300,000-unit level within 18 to 24 months, we will be able to spread 300,000 units over our total fixed costs of $1.2 million ($6.00 × 200,000) and, therefore, reduce our per unit fixed costs to $4.00 per unit or a total per unit cost of $18.00.

V.   Research and Development Plan

The investor will want to know the extent and nature of any research and development underway and the costs and time required for a marketable product. Such research and development might include additional design and testing to convert a laboratory prototype to a production prototype, or it might entail the development of artistic packaging for an existing product, or it might be a major change in special effects and lighting for a new concert tour or the retooling of production facilities or the modification of a previously successful product to meet increasing competition. Also, name the main members of the research and development team and their responsibilities.

Where research and development prove to be a heavy budget user, the investor wants to deal with a true inventrepreneur, one who knows how to perform or manage research and development and one who also can bring into production a viable, marketable product or service. The key to a business venture's success, from the investor's viewpoint, is a happy, profitable blend of research and development, production, and marketing. With venture capitalists, it is common to back engineer-inventor types who become chief executives of their fledgling companies. It is almost as common for these executives to fail after a product or service is selling and the company is growing rapidly because these people have little interest in management. They feel more comfortable in the lab. They want to create a product that is so good they won't have to depend on salespeople and all their nonsense. The product will sell itself. On the other hand, a chief executive with a marketing background just as readily slashes R and D to hire more salespeople and increase the advertising budget. Such a chief executive tries to sell his or her way out of problems. The test of a strong, successful chief executive is balance and a strong sense of reality[2]—a true inventrepreneur.

Following is an example of how this section may be written.

Since its start in 19X1, Sofpro has maintained a preeminence in accounting and business software packages, especially our ACC-REC program, which remains our hallmark product to this day. Its development took 18 months with a total expenditure of $500,000.00 for R and D. Total sales for ACC-REC to date is $6.8 million.

Sofpro has also created two other innovative and economically successful packages for the banking industry, Loan-Analyzer and Stock-Quote. Both are being revised to include graphic presentation and to increase computer compatibility. These changes will cost $100,000.00 and will require six months to complete. Initial R and D expenditures for these packages were $400,000.00. We license these packages, and total royalty revenue to date is $3.9 million. We project that the revised packages will increase their past revenue by 20 percent per year for the next five years.

Our most ambitious program to date is Inventory-Control, a package that will revolutionize the management of inventory for any organization that is inventory-intensive. The introduction of Inventory-Control will establish Sofpro as the leader

---

[2]Thomas P. Murphy, " 'Pluck it Out,' " *Forbes*, September 24, 1984, p. 258. This material is used with permission.

in computer-based inventory control systems. In one program, it provides complete accountability, costing with a variety of cost-flow methods (e.g., FIFO, LIFO), forecasting, automatic reordering, safety stocks, and economic order quantities. Moreover, on the computer technical side, the total program will be on a chip in programmable read-only memory (PROM). Using chips or firmware for storage of programs works better than storing them on a floppy or hard disk. The PROM approach is simpler, more durable, and easier to intall; moreover, PROM prevents or, at least, discourages copying of the program. Even though all our programs are copyrighted, the unlawful copying of programs is still a major problem for all software vendors. The use of PROM and an encryption module will significantly increase security for Inventory-Control.

The current research and development status of Inventory-Control is as follows: (1) logic and systems design—80 percent complete, (2) coding—50 percent complete, (3) testing—15 percent complete, (4) PROM technology development and testing—20 percent complete, (5) encryption module development—10 percent complete, (6) documentation preparation—5 percent complete, and (7) package design—10 percent complete. We have budgeted $900,000.00 and nine months to complete all research and development, at which time, Inventory-Control will be ready for marketing.

To reflect the importance of, and commitment to, new software product development, Yolanda Valenzuela joins us next month as vice president of R and D. Yolanda held a similar position at Micro-Sof, where she was instrumental in the development of Petunia 4-5-6, one of the top-selling spread-sheet programs of the early 1980s. Yolanda is backed up by a group of high-level support people. Sally Higgins is chief systems analyst. She is the developer of Stock-Quote. Jorge Navarro is lead programmer and has been the main programmer for all Sofpro programs. Marvin Stein is in charge of PROM development and testing. Steve Majinsky heads up our documentation and maintenance group. He comes to us from Sparta, where he was senior documentation writer. Tony Silvio is developing the encryption module. He was a major in the U.S. Army, where he had 20 years of experience in the development of security programs, especially scramblers for telecommunications. Jim Parsons is from our marketing department and is working one-half time in research and development to design packaging and brochures for Inventory-Control. The people are superbly supported by a team of 20 technicians.

Within the next nine months we feel confident that this highly capable team will bring to market a top Inventory-Control program that will eclipse the competition. Moreover, they now have on the drawing board several other business packages that show a lot of promise. We fully expect that products coming from this group will invigorate company growth in years to come.

Today Sofpro stands positioned at its moment of greatest opportunity. With the necessary R and D funds forthcoming and properly marshaled, an explosion of growth is expected. Inventory-Control alone should generate over $4 million within three years after its introduction to the marketplace. Based on our strong R and D team, the years ahead will be a period of great excitement and reward for Sofpro shareholders.

VI. Manufacturing and Operations

This section describes the operating side of your business venture. For a manufacturer, you need to describe your production characteristics, labor force, key suppliers, or subcontractors, equipment, property and facilities, and manufacturing cost data. If your business venture is something other than manufacturing, such as retailing or service, similar data should be furnished where applicable. If your business venture is already set up or is a buyout, describe what exists. If it is a start-up, describe what you have planned.

A. Production Characteristics. If you are a manufacturer, what is the mode of the conversion process? Are you a continuous process manufacturer like cement producers? Or is your product custom-made to order as in a job shop operation? Are you an assembler of a few ready-made components into a finished product? Are you a processor, such as a food processor? Are there any health and safety problems connected with your production process? How important is quality control? Are there any major bottlenecks in your operation? What is your present production backlog?

B. Labor Force. Describe the number of employees you have (or need) and whether they are union or nonunion employees. If union, describe the contract and when it expires. Describe the supply and quality of labor. Must your labor force be trained? Exactly what is the breakdown of your labor force, such as full-time, part-time, white-collar, blue-collar, technical, nontechnical, degreed, and non-degreed? What kind of pension and profit-sharing plan do you have or envision?

C. Suppliers. In any business that uses products or services of other suppliers or subcontractors, the relationship with, and dependability of, these people can be a key to the success and growth of your business venture. A good working relationship with, and total commitment from, your suppliers and subcontractors to provide you with a consistent stream of material decreases the probability of production delays and interruptions. Some businesses are plagued with shortages of raw materials that wreck manufacturing schedules and that, if of long enough duration, can cause you to have problems servicing your customers. Include in your business plan a list of your key suppliers or subcontractors, items supplied, dollar volume, lead time, and backup. An example follows.

Supplier	Item Supplied	Dollar Volume	Lead Time	Backup
ACME	Power converter	$1,000,000.00	60 days	DYSAN
TREK	Module-A	900,000.00	120 days	LISA
PIEZO	T-Frame	750,000.00	90 days	—

D. Equipment. Most manufacturing businesses require certain kinds of machine tools to effect the manufacturing process. These machine tools may be special molding and extrusion equipment, grinders and polishers, and power tools of all kinds. Are you set up to use this equipment on a continual basis? High output means low unit overhead and substantial cost savings. Do you plan to operate three shifts? Is your equipment used for specialized purposes? What is its life and resale value? Here is an example.

Proposed Plastic Extruder Vendor: Acme Cleveland

List price	$100,000.00
Cost to install	$5,000.00
Lead time to install	6 months
Expected life	5 years
Scrap value in 5 years	$2,000.00
Resale or collateral value	$6,000.00[a]
Annual variable expenses to operate (3 shifts)	$70,000.00
Annual revenue from sales	$400,000.00

[a]Highly specialized equipment with minimal resale value.

E. Property and Facilities. Describe the property and facilities currently used to conduct your business or that planned for a start-up. If your business entails a plant and warehouses, give location, square feet, type of construction, acres of land, and the like. An example follows.

In September 19X1, the expansion to SURETHING Company's factory and offices in Portland, Oregon, was completed and occupied. The building stands on 80 acres of land adjacent to a major railroad spur. The total cost for the land and building was $900,000.00, of which $500,000.00 is still owed. Mortgage payments, including interest, are $86,000.00 per year for the next 10 years. The location is ideal to serve our market.

With this new facility, SURETHING now operates out of a modern 42,000-square-foot building containing one of the most complete calibration operations found anywhere in the industry. The building design includes an air-supported roof membrane with clear spans that are 200 feet wide and sufficient solar-collector surfaces that totally eliminate the need for conventional heating and cooling systems. Moreover, the building is designed for expansion where modules can be conveniently added as required to meet sales growth for the foreseeable future.

We project that every increase of $500,000.00 in sales will require a 5000-square-foot module that costs $100,000.00 plus $60,000.00 for additional production equipment and support facilities. With the 80 acres we now have and an option on a contiguous 100-acre tract, we have the room to grow to a 200,000-square-foot plant along with sufficient warehouses and office space. We, therefore, project the useful life of this location at 20 years minimum. In other words, we do not project any need to change location in the foreseeable future.

F. Manufacturing Cost Data. If you plan to start a merchandising operation, your product costs are simply what you have to pay your suppliers to get the product on your shelves. If, on the other hand, your business venture entails manufacturing, then your cost to manufacture the product includes direct materials, direct labor, and factory overhead. Presentation of manufacturing costs should be included in your business plan. An example follows.

In AUTO-MIRROR, the number of mirrors manufactured is as low as 30,000 in some years and as high as 60,000 in other years but is 40,000 in an average year. Fixed costs are $120,000.00 a year regardless of the volume for that year. Variable costs are $6.00 per unit broken down as follows: $3.00 for direct material, $2.00 for direct labor, and $1.00 for variable overhead. Following is a cost schedule at different volume levels.

	High-Volume Year	Average Year	Low-Volume Year
Units manufactured	60,000	40,000	30,000
Total fixed costs	$180,000.00	$180,000.00	$180,000.00
Unit costs			
Variable costs	$6.00	$6.00	$6.00
Fixed cost	3.00	4.50	6.00
Total cost per unit	$9.00	$10.50	$12.00

Our aim is to strengthen our marketing department to provide us with a higher and more consistent product demand. If our new sales force can create unit sales of 60,000 annually, we can cut our unit fixed cost by one half.

VII. The Key People

As stressed throughout this text, the management team and directors are keys to the business venture's success. The main questions that most investors ask are, "Who are the key people, and what are their qualifications?" "What are they being paid?" State who is going to do what. Who has overall authority? Who is responsible for research and development, for production, for sales? Who is in charge of accounting and financial control? Be specific about these people's skills, education, and experience. The investor wants to see logical connections of people, qualifications, and responsibilities. A person with a marketing background, for example, would probably not be able to head production. Also, the investor may ask about directors. He or she will want to know why certain people are directors if they have no obvious connection with the company. Why is a spouse a director or officer of the company? Why is your lawyer a director? Most investors strongly believe that lawyers make poor directors because lawyers are conflict-oriented. Try to get directors who can give sound business advice and help the company in its dealings with others. Also, list consultants, if any.

Generally, there are no more than two or three key people in a small business and six or seven in a large one. In describing these people, be brief and to the point. Stress achievements and results; go easy on superlatives. Disclose any agreements the company has with these people, their ownership, and their remuneration. These people should be ready to answer very personal questions. In some instances, also be prepared to deal with "off-the-wall" questions. Examples: "Why did you get a divorce?" "Have you ever stolen anything?" "What was your childhood like?" "Explain the trouble you had with John Smith at ABC Company." "The GIZMO that you are working on seems to be very much like ABC's GIZMO; is there a problem with trade secret or patent infringement here?" "Can you explain the difference between research and development (R and D) and theft and guile (T and G) in product design?"

A.   Description of Management Team and Directors.   Before agreeing to back your business venture, the prospective investor will conduct a thorough and exhaustive background check on you and each member of your team. If everything doesn't check out, you will have a tough time raising capital. For the investor's convenience, prepare a brief résumé of each member of your team, including employment experience, achievement, education, age, and marital status. More lengthy résumés belong in the appendix. They should include sufficient detail to permit the investor to make a thorough background check. For example, employment information should include positions held, job descriptions, where employed, immediate supervisors, dates of employment, salary, and reason for leaving. Educational background includes schools attended, degrees awarded, and dates. Include character references, their position, and address. Also include information about your personal side, such as your hobbies and leisure-time activities. Here are examples of résumés included in the body of the business plan.

The principal directors and executive officers of Nucor are as follows.

Name	Office
Tim Kelly	chairman of the board, chief executive officer, president, treasurer, and secretary
Robert Montgomery	vice president of information systems and accounting and director
Vincent Skorus	vice president of marketing and director
Amy Rabb	vice president of production and director
Milton Friedman	director and president of Western Bank
Willy Kohl	director and president of Simplex, Incorporated

Tim Kelly, 45, is the founder of Nucor. He received a B.S. degree in mechanical engineering from the University of Illinois. He worked for 10 years for Maxim in various positions related to the management of research activities related to development of core testing equipment. After leaving Maxim, he joined Macore as manager of their research and development department. For the last six years, he has served as president of Test-Core, a major division of Macore. Under Tim's management, Test-Core grew to a $500 million company, four times its sales before he took over. In addition, two major products were brought to market by Test-Core during his tenure. Both have received engineering awards and are considered in the trade as state-of-the-art. Kelly is married to Stella and has three children. He is in excellent health, enjoys golf, swimming, and reading.

Robert Montgomery, 38, received a B.B.A. in accounting from Ohio State University. He started with Tri-Test as a junior accountant and rose to be manager of information systems. He was in charge of converting Tri-Test's information system from a manual-based to a computer-based system. He left Tri-Test on the first of this year to join Nucor. He still has a one-year agreement with Tri-Test to act as their consultant to help find and orient his replacement. He is presently a director of North Rim Savings and Loan. Montgomery is single and in good health. His hobbies include photography and cross-country skiing.

Vincent Skorus, 32, earned a B.S. in marketing from UCLA. Prior to joining Nucor, Skorus was employed by Agnico, serving first as a public relations specialist in southern California. Subsequently, he became director of marketing for the Southwest. In the latter position, Skorus was the top marketing executive for the largest region of Agnico with full marketing responsibility from start-up to implementation. Last year, Skorus was recognized for outstanding marketing achievement, receiving the "Tommy" Award from the Los Angeles Sales and Marketing Executives Club. Vincent is married to Tanya and has two children. He is in excellent health, and his main hobbies are jogging and tennis.

Amy Rabb, 30 received a B.S. in industrial engineering from Penn State. She was hired by EROX to help implement a computer-assisted manufacturing (CAM) system. After this was accomplished, she was put in charge of the system, a position she held until joining Nucor the first of this year. She is married to Fred and has one child. Her main hobby is skydiving.

Milton Friedman, 59, is an outside director of Nucor. He has been in banking all of his adult life and has worked in all of its areas. After earning an M.B.A. from Wharton, he joined Republic Bank in Philadelphia, where he rose to senior vice president. He joined Western Bank five years ago and now serves as its president. He is a director of several charitable organizations, including Mount Haven Hospital. Friedman is listed in *Who's Who in Finance and Industry*. He is married to Mildred and has four children. His hobbies include landscape painting and hiking.

Willy Kohl, 45, is an outside director of Nucor. He has over 25 years of experience in manufacturing. He started Simplex, Incorporated, 20 years ago in a small machine shop in Tucson, Arizona. For the previous five years, he had served as a shop supervisor for Ansco. Today Simplex is the leading manufacturer of portable cement mixers with annual sales of $100 million. He is international director of the Industrial Society and is listed in *Who's Who in Finance and Industry*. He is married to Agnes and has two children. His hobby is moose hunting.

B. Remuneration. List all executives and directors who will receive fees and salaries. An example follows.

Name	Position	Remuneration
Tim Kelly	chief officer	$75,000.00
Robert Montgomery	chief accountant	$60,000.00
Vincent Skorus	vice president—marketing	$55,000.00
Amy Rabb	vice president—production	$55,000.00
Milton Friedman	outside director	$4,000.00
Willy Kohl	outside director	$4,000.00

The chances of obtaining financing for a start-up are quite small when the founding management team is not prepared to accept initial modest salaries. Be specific on your plans about employee benefits, stock options, or profit-sharing programs you expect to offer.

C. Shareholders. List the name of the individual, the amount of shares owned, the percentage of ownership, and the price paid. Here is an example.

Name	Number of Shares	Percentage of Ownership Before Financing	Percentage of Ownership After Financing	Price Paid
Kelly	500,000	25	20	$ 500,000.00
Montgomery	300,000	15	12	300,000.00
Skorus	200,000	10	8	600,000.00
Rabb	200,000	10	8	600,000.00
Friedman	400,000	20	16	2,000,000.00
Kohl	400,000	20	16	2,000,000.00
"Investor"	500,000	—	20	5,000,000.00

D. Employment Agreements Describe in detail any employment agreements that the company has with any officers, directors, or employees. Be careful to spell out those areas that contain special perquisites such as golden parachutes and job security arrangements. Such agreements are generally not approved by most investors. They believe that to assure any manager that he or she will not be fired for poor performance and will continue to get a high salary is not good management. In this section, also include a description of any agreements not to compete that your employees have with your company and especially those made with other companies before joining you. If any of your people have noncompete agreements with other companies that are still in effect, make sure that you can demonstrate that your company is free and clear of any liability, as for stealing trade secrets, unfair competition, or product-service infringement.

E. Consultants. List the names of your consultants, if any, such as accountants, lawyers, bankers, or engineers. Give their addresses, and describe precisely what kind of consulting they do and why. Disclose any fees or retainers paid.

VIII. Overall Schedule, Major Events, and Risks

A schedule that shows the timing and interrelationship of the major events necessary to launch the business venture and realize its objectives is an essential part of a business plan. An example of how a schedule can be designed is displayed as follows.

Major Activities and Events

1 Incorporation.
2 Completion of demonstration and production prototypes.
3 Recruiting and hiring of sales representatives.
4 Attend Chicago Trade Show.
5 Order and receive three tons of graphite.
6 Hiring and training 10 Static-X operators.
7 Installation and testing of Static-X equipment.
8 Full production.
9 First orders.
10 First deliveries.
11 First payments on accounts receivable.

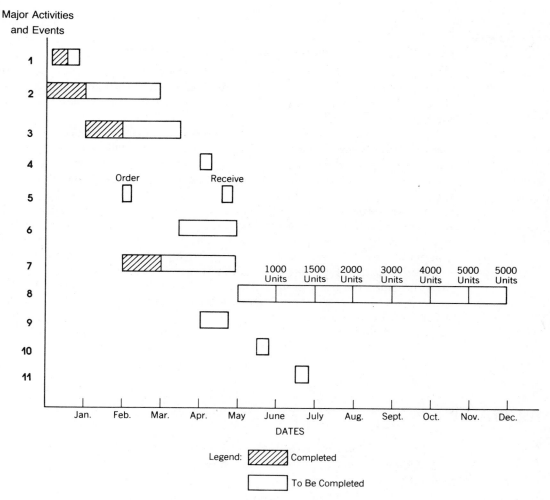

Schedule of activities and major events for the year.

In addition to potential slippages, development of a business has other risks and problems. As a philosopher once said, "There was never a whaling voyage that didn't run into a storm." The investor wants to know what the storms might be and if you are the sailor who can see the "signs" and steer the vessel to a safe harbor. Taking the initiative to identify and discuss risks helps you demonstrate to the investor that you have realistically thought about them and can handle them. Risks then tend not to loom as large black clouds in the investor's thinking about your venture. Examples of risks that should be disclosed are pending price wars, expenses greater than estimates, credit problems, and slippages in the schedule.

SUMMARY

The business plan is the key entrepreneurial document, which includes sufficient information to answer most questions that lenders and investors interested in providing you with capital might ask. It also serves as a major planning and control tool once your business is operative.

Every element of the business plan serves a special purpose. For example, the letter of transmittal "shakes hands" with readers and tells them why they should read your business plan. The summary, however, is the "grabber" of the business plan. Without a good, catchy summary, the chances are slim that anyone will read the rest of your business plan.

Other key elements of your business plan describe your business in detail where readers can understand it clearly and know what your product or service is and how it works. Readers also want to know the market for your product or service and how you plan to sell it. Moreover, if you plan to manufacture your own product or do any research and development, the reader wants to know about this. Another very important element is a description of the management team—those key people who are really going to run the business. Following this should be a schedule that discloses when certain major events will take place and also the risks of delays and problems inherent in the schedule.

ASSIGNMENT

1 Prepare all the elements up to the financing program of a business plan for your venture.

2 What is the purpose of a letter of transmittal?

3 Interpret the "private placement disclaimer" contained in the title page.

4 Explain the purpose of a summary. What is the summary format?

5 How are computers being used to bring the entrepreneur and investor together?

6 Give the purpose of the business description and each topic included in this section.

7 What do market research and analysis entail? What is their purpose in the business plan?

8 Describe and give the purpose of the marketing plan.

9 Why might an investor be interested in your research and development plans?

10 What is the purpose of the manufacturing and operations section? How would you change this section to fit a business plan for a nonmanufacturing business.

11 Why is the section on key people one of the most important sections of the business plan? What should be included in this section?

12 What is the purpose of the section on overall schedule, major events, and risks?

BIBLIOGRAPHY

Anthony, Robert N., John Dearden, and Norton M. Bedford. *Management Control Systems*, 5th ed. Homewood, Ill.: Richard D. Irwin, 1984.

Dible, Donald M. (ed.). *Winning The Money Game*. Santa Clara, Calif.: Entrepreneur Press, 1975.

Gladstone, David J. *Venture Capital Handbook*. Reston, Va.: Reston Publishing Company, 1983.

Haslett, Brian, and Leonard E. Smollen. "Preparing a Business Plan." In Stanley E. Pratt (ed.), *Guide to Venture Capital Sources*, 7th ed. Wellesley Hills, Mass.: Capital Hills Publishing, 1983.

Kramer, Donald J. "The Entrepreneur's Perspective." In Stanley E. Pratt (ed.), *Guide to Venture Capital Sources*, 7th ed. Wellesley Hills, Mass.: Capital Publishing, 1983.

Liles, Patrick R. *New Business Ventures and the Entrepreneur*. Homewood, Ill.: Richard D. Irwin, 1974.

Mancuso, Joseph R. *How to Prepare and Present a Business Plan*. Englewood Cliffs, N.J.: Prentice-Hall, a Spectrum Book, 1983.

Murphy, Thomas, P. " 'Pluck it Out.' " *Forbes*. September 24, 1984.

Pearsall, Thomas E., and Donald H. Cunningham. *How to Write for the World of Work*, 2d ed. New York: Holt, Rinehart and Winston, 1982.

Pratt, Stanley E. (ed.), *Guide to Venture Capital Sources*, 7th ed. Wellesley Hills, Mass.: Capital Publishing, 1983.

Sanger, Elizabeth. "Mating by Computer." *Barron's*. September 3, 1984.

Shaffer, Richard A. "Venture Capital Firms Are Hit by Slower Growth in Financing." *The Wall Street Journal*. Section 2, August 17, 1984.

Silver, A. David. *The Entrepreneurial Life*. New York: Wiley, 1983.

Tootelian, Dennis H., and Ralph M. Gaedeke. *Small Business Management Operations and Profiles*, 2d ed. Glenview, Ill.: Scott, Foresman, 1985.

Welsh, John A., and Jerry F. White. *The Entrepreneur's Master Planning Guide*. Englewood Cliffs, N.J.: Prentice-Hall, Spectrum Book, 1983.

Williams, Edward E., and Salvatore E. Manzo. *Business Planning for the Entrepreneur*. New York: Van Nostrand Reinhold, 1983.

CHAPTER 18

Elements of the
Business Plan—Part II

INTRODUCTION

A key element of the business plan deals with the actual financing of your venture. All the other elements support this part of your business plan. The objectives of this chapter are the following.

1 To analyze and present the main ingredients of the financial part of the business plan.

2 To mention briefly the appendixes and bibliography, the last two elements of the business plan.

THE FINANCIAL PART OF THE BUSINESS PLAN

The two key elements of the financial part are (1) the financial program and (2) the financial plan and projections. Both are now discussed.

IX. The Financing Program (continued from the preceding chapter)

This section of your business plan answers seven fundamental questions: (1) What do I need the money for? (2) How much money do I need now and in the future? (3) Where am I going to get it? (4) What financial structure will I use? (5) How and when will I repay the investors? (6) What are the risks? (7) Can I afford the cost of money? Surprisingly, many people going into business are not very precise in asking or answering these questions. The following material helps in this area. In the final analysis, however, it is up to you to *negotiate* the best deal.

A. Reason for Financing. You need to know exactly why you are requesting the money and how much to get. Inadequate capital is one of the chief causes of business failure. Are you seeking seed money to bring a "garage-idea" to a full production prototype? Have you already started a business but need a significant injection of money to get it going? Are you embarking on a major expansion of your present business or bringing on board a major new product line? Are you purchasing new production facilities? Are you planning to buy an existing business? Example: Madame's Slipper Shoppe is for sale at a price of $200,000.00. I need a five-year loan of $80,000.00 at a fixed rate of 14 percent to close the deal. I will put up $20,000.00 of my money and finance the remaining $100,000.00 with the owner for 10 years at a fixed interest rate of 14 percent. Next February I will need an additional $10,000.00 for working capital. Thereafter, all debt service and financing needs will come from sales."

B. Sources of Financing. Unless you can finance your business venture yourself, you will have to go to an outside source. When going to an outside source, remember the "golden rule of financing," which simply put is this: "The individual who has the gold rules." The more money he or she puts into your business, the more ownership and control the financer expects. These financing sources fall into two broad categories: lenders and investors. Lenders are primarily looking for capital preservation, income, tax benefits, and security. Investors are primarily looking for wealth accumulation. Let us quickly review sources of financing starting with yourself.

1 *Bootstrap.* You furnish your own capital through savings or from internal financing of an existing business. You may, for example, take on a second job and salt away the money you make until you have accumulated sufficient capital to get started. Or you may have started a business on a shoestring and expand only when you have generated enough capital to do so. For the entrepreneurs who love their freedom and independence, this is the best way to go. You still, however, need a business plan for yourself if for no one else.

2 *Relatives.* Mom or Dad or Uncle Clyde or Aunt Gladys may put up the money. This can be the best and easiest way to get financing; it can also be the worst. Unless your relatives can afford to lose what they lend you, this method of financing is generally not recommended.

3 *Angel.* In some instances, a wealthy person who has "made it" may be willing to back you if you and your business plan touches his or her fancy. This "business angel" may not only back you but take an active interest in your venture to help ensure its success. Other seemingly potential business angels are those who have inherited vast wealth. Such people do not generally make good sources of financing because they have little knowledge of what it takes to make a business work. They are wealth maintainers rather than wealth makers.

4 *Professional.* As discussed earlier in this text, there are a number of professional sources of financing. These include trade credit through suppliers; installments or prepayments from customers; mortgages or commercial or industrial property or a second mortgage on residential property (e.g., your house); loans on equipment or equipment leasing; equity financing from venture capitalists through the issue of common stock, preferred stock, convertible debentures, or debt with warrants; use of government-supported sources, such as Small Business Investment Companies (SBICs), Minority Enterprise Small Business Investment Companies (MESBICs), Small Business Administration (SBA), Economic Development Administration (EDA) of the United States Department of Commerce, Local Development Companies (LDCs) formed by communities and cities, and the Farmers Home Administration (FmHA) of the United States Department of Agriculture; and loans from commercial banks, investment bankers, consumer finance companies, savings and loan associations, and insurance companies; the use of factors; and the sale of franchises.

C.   Financial Package.   Let us look at a complete financing package that uses both lenders and investors, as illustrated in Table 18.1.

In deciding the mix of debt and equity capital to have in your financing package, you have many trade-offs to consider. Debt capital is usually cheaper and gives you more control, but obtaining this kind of capital depends on your ability to repay or generate enough cash over a short period of time to service the debt, both interest and principal. Moreover, it generally requires significant security or collateral. Equity gives you more time and breathing room but less control. The major point to remember at this stage is to be careful that you do not become too leveraged, that is, a high debt to equity ratio. You will be a much riskier company and will consequently lose some of your flexibility because you will have used up much of your debt capacity and will not be able to borrow additional funds for second- and third-round financing. An example of a high-leveraged company and a low-leveraged company is shown in Table 18.2.

Don't tell the investor that you simply need X dollars. Outline specifically the complete financing package although he or she may be only one source of several sources you intend to use. If you want a loan, describe the terms you are seeking. What is the period: 3, 5, 10 years? Do you need an interest-only period? What interest rate do you desire? Will the interest rate be variable or fixed? Will the loan include any conversion privileges? If you expect some suggestions and modifications from the lender, then leave some room to accommodate such changes.

If you are offering preferred stock, what is the price and what dividend will you pay? Will the dividend be cumulative? This means that if you miss a period, you will make it up in another period. After a set period, will you redeem the stock? Is the preferred stock convertible to common stock? If so, what is the conversion ratio, for example, one share of preferred for three shares of common. What are the voting rights? Specifically, what preferential treatment will the preferred shareholders have?

If you are offering common stock, what is the dividend? Is the dividend cumulative? Will a redemption of the common stock be required after a period of time to give the investor his or her money back? What is the price of the stock per share? What are the voting rights? What registration rights will shareholders have? Can the investors make you register the stock and in so doing make you become a public company?

D.   Timing and Stages of Financing.   Another important consideration in building the financial package is the timing and stages of financing. One method is the "all or nothing" approach where you try to raise enough money the first time to finance your business venture to a point several years down the road. This approach requires a significant amount of money up-front without much of a track record and, therefore, presents a higher risk to the investors. Generally, to offset this higher risk, the investors will require a higher rate of return and, therefore, a larger percentage ownership of the company. The result is a lower price you get for the stock you sell investors.

TABLE 18.1

Complete Financing Package

Layer	Lenders/Investors	Loans/Securities
S E N I O R D E B T L A Y E R	Commercial banks	1. Revolving line of credit—unsecured
	Suppliers/vendors	2. Revolving line of credit—secured by: a. Accounts receivable b. Inventory
	Factors	3. Fixed asset loans or leases secured by: a. Machinery and equipment b. Real estate
	Leasing companies	4. Senior notes—unsecured
S U B O R D I N A T E D D E B T L A Y E R	Insurance companies	1. Senior subordinate notes
	SBIC	2. Junior subordinate notes
	Venture capital firms	3. Debt with warrants
	Investment bankers	4. Convertibles
E Q U I T Y L A Y E R	Insurance companies	1. Preferred stock
	Investment bankers SBIC Venture capital firms Relatives/angels Bootstrap	2. Common stock

TABLE 18.2
Example of Leverage

A highly leveraged example of a financing package may include these.

Accounts payable	$ 20,000.00	
Equipment lease ($1,000 per month)	12,000.00	
Secured revolving line of credit	10,000.00	
SBIC 10-year subordinated loan	30,000.00	
Debt		$ 72,000.00
SBIC preferred stock	$ 15,000.00	
Bootstrap common stock	10,000.00	
Equity		$ 25,000.00
Total sources of capital		$ 97,000.00
A less leveraged example follows.		
Senior bank term loan[a]	$ 90,000.00	
10-year subordinated loan	90,000.00	
Debt		$180,000.00
Preferred stock	$ 50,000.00	
Common stock	350,000.00	
Equity		400,000.00
Total sources of capital		$580,000.00

[a]Assignment of $90,000.00 life insurance to be kept in force during the term of the loan.

The main advantage of this approach is that it reduces the chance of running out of money at critical times during the venture's development. Furthermore, it reduces the time you need to spend to raise more money. Each round of financing requires a considerable amount of time that you could spend on the management of the company and its operations.

A better approach may be staged financing, where further financing is available on reaching a major milestone, such as sales of $1 million, annual production of 10,000 units, and plant capacity of 95 percent. This approach has benefits for both you and the investors. You can focus your energy and talents to running the business and meeting milestones and not worrying about financing. For the investors, each milestone represents results from earlier projections and a reduction in risk. Results mean that the venture is achieving various goals, and the chances of the venture's succeeding increase. Meeting or exceeding projections and meeting milestones build credibility. You are doing what you said you would do.

There are two disadvantages, however, with this approach. First, unless you have an agreement that guarantees automatic financing at subsequent phases, some or all of the investors may drop out leaving you to scramble for new investors. Second, the amount of money raised at any stage may not be enough to achieve the next milestone if unexpected problems or delays occur. You may have to go to a bank for a loan to fill in the gaps, which may result in expensive financing, or—what is worse—it could result in a situation where adequate financing is not readily available.

E. Equity, Control, and Valuation-Pricing.   One of the first questions a venture capitalist will ask is, "How much equity and control are you willing to give up?" Some people believe control to be very important; others don't put much stock in it. They say that once you have to worry about control, the "ball game's over."

The true value or fair price for an investment is a function of numerous variables, such as the business venture's future growth outlook, the quality of the management team, the strength of the company's market position, the uniqueness of the product or service, the stabiltiy of earnings and cash flow, and the number of other investors vying for the business venture.

Clearly, investors consider all these variables in addition to a variety of valuation yardsticks, including book value, replacement value of assets, historical earnings (if available), and so forth. Projected after-tax earnings, however, are the critical determinant from the venture capitalist's viewpoint. As a very general rule, a venture capitalist will pay a price of 5 times to 12 times earnings. If, for example, your projected after-tax earnings are $50,000.00, then the value of your company may be determined to be $500,000.00 (10 times $50,000.00). If you have incorporated and have 100,000 shares authorized, then the venture capitalist would be willing to pay $5.00 per share. Let us investigate further the equity, control, and valuation part of business plans.

Equity.   The percentage of equity that venture capitalists request is directly proportional to the risk involved. Typically, companies with young or unproved management teams or both represent greater risk. If your management team is inexperienced, venture capitalists may request a greater share of the equity to compensate for greater risk. Another area of risk that will concern investors is your market. Generally, introducing a new product into a proved market is less risky than trying to create a new market for a new product. If both your product and your market are new, a venture capital group may again request a higher share of the equity. Often the biggest reason why a deal falls through is the entrepreneur's unwillingness to give up a reasonable amount of equity. Entrepreneurs will think of a number of persuasive arguments to prove why an investor should own a small percentage of the company. Some entrepreneurs start by discussing the return on investment (ROI) that the investor will receive if he or she invests. According to Gladstone, the discussion usually proceeds as follows[1].

Entrepreneur: If you invest $300,000.00 and you get 10 percent of the company you will make a fortune.

Venture capitalist: But if I get only 10 percent of the company for $300,000.00, this means that 100 percent of the company is currently worth $2.7 million. I don't see how a company at this stage of development is worth $2.7 million because of an idea.

[1]David J. Gladstone, *Venture Capital Handbook* (Reston, Va.: Reston Publishing Company, 1983), p. 116. This material is adapted by permission of Reston Publishing Company, Prentice-Hall Company, 11480 Sunset Hills Road, Reston, Va. 22090.

Entrepreneur: Wait. Let me finish. When we hit the projections that we are shooting for in three years, the company will be earning about $3 million before taxes. Using a price-earnings ratio of 10 to 1 on pretax dollars, which is, of course, 20 to 1 after tax, the company will be worth $30 million. Your 10 percent will be worth $3 million. You will have received a 10 to 1 return on your investment in only three years. That seems to be super.

Venture capitalist: And if your company fails, I lose $300,000.00, and you lose very little. And if the company goes as you say it is going to go, you will have made $27 million and invested a small amount, whereas I invested $300,000.00 and received $3 million. This is just not an equitable distribution of the potential return if you consider the risk you are asking me to take on my $300,000.00.

If you do not intend to put up any of your own money, the deal will have to be extremely attractive before any venture capitalist will wish to invest in your business venture. Most aspiring entrepreneurs don't have much money to put into a business, but taking out a second mortgage on your house or borrowing the cash value of your life insurance or selling some personal assets will be a sign of your commitment to the venture capitalist. The venture capitalist realizes that you are putting your talents and "sweat, blood, and tears" into the venture. Furthermore, he or she realizes that if it fails, you will have a black mark on your record, and you will be set back for many years of your life. But he or she also does not want you to be able to walk away from the deal without suffering some economic loss. In the preceding example, where the entrepreneur is seeking $300,000.00 with only a small personal investment, the venture capitalist will want at least 80 percent ownership in the company. With an investment of $30,000.00 (10 percent of the deal), the entrepreneur is probably in a position to negotiate 50 percent of the equity for himself or herself. If he or she invests one third, then he or she can probably obtain two thirds of the equity.[2]

The distribution of ownership in any deal depends largely on a measure of the total contribution of the parties involved and the amount of risk assumed by each. That is, the pie is divided according to what each participant brings to the party. Simply put, one furnishes the recipe, one furnishes the cooking ability, and another furnishes the ingredients. Typical ranges of equity for different situations are roughly estimated to be as follows.[3]

1 From 10 to 20 percent for the entrepreneur when the venture capitalist puts up all the money and the venture is still in the seed capital stage.

2 From 30 to 80 percent for the entrepreneur when the seed capital stage is over, depending on the amount invested by the venture capitalist.

[2]Ibid., p. 117.

[3]Patrick R. Liles, *New Business Ventures And The Entrepreneur* (Homewood, Ill.: Richard D. Irwin, 1974), p. 485. This material is used with permission.

3 From 10 to 50 percent for the venture capitalist in a mature venture where substantial capital has already been invested and the funds are for expansion.

Generally, if the investor is putting up most of the capital in a start-up, he or she will probably want voting control of the venture. In some notable exceptions involving high-tech ventures, investments have been made by venture capitalists who received only 30 or 40 percent of equity after putting up all the capital. Such deals were usually struck during extremely bullish stock markets, especially those dealing in "hot" new issues.

In the more general cases, the greater the amount of his or her own money that the entrepreneur puts up, the less equity will be requested by the venture capitalist. For example, if you put up 20 or 30 percent of the capital, the investor might require only a 30 or 40 percent equity interest. As always with any investment decision, the key factors are potential, quality, and risk. For example, the greater the quality and potential of the deal and the less risk, the less equity the venture capitalist will demand. There is also a motivational side to the equity and control question. The venture capitalist normally wants the entrepreneur and his or her team to retain sufficient equity to ensure that they will be properly motivated to perform and feel as if they have a significant stake in the venture. At the same time, if members of the entrepreneurial team or even the lead entrepreneur prove to be lacking, venture capitalists want the power to "get them out of the system."

Control.   If control becomes a sticky point during your negotiations, you might suggest that the managers retain control but that the board of directors be composed of an equal number of representatives from management and investors, with a neutral outside board member to serve as a tiebreaker. Or a proposal may be made that when certain projections are achieved, then the venture capitalist will relinquish a part of his or her control.

Valuation-pricing.   The venture capitalist looks at your projected after-tax earnings at the end of a certain period, usually from three to five years, and multiplies these earnings by a factor that he or she deems relevant. This factor is not a standard. If your business venture is in a growth industry such as cellular communications or biotechnology, investors could use an earnings multiple of 15 to 30. If your venture is a consumer-oriented business, investors may use a multiple of 5 to 10. A multiple will determine the future value of your company. For example, if you project annual after-tax earnings of $500,000.00 and you are in a hot growth industry, a venture capitalist might multiply your projected earnings of $500,000.00 by 20 and come up with a value of $10 million. This is the value one could assume your company would have if it went public or were sold. It's important for the venture capitalist to know this figure for two reasons: (1) The venture capitalist will want to be sure your company will be big enough someday to make his or her investment worthwhile, and (2) the venture capitalist will use this figure to determine how much ownership in the company is needed to meet his or her goals for return on investment.

In pricing the deal, the venture capitalist decides what return on investment he or she wants when cashing in on his or her investment at the end of three to five years. For example, he or she may want six times an investment of $1 million in three years, or $6 million. His or her next step then is to multiply a price-earnings multiple to third-year earnings, which is appropriate to the industry and the risk involved in the deal. For example, if a 10 times multiple is applicable, he or she multiplies projected earnings of $2 million by 10 and then divides the resulting figure of $20 million into his or her targeted return of $6 million. The result is 0.30; therefore, he or she will seek 30 percent equity in the company.

Remember this: A deal should be simple and agreeable to all parties for it to work. Neither the management team nor venture capitalists should feel that they are in an adversary position. Although some venture capitalists may prefer a combination of both debt and equity, many feel that paying themselves interest out of their own capital doesn't make sense. They may, for example, want preferred stock or convertible notes with interest forgiven until the company is expected to be profitable. If, however, convertible notes are offered, this can have the disadvantage of making the venture capitalist a creditor and thereby complicate the relationship between the management team and the venture capitalist.

In some situations, a pricing deadlock may develop. One way to break this deadlock is to propose a performance deal. For example, if a price of $10.00 per share is wanted by the entrepreneurial team, but the venture capitalist considers it too high, an agreement could be written where the price would be paid subject to downward adjustment if the venture did not meet its projections, thereby increasing the venture capitalist's ownership of the company. If, on the other hand, the management team performed at or above projections, then they would receive the asking price. This approach attempts to bring the valuation of the venture in line with its real value.

X. Financial Plan and Projections

Investors and lenders want to know how their money is going to be spent and how you are going to make money with the capital they furnish. These questions are answered by disclosing your budget, income statement, balance sheet, and cash flow statement for the next three to five years. It doesn't make any difference whether you are raising seed, start-up, buyout, or expansion capital, you must describe in detail your financial plan for now and the future. To do this, you will have to make key assumptions and forecasts. If you don't know what you plan to do and how much in sales and profits you plan to make and how you plan to put capital to work, then the obvious question is: Why are you trying to raise money in the first place? Furthermore, the financial plan is for you and your management team. It serves as a road map, as an operating plan for financial management of your business venture.

Two key things to remember when preparing your financial plan are (1) to be conservative and (2) to disclose fully what you plan to do with the money. To overestimate your earnings, for example, will diminish, if not destroy, your credibility and will consequently make it exceedingly difficult to get future-stage financing. Try to be on the mark or close to it. If anything, underestimate. Also, don't hide anything. Investors and lenders don't like surprises. They, indeed, expect you to be prudent and to spend the money the way you said you would. There are a number of stories in the investment community about new, hotshot presidents who, as soon as they got their hands on the money, bought jets, moved to luxurious offices, or some other downright stupid or shady thing. Some of these people are now on the outside looking in; others are in court with a cadre of high-priced lawyers at their side.

A. The Budget.   The budget is a plan expressed in unit and dollar terms that covers a specified period, usually one year. It describes how capital and other resources will be acquired and used over some specific time interval. It is a plan for the future expressed in formal, quantitative terms. It shows a relationship and summary of all phases of your company's plans and goals for the future. It sets specific targets for sales, production, marketing, and administration and culminates in projected or budgeted earnings, balance sheet, and cash flow statements. The complete budget picture is shown in Figure 18.1. The same kind of budget relationship would be appropriate for retail and service businesses. For retail, the production budget is eliminated. For a service business, both the inventory and production components are eliminated.

Programming and strategic planning are the process of selecting specific programs for action. Introducing a new product or service is a program. Research and development projects represent another program. Installation of new production facilities represents still another example of a program. The budget describes which, when, and what amounts of resources will be used for each program and how certain programs will generate sales.

On the following pages is an example of how these budgeting components are used to create an overall financial plan. This example breaks the first year's operation into quarters. In some situations, you would develop a financial plan for a three- to five-year period, with the first year on a monthly basis, year two on a quarterly basis, and the remaining years on an annual basis. In the following example, assume a small manufacturing company just getting started with a $30,000.00 loan from a bank and $100,000.00 from a common stock offering.

If these financial projections are to be useful to investors and to you, they must represent your best estimate of probable operating results. It is important to understand, however, that too much financial information can be worse than too little. The budget and financial model presented here and in Figure 18.1 seem to be appropriate for most cases if extended over a three- to five-year-period and set up side by side on a foldout sheet. If you need to highlight or explain certain areas such as sales forecast, cost of goods sold, and the like, include such technical documentation in the appendixes. The same statements can be used for retail and service business with appropriate modifications. For example, these kinds of businesses would not include production data.

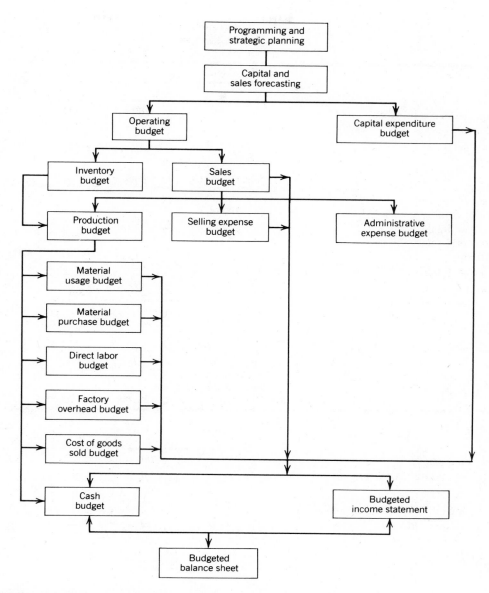

FIGURE 18.1 *A complete budget program for manufacturing.*

Your Company
Sales Budget
for the Year Ending December 31, 19X1

	Quarter				Total
	1	2	3	4	
Expected sales in units	800	700	900	800	3,200
Unit sales price	×$80	×$80	×$80	×$80	×$80
Total sales	$ 64,000	$56,000	$72,000	$64,000	$256,000

Schedule of Expected Cash Inflow

	Quarter				Total
Loan from bank	$ 30,000				$ 30,000
Sell of common stock	100,000				100,000
Quarter 1 sales ($64,000)	25,000	$27,000			52,000
Quarter 2 sales ($56,000)		39,000	$16,000		55,000
Quarter 3 sales ($72,000)			50,000	$20,000	70,000
Quarter 4 sales ($64,000)				45,000	45,000
Total cash inflow	$155,000	$66,000	$66,000	$65,000	$352,000

Your Company
Production Budget-Units
for the Year Ending December 31, 19X1

	Quarter				Total
	1	2	3	4	
Projected sales	800	700	900	800	3,200
Desired ending inventory	70	90	80	100	100
Total needs	870	790	980	900	3,300
Less: Beginning inventory	80	70	90	80	80
Units to be produced	790	720	890	820	3,220

Your Company
Direct Material Budget
for the Year Ending December 31, 19X1

	Quarter				
	1	2	3	4	Total
Units to be produced	790	720	890	820	3,220
Raw material per unit	× 3	× 3	× 3	× 3	× 3
Raw material needed for production	2,370	2,160	2,670	2,460	9,660
Desired ending inventory	216	267	246	250	250
Total needs	2,586	2,427	2,916	2,710	9,910
Less: Beginning inventory	237	216	267	246	237
Raw materials to be used	2,349	2,211	2,649	2,464	9,673
Unit price	× $3	× $3	× $3	× $3	× $3
	$7,047	$6,633	$7,947	$7,392	$29,019

Schedule of Expected Cash Payments

19X0 Accounts payable	$20,000[a]				$20,000
Quarter 1 purchases ($7,047)	3,500	$3,547			7,047
Quarter 2 purchases ($6,633)		3,311	$3,322		6,633
Quarter 3 purchases ($7,947)			3,973	$3,974	7,947
Quarter 4 purchases ($7,392)				3,696	3,696
	$23,500	$6,858	$7,295	$7,670	$45,323

[a]This $20,000 is to pay off trade accounts of 19X0. The amount of $20,000 of the $30,000 loan will be used for this purpose.

Your Company
Direct Labor Budget
For the Year Ending December 31, 19X1

	Quarter				
	1	2	3	4	Total
Units to be produced	790	720	890	820	3,220
Direct labor hours per unit	× 4	× 4	× 4	× 4	× 4
Total hours	3,160	2,880	3,560	3,280	12,880
Direct labor cost per hour	× $6	× $6	× $6	× $6	× $6
Total direct labor cost	$18,960	$17,280	$21,360	$19,680	$77,280

Your Company
Factory Overhead Budget
for the Year Ending December 31, 19X1

| | Quarter | | | | |
	1	2	3	4	Total
Budgeted direct labor hours	3,160	2,880	3,560	3,280	12,880
Variable overhead rate	× $3	× $3	× $3	× $3	× $3
Variable overhead budgeted	$ 9,480	$ 8,640	$10,680	$ 9,840	$38,640
Fixed overhead budgeted	4,000	4,000	4,000	4,000	16,000
Total budgeted overhead	$13,480	$12,640	$14,680	$13,840	$54,640
Less: Depreciation	8,000	8,000	8,000	8,000	32,000
Cash disbursements for overhead	$ 5,480	$ 4,640	$ 6,680	$ 5,840	$22,640

Your Company
Selling and Administrative Expense Budget
for the Year Ending December 31, 19X1

| | Quarter | | | | |
	1	2	3	4	Total
Expected sales in units	800	700	900	800	3,200
Variable selling and administrative expenses per unit	×$4	×$4	×$4	×$4	×$4
Budgeted variable expense	$ 3,200	$ 2,800	$ 3,600	$ 3,200	$12,800
Fixed selling and administrative expenses					
Promotion and advertising	1,200	1,200	1,200	1,200	4,800
Insurance	3,000				3,000
Office salaries	8,000	8,000	8,000	8,000	32,000
Rent	500	500	500	500	2,000
Taxes	400	400	400	400	1,600
Total budgeted selling and administrative expenses	$16,300	$12,900	$13,700	$13,300	$56,200

Your Company
Cash Budget
for the Year Ending December 31, 19X1

| | Quarter | | | | |
	1	2	3	4	Total
Cash balance, beginning	$ 1,000	$(8,240)	$16,082	$33,047	$ 1,000
Add receipts					
From customers	25,000	66,000	66,000	65,000	
From loan	30,000				
From sale of common stock	100,000				$352,000
Total cash available	$156,000	$57,760	$82,082	$98,047	$353,000
Less cash disbursements					
Direct materials	$ 23,500	$ 6,858	$ 7,295	$ 7,670	$ 45,323
Direct labor	18,960	17,280	21,360	19,680	77,280
Factory overhead	5,480	4,640	6,680	5,840	22,640
Selling and administrative	16,300	12,900	13,700	13,300	56,200
Equipment purchase[a]	100,000				100,000
Income tax				10,000	10,000
Interest				4,500	4,500
Cash balance, ending	($ 8,240)	$16,082	$33,047	$37,057	$ 37,057

[a]Equipment purchased for $100,000 from sale of common stock.

Your Company
Budgeted Income Statement
for the Year Ending December 31, 19X1

Sales (3,200 units @ $80)		$256,000
Less variable expenses		
Variable cost of goods sold		
(3,200 units @ $45)	$144,000	
Variable selling and administrative	12,800	156,800
Contribution margin		$ 99,200
Less fixed expenses		
Factory overhead	$ 16,000	
Selling and administrative	43,400	59,400
Net operating income		$ 39,800
Less interest expense		4,500
Net income before income taxes		$ 35,300
Less income taxes		10,000
Net income		$ 25,300

Your Company
Balance Sheet
for the Year Ending December 31, 19X1

Assets

Current assets		
Cash		$ 37,057
Accounts receivable		34,000
Materials inventory (250 @ $3)		750
Finished goods inventory (100 @ $45)		4,500
Total current assets		$ 76,307
Fixed assets		
Land		$ 60,000
Building and equipment	$160,000	
Less accumulated depreciation	32,000	
Net building and equipment		128,000
Total fixed assets		$188,000
Total assets		$264,307

Liability and Shareholders' Equity

Current liabilities	
Accounts payable	$ 3,696
Long-term liabilities	
Bank loan for 7 years @ 15 percent	30,000
Total Liabilities	$ 33,696
Shareholders' equity	
Common stock (120,000 shares @ $1)	120,000
Common stock offered (100,000 shares @ $1)	100,000
Retained earnings (income of $25,300	
less last year's deficit of $14,689)	10,611
	$264,307

B. Key Assumptions and Estimates.   The budgeted statements and projections should be solidly based on a foundation of well-researched and reasonable assumptions. The assumptions should reflect industry performance, and, if not, specific justification should be given. You may give "worst case" and "best case" numbers along with the "most likely" numbers if you like. Trying to set the most likely mark and then hit it is the best way to go, however.

The entire budget and your financial plans revolve around and are based on a sales forecast—the units you will sell *and* the price you will get per unit. Sales forecasting is the main gear that drives all the other gears, and it is the most uncertain part of your financial plan. It must be supported by a combination of facts, market surveys, detailed analysis, and assumptions and be typical of your industry. You should explain the basis used for forecasting sales. Your sales forecast should conform to your description of the market, your market strategy, your advertising and promotion plans, and your anticipated position in the market, as described in the marketing section of your business plan. For example, your market share should be consistent with your estimate of the total market and your competitive advantage over others in that market. If you have more than one product or service line and the composition of sales by product-service line will change over time, show separate projections and assumptions for each line. Similarly, if you have a product or service targeted for one market segment, show each segment separately.

Other areas where key assumptions and estimates must be made are (1) cash, (2) accounts receivable, (3) inventory, (4) cost of goods manufactured and sold, (5) plant and equipment, (6) marketing expense, (7) accounts payable, and (8) administrative expenses. This list, however, is not exhaustive.

1 *Cash.*   Estimate the minimum amount of cash needed to operate the company. This will serve as the basis for setting the amount of cash you need to borrow or get through the sale of stock. Moreover, you will normally need enough cash on hand to cover at least two months' disbursements. Always allow yourself a cushion for unexpected problems and additional expenses.

2 *Accounts receivable.*   Never assume that accounts receivable are going to be collected in less than 30 days. Collections more likely will be in the 60- to 90-day range with some percentage of your accounts receivable never collected. Industry statistics may give you a fairly good indication of the length of collection period to expect. Note, however, that start-up businesses normally do not have strong leverage in collecting from new customers, so you may want to lengthen your estimated collection period accordingly.

3 *Inventory.*   The amount of inventory of raw materials you need is the amount necessary to support your forecast sales volume plus allowance for waste and scrap. The timing of your inventory purchases will be a major factor in your cash flow budget.

4 *Cost of goods manufactured and sold.*   Make engineering and statistical analyses to establish direct labor, direct material, and factory overhead costs that go into manufacturing your product. Labor costs are based on standard production time and an estimated hourly wage. Direct materials costs are based on material usage that goes into making finished units and supplier quotations. Factory overhead is an estimate of annual costs applied on each unit as a percentage of direct labor amounts (factory overhead can also be applied by other methods such as a factory overhead rate times so many labor hours or machine hours per unit of output).

5 *Plant and equipment.*   Describe what major assets you plan to acquire and why. This area has already been explained in another area of your business plan. You will, however, show the acquisition cost and depreciation in your financial statements.

6 *Marketing expenses.* Your marketing plan has been explained elsewhere in your business plan. Include the appropriate expenses in your financial statements.

7 *Accounts payable.* One of the reasons you may be trying to raise long-term capital is to pay past due accounts payable. Or it could be that because you are a start-up, you cannot get credit until you have established a good credit history. Even if you can get credit, you should probably assume that your payment period will generally be shorter than the industry average during your early years. Another good assumption is that your payment terms may be 30 days or less, and your receivables may have an average collection period of 30 days or more. This situation can cause cash flow anemia.

8 *Administrative expenses.* Prepare a schedule of the major administrative and support personnel, rent, insurance, office furniture and fixtures, supplies, and the like. Include all of these expenses in your budgeted statements.

XI. Appendixes

The appendixes are prepared to explain, support, and augment the main body of the business plan. When preparing the appendixes, arrange the material in the same sequence as the business plan. If the appendix is not voluminous, it may be attached to the back of the business plan. If, on the other hand, it is lengthy and detailed, it should be prepared separately and furnished to lenders and investors if they want it.

Some examples of materials included in the appendixes are product drawings and specifications; blueprints; pictures; detailed résumés; letters of reference; credit reports; marketing surveys; articles from trade journals; job descriptions; legal documents; copies of leases; franchise agreements; all types of contracts; licenses and permits; articles of incorporation and charter; tax records; patents, copyrights, trademarks, and other protective material; insurance policies and certificates; and financial analysis and ratios.

XII. Bibliography

The bibliography is a list of writings relating to a particular author and subject. These works are referred to in the business plan or consulted by you in the production of it.

SUMMARY

Money is what makes things happen, and people who furnish this money want to know in detail why you are trying to raise money and what you intend to do with it. They also want to know how you plan to pay it back and why your business venture will provide them with a high return on their investment. And, finally, some readers have a greater need for detail, exhibits, and documents to support and explain the main elements of your business plan. Have this material available when needed.

ASSIGNMENT

1 Prepare the financial part of your business plan.

2 What is the difference between debt and equity?

3 Describe the main differences between senior debt, subordinated debt, and equity. Be specific and give examples.

4 Compare and contrast equity, control, and valuation-pricing. Give an example.

5 What are the key components of the financial plan and projections? Give a brief example of each. What are pro forma statements?

BIBLIOGRAPHY

Anthony, Robert N., John Dearden, and Norton M. Bedford. *Management Control Systems*, 5th ed. Homewood, Ill.: Richard D. Irwin, 1984.

Dible, Donald M. (ed.). *Winning the Money Game*. Santa Clara, Calif.: Entrepreneur Press, 1975.

Gladstone, David J. *Venture Capital Handbook*. Reston, Va.: Reston Publishing Company, 1983.

Haslett, Brian, and Leonard E. Smollen. "Preparing a Business Plan." In Stanley E. Pratt (ed.). *Guide to Venture Capital Sources*, 7th ed. Wellesley Hills, Mass.: Capital Hills Publishing, 1983.

Kramer, Donald J. "The Entrepreneur's Perspective." In Stanley E. Pratt (ed.). *Guide to Venture Capital Sources*, 7th ed. Wellesley Hills, Mass.: Capital Publishing, 1983.

Liles, Patrick R. *New Business Ventures and the Entrepreneur*. Homewood, Ill.: Richard D. Irwin, 1974.

Mancuso, Joseph R. *How to Prepare and Present a Business Plan*. Englewood Cliffs, N.J.: Prentice-Hall, Spectrum Book, 1983.

Murphy, Thomas, P. " 'Pluck it Out.' " *Forbes*. September 24, 1984.

Pearsall, Thomas E., and Donald H. Cunningham. *How to Write for the World of Work*, 2d ed. New York: Holt, Rinehart and Winston, 1982.

Pratt, Stanley E. (ed.). *Guide to Venture Capital Sources*, 7th ed. Wellesley Hills, Mass.: Capital Publishing, 1983.

Sanger, Elizabeth. "Mating by Computer." *Barron's*. September 3, 1984.

Shaffer, Richard A. "Venture Capital Firms Are Hit by Slower Growth in Financing." *The Wall Street Journal*. Section 2, August 17, 1984.

Silver, A. David. *The Entrepreneurial Life*. New York: Wiley, 1983.

Tootelian, Dennis H., and Ralph M. Gaedeke. *Small Business Management Operations and Profiles*, 2d ed. Glenview, Ill.: Scott, Foresman, 1985.

Welsh, John A., and Jerry F. White. *The Entrepreneur's Master Planning Guide*. Englewood Cliffs, N.J.: Prentice-Hall, Spectrum Book, 1983.

CHAPTER 19

Presentation of
the Business Plan

INTRODUCTION

After the business plan is prepared, a critical decision is to find the right investor to back your venture. Once the right investor is found, the next step is to get an interview where you can make a personal, oral presentation. The presentation is where everything comes together, an opportunity to finalize the deal and end the long hours of research and preparation. It is the opportunity to raise the capital you need to start or expand your business venture. If you are successful, here is where your venturing ends and the start of your business begins. The objectives of this chapter follow.

1 To present some guidelines that will help you make a successful presentation of your business plan.
2 To discuss ethics and rules of conduct.

CHOOSING THE RIGHT INVESTOR

In choosing the right investor, you are looking for a *backer*, someone who will give capital, counseling, and support to launch your business venture; stand with you through the hard times; and help you to achieve success eventually. You have to look at choosing your investor as carefully as you would in choosing a spouse because in effect it has characteristics similar to a marriage. Indeed, compatibiltiy in attitude, goals, ethics, and management style is imperative. Choosing the right investor requires a good match between your business plan and the investor's background, credentials, financial capacity, and reputation. Once such an investor is found, an interview should be arranged to give you a chance to present and defend your business plan.

Matching the Investor with the Business Plan

The first thing you want to do in selecting an investor is to consider those located close to your business or where your business will be. If you are unable to raise capital from local investors, you will have to explain why you are seeking capital outside your geographic area. Generally, investors like to invest in ventures within 400 to 500 miles of their firm. A few of the larger investment bankers or venture capitalist firms are national in scope and will consider backing ventures in other areas of the country.

All investors in your area or three thousand miles away, large or small, are looking for capable entrepreneurs with ventures that promise strong markets, growth, and big returns. Unless you can show exceptional profits, you should not approach the venture capitalist investor or any other potential backer. These people are not interested in backing a "good cause" or ventures that will revolutionize the marketplace but have little payoff; they are generally not interested in meeting glamorous people unless they have a glamorous business deal to offer; they don't want their names inscribed on a plaque; and they don't want to be part of history unless they are written up in *Forbes 400*. None of these things will induce venture capitalists to back you. The promise of substantial returns for them and you will be of interest—a partnership in a deal that will make big money.

Several other variables should be considered when trying to match the right investor with your business plan. Most investors, for example, develop a dollar range of investments that they prefer. Some like $50,000.00 to $100,000.00 deals. Others don't even want to talk to you unless you can offer a deal of over $1 million. Most investors also have their favorite fields that they invest in. Indeed, most will not invest in any deal in a field with which they are unfamiliar. Some specialize in launching state-of-the-art, high-technology start-ups; some like fast-food restaurants; some like health services; some like retailing and wholesaling; some like movie production; some like computer software; some like construction; and so forth. Some investors like to provide expansion capital; some like to participate in leveraged buyouts; still others like to provide seed or start-up capital. Some want only common stock; others want a combination of convertible debentures and preferred stock with conversion rights. Some investors like revolutionary and innovative products and services; still others prefer evolutionary or substitution products and services.

Reputation and Credibility of the Investor

Assume that you find several investors who meet the characteristics and needs of your business plan. Does the investor have the reputation and credibility that you desire? Choosing a reputable investor is a critical decision. You will be choosing someone who will be working closely with you over a long period of time; someone who will be involved in your operations; and someone who will require periodic budgets, financial statements, and other reports—in effect, it will become a business marriage.

Clearly, subsequent rounds of financing will be needed as the venture grows. The access to later-stage financing, to be sure, will depend on the stability and strength of the investor whom you choose. You certainly don't want a backer with a weak vision, a weak heart, and a weak pocketbook. Can he or she stay with you through the difficult times? Do they have skilled personnel who can help you solve problems? Do they have influence that can help you with suppliers, bankers, regulators, and so forth?

How do you find the right investor for your venture? You can do it yourself, or you can use your banker or an investment banker or your lawyer or your accountant. In most instances, you will be better off by getting help. Sometimes one of these persons may be able to set up a meeting with a venture capitalist or several at one time to make a simultaneous presentation of your business plan.

If you have already met with several investors and these meetings have progressed to the point where they are seriously interested in you, they will welcome a thorough investigation of their background, credentials, and track record. You can be assured that they will investigate you. In early conversations with them, find out whom they have invested in, and call these entrepreneurs to determine how they are being treated. Indeed, one of the most important things you can do is talk to entrepreneurs whom they have backed.

Furthermore, determine if they are involved in a lot of litigation. Check the courthouse to see if they have suits against them. Run a credit report on them to see what is in their credit file. Also, ask for bank and other references. Check with the venture capital industry's trade associations, such as the American Association of Minority Enterprise Small Business Investment Companies (AAMESBIC), the National Association of Small Business Investment Companies (NASBIC), the National Venture Capital Association (NVCA), the Western Association of Venture Capitalists (WAVC), and the Council for Entrepreneurial Development (CED). Also, you might want to subscribe to the *Venture Capital Journal* for general information.

Getting the Interview

There are basically three ways to contact your selected investor: by phone, by mail, and by an intermediary. If you call, remember that most investors are under severe time pressures; therefore, be brief and to the point. Explain the deal you are trying to finance, ask if funds are available, and ask if they can review your business plan within the next week. If so, send them your business plan. Some investors will not talk to you but will have their secretary ask you to mail the business plan (maybe only the summary). Investors who use this approach are trying to weed out crackpots with crazy ideas and to manage their time better. Don't be discouraged by this kind of treatment; mail them your business plan. If they have not responded within a couple of weeks, then move on to other investors.

The indiscriminate mailing of your business plan to a large group of investors is generally counterproductive, a waste of time and money, and may be illegal as we will see later. The advice is this: Do not use a mass-mailing list to send unsolicited business plans. Investors will get the impression that you are "shopping around" and, generally, will not respond. Eventually, this approach is likely to weaken your chances of ever raising capital from anyone because what you are doing gets around quickly in the investment community.

Probably the most desirable way to approach a venture capitalist for an interview is through an introduction from an individual who is known and respected by the venture capitalist. For example, this intermediary may be a banker, lawyer, or accountant. The introduction, however, is all they can do for you. From there on, it is up to you. Generally, investors will want to see something in writing first, so send them a summary of your business plan or maybe the entire plan if that is what they want and then follow up with a phone call within a week for a formal interview and presentation.

Even with a good introduction to an investor, you still may not get the interview. For a variety of reasons, most business plans are turned down before entrepreneurs get a chance to present and defend them. For those plans that are considered for further investigation, you will receive a phone call. After a few more details are checked, the deal may then be turned down. If you are among the few who remain, you will be invited to the office for a detailed presentation and conference. This is your chance. Be ready. Do your homework.

Legal Considerations

You should realize at this point that offering your business plan makes you subject to a number of securities laws, especially if you are using mass-mailing techniques and showing your business plan to "too many" investors. For example, the Securities and Exchange Commission (SEC) frowns on offering your business plan to more than 35 potential investors. Moreover, state laws, often called blue-sky laws, may even be tougher. For instance, in Massachusetts, a business plan can be shown to only 25 potential investors. If you solicit backing only from residents of the state in which you will be operating in, then you must be in compliance with the securities laws of that state. If you cross state lines, then you must satisfy both state and federal laws.

Before showing or mailing your plan to a potential investor, enlist the services of a lawyer who is experienced in securities laws for guidance. Also, be sure to enclose a disclaimer prominently displayed on the title page. Moreover, keep track of all copies of the business plan, who has received copies, and those copies returned and from whom. Set up your control system like a library checkout system.

THE INITIAL MEETING

The initial meeting is generally in the prospective investor's office and will usually last from 30 minutes to an all-day affair, depending on the length of the presentation and depth of discussion. Normally, the meeting will last from one to two hours. In most instances, the investor sees your business plan before he or she sees you. During this first meeting, the investor will attempt to read you, to size you up, and to get a gut feel of the venture and its potential for success. He or she will be judging your ability as an entrepreneur-manager and your potential in making it work. A first impression is extremely important. If it is a bad one, the deal will probably never get off the ground. So the meeting has three objectives: (1) to obtain more information about the business plan and to understand from you how it will make money, (2) to size you up by an eyeball-to-eyeball meeting, and (3) to begin negotiations to work out a financial package.

Making a Good First Impression

When you first meet your selected investor, the initial impression you make is based on appearance and attitude. If this impression is favorable, your investor is more likely to listen to you; but if it is not favorable, your prospective investor may put up communication barriers that can be difficult to overcome. Here are some suggestions for making a favorable first impression.

1 Dress appropriately by wearing clothes that are fairly conservative.
2 Be neat, clean, and well groomed.
3 Do not smoke, chew gum, or drink when in your prospective investor's office.
4 Show enthusiasm and energy. Display a good sense of humor.
5 Be straightforward and honest. Do not try to act like someone's stereotype of an entrepreneur. Do not exaggerate, and do not hide anything.
6 Be confident and slightly aggressive, and sell yourself and your venture. The main thing is to have good answers for the questions asked. Know your business plan in detail.
7 A smile is the universal act of warmth and friendliness. Like the successful salesperson, you should have "a shine on your shoes and a smile on your face."
8 Use terms that everyone understands. If you use a special term, be sure it is used and pronounced correctly.
9 Do not apologize for taking the investor's time.
10 Maintain eye contact with all those in attendance.
11 If the investor offers to shake hands, do so with a firm grip while continuing to maintain eye contact.
12 Learn how to pronounce your prospective investor's name correctly *before* meeting him or her.
13 Leave all unnecessary materials outside the office such as your overcoat and umbrella.
14 Do not let a third person represent you or try to sell your business plan.
15 Do not bring your accountant or lawyer at the early meetings. In fact, do not bring anyone with you unless another person has an equal or substantial interest in the venture. Ideally, keep the first meeting to just you and the prospective investor.

From the Investor's Viewpoint

Try to look at the business plan and what you are offering from the investor's viewpoint. Most venture capitalists as well as other potential backers strongly believe that a good entrepreneur-manager is at the heart of a successful investment. They want to make sure that they are backing the right person with the right idea at the right time in the right marketplace. They want to become shareholders in a well-run, profitable business, not a "stuckholder" in a loser.

Lenders and investors also realize that the task of identifying exceptional entrepreneurs to back is difficult. Still, they must make judgments about the business plan, projections, and your ability to perform. Does the business plan have potential? Are the projections feasible? Are they based on sound assumptions? Do you have the ability to make the projections come true? What are the reputation, quality, and experience of the entrepreneurial team? Unfortunately (or fortunately), this is a subjective area, not applicable to a scientific approach. A lot of it is like trying to shovel smoke. The evaluation process is open to a wide range of interpretations, but all investors try, and all of them have "their ways."

Some want to meet you privately in their office; some may want to meet in a conference room with several others in attendance; some may want to see you out in the field or on the shop floor; still others may want you to deliver a very formal presentation to a select audience, maybe even including an in-house psychologist. No matter, they are looking for *clues* to help them to decide whether or not they will back you. They may probe, aggravate, and irritate to determine your "hot spots," to see how you react. They want to see if you are a buck passer by giving excuses, covering up, or blaming others. They want to see if you exaggerate. Are you a big talker and small achiever? Are you a money-waster? Are you overly concerned with the size of your office, perquisites, and a big salary? Do you think like an owner-partner or an employee? Do you have a welfare attitude toward employees? Can you fire people if you have to? Can you bite the bullet and make deep cuts if necessary? Do you flit from one idea to another? Can you get the product out of R and D and into the marketplace?

Lenders and investors want to back a person with good management abilities—someone who has got it together. They want someone who is hungry, who wants to make big money, maybe someone who is even a little greedy, but also someone who is honest, committed, and loyal. They want someone who is enthusiastic and has the energy to deal with and overcome problems and setbacks. They want someone who is dependable, who will stay with the venture day-by-day and month-by-month and not fall by the wayside when the going gets tough. Are you dedicated? Do you have a nurturing quality? What will you do if the venture gets sick and falters? If the business has a problem will you stay up all night to get it solved, or will you go home at five? All lenders and investors know from experience, sometimes bitter experience, that it is exceedingly difficult to start a new business and make it successful. The time and patience commitment is immense, and the personal price that you must pay is extremely high. Are you willing to pay it?

If someone else is going to back you, then you must be able to take advice. Can you take advice without being a "yes" person? If there is an entrepreneurial team, is there a lead person, someone who is clearly in charge? Is each team member's capabilities matched to responsibilities? How long have the team members known each other? How long have they worked together? Do they work well together? Are there any weak links?

One of the principal and recurring questions is going to be this: "OK, if things don't work out as you say they are, then what?" Indeed, you better have a reasonable and logical answer to this question. Have ready several contingency plans to protect the venture's downside. Your attitude must be to treat failure as an enemy that is always in the rocks and hedges ready to ambush you and your venture. Have well-conceived tactics and strategies for beating this enemy.

Are you mentally tough? Do you have a strong ego and high level of confidence, or are you trying to become someone's poodle? Do you have a venturesome spirit? Are you someone who is willing to take chances without being reckless? Nolan Bushnell, entrepreneur *extraordinaire* of Atari and Pizza Time Theatre fame, among other things, has started a venture capital firm, Catalyst Technologies. He is trying to incubate a new generation of products and businesses for the marketplace, such as on-board navigational equipment for automobiles and devices that allow viewers to intervene in television programs to customize the content. What does he look for in an aspiring entrepreneur? He says he looks for *daring*, saying that it really shouldn't matter if you lose a little now and then, that the real problem is the little M.B.A. bastards who are ruining venture capital by not being venturesome enough.[1]

The late André Meyer, an entrepreneurial prototype somewhat different from Bushnell and a true legend in investment circles, always trusted his judgment completely and had his way of sizing up entrepreneurs seeking capital. He told an entrepreneur once that one hour was all that he needed because "I can tell within 15 minutes by listening to you if you are smart. I can tell within 30 minutes of hearing the description of the business if the product is good and the market is ready. If it is too technical, I can describe it to a technical consultant within 30 minutes and have an answer. Then, to find out if you are honest, I need to call some of your references, and that takes another 30 minutes."[2]

You may gain a little insight into the way venture capitalists think from the following epigrams of Fred Adler, a leading venture capitalist. He calls them Adler's laws.[3]

1 The probability of a company's succeeding is inversely proportional to the amount of publicity it receives before it manufactures its first product.

2 An investor's ability to talk about his or her winners is an order of magnitude greater than his or her ability to remember his or her losers.

3 If you don't think you have a problem, you have a big problem.

4 Happiness is positive cash flow. Everything else will come later.

5 The probability of the success of a small company is inversely proportional to the size of the president's office.

---

[1]Stephen Kindel, "Counselor/Coach Syndrome," *Forbes 400*, October 1, 1984. pp. 240–48. This material is used with permission.

[2]Quoted from A. David Silver, *The Entrepreneurial Life* (New York: Wiley, 1983), p. 136. This material is used with permission.

[3]Quoted from Gordon B. Baty, *Entrepreneurship for the Eighties* (Reston, Va.: Reston Publishing Company, 1981), p. 105. This material is adapted by permission of Reston Publishing Company, a Prentice-Hall company, 11480 Sunset Hills Road, Reston, Va. 22090.

6 Would-be entrepreneurs who pick up the check after luncheon discussions are usually losers.

7 The longer the investment proposal, the shorter the odds of success.

8 There is no such thing as an overfinanced company.

9 Managers who worry a lot about voting control usually have nothing worth controlling.

10 There's no limit on what an individual can do or where he or she can go, if he or she doesn't mind who gets the credit.

11 The conventional wisdom is that you shouldn't shop the deal; the reality is that you have to shop the deal.

PRESENTING THE BUSINESS PLAN

An even bigger problem than *preparing* the business plan is *presenting* it, the eyeball-to-eyeball interaction with a prospective investor to explain the business plan and to persuade him or her to give you some hard, cold cash. If you get the chance to make an oral presentation, probably all you have done up to that point is generated some interest in your venture, at least enough to get the interview. From here on it is up to you—the total you. The total you is how you look, how you dress, how you talk, how you act, how you react, the general impression that you make. Indeed, the burden of persuading the investor to back you cannot be supported by the business plan alone; you must prepare a well-structured and rehearsed oral presentation. The oral presentation is the key to persuading the investor to back you.

Nonverbal Messages

The investor has a rational and emotional side; you must consider both. One cannot dispute the importance of your business plan, the text of your business plan, and the words you use to explain it, but most communication is nonverbal. A lot depends not so much on "what" you say but "how" you say it. People receive your ideas and information through both sight and hearing and crank this through the rational and emotional mind. Vocal qualities and diction are nonverbal; certain sounds such as grunts, groans, sighs, and throat clearings are nonverbal; a shrug, a stutter, and posture are nonverbal; dress, grooming, and gestures are nonverbal; but any one or all may convey messages open to a wide range of interpretations; a smile or a frown can signal a host of nonverbal messages. Most people react strongly to what they hear, what they think they hear, and what they see. A person's appearance is a veritable signpost of messages. Appearance along with body stance and movements can "say" a lot to those who are "listening."

When verbal and nonverbal messages contradict each other, the listener will normally pay more attention and believe the nonverbal message. Ideally, you should try to make the two consistent. Use appropriate hand gestures to stress a significant point. Be presentable by being as neat, clean, and attractive as possible. Offer a friendly smile and a firm handshake. Leave out the grunts, sighs, and the vocalizers such as "um," "uh," "er," "heh," "you know," and "like." Don't invade the investor's space such as putting your feet on the rung of his or her chair or going to his or her side of the desk. Give the investor plenty of time to interact. Besides its persuasive powers, eye contact helps hold the investor's attention and gain support.

Basic Presentation Methods

There are four basic ways of orally delivering your business plan, which are memorization, off-the-cuff presentation, reading, and extemporaneous. Each has its place, but generally the extemporaneous method is the most effective.

A memorized presentation is somewhat effective and gives you a feeling of security, but it sacrifices freedom and freshness. Even with a memorized presentation, you need an outline in case you become lost.

An off-the-cuff presentation is unrehearsed and is absolutely not recommended as a way to present your business plan. You are the author of the business plan, and it seems that you would not need to review it; but if you don't you will forget major points and tend to ramble.

Reading from your business plan can be described in two words: *ho* and *hum*; it is an effective sleeping pill. It has all the drawbacks of memorization plus the inability to maintain eye contact.

The extemporaneous method is the best way to present your business plan. If you have done your homework and know your business plan inside out, then this is the most versatile and expressive method of delivery. You are more spontaneous and energetic. You can more readily adapt to topics and situations for which you had not planned. This method gives you the best way to maintain eye contact and establish rapport. You can keep your prospective investors interested and personalize your presentation. All this, however, depends on you having done your homework thoroughly. Master your material thoroughly, develop an outline, and go from there. With this method, you have strong organization on one side and flexibility and energy on the other.

Rehearsing the Presentation

A presentation to an audience is a thought transference process with certain supporting behavior. It is thinking in public. Rehearsal, therefore, more than anything else, is thinking. It is the process of doing and practicing in private what you will do in public. Do not, however, memorize. The following suggestion may be helpful.[4]

---

[4]W. A. Mambert, *Effective Presentation* (New York: Wiley, 1976), pp. 250–51. This material is used with permission.

1 Know the outline of your presentation inside out. Make it a mental picture or pathway in your mind (which is what you want it to become for your audience, also).

2 Repeatedly travel this mental pathway. Become totally familiar with each "signpost," that is, your notes, supportive devices, visual aids, and so forth.

3 As you come to each element along the pathway, envision yourself actually reliving and retelling what you are mentally experiencing to your audience.

4 Test yourself to see if a key word will trigger your recall of a specific element, for example, an anecdote, an example, or a list of details. From this point, you can retell in your own words without further reference to written notes.

5 Some other things may be committed to memory: (a) your very first statement to your audience, (b) your very last statement to your audience, and (c) any special quotations or similar material that you want to quote verbatim.

6 Be thoroughly familiar with the content of each individual aid.

7 Actually practice the use of any equipment to be used.

8 Actually perform any act to be performed during the presentation. For example, if a blackboard illustration is to be drawn, it should be practiced at least once in advance on the blackboard.

9 Any demonstration should be rehearsed from beginning to end at least once.[5]

Rehearsing too much, however, can become the same as memorization, which puts you in a straitjacket. Losing your adaptability can boomerang on you if anything unexpected happens. The recommendation, therefore, is to be well prepared but stay loose. To show how you should be prepared for anything, note this following story: The presenter discovered that the holes in his charts did not match the pegs on the easel he was promised. All eyes were immediately on him, all aware of his dilemma. He glanced around with barely a moment's hesitation, bent down, removed his shoe laces and, to the accompaniment of a hearty round of applause, used them to tie his charts to the easel. Turning to his audience, he quipped, "This is operating on a shoestring."[6] No matter how well you plan, some things are going awry. Be ready to adapt when they do.

Moreover, you must be able to maintain control of the presentation if last-minute changes in allotted time and interruptions occur, and they usually will. If you have memorized a 30-minute presentation and time constraints reduce it to 15 minutes, what do you leave out? In fact, if you give a good presentation, you will probably get a number of questions from your listeners. Such feedback can be effectively used by you to tailor your presentation to fit the feedback and to determine to what extent the investor is accepting or rejecting your presentation. Moreover, you want to encourage participation because generally people become alienated if they are not given a chance to ask questions. Unwelcome interruptions come

[5]Ibid.
[6]Ibid.

from outside sources such as the telephone, a real presentation killer unless you can adapt to such interruptions and keep things moving and on track. If an outside interruption has, however, caused a significant distraction, you may be better off by suggesting that another meeting be scheduled.

Preparing Notes

Generally speaking, the fewer notes, the better your delivery. The function of notes should not be so much to help remember information as to remember to include activities and ideas already stored in your memory or to direct you to do something that you might forget to do in the general press of time and place. Your notes should contain the following.

1 The subject matter of your presentation in abbreviated form.
2 Directions for movements, gestures, readings, passing out handouts, use of the blackboard, and similar stage activities.
3 Cue for the use of visual aids such as charts or slides. You should also keep on the podium with you a copy of each individual aid.
4 Any information to be written on a blackboard, easel, chart, or similar medium during the presentation.

Never mention your notes to an audience. "It says here in my notes . . . ," "I lost my place in the notes," and similar comments are made only by amateurs. You should actually play down and screen from your audience the fact that you are using notes. Don't cover up; just don't call undue attention to them.

The symbols and other "memory joggers" you use in your notes are personal. But standardizing your system will help. You can use color codes, for example. If you know that a red arrow is always your reminder to walk to the blackboard, you will be able to look ahead in your notes and always stay on track. Similarly, if you always start a major point on a new card, you will have better transition and a smoother flow.

Use of Visual Aids

The use of pictures, graphics, handouts, and the like becomes an integral part of your presentation and helps to support it. These, if well prepared and handled, increase the listener's understanding and make you more credible. Thousands of bits of data about sales projections can be captured and clearly presented in a bar chart, for example; or percentage of different expenses to sales can be effectively compared and presented in a pie chart.

There are a number of aids at your disposal, such as pictures, blackboards and flip charts, films, audio aids, written handouts, videotapes, graphs, prototypes, full-scale models, charts and diagrams, and samples (e.g., tactile aids). If, for example, you are using a special material that has a smooth, woodlike surface and is fireproof, then pass it around, and let the audience get a closer look at it, touch it, and try to set it on fire. One of the most effective aids, however, that most presenters do not think of is people. They can be used in countless ways and in some situations make the most effective visual aid. For example, you might hire a person or select someone from the audience to model or use your product while you are describing it. Sometimes aids can achieve what words alone cannot. A little showmanship and pizzazz don't hurt. If you are manufacturing durable suitcases, have some bruiser jump up and down on one, and allow the "silent language" to make impressive points about your product.

When deciding whether to use visual aids, you should make sure that they fit your business plan, your listeners, and enhance understanding. Aids work only when they further communication between you and your listeners. You should use aids competently (e.g., know how to work the projector or viewgraph). Make sure that the aids can be seen or heard by everyone in the room. Don't let anyone feel "left out." Aids should be more than decoration and show. They should augment, clarify, and support the presentation, not detract from it. Remember that visual aids are for *vision*; the less "busy" they are and the less copy they contain, the better. And consider people with poor eyesight; make the symbols and data large enough and clear enough so that even people with poor eyesight can see them. Furthermore, don't be too quick to move to the next aid. Nothing is more disconcerting than to see a graph flash across a screen before the viewer has had a chance to understand it.

Dealing with Stage Fright

There are many cases of stage fright, or "buck fever" as it is also called. Most people, even professionals, suffer from butterflies. In most cases, it is not beneficial to overcome such feelings completely for two reasons. First, it is beneficial to maintain a certain amount of tension in the human mechanism. People usually function better when they are keyed up. Second, a complete absence of such tension can result in laxness, which can result in an ineffective presentation. If you have done your homework, rehearsed your presentation, and believe in what you are doing, stage fright should be of little concern to you.[7]

Motivational Countdown

When you arrive at the place of presentation, you want to be ready to perform at a peak effectiveness. Here are some suggestions to motivate yourself in those final moments before delivery.

[7]Ibid., pp. 260–65.

1 Be fully prepared and rehearsed at least 12 hours before the presentation, with notes complete and in their final form and all aids, equipment, and other matters finally arranged.

2 If the presentation is to be given in the morning, do nothing more to it or with it after the close of activity on the preceding day. Use the evening for recreation or some activity entirely unrelated to the presentation.

3 If it is to be later in the day, do essentially the same, routine things that you normally do during the day.

4 Two hours before going on, take one last look through the notes. Make sure your note cards are in order, and briefly run through the thought sequence pattern. Then put them away, and do not look at them again before going on.

5 From here on, think only in a generalized way of how valid the message is, how much it needs to be told, and how important it is to the audience. Attempt to build a militant, motivated feeling about the whole matter.

6 Visit a valet shop, shoeshine parlor, or barber shop. If possible, change into fresh clothes, take a shower, or even drop into a store and buy something new. In short, perform some kind of "freshening up" exercise.

7 Then take a walk, read an inspirational passage, listen to some music, or engage in a light conversation unconnected with the subject.

8 Plan on arriving for the presentation about 15 minutes early, no earlier, for waiting can build tension. Take a look around to be sure that everything is in order.

9 When called on or announced, walk slowly and confidently to the head of the conference table or to the podium if one is furnished. Hold your notes in your hand, or set them on the rostrum; pause for 5 or 10 seconds, look directly and pleasantly at the audience, and begin. If the presentation is a little less structured, adapt accordingly.[8]

Improving Voice and Speech Pattern

The voice and speech are the primary tools used in oral presentation and as such ought to receive consideration and practice in improvement. Here are some helpful suggestions.[9]

1 Use pauses as a tool for emphasis.

2 Breathing and posture are important. To breathe deeply, stand erect with shoulders thrown comfortably back and chin inclined slightly above the hori-

[8]Ibid., pp. 266–69.
[9]Ibid., pp. 270–79.

zontal. This should be a natural posture and not exaggerated. Then simply draw air deeply into the body. Hold the breath for a few seconds, and begin to speak. It is not necessary to wait for the air supply to become exhausted before replenishing it. Air should be inhaled at normal pauses in speech.

3 Eating a large meal before a presentation diminishes body resonance and also will tend to dull your thinking and action.

4 Vary speaking speed as your intended effects vary.

5 Pay full attention to the pronunciation of word prefixes and suffixes. It is important to your credibility to pronounce words properly.

6 A cultured, educated voice is always to be desired although at times you might intentionally lapse into colloquialism or informal delivery. (Normally, not recommended.)

At the Podium

The oral delivery of your business plan is the "moment of truth." Practiced natural-ness and the ability to feel what you are saying are the best guarantees of a successful delivery. Here are some additional suggestions:[10]

1 Watch your posture. Do not lean on anything. Stand with both legs straight, knees relaxed, shoulders back, and chin slightly higher than horizontal.

2 Avoid first-person pronouns and personal references. Unless absolutely perti-nent to the presentation, do not include personal stories.

3 Use humor wisely. Avoid reference to race, religion, personal beliefs, and special interest groups.

4 Generally avoid apologies. Never start a presentation by apologizing for lack of preparation, dropped items, or confused notes. If you have to apologize for this, you shouldn't be up there.

5 If you lose your place, stop and find it. Don't continue in a hopeless fumble.

6 Pace your delivery to the audience. Watch for responses. If eyes, questions, or other reactions indicate that an idea is not getting across, slow down. Ask questions to see if you are being understood.

7 Never argue with an audience member, no matter who is right.

Closing the Presentation

When to ask for the money is just as important as *how* to ask for it. In the business plan you were asking for it indirectly. During or at the end of your presentation, the prospective investor will generally indicate if he or she plans to back you, so the

[10]Ibid., pp. 283–94.

"when to ask for the money" question may be a moot issue. In some instances, however, you have to become something of a salesperson and actually pin the investor down as to what his or her intentions are—like a salesperson closing a sale. Although salespeople have a number of closing methods, the one that seems particularly appropriate to your request for backing is called a "summary close." After your presentation, you simply summarize all the main points of the business plan and the benefits that the prospective investor will enjoy. This prepares the investor to make a decision. Clearly, the desired decision will normally be expressed as, "I like your plan, and I am pretty sure that we will back you. Let's get together next Monday and work out the details." But the comment may be somewhat nebulous: "Sounds pretty good to me; we sure need more businesses like that." This response paves the way for your actual close such as, "Fine. When can we get together to work out the details?"

Another situation that you may find yourself in is a "contingent close," which involves getting a commitment from the prospective investor that he or she will back you if you can prove a point or perform something. For example, the investor may say, "Everything you have said sounds OK, but I don't believe you can get your product ready for production by June." Your response might be, "If I get a production prototype ready for demonstration in my shop by May 15, will you back me?" The investor may respond by saying, "As I said before, getting the product out of R and D is my only concern. If you can show me a production prototype by a week or two before June, you've got a deal." Your response then is, "Good, we will start this afternoon, and I will call you Tuesday to set a time for demonstration."

Generally, simple, logical persuasion is appropriate in dealing with most investors. Persistence is important, but you will not be able to browbeat these people into submission, nor would you want to because you are going to have to live with each other for a long time after the deal is over. If the investor says, "We'll have to look at your proposal further and get back to you in a few days," it is probably a nice "no," and you should move on to another prospective investor. After a complete presentation you probably will not get "We have a deal," but you should at least get a fairly firm commitment and indication of strong interest.

FINALIZING THE DEAL

By the time the investor has come to the point of negotiating investment terms, he or she has a pretty good idea of what it will take before he or she invests his or her money. If he or she cannot move you close to his or her terms, the deal will fall through. The experienced investor will not try to browbeat you because he or she wants you also to be satisfied with the deal.

Once all parties have agreed in principle, the investor will give you a draft of the agreement. It contains a number of covenants, operating rules, restrictions, reporting conventions, personal warranties, and so forth. You, your accountant, and your lawyer should go over it with care, because it may be necessary to start an entire new round of negotiation to get it acceptable to you, your investor, and other lenders or investors.

If you were short of cash when you started your capital-raising process, your investor may offer to provide you some "bridge capital" to tide you over until all the details are worked out and the final funds are provided. Unless you are firmly convinced that the deal will go through and you are completely satisfied, do not accept bridge capital if possible. If you accept the bridge capital and the deal falls through, you may be in a default condition, and the business may become the investor's for a tiny fraction of its value. Moreover, accepting bridge capital puts tremendous pressure on you to concede a number of negotiating points just to keep the deal from "falling out of bed."

Every investor has a different way of making a commitment to you. Some will issue a commitment letter; others will not. Once you have reached an oral agreement with your investor, he or she may begin to draw up the legal documents and attempt to close on the investment on the basis of the oral understanding you have reached. Some people prefer a commitment letter as an intermediate step between oral understanding and legal documents. Indeed, if neither party can agree on the terms and conditions of a letter, then obviously legal documents cannot be drawn.

The Commitment Letter

The commitment letter contains five basic segments. The first segment states the terms on which the loan is being made to your company and the terms of the equity option. The second section states the collateral for the loan. The third part talks about the conditions of the loan, both negative and positive. The fourth outlines the representations you have made that have induced the investor or lender to make a commitment. The fifth part deals with the conditions on which the commitment was made. Each part is now discussed.[11]

1 *Terms of the investment.* In this section, the investor will try to state in clear terms precisely what he or she intends to do. Example: "The investor will make a loan of $100,000.00 for five years at an interest rate of 15 percent per annum paid monthly on the first of each month. Disbursement and takedown of the loan shall be 100 percent of the loan at closing. In connection with this financing, the investor will receive at the closing separate stock options to purchase stock in the company. The cost of the options to the investor will be $100.00. These options, when exercised, will provide stock ownership in the company of 20 percent at the time of exercise. The exercise price will be $20,000.00. The options will expire five years from closing. Any time after five years from the closing, the

[11]Parts summarized from David Gladstone, *Venture Capital Handbook* (Reston, Va.: Reston Publishing Company, 1983), pp. 27–43. This material is adapted by permission of Reston Publishing Company, a Prentice-Hall company, 11480 Sunset Hills Road, Reston, Va. 22090.

investor may require a registration and public offering of the shares owned by the investor at the company's expense.''

2 *Collateral and security.* This section of the commitment letter sets out the collateralization of the loan with certain assets of the company, and, in some cases, your own personal assets. Examples of provisions include ''A second secured interest in all the tangible and intangible assets of the company, including but not limited to inventory, machinery, equipment, furniture, fixtures, and accounts receivable subordinated as to collateral to a first secured bank loan of $50,000.00 on terms acceptable to the investor. Pledge and assignment of all the stock of the company and assignment of any and all leases of the company. Personal signature and guarantees of you and your spouse. Assignment of a life insurance policy on your life for the amount of the loan outstanding with the investor listed as the loss payee. Adequate hazard and business insurance, which shall include all perils and liabilities. All such insurance shall be assigned to the investor who shall be listed as the loss payee to the extent of his or her interest.''

3 *Conditions of the loan.* This section enumerates the conditions under which the loan will exist. Example: ''The company will provide the investor with monthly financial statements prepared in accordance with generally accepted accounting principles. The company will provide the investor with a monthly two-page summary of operations included with the financial statements. Within 90 days after the year end the company will provide financial statements audited by a CPA acceptable to the investor. The president of the company will provide the investor with a certificate each quarter stating that no default has occurred in the terms and conditions of this loan. In accordance with generally accepted accounting principles, the company will maintain (a) a current ratio of not less than 2 to 1, (b) accounts receivable turnover of not less than 10, (c) inventory turnover of not less than 3.5, (d) sales of not less than $500,000.00 per year, and (e) net worth of at least $200,000.00. Management will not sell, assign, or transfer any shares it owns in the company without written approval of the investor. The company will have board meetings at least once each quarter at the company's business office. The investor or his or her representative will have the right to attend each meeting at the company's expense, and the investor shall be notified of each meeting at least two weeks before it is to occur. The company will pay no cash dividends, and the company will not sell any assets of the business that are not part of the regular course of business without the investor's approval. The company will not expend funds in excess of $10,000.00 per year for capital improvements without written approval from the investor. The management team, including you, will live in the metropolitan area where the business is located. The company will not be relocated without the express written permission of the investor. The company will not pay any employee, nor will it loan or advance to any employee money that in total exceeds $60,000.00 per year without the written approval of the investor. The company will not pay any brokerage fees, legal fees, or consulting fees in excess of $10,000.00 per year without the written approval of the investor. The company will pay all closing costs and recording fees, which include all attorney's fees, even those of the investor's attorney."

4 *Representations.* The representations you made through your business plan and the presentation of your business plan were inducements to the investor to make the commitment. If any of these representations are not true, this commitment letter may be declared void by the investor. The point is this: Do not sign a representation you cannot fulfill. Examples of representations: "The company is a corporation in good standing in [your state]. The company will provide the investor with a certificate of good standing and a copy of the charter, the bylaws, and the organizing minutes of the company. There are no lawsuits against the company, its directors, or its officers, nor do you know of any that may be contemplated. The company is current on all taxes owed. The financial statements are true and correct. The company has a net worth of $80,000.00. The money borrowed will be used as follows: (1) $50,000.00 to pay accounts payable and (2) $50,000.00 for working capital. On closing the investor's loan, the company will have approximately the following assets: (1) cash, $130,000.00; (2) inventory, $200,000.00; (3) accounts receivable, $220,000.00; (4) machinery and equipment, $400,000.00; and (5) land and building, $250,000.00. During the past 10 years none of the directors, officers, or management has been arrested or convicted of a material crime or a material matter."

5 *Conditions of commitment.* Certain conditions must be achieved, or the investor's commitment will be void. Examples: "All legal documents must be acceptable to the investor. A favorable credit check of you and your business and a favorable 'due diligence' review of you, your business, and your industry must take place with no adverse occurrences before closing. A favorable visit to your business operation or proposed location by the investor must take place. The entire funds from all financing sources as set forth in this commitment letter must be raised."

The reasons behind each of the preceding items are self-evident. To the extent that you can remove some of these items (or others) from the commitment letter or keep them from being added to the legal documents, you will simplify the relationship between you and the investor. The investor's lawyer will make sure that whatever is in the commitment letter is in the legal documents, so remove troublesome items before you sign the letter. The preceding examples, however, are representative of items that most investors will ask for. Negotiate every point in the letter, but do not quibble over details. It is important that the commitment letter spell out the business deal, not the legal deal, between the two of you. Once a commitment letter is signed, it is usually given to the lawyers to use in drawing up the legal documents.[12]

[12]Ibid.

In reality, the commitment letter is not a commitment at all. The investor can have a change of heart and simply say that he or she does not believe the business venture will make it. You don't really have a commitment until you have the money in hand. Most investors are reputable and will honor their commitments. If they want to get out of the deal, they will. Your objective, however, is to get the commitment letter and continue to push for closing. When you get the money, you know that the investor has made a real commitment.[13]

The Investment Memorandum

For some strange reason, when an investor, such as a venture capital firm, purchases stock in your new business venture, he or she does not call the commitment letter a commitment letter. The firm calls this letter an investment memorandum or a term sheet even though it is in the form of a letter.[14] An investment memorandum usually states all the terms and conditions of the stock purchase.

The five categories in an investment memorandum for the purchase of stock are virtually the same as those covered in the commitment letter. The items included in the "terms of the investment" category, however, will naturally differ. Examples of some items included in this category are these: "The investor will purchase 100,000 shares of common stock in the company at $5.00 per share. All shares will be purchased at closing. If the company has not had a public offering of its stock within five years from the closing date, then the investor will have a 'put' provision whereby the investor can require the company to redeem the shares resulting from this purchase at the higher of the following: (1) book value per share, (2) earnings per share times 10, (3) $10.00 per share. Any time after five years from closing, the investor may require a registration and public offering of the shares owned by the investor at the company's expense. The investor will have full 'piggyback' rights to register shares any time the company or its management is registering shares for sale, and such registration of the investor's shares shall be paid by your company."[15]

When you and your investor have reached an understanding on the terms and conditions of the investment, the investor must begin what is known in his or her world as "due diligence." *Due diligence* simply means that the investor will conduct a background check on you and your management team and try to verify the key points in your business plan. Some investors will not issue a commitment letter (or investment memorandum) until they have performed due diligence.[16]

[13]Ibid., p. 151.
[14]Ibid., pp. 143–48.
[15]Ibid.
[16]Ibid. p. 153.

The Closing

Sometime after the due diligence is completed and the visit to the business is past, the investor's lawyer will contact you about closing the deal. You should also have a lawyer to represent you. The investor's lawyer will draw up the legal documents that are necessary for closing. The legal documents should follow the commitment letter or investment memorandum. The legal documents will contain both standard paragraphs known as "boilerplate" paragraphs and special stipulations. There are two types of closings, a loan with options to own stock and an agreement to purchase stock.[17] Because the stock purchase is similar to the loan agreement, it will not be repeated.

Legal documents for loans with options include a loan agreement, a note, and a stock purchase option. Each document has specific objectives and each covers separate ground. These are summarized as follows.[18]

1 *The loan agreement.* To some extent, the loan agreement will include the items in the commitment letter plus items standard for loan agreements. There are 10 sections to the loan agreement, which are (1) purchase and sale, which describes terms, conditions, and securities to be purchased; (2) collateral and security; (3) affirmative covenants, which cover all the items you agreed you would do as long as the loan or option to own stock is outstanding; (4) negative covenants, which are those things you agreed not to do; (5) events of default, which describe terms that will cause a default of the loan; (6) equity rights, which cover a wide range of items relating to the equity of the company, the equity of the investor, or option to own equity held by the investor; (7) representations and warranties; (8) fees and expenses; (9) definitions that define every technical or legal term appearing in the document; and (10) conditions of closing, which include such things as certificate of incorporation, opinion of your lawyer, certified audit, a copy of a letter from the senior lender consenting to this transaction.

2 *The note.* The note is a detailed statement of the terms of the loan, including how much money is being loaned, when it is to be repaid, the interest rate, what day of the month it is to be paid, guarantors, conditions of prepayment of the loan, collateral of the loan, subordination of the loan to other loans, references to covenants in the loan agreement, a complete list of defaults, and waivers and amendments.

3 *The stock purchase option.* This document provides the following details: duration of the stock option; any covenants of the company during ownership of the stock option; the mechanism for surrendering the option in exchange for stock; the exact price that must be paid when the option is exercised; adjustments to the exercise price, that is, the formula that will be used in case shares are sold at a

[17]Ibid., p. 175.
[18]Ibid., pp. 176–84.

low price or additional shares are issued by the company; the availability of shares owned by the company to be issued if the option is exercised; any written notices that must be given; a definition of common stock; expiration date of the stock option; and transferability of the option. Your objective throughout the entire process is to obtain legal documents acceptable to the investor and to the investor's lawyer. As soon as that process is complete, you and the investor can sign the legal documents. At that point, you have your money. Indeed, the quicker you can go through the legal documents and the harder you can push your lawyer to review them and get them back to the investor's lawyer, the sooner you will get your money.[19]

ETHICS AND RULES OF CONDUCT

You have raised the money and you are ready to embark on the biggest project of your life, a full-fledged entrepreneur who has a chance to rise to power and status and amass a fortune. You are the real hero of economic growth. You help distribute wealth; you provide jobs; you serve customers' needs and wants; you are instrumental in improving the standard of living of all members of society. Many eyes are now on you, many with hope and trust, some with envy, and still others looking for a weakness. You are going to be embattled, tempted, and praised. Now is the time to think seriously about setting for yourself a code of ethics and rules of conduct that you will live by as an entrepreneur and businessperson.

Overview

The Greek word for ethics and the Latin term for morals both came from the same root, the Greek word *ethos*, meaning "custom" or "a habitual mode of conduct." Ethics bases itself on a reflective analysis of moral experience and gives us some general knowledge of right and wrong conduct. But we must still make personal decisions that apply this knowledge to particular cases. In the case of ethical reflection, we encounter a number of certain situations with no clear-cut answers. We are not always sure about what moral principle should govern a particular decision. Do you default on a debt to apply this money to pay for an operation to save your child's life? Do you fire a nonproductive employee six months before retirement? How practical are you? How compassionate are you? Did you exaggerate or lie about some item in your business plan? Do you plan to produce products of poor quality? Have you stolen trade secrets or confidential information from your employer to base your business venture on? Clearly, the executive is in a fiduciary relationship with his or her company that imposes restitutions on conflicts of interest. In this capacity, ethics prevents one from self-serving ventures.

A code of ethics is supposed to develop a way of dealing with these difficult

---

[19]Ibid., p. 194.

conflicts and reach a systematic general doctrine on moral life. Without some virtues and ethics in men and women, our world, indeed, would be utterly chaotic.

Ethical philosophers in early times included Socrates, Plato, Aristotle, the Epicureans, and the Stoics. All engaged in persistent questioning to define the virtuous man. Some said the highest good was in pleasrue, especially pleasure of the mind. Others believed that the truly ethical person cultivates the virtues of prudence, temperance, courage, and justice; or virtues of faith, hope, and charity. All these philosophers stressed that the ultimate reward of ethical conduct was peace of mind.

Later, ethical philosophers seemed to offer a metaphysical kind of ethics. Kant believed that an act is genuinely moral only when it is done out of pure respect for duty. Mill took a more utilitarian view; he believed that decisions should be guided by the principle of achieving the greatest happiness for the greatest number of people.

Humanism strives to set up an ethical system apart from religious authority. Ethical reflection and the setting of ethical standards through the ages have seldom, however, been carried on in isolation from religious convictions. One reason is that religion strongly affects the moral judgments of individuals and communities. The Ten Commandments are the best-known example of how religious belief shaped private and public morality of Judaism and the Christian religion. Harry Truman said, "The Sermon on the Mount and The Ten Commandments are enough code of ethics for anybody." He was probably right.

Other religions vary in their emphasis on ethical systems. For example, problems of conduct have much more significance for Moslems than for Hindus. Islam, through the Koran, teaches Moslems certain laws for everyday life. Hinduism, however, stresses the soul's release from this world and preaches complete detachment from the affairs of this life. America draws its ethical standards from a variety of sources, but mainly from the English common law and the Judaic-Christian ethical tradition. Some rules in the Code of Hammurabi and some Egyptian writings were similar to the Old Testament. Greek and Roman law, chiefly the latter, had real influence on common law and on the canon or church law that ruled some British activities into the nineteenth century. Saint Thomas Aquinas wrote out many ethical precepts that were repeated in canon and in common law; he drew his maxims principally from the Old and New Testaments, from Roman law, and from Aristotle.[20]

Some ethical precepts that are especially applicable to the entrepreneur follow.[21]

1 Public health and safety are the supreme law.

2 Property should be used so that it does not damage others.

[20]George C. S. Benson, *Business Ethics in America* (Lexington, Mass.: Lexington Books, D. C. Heath, 1982), p. 1. This material is used by permission of the publisher.
[21]Ibid., pp. 1–2.

3 Manufacturers and artisans should maintain the quality of products.

4 Business has some responsibility for charitable giving.

5 The law should be obeyed.

6 Commercial transactions should be conducted without deception.

7 Reporting of truth must be systematic; weights and measures and accounting are two systems toward that end.

8 The obligation of contracts must be respected.

The Real Business World

Often entrepreneurs have only God to turn to. They cannot completely trust anyone. They expect the best, have to be ready for the worst. They have to construct an alert defensive posture. In business, the name of the game is money, and lots of people out there will cut your throat in more ways than one over a few dollars. It isn't pretty, but that is the way it is.

All the legal and organizational aspects are certainly important. But all this will carry you only so far. In the rough and tumble business world, there is often a big difference between what ought to be and what is. Most of the time, there is a conflict between morality, religion, conscience, and your instinct to survive. Every penny you don't pay the IRS is one more penny you can use to turn your business around, for example.

As an entrepreneur, you will not always be able to hide behind the veil of law, stand on the Holy Bible, or live by philosophical platitudes. At some point, you will have to step in the arena and perform. One thing is sure; as an entrepreneur, you will have to make some tough decisions. Now is a good time to think about how you might deal with complex, conflicting problems and make the tough decision. Certainly, an unquestioning reliance on legalities only is inadequate in today's world.

A Meshing and Matching of Ethics

Because ethics are personal and internalized, many of us may not be aware of how we would make tough decisions under pressure. The success of our business and a happy, viable marriage of the entrepreneurial team and investors depend on the compatibility of ethics. A significant clash in individual ethics can cause a team to rupture and a business to fail before it even gets started. It is, therefore, imperative that all members of a team determine as soon as possible the mesh and match of ethics. It is extremely difficult for persons with different codes of ethics to agree on what to do when the tough times come, and they will come.

The range of ethics is probably different for each individual; that is, no one's will match point for point. Closeness of match is desirable, however, among your entrepreneurial team members, board of directors, and investors, especially venture capitalists. It is worth noting that venture capitalists are good at spotting promoters who conduct themselves a lot in the amoral or illegal end of the ethical continuum. If you are to raise capital and succeed in building your business, your reputation as an entrepreneur is a valuable asset. Investors, government, and consumers are increasingly intolerant of unethical entrepreneurs or promoters.

A Potpourri of Advice

In the final analysis, ethics, morality, and religion are very personal things. All humankind is in a dilemma as to what is right and wrong conduct. Entrepreneurs are in the middle of this dilemma because they are people of energy and action; they are innovators; they are always striving and moving ahead. They are in a milieu within which one must compete to survive.

When it comes to advice on how one should conduct oneself, most people are only too willing to give it. I am no exception. From strictly a business viewpoint, a potpourri of advice is offered in the following comments. Much of it, if not all of it, you have heard before, but this time, view it from the perspective of a budding entrepreneur trying to get off to a good start.

First, be willing to work and get the job done. If you are not willing to work at least 60 hours a week, then go to work at the post office and give up on entrepreneurship. Survive. If you believe that what you're doing is worthwhile, then you do what it takes to survive. Be trustworthy. If you tell someone something, he or she will be able to carve it in stone. If you see that you can't honor a commitment, let appropriate people know that you can't in plenty of time so that they can make other plans. Produce good quality products and services, and stand behind what you sell. Keep your customers satisfied. Strive to be respected by all your peers and others with interest in your business.

If you are the chief officer of your business, it is up to you to create an atmosphere of excellence, integrity, and performance that reflects strong ethical standards of behavior. It must start with you, at the top; writing it down on paper is not enough; exemplary action is required. Be provident in your use of resources, and develop habits of self-control and tolerance. Limit your involvement in "puffing the goods," silly hype, and bluffing. Maintain a high standard of integrity and honesty. Always ask yourself what effect a particular decision will have on your sensibilities and peace of mind in the long run. If you believe that it is expedient and the price you pay is too high, then don't do it.

An excellent article by Laura R. Nash includes the following 12 questions to ask yourself when trying to make an ethical decision.[22]

1 Have you defined the problem accurately?

2 How would you define the problem if you stood on the other side of the fence?

---

[22]An exhibit from Laura L. Nash, "Ethics Without The Sermon," *Harvard Business Review*, November–December 1981, p. 81. Reprinted by permission of the Harvard Business Review. Copyright © 1981 by the President and Fellows of Harvard College; all rights reserved.

3 How did this situation occur in the first place?

4 To whom and to what do you give your loyalty as a person and as a member of the corporation?

5 What is your intention in making this decision?

6 How does this intention compare with the probable results?

7 Whom could your decision or action injure?

8 Can you discuss the problem with the affected parties before you make your decision?

9 Are you confident that your position will be as valid over a long period of time as it seems now?

10 Could you disclose without qualm your decision or action to your boss, your CEO, the board of directors, your family, society as a whole?

11 What is the symbolic potential of your action if understood? if misunderstood?

12 Under what conditions would you allow exceptions to your stand?

If you can deal with these questions and manage all of this advice and put it to work, most people will consider you ethical. Clearly, if you can gain the respect from your customers, creditors, competitors, investors, bankers, employees, partners, and family, you must be doing something right.

The Goodness of Profit

A final word on ethics: Making money is ethical if done honestly. From time to time, one hears members of the clergy, philosophy professors, and others speak of "filthy lucre." Many pastors preach against the "almighty dollar." They stand in the pulpit and state that money is the root of all evil, and those who have it are wicked until the collection plate goes around. Then they scream if the plate's not overflowing. There is an inconsistency in this doctrine.

There are a lot of things better than money, but money is power, and you ought to strive to earn some; you can do more good with it than without it. Money builds churches, synagogues, schools, and hospitals and helps crippled children and brings together factors of production for employment. It also pays preachers, priests, and rabbis. It is wrong to think you have to be poor to be pious. The Holy Bible does not say that money is the root of all evil, but that the love of money is the root of all evil.

Some people think it is unethical to make a profit on anything that you sell. Profit is the compensation that accrues to you for the assumption of risk in business enterprise as distinguished from rent or wages. Indeed, it would be almost criminal, stupid, and dysfunctional to sell products or services for less than cost. You have to be true to yourself, to your investors, to your creditors, and certainly to your family who depend on you. A person who owns a business that is not making money ought to get out and let someone else take over. Such a person is not doing anyone any good, not customers, family, or self. As an entrepreneur, many hold you in trust. Honor this trust always.

SUMMARY

The kind of investor you choose to back you will be one of the key success factors. Choose someone who is compatible with you and your business plan and someone who will stay with you through thick and thin. When meeting with your prospective investor, do everything possible to make a good impression. Venture capitalists and other investors are just like people everywhere; they often pay an inordinate amount of attention to nonverbal messages and appearance. Often it is not so much what you say but how you say it, or not who you are in reality but how you appear. Once given the chance to present your business plan, use an extemporaneous method of delivery and other techniques such as visual aids that will increase understanding. Once the presentation is made, try to get some kind of a commitment from the prospective investor, such as a commitment letter or investment memorandum. From these, legal documents are drawn up that become instruments for closing the deal and getting your money.

The business plan is a road map for operating your business. Ethics and rules of conduct serve as a road map that guides you in your connections and dealings with your investor, banker, employees, customers, suppliers, and others. Ethical conduct fosters better human relations and, in the long run, a stronger economic system. Without ethics, chaos would abound. For the marketplace to work, there must be trust; people must meet their oral commitments; people must be prudent. Businesspeople who are unethical are detrimental to their peers and to business in general.

ASSIGNMENT

1 Why is it important to choose the right investor? Explain fully. How do you match the investor with the business plan?

2 How do you check the reputation and credibility of the investor?

3 Describe ways to get the interview. Include some ways not discussed in the text.

4 What are the legal problems that you might run into while showing your business plan?

5 Outline how you would prepare for your initial meeting with your prospective investor. What is the investor looking for in you?

6 What are nonverbal messages? What do they have to do with presenting your business plan?

7 List the basic presentation methods. What method do you recommend? Why?

8 Explain how you would prepare for a presentation of your business plan. What kind of visual aids do you plan to use? Explain how you plan to close the presentation.

9 What is a commitment letter? What is an investment memorandum? What are they used for?

10 What are the legal instruments of closing? What do they include?

11 Why are ethics and rules of conduct important to an entrepreneur?

12 What are the source of ethical precepts?

13 Outline a code of ethics you are now living by or plan to live by as an entrepreneur.

14 Is profit good or bad? Explain fully.

15 The following exercises involve a number of situations that require tough decisions. Choose the one, or offer one of your own, that represents the decision you would make. Make any assumptions that you deem necessary. Above all, try to put yourself in the situation where you feel that you are really facing this in life. Don't worry about wrong or right answers as far as this course is concerned.

(a) You are in the shipping office of your major supplier. You and Joe, the office manager, are alone. Joe says he's going out to check on some things and get a cup of coffee. When he leaves, you notice a proposal and list of specifications of a new product that your competitor is coming out with later this year. What would you do?

———Ignore them and do nothing.

———Sneak a peek to get some general, key figures.

———Put a copy in your briefcase.

———Other. Explain.

(b) A large chain of nursing homes bought and installed over $2 million worth of your company's smoke detection and fire suppression systems. Harry Hingle, one of the founders and members of the entrepreneurial team of your company, tells you confidentially that he has found out that some of the detection and switching devices are defective. He also adds that you and he are the only ones who know about this. You ask him what would happen if one of the nursing homes had a fire. Harry states that there are only a 20 percent probability of smoke detection and a 40 percent probability that the switching system would turn on the sprinklers. You ask him what this all means in human terms. His response is that it would be grim; a lot of people would die if a fire broke out. Harry also tells you that at minimum it would cost $200,000 to correct these defects. Your company has just expanded and is presently cash anemic. Such an outlay at this time would spell disaster for your company. What would you do?

———You and Harry swear to secrecy and do nothing.

———Start juggling resources and map out a plan to correct all defects.

———Other. Explain.

(c) You are a noted and respected breeder of registered beef cattle. The breeding association of which you are both a charter member and director has a Code of Professional Ethics that all members swear to and sign. You were one of the founding members who helped prepare this code. Part of this code includes explicit instructions for using artificial insemination. For example, the sire must be registered with the association, blood-tested, and the like. Also, when preparing breeding certificates and pedigrees, the breeder is trusted to show the correct dam and sire of the progeny being registered. An important and influential friend of yours from Brazil mentions to you that he can get you some ampules of semen from El Capitan, a "perfect," but little-known bull owned by a small rancher in an obscure part of Brazil. On one of your visits to Brazil, you found this bull by accident and knew in an instant that he had all the great characteristics that would match perfectly with a special herd of your heifers. But he cannot be registered by the association because of sketchy breeding records. Moreover, federal law restricts the importation of untested cattle and semen into the United States. What would you do?

————You have got to have this bull. Period. To mate him with your special herd of heifers will put you on the front row of superbeef genetics. You can assign some great bulls as sires of the resulting progeny. A few top breeders may suspect something, but you can probably explain that these particular matings resulted in a special genetic nick. Anyway, if anyone ever does find out, it won't be that easy for them to prove, and by then you'll be so far ahead of the pack that it really won't make much difference anyway. You call your friend back, and tell him to meet you at the El Paso Airport with a nitrogen tank full of semen ampules of El Capitan and that you will have the cash.

————Tell your friend that you would really like to use El Capitan but you must pass on the offer.

————Other. Explain.

(d) An unqualified opinion rendered by your CPA on your financial statements is imperative for you to receive a critical loan from the bank. Your own internal accountant, per your instructions, prepared your balance sheet on a current value basis versus using the cost basis. To convert it back to the cost basis would reduce the assets by $200,000, enough to prevent you from getting a loan. Your CPA informs you that for him to render an unqualified opinion, the cost basis must be used.

————You offer the CPA $1,000 to go along with your accounting procedure.

————You tell your CPA that if he does not go along with your accounting methods, he is fired.

————You abide by your CPA's instructions and prepare the statements accordingly.

————Other. Explain.

(e) You know that one of your major competitors is ripe for a buyout. You hire a buyer and instruct him to

————Give the best deal—whatever is fair.

————Pretend to be a serious buyer who is interested in buying. Get into protracted negotiations and continue to plot better offers to extend the seller to a point of no return after other buyers have been closed out. Then bail out and come back later and buy out your competitor at a huge discount.

————Other. Explain.

(f) Your business is failing because it cannot meet contracts, lease agreements, and amounts owed trade creditors and bankers. What would you do?

————Fight it to the bitter end.

————Petition for Chapter 7 treatment of the Bankruptcy Code.

————Petition for Chapter 11 treatment of the Bankruptcy Code.

————Let your business fail, form a corporation, and then buy back the assets for a few cents on the dollar and start all over again with a clean slate. (See the following note.)

If you cannot decide, think about these advantages of the dump-buy-back method. You end up with little or no liabilities. Under a Chapter 11, you still have reduced creditor claims to deal with. It is simpler and less costly than a Chapter 11. Starting over is faster. The legal hassle of a Chapter 11 can drag on for months. You enjoy more control because a Chapter 11 puts your assets under the supervision and control of the bankruptcy trustee and your creditors. Remember that if your location has value, make sure you control it by signing a new lease agreement a few days before you employ the dump-buy-back method. With the location tied up, the assignee can only inform prospective bidders that they will have to remove the assets. This condition usually discourages most bidders. (This note is for clarification only.)

————Other. Explain.

(g) You display your prototype at several trade shows. It is a big hit, and you receive a flood of orders, but you have not made arrangements to mass-produce it yet. Most of the people ordering your product indicate that they need 60-day delivery, but you know that, at best, you cannot make any shipments for 6 months, and you are not really sure about that. What do you do? You know that they will not give you an order if you let them know the real situation.

————Turn down the orders.

————Take the orders, and commit to their delivery dates.

————Take the orders, and try to weasel out of making delivery commitments.

————Other. Explain.

(h) One of your big customers is delinquent in paying his bill for $20,000.00. You are in desperate need of a cash transfusion, and you try to make a deal with him to pay his bill within seven days and get a 10 percent discount; otherwise, you will sue. He says that if he pays you, he will have to forego an operation that may save his life. What do you do?

————Sue.

————Forgive the debt, and right it off with the knowledge that you may lose your business.

————Tell him to pay when he can.

————Other. Explain.

(i) Your company is suffering from severe cash anemia. You "encourage" your employees to lend 15 percent of their wages to the company in return for a 14 percent note. Four of your employees refuse to participate. What do you do?

————Fire them.

————Demote them.

————Do nothing.

————Other. Explain.

(j) At the Spring market in Dallas, you placed a $100,000.00 order with XYZ Company. In the meantime, you have become insolvent, and you see little chance that you can pay XYZ, but the goods from them may help you survive and get you off the hook with some other creditors. You

————Call XYZ and tell them to cancel the order because you will not be able to pay them.

————Tell XYZ nothing. Let them ship the order and hope that you can negotiate with them later.

————Other. Explain.

(k) You realize that you can't pay your debts, and you set up meetings with your five major creditors. During the negotiation you

————Tell them that you are sorry and give them a lien against all your personal property to safeguard the amounts owed them.

————Knowing that they may not get much more than three or four cents on the dollar if you fail, you tell them you will settle for four cents on the dollar. To sweeten the deal, you promise them a check next week for full settlement. While they are thinking about your offer, you pop a few sugar pills and tug at your heart. The creditors will probably assume these pills are heart medicine.

————Throw the keys on the table and tell them it's their red wagon, that you're going to pick apples in Washington. Then let them react.

————Other. Explain.

(l) A few minutes after receiving a $1 million order for mufflers from a jobber in Hong Kong, you learn that the alloy used for the manufacture of these mufflers is defective and will rupture during normal driving conditions. The supplier of your alloy is no longer in business. Your lawyer tells you that the jobber in Hong Kong will not have any recourse against you. What do you do?

————Cancel the present order with the jobber, and try to fill this order with future production of a nondefective alloy.

————Ship the order without saying anything.

————Tell the jobber that the mufflers are made with defective material, and try to negotiate a reduced price.

————Other. Explain.

BIBLIOGRAPHY

Arthur Young and Company. *Outline for a New High Technology Business Plan*. New York: Arthur Young and Company, 1983.

Baty, Gordon B. *Entrepreneurship for the Eighties*. Reston, Va.: Reston Publishing Company, 1981.

Benson, George C. S. *Business Ethics in America*. Lexington, Mass.: Lexington Books, D. C. Heath, 1982.

Brandt, Steven C. *Entrepreneuring*. Reading, Mass.: Addison-Wesley, 1982.

Braybrooke, David. *Ethics in the World of Business*. Totowa, N.J.: Rowman & Allanheld, 1983.

Brown, J. W., and R. B. Lewis. *Audio-Visual Instruction: Technology, Media, and Method*, 5th ed. New York: McGraw-Hill, 1976.

Deloitte, Haskins, and Sells. *Raising Venture Capital*. New York: Deloitte, Haskins, and Sells, 1982.

Gilder, George. *The Spirit of Enterprise*. New York: Simon & Schuster, 1984.

Gladstone, David. *Venture Capital Handbook*. Reston, Va.: Reston Publishing Company, 1983.

Goldstein, Arnold S. *How to Save Your Business*. Wilmington, Del.: Enterprise Publishing, 1983.

Gorman, Walter F. *Selling: Personality, Persuasion, and Strategy*. New York: Random House, 1979.

Jacobs, Leslie W. "Business Ethics and the Law: Obligations of a Corporate Executive." *The Business Lawyer*. July 1973.

Kant, Immanuel. *Groundwork of the Metaphysic of Morals*. Translated by H. J. Paton. New York: Harper & Row, 1964.

Kindel, Stephen. "Counselor/Coach Syndrome." *Forbes 400*. October 1, 1984.

Kravitt, Gregory I. *How to Raise Capital*. Homewood, Ill.: Dow Jones-Irwin, 1984.

Mambert, W. A. *Effective Presentation*. New York: Wiley, 1976.

Nash, Laura L. "Ethics Without the Sermon." *Harvard Business Review*. November–December 1981.

Silver, A. David. *The Entrepreneurial Life*. New York: Wiley, 1983.

Stancill, James McNeill. "Realistic Criteria For Judging New Ventures." *Harvard Business Review*. November–December 1981.

Timmons, Jeffrey A., Leonard E. Smollen, and Alexander L. M. Dingee, Jr. *New Venture Creation: A Guide to Small Business Development*. Homewood, Ill.: Richard D. Irwin, 1977.

Venture Capital Journal. Published monthly by Venture Economics, Inc.; P.O. Box 348, 16 Laurel Avenue, Wellesley Hills, Mass. 02181.

INDEX